Sabine Wieduwilt (Ed.)

Real Estate Investment and ESG

A guide and toolkit for practitioners across the globe

1st Edition

Haufe

Bibliographical Information of the German National Library

The German National Library lists this publication in the German National Bibliography.
Detailed bibliographical data can be accessed on the internet at http://dnb.dnb.de.

Print: ISBN 978-3-648-19286-3 Order no. 16125-0001
ePub: ISBN 978-3-648-19287-0 Order no. 16125-0100
ePDF: ISBN 978-3-648-19288-7 Order no. 16125-0150

Sabine Wieduwilt (Ed.)
Real Estate Investment and ESG
1st Edition, January 2026

Munzinger Str. 9, 79111 Freiburg, Germany
www.haufe.de | info@haufe.de

Photo credit (cover): ©Valentina Shilkina, iStock

Product Management: Bettina Noé

Table of Contents

Preface

Sabine Wieduwilt

»The flap of a butterfly's wings in Brazil can set off a tornado in Texas.«[1]

The power of transformation, or the »butterfly effect«

The real estate investment sector is experiencing significant transformation as environmental, social, and governance (ESG) issues gain global prominence. Once a niche concern, ESG is now central to investment strategy, risk management, and value creation, driven by the increasing demand for responsibility and transparency from investors, regulators, and communities. While perspectives on sustainability and ESG shift due to geopolitical or economic or other factors, and the debate continues whether it is appropriate to use these terms or concepts to shape our business dealings, the practical challenge remains: how can we effectively implement ESG in real estate projects, if we decide to do so?

Sometimes, whether as an individual, a company, a country or even a continent, we feel that we lack the power to change things. Does it then make sense to do anything? Why not continue acting, using, misusing, and spoiling in the same way as before?

This metaphor *»The flap of a butterfly's wings in Brazil can set off a tornado in Texas.«* illustrates how small actions or events can have significant, far-reaching consequences, especially in complex systems.

©Judith Carla Wieduwilt (2025)[2]

Consider reading this book with the intention of changing one small aspect of the way you handle projects right now.

1 The concept originates from chaos theory and is often attributed to meteorologist Edward Lorenz, who used it to explain how tiny changes in initial conditions can lead to vastly different outcomes in weather systems. The phrase has since become a popular way to express the idea that minor events can have significant and unpredictable impacts.

2 Each author holds the rights to all illustrations in their respective subchapters, with the exception of illustrations that are marked separately (such as his first »butterfly effect« from Judith Carla Wieduwilt), and the illustrations referring to official sites, such as eurolex.

The intention, chapters and structure of this book

> *»We may well be the last generation with an opportunity to act.«* Is that how we want to think? *Let us reframe sustainability not as a sacrifice, but as an opportunity.*[3]

»Real Estate Investment and ESG: A Guide and Toolkit for Practitioners Across the Globe« intends to serve as a resource for professionals – including investors, asset managers, legal advisors, and policymakers – seeking to understand and apply ESG considerations in real estate investment. As global stakeholders increasingly demand more accountability, transparency, and sustainability from the sector, this book strives to provide knowledge, context, frameworks, and practical tools that can be used to meet new standards and expectations.

Our goal throughout the book is to bridge the gap between theory and practice. We intend to demystify ESG terminology and acronyms to make the subject more accessible.

What could be a relevant scenario or use case? Let's say Global Asset Partners (GAP)[4], a multinational real estate investment firm that manages properties worldwide and faces the challenge of aligning its ESG strategy with diverse regional regulations and global standards. In order to meet regulatory demands and gain a competitive edge as well as create long-term value through responsible investment practices, GAP goes ahead to map regulatory requirements in each jurisdiction, adopting international frameworks like TCFD and ISSB and engages stakeholders to tailor ESG initiatives and integrate ESG considerations throughout the investment process. This ensures compliance, operational improvements, and enhanced investor trust.

The intention of this book was to gather insights and generate ideas for implementing ESG into real estate investment practice.

The structure of this book mirrors the complexity of ESG in real estate. It starts with an examination of the global forces, standards, and historical context behind the ESG movement, clarifying key terms and international agreements. Subsequent chapters explore how ESG factors shape investment strategies, financing, and the rise of impact investing. The book then covers essential processes like due diligence, valuation, greenwashing risks, and operational challenges such as stranded assets, carbon emissions, and the circular economy. It also discusses the increasing role of data, AI, contracts, procurement, regulations, and post-merger integration in ESG. The final section provides regional and local perspectives, highlighting unique challenges and opportunities in different markets, giving readers both a comprehensive and practical understanding of ESG in real estate worldwide.

---

3 Ritchie, Hannah, Are We the Last Generation, or the First Sustainable One, TED, https://www.youtube.com/watch?v=Kl3VVrggKz4, accessed 16.08.2025.

4 Global Asset Partners (GAP) is only a fictitious firm that has not been researched. This is not a real-life example or setting.

Here is an overview of the chapters:

Chapter 1: ESG global dynamics and standards – This chapter sets the stage by tracing the historical development of sustainability/CSR/ESG in real estate, examining international treaties, global dynamics, and the shift in focus towards sustainability/CSR/ESG. It seeks to entangle the terminology and acronyms that permeate ESG discussions. It then covers international treaties and conventions focusing on environmental and human rights, as a key area of the normative framework. It also explores the interplay with the instruments, standards, and frameworks that guide implementation. The chapter also delves into the three pillars of ESG: environmental (with a focus on climate, the IPFCC report, and litigation risks), social (emphasizing sustainable supply chains), and governance (addressing anti-bribery and corruption and anti-money laundering (ABC & AML)).

Chapter 2: The real estate investment market, ESG & investment, finance, greenwashing – Here, the book explores the intersection of ESG and real estate investment. It provides an overview of the global investment market, focusing on megatrends, terms, and acronyms related to responsible investment, and different investor types. The chapter discusses various investment approaches, including impact investing and the integration of ESG into real estate financing, and guidance on drafting clauses and otherwise preparing for financing linked to ESG principles and the risks of greenwashing, and provides an overview of thematic bonds.

Chapter 3: Due diligence, valuation, and user perspective – This chapter offers a deep dive into the practical aspects of ESG factors in real estate transactions for the investment process. It covers environmental due diligence (EDD), ESG-specific due diligence process, and the legal considerations involved. The chapter also addresses valuation methodologies that incorporate ESG factors, and discusses whether ESG affects valuation. Additionally, it looks at carbon accounting as business-critical for tenants and a strategic imperative for landlords.

Chapter 4: Further details and perspectives – Focusing on the operational side, this chapter discusses details that may be of interest for real estate investments, such as the Carbon Risk Real Estate Monitoring (CRREM) framework, and the impact of greenhouse gas emissions – including embodied carbon and resource depletion – on real estate. It explores water and health, with a deep dive into a water-cleansing tool in real estate projects, brownfield investments, and the role of insurance and climate adaptation. The chapter concludes with data and artificial intelligence.

Chapter 5: Contracts, procurement, and regulatory frameworks – This chapter addresses the legal and regulatory dimensions of ESG factors in real estate transactions. It covers various deal structures (for example asset and share deals, forward deals, joint ventures, and cross-border deals), the evolution of EU procurement from a sustainability focus to strategic autonomy, real estate investment and funds, and competition. The chapter also explores ESG and different types of management contracts and post-merger integration.

Chapter 6: Global, regional and local perspectives – Recognizing the global nature of real estate investment, the final chapter provides a review of ESG practices and challenges across different continents or regions. It offers deep dives into Africa, Asia, Europe (the EU and the U.K.), the U.S., and Latin America, highlighting regional nuances, regulatory environments, and market-specific opportunities and risks.

Each of the six chapters is divided into six subchapters. The subchapters are written by different authors. There is no need to read the book or any chapter in the linear order. Additionally, each author may have a different view and interpret ESG and real estate investment differently.

Why collaboration is essential. An invitation to explore and transform

»*The greatest threat to our planet is the belief that someone else will save it.*«[5] – This underscores the necessity of both individual and collective action for sustainability. No single company can address complex environmental challenges alone. Instead, innovative collaboration is vital for protecting natural resources and creating business value. The Earth's shared resources – air, forests, and oceans – are being depleted by fragmented, self-interested actions. Only systemic, collaborative solutions can preserve them while unlocking their potential. As collaborative practices and market incentives increase, aligning business interests with environmental preservation will drive progress for both the economy and the planet.[6] We think we're revolutionizing the way we develop cement by developing »green cement«, but we're still using sand from the beaches. However, instead of becoming hopeless, we have the opportunity to collaborate more and better.

»Addressing diverse perspectives is crucial for effective global communication and stakeholder engagement, leading to more impactful solutions.«[7] Implementing ESG in real estate investment is a journey, not a destination. It demands leadership, collaboration, and a willingness to challenge established norms. The intention of this book project is to gather meaningful and respectful content.

With the goal of reaching many practitioners, we aim for a global or international view. Even when we strive to be broad, holistic and all-encompassing, we're well aware that we tend to block other views and perspectives. For example the United Nations (UN) seems to cover the globe; however, not all of its initiatives or agreements have been adopted or are being followed worldwide. The Organisation for Economic Co-operation and Development (OECD) covers only

5 Robert Swan, Author and the first person to walk to both poles, https://www.activesustainability.com/environment/robert-swan-and-our-planet/, accessed 31.08.2025.

6 Nidumolu/Ellison/Whalen/Billman, The Collaboration Imperative for Sustainable Business Practices, 2014, https://hbr.org/2014/04/the-collaboration-imperative-2, accessed 29.05.2025.

7 Nidumolu/Ellison/Whalen/Billman, The Collaboration Imperative for Sustainable Business Practices, https://hbr.org/2014/04/the-collaboration-imperative-2, 2014, accessed 29.05.2025.

38 countries[8], excluding middle and Latin America, Africa, and Asia. Please always question whether we have covered every aspect.

Also, we are working against a moving target. When I asked practitioners to join the project, one of the key reasons for declining was »there is too much changing right now; this is not the time«. Buildings have a longer lifespan than politicians, the ground they stand on has an even longer lifespan, and our planet will hopefully remain habitable for humans for centuries to come.

We invite you to explore, question, engage with and apply the insights and tools contained within these pages, and to contribute to the global movement toward a more sustainable and responsible real estate sector.

Please see this as an invitation to write our future.[9]

> *»No matter what people tell you, words and ideas can change the world.«*[10]

8 OECD, Members and partners, https://www.oecd.org/en/about/members-partners.html, accessed 13.09.2025.

9 This book is also a tribute to Wolfgang Lucas, my father who died two weeks before we handed in the book, who was a victim and a survivor of war, believed in peace, never made a difference between anybody's origins or background, lived two sides of Germany and never believed in a wall, loved the African continent and the people on it, especially from Benin, and who discussed and lived sustainable development while politicians were introducing it at global level.

10 John Keating (Robin Williams) in Dead Poets Society, a screenplay by Tom Schulman, directed by Peter Weir, 1989.

1 ESG global dynamics and standards – including a spotlight on E (climate), S (supply chains) and G (ABC & AML)

1.1 Introduction to Chapter #1

Sabine Wieduwilt

»Start by doing what is necessary, then do what is possible, and suddenly you are doing the impossible.«[11]

1.1.1 Setting the scene – finding the meaning of ESG. Chapter #1 overview

We are writing this book in 2025, it's a time of extreme events, turmoil, criticism against the acronym ESG, and a divide of opinions on its relevance.

When this book is published at the beginning of 2026, will ESG be just three letters that used to belong together with a sense of urgency, but are now a shadow of the past?

What's the catch with ESG and real estate investment?

What does ESG actually mean? Sometimes it feels nebulous and vague; we feel like we're poking around in the fog.

This chapter #1 will hopefully lift some of the fog by providing context and meaning.

11 This quote from a Bizcommunity article encourages taking incremental steps towards sustainability and ESG goals. Bizzcommunity, ESG Quotes, St. Francis of Assisi, https://www.bizcommunity.com/Quotes/196/348.html, accessed 31.05.2025.

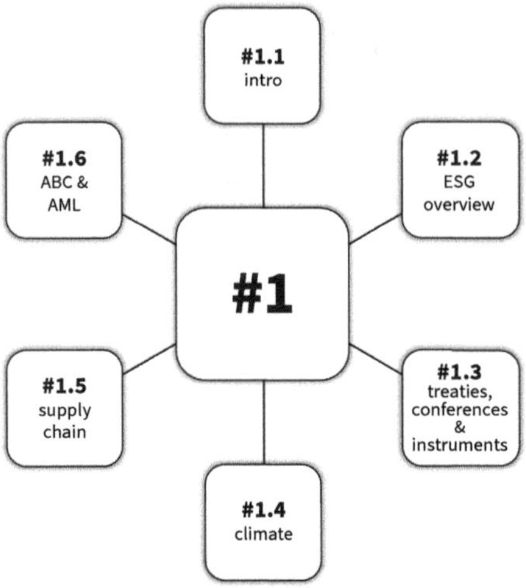

Chapter #1 opens with a general introduction to the terms sustainability/CSR/ESG (#1.2), followed by international conferences, treaties and agreements, a structural review of rule-givers in the sustainability/CSR/ESG arena, with a brief differentiation between principles and implementation, and some examples of institutions, standards, initiatives (#1.3), including a peak at climate issues, specifically the 6th IPCC report and the built environment, as well as related litigation risks (#1.4), followed up by a discussion of the invisible workforce in global supply chains (#1.5), then concluding with anti-bribery and corruption (»ABC«) and anti-money laundering (»AML«) and practical guidance (#1.6).

On a side note: It would not do justice to the authors of this book to frame their contributions solely as disciplines under the umbrella of sustainability/CSR/ESG.

In any case, I am convinced that regardless of our views on sustainability/CSR/ESG, we can work to reduce the risks, enhance opportunities, and have a positive impact.

With this first chapter #1, we begin by exploring sustainability/CSR/ESG issues from a global perspective, before narrowing our focus to real estate and real estate investment.

1.1.2 Milestones – tabular overview

Before we dive into the details, please take a look at **Table 1**, which provides a non-comprehensive **overview of the milestones** for those who prefer chronological tables.

Year	*Title*	*Information*
1972	**United Nations Conference on the Human Environment (Stockholm Conference)**	The first major international conference to focus on global environmental issues, leading to the Stockholm Declaration and the establishment of the United Nations Environment Programme (UNEP).
1976	**OECD Guidelines for Multinational Enterprises**	The Organisation for Economic Co-operation and Development (OECD) adopted its Guidelines for Multinational Enterprises, providing voluntary principles and standards for responsible business conduct. See 2011 MNE; 2018 RBC; 2023 MNE for updates.
1987	**Brundtland Report (»Our Common Future«)**	The World Commission on Environment and Development (WCED) published the Brundtland Report, thereby introducing the concept of »sustainable development.«
1987	**OECD**	The OECD published »Environmental Policies for a Sustainable Development,« further integrating sustainability into its policy framework.
1992	**United Nations Conference on Environment and Development (UNCED, »Rio Earth Summit«)**	A landmark event held in Rio de Janeiro, resulting in several foundational agreements: Rio Declaration on Environment and Development, Agenda 21 (a comprehensive plan of action for sustainable development), United Nations Framework Convention on Climate Change (UNFCCC), Convention on Biological Diversity (CBD), United Nations Convention to Combat Desertification (UNCCD), Forest Principles.
1998	**International Labour Organization (ILO) Declaration on Fundamental Principles and Rights at Work**	The ILO adopted this declaration, thereby identifying core labor standards that all member states are expected to respect and promote.
2000	**United Nations Global Compact**	Launched to encourage businesses worldwide to adopt sustainable and socially responsible policies, based on ten principles in the areas of human rights, labor, environment, and anti-corruption.
2003	**Equator Principles**	A risk management framework adopted by financial institutions for determining, assessing, and managing environmental and social risk in projects.
2006	**UN Principles for Responsible Investment (PRI)**	An investor initiative in partnership with UNEP Finance Initiative and the UN Global Compact, promoting the incorporation of environmental, social, and governance (ESG) factors into investment decision-making.
2008	**ISO 26000 Guidance on Social Responsibility**	The development of the standard began in 2008, and it was published in 2010, providing guidance on how businesses and organizations can operate in a socially responsible way.

Year	*Title*	*Information*
2011	**United Nations Guiding Principles on Business and Human Rights (UNGP)**	Endorsed by the UN Human Rights Council, these principles clarify the duties and responsibilities of states and businesses to prevent, address, and remedy human rights abuses committed in business operations.
2015	**Agenda 2030 – United Nations Sustainable Development Goals (SDGs)**	The UN adopted 17 SDGs as part of the 2030 Agenda for Sustainable Development, providing a global blueprint for peace and prosperity for people and the planet.
2015	**Paris Agreement (under the UNFCCC)**	A legally binding international treaty on climate change, adopted at COP21 in Paris, aiming to limit global warming to well below 2°C.

Table 1: Overview of milestones (non-comprehensive)

1.2 Sustainability/CSR/ESG

Sabine Wieduwilt

»You cannot get through a single day without having an impact on the world around you. What you do makes a difference and you have to decide what kind of a difference you want to make.«[12]

1.2.1 Introduction to #1.2

Do I have to get through the jungle of sustainability/CSR/ESG in order to make a difference? Of course not.

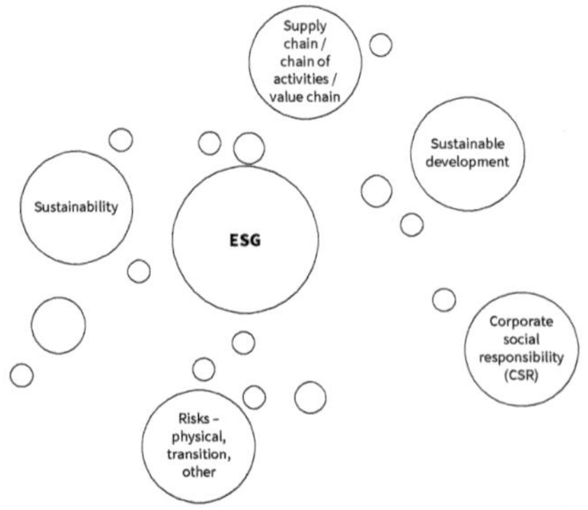

We sometimes get so tangled up in trying to define sustainability/CSR/ESG, that we lose interest before understanding the terminology or global dynamics.

There are as many meanings of sustainability/CSR/ESG as there are people who use the acronyms. ESG is often used interchangeably with »sustainability« and »sustainable development,« as well as »CSR«. With this book, we don't aim for perfection in delineating the terms, we don't want to get wrapped up in that.

12 Goodall, Jane, quote on goodreads.com, https://www.goodreads.com/quotes/511077-you-cannot-get-through-a-single-day-without-having-an, accessed 12.09.2025.

#1.2 ESG overview	**#1.2.1 - intro to #1.2**	
	#1.2.2 - sustainability / sustainable development	
	#1.2.3 - CSR	
	#1.2.4 - ESG	
	#1.2.5 - ESG & real estate	

Subchapter #1.2 compiles a selection of publications, reports, models, conferences, and other materials associated with the terms, sustainability and sustainable development (#1.2.2), CSR (#1.2.3) and ESG issues, including discussions around ESG (#1.2.4)[13]. It then provides a tabular overview of ESG and real estate (#1.2.5).

1.2.2 Sustainability, sustainable development

The concept of **sustainability** has been a guiding principle for political, economic and ecological action.

Traditional societies and indigenous peoples: Long before the modern term existed, many ancient cultures and indigenous communities practiced forms of resource management that prioritized the long-term capacity of their environment to sustain them.[14]

1713 – The term **sustainability** comes from the **Latin word »sustinere«**, meaning to maintain, support, uphold, or endure.

Hans Carl **von Carlowitz**, a Saxon tax accountant and mining administrator, introduced the concept of »sustainability« in his book **»Sylvicultura oeconomica«**.[15] Excessive logging in Saxony (now in Germany) to supply wood for mining and other uses led to visible forest depletion. Carlowitz advocated for the responsible, long-term use and replanting of timber to ensure the continuous and sustainable use of forests.[16] This prompted the search for better wood management.

13 For a brief tabular overview of sustainability/CSR/ESG see for example: Wieduwilt, Sabine, in: Wieduwilt, Sabine, Implementing ESG into Real Estate Contracts. A guide and toolkit for practitioners from a European perspective 2025, #1.1.3(a), 22, 23.

14 Redvers/Aubrey/Celidwen/Hill, Indigenous Peoples: Traditional knowledges, climate change, and health, 2023, https://pmc.ncbi.nlm.nih.gov/articles/PMC10575522/, accessed 11.09.2025.

15 Università di Macerata, What is Sustainability?, https://www.unimc.it/farminc/en/mod4/unit4.html, accessed 11.09.2025; Nachhaltigkeit, Begriffsentwicklung, Lexikon der Nachhaltigkeit, 2015, https://www.nachhaltigkeit.info/artikel/begriffsentwicklung_1729.htm, accessed 03.08.2025; Grunwald/ Kopfmüller, Nachhaltigkeit, 3., aktualisierte und erweiterte Auflage, 2022, 21f; von Carlowitz, Hanns Carl Sylvicultura oeconomica, 1713.

16 The term »sustainability« is first mentioned in Carlowitz's work on page 105: »Wird derhalben die gröste Kunst/ Wissenschaft/ Fleiß/ und Einrichtung hiesiger Lande darinnen beruhen/ wie eine sothane Conservation und Anbau des Holtzes anzustellen/ daß es eine continuirliche beständige und nachhaltende Nutzung gebe/ weiln es eine unentberliche Sache ist/ ohne welche das Land in seinem Esse [Existenz] nicht bleiben mag. citation from: Huss/von Gadow, Einführung in das Faksimile der Erstausgabe der Sylvicultura oeconomica von H. C. von Carlowitz, 1713, 2012, https://www.forstbuch.de/wp-content/uploads/2018/04/Carlowitz_1713_Einleitung.pdf, accessed 11.09.2025, 27.

1798 – Thomas **Malthus**, an English economist, proposed the concept of the »**Malthusian trap,**« warning of an impending imbalance between population growth and food resources.[17]

1962 – Rachel **Carson**, a U.S. marine biologist, writer, and conservationist, published »**Silent Spring**«,[18] a book that raised public awareness about the dangers of pesticides and sparked the modern environmental movement.

1969, 1970 – as a result of environmental debate in the U.S., **The National Environmental Policy Act (NEPA, U.S.)** was passed in 1969 and took effect in 1970 and was one of the first laws worldwide to require **systematic environmental impact assessments** for federal projects. This established a foundation for considering environmental effects in project planning.

1968, 1972 – The **Club of Rome** – an informal international association formed in 1968 to foster understanding of the interconnected global challenges facing humanity – commissioned the book »**The Limits to Growth**« in 1972. The book used systems dynamics modeling to warn that unchecked exponential growth in population, industrialization, resource consumption, and pollution would likely exceed the planet's physical limits within a century, leading to potential collapse unless deliberate action was taken to achieve a sustainable global equilibrium.[19]

1972 – At the **United Nations Conference on the Human Environment** in **Stockholm**, the first world conference to make environmental issues a major concern, participants adopted a **series of principles for the sound management of the environment**, including the Stockholm Declaration, the Action Plan for the Human Environment, and several resolutions. The **Stockholm Declaration** contained 26 principles and elevated environmental issues to the forefront of international concerns. It also marked the start of a dialogue between industrialized and developing countries regarding the link between economic growth, air and water pollution, and the well-being of people worldwide. The **Action Plan** contained three main categories, which were broken down into 109 recommendations: (1) Global Environmental Assessment Programme (watch plan); (2) Environmental management activities; (3) International measures to support assessment and management activities carried out at the national and international levels.[20]

---

17 Del Sarto, Nicola, ESG Factors and Financial Outcomes in Banks. Quantitative Insights into the ESG-Cost of Debt Relationship, 2025, 2; thwink.org, Finding and Resolving the Root Causes of the Sustainability Problem, The Malthusian Trap, https://www.thwink.org/sustain/glossary/MalthusianTrap.htm, accessed 11.09.2025.

18 Carson, Rachel, Silent Spring, 1962.

19 Meadows, D H/Meadows, D L/Randers/Behrens, The Limits to Growth. A report for the Club of Rome's project on the predicament of mankind, 1972, https://www.donellameadows.org/wp-content/userfiles/Limits-to-Growth-digital-scan-version.pdf, accessed 03.08.2025; The Origin of »Limits to Growth« – Interview with Dennis Meadows, 14.07.2016, https://www.youtube.com/watch?v=U7Z6h-U4CmI, accessed 12.09.2025.

20 United Nations, Conferences, Environment and Sustainable Development, United Nations Conference on the Human Environment, 5–16 June 1972, Stockholm, https://www.un.org/en/conferences/environment/stockholm1972, accessed 03.08.2025.

1972 – In his lectures at **M.I.T. Ernst Basler's** (company founder and sustainability pioneer[21]) focused on expanding the concept of sustainability. He discussed the need to manage not just forests, but all environmental resources – such as water, soil, air, and biodiversity – in a way that would ensure their availability and health for future generations. Basler emphasized the **interconnectedness of ecological systems** and the importance of **considering long-term impacts** when making decisions about resource use.[22]

1983, 1987 – Within the Framework of the United Nations, the **World Commission on Environment and Development (WCED)** was established. Gro Harlem Brundtland was appointed to chair the commission (»Brundtland Commission«). In 1987 the commission issued the **Brundtland Report**, titled »**Our Common Future**«, intending to address the conflict between globalized economic growth and accelerating ecological degradation by redefining »economic development« in terms of »sustainable development.«[23]

»**Sustainable development** is development that meets the needs of the present without compromising the ability of future generations to meet their own needs.«[24]

According to the report, »sustainable development« requires an integrated approach that considers environmental concerns alongside economic development.[25] Some have stated that sustainability is also defined in the report:

Sustainability can be defined as »meeting the needs of the present without compromising the ability of future generations to meet their own needs«[26], which broadens the scope of sustainability beyond environmental concerns.[27]

The document defines »sustainable development« and uses this as the operative concept, with »sustainability« being an attribute applied to specific systems or processes, rather than a term

21 Basler, Ernst, Our living space is finite, but our capacity for innovation is not, https://www.ebp.global/ch-de/about-ebp/unsere-geschichte, accessed 08.09.2025.

22 Basler, Ernst, Strategy of Progress: Environmental Pollution, Habitat Scarcity and Future Research, 1973 (Strategie des Fortschritts: Umweltbelastung Lebensraumverknappung and Zukunftsforshung, 1973).

23 International Development Research Centre (IDRC) Digital Library/Bibliothèque numérique du CRDI, Brundtland Commission/Commission Brundtland (WCED), https://hdl.handle.net/10625/53401, accessed 11.09.2025.

24 World Commission on Environment and Development (WCED), Our Common Future, 1987, Internet: https://sustainabledevelopment.un.org/content/documents/5987our-common-future.pdf, accessed 03.08.2025, 41; The term »sustainable development« was shaped significantly by the so-called Brundtland Report. Nachhaltigkeit, Begriffsentwicklung, Lexikon der Nachhaltigkeit, 2015, https://www.nachhaltigkeit.info/artikel/begriffsentwicklung_1729.htm, accessed 03.08.2025.

25 United Nations Academic Impact (UNAI), Sustainability, https://www.un.org/en/academic-impact/sustainability, accessed 29.07.2025; United Nations (ed.), Report of the World Commission on Environment and Development: Our Common Future, 1987, accessed 11.09.2025.

26 United Nations Academic Impact (UNAI), Sustainability, https://www.un.org/en/academic-impact/sustainability, accessed 29.07.2025; United Nations (ed.), Report of the World Commission on Environment and Development: Our Common Future, 1987, https://sustainabledevelopment.un.org/content/documents/5987our-common-future.pdf, accessed 11.09.2025.

27 Del Sarto, Nicola, ESG Factors and Financial Outcomes in Banks. Quantitative Insights into the ESG-Cost of Debt Relationship, 2025, 3.

with a separate definition. In the report, the meaning of »sustainability« is always contextual – linked to the ability of systems, resources, or development paths to endure and support both present and future needs. The term »sustainability« is used throughout the report in relation to development, resource use, or specific sectors (e.g., »sustainable energy pathway,« »sustainable industrial development«). While the report discusses the need for »sustainability« in various contexts, such as agriculture, industry, and population, it does not isolate or define »sustainability« as an abstract concept independent of development or sector-specific applications.

There have been numerous attempts to define **sustainability**, which are often very similar in essence.[28] See **three common visualizations of sustainability** in **Table 2**[29] (they are not conclusive).

Figure 1: Three intersecting circles (Venn Diagram)
(Edward Barbier, 1987)[30]

Sustainability is represented by three intersecting circles for environment, economy, and society. Sustainability is where all three overlap.

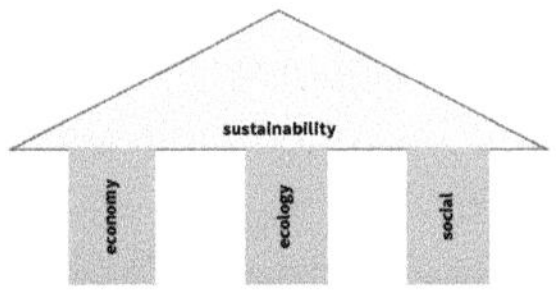

Figure 2: Three Pillars Model (early 1990s, popularized in 1992 with the UN Rio Declaration and Agenda 21, sustainability literature)

There are three pillars of sustainability: environmental, economic, and social; each pillar is equal in rank and supports the overall structure.

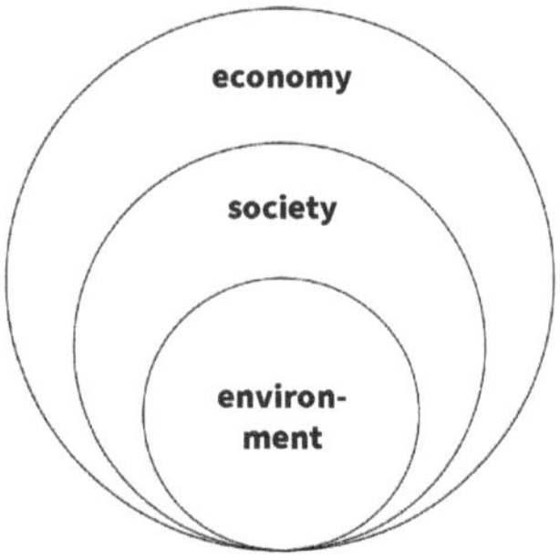

Figure 3: Nested Approach (Nested Ellipses)
(Mary Scott Cato, 2009)[31]

The environment as the foundation, with society nested within it, and the economy nested within society. The nested ellipses emphasize the hierarchy of these dimensions, placing the *environment* at the foundation and highlighting that both society and the economy are constrained by environmental limits.

Table 2: Three common visualizations of sustainability

28 Lexikon der Nachhaltigkeit, Nachhaltigkeit Definition, 2015, https://www.nachhaltigkeit.info/artikel/definitionen_1382.htm, accessed 03.08.2025.

29 For further visualizations of the 3-pillar model, see for example: Lexikon der Nachhaltigkeit, 2016, https://www.nachhaltigkeit.info/artikel/1_3_a_drei_saeulen_modell_1531.htm, accessed 03.08.2025.

30 Barbier, Edward, The Concept of Sustainable Economic Development, in: Environmental Conservation, 1987, vol. 14, issue 2, 101–110

31 Cato, Scott, Green Economics, 2009, 36–37.

1992 – At the **United Nations Conference on Environment and Development (UNCED)** in **Rio de Janeiro** in **1992**, The **Agenda 21** was adopted, a comprehensive action plan for achieving sustainable development globally, nationally, and locally. ‹Integration of Environment and Development: Agenda 21 opens with a clear statement of the need for integration: »Humanity stands at a defining moment in history. We are confronted with a perpetuation of disparities between and within nations, a worsening of poverty, hunger, ill health and illiteracy, and the continuing deterioration of the ecosystems on which we depend for our well-being. However, integration of environment and development concerns and greater attention to them will lead to the fulfilment of basic needs, improved living standards for all, better protected and managed ecosystems and a safer, more prosperous future.«[32] Both the Agenda 21 and the **Rio Declaration** emphasized the integration of the three dimensions environmental, economic, and social into sustainable development policy.

2000 – Building upon a decade of United Nations conferences and summits, world leaders gathered at the United Nations Headquarters in New York to adopt the United Nations Millennium Declaration. This declaration committed their nations to a new global partnership to reduce extreme poverty and set out a series of time-bound targets – with a deadline of 2015 – that have become known as the **Millennium Development Goals.**[33]

2015 – The United Nations General Assembly adopted the resolution »Transforming our world: the 2030 Agenda for Sustainable Development« (**Agenda 2030**), which sets out a **15-year plan** for global sustainable development under the guiding motto »**Transforming our World,**« paraphrased as »**People, Planet, Prosperity, Peace and Partnership**« (see **Figure 4**).

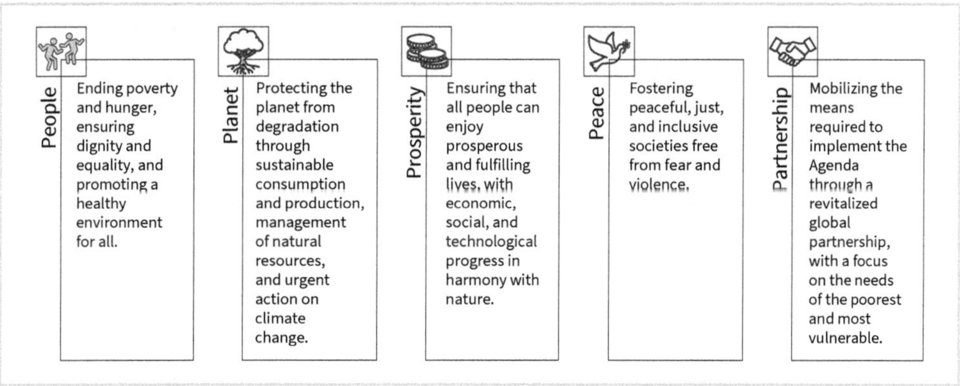

Figure 4: Agenda 2030 – 5 Ps

32 UNCED, Agenda 21: Program of Action for Sustainable Development, 1992, https://sustainabledevelopment.un.org/outcomedocuments/agenda21, accessed 03.08.2025, Preamble, 1.1.

33 United Nations, Millenium Development Goals and Beyond 2015, https://www.un.org/millenniumgoals/bkgd.shtml, accessed 03.08.2025.

Figure 5: UN SDGs

At the heart of this agenda are the **17 Sustainable Development Goals (SDGs)**, with 169 targets, providing a comprehensive framework for advancing sustainability worldwide. The SDGs are a call to action for all countries – rich, poor, and middle-income – to promote prosperity while protecting the planet. They recognize that ending poverty must go hand in hand with strategies that stimulate economic growth and address a range of social needs, including education, health, social protection, and job opportunities, while tackling climate change and protecting the environment.[34]

The Agenda 2030 further states that sustainable development aims to ensure that »all human beings can fulfil their potential in dignity and equality and in a healthy environment,« while also protecting the planet from degradation, ensuring prosperity, fostering peaceful and inclusive societies, and revitalizing global partnerships. Implementation of the 2030 Agenda is country-led; each nation is responsible for integrating the Sustainable Development Goals into national strategies and policies, while systematic reporting and follow-up are ensured through regular national, regional, and global reviews. The High-Level Political Forum oversees global progress using a framework of indicators and high-quality, timely, and disaggregated data to track and assess achievement of the goals.[35] While the Agenda 2030 does not offer a concise, standalone definition of »sustainability« or »sustainable development,« it thoroughly describes these concepts as a holistic, integrated approach to advancing the economic, social, and environmental well-being of present and future generations while ensuring that »no one is left behind.«

34 United Nations (ed.), Transforming our world: the 2030 Agenda for Sustainable Development, https://sdgs.un.org/2030agenda, accessed 12.09.2025; UN, UN Sustainable Development Goals, https://www.un.org/sustainabledevelopment/, accessed 29.07.2025.

35 United Nations, Transforming our world: the 2030 Agenda for Sustainable Development, https://sdgs.un.org/2030agenda; United Nations Academic Impact (UNAI), Sustainability, https://www.un.org/en/academic-impact/sustainability, accessed 29.07.2025.

Conrads/Serode/Sauer/Tauberschmitt[36] have described **three phases** of the development of sustainability. The concept of sustainability has evolved through these three distinct phases, each reflecting a deeper understanding of the interconnectedness of environmental, social, and economic factors.

The **first phase** emerged in the **early 1970s** and focused on resource constraints and the potential limits to economic development. Influenced by the Club of Rome's 1972 report »**The Limits to Growth,**« this phase emphasized the finite nature of Earth's resources and the necessity of prudent management to prevent depletion and environmental degradation. It marked the beginning of global awareness and advocacy for sustainable resource use.

The **second phase gained prominence in the 1980s** and expanded the focus to include the environmental impacts of human activities and the responsibility toward future generations. This phase highlighted the negative effects of pollution, deforestation, and other forms of environmental degradation, emphasizing the concept of intergenerational equity. It underscored the need to address short- and medium-term environmental challenges while considering their long-term implications for future generations.

The **third phase, which began in the late 1980s and continues to this day**, takes **a holistic and long-term approach to sustainability.** Influenced by the Brundtland Commission's 1987 report »Our Common Future,« this phase integrates economic, social, and environmental dimensions into a comprehensive framework for sustainable development. It emphasizes long-term planning and considering sustainability impacts over extended time horizons and recognizes sustainability as a global guiding principle. This phase underscores the importance of continuous adaptation and innovation in sustainability practices to address emerging challenges and ensure a resilient and equitable future for all.

1.2.3 Corporate Social Responsibility (CSR)

According to *Del Sarto,* Corporate Social Responsibility (CSR) is a concept intimately connected to sustainability, reputation, and the role of companies in society.[37] According to *Dathe et al.*, the fundamental concept of CSR is based on the idea that businesses have the responsibility to ensure that their operations do not negatively impact society or the environment.[38]

36 Conrads/Serode/Sauer/Tauberschmitt: Vier Grundprinzipien der ESG-Transformation als Basis der teleologischen Auslegung – Teil 1 ESG 2023, 168; Conrads/Wilke/Sauer: Vier Grundprinzipien der ESG-Transformation als Basis der teleologischen Auslegung – Teil 2 ESG 2023, 292.

37 Del Sarto, Nicola, ESG Factors and Financial Outcomes in Banks. Quantitative Insights into the ESG-Cost of Debt Relationship, 2025, 23.

38 Dathe, T/Helmhold, M/Dathe, R/Dathe, I, Implementing Environmental, Social and Governance (ESG) Principles for Sustainable Businesses, 2024, 24.

1953 – The term Corporate Social Responsibility (CSR) was mentioned by *Howard R.* ***Bowen*** in his book »**Social Responsibilities of the Businessman**«, in which he advocated large corporations in the United States to contribute more to civil society. Bowen raised the question of what responsibilities society could reasonably expect from business leaders.[39]

1960s, 1970s – **Social movements** such as the civil rights, the consumer, the environmental and the women's movements played an important role in shaping the development of societal expectations towards corporations.[40] In 1960, Keith Davis argued that social considerations should take precedence over pure profit motives.[41]

For three **CSR models** to visualize the concept: 1971–1979/1983/1991–1997, see **Table 3**.

<table>
<tr>
<td>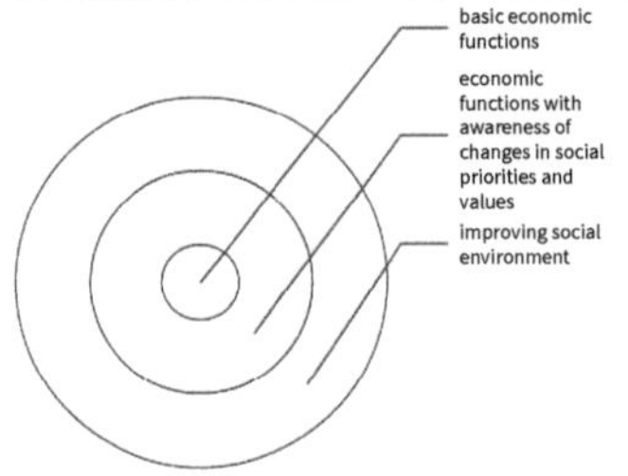

Figure 6: Social Responsibilities of Business Corporations (Del Sarto, based on CED report, 1971)</td>
<td>

Figure 7: Pyramid of Corporate Social Responsibility (Archie B. Carroll, 1991)</td>
<td>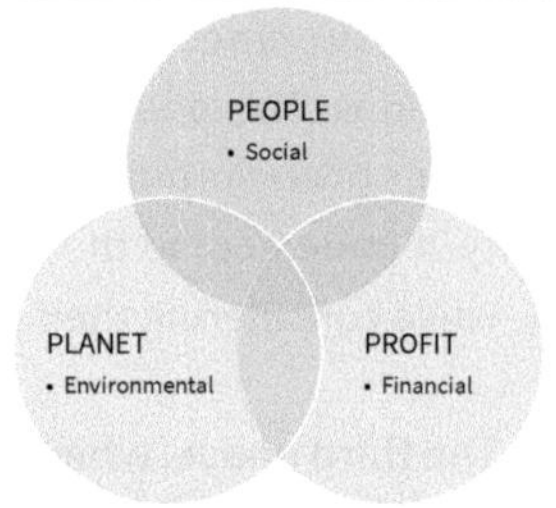

Figure 8: Triple Bottom Line (TBL, John Elkington, 1997)</td>
</tr>
<tr>
<td>CSR as a multi-layered concept consisting of three concentric circles: core economic responsibilities, broader societal expectations and addressing emerging social issues.</td>
<td>»Stated in more pragmatic and managerial terms, the CSR firm should strive to make a profit, obey the law, be ethical and be a good corporate citizen.«</td>
<td>Companies should measure success not only in terms of economic performance, but also in terms of environmental and social impact.[42]</td>
</tr>
</table>

Table 3: Three models to visualize the concept of CSR

1971 – The **Committee for Economic Development (CED)**, a U.S.-based nonprofit public policy think tank, issued a report titled »Social Responsibilities of Business Corporations«. The report called to redefine the corporate mission, proposing that businesses support »human values« by contributing to social progress, even at the expense of short-term profits. In this report, CED introduced the idea of CSR as a multi-layered concept consisting of three concentric circles: the innermost circle representing core economic responsibilities; the intermediate circle representing broader societal expectations; and the outermost circle representing emerging social issues.[43]

---

39 Spießhofer, Birgit, § 5 Corporate Social Responsibility – neue Formen normativer Steuerung im globalen Ordnungsrahmen, in: Burgi/Habersack, Handbuch Öffentliches Recht des Unternehmens, 1. Auflage 2023, Rn. 3.

40 Dathe, T/Helmhold, M/Dathe, R/Dathe, I, Implementing Environmental, Social and Governance (ESG) Principles for Sustainable Businesses, 2024, 25.

41 Del Sarto, Nicola, ESG Factors and Financial Outcomes in Banks. Quantitative Insights into the ESG-Cost of Debt Relationship, 2025, 24.

42 Del Sarto, Nicola, ESG Factors and Financial Outcomes in Banks. Quantitative Insights into the ESG-Cost of Debt Relationship, 2025, 30.

43 Del Sarto, Nicola, ESG Factors, 24, 25–27.

1979 – A shift was noted (i.a. by Carroll) in the strategic placement of CSR in organizational policy. **Carroll** developed a three-dimensional conceptual model of corporate social performance, proposing a four-part-definition. According to this definition, businesses must address a range of obligations toward society. Social responsibility must comprise all four categories of responsibilities: economic, legal, ethical, and discretionary. Carroll revisited his four-part definition of CSR in 1983, repositioning the discretionary component to include volunteerism and/or philanthropy. In 1991, Carroll redesigned the model into the »**Pyramid of Corporate Social Responsibility.**« See Figure 7, as a metaphor for the economic responsibilities being the foundation.[44]

1997 – The emphasis on environmental sustainability paralleled with the development of CSR, leading to the establishment of frameworks such as **Elkington's Triple Bottom Line (TBL)** (see Figure 8). This framework proposes that companies measure success not only by economic performance, but also by environmental and social impact.[45]

In the **1990s**, there was a growing discussion about accountability and the need for formal reporting and transparent communication of a company's commitments and achievements in the context of social responsibility towards all stakeholders.[46]

2000s – The turn of the millennium brought heightened attention to the environmental impact of human activities, prompting **Stoermer** to introduce the term »**Anthropocene**«.[47]

21st century – CSR expanded to encompass sustainability as the concept of ESG gained prominence.[48]

2001 – The OECD published »**OECD Guidelines and Corporate Social Responsibility in a Global Economy,**«[49] defining CSR as an evolving, holistic approach in which businesses integrate social, environmental, and ethical responsibilities into their core strategies. The report emphasized that CSR goes beyond philanthropy, requiring responsible governance, transparent reporting, and sustainable development, and highlighted the need for voluntary initiatives, supportive public policy, and global standards to guide responsible business conduct. The document aimed to promote CSR as essential for sustainable growth and long-term business success in a globalized world. **Figure 9**, based on the **OECD's 2001 document** for **key content of CSR**, illustrates its **role in the global economy**, and **implementation and challenges**. According to the document, CSR was anticipated to become a core component of business strategy and operations, driving sustainable development and long-term success through innovation,

44 Del Sarto, Nicola, ESG Factors, 25, 27–30. See Carroll revisiting the pyramid of CSR in 2016: Carroll, Archie B, Carroll's pyramid of CSR: taking another look. International Journal of Corporate Social Responsibility, International Journal of Corporate Social Responsibility, 2016, https://jcsr.springeropen.com/articles/10.1186/s40991-016-0004-6#citeas, accessed 29.10.2025.

45 Del Sarto, Nicola, ESG Factors, 25.

46 Del Sarto, Nicola, ESG Factors, 30.

47 Del Sarto, Nicola, ESG Factors, 30.

48 Del Sarto, Nicola, ESG Factors, 25.

49 Organisation for Economic Co-operation and Development (OECD), OECD Guidelines and Corporate Social Responsibility in a Global Economy, 2001.

transparency, and collaboration among all stakeholders. The OECD's 2001 document also differentiates between normative frameworks and instruments and delineates as well as provides examples of each (see subchapter #1.3 for more detail).

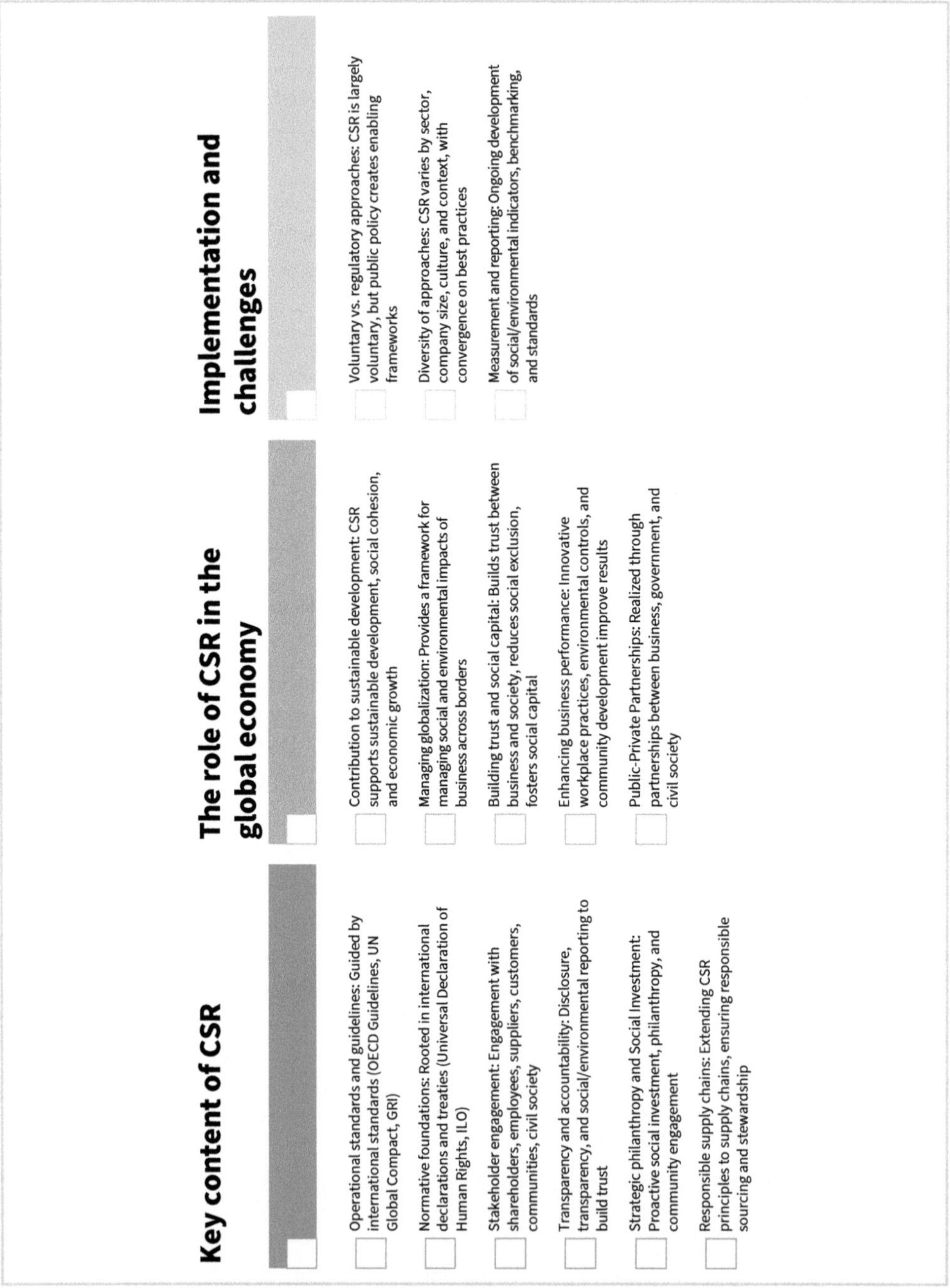

Figure 9: CSR – key content, role in global economy, implementation and challenges (based on OECD 2001)

2001 – In the **European Union's (EU) Green Paper on CSR »Promoting a European framework for Corporate Social Responsibility«**[50], the EU formally adopts CSR, defining it as a concept whereby companies voluntarily integrate social and environmental concerns into their business operations and stakeholder interactions.[51]

> *Spießhofer*[52] – CSR was developed in response to the limitations of traditional legal frameworks. The globalization of the economy and the growing power of corporations create a demand for a corresponding assumption of responsibility. There is a recognized need for a global eco-social regulatory framework that can effectively govern transnational business activities and establish a »level playing field« for all market participants. While setting standards for responsible business conduct, these legal frameworks, especially national laws, are limited by their territorial scope and lack of extraterritorial effect, unable to adequately regulate global business processes. The idea of a world government or world law is neither feasible nor desirable. International treaties are often slow to negotiate, depend on state ratification, and typically result in only minimal consensus.[53]
>
> The concept of CSR began as a voluntary commitment by businesses to address social and environmental issues, with a focus on individual ethical responsibility. Over time, the focus shifted from individual to corporate responsibility, with increasing attention being given to the collective obligations of companies.[54]

2011 – In its **strategy for 2011–2014**, the **Commission (EU) redefined CSR** as the responsibility of enterprises for their impact on society and, therefore, it should be company-led. Companies can become socially responsible by (i) integrating social, environmental, ethical, consumer, and human rights concerns into their business strategy and operations; and (ii) following the law,[55] in short:

»**Corporate social responsibility (CSR)**«, is »the responsibility of enterprises for their impacts on society«.[56]

---

50 Commission of the European Communities, Green Paper: Promoting a European Framework for Corporate Social Responsibility, 18.07.2001, https://eur-lex.europa.eu/LexUriServ/LexUriServ.do?uri=COM:2001:0366:FIN:en:PDF, accessed 06.09.2025; see summary: European Union, eurolex, Summaries of EU Legislation, Green Paper on corporate social responsibility, https://eur-lex.europa.eu/EN/legal-content/summary/green-paper-on-corporate-social-responsibility.html, accessed 06.09.2025.

51 Spießhofer, Birgit, § 5 Corporate Social Responsibility – neue Formen normativer Steuerung im globalen Ordnungsrahmen, in: Burgi/Habersack, Handbuch Öffentliches Recht des Unternehmens, 1. Auflage 2023, Rn. 4.

52 Spießhofer, § 5 Corporate Social Responsibility, Rn. 1.

53 Spießhofer, § 5 Corporate Social Responsibility, Rn. 1; Organisation for Economic Co-operation and Development (OECD), OECD Guidelines and Corporate Social Responsibility in a Global Economy, 2001.

54 Spießhofer, § 5 Corporate Social Responsibility, Rn. 4.

55 EC, Corporate sustainability and responsibility, https://single-market-economy.ec.europa.eu/industry/sustainability/corporate-sustainability-and-responsibility_en, accessed 03.08.2025.

56 Spießhofer, § 5 Corporate Social Responsibility, Rn. 4.

While compliance with applicable law is established as the minimum standard, companies are also expected to implement processes that integrate social, environmental, ethical, human rights, and consumer concerns into their strategies and operations, in close cooperation with stakeholders.[57] »Corporate Social Responsibility (CSR) refers to the comprehensive responsibility of companies for the social, ecological, and economic impacts of their core business activities, emphasizing that responsible and sustainable business practices should be integrated into all operations and go beyond mere philanthropy or compliance with legal requirements. The EU Commission now supports a broader, more binding approach to CSR, advocating for legal measures such as mandatory disclosure of social and environmental information and the application of high standards throughout the entire value chain, both domestically and internationally.«[58]

2011 – The Organization for Economic Co-operation and Development (OECD) used the term **Responsible Business Conduct (RBC)** in its update of the OECD Guidelines for Multinational Enterprises. This change from »Corporate Social Responsibility (CSR)« to the broader and more actionable concept of »Responsible Business Conduct (RBC)« reflected a move toward integrating responsible practices into all aspects of business operations, emphasizing not just voluntary initiatives but also the expectation that companies avoid and address adverse impacts related to human rights, labor, environment, and anti-corruption throughout their global operations and supply chains.[59] The OECD has defined RBC as follows:

»**Responsible Business Conduct (RBC)**« is defined as »making a positive contribution to economic, environmental and social progress with a view to achieving sustainable development and avoiding and addressing adverse impacts related to an enterprise's direct and indirect operations, products or services.«[60,61]

2011 – **John Ruggie** presented his **final report as the Special Representative of the Secretary General on the issue of human rights and transnational corporations and other business enterprises.** It summarizes his work from 2005 to 2011 and **presents the »Guiding Principles on Business and Human Rights: Implementing the United Nations ›Protect, Respect and Remedy« Framework«** for consideration by the Human Rights Council. No. 6 of the Introduction to the Guiding Principles states: »**The Framework rests on three pillars.** The first is the **State duty to protect** against human rights abuses by third parties, including

57 Spießhofer, § 5 Corporate Social Responsibility, Rn. 4.

58 Lexikon der Nachhaltigkeit, Corporate Social Responsibility (CSR), https://www.nachhaltigkeit.info/artikel/corporate_social_responsibility_unternehmerische_1499.htm, accessed 03.08.2025.

59 According to the Commission (EU), Responsible Business Conduct (RBC) is an alternative term introduced by the OECD in close cooperation with business, trade unions and non-governmental organisations: EC, Corporate sustainability and responsibility, https://single-market-economy.ec.europa.eu/industry/sustainability/corporate-sustainability-and-responsibility_en, accessed 03.08.2025.

60 OECD, Responsible Business Conduct, https://www.oecd.org/en/topics/responsible-business-conduct.html, accessed 12.09.2025.

61 EC, Corporate sustainability and responsibility, https://single-market-economy.ec.europa.eu/industry/sustainability/corporate-sustainability-and-responsibility_en, accessed 03.08.2025.

business enterprises, through appropriate policies, regulation, and adjudication. The second is the **corporate responsibility to respect** human rights, which means that business enterprises should act with due diligence to avoid infringing on the rights of others and to address adverse impacts with which they are involved. The third is the **need for greater access by victims to effective remedy**, both judicial and non-judicial. Each pillar is an essential component in an inter-related and dynamic system of preventative and remedial measures: the State duty to protect because it lies at the very core of the international human rights regime; the corporate responsibility to respect because it is the basic expectation society has of business in relation to human rights; and access to remedy because even the most concerted efforts cannot prevent all abuse«[62]. The UN Guiding Principles on Business and Human Rights (UNGP) were annexed to the report. The Commission (EU) states in relation to the UNGP: »Human rights are an increasingly important aspect of CSR/RBC, especially when it comes to businesses' global supply chains. The UN guiding principles on business and human rights (UNGPs) define what companies and governments should do so businesses don't have a negative impact on human rights. These guiding principles were endorsed by the UN Human Rights Council in 2011, stating that business enterprises are specialized organs of society, which requires them to comply with all applicable laws and to respect human rights.«[63] The UNGP expand the responsibilities beyond the internal sphere of the company – »piercing the corporate veil«. This concept was also introduced in the OECD.

62 Human Rights Council, Report of the Special Representative of the Secretary General on the issue of human rights and transnational corporations and other business enterprises, John Ruggie. Guiding Principles on Business and Human Rights: Implementing the United Nations »Protect, Respect and Remedy« Framework, 2011, https://www.ohchr.org/sites/default/files/Documents/Issues/Business/A-HRC-17-31_AEV.pdf, accessed 06.09.2025; see separate UNGP, https://www.ohchr.org/sites/default/files/documents/publications/guidingprinciplesbusinesshr_en.pdf, accessed 06.09.2025.

63 EC, Corporate sustainability and responsibility, https://single-market-economy.ec.europa.eu/industry/sustainability/corporate-sustainability-and-responsibility_en, accessed 03.08.2025.

The role of international organizations: The United Nations (UN), the Organization for Economic Cooperation and Development (OECD), and the International Organization for Standardization (ISO) develop key frameworks and guidelines, such as the UN Global Compact, the OECD Guidelines for Multinational Enterprises, and ISO 26000, which set out principles for responsible business conduct on a global scale.[64]

Regarding sustainability and CSR, the German Federal Ministry of Labor and Social Affairs states that »CSR refers to a company's responsibility for its impact on society. This includes social, environmental and economic aspects, as for example outlined in the internationally recognized reference documents on CSR, chief among them the fundamental ILO declaration on multinational enterprises and social policy, the OECD Guidelines for Multinational enterprises, the UN Guiding Principles on Business and Human Rights, the UN Global Compact and ISO 26000. More specifically, CSR for example involves fair business practices, staff-oriented human resource management, economical use of natural resources, protection of the climate and environment, sincere commitment to the local community and also responsibility along the global supply chain.«[65]

> *Spießhofer*[66] – Corporate responsibility is viewed as both a positive goal of maximizing shared value for owners, stakeholders, and society, and a negative obligation of preventing and mitigating harm. CSR is not considered to be in opposition to shareholder value, but rather as being essential to its long-term promotion and sustainability. The boundaries of corporate conduct are shifting from mere legality to legitimacy, evolving from a »legal license to operate« to a »social license to operate.« Companies are increasingly expected to meet societal expectations and normative standards, rather than just legal requirements. CSR is characterized by a »smart mix« of voluntary measures, regulations,

64 Spießhofer, Birgit, Sustainable Corporate Governance, NZG 2022, 435, 438; Spießhofer, Birgit § 5 Corporate Social Responsibility – neue Formen normativer Steuerung im globalen Ordnungsrahmen, in: Burgi/Habersack, Handbuch Öffentliches Recht des Unternehmens, 1. Auflage 2023, Rn. 25, 86.

65 CSR, (initiative by) German Federal Ministry of Labour and Social Affairs, Sustainability and CSR, https://www.csr-in-deutschland.de/EN/CSR/Background/Sustainability-and-CSR/sustainability-and-csr.html, accessed 29.07.2025; United Nations Human Rights Office of the High Commissioner, Guiding Principles on Business Human Rights, http://www.ohchr.org/Documents/Publications/GuidingPrinciplesBusinessHR_EN.pdf, accessed 13.09.2025; UN, UN 2030 agenda for sustainable development, https://www.un.org/sustainabledevelopment/development-goals/, accessed 13.09.2025; UN Global Compact, https://unglobalcompact.org/, accessed 13.09.2025; International Standard for Organization (ISO), ISO 26000 Social responsibility, https://www.iso.org/iso-26000-social-responsibility.html, accessed 13.09.2025; OECD, Responsible Business Conduct, 2018, https://www.oecd.org/en/topics/policy-issues/responsible-business-conduct.html, accessed 13.09.2025; OECD, OECD Due Diligence Guidance for Responsible Business Conduct, https://www.oecd.org/en/publications/oecd-due-diligence-guidance-for-responsible-business-conduct_15f5f4b3-en.html, accessed 13.09.2025; International Labour Organization (ILO), Tripartite declaration of principles concerning multinational enterprises and social policy (MNE Declaration), 2022, https://www.ilo.org/publications/tripartite-declaration-principles-concerning-multinational-enterprises-and-3, accessed 13.09.2025.

66 Spießhofer, Birgit, § 5 Corporate Social Responsibility, Rn. 2, 42, 58, Spießhofer, Birgit, Sustainable Corporate Governance, NZG 2022, 435, 436.

market incentives, and accountability mechanisms. Companies are expected to take the lead in developing CSR strategies, with support from governments, civil society, consumers, investors, and the media. The area of responsibility for companies is significantly broadened, extending beyond the internal sphere to include the entire value chain and supply network. The UN Guiding Principles on Business and Human Rights (UNGP) and the OECD Guidelines introduce the concept of due diligence, which requires companies to address risks to human rights and the environment throughout their operations and business relationships. With the adoption of the EU CSR-Reporting Directive (2014/95/EU)[67], corporate reporting underwent a paradigm shift. Reporting is no longer just about financial value but also about the company's social and environmental impacts, thereby extending accountability to the public and civil society. The scope of CSR has broadened to include not only compliance with legal requirements but also the proactive identification, prevention, minimization, and compensation of potential negative impacts.

Spießhofer[68] highlights the following regarding the nature of CSR:

Polycentric and pluralistic governance: The regulatory framework for CSR is polycentric, involving multiple actors (both public and private) and various instruments, hard and soft law, education, reputation, and market mechanisms. The distinction between private and public governance is becoming increasingly blurred.

Challenges of fragmentation and complexity: The current landscape of CSR regulation is fragmented and complex, with overlapping standards and actors. This creates challenges for legal certainty, harmonization, and effective implementation.

CSR as a key concept and guiding principle: Rather than having a fixed definition, CSR serves as a key concept and orienting principle in the ongoing debate about the role and responsibility of companies in a globalized world. The underlying normative and cultural expectations are decisive for shaping the content and enforcement of corporate responsibility.

Ongoing evolution: The development of CSR continues to be shaped by new forms of normative regulation, the interplay between soft and hard law, and the dynamic involvement of a wide range of stakeholders at the national, European, and global levels.

67 NFRD, now CSRD, see #6.4.2(c) and (f).

68 Spießhofer, Birgit, § 5 Corporate Social Responsibility, Rn. 9, 18, 42, 45; Spießhofer, Birgit, Sustainable Corporate Governance, NZG 2022, 435, 436.

The concept of Environment, Social, Governance (ESG) has become widely used, often interchangeably with CSR.[69]

1.2.4 Environmental, Social, and Governance (ESG)

What's ESG? See exemplary for introductory purposes a definition from the Commission's (EU) website:

> »ESG can be a framework or criteria to measure the sustainability and ethical impact of an investment or a company focusing on three fields: Environmental, Social and Corporate Governance. While the term ESG is often used in the context of investing, stakeholders include also customers, suppliers, and employees, all of whom are increasingly interested in how sustainable an organization's operations are.«[70]

ESG was first mentioned in the early 2000s, formally introduced in the »Who Cares Wins« report (see below under (b)). However, let's take a step back again (below under (a)).

(a) Pre-ESG

> It is worth mentioning the economic theories, practices, and the paradigm shift that occurred before the 2000s.

1970s–1980s – During this period, economist Milton Friedman articulated the shareholder primacy doctrine,[71] arguing that the only social responsibility of a business is to maximize its profits. Friedman warned that social responsibility initiatives could harm financial performance and that government regulation would damage the macroeconomy. This perspective, known as the Friedman Doctrine, dominated corporate and investment thinking throughout the late 20th century.[72] In the context of the shift from traditional to sustainable finance, Del Sarto[73] describes the economic theories of **shareholder primacy, stakeholder theory** and **shared value theory** (illustrated in **Figure 10**) as the »**theoretical frameworks that support this paradigm shift** toward sustainability, which form the foundation for understanding how and why companies are increasingly expected to adopt socially and environmentally responsible practices«.

69 Spießhofer, Birgit, § 5 Corporate Social Responsibility, Rn. 4. In the publications, the terms »Sustainable Corporate Governance« and »Corporate Political Responsibility« are also used or discussed. We have refrained from introducing or differentiating those terms.

70 EC, Corporate sustainability and responsibility, https://single-market-economy.ec.europa.eu/industry/sustainability/corporate-sustainability-and-responsibility_en, accessed 03.08.2025.

71 CFI Team, Friedman Doctrine, https://corporatefinanceinstitute.com/resources/equities/friedman-doctrine/, accessed 13.09.2025.

72 Wikipedia, Environmental, social, and governance, https://en.wikipedia.org/wiki/Environmental,_social,_and_governance, accessed 06.08.2025.

73 Del Sarto, ESG Factors and Financial Outcomes in Banks, 2025, 32.

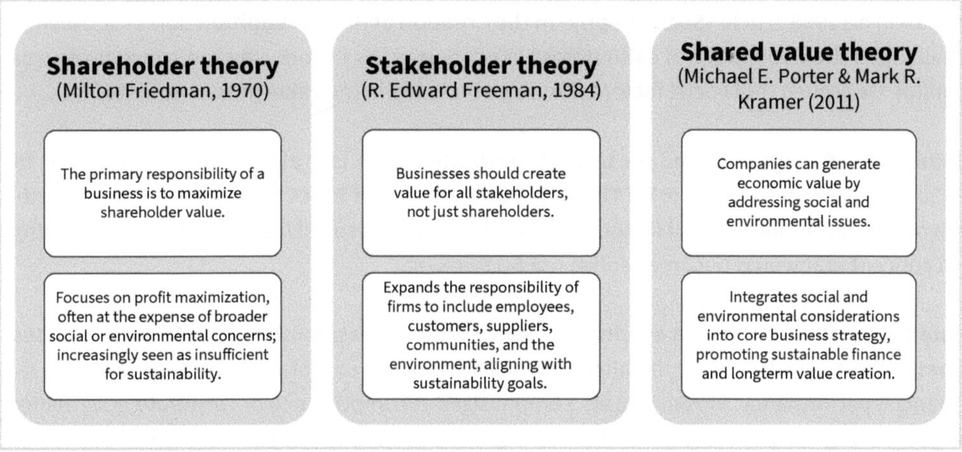

Figure 10: Economic theories »supporting paradigm shift«

The concept of ESG is based on the broader tradition of sustainable and responsible investment (RI) and its variations, such as ethical and socially responsible investing (SRI).

1970s – The origins of ESG investing can be tracked back to the broader movement of **ethical and socially responsible investing (SRI).** In the 1970s, global opposition to South African apartheid led to selective disinvestment, as examples of decisions being guided by ethical and social considerations rather than purely financial ones.[74]

1977 – *The **Sullivan Principles***[75], introduced by Leon Sullivan in 1977, provided a code of conduct for companies operating in apartheid-era South Africa. These principles became a benchmark for ethical investing, encouraging companies and investors to consider social justice and human rights in their business and investment decisions.

1981 – Freer **Spreckley** introduced the **concept of social accounting and auditing**, proposing that organizations should use internal criteria such as financial viability, social wealth creation, organizational governance, and environmental responsibility in their annual planning and reporting. This emphasized the importance of non-financial factors in organizational assessment.[76]

74 Wikipedia, Environmental, social, and governance, https://en.wikipedia.org/wiki/Environmental,_social,_and_governance, accessed 06.08.2025.

75 Quellen zur Geschichte der Menschenrechte, The Sullivan Principles, https://www.geschichte-menschenrechte.de/fileadmin/editorial/download/Sullivan_Principles.pdf, accessed 13.09.2025.

76 Freer Spreckley, Social Enterprise Planning Toolkit, 2011, https://locallivelihoods.com/wp-content/uploads/2020/06/Social-Enterprise-Planning-Toolkit.pdf, accessed 13.09.2025.

1988 – In his 1988 article »**Social Capital in the Creation of Human Capital,**« James S. Coleman challenged the dominance of self-interest in economics by introducing the concept of social capital. He argued that social factors should be included in the value measurements.[77]

1998 – John **Elkington** coined the term »triple bottom line« (see also under CSR, #1.2.3) in his 1998 book **Cannibals with Forks: The Triple Bottom Line of 21st Century Business.** Elkington advocated for the inclusion of financial, environmental, and social factors in business valuation – a concept that would become central to ESG thinking.[78]

Late 1990s–2000s – Robert **Levering** and Milton **Moskowitz** published the »**Fortune 100 Best Companies to Work For« list**, highlighting the link between corporate social responsibility and financial performance. Moskowitz also emphasized the importance of corporate governance, arguing that good governance maximizes productivity and efficiency without harming financial performance.[79]

2000 – **UN Global Compact**, a voluntary corporate responsibility initiative, was launched by Secretary-General of the United Nations Kofi **Annan**. Its primary goal was to implement universal principles in business and encourage businesses to adopt sustainable and socially responsible policies, as well as report on their implementation. This marked a significant shift in the UN's approach, moving from an adversarial stance toward businesses to a more collaborative one, aiming to harness the power of the private sector for global development, human rights, labor standards, and environmental protection.[80]

2003 – The UN convened the **first Institutional Investor Summit on Climate Risk**, which resulted in the creation of the **Investor Network on Climate Risk**, a group of seventy investors with seven trillion dollars in assets. This initiative reflected a growing concern about the financial implications of climate change and the need for investor engagement.[81]

---

77 Coleman, James S, Social Capital in the Creation of Human Capital, https://www.jstor.org/stable/2780243, accessed 13.09.2025.

78 Wikipedia, Environmental, social, and governance, https://en.wikipedia.org/wiki/Environmental,_social,_and_governance, accessed 06.08.2025.

79 Wikipedia, Environmental, social, and governance, https://en.wikipedia.org/wiki/Environmental,_social,_and_governance, accessed 06.08.2025.

80 Ruggie, John Gerard, The United Nations and Globalization: Patterns and Limits of Institutional Adaptation, Global Governance 9, no. 3, 2003, 301–321, https://www.jstor.org/stable/27800413; Thérien/Pouliot, The Global Compact: Shifting the Politics of International Development?, Global Governance 12, no. 1, 2006, 55–75, https://www.jstor.org/stable/27800613; United Nations Global Compact, Our Mission, https://www.unglobalcompact.org/what-is-gc/mission; Pollman, Elizabeth, The Making and Meaning of ESG, Harvard Business Law Review 14, 2024, 404–453, https://ssrn.com/abstract=4219857.

81 Pollman, Elizabeth, The Making and Meaning of ESG, Harvard Business Law Review 14, 2024, 404–453, https://ssrn.com/abstract=4219857; Pargendler, Mariana, The Rise of International Corporate Law, Washington University Law Review 98, no. 6, 2021, 1765–1817, https://openscholarship.wustl.edu/law_lawreview/vol98/iss6/6.

2003 – The **Equator Principles**[82] were launched. Based on existing environmental and social policy frameworks established by the International Finance Corporation,[83] the Equator Principles became a global benchmark for managing environmental and social risk in project finance.

(b) ESG

Introduction of the acronym ESG – According to Del Sarto,[84] the concept of ESG builds on the broader tradition of sustainable and responsible investment (SRI)[85], which has existed much longer. Unlike SRI, however, which is based on ethical principles and moral criteria and often employs negative screening (e.g., avoiding investments in companies involved in alcohol, tobacco, or firearms), ESG investments are founded on the premise that ESG factors are financially relevant. ESG factors cover a wide range of issues that are traditionally outside the scope of financial analysis but that can have a significant financial impact.

According to *Del Sarto*[86], ESG is a widely used yet variably defined framework for evaluating companies and investments based on environmental, social, and governance criteria, and is considered an evolution of CSR that reflects modern social responsibility. The UN Principles for Responsible Investment (UN PRI) offer a leading framework for ESG that is now central to measuring long-term sustainability and signals a broader green transition in markets and society.

2004 – The **term/acronym ESG** was **formally introduced in the United Nations report »Who Cares Wins,«** which was a **joint initiative of financial institutions**. The initiative was launched at the invitation of former UN Secretary-General Kofi Annan, who wrote to the CEOs of 55 of the world's leading financial institutions, inviting them to participate, under the auspices of the UN Global Compact. The report's expressed goal was: »By establishing the link between environmental, social and governance issues and investment decisions, this report wishes to contribute to better integration of these factors in investment decisions which will ultimately support the implementation of the Global Compact principles throughout the business world.«[87] The report emphasized the importance of ESG factors for long-term value creation, risk management, and sustainable development. It advocated for improved disclosure, the integration of ESG into research and investment processes, and the collaboration among market actors, including regulators, companies, investors, and NGOs, to foster more resilient and responsible financial markets. This report marked the transition from the general concept of responsible

82 Equator Principles Association, About the Equator Principles, https://equator-principles.com/about-the-equator-principles/, accessed 07.08.2025.

83 Wikipedia, Equator Principles, https://en.wikipedia.org/wiki/Equator_Principles, accessed 06.08.2025.

84 Del Sarto, Nicola, ESG Factors and Financial Outcomes in Banks. Quantitative Insights into the ESG-Cost of Debt Relationship, 2025, 44.

85 See above under (a) the term for SRI: »*ethical and socially responsible investing (SRI)*«, for a gathering of further terms, see #2.3.2(c).

86 Del Sarto, Nicola, ESG Factors and Financial Outcomes in Banks. Quantitative Insights into the ESG-Cost of Debt Relationship, 2025, 44, 45, 46.

87 Swiss Federal Department of Foreign Affairs/United Nations, Who Cares Wins. Connecting Financial Markets to a Changing World, https://documents1.worldbank.org/curated/en/280911488968799581/pdf/113237-WP-WhoCaresWins-2004.pdf, accessed 07.09.2025.

investing to a more structured framework that focuses on environmental, social, and governance factors.[88]

2005 – The **United Nations Environment Programme Finance Initiative (UNEP FI)** commissioned the law firm Freshfields Bruckhaus Deringer to analyze the legal framework for integrating ESG issues into institutional investment. Freshfields Bruckhaus Deringer then issued a report for UNEP FI. The report concluded that integrating ESG issues into investment analysis was not only permissible and arguably part of the fiduciary duty. It also explored how ESG considerations could be incorporated into legal obligations to benefit beneficiaries and society. The report emphasized that responsible investment that aligns with ESG factors is permissible and increasingly recognized as compatible with fiduciary duties. This legal interpretation helped legitimize ESG integration in mainstream investment practices.[89]

2006 – The **Principles for Responsible Investment (PRI)**, launched by the UN Environment Programme Finance Initiative and the UN Global Compact at the New York Stock Exchange provided a framework for integrating ESG into investment processes, promoting responsible investment practices globally. The initiative was founded on the conviction that ESG issues can affect the financial interests of investors and the performance of investment portfolios and are therefore important to fiduciary duty. The PRI encourages its signatories to incorporate ESG analysis, active ownership, transparency, industry collaboration, and reporting, aiming to foster sustainable capital markets and support UN initiatives, such as the Global Compact and UNEP FI. According to Del Sarto,[90] the »Freshfields Report« demonstrated that ESG issues are relevant to financial evaluations, and numerous academic studies in the following years confirmed that strong corporate sustainability performance is associated with positive financial outcomes.

2006 – Michael **Barnett** and Robert **Salomon** published a **study in 2006** proposing that social responsibility and financial performance could be complementary. They suggested a non-linear, inverted U-shaped relationship between ESG and financial returns. This challenged the assumption that ESG always helps or hurts financial performance. Instead, they posited an optimal level of ESG investment.

2008 – The »**Who Cares Wins**« initiative concluded with a **final report** noting that ESG integration was becoming mainstream, though progress was uneven across environmental, social, and governance issues. The report highlighted that, although corporate governance and

88 United Nations Global Compact et al., Who Cares Wins: Connecting Financial Markets to a Changing World, 2004, https://press.un.org/en/2006/sg2111.doc.htm, accessed 07.09.2025. https://documents1.worldbank.org/curated/en/280911488968799581/pdf/113237-WP-WhoCaresWins-2004.pdf, accessed 07.09.2025.

89 United Nations Environment Programme Finance Initiative (UNEP FI), Asset Management Working Group (AMWG), Freshfields Bruckhaus Deringer, Fiduciary Responsibilities and Responsible Investment Practices, 2005.

90 Del Sarto, Nicola, ESG Factors and Financial Outcomes in Banks. Quantitative Insights into the ESG-Cost of Debt Relationship, 2025, 44.

environmental issues had advanced, social and stakeholder issues lagged behind. The global financial crisis reinforced the need for better risk management, including ESG-related risks.[91]

2010s – ESG terminology and practices spread rapidly, aided by the growing influence of large institutional investors and asset managers.[92] The **Global Reporting Initiative (GRI)** expanded its guidelines to cover ESG issues, and the **PRI's** signatory base grew to include thousands of investors worldwide.[93] ESG became a central theme in corporate governance, investment products, and regulatory discussions.[94]

2011 – Alex **Edmans** demonstrated in a 2011 study, that companies with high employee satisfaction (a social factor) outperformed their peers in terms of stock returns, providing empirical support for the idea that social factors within ESG can have a measurable impact on financial performance.

2014 – The **Law Commission (England and Wales)** confirmed in 2014 that pension trustees could consider ESG factors in investment decisions, further embedding ESG considerations into the legal and regulatory framework for institutional investors.

2015 – A study by **Fried, Bush & Bassen** found a positive link between ESG performance and financial performance in 90 % of cases, suggesting that integrating ESG criteria can reduce risk exposure and improve financial outcomes.

2010s–2020s – The distinction between **ESG risk rating agencies** (such as MSCI and Sustainalytics) and **ESG effectiveness rating agencies** (such as Refinitiv and Moody's) has become important for understanding the difference between measuring exposure to ESG risks and actual ESG impact, reflecting the growing complexity and sophistication of ESG models in the investment industry.

2017 – BlackRock CEO Larry Fink referenced ESG in his annual letter to CEOs, signaling the mainstreaming of ESG considerations among the world's largest asset managers.[95] The »Big

91 IFC/FDFA/UN Global Compact, Outcomes of the Who Cares Wins Initiative 2004–2008: Future Proof? Embedding Environmental, Social and Governance Issues in Investment Markets, 2009, https://documents1.worldbank.org/curated/en/476811468158704493/pdf/476600WP0Futur10Box338858B01PUBLIC1.pdf; Pollman, Elizabeth, The Making and Meaning of ESG, Harvard Business Law Review 14, 2024, 404–453, https://ssrn.com/abstract=4219857.

92 Lund/Pollman, The Corporate Governance Machine, Columbia Law Review 121, no. 7, 2021, 2563–2625, https://columbialawreview.org/content/the-corporate-governance-machine/; Pollman, Elizabeth, The Making and Meaning of ESG, Harvard Business Law Review 14, 2024, 404–453, https://ssrn.com/abstract=4219857; Eccles/Stroehle, Exploring Social Origins in the Construction of ESG Measures, SSRN, 12.07.2018, https://papers.ssrn.com/sol3/papers.cfm?abstract_id=3212685.

93 Global Reporting Initiative (GRI), Our Mission and History, https://www.globalreporting.org/about-gri/mission-history/.

94 Lund/Pollman, The Corporate Governance Machine, Columbia Law Review 121, no. 7, 2021, 2563–2625. https://columbialawreview.org/content/the-corporate-governance-machine/; Pollman, Elizabeth, The Making and Meaning of ESG, Harvard Business Law Review 14, 2024, 404–453, https://ssrn.com/abstract=4219857.

95 BlackRock. Larry Fink's 2017 Letter to CEOs, https://www.blackrock.com/corporate/investor-relations/2017-larry-fink-ceo-letter, accessed 29.10.2025.

Three« (BlackRock, Vanguard, and State Street) began offering ESG funds and engaging with portfolio companies on ESG issues, which further accelerated the adoption of ESG practices.[96]

2020 – BlackRock published one of several surveys, titled »Sustainability Goes Mainstream: 2020 Global Sustainable Investing Survey«, which analyzed global investor attitudes and behaviors regarding sustainable investing. The survey revealed that sustainability considerations were becoming central to investment decisions, with the environmental dimension emerging as the most prominent ESG factor.[97]

2020s – ESG became a ubiquitous term in global finance, corporate governance, and regulatory policy. However, its flexible and evolving definition has led to challenges, including confusion over its meaning, the proliferation of inconsistent ESG ratings, and criticism regarding greenwashing and the effectiveness of ESG investing. Political backlash, particularly in the United States, intensified, with some viewing ESG as ideologically driven or »woke capitalism«. Regulatory efforts to standardize ESG disclosures, such as the SEC's climate disclosure rules and the EU's Corporate Sustainability Reporting Directive, have faced both support and legal challenges (SEC 2022; EU Commission 2024).[98]

2021 – The **EU Sustainable Finance Disclosure Regulation (SFDR)** advanced ESG disclosure and standardization further.

2024 – Recent research by **Susen & Etter** (2024) found that higher levels of ESG performance (ESG tilt) and changes in ESG performance over time (ESG momentum) are positively correlated with increased employee satisfaction in S&P 500 companies. This correlation is mediated by perceptions of organizational justice and expectations of future rewards.

2024 – The debate over the meaning, utility, and future of ESG continued, with proposals to redefine, narrow, or even abandon the term[99]. The flexibility that enabled the global spread of ESG is now seen as a source of both its strength and its most significant challenges.[100]

---

96 Lund, Dorothy S, Asset Managers as Regulators, University of Pennsylvania Law Review 171, no. 1, 2022, 77–144. https://scholarship.law.upenn.edu/penn_law_review/vol171/iss1/2; Barzuza/Curtis/Webber, Shareholder Value(s): Index Fund ESG Activism and the New Millennial Corporate Governance, Southern California Law Review 93, no. 6, 2020, 1243–1296, https://southerncalifornialawreview.com/2020/09/01/shareholder-values-index-fund-esg-activism-and-the-new-millennial-corporate-governance-article-by-michal-barzuza-quinn-curtis-david-h-webber/.

97 See #6.5 on changes of Blackrock's position.

98 Pollman, Elizabeth, The Making and Meaning of ESG, Harvard Business Law Review 14, 2024, 404–453, https://ssrn.com/abstract=4219857.

99 The Economist, Measure Less, But Better, 21.07.2022, https://www.economist.com/special-report/2022/07/21/measure-less-but-better; Edmans, Alex, The End of ESG, European Corporate Governance Institute (ECGI) Working Paper No. 847, 2022, https://papers.ssrn.com/sol3/papers.cfm?abstract_id=4221990.

100 Pollman, Elizabeth, The Making and Meaning of ESG, Harvard Business Law Review 14, 2024, 404–453, https://ssrn.com/abstract=4219857.

(c) Discussion, critique and trends

Trends

From **voluntary to mandatory standards** and **back to voluntary again**: the EU's Sustainable Finance Disclosure Regulation (SFDR) and the Corporate Sustainability Due Diligence Directive (CSDDD) are examples of increasing regulatory requirements. With the EU's simplification package, the EU is partly reverting to voluntary standards again or at least reducing the mandatory requirements.[101]

The alignment and interoperability of standards are being promoted through international cooperation with organizations such as the IPSF and ISSB, which work to harmonize frameworks.

ESG criticism

The term/acronym ESG is being questioned. Are new acronyms introduced to replace ESG? For example: Geopolitics Sustainability Economics (GSE)[102].

Pollman[103], in her Harvard Business Review article »Summary of« The Making and Meaning of ESG'« took a critical stance to the current use of ESG. The article explores the term's history, diverse usages, and implications in corporate governance and investment. It traces ESG's origins to United Nations initiatives and highlights how the term was coined through collaboration between the UN and major financial industry players without a precise definition or clear normative goals.

Over time, ESG has evolved to encompass a wide range of meanings, from a set of factors for investment analysis and risk management to a synonym for corporate social responsibility (CSR), sustainability, or even an ideological or political stance. This flexibility has contributed to the global spread and mainstream adoption of ESG, attracting trillions of dollars in investment and prompting companies and regulators to develop ESG policies.

However, the article critiques the broad and unfixed definition of ESG, arguing that combining environmental, social, and governance factors into one term has led to confusion, unrealistic expectations, and challenges such as greenwashing and »sustainability arbitrage.« This lack of clarity makes it difficult to empirically demonstrate a causal relationship between ESG and financial performance and has resulted in a proliferation of inconsistent ESG ratings.

The article also discusses the political and ideological backlash against ESG, particularly in the United States, where the term has become »weaponized« and is facing regulatory and legisla-

101 See also chapters #6.4.2; #5.3.

102 Steinmüller, Thomas, ESG is out, GSE is in, May 2025, https://www.linkedin.com/feed/update/urn:li:activity:7331911204061200384/, accessed 31.05.2025.

103 Pollman, Elizabeth, The Making and Meaning of ESG, Harvard Business Law Review 14, 2022, 404.

tive challenges. These critiques are intertwined with the original flexibility and ambiguity of ESG, creating obstacles for the future of the ESG movement and regulatory reform.

Ultimately, the article emphasizes the need for greater clarity and careful consideration of ESG's future role in corporate and financial practices, noting that the ambiguity of its normative goals must be resolved to address ongoing challenges and critiques.

Defenders of the concept

Highlighting the benefits for companies

CSR initiative by German Federal Ministry of Labour and Social Affairs:

Sustainably managed companies tend to *achieve greater long-term success* due to an enhanced reputation, increased efficiency, reduced risks, and improved innovation, while also *attracting institutional investors* who increasingly prioritize sustainability in their investment decisions.[104]

Three UN PRI blogs 2021, 2023, 2024:

2021 – Industry research shows correlations between higher ESG rankings and better risk-adjusted equity returns. However, results vary by geography, sector, company size, and quality. Governance factors are most consistently linked to performance, while environmental and social impacts differ by context.[105]

2023 – Climate risk is increasingly recognized as central to investment risk, though challenges in measurement persist. Governance remains the strongest ESG predictor of returns, and ESG funds – particularly those with higher ESG rankings – demonstrated resilience during the recent market volatility. However, sector exposures, such as underweighting energy, affected outcomes.[106]

2024 – While ESG factors have historically been associated with strong investment performance, recent market shifts have complicated this relationship. Some studies show that -ESG companies continue to outperform, while others find little or no link. Overall, ESG's impact on returns remains nuanced and context-dependent. Integrating ESG factors can offer potential downside protection and lower risk.[107]

---

104 CSR, (initiative by) German Federal Ministry of Labour and Social Affairs, CSR, Benefits for companies, https://www.csr-in-deutschland.de/EN/CSR/Benefits-for-Companies/benefits-for-companies-article.html, accessed 29.07.2025.

105 Belsom, Toby, UN PRI, PRI Blog, ESG factors and equity returns – a review of recent industry research, 2021, https://www.unpri.org/pri-blog/esg-factors-and-equity-returns-a-review-of-recent-industry-research/7867.article, accessed 07.09.2025.

106 Belsom, Toby, UN PRI, PRI Blog, Part II: ESG factors and returns – a review of industry research since 2021, 2023, https://www.unpri.org/pri-blog/part-ii-esg-factors-and-returns-a-review-of-industry-research-since-2021/11113.article, accessed 07.09.2025.

107 Bartek, Michal, UN PRI, PRI Blog, Part III: ESG factors and returns – a review of recent research, 2024, https://www.unpri.org/pri-blog/part-iii-esg-factors-and-returns-a-review-of-recent-research/12728.article, accessed 07.09.2025.

About the critical assessment of ESG

There's the fashionable phrase that keeps ringing in my ears »*sustainability/CSR/ESG is too expensive*«. Instead of indulging on whether this is right or wrong, I'll add a quote from Carroll on »CSR«: »*The traditional thought is that resources spent for legal ethical and philanthropic purposes might necessarily detract from profitability. But according to this case for CSR this is not a valid assumption or conclusion.*«[108]

»*Policy incoherence*« is not based on the term being unclear. If we don't understand how sustainable finance laws and standards are supposed to work together, it may be based on the evolving nature of the concept and that the practical implications still need to be further refined. Sometimes, they are not well-interlinked, sometimes, we have too many different rules from various rule-setters at various levels[109], tending to push »greenwashing« risks to businesses, when those setting the rules have themselves not set completely clear, coherent, or practical rules, or set rules in isolation to the other rules »out there«, leaving some questions about coherence unanswered when the industry has put a lot of effort into coming together. If this is correct, what do we do about it?

In any case, we may have to be careful about *one-sided views* when thinking about policing others, *moralizing business* – other businesses or regions because we think we're the only ones knowing what's right[110]. We can perhaps act on this by starting to change our own – personal, company's, state's, etc. – actions before we change others, or at least think twice before we become too judgmental.

»*Unclear and hence does not make sense*« – If we look into the background of sustainability/CSR/ESG, we will see that there was never an intention to provide one definition for these terms and acronyms or to provide clear delimitations between them. As there is no single definition, but rather 1001 definitions, moreover, since sustainability/CSR/ESG are concepts, »*we have to take a conceptual approach*«[111]. There are regional and sector-specific topics, as well as practice area specifics. Not to mention the legal side – there are so many complex relations that do not fit into a simple definition.

Staying ahead of the curve – No matter what we call it or how we think or feel about the concepts in the short term – if we stop now or lose sight of sustainability/CSR/ESG in favor of short-term goals, we need to consider the medium- and long-term effects.

108 Carroll, Archie B, Carroll's pyramid of CSR: taking another look. International Journal of Corporate Social Responsibility, International Journal of Corporate Social Responsibility, 2016, https://jcsr.springeropen.com/articles/10.1186/s40991-016-0004-6#citeas, accessed 29.10.2025.

109 See discussion for CSR under #1.2.3.

110 Spießhofer, Birgit, Corporate Political Responsibility – Handel nur mit Freunden, IWRZ 2024, 259.

111 Spießhofer, Birgit and others.

1.2.5 ESG and real estate

Because there is no single definition of ESG, a conceptual approach is necessary to understand its diverse and far-reaching implications for real estate. Rather than attempting a detailed classification, which could lead to more confusion, **Table 4** presents **selected topics** covered by ESG. It references some global standards or initiatives and highlights some specific implications for the real estate sector.

ESG Component	Global Level	Real Estate Implications
Environmental	• Climate change mitigation • Renewable energy • Resource efficiency • Pollution control • Biodiversity conservation[112] • Global treaties (e.g., Paris Agreement) • Reporting and disclosure rules and standards (e.g., GRI, CDP)[113]	• Energy-efficient buildings • Sustainable construction materials • Green building certifications (e.g., LEED, BREEAM) • Reducing carbon footprint • Enhancing resilience to climate change • Standards and treaties for sustainable urban development (e.g., the New Urban Agenda)
Social	• Human rights • Labor practices • Community engagement • Diversity and inclusion • Health and safety • UN Guiding Principles on Business and Human Rights (UNGP) • OECD Guidelines for Multinational Enterprises	• Promoting social well-being • Ensuring affordable housing • Creating inclusive communities • Engaging with local stakeholders • Health and safety standards for construction workers and building occupants
Governance	• Board diversity • Executive compensation • Anti-corruption measures • Shareholder rights • Transparency and disclosure • UN Global Compact • Principles for Responsible Investment (UNPRI)	• Transparent decision-making • Ethical business conduct • Accountability to investors and stakeholders • Robust risk management • Compliance with regulations • Fostering diversity in leadership

Table 4: ESG and real estate – selected topics

112 See details on biodiversity: Pwc, Real estate and biodiversity: a critical nexus
A global thought leadership report on nature-positive strategies for the built environment, June 2025, https://www.pwc.de/en/real-estate/pwc-study-real-estate-and-biodiversity-a-critical-nexus.pdf, accessed 29.06.2025.

113 OECD, Global Corporate Sustainability Report 2025, 29.10.2025, 14, https://www.oecd.org/en/publications/2025/10/global-corporate-sustainability-report-2025_57b105f2.html, accessed 30.11.2025: real estate sector has the lowest level of disclosure.

The following standards should also be considered:

- GRESB: ESG benchmarking and reporting for real estate and infrastructure assets
- World Green Building Council: Global advocacy and standards for sustainable buildings
- GRI (Global Reporting Initiative): Sustainability reporting framework, including real estate sector disclosures
- CDP (Carbon Disclosure Project): Disclosure of environmental impact, especially carbon emissions, for real estate and other sectors.

1.3 The global normative framework and instruments

Sabine Wieduwilt

»Making peace with nature is the defining task of the 21st century.«[114] *»To deny people their human rights is to challenge their very humanity.«*[115]

1.3.1 Introduction to #1.3

Who sets and enforces the rules in the realm of CSR/ESG? Historically, soft law has played a major role. More recently, hard law expanded but faced pushback. *Spießhofer*[116] offers an overview of rule-setters and enforcers in her work. Her overview shows that an enterprise is not governed only by traditional national law; it must follow many rules from diverse rule-givers. These include states, regional bodies such as the EU/OHADA, IGOs (UN, OECD, ILO), NGOs, investors and financiers, export credit agencies, industry associations, private standard-setters (ISO, IdW), contractual counterparties (suppliers, clients, and lawyers), and ratings agencies.

That's a lot to digest. The OECD's 2001 CSR guidance, for example, translates very decently what's relevant to understand the structure of rules – including the principles and the normative framework and the implementation.

There are principles and normative frameworks. A key area of that, for sustainability/CSR/ESG, comes from international treaties, other agreements, and global conferences. Major agreements, such as the Paris Agreement and the Convention on Biological Diversity (CBD), as well

114 António Guterres, Secretary General of the United Nations, https://unfccc.int/news/un-secretary-general-making-peace-with-nature-is-the-defining-task-of-the-21st-century, accessed 12.09.2025.

115 Nelson Mandela at a joint meeting of the United States Congress, Washington DC, 1990, https://www.un.org/en/exhibits/page/building-legacy-nelson-mandela, accessed 12.09.2025.

116 Spießhofer, Birgit, Sustainable Corporate Governance, NZG 2022, 435; copied also in Wieduwilt, Sabine, in: Wieduwilt, Sabine, Implementing ESG into Real Estate Contracts. A guide and toolkit for practitioners from a European perspective, 2025, #1.1.3(c), 26.

as key human rights treaties such as the International Covenant on Civil and Political Rights (ICCPR) and the International Covenant on Economic, Social and Cultural Rights (ICESCR), shape national laws by requiring environmental impact assessments, sustainable resource management, pollution reduction, and the protection of fundamental human rights. Further agreements and conferences – including the UNFCCC COPs, CBD COPs, the Stockholm Conference (1972), the Rio Earth Summit (1992), and major human rights conferences, such as the Vienna World Conference on Human Rights (1993) – have established environmental and human rights governance frameworks at the international level. These agreements and conferences drive energy efficiency, renewable energy, climate resilience, and respect for human rights in real estate and other sectors. They are also referenced in CSR/ESG instruments and standards. The 2030 Agenda for Sustainable Development includes 17 SDGs; several focus on environmental protection and human rights, drawing from these normative frameworks. The OECD MNE[117] and other instruments are based on international agreements[118]. The same applies to sustainable finance frameworks.

Then, it may be helpful to list some institutions and examples of standards with relevance on a global scale.

#1.3 **Conferences and agreements – principles for normative framework versus instruments for implementation, institutions, etc.**	**#1.3.1 – intro to #1.3**
	#1.3.2 – environmental agreements and conferences
	#1.3.3 – human rights treaties
	#1.3.4 – structure – international law, agreements
	#1.3.5 – normative framework versus instruments
	#1.3.6 – institutions, initiatives, standards

This chapter delves into international agreements and conferences, focusing on environmental aspects, objectives and types and structures of environmental laws (#1.3.2) and lists some of the key human rights treaties (#1.3.3). The chapter also provides structural information about international law, including sources of international law, non-binding instruments versus legally binding treaties and customary law and types of agreements (#1.3.4). It then discusses the perspective of this global normative framework versus global instruments (#1.3.5) and concludes with examples of global institutions, initiatives, and standards (#1.3.6).

1.3.2 Environmental agreements and conferences, environmental law

Major agreements such as the Paris Agreement and the Convention on Biological Diversity (CBD) shape national laws by requiring environmental impact assessments, sustainable resource

117 See for example reference to environmental objectives, building on environmental agreements, OECD, OECD Guidelines for Multinational Enterprises on Responsible Business Conduct, 2023, https://www.oecd.org/en/publications/oecd-guidelines-for-multinational-enterprises-on-responsible-business-conduct_81f92357-en.html, accessed 30.08.2025, 33, 35.

118 See for example the EU Taxonomy Regulation as one of the regional taxonomies: Regulation (EU) 2020/852 of the European Parliament and of the Council of 18 June 2020 on the establishment of a framework to facilitate sustainable investment, and amending Regulation (EU) 2019/2088, https://eur-lex.europa.eu/eli/reg/2020/852/oj/eng, accessed 07.06.2025, Art. 10–16.

management, and pollution reduction. These agreements drive energy efficiency, renewable energy, and climate resilience in real estate and other sectors. They are also referenced in CSR/ESG instruments and standards. The **2030 Agenda for Sustainable Development** includes 17 SDGs, several of which focus on environmental protection.

Section #1.3.2 provides an overview of conferences (under (a)), environmental objectives and agreements (under (b)), to conclude with types and structures of environmental law (under (c)).

(a) Conferences

Below is a list of key **international climate conferences and agreements** in chronological order from 1972 to 2012[119]:

Year	*Title*	*Information*
1972	**Stockholm Conference**	The first global environmental conference, which led to the adoption of the Stockholm Declaration, setting forth principles for sustainable development and environmental protection, and the establishment of the United Nations Environment Programme (UNEP).
1979	**World Climate Conference**	One of the first major international meetings of scientists to discuss climate change, resulting in the establishment of the World Climate Programme (WCP), which coordinates climate research and monitoring.
1992	**Earth Summit (Rio de Janeiro)**	The United Nations Conference on Environment and Development (UNCED) introduced the concept of sustainable development. This conference resulted in key documents, including the Rio Declaration, Agenda 21 (a non-binding sustainable development plan), the Convention on Biological Diversity, the Forest Principles, the United Nations Framework Convention on Climate Change (UNFCCC), and the Convention to Combat Desertification.
2002	**Johannesburg Summit**	The United Nations Conference on Sustainable Development (UNCSD) aimed to implement the outcomes of the Rio Summit. The conference emphasized the importance of public-private partnerships, precise timelines, and binding agreements to achieve sustainability goals.

119 See also: UN Climate Change, Chronological Overview of Key Climate Conferences and Agreements: UNFCCC, Past conferences overview, https://unfccc.int/process-and-meetings/conferences/past-conferences/past-conferences-overview, accessed 21.04.2025; European Parliament (EP), Interactive timeline. A guide to climate change negotiations – infographic containing a timeline listing milestones and key initiatives in the global fight against climate change. EP, Interactive timeline. A guide to climate change negotiations, https://www.europarl.europa.eu/topics/en/article/20180404STO00910/infographic-timeline-of-climate-change-negotiations, accessed 21.04.2025; Climate Club, The History of Climate Conferences in 13 minutes, YouTube, 2024, https://www.youtube.com/watch?v=aPV2nVcflo4, accessed 08.06.2025; Climate Club, The History of Climate Conferences in 10 minutes, Part 2, YouTube, 2024, https://www.youtube.com/watch?v=Hi8xPSK4AWE, accessed 08.06.2025.

Year	Title	Information
2009	**Copenhagen Conference**	The 15th Conference of the Parties (COP15) to the UNFCCC resulted in the Copenhagen Accord. The accord recognized the need to limit the global temperature rise to below 2 degrees Celsius and committed financial support to developing countries. However, it did not produce a legally binding treaty.
2012	**Rio+20 Conference**	The United Nations Conference on Sustainable Development revisited the themes from the 1992 Earth Summit. It discussed political issues, such as the »green economy,« and led to the further development of UNEP.

Table 5: International climate conferences and agreements

Conferences of the Parties (COPs) are regular meetings of signatory countries that review and advance agreements. Notably under the UNFCCC (annual climate COPs since 1995), COP21 (2015) produced the Paris Agreement and the CBD (biodiversity COPs), with COP15 (2022) that set new biodiversity goals. These conferences rotate locations and involve governments, civil society, and the media in negotiations and progress review.[120] The **conventions established at the 1992 Rio Conference** formed the basis for ongoing **Conferences of the Parties (COPs)**, where signatory countries regularly meet to review and advance major environmental agreements. The most prominent are the climate change COPs, which have convened annually since 1995 under the UNFCCC[121], resulting in milestones like the **2015 Paris Agreement (COP21)**. Biodiversity COPs have also been significant, with the 2022 Kunming-Montreal Global Biodiversity Framework (COP15) setting ambitious conservation goals. UN Climate Change Conferences rotate among UN regional groups and serve as the main global forum for negotiating and reviewing the implementation of the UNFCCC, the Kyoto Protocol (through the **Conference of the Parties serving as the Meeting of the Parties to the Kyoto Protocol, »CMP«**), and the Paris Agreement (through the **Conference of the Parties serving as the Meeting of the Parties to the Paris Agreement, »CMA«**). These meetings bring together government officials, civil society, and the media to assess progress, adopt new decisions, and negotiate further legal instruments. The process involves complex negotiations and consensus-building to advance global climate and biodiversity action.

(b) Environmental objectives, environmental agreements (IEAs), and bodies

Conferences, treaties, and further agreements relating to different objectives – Major international treaties and conferences, such as the United Nations Framework Convention on Climate Change (UNFCCC), the Convention on Biological Diversity (CBD), and the Stockholm and

120 UNFCCC, What are United Nations Climate Change Conferences?, https://unfccc.int/process-and-meetings/what-are-united-nations-climate-change-conferences, accessed 21.04.2025; UNFCC, Documents and decisions, https://unfccc.int/decisions?gad_source=1&gclid=EAIaIQobChMIjafvzLDHhwMVFKKDBx2ANANpEAAYASABEgLn1_D_BwE, accessed 08.06.2025.

121 UNFCCC, What are United Nations Climate Change Conferences?, https://unfccc.int/process-and-meetings/what-are-united-nations-climate-change-conferences, accessed 21.04.2025; UNFCC, Documents and decisions, https://unfccc.int/decisions?gad_source=1&gclid=EAIaIQobChMIjafvzLDHhwMVFKKDBx2ANANpEAAYASABEgLn1_D_BwE, accessed 08.06.2025.

Rio Declarations set environmental aims. These documents often focus on specific issues, such as climate change mitigation and adaptation, the sustainable use and protection of water and marine resources, the transition to a circular economy, pollution prevention and control and the protection and restoration of biodiversity and ecosystems. Below are **examples of Multilateral Environmental Agreements (MEAs)**[122] and further agreements, **sorted by environmental objectives**, whereby there may be overlaps, as the objectives are connected:

Climate change mitigation and adaptation	UNFCCC Vienna Convention MONTREAL PROTOCOL
1985 – The Vienna Convention for the Protection of the Ozone Layer and its 1987 Montreal Protocol on Substances that Deplete the Ozone Layer	The Vienna Convention provides a framework for international efforts to protect the ozone layer, while the Montreal Protocol establishes binding obligations to phase out the production and consumption of ozone-depleting substances.
1992 – United Nations Framework Convention on Climate Change (UNFCCC) and its 1997 Kyoto Protocol and 2015 Paris Agreement	The UNFCCC provides the legal framework for international cooperation to stabilize greenhouse gas concentrations and prevent dangerous climate change, establishing foundational obligations for all countries and requiring developed nations to lead the way in emissions reductions and support for developing countries. The Kyoto Protocol (1997) set legally binding emission reduction targets for developed countries and introduced mechanisms, such as emissions trading, the Clean Development Mechanism, and Joint Implementation to facilitate cost-effective compliance. The Paris Agreement (2015, adopted at COP21) commits all countries to limiting warming to well below 2°C towards pre-industrial levels (ideally 1.5°C). It requires regular updates of nationally determined contributions (NDCs), and emphasizes transparency, accountability, and support for adaptation and climate finance. Progress is assessed through regular global stocktakes.[123]

122 UNEP, Secretariats and Conventions, GlobalMEAs, https://www.unep.org/about-un-environment/why-does-un-environment-matter/secretariats-and-conventions#global, accessed 08.06.2025. Not covered are conventions addressing desertification, which have been on the international agenda for a long time.

123 Paris Agreement, Art. 14; United Nations, NDC 3.0, 2024, https://unfccc.int/ndc-3.0, accessed 22.08.2024; See UN documents on Climate Change, https://unfccc.int/decisions?gad_source=1&gclid=EAIaIQobChMIjafvzLDHhwMVFKKDBx2ANANpEAAYASABEgLn1_D_BwE, accessed 27.07.2024; United Nations, Climate Action, The Paris Agreement, https://www.un.org/en/climatechange/paris-agreement, accessed 03.08.2025.

Water and marine resources	
1982 – UN Convention on the Law of the Sea (UNCLOS)	This convention establishes the legal framework for marine conservation, sustainable use of ocean resources, and governance of activities in international waters.
2023 – High Seas Treaty	This treaty aims to protect marine biodiversity and promote the sustainable use of resources in areas beyond national jurisdiction by establishing new conservation and management measures.
Transition to a circular economy	
See below pollution prevention and control (Basel, Minamata, Stockholm)	There is no comprehensive international treaty solely dedicated to the circular economy. However, several multilateral environmental agreements and global initiatives incorporate circular economy principles, particularly regarding waste, chemicals, and resource management.[124]
Pollution prevention and control	
1989 – Basel Convention on the Control of Transboundary Movements of Hazardous Wastes and their Disposal	This treaty is designed to reduce the movement of hazardous waste between countries, particularly from developed to less developed countries, and to ensure the environmentally sound management of such waste.
1998 – Rotterdam Convention on the Prior Informed Consent Procedure for Certain Hazardous Chemicals and Pesticides in International Trade	This agreement promotes shared responsibilities and cooperative efforts in the international trade of certain hazardous chemicals, ensuring that importing countries are informed about the risks.
2001 – Stockholm Convention on Persistent Organic Pollutants	This is a global treaty designed to protect human health and the environment from chemicals that remain intact in the environment for long periods of time, spread widely across geographical areas and accumulate in living organisms.
2013 – Minamata Convention on Mercury	An international treaty aimed at protecting human health and the environment from anthropogenic emissions and releases of mercury and mercury compounds.

124 See regional initiatives for example: The European Union's New Circular Economy Action Plan, Communication from the Commission to the European Parliament, the Council, the European Economic and Social Committee and the Committee of the Regions. A new Circular Economy Action Plan For a cleaner and more competitive Europe, COM/2020/98 final, https://eur-lex.europa.eu/legal-content/EN/TXT/?uri=celex:52020DC0098, accessed 07.09.2025 (the New Circular Economy Action Plan was already addressed in the EU Green Deal, further defined in the Action Plan) and similar strategies in other regions are influential but not international treaties. See especially section 3.6 of the EU's Circular Economy Action Plan, which provides details on the following: The EU's new Circular Economy Action Plan aims to increase material efficiency and reduce climate impacts in the construction sector by launching a comprehensive Strategy for a Sustainable Built Environment, promoting circularity throughout building lifecycles, revising regulations to encourage recycled content and durability, integrating life cycle assessment, and improving waste management and soil use.

Biodiversity and ecosystems	
1973 – Convention on International Trade in Endangered Species of Wild Fauna and Flora (CITES)	This is a global agreement that aims to ensure that international trade in specimens of wild animals and plants does not threaten their survival.
1992 – Convention on Biological Diversity (CBD) – especially the Nagoya Protocol (2010) and Kunming-Montreal Global Biodiversity Framework (2022)	This is an international treaty aimed at conserving biological diversity, promoting the sustainable use of its components and ensuring the fair and equitable sharing of benefits arising from genetic resources. **The Nagoya Protocol (2010)**: Adopted under the Convention on Biological Diversity (CBD), it establishes a framework for the fair and equitable sharing of benefits arising from the use of genetic resources, promoting access and supporting biodiversity conservation. **The Kunming-Montreal Global Biodiversity Framework (2022)**[125]: Adopted at COP15 of the CBD, it sets global goals and targets to halt and reverse biodiversity loss by 2030, focusing on the conservation, restoration, and sustainable use of ecosystems.

Table 6: MEAs sorted by environmental objectives

International environmental agreements (IEAs) are treaties that are binding under international law and aim to manage the human impact on natural resources and the environment. **Bilateral agreements** involve two nations, while **multilateral environmental agreements (MEAs)** involve three or more, often under the auspices of the United Nations. **MEAs** address issues such as climate change, biodiversity, hazardous waste, and marine protection.

History and Use

The use of MEAs began in 1857 with a German agreement regulating water flow from Lake Constance. International environmental protocols gained prominence in the 1960s due to transboundary environmental issues. The 1972 Stockholm Conference led to a significant increase in the number of international environmental agreements, with the Stockholm Declaration being the first universal document on an environmental issue. An effective MEA system requires a complex network, as conflicting internal views can impede implementation and affect external relationships. MEAs can influence each other positively or negatively, impacting their effectiveness. Policies are determined by participating countries, with the United Nations and the World Trade Organization playing key roles in forging and implementing agreements. There has

125 The Convention on Biological Diversity (CBD), 1992, https://www.cbd.int/convention/text, see also 2024: https://www.cbd.int/convention, and for conference 12–16 August 2024: The Convention on Biological Diversity, Ad Hoc Open-ended Working Group on Benefit-sharing from the Use of Digital Sequence Information (DSI) on Genetic Resources, 2024, https://www.cbd.int/conferences/wgdsi-2, accessed 10.08.2024 and 08.09.2024.

been an increasing use of environmental provisions in bilateral environmental agreements and international investment agreements.[126]

»Since the founding of the United Nations in 1945, countries have worked together to forge groundbreaking agreements to safeguard the environment. From protecting species to repairing the ozone layer, these accords reflect the power of international cooperation even in challenging times. A subset of these pacts, known as Multilateral Environmental Agreements (MEAs), underpin the global environmental movement.«[127]

The role of international organizations

The **United Nations (UN)** leads in negotiating and implementing MEAs. The **United Nations Environment Programme (UNEP)** is the leading global environmental authority, administering and supporting MEAs and promoting international cooperation on issues such as climate change, ecosystem management, and resource efficiency[128]. **UNEP** promotes environmental objectives, typically presented as thematic priorities, through its programs and reports. Its work covers climate change, ecosystem management, resource efficiency, chemicals and waste, and environmental governance, among others. The **UN's InforMEA** portal compiles MEA information for parties and stakeholders. The **World Trade Organization (WTO)** participates in MEA negotiations to align trade and environmental policies.[129]

(c) Environmental law – types and principles

Cheever and Campbell-Mohn refer to »environmental law« as »environmental law, principles, policies, directives, and regulations enacted and enforced by local, national, or international entities to regulate human treatment of the nonhuman world. [...]«[130]

126 Conferences further history: Wikipedia, International environmental agreement, https://en.wikipedia.org/wiki/International_environmental_agreement, accessed 21.04.2025.

127 UNEP, Secretariats and Conventions, https://www.unep.org/about-un-environment/why-does-un-environment-matter/secretariats-and-conventions, accessed 30.08.2025.

128 UNEP, Secretariats and Conventions, https://www.unep.org/about-un-environment/why-does-un-environment-matter/secretariats-and-conventions, accessed 30.08.2025.

129 WTO, The Doha mandate on multilateral environmental agreements (MEAs), https://www.wto.org/english/tratop_e/envir_e/envir_neg_mea_e.htm, accessed 30.08.2025.

130 Cheever/Campbell-Mohn, environmental law, in: Brittanica, https://www.britannica.com/topic/environmental-law, accessed 07.06.2025.

Types of environmental law

Command-and-control legislation	»Such laws typically involve three elements: (1) identification of a type of environmentally harmful activity, (2) imposition of specific conditions or standards on that activity, and (3) prohibition of forms of the activity that fail to comply with the imposed conditions or standards.«[131]
Environmental assessment mandates	»Such mandates generally perform three functions: (1) identification of a level or threshold of potential environmental impact at which a contemplated action is significant enough to require the preparation of an assessment, (2) establishment of specific goals for the assessment mandated, and (3) setting of requirements to ensure that the assessment will be considered in determining whether to proceed with the action as originally contemplated or to pursue an alternative action.«[132]
Economic incentives	»The use of economic instruments to create incentives for environmental protection […]. Such incentives include pollution taxes, subsidies for clean technologies and practices, and the creation of markets in either environmental protection or pollution.«[133]
Set-aside schemes	»[...] setting aside of lands and waters in their natural state. In the United States, for example, the vast majority of the land owned by the federal government (about one-third of the total land area of the country) can be developed only with the approval of a federal agency.«[134]

Table 7: Types of environmental law

131 Cheever/Campbell-Mohn, environmental law, in: Brittanica, https://www.britannica.com/topic/environmental-law, accessed 07.06.2025. Example of command and control legislation: »Another type of activity regulated by command-and-control legislation is environmentally harmful trade. Among the most-developed regulations are those on trade in wildlife. The Convention on International Trade in Endangered Species of Wild Fauna and Flora (CITES, 1973), for example, authorizes signatories to the convention to designate species »threatened with extinction which are or may be affected by trade.« Once a plant or animal species has been designated as endangered, countries generally are bound to prohibit import or export of that species except in specific limited circumstances.«

132 Cheever/Campbell-Mohn, environmental law, in: Brittanica, https://www.britannica.com/topic/environmental-law, accessed 07.06.2025. Example of environmental assessment mandates: »Unlike command-and-control regulations, which may directly limit discharges into the environment, mandated environmental assessments protect the environment indirectly by increasing the quantity and quality of publicly available information on the environmental consequences of contemplated actions. This information potentially improves the decision making of government officials and increases the public's involvement in the creation of environmental policy. [examples: United States National Environmental Policy Act (1969);] Similarly, the European Union (EU) requires an environmental impact assessment for two types of projects. So-called ›annex-I Projects‹ (e.g., oil refineries, toxic waste landfills, and thermal power stations with heat output of 300 or more megawatts) are generally subject to the requirement, and ›annex-II Projects‹ (e.g., activities in chemical, food, textile, leather, wood, and paper industries) are subject to an environmental impact assessment only where »member states consider that their characteristics so require.« Such assessments must describe and evaluate the direct and indirect effects of the project on humans, fauna, flora, soil, water, air, climate, and landscape and the interaction between them.«

133 Cheever/Campbell-Mohn, environmental law, in: Brittanica, https://www.britannica.com/topic/environmental-law, accessed 07.06.2025.

134 Cheever/Campbell-Mohn, environmental law, in: Brittanica, https://www.britannica.com/topic/environmental-law, accessed 07.06.2025.

Principles of environmental law[135]

Modern environmental law is shaped by key principles outlined in documents like Our Common Future (1987) and the Rio Declaration (1992):

Precautionary principle	If an activity is suspected of causing environmental harm, it should be controlled even without full scientific certainty. The Rio Declaration states that the lack of certainty should not delay the implementation of cost-effective measures to prevent environmental degradation.
Prevention principle	Preventing environmental harm is more effective and less costly than responding after damage occurs. This principle underpins laws on hazardous waste and pesticides, and was central to the Basel Convention (1989).
Polluter pays principle	Since the 1970s, this principle has held that those who cause pollution should bear the costs, rather than shifting them to society. Environmental regulations aim to ensure that polluters pay for the real costs of their actions.
Integration principle	Environmental considerations should be integrated into decision-making processes, such as through environmental impact assessments, to ensure that the potential consequences are fully considered.
Public participation principle	The public should have opportunities to influence environmental decisions, often through comments, hearings, or legal challenges. This principle is supported by laws and international agreements, such as the Rio Declaration and the Århus Convention.
Sustainable development	This approach seeks economic growth while preserving the environment for future generations. Although it is widely endorsed, achieving sustainability can be complex, because it depends on the resources and context involved. The concept was a major focus of the 1992 Earth Summit.

Table 8: Principles of environmental law

1.3.3 Human rights declarations and treaties

»Even if women can contribute to lasting peace, there are few involved in peace negotiations.«[136]

The international human rights framework is built on core treaties, declarations, and monitoring bodies that establish and protect fundamental rights and freedoms.

Human rights frameworks, such as the Universal Declaration of Human Rights and the UN Guiding Principles on Business and Human Rights, emphasize the right to adequate housing, protection against forced evictions, and respect for indigenous and local communities. These standards require fair compensation, non-discrimination, and community engagement.

135 Cheever/Campbell-Mohn, environmental law, in: Brittanica, https://www.britannica.com/topic/environmental-law, accessed 07.06.2025.

136 EP, Women in peace building: why and how to increase their role, 2025, https://www.europarl.europa.eu/topics/en/article/20250227STO27080/women-in-peace-building-why-and-how-to-increase-their-role, accessed 21.04.2025.

There are nine core international human rights treaties[137], each of which is monitored by a committee of experts to ensure that states comply with their obligations. The international human rights framework was significantly advanced by the 1948 Universal Declaration of Human Rights (UDHR), which, along with the International Covenants on Civil and Political Rights (and its two Optional Protocols) and on Economic, Social and Cultural Rights, forms the **International Bill of Human Rights.**

Since 1945, additional treaties and instruments – both international and regional – have further developed human rights protections. States that ratify these treaties are legally bound to respect, protect, and fulfill human rights, often by enacting compatible domestic laws. When national remedies fail, individuals can seek recourse through regional or international mechanisms to uphold these rights (international human rights law[138]; see also UN, OHCR, human rights law[139]).

See below a **chronological overview of key human rights declarations and treaties:**[140]

Year	*Title*	*Information*
1948	*Universal Declaration of Human Rights (UDHR)*	Adopted by the United Nations General Assembly, this declaration sets forth fundamental human rights to be universally protected.
1965	*International Convention on the Elimination of All Forms of Racial Discrimination (ICERD)*	Aims to eliminate racial discrimination and promote understanding among all races.
1966	*International Covenant on Economic, Social and Cultural Rights (ICESCR)*	Ensures the protection of economic, social, and cultural rights, including the rights to work, social security, and education.
1966	*International Covenant on Civil and Political Rights (ICCPR)*	Protects civil and political rights, such as the rights to life, freedom of speech, and freedom of religion.
1979	*Convention on the Elimination of All Forms of Discrimination against Women (CEDAW)*	Focuses on eliminating discrimination against women and ensuring women's equal rights.
1984	*Convention against Torture and Other Cruel, Inhuman or Degrading Treatment or Punishment (CAT)*	Aims to prevent torture and other cruel, inhuman, or degrading treatment or punishment.
1989	*Convention on the Rights of the Child (CRC)*	Protects the rights of children, ensuring their well-being and development.

137 UN, OHCR, Complaints about human rights violations, Treaty Bodies, https://www.ohchr.org/en/treaty-bodies/complaints-about-human-rights-violations, accessed 21.04.2025.

138 UN, OHCR, International Human Rights Law, https://www.ohchr.org/en/instruments-and-mechanisms/international-human-rights-law, accessed 21.04.2025; UN, The Core International Human Rights Instruments and their monitoring bodies, https://www.ohchr.org/en/core-international-human-rights-instruments-and-their-monitoring-bodies, accessed 30.08.2025.

139 UN, OHCR, What are human rights, https://www.ohchr.org/en/what-are-human-rights, accessed 21.04.2025.

140 See including protocols and further details: UN, OHCR, The Core International Human Rights Instruments and their monitoring bodies, https://www.ohchr.org/en/core-international-human-rights-instruments-and-their-monitoring-bodies, accessed 08.06.2025.

Year	*Title*	*Information*
1990	*International Convention on the Protection of the Rights of All Migrant Workers and Members of Their Families (ICMW)*	Protects the rights of migrant workers and their families.
2006	*Convention on the Rights of Persons with Disabilities (CRPD)*	Promotes and protects the rights of persons with disabilities, ensuring their full and equal participation in society.
2006	*International Convention for the Protection of All Persons from Enforced Disappearance (CPED)*	Aims to prevent enforced disappearances and ensure justice for victims and their families.

Table 9: Human rights declarations and treaties

1.3.4 International law, sources of international law, treaties, conferences, non-binding instruments

For context, chapter #1.3.4 addresses the terms »international law« (under (a)), and »sources of international law« (under (b)), non-binding agreements versus legally binding treaties (under (c)), and types of agreements in international law and their terminology (under (d)).

(a) International law: definition and distinctions

International law is often referred to as the »**law of nations**« or »public international law,« the collection of legal rules, principles, and standards that govern the relations between sovereign states and other entities recognized as international actors. The term was coined by the English philosopher Jeremy Bentham (1748–1832). International law is fundamentally different from **international comity,** which consists of nonbinding practices that states adopt out of courtesy, such as the tradition of saluting foreign warships at sea. Furthermore, public international law should not be confused with the field of **conflict of laws**, also known as **private international law**. Public international law addresses the legal framework between states and international entities, while conflict of laws deals with the rules that determine which domestic legal system applies when a case involves foreign elements. In this context, »municipal law« refers to the domestic law of individual states. International law operates as an independent legal system, separate from the internal legal orders of individual countries. Unlike **domestic legal systems,** international law lacks a central legislative authority. For example, the United Nations General Assembly, despite its resemblance to a legislative body and its representation of nearly **193 countries**, does not have the authority to enact binding laws. Its resolutions are generally recommendations, except in certain circumstances within the UN framework.[141]

141 Shaw, Malcolm, International law, in: Brittanica, https://www.britannica.com/topic/international-law, accessed 07.06.2025; UN, International Law and Justice, https://www.un.org/en/global-issues/international-law-and-justice, accessed 7.06.2025; Wikipedia, International law, https://en.wikipedia.org/wiki/International_law, accessed 07.06.2025; Wikipedia, Conflict of laws, https://en.wikipedia.org/wiki/Conflict_of_laws, accessed 07.06.2025.

(b) Sources of international law

Article 38 of the Statute of the International Court of Justice (ICJ) lists the following sources of international law upon which the ICJ decides:

> *a.* ***international conventions,*** *whether general or particular, establishing rules expressly recognized by the contesting states;*
>
> *b.* ***international custom,*** *as evidence of a general practice accepted as law;*
>
> *c. the* ***general principles of law recognized by civilized nations;***
>
> *d. [...],* ***judicial decisions and the teachings of the most highly qualified publicists of the various nations,*** *as subsidiary means for the determination of rules of law.*[142]

(c) Non-binding instruments versus legally binding treaties

Non-binding instruments differ from legally binding treaties in their legal enforceability.[143]

Non-binding instruments are agreements that outline political commitments without legally binding member states. They can influence legal outcomes, but they do not impose legal obligations. One example is the 1972 Stockholm Declaration, which led to the creation of the United Nations Environment Program. Similarly, the Rio+20 Conference in 2012 resulted in a vision for sustainable development that balances economic, social, and environmental needs. Although there are no legal penalties for noncompliance, member states are politically committed to achieving the goals and avoiding actions contrary to the agreements.[144]

Legally binding treaties, including conventions, are agreements between member states or international organizations that impose legal obligations. The United Nations administers many such treaties, such as the Convention on Biological Diversity. This convention mandates countries to conserve biodiversity, promote sustainable use, and ensure fair sharing of genetic resources. **For an agreement to be considered a treaty or convention**, it must be **(i) legally binding, (ii) agreed upon by authorized entities, (iii) follow international law, and (iv) in writing**. While signing indicates support and the intention to ratify, but it becomes legally binding only upon ratification, which typically involves a formal process within a country, such as approval by the national legislature or another government body. Once approved, the member

142 UN, Statute of the International Court of Justice, https://www.un.org/en/about-us/un-charter/statute-of-the-international-court-of-justice, accessed 01.06.2025; see also: Wolfrum, Rüdiger, Sources of International Law, Oxford Public International Law: Sources of International Law, 2011, https://opil.ouplaw.com/display/10.1093/law:epil/9780199231690/law-9780199231690-e1471, accessed 07.06.2025; Greenwood, Christopher, Sources of International Law: An Introduction, https://legal.un.org/avl/pdf/ls/greenwood_outline.pdf, accessed 07.06.2025; Wikipedia, Sources of International Law, https://en.wikipedia.org/wiki/Sources_of_international_law, accessed 07.06.2025; Soft law: Thürer, Daniel, Soft Law, 2009, in: Oxford Public International Law, https://opil.ouplaw.com/display/10.1093/law:epil/9780199231690/law-9780199231690-e1469, accessed 07.06.2025. Art. 38 in addition states that the provision shall not prejudice the power of the Court to decide a case ex aequo et bono, if the parties agree thereto.

143 UN, OHCR, Understanding international agreements, 2024, https://www.unep.org/news-and-stories/video/understanding-international-agreements, accessed 21.04.2025.

144 UN, OHCR, Understanding international agreements, 2024, https://www.unep.org/news-and-stories/video/understanding-international-agreements, accessed 21.04.2025.

state formally agrees to be bound by the treaty's terms. The primary **source** for definitions and rules regarding **treaties and binding international agreements** is the **Vienna Convention on the Law of Treaties (VCLT, 1969)**[145]. The **Vienna Convention on the Law of Treaties (VCLT)** is an international agreement that regulates treaties among sovereign states. Known as the »treaty on treaties«, the VCLT establishes comprehensive, operational guidelines, rules, and procedures for how treaties are drafted, defined, amended, and interpreted. **According to the VCLT** (Article 2)[146], a »**treaty**« is »an international agreement concluded between States in written form and governed by international law, whether embodied in a single instrument or in two or more related instruments and whatever its particular designation.« The Vienna Convention on the Law of Treaties (VCLT) was drafted by the International Law Commission (ILC) of the United Nations, which began work on the convention in 1949. Non-ratifying parties, such as the U.S., have recognized parts of the VCLT as a restatement of customary international law. The so-called »Freshfields Report« for **UNEP FI**[147] includes a description of sources of international law, especially treaties and customary law: »***International law*** *derives from a number of* ***sources****. The most important are* ***treaties*** *(sometimes called conventions, agreements, memoranda of understanding or protocols). These treaties (especially the very widely accepted ones, like the UN Charter) look like legislation, but, as States are all sovereigns and there is no international equivalent of a parliament, the true analogy in domestic law is a* ***contract****. Indeed, most treaties only bind the States which are parties to them –* ***very few treaties have a third-party effect****. For some States, international treaties form an integral part of the national legal system, being in a sense ›directly applicable‹. For others, a confirmatory act by the national legislature is required. Whatever the national system, however, at the international level, adherence to a treaty creates binding legal obligations on the State towards other States party to the same treaty. The other important source of international law is* ***customary law****. This does not derive from treaties, but* ***from the way that civilised States behave towards one another****. Custom, it might be said, is not what States say, but what they do – although it also includes what they say they do! Customary law must be consistently and uniformly accepted and applied by a State and the State must apply the custom because it feels that it is legally obliged to do so. Acceptance as custom is one of the routes by which ›soft law‹ instruments (such as the Declarations of UN conferences, like those of Stockholm and Rio de Janeiro discussed below) can ›graduate‹ to become binding international law norms.*«

145 United Nations Treaty Collection, Vienna Convention on the Law of Treaties (VCLT), https://treaties.un.org/pages/ViewDetailsIII.aspx?src=TREATY&mtdsg_no=XXIII-1&chapter=23&Temp=mtdsg3&clang=_en, accessed 01.06.2025. UN, Vienna Convention on the Law of Treaties 1969, https://legal.un.org/ilc/texts/instruments/english/conventions/1_1_1969.pdf, accessed 13.09.2025; information for the following lines are also partly taken from: Wikipedia, Vienna Convention on the Law of Treaties, https://en.wikipedia.org/wiki/Vienna_Convention_on_the_Law_of_Treaties, accessed 25.10.2025.

146 Vienna Convention on the Law of Treaties, 1969, https://legal.un.org/ilc/texts/instruments/english/conventions/1_1_1969.pdf, accessed 07.06.2025, Art. 2(1)(a).

147 UNEP FI, A legal framework for the integration of environmental, social and governance issues into institutional investment, 2005, https://www.unepfi.org/wordpress/wp-content/uploads/2022/07/Freshfields-A-legal-framework-for-the-integration-of-ESG-issues-into-institutional-investment.pdf, accessed 24.07.2025, see footnote 65 of this report, which is introduced in #1.2.4.

(d) Types of agreements in international law and their terminology

The main parties to international agreements are states[148] and, in some cases, international organizations or other recognized subjects of international law. International agreements are essential in shaping global relations, but their nuances can be complex. The term »agreement« is generic and can refer to both binding and non-binding instruments, depending on the context and intention of the parties. International law recognizes a various types of agreements between states and other international actors. These agreements differ in their legal effect, formality, and the terminology used to describe them. The following summary outlines the main types, the terms commonly used to describe them, and the key documents in which they are generally described or defined.[149]

Type	*Common Terms Used*	*Binding?*	*Key Document/Definition Source*
Treaty	Treaty, Convention, Protocol, Charter	Yes	Vienna Convention on the Law of Treaties (VCLT)
Non-Binding	Declaration, MoU, Joint Statement	No	Not defined in VCLT; recognized in practice
Protocol	Protocol	Yes	VCLT, main treaty it supplements
Convention	Convention	Yes	VCLT, specific conventions
Charter/Statute	Charter, Statute	Yes	Foundational treaties (e.g., UN Charter)
Agreement	Agreement	Yes/No	VCLT, context-dependent

Table 10: Agreements in international law

1.3.5 The normative framework versus instruments

Who sets the rules, who translates the rules for implementation, at what levels?

International treaties and agreements are formal, binding agreements between countries that establish standards, obligations, or cooperation in various fields, including environmental protection, human rights, labor standards, and anti-corruption. Examples include the Paris Agreement on climate change, the Universal Declaration of Human Rights, and International Labour Organization (ILO) conventions.

148 See also for the EU as signatory to international treaties (»völkerrechtliche Abkommen«): Umweltvölkerrecht, deutsche Sicht: Stüer/Beckmann, BauR-HdB, 6. Aufl. 2025, Rn. 5235–5236; In the EU: Grabitz/Hilf/Nettesheim/Winkler, 84. EL Januar 2025, AEUV Art. 191 Rn. 38.

149 Specific type of agreement which can include sustainability-related provisions: International Investment Agreements (IIAs), see for IIAs and investment-related instruments (IRIs): UNCTAD, International Investment Agreements Navigator, Trade and Development, https://investmentpolicy.unctad.org/international-investment-agreements, accessed 30.08.2025. See also: OECD, Strengthening Sustainable Investment through International Investment Agreements, 2024, https://www.oecd.org/content/dam/oecd/en/publications/reports/2024/10/strengthening-sustainable-investment-through-international-investment-agreements_b8772cb7/a8729c98-en.pdf, accessed 24.07.2025.

How do we implement? Where do we start?

These treaties, agreements, and conferences are part of the framework that set out the principles for responsible investment, sustainable development, and ethical business practices in the real estate sector. While there is **not always a direct, one-to-one link** between international treaties or agreements and the specific ESG standards in real estate investment, there is a clear relationship. International treaties and agreements establish the high-level principles, goals, and obligations that inform and inspire the development of more detailed, actionable standards and frameworks. These standards then translate the broad commitments of treaties into practical requirements and metrics for investors and companies.

Level	*Example (Environmental)*	*Example (Social)*	*Example (Governance)*
Treaty/Agreement	Paris Agreement	ILO Conventions	UNCAC, OECD Anti-Bribery
National/Regional Law	EPBD, Building Codes	National labor laws	Anti-corruption laws
ESG Standard/Framework	TCFD, GRI, PRI	GRI, UN Guiding Principles	GRI, PRI, TCFD
Investment Practice	Energy efficiency reporting	Labor rights due diligence	Anti-bribery compliance

Table 11: From treaties to standards

Companies engage with and apply CSR/ESG in various ways. Then there is the foundation, the broader international consensus and legitimacy for the issues addressed by these instruments.

In its 2001 working paper, »OECD Guidelines and Corporate Social Responsibility in a Global Economy,«[150] the OECD described these means by which companies engage with CSR as global instruments, which include operational standards and guidelines and practical tools and standards for companies to implement CSR. These instruments focus on specific guidance, reporting, and certification, including for example the OECD Guidelines for Multinational Enterprises, the UN Global Compact, and the Global Reporting Initiative (GRI).

instruments –	**practical, operational tools and standards for implementation**
operational standards and guidelines	focus on specific guidance, reporting, and certification, for example, the OECD Guidelines for Multinational Enterprises, the UN Global Compact, and the Global Reporting Initiative (GRI)
foundation —	**underlying principles, rights and values,**
normative framework	for example, international declarations and treaties, Universal Declaration of Human Rights and ILO Conventions

Table 12: Instruments and foundation

150 Organisation for Economic Co-operation and Development (OECD), OECD Guidelines and Corporate Social Responsibility in a Global Economy, 2001.

The OECD (Table 12) differentiates between these **instruments**, means, and operational standards and guidelines and the **normative framework** – the broader international consensus and legitimacy for the issues addressed by these instruments, as well as the foundational international declarations and treaties that provide the underlying principles, rights, and values that CSR instruments aim to implement. According to the OECD, CSR is rooted in international declarations and treaties, such as the Universal Declaration of Human Rights and ILO Conventions.

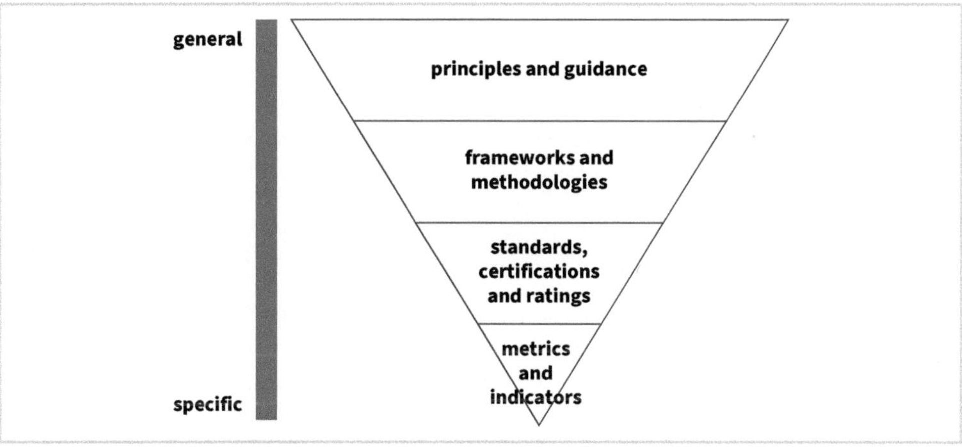

Figure 11: Categorizing impact management and measurement

The relationship is one of foundation and application within the CSR (or ESG) framework. In a report on social impact investment, the **OECD categorizes** existing **impact management and measurement initiatives**[151] by drawing an inverted pyramid (Figure 11) ranging from broad, high-level principles at the top, down to specific, granular metrics at the bottom. The report also discusses the challenges to harmonization and standardization, as one moves down the pyramid.[152]

Returning to the instruments and normative framework in sections #1.3.2 to #1.3.4 of chapter #1.3, we see that it works at the very top of the inverted pyramid, or, looking at this from a different perspective, at the very bottom, laying the foundation. In #1.3.5, however, we direct our attention to implementation.

For a broader view of the normative frameworks and instruments, refer to the 2001 working paper »OECD Guidelines and Corporate Social Responsibility in a Global Economy«[153], boxes 2 and 3, many of which are mentioned below under #1.3.6 and throughout this book.

---

151 OECD, Social Impact Investment 2019: The Impact Imperative for Sustainable Development, 2019, https://doi.org/10.1787/9789264311299-en, accessed 10.08.2025.

152 OECD, Social Impact Investment 2019: The Impact Imperative for Sustainable Development, 2019, https://doi.org/10.1787/9789264311299-en, accessed 10.08.2025.

153 Organisation for Economic Co-operation and Development (OECD), OECD Guidelines and Corporate Social Responsibility in a Global Economy, 2001.

- Box 2 (CSR Instruments): Practical, operational tools and standards for companies to implement CSR, with a focus on specific guidance, reporting, and certification.
- Box 3 (Normative Framework): Foundational international declarations and treaties that provide the underlying principles, rights, and values that CSR instruments seek to realize in practice.

1.3.6 Institutions and standards

A broad array of global institutions and standards exist that continue to shape the framework for sustainability, Corporate Social Responsibility (CSR), and Environmental, Social, and Governance (ESG) on a horizontal level across sectors and also for the real estate sector, namely in real estate investment.

(a) Key Global Institutions are:

- **United Nations (UN):** Through bodies such as the United Nations Environment Programme (UNEP), UN-Habitat, and the Intergovernmental Panel on Climate Change (IPCC), the UN sets global agendas and provides scientific assessments and policy guidance on sustainability and climate change. The UNEP also partners with the financial sector through the UNEP Finance Initiative (UNEP FI) to encourage sustainable financing and develop principles for responsible banking, insurance, and investment.
  United Nations Global Compact

Aspect	Description
Launch	2000 (UN Secretary-General initiative).
Legal nature	Voluntary corporate sustainability platform; not a treaty or UN General Assembly resolution.
Ten principles	Derived from the Universal Declaration of Human Rights (Principles 1–2); the ILO Core Conventions (3–6); the Rio Declaration on Environment and Development (7–9); and the UN Convention Against Corruption (10).
Participation commitments	Integrate the Ten Principles into strategy and operations; submit an annual Communication on Progress (COP).
Accountability & transparency	Public COP database; failure to report leads to »Non-communicating« status and eventual delisting.
Support structure	UN Global Compact Office (New York) and over 60 local networks facilitating peer learning, partnerships and policy dialogue.
Stakeholder engagement	Businesses, UN agencies, labor organizations, civil society, and academia collaborating on thematic and country programs.
Objective	Mobilize a global movement of responsible companies to advance a sustainable and inclusive world economy.

Table 13: UN Global Compact

- **Organisation for Economic Co-operation and Development (OECD):** The OECD issues guidelines for multinational enterprises, including recommendations for responsible business conduct. Examples of standards:
  OECD Guidelines for Multinational Enterprises and Responsible Business Conduct Due Diligence Guidance

Aspect	Description
Launch & evolution	First adopted in 1976; with major revisions in 2000, 2011, and 2023.
Legal nature	Non-binding recommendations addressed by adhering governments to multinational enterprises.
Thematic pillars	Human rights, labour, environment, anti-bribery, consumer interests, disclosure, taxation, competition, science and technology.
Due diligence focus	The 2011 revision was aligned with the UNGPs on Business & Human Rights, and the 2023 revision provided more detailed guidance on risk-based due diligence across operations, the supply chain, and business relationships, including the impacts of climate and technology.
Implementation architecture	Over 50 adhering governments have established National Contact Points (NCPs) to promote the Guidelines, facilitate mediation, and provide a non-judicial grievance mechanism.
Reporting and accountability	There is no mandatory reporting; enterprises are expected to conduct and communicate risk-based due diligence; and NCPs publish final statements on specific instances.
Geographic reach	All OECD members plus several non-members; applies to companies operating in or from those jurisdictions.
Purpose	Encourage the avoidance and remediation of adverse impacts, foster sustainable, inclusive growth, and harmonize corporate conduct with societal expectations.

Table 14: OECD MNE

- **International Labour Organization (ILO):** The ILO sets international labor standards, that contribute to the social dimension of ESG and CSR, with conventions that address labor rights, equality, and working conditions.
- **World Trade Organization (WTO):** The WTO provides a framework for international trade, including provisions for environmental protection and sustainable development.
- **International Organization for Standardization (ISO):** The ISO develops and publishes international standards, such as ISO 14001 (environmental management) and ISO 26000 (social responsibility), which are widely adopted in real estate and investment.

(b) Key standards[154] and frameworks

- **Principles for Responsible Investment (PRI):** A UN-supported network that guides institutional investors in integrating ESG factors into investment and ownership decisions, including real estate.
- **Global Reporting Initiative (GRI):** Provides a widely used sustainability reporting framework that enables organizations to communicate their environmental, social, and governance impacts.
- **Task Force on Climate-related Financial Disclosures (TCFD):** Established by the Financial Stability Board (FSB), the TCFD develops recommendations for climate-related financial risk disclosures, which are increasingly becoming mandatory in several jurisdictions.
- **International Sustainability Standards Board (ISSB):** As part of the IFRS Foundation, the ISSB is developing global sustainability-related financial reporting standards, consolidating previous initiatives such as the SASB and the CDSB.
- **Sustainability Accounting Standards Board (SASB):** Sets sector-specific standards for the disclosure of financially material sustainability information, including for real estate.
- **Carbon Disclosure Project (CDP):** Operates a global disclosure system for environmental impacts that is widely used by real estate companies and investors.
- **GRESB (Global Real Estate Sustainability Benchmark):** Provides ESG data and benchmarks specifically for real estate portfolios and infrastructure assets, supporting investor decision-making.

(c) Other Notable Initiatives

- **International Platform on Sustainable Finance (IPSF):** This is a forum where policymakers can align and compare sustainable finance initiatives, aiming to scale up private capital for sustainable investments.
- **International Sustainable Finance Centre (ISFC):** A think tank that focuses on research, capacity building, and convening stakeholders around sustainable finance and standardization.

1.4 The ›E‹ in ESG – focus on the IPCC report and climate-related litigation risks

Alexander McGregor, LLM

Environmental factors in the built environment are crucial to the long-term value of real estate and mitigating litigation risk.

154 Notable for real estate – see tabular overviews in subchapter #4.1.2.

1.4.1 Introduction to #1.4

The ›E‹ for ‚Environmental‹ in – the widely used but expansive acronym – ESG has emerged as a critically relevant issue in the real estate and construction sectors, and an important factor in the long-term value of real estate and mitigating legal risk.

The built environment is notably one of the most carbon-intensive sectors, accounting for approximately two-fifths of global greenhouse gas emissions.[155] With global building stock expected to double in floor area by the midcentury, the decisions taken by investors, developers and policymakers today, particularly those related to climate mitigation measures, will influence the sector's contribution to climate stability.[156]

The Intergovernmental Panel on Climate Change (IPCC) is the United Nation's body that assesses science related to climate change and »*was created to provide policymakers with regular scientific assessments on climate change, its implications and potential future risks, as well as to put forward adaptation and mitigation options.*«[157] The IPCC's Sixth Assessment Report provides a detailed vision for the real estate sector to achieve the decarbonization goals of the 2015 Paris Agreement.[158] Environmental considerations are not new to the real estate sector and are already incorporated into permitting and building energy efficiency ratings. However, the IPCC calls for rapid, systemic upscaling and advances in energy-efficient design and the use of low-carbon materials and smart building systems. The IPCC Report can be viewed as a key policy document and playbook for industry stakeholders, not only to support climate-resilient development and proactively align with emerging environmental benchmarks, but to mitigate transition risk and legal exposure.

Litigation risk for sectoral stakeholders is varied and draws on trends seen in other carbon-intensive sectors that are becoming increasingly relevant to real estate. Claims relating to greenwashing, breach of fiduciary duty, climate change and biodiversity loss, strategic claims (for example, aimed at driving change in line with the Paris Agreement and IPCC recommendations), and consumer and investor lawsuits, are likely to be seen as the effects of climate change materialize.

Real estate stakeholders who pay close attention to the IPCC Report will be best positioned to mitigate legal risk, realize value and thrive in a transformed sector.

155 World Green Building Council (WGBC), Bringing Embodied Carbon Upfront, https://worldgbc.s3.eu-west-2.amazonaws.com/wp-content/uploads/2022/09/22123951/WorldGBC_Bringing_Embodied_Carbon_Upfront.pdf, accessed 14.08.2025.

156 World Green Building Council (WGBC), Bringing Embodied Carbon Upfront, https://worldgbc.s3.eu-west-2.amazonaws.com/wp-content/uploads/2022/09/22123951/WorldGBC_Bringing_Embodied_Carbon_Upfront.pdf, accessed 14.08.2025.

157 The Intergovernmental Panel on Climate Change (IPCC), https://www.ipcc.ch/, accessed 14.08.2025.

158 This third and final part of the Sixth Assessment Report published in March 2022 focuses on climate change mitigation across various economic sectors including buildings (Chapter 9).

#1.4 "E" – climate & IPCC report, litigation risk	
	#1.4.1 – intro to #1.4
	#1.4.2 – the IPCC report in more detail
	#1.4.3 – global differences
	#1.4.4 – litigation risk
	#1.4.5 – mitigating risk

In this subchapter #1.4 we discuss the **IPCC report** (#1.4.2), global differences (#1.4.3), the litigation risk involved (#1.4.4), and general principles to mitigate those risks (#1.4.5).

1.4.2 The IPCC report in more detail

The UN warns that the building sector is not on track for decarbonization by 2050.[159] Furthermore, due to the long lifespan of buildings, today's construction and retrofitting decisions can »lock in« carbon emissions (or savings) for decades.[160] According to the IPCC, immediate action is required.

Carbon mitigation in the building sector involves two distinct emissions streams:[161]

- **Operational carbon** – from heating, cooling, lighting and appliance use (comprising approximately 28 % of global carbon emissions); and
- **Embodied carbon** – from producing and transporting construction materials, such as cement and steel (accounting for 11 % of global emissions).[162]

The IPCC Report offers recommendations for addressing both operational and embodied carbon.

> **Renovation or refurbishment of existing buildings** – The IPCC identifies the retrofitting and repurposing of existing buildings, making better use of the circular economy, as vital to reducing sectoral emissions. Low renovation rates and insufficient ambition in existing building renovations are key drivers of continued emissions, especially in developed economies.[163] While retrofitting is technically feasible and economically rational, it presents challenges such as financing upfront costs, minimizing disruption to occupants, and overcoming technical limitations in old buildings. From an investment standpoint, retrofitting

159 UN Environment Programme, Global Status Report for Buildings and Construction, https://wedocs.unep.org/bitstream/handle/20.500.11822/45095/global_status_report_buildings_construction_2023.pdf, accessed 14.08.2025.

160 Sandberg, Nina Holck, et al., Large potentials for energy saving and greenhouse gas emission reductions from large-scale deployment of zero emission building technologies in a national building stock, 2021.

161 World Green Building Council (WGBC), Bringing Embodied Carbon Upfront, https://worldgbc.s3.eu-west-2.amazonaws.com/wp-content/uploads/2022/09/22123951/WorldGBC_Bringing_Embodied_Carbon_Upfront.pdf, accessed 14.08.2025.

162 57 % of buildings' greenhouse gas emissions were indirect (from electricity and district heat), 24 % were direct on-site emissions, and about 18 % were from embodied carbon in building materials from the use of cement and steel: IPCC Report, Chapter 9: Buildings, p. 955.

163 Cabeza/Bai/Bertoldi/Kihila/Lucena/Mata/Mirasgedis/Novikova/Saheb, Buildings. In IPCC, Climate Change 2022: Mitigation of Climate Change. Contribution of Working Group III to the Sixth Assessment Report of the Intergovernmental Panel on Climate Change, 2022, p. 955.

can extend asset life, reduce operational carbon emissions, mitigate transition risk, and align portfolios with regulatory and investor expectations.[164]

Technology and innovation – The IPCC refers to a new generation of »smart« buildings and urban energy systems that can significantly reduce operational emissions. These systems effectively turn previously passive energy consumers into active participants (»prosumers«) in the energy system.[165]

Policy interventions to drive decarbonization – The ›E‹ in ESG is particularly relevant to the energy efficiency of buildings, which are evaluated using »green« rating systems.[166] The IPCC encourages policy interventions[167] to drive building sector decarbonization, with energy codes identified as being the »*main regulatory instrument*« to reduce carbon emissions from buildings.[168] Currently, rating systems and energy codes are localized to specific countries and regions. The development of clearer and consistent codes and legal obligations globally will ensure that new buildings are built to high-efficiency standards and prevent low-efficiency lock-in.

Emission targets and reporting – The IPCC emphasizes the importance of accurate reporting of direct, indirect and embodied emissions. As in other sectors, there is a lack of reliable data and harmonization across key metrics.[169] For example, there is no internationally agreed definition of a net-zero building – e.g., whether this entails a comprehensive assessment of the entire life cycle for operational and embodied carbon. This is gradually changing as regulators strive to ensure the availability of meaningful and comparable data sets and companies voluntarily adhere to reporting standards to boost their sustainability credentials. Meanwhile, rules governing the reporting of environmental impacts for the real estate sector are crystalizing. Notably, legislation such as the EU's Corporate Sustainability Reporting Directive (CSRD) requires larger companies to report climate-related risks and mitigations.

---

164 The European Commission's Renovation Wave initiative, for example, aims to at least double annual renovation rates and retrofit 35 million buildings by 2030, which is predicted to cut building energy use and create jobs. Communication from the Commission to the European Parliament, the Council, the European Economic and Social Committee and the Committee of the Regions. A Renovation Wave for Europe – greening our buildings, creating jobs, improving lives, COM/2020/662 final, https://energy.ec.europa.eu/topics/energy-efficiency/energy-performance-buildings/renovation-wave_en, accessed 14.08.2025.

165 Cabeza/Bai/Bertoldi/Kihila/Lucena/Mata/Mirasgedis/Novikova/Saheb, Buildings. In IPCC, 2022: Climate Change 2022: Mitigation of Climate Change. Contribution of Working Group III to the Sixth Assessment Report of the Intergovernmental Panel on Climate Change, 2022, p. 981.

166 According to the International Energy Agency (IEA), about 80 countries now have some form of building energy code in place, a 30 % increase in adoption since the Paris Agreement in 2015, https://www.iea.org/reports/technology-and-innovation-pathways-for-zero-carbon-ready-buildings-by-2030, accessed 14.08.2025.

167 For example, the IPCC refers to policy packages based on the SER (Sufficiency, Efficiency, Renewables) framework to grasp the full mitigation potential of the global building stock.

168 IPCC, Climate Change 2022: Mitigation of Climate Change. Contribution of Working Group III to the Sixth Assessment Report of the Intergovernmental Panel on Climate Change, 2022, p. 956.

169 IPCC, Climate Change 2022: Mitigation of Climate Change. Contribution of Working Group III to the Sixth Assessment Report of the Intergovernmental Panel on Climate Change, 2022, pp. 960, 983, 1009 and 1016.

1.4.3 Global differences

Climate mitigation in buildings is a global imperative according to the IPCC, but the challenges and strategies vary by region:

EU – The EU is generally considered to be at the forefront of building climate policy. As part of the European Green Deal, it aims to reach net-zero by 2050, and it addresses buildings through directives such as the Energy Performance of Buildings Directive (EPBD) and the Renovation Wave strategy.

UK – The UK has a net-zero goal by 2050 (enshrined in the Climate Change Act 2008). However, the government has recently scrapped plans to ban the sale of new gas boilers in 2035.[170]

North America – Efforts are more localized. New York (via Local Law 97) is pioneering carbon caps, while California, USA, and British Columbia, Canada, have advanced energy codes. Federal incentives for homeowners to retrofit in the USA are under government review and legal challenge.

Asia and Global South – Financing is a major constraint – the upfront cost of efficient buildings can be a barrier in lower-income regions, so international support is needed. The IPCC notes the »limited flow of finance« for building efficiency as a key obstacle and calls for knowledge transfer to the Global South.[171]

Investors with international interests must now also consider the varying speeds and directions of governments and regulators worldwide and respond to diverging expectations regarding sustainability, as well as the countervailing risks this creates.

1.4.4 Litigation risk

As sustainability standards become ingrained in regulatory frameworks and form part of investor expectations in certain parts of the world, the litigation risks for various stakeholders in the real estate sector are becoming more varied and complex. The following section is not exhaustive but identifies emerging risks in the sector.

170 Development and building standards in the UK are particularly contentious, with activism targeting the stated need for the insulation of housing stock and long running public debate over the use of green spaces for new housing developments.

171 IPCC, Climate Change 2022: Mitigation of Climate Change. Contribution of Working Group III to the Sixth Assessment Report of the Intergovernmental Panel on Climate Change, 2022, pp. 956 and 1016.

(a) Breach of fiduciary duty claims

It is estimated that over 20 % of real estate portfolios in various developed countries are at risk of becoming stranded assets in the coming years.[172] This could be for various climate-related reasons, for example:

- Lack of alignment with net-zero pathways, such as the use of insulation and »smart design« features in new and retrofitted buildings and transparency in emissions reporting.
- Adoption of stricter building codes and minimum sustainability standards for property, which could lead to operational restrictions, forced upgrades or fines for noncompliance.
- Failure to respond to physical climate risks, such as extreme weather events.

Each of these reasons could lead to financial losses and potential claims for breach of fiduciary duty against company directors of real estate and construction businesses.

Notably, claimants and NGOs bringing strategic claims[173] are focusing on whether transition plans adequately address the financial risks associated with climate change. For example, in 2023, the environmental NGO ClientEarth filed a derivative action lawsuit against the directors of the energy company Shell plc in the English High Court.[174] ClientEarth (unsuccessfully) argued that Shell's climate strategy failed adequately to mitigate the risk of stranded assets and therefore its directors breached their duties under the UK Companies Act.[175] This type of claim, brought by affected investors and NGOs, is also conceivable in a real estate context.

(b) Claims for climate- and biodiversity-related damages

Although climate- and biodiversity-related litigation is not a new phenomenon, most historical claims have been against governments and private organizations to prevent carbon intensive projects and nature loss, and to hold them accountable for failing to reduce emissions in line with the Paris Agreement. Claims for climate-related *damages* against private organizations are less common and have primarily targeted energy companies in the USA.

However, there are signs that the sectoral and jurisdictional focus of claimants and NGOs (and their litigation funders) is shifting. For example, in 2022 a group of Indonesian fishermen filed an ongoing claim against Holcim – the world's largest manufacturer of building materials – in Switzerland, demanding that Holcim reduce its carbon emissions and co-finance climate change adaptation measures in Indonesia proportionate to Holcim's historical contribution to overall global emissions.[176]

---

172 Wintermeyer, Lawrence, Time To Get Real On Real Estate Net Zero With Talent, Technology, And Tokenization, 02.05, 2024, https://www.forbes.com/sites/lawrencewintermeyer/2024/05/02/time-to-get-real-on-real-estate-net-zero-with-talent-technology-and-tokenization/, accessed 14.08.2025.

173 Given the breadth of issues incorporated within the term »ESG« and the absence of a specific self-contained liability system for related claims, claimants are bringing more creative, »strategic« claims – including claims against directors – with the aim of influencing the broader debate around sustainability issues and corporate decision-making.

174 ClientEarth v Shell plc [2023] EWHC 1897 (Ch).

175 Companies Act 2006, sections 172 and 174.

176 Asmania et al. v. Holcim.

While the jurisprudence regarding transnational climate-related damages is developing and the procedural, legal and evidential pathways to success narrow, this example illustrates how climate litigation is increasingly relevant to developers with high historical emissions and embodied carbon footprints. If emitter liability is ultimately established in this context, it will likely affect legal risk across the entire real estate value chain.

(c) Greenwashing and climatewashing claims

Simply put, greenwashing occurs when there is a discrepancy between what a business claims about its sustainability practices and its actions.[177] For example, asset managers and developers may face lawsuits and suffer reputational damage for deliberately or negligently misrepresenting the sustainability of buildings, failing to disclose climate-related risks, or failing to meet stated emission reduction targets.

Establishing greenwashing claims in the real estate sector will be highly context dependent given the lack of uniform sustainability definitions.[178] However, as in other sectors, consumers, investors and regulators are increasingly scrutinizing »green claims« in marketing and reporting.[179] Mandatory disclosure rules pervading the real estate sector also provide interested parties with access to more emissions data for analysis and evidence to support complaints. This area warrants monitoring and risk mitigation.

(d) Claims by investor and building users

Larger and publicly traded real estate and construction businesses may have regulatory obligations to disclose information regarding sustainability goals in marketing and statutory reports. If this information is misleading or overstates sustainability credentials, leading to investor losses or consumer damages, there is potential for class action claims, especially in jurisdictions with an established plaintiff bar and mass claim procedures, such as the USA. These claims could be coupled with allegations of securities fraud, greenwashing, and breaches of fiduciary duty.

1.4.5 Mitigating risk

The convergence of climate mitigation and environmental performance measures, as outlined in the IPCC Report, as well as various litigation risks, demands proactive planning. For every risk, there is a mitigation strategy. However, there is no one-size-fits-all approach. The appro-

177 Relevant in this context are related claims of »greenlighting« – i.e. shining light on a product or business's positive environmental attributes while concealing or ignoring (more) significant negative features – and »greenhushing« – where a business is deliberately silent on green issues to avoid scrutiny.

178 Note that some countries like France regulate particular green claims wording, for example, »carbon-neutral« or »zero-emission« claims – see, e.g., Decree No. 2022–539.

179 For example, the German NGO Deutsche Umwelthilfe (DUH) challenged TotalEnergies over ›climate-neutral‹ and ›CO_2-compensated‹ claims relating to heating oil marketed for residential use (Deutsche Umwelthilfe v. TotalEnergies Wärme & Kraftstoff Deutschland GmbH, 2022).

priate mitigation strategy depends on a business's activities, location, and the regulatory and litigation environment in which it operates, among other things.

There are some **general principles that can help businesses navigate litigation risks** and **take advantage of opportunities related to climate mitigation in buildings.** These include:

- Carrying out comprehensive sustainability due diligence on assets, projects, and counterparties that promise to deliver climate mitigations, and ensuring suitable contractual protections.
- Ensuring that sustainability statements are accurate, transparent, and supported by evidence, ideally in accordance with recognized international standards.
- Recording and tracking progress and delivery on climate commitments.
- Managing investor and consumer expectations through timely and transparent updates and disclosures.
- Integrating climate risk assessments into development and investment decisions.
- Monitoring evolving regulatory and litigation trends.

By aligning with the IPCC's recommendations and anticipating legal risks, stakeholders in the sector can mitigate potential liabilities and contribute meaningfully to global climate goals.

1.5 The ›S‹ in ESG – the pursuit of profit: The invisible workforce in global supply chains

Eriphyle Mitakidou-Ghabel

1.5.1 Introduction to #1.5: The hidden cost of flexibility and efficiency

Global supply chains are valued for their flexibility, efficiency and ability to scale production while reducing costs. However, this value often comes at a significant »human cost«: the invisible workforce. This refers to those whose work is critical to the supply chain, but whose contributions are neither directly visible nor traceable.

This invisibility is not due to their work being unimportant, but because global supply chains are often designed in a way to obscure them. Two of the most prominent practices that create sufficient distance between a company and the people performing the work are subcontracting and the use of on-demand or temporary workers. Both practices will be examined in greater detail to demonstrate that they are not merely an operational choice, but a high-risk strategy that facilitates profit by externalizing risk and responsibilities[180]. A narrow focus on direct sup-

180 LeBaron, Genevieve, Subcontracting Is Not Illegal, But Is It Unethical? Business Ethics, Forced Labor, and Economic Success, in The Brown Journal of World Affairs Vol. 20, No. 2, 237, 242.

pliers – common in both national and European due diligence legislation[181] – therefore, fails to reveal the most severe risks inherent to deeper supply chain levels.

While the governance of global supply chains is undeniably complex, »meaningful« due diligence must go beyond direct suppliers to address the systemic invisibility of labor embedded in today's global supply chains.

#1.5 "S" – invisible workforce, global supply chains	**#1.5.1 – intro to #1.5**
	#1.5.2 – subcontracting
	#1.5.3 – on-demand workers
	#1.5.4 – meaningful due diligence
	#1.5.5 – conclusion

This subchapter #1.5 **on the invisible workforce of global supply chains** covers subcontracting (#1.5.2), on-demand workers (#1.5.3), making invisible labor visible, conducting meaningful due diligence (#1.5.4), and concluding remarks (#1.5.5).

1.5.2 Subcontracting: The invisible workforce in supply chains

In the case of subcontracting, suppliers (contractors) employ additional individuals or companies[182], called subcontractors, from outside their organization[183] to perform their contractual work or services, either partially or entirely. In this context, a subcontractor is obligated to provide its work or services solely to the contractor, even though they ultimately operate within the principal's (e.g., buyer) scope of responsibility[184]. While subcontracting is not illegal per se – unless it is explicitly prohibited by contract – it has repeatedly been proven to facilitate human rights violations[185]. This often occurs when contractors transfer assigned work to unregistered workshops or informal enterprises without informing the principal. These subcontracted entities are usually smaller and lack the same standards regarding labor regulations[186], documentation, wage, working conditions, working hours[187], and occupational health and safety as the

181 German Supply Chain Act (Lieferkettensorgfaltspflichtengesetz), French Supply Chain Act (Loi de vigilance), EU's Corporate Sustainability Due Diligence Directive with its proposed amendments under Omnibus I.

182 Policy Department for Citizens' Rights and Constitutional Affairs, Liability in Subcontracting Chains: National Rules and the Need for a European Framework, https://www.europarl.europa.eu/RegData/etudes/STUD/2017/596798/IPOL_STU(2017)596798_EN.pdf, accessed 19.08.2025, 19.

183 European Commission, Directorate-General for Employment, Social Affairs & Inclusion Directorate D — Labour Mobility, Unit Unit D-1: Free movement of Workers and EURES, European Platform tackling undeclared work, Glossary of Terms, October 2018, https://www.ela.europa.eu/sites/default/files/2021-09/Glossary%20v6-final_0.pdf, accessed 20.08.2025, 5.

184 Haak, Andreas, Unternehmerische Zusammenarbeit in der öffentlichen Auftragsvergabe, https://www.vdz.org/vergabe-beschaffung/unternehmerische-zusammenarbeit-der-oeffentlichen-auftragsvergabe, accessed 08.08.2025.

185 LeBaron, Genevieve, Subcontracting Is Not Illegal, But Is It Unethical? Business Ethics, Forced Labor, and Economic Success, in The Brown Journal of World Affairs Vol. 20, No. 2, pp. 237 et seq.

186 Mosely, Layna, Labor Rights and Multinational Production, Cambridge University Press, https://scispace.com/pdf/labor-rights-and-multinational-production-390o8as1aa.pdf, accessed 08.08.2025.

187 Labowitz/Baumann-Pauly, Business as usual is not an option: Supply chains and sourcing after Rana Plaza, https://bhr.stern.nyu.edu/publication/business-as-usual-is-not-an-option-supply-chains-and-sourcing-after-rana-plaza/, accessed 11.08.2025.

contractor[188]. This practice is commonly driven by tight deadlines, the high product demand, or unanticipated orders that suppliers are required to fulfill[189]. However, subcontracting also serves the contractor's interests, as it is frequently used as a deliberate strategy to increase profits and remain competitive on the market. As a result, subcontracting is widespread, particularly in sectors such as agriculture and food processing, textiles, road transport, and construction. Further down the supply chain, workers are often unaware of their rights or of the grievance mechanisms[190] that contractors or principals may have established. Consequently, many choose to tolerate rights violations in order secure a steady income[191]. Moreover, amid the complex web of contractors and subcontractors, it is challenging for workers to determine who is legally responsible for their employment conditions[192]. Hence, although subcontracting is not illegal per se, it fuels illegal practices.

1.5.3 On-demand workers: Flexibility at the expense of protection

On-demand or temporary workers are typically hired through agencies or digital platforms and can be deployed flexibly as needed. This practice has enabled suppliers to respond rapidly to buyer demand and is prevalent in sectors, such as logistics, warehousing, agriculture, and manufacturing. Suppliers benefit from cost savings, reduced recruitment overhead, and scalable workforce capacity. However, this flexibility often comes at the expense of workers. Many are excluded from benefits, sick leave, and collective bargaining[193]. Wages often exclude compensation for overtime, and working hours are frequently irregular and unpredictable. Workers may also receive little to no adequate training on their rights and responsibilities or health and safety. Temporary workers may also lack knowledge of grievance mechanisms or may not be eligible to use them. They often fear retaliation if they speak up.

Similar to illegal subcontracting, on-demand labor externalizes risk and responsibility while offering increased flexibility.

188 SOMO and CCC, Fatal Fashion – Analysis of recent factory fires in Pakistan and Bangladesh: a call to protect and respect garment workers' lives, https://www.somo.nl/fatal-fashion-2/, accessed 10.08.2025; https://www.etuc.org/en/securing-workers-rights-subcontracting-chains, accessed 10.08.2025.

189 SOMO, Fact Sheet, Hidden subcontracting in the garment industry, Zooming in on the role of buying companies, https://www.somo.nl/wp-content/uploads/2015/09/Hidden-subcontracting.pdf, accessed 20.08.2025, 1.

190 Syndicate European Trade Union, Securing Workers' Rights in Subcontracting Chains, https://www.etuc.org/sites/default/files/2021-10/Securing%20workers%20rights%20brochure_v4-spreads.pdf, accessed 19.08.2025, 11.

191 Syndicate European Trade Union, Securing Workers' Rights in Subcontracting Chains, https://www.etuc.org/sites/default/files/2021-10/Securing%20workers%20rights%20brochure_v4-spreads.pdf, accessed 19.08.2025, 11.

192 Policy Department for Citizens' Rights and Constitutional Affairs, Liability in Subcontracting Chains: National Rules and the Need for a European Framework, 2017, https://www.europarl.europa.eu/RegData/etudes/STUD/2017/596798/IPOL_STU(2017)596798_EN.pdf, accessed 19.08.2025, 10.

193 Faris Natour, Respecting Human Rights in the On-Demand Economy: Closing the New Governance Gap, https://www.cambridge.org/core/services/aop-cambridge-core/content/view/D449DF0A9E34E3D56A3C2361551DB551/S2057019816000079a.pdf/respecting-human-rights-in-the-on-demand-economy-closing-the-new-governance-gap.pdf, accessed 13.08.2025, p. 317.

1.5.4 Making invisible labor visible

Though different in form, both subcontracting and on-demand labor share a key characteristic: they enable companies to benefit from labor while distancing themselves from responsibility for the conditions under which that labor is performed. Mandatory due diligence obligations exist and already apply to many companies, yet both practices remain invisible due to a narrow, contract-focused approach that is unable to capture workers' actual conditions. Therefore, national and European due diligence legislation, with their focus on direct suppliers, has proven insufficient to deliver meaningful impact. This underscores the necessity of revisiting the foundational documents that have guided the development of such mandatory legislation over the past decade: the United Nations Guiding Principles (UNGPs) and the OECD Guidelines for Multinational Enterprises (OECD Guidelines). The UNGPs establish a global standard outlining the corporate responsibility to respect human rights and the state's duty to protect against abuses, while the OECD Guidelines offer detailed recommendations for responsible business conduct, including human rights, labor rights, and environmental stewardship, specifically tailored for multinational corporations. Both the UNGPs and the OECD Guidelines demand more than contractual compliance. They require companies to respect human rights and to adopt a risk-based approach to due diligence, prioritizing the most severe risks to people regardless of where they occur in the supply chain[194]. Hence, conducting »meaningful« due diligence requires companies to map their entire supply chain and identify all pain points.[195] To tackle this challenge, the following key measures should be considered by a principal (e.g., a buyer):

a) **Responsible business practices**: Align purchasing and production timelines to avoid cost and time pressures that incentivize subcontracting. Purchasing practices should promote respect for human and labor rights at all levels of the supply chain[196], including anticipating demand and checking supplier capacity.
b) **Authorization of subcontractors**: The use of subcontractors to fulfill assigned orders should be contractually prohibited unless authorized by the principal or limited to a pre-approved list of subcontractors, in order to maintain transparency and control[197]. In any case, the principal should receive key information about the subcontractor. This could include the subcontractor's legal name, business registration number, location of operations, number of employees, and details on compliance with labor standards.
c) **Traceability**: Companies should go beyond direct contractual suppliers and trace the entire supply chain, including intermediaries, agencies, and hidden workshops. Companies must map the actual production processes and engage with workers directly, instead of merely relying on contracts. Traceability includes both products and the labor behind them.

194 UNGPs, Commentary to Principle 17, https://www.ohchr.org/sites/default/files/documents/publications/guidingprinciplesbusinesshr_en.pdf, accessed 20.08.2025.

195 SOMO, Fact Sheet, Hidden subcontracting in the garment industry, Zooming in on the role of buying companies, https://www.somo.nl/wp-content/uploads/2015/09/Hidden-subcontracting.pdf, accessed 20.08.2025, 3.

196 SOMO, Fact Sheet, Hidden subcontracting in the garment industry, Zooming in on the role of buying companies, https://www.somo.nl/wp-content/uploads/2015/09/Hidden-subcontracting.pdf, accessed 20.08.2025, p. 5.

197 Syndicate European Trade Union, Securing Workers' Rights in Subcontracting Chains, https://www.etuc.org/sites/default/files/2021-10/Securing%20workers%20rights%20brochure_v4-spreads.pdf, accessed 19.08.2025, 15.

d) **Supplier training and onboarding**: Ensure that training on health and safety, fair wages, and workers' rights applies equally to temporary and subcontracted workers.
e) **Oversight and verification**: Traditional audits focusing on direct suppliers are insufficient. Regular unannounced visits and direct engagement with workers are essential to detecting hidden workers and preventing abuse. Otherwise, a supplier can easily change production arrangements without this being noticed.
f) **Access to remedy**: Guarantee accessible grievance mechanisms for all workers, regardless of employment status, and ensure these mechanisms are communicated throughout the supply chain.

1.5.5 Conclusion

Cases of illegal subcontracting and on-demand labor illustrate how the pursuit of profit in global supply chains can result in invisible workers and hidden workshops. These practices demonstrate why due diligence must extend beyond direct suppliers and formal contracts. The challenge ahead is not to abandon flexibility, but rather to ensure that it no longer comes at the expense of human rights by integrating »meaningful« due diligence throughout the supply chain.

1.6 The ›G‹ in ESG – governance in the real estate industry: Anti-bribery and corruption (ABC) and anti-money laundering (AML)

Dr. Matthias Brockhaus

1.6.1 Introduction to #1.6

In the globally networked real estate industry, integrity and transparency are considered foundational principles of any sustainable business relationship. In this context, good corporate governance plays a particularly important role, as continuously increasing compliance requirements must be observed and implemented. In this context, governance is generally understood as adherence to the standards of good corporate management, which is primarily reflected in the establishment of an appropriate corporate structure and the implementation of a compliance management system.[198] In Germany, for example, the German Corporate Governance Code (»DCGK«) is intended to ensure a collection of principles, recommendations, and

198 Roeder/Werthmüller/Schlutz/Havlik, Compliance (due diligence) in the context of transactions – ESG due diligence, CCZ 2024, 13; Keilich, Jochen ESG reporting obligations and their impact on labour law, SPA, 2024, 73.

suggestions for »good corporate governance.«[199] In addition, the requirements of anti-bribery and corruption (ABC) and anti-money laundering (AML) legislation in general and across countries must be complied with in the area of criminal law. It should be noted that the implementation of compliance requirements applies not only to large companies and banks, but also to all smaller players in the real estate sector, such as real estate agents.

#1.6	**#1.6.1 - intro to #1.6**
"G" - ABC & AML	**#1.6.2 - concept and meaning of "ABC"**
	#1.6.3 - term and meaning of "AML"
	#1.6.4 - relevance for the real estate industry
	#1.6.5 - legal obligations and possible consequences
	#1.6.6 - conclusion

This subchapter #1.6 on **governance in the real estate industry** covers the concept and meaning of »ABC« (#1.6.2), the term and meaning of »AML« (#1.6.3), the relevance for the real estate industry (#1.6.4), legal obligations and possible consequences (#1.6.5) followed by concluding remarks (#1.6.6).

1.6.2 Concept and meaning of »ABC«

One aspect of criminal compliance that companies must pay particular attention to is the fight against corruption. Corruption disrupts fair competition, undermines trust, endangers the reputation of those involved, and can have serious civil and, in particular, criminal consequences. In principle, companies issue a so-called »ABC policy« for this purpose, which may include a »code of ethics« and an »anti-bribery and anti-corruption policy.«[200] The aim of these regulations is to identify and reduce potential corruption risks for employees in the company, for which rules of conduct are established that usually go well beyond the standard legal requirements.[201] For example, anti-corruption guidelines may specify strict value limits and approval requirements for the granting and acceptance of gifts.[202]

In the real estate industry, corruption can manifest itself in the distribution of subsidies, in approval procedures, in government procurement processes, or through inadmissible donations to decision-makers.[203] Since corruption is a global problem, efforts to fight it are already being made at international level, which in Germany is happening through the ratification and implementation of international agreements and at European level through the adoption of

199 Thoms, Anahita, in: Moosmayer/Lösler, Corporate Compliance, § 17 ESG – Legal and Regulatory Foundations, margin note 26.

200 Wolfram/Peukert, Impact of the ›new‹ Section 299 of the German Criminal Code (StGB) on compliance practice, NZWiSt 2017, 208.

201 Schoop/Ballo, in: Volk/Beukelmann, Munich Lawyers' Handbook: Defence in Commercial and Tax Criminal Matters, 3rd edition 2020, section 20 corruption, margin note 20.

202 Wolfram/Peukert, NZWiSt 2017, 208, 209.

203 Schoop/Ballo, in: Volk/Beukelmann, section 20 corruption, margin note 18.

an anti-corruption package of measures.[204] Of particular relevance is the draft EU directive (EU Anti-Corruption Directive).[205]

1.6.3 Term and meaning of »AML«

Another important aspect is the fight against money laundering, which also poses new challenges for companies due to global networking and cross-border financial crime. Money laundering involves infiltrating illegally obtained assets – for example from crimes such as fraud, drug trafficking or tax evasion – into the legal economic cycle to hide their criminal origin. The area of AML (›Anti-Money Laundering‹) refers to measures designed to make money laundering more difficult or prevent it altogether. At EU level, numerous legal acts have already been enacted in this area, which, in addition to fighting money laundering, also deal with the establishment of a separate EU supervisory authority.[206] This alone demonstrates the urgency of the issue.

1.6.4 Relevance for the real estate industry

The real estate sector is particularly affected by this area, as the high transaction volume and complex corporate structures can often obscure the origin of monetary values. Caution is advised, especially in the case of large cash payments and the involvement of foreign companies. From a European perspective, a higher risk of money laundering is assumed in particular when there is a cross-border correspondence relationship.[207] The area of public procurement is also affected when decision-makers demand substantial personal benefits in order to select a particular candidate.[208] Violations of the regulations can result in both significant financial penalties and administrative measures.[209]

204 Grützner/Behr, in: Momsen, Carsten, WirtschaftsSteuerStrafR-HdB/Grützner/Behr, 2. Ed. 2020, section 30, margin note 377; Volk/Beukelmann/Schoop/Ballo, section 20 corruption, margin note 71.

205 Anti-Corruption Directive (2023/0135(COD)) – proposal: Proposal for a Directive of the European Parliament and of the Council on combating corruption, replacing Council Framework Decision 2003/568/JHA and the Convention on the fight against corruption involving officials of the European Communities or officials of Member States of the European Union and amending Directive (EU) 2017/1371 of the European Parliament and of the Council, https://eur-lex.europa.eu/legal-content/EN/TXT/?uri=celex%3A52023PC0234, accessed 29.10.2025.

206 Haufellner/Haffke/Heinrichs, Current developments in money laundering law, BKR 2025, 392, 393.

207 Bauerfeind/Hille, The future of money laundering supervision, GWR 2024, 33, 34.

208 Schoop/Ballo, Volk/Beukelmann, section 20 corruption, margin note 18.

209 Achtelik, Olaf, The new EU legislation to combat money laundering and terrorist financing, BKR 2024, 353, 360.

1.6.5 Legal obligations and possible consequences

The legal requirements for preventing corruption and money laundering are far-reaching in the real estate sector. Each measure aims to ensure market transparency and to prevent illegal assets from entering the legal economic cycle or gaining a competitive advantage through corruption.

The **essential duties include** the following:

a) **Know Your Customer (»KYC«)**: A key component of AML measures is the application of customer due diligence obligations.[210] A number of due diligence obligations must be complied with in relation to contracting parties. In particular, the parties must be clearly identified, the beneficial owners must be determined, and the purpose of the intended business relationship must be assessed.[211] Contractual partners of companies must submit to far-reaching contractual provisions and self-disclosures for this purpose.[212] The aim is to reveal not only the formal contractual partners, but also the individuals behind a company. Furthermore, all collected information must be documented in a clear and transparent way.
b) **Suspicious activity reports**: Companies have to exercise greater due diligence if their risk analysis indicates that there may be an increased risk of money laundering.[213] If suspicions arise in connection with a real estate transaction, the facts must be forwarded to a central reporting office – in Germany, the Financial Intelligence Unit – for analysis and further investigation.[214]
c) **Documentation and retention obligations**: In addition, all details and information obtained in the course of fulfilling due diligence obligations must be recorded and retained by the obligated parties. This is intended in particular to prevent the person behind the company from hiding and to enable them to be investigated by the investigating authorities at a later date.[215]
d) **Internal organization and employee training**: Furthermore, there must be a compliance manager who is responsible for ensuring compliance with relevant legal provisions and official orders.[216] Companies are obliged to set up internal control mechanisms in order to identify and minimize risks at an early stage. Moreover, a money laundering officer at management level must be appointed, who is responsible for ensuring compliance with money laundering regulations.[217] In addition, regular training of employees on typical risk scenarios and legal requirements must be conducted.

210 Bauerfeind/Hille, The future of money laundering supervision, GWR 2024, 33, 34.
211 Figura, Julia, in: Herzog/Achtelik, Money Laundering Act, 5. Ed. 2023, section 10, margin note 5.
212 Schoop/Ballo, in: Volk/Beukelmann, section 20 corruption, margin note 20.
213 Achtelik, Olaf, in: Herzog/Achtelik, Money Laundering Act, section 15, margin note 4.
214 Achtelik, Olaf, The new EU legislation to combat money laundering and terrorist financing, BKR 2024, 353, 360.
215 Herzog, Felix, in: Herzog/Achtelik, Money Laundering Act, section 8, margin note 3.
216 Achtelik, Olaf, The new EU legislation to combat money laundering and terrorist financing, BKR 2024, 353, 356.
217 Herzog, Felix, in: Herzog/Achtelik, Money Laundering Act, section 7, margin note 1.

*The following **practical example** illustrates the implications: If a buyer acquires a commercial property through a non-transparent offshore structure and pays the purchase price mainly in cash, they should expect a suspicious transaction report. If the case is taken up by the authorities, there is a risk not only of confiscation of the property, but also of criminal consequences for all parties involved, including the broker, the notary, and managing directors of the company.*

1.6.6 Conclusion

The fight against corruption and money laundering is not a temporary phenomenon or mere bureaucratic duty, but a central element of sustainable corporate governance. If companies fail to implement governance criteria, they must accept reputational damage, loss of value and increasingly difficult refinancing.[218] In addition, there is a risk of criminal consequences such as heavy fines and criminal proceedings against those responsible. Companies are therefore well advised to incorporate all ABC and AML structures into their compliance systems so that they are ultimately rewarded with increased efficiency, value enhancement and future viability.[219]

218 Roeder/Werthmüller/Schlutz/Havlik, Compliance (due diligence) in the context of transactions – ESG due diligence, CCZ 2024, 13.

219 Roeder/Werthmüller/Schlutz/Havlik, Compliance (due diligence) in the context of transactions – ESG due diligence, CCZ 2024, 13.

2 Real estate investment – market, responsible investment, approaches, investor types, impact investing, financing and ESG

2.1 Introduction to Chapter #2

Sabine Wieduwilt

»The best investment on Earth is earth.«
– Louis Glickman[220]

2.1.1 Content of Chapter #2

This book is about real estate investment and ESG.

There are as many ways to incorporate ESG into real estate investment, to invest responsibly as there are definitions of ESG. In the previous chapter, we approached the topic from the perspective of ESG. In this chapter, we start with the angle of real estate investment, setting the stage with market insights.

This chapter focuses on the investment market (#2.2), looks into (sustainable and) responsible investment (#2.3), real estate investment approaches, with a view to investor types and deal structures (#2.4), then looks a bit closer at impact investing (#2.5), and closes with ESG and finance, including notes on greenwashing (#2.6).

220 Glickman, Louis, real estate investor, from: Realty Mogul, 20 Famous Real Estate Investing Quotes, https://www.realtymogul.com/knowledge-center/article/20-famous-real-estate-investing-quotes, accessed 10.08.2025.

2.1.2 Real estate investment

Before we dive into all of this: *What are we talking about when we talk about real estate investment?*

©Judith Carla Wieduwilt (2025)

Working as a lawyer with 20 years of experience in real estate from the legal side, I'm still not the market professional, hence I need to keep my insights on real estate investment from a market perspective very basic in this introduction. Please skip to chapter #2.2 if you want to read market insights about the global real estate market from market intelligence, data, and foresight professionals.

What is real estate investment? It involves the purchase, ownership, management, rental, and/or sale of real estate for profit. Real estate is a tangible asset class that offers investors the potential for capital appreciation, income generation, and portfolio diversification. Real estate investment is a dynamic and diverse field, encompassing a wide range of strategies and investor profiles. From individual investors seeking passive income through rental properties to institutional investors managing large portfolios of commercial real estate, the approaches to real estate investment are as varied as the investors themselves. Real estate investment spans several distinct asset classes, each with its own risk profile, return potential, and market dynamics.

Table 15 provides a general overview of **real estate investment concepts, including investment approaches, types of investors, deal types, and asset classes.** If offers a short description of each category without regard for completeness. Successful investors carefully consider these characteristics when constructing and managing their real estate portfolios. See also **Table 16**, which includes notes on **capital markets, securities markets, and financing structures.** For a more complete and nuanced overview, we could also address core investment vehicles and markets of the real estate investment landscape. We could also add strategic, structural, risk, exit, tax, and sustainability considerations which are increasingly important in today's market.

Section	Category	Description
Investment approaches	**Direct investment**	Involves purchasing physical properties directly. Investors have full control over the property but also bear all the risks and responsibilities associated with ownership.
	Indirect investment	Involves investing in real estate through vehicles such as Real Estate Investment Trusts (REITs), real estate mutual funds, or private equity funds. This approach offers diversification and professional management, but less control over individual properties.
Investor types	**Individual investors**	These investors typically invest in residential or small commercial properties. They may seek rental income, capital appreciation, or both.
	Institutional investors	Investors may include pension funds, insurance companies, and investment firms. They often invest in large-scale commercial properties and have a long-term investment horizon.
	Private equity firms	They raise capital from investors to acquire, manage, and sell real estate assets. They often focus on value-add and opportunistic strategies.
Deal types	**Core**	Low-risk, stable income properties in prime locations with high occupancy rates.
	Core-plus	Slightly higher risk than core properties, but have potential for value-add through property improvements.
	Value-add	Properties that require significant improvements or repositioning to increase value.
	Opportunistic	High-risk, high-reward investments, often involving distressed properties or development projects.
Asset classes	**Residential**	Includes single-family homes, multi-family apartment buildings, condominiums, and townhouses. Residential properties are often favored by individual investors due to their familiarity and the potential for steady rental income. Market dynamics are influenced by demographic trends, local employment rates, and supply and demand of housing.
	Office	Office properties range from small professional buildings to large skyscrapers in central business districts. These assets are typically favored by institutional investors and are sensitive to economic cycles, employment trends, and shifts in workplace practices such as remote work.
	Retail	Retail real estate includes shopping centers, strip malls, standalone stores, and large regional malls. The performance of these assets is closely tied to consumer spending patterns and the evolving landscape of e-commerce, which has prompted significant changes in tenant mix and property usage.

Section	Category	Description
Asset classes	**Industrial**	This category encompasses warehouses, distribution centers, manufacturing facilities, and flex spaces. In recent years, industrial real estate has seen strong demand, driven by the growth of e-commerce and the need for efficient supply chain logistics.
	Hospitality	Hospitality assets include hotels, resorts, and short-term rental properties. Due to their high sensitivity to economic cycles, travel trends, and global events, these investments are more volatile but potentially lucrative during periods of high demand.
	Specialty and Alternative Assets	This broad category covers properties such as student housing, senior living facilities, self-storage facilities, data centers, and healthcare real estate. These assets often cater to specific demographic or industry needs and can offer diversification benefits within a real estate portfolio.

Table 15: Concepts in real estate investment

Section	Category	Description
Capital markets	Equity markets	Platforms for buying/selling ownership interests (e.g., shares in REITs, real estate companies).
	Debt markets	Markets for trading real estate debt instruments (e.g., mortgage-backed securities, bonds).
	Public vs. private Markets	Public markets are traded on exchanges (REITs, listed companies), while private markets involve direct transactions and private funds.
Securities markets	Stocks	Shares in real estate companies or REITs, traded on public exchanges.
	Bonds	Debt securities issued by real estate companies or for property financing.
	REITs	Publicly traded trusts investing in real estate assets, offering liquidity and diversification.
	Mortgage-Backed Securities (MBS)	Securities backed by pools of mortgages, providing exposure to real estate debt.
Financing structures	Traditional mortgages	Standard loans secured by real estate, typically with fixed or variable rates.
	Mezzanine financing	A hybrid of debt and equity; subordinate to senior debt, higher risk and return.
	Preferred equity	An equity investment with priority over common equity in distributions, but below debt.
	Syndicated loans	Loans provided by a group of lenders, spreading risk for large transactions.

Table 16: Capital markets, securities markets and financing structures

2.2 The global investment market

Andreas Trumpp/Tobias Dichtl

2.2.1 Introduction to #2.2

This chapter opens with a map of the global investable property landscape and its broad classifications, then drills into the forces that shape returns. It walks through five global megatrends – demographics, decarbonization, digitalization, supply-chain realignment, and the emerging defense buildup – before laying out how monetary policy, the real-economy backdrop, and shifting geopolitical and geoeconomic sands filter risk and capital. The discussion then turns to today's market mechanics, highlighting the steady rise in transparency, the patchy recovery in liquidity, and the state of capital flows, deal volumes and pricing as of mid-2025. Each section concludes with a brief »why investors should care« take-away, keeping the focus on practical implications rather than theory.

#2.2	**#2.2.1 - intro to #2.2**
Global real estate investment market & megatrends	**#2.2.2 - global property investment market**
	#2.2.3 - global megatrends
	#2.2.4 - monetary and financial policy
	#2.2.5 - economic environment
	#2.2.6 - geopolitics and geoeconomics
	#2.2.7 - today's real estate markets

In this subchapter #2.2 on the **global real estate investment market**, we classify the market (#2.2.2), then continue with factors influencing the market, starting with global megatrends (#2.2.3), then following up with the monetary and financial policy (#2.2.4), the economic environment (#2.2.5) and geopolitics and geoeconomics (#2.2.6). After discussing the influencing factors, we look into today's real estate markets (#2.2.7).

2.2.2 Classification and size of the global property investment market

MSCI estimates the broader »investable« market (including owner-occupied & small landlords) to be around USD 19 trillion. The professionally managed universe amounts to USD 12.5 trillion, underscoring how much stock remains outside of institutional hands. The Americas remain the deepest hunting ground at USD 5.3 trillion, yet EMEA's USD 3.8 trillion offers the broadest country diversification, while APAC's USD 3.3 trillion is the fastest institutionalizing.[221] Investors seeking large-scale residential exposure gravitate to the U.S., while office-to-green-conversion plays are most prevalent in Europe. APAC offers the clearest hospitality and data center pipelines. Note that currency swings can mask reality: The modest global shrinkage in 2024 compared to 2023 was mostly a USD story. Recovery is the base case, not a given. Major forecasters

221 Neshat/Patkar/Hariharan, MSCI Real Estate Market Size Report – The size of the professionally managed global real estate investment market in 2024, 2025.

(MSCI, JLL, CBRE, Savills among others) predict rising volumes and values through 2025, but all highlight refinancing risk, policy shocks, and a still-fragile China as potential spoilers.[222]

Why should investors care?

Market size is an important factor in portfolio construction for institutional investors who want to avoid over-allocating to specific countries or regions. Some investors focus on regions with which they are more familiar and whose regulatory framework suits them best. Global portfolios usually reflect market size in their allocation.

Different regions have historically shown different market cycles and developments. This enables diversification across the portfolio, which mitigates risks that could materialize in a country or region. While country- or region-specific risks can be diversified, structural trends or external shocks with an impact on a global level cannot be mitigated.

2.2.3 The influence of global megatrends on the investment market

(a) Demographic shift

All available figures sketch a world in which the Global North must retrofit for an aging population and smaller households, while the Global South scrambles to house and service hundreds of millions of new urban consumers – a demographic fork that shapes every regional investment strategy.

The U.S. already has 17.6% of its population aged 65 and older (54 million people) – up from 12.4% in 2000.[223] Retirees and job seekers alike are migrating to the Sun Belt, where midsized southern cities are growing at a rate of about 1.5% per year – the fastest of any U.S. region.[224] Europe is the world's oldest large economic bloc: 21.6% of EU residents are over 65, and the median age is 44.7 years.[225] At the same time, household structures are fragmenting: 75 million EU adults now live alone, up 17% since 2015.[226] The pairing of an ageing population and smaller households is driving secular demand for rental housing and senior living facilities, while stringent energy performance rules keep supply tight and rents firm. Japan remains the poster child of ageing, with almost one-third of its citizens (36 million) already over 65, a pillar for

222 CBRE, 2025 Global Investor Intentions Survey, 2025, https://www.cbre.com/insights/viewpoints/2025-global-investor-intentions-survey, accessed 08.09.2025; Savills, 2025 Global Investment Outlook, 2025, https://impacts.savills.com/market-trends/2025-investment-outlook.html, accessed 08.09.2025; JLL, Global Real Estate Perspective, May 2025, https://www.jll.com/en-us/insights/market-perspectives/global, accessed 29.07.2025.

223 World Bank Group, 2025, https://data.worldbank.org/indicator/SP.POP.65UP.TO.ZS, accessed 30.07.2025.

224 United States Census Bureau, Sun Belt Cities and Towns Led Nation in Population Growth, 2024, https://www.census.gov/library/stories/2024/05/sun-belt-cities-and-towns.html, accessed 30.07.2025.

225 Eurostat, Population structure and ageing, 2025, https://ec.europa.eu/eurostat/statistics-explained/index.php/Population_structure_and_ageing, accessed 30.07.2025.

226 Eurostat, Household composition statistics, 2025, https://ec.europa.eu/eurostat/statistics-explained/index.php/Household_composition_statistics, accessed 30.07.2025.

healthcare REITs and senior housing.[227] At the other extreme, emerging Asia is urbanizing at breakneck speed: the UN projects that India alone will add 416 million urban dwellers by 2050, while its current urban population is expanding by roughly 2% per year.[228] Indonesia's cities are growing by 1.9% annually and the Philippines by 1.5%, channeling capital toward mass-market residential housing and modern warehouses needed to serve a swelling urban middle class.[229]

(b) Sustainability and decarbonization

Every major capital provider now prices climate risk and carbon performance, and regulators are tightening building efficiency rules. The cost of ***not*** decarbonizing is now explicit: insurance premiums, brown discounts, and refinancing spreads all punish laggards. Europe is regulation-led; the Americas are insurance- and litigation-led; APAC is bifurcated between top-tier net-zero adopters and undervalued emerging-market risk. Green-capital supply is ample. In 2024 USD 1 trillion in sustainable bonds were issued, with EMEA still leading and APAC closing in fast.[230]

Climate risk is finally being priced. In the U.S., homeowners in the top-risk ZIP codes pay 82% higher home-insurance premiums and face non-renewal rates 80% higher that those in low-risk areas. Excess-&-surplus (E&S) premiums in catastrophe-exposed states have jumped to USD 3 billion in 2024 from USD 1.2 billion in 2018.[231] Capital is tilting toward inland »climate-haven« metros, code-plus logistics, and multifamily properties that are above the revised Federal Emergency Management Agency (FEMA) flood or wildfire thresholds. REIT green-bond issuance (USD 4.25 billion in 2024) is funding retrofits.[232] EMEA still issues 42% of all global green bonds and 51.7% of green bonds specifically. APAC accounted for 30% of all sustainable bonds and 27.2% of green bonds in 2024.[233]

Furthermore, regulation is the hammer. The 2024 recast of the Energy Performance of Buildings Directive (EPBD) establishes zero-emission as the standard for new public buildings starting

227 World Economic Forum, More than 1 in 10 people in Japan are aged 80 or over. Here's how its ageing population is reshaping the country, 2023, https://www.weforum.org/stories/2023/09/elderly-oldest-population-world-japan, accessed 30.07.2025.

228 United Nations, 68% of the world population projected to live in urban areas by 2050, 2018, https://www.un.org/uk/desa/68-world-population-projected-live-urban-areas-2050-says-un; macrotrends, India Urban Population, 2023. https://www.macrotrends.net/global-metrics/countries/ind/india/urban-population, accessed 30.07.2025.

229 Trading Economics, Indonesia – Urban Population Growth in %, 2024, https://tradingeconomics.com/indonesia/urban-population-growth-annual-percent-wb-data.html; macrotrends, Philippines Urban Population, 2023, https://www.macrotrends.net/global-metrics/countries/phl/philippines/urban-population, accessed 30.07.2025.

230 Intercontinental Exchange, Sustainable Bond Analysis, 2024, https://www.ice.com/insights/sustainable-bond-report-2024, accessed 30.07.2025.

231 Reuters, International, domestic insurers push into catastrophe-hit US property markets, 2024, https://www.reuters.com/markets/us/international-domestic-insurers-push-into-catastrophe-hit-us-property-markets-2024-12-16, accessed 30.07.2025.

232 S&P Global, Green bond issuance by US REITs picks up in 2024, 2025, https://www.spglobal.com/market-intelligence/en/news-insights/articles/2025/1/green-bond-issuance-by-us-reits-picks-up-in-2024-87195777, accessed 30.07.2025.

233 Intercontinental Exchange, Sustainable Bond Analysis, 2024, https://www.ice.com/insights/sustainable-bond-report-2024, accessed 30.07.2025.

in 2028 and for all new constructions beginning in 2030.[234] In a recent paper, JLL notes that 69 % of investors report price reductions (0–100 bp) on inefficient assets, and 76 % say they walked away from or bid lower on brown stock.[235] In APAC, we notice a two-speed race. Mature markets, such as Japan, Australia, and Singapore, have set hard net-zero dates, while physical-risk pricing is still catching up in parts of ASEAN. Core capital demands green-certified towers in mature markets. Early-stage investors are funding elevated-floor, solar-powered logistics hubs in Vietnam, Thailand, and Indonesia, betting that physical-risk pricing will tighten. Japan's cheap transition financing is underwriting mass heat-pump and solar retrofits.

(c) Digitalization and data economy

The digital economy megatrend is no longer merely supportive; it is foundational, and the race is on to secure power-dense sites across all three regions before artificial intelligence's (AI) electrical appetite overtakes the grid. The AI boom has transformed data-infrastructure from a niche »alternative« into the hottest slice of global real estate. Two structural facts frame every regional story. First, it is about power and capital expenditures (CapEx): McKinsey estimates that USD 6.7 trillion must be spent on data center capacity by 2030 just to keep pace with AI workloads.[236] Second, it is about energy draw: The IEA projects that data center electricity use will more than double to about 945 TWh by 2030. That accounts for about 3 % of all power consumed on the planet and slightly more than Japan uses today.[237]

JLL reports that North American colocation vacancy hit a record low 2.6% in 2024 as AI demand sent absorption to 4.4 gigawatts – i. e. four times the level in 2020. The under-construction pipeline is 6.6 gigawatts (GW), 78 % of which is already pre-leased.[238] This indicates that growth is guaranteed, but grid access is the new permit requirement. This is why developers pay premiums for on-site generation or utility joint ventures. In EMEA, current demand far exceeds supply. In the core FLAP-D markets (Frankfurt, London, Amsterdam, Paris, and Dublin), 2024's take-up was 344 MW versus 306 MW of new supply, and pre-lets doubled to 702 MW. JLL forecasts that the region will outpace the rest of the world, growing at a compound rate of 25 % through 2027 as AI cloud nodes proliferate.[239] This is why pricing is power-constrained, not demand-constrained. CBRE expects regional capacity in APAC to double within three years,

---

234 European Commission, Nearly-zero energy and zero-emission buildings, 2025, https://energy.ec.europa.eu/topics/energy-efficiency/energy-performance-buildings/nearly-zero-energy-and-zero-emission-buildings_en, accessed 30.07.2025.

235 JLL, Sustainability remains a key driver for European real estate investors, 2025, https://www.jll.com/en-belux/insights/sustainability-remains-a-key-driver-for-european-real-estate-investors, accessed 30.07.2025.

236 McKinsey & Company, The cost of compute: A $7 trillion race to scale data centers, 2025, https://www.mckinsey.com/industries/technology-media-and-telecommunications/our-insights/the-cost-of-compute-a-7-trillion-dollar-race-to-scale-data-centers, accessed 30.07.2025.

237 International Energy Agency (IEA), Energy demand from AI, 2025, https://www.iea.org/reports/energy-and-ai/energy-demand-from-ai, accessed 30.07.2025.

238 JLL, Record-low data center vacancy fuels modern-day »gold rush«, 2025, https://www.jll.com/en-us/newsroom/record-low-data-center-vacancy-fuels-modern-day-gold-rush, accessed 30.07.2025.

239 JLL, EMEA Data Centre Report Q4 2024, 2024, https://www.jll.com/en-de/insights/emea-data-centre-report, accessed 30.07.2025.

yet still run a 15–25 GW deficit by 2028 because most builds aren't AI-spec. Overall, capital is pivoting to cheaper, power-available satellites.[240]

(d) Deglobalization and supply chain reconfiguration

Geopolitics, tariff risk, pandemic scars and green industrial policy have taught multinational corporations that »just-in-case« beats »just-in-time«. This means moving trillions of Euros of plant, inventory and logistics spending, as well as the real estate that houses them, closer to end markets or allied countries. In other words: Deglobalization is not shrinking trade; it is reshaping it. From the U.S.–Mexico–Canada rail spine to Europe's »Made-in-EU« battery belt and the factory corridors of India and ASEAN, real estate capital is redeploying toward locations that offer resilience, green power, and fast market access. Investors who secure land, power grids, and labor today stand to benefit from the structural rent growth baked into this supply chain realignment.

In the Americas, companies are betting that nearshoring trends will outweigh potential showdowns over U.S.-Mexico trade. While logistics companies prepare for tariffs, they maintain their investments at the border.[241] In EMEA, a »Made-in-Europe« push is possible. In addition, the EU's strategic autonomy agenda may particularly boost demand for urban logistics and light manufacturing hubs. The APAC region is also undergoing a major transition, diversifying away from single-country manufacturing in China to a more diverse manufacturing base that includes countries such as India, Vietnam, and Malaysia, which are absorbing Chinese capacity.[242]

(e) Defense

Defense and security have evolved from a policy footnote to a major investment theme. Whether it is the modernization of U.S. bases, the construction of factories for Europe's strategic autonomy or the development of AUKUS submarine yards, the cash now flowing into the sector is large enough to affect local real estate demand curves – especially in industrial, logistics, specialized R&D and mission-critical housing. World military expenditure reached an all-time high of USD 2.72 trillion in 2024, up 9.4% YoY – the steepest jump since the Cold War. Every region increased its budgets, led by the U.S. (USD 997 billion), Europe (up 17%) and the Middle East (up 21%).[243] Funding is no longer allocated just to weapons: modernization programs now carve out tens of billions for sites, depots, R&D labs, housing, energy resilience and logistics corridors – all of which are property-heavy projects. In EMEA, the EU's first Defense Industrial Strategy (EDIS) and NATO's pledge to spend 1.5% of GDP on defense-related infrastructure by 2035

240 CBRE, AI Boom Drives Data Centre Demand Amid Supply and Power Challenges, 2025, https://www.cbre.com/press-releases/ai-boom-drives-data-centre-demand-amid-supply-and-power-challenges-cbre, accessed 30.07.2025.

241 The Wall Street Journal, Bracing for Tariffs, Logistics Operators Stand by Their Border Investments, 2025, https://www.wsj.com/articles/bracing-for-tariffs-logistics-operators-stand-by-their-border-investments-3b1b1054, accessed 30.07.2025.

242 The Economic Times, Healthy inflows into India to continue in 2025, 2025, https://economictimes.indiatimes.com/markets/stocks/news/inflows-into-india-to-continue-in-2025/articleshow/116649887.cms, accessed 30.07.2025.

243 Reuters, World military spending hits $2.7 trillion in record 2024 surge, 2025, https://www.reuters.com/business/aerospace-defense/world-military-spending-hits-27-trillion-record-2024-surge-2025-04-27, accessed 30.07.2025.

are directing funds toward depots, ports, railways, and stockpiling.[244] In APAC, we see countermeasures against China's military buildup in Japan and Australia, as well as increased support for the manufacturing industry in India/ASEAN.[245] The U.S. continues to spend the most money globally on its military. In 2024, spending totaled nearly one trillion USD.[246]

Why investors should care about megatrends

Real estate investments are driven by long-term market fundamentals as most investors underwrite longer holding periods and the limited liquidity of investment products restricts the ability for short-term reactions. Therefore, megatrends are a key component of strategic decision regarding portfolio allocation and individual investments. In response to demographic changes and digitization, a reweighting of portfolios toward alternative sectors (data centers, life science, BTR, senior living) can be observed over the last couple of years. This process will most likely continue, given the increasing speed of change. For existing properties which are negatively impacted by megatrends, an active asset management – i. e. retrofit, reposition, or convert – becomes more important to capture the »brown to green« upside and mitigate obsolescence risk.

Ultimately, all of these megatrends have an effect on pricing. Risk-adjusted pricing that reflects these developments leads to discounts for stranded and climate-exposed assets, while cap rate compression persists in the living and logistics sectors, even as policy rates fall. The impact is also clearly visible in product development and capital raising. Thematic funds and joint venture platforms targeting supply chain nodes (logistics), digital infrastructure, and regulated housing niches are raising capital, while the inflow into legacy funds with large allocations to traditional sectors, such as offices, are drying up.

2.2.4 The influence of monetary and financial policy on the investment market

Real estate cycles never unfold in isolation. They are largely shaped by the policy environment in which buyers, sellers, and developers make decisions. Two levers matter most. First, fiscal policy directly affects the after-tax return on property and the attractiveness of specific locations. Mortgage-interest deductions, capital-gains relief, housing vouchers, or new transportation links can all ignite demand and increase land values, while higher property or income taxes can quickly reduce activity. Second, monetary policy determines the cost and availability of credit. Because real estate is typically purchased with leverage and long maturities, changes in policy rates,

244 European Parliament, European defence industrial strategy, 2025, https://www.europarl.europa.eu/RegData/etudes/BRIE/2024/762402/EPRS_BRI%282024%29762402_EN.pdf, accessed 30.07.2025.

245 The Guardian, UK and Australia sign Aukus treaty to build nuclear submarines as Lammy downplays US doubts, 2025, https://www.theguardian.com/australia-news/2025/jul/26/uk-and-australia-sign-aukus-treaty-to-build-nuclear-submarines-as-lammy-downplays-us-doubts, accessed 30.07.2025.

246 Statista, USA: Militärausgaben von 2008 bis 2024, 2025, https://de.statista.com/statistik/daten/studie/183059/umfrage/militaerausgaben-der-usa/, accessed 30.07.2025.

quantitative easing programs, or macroprudential rules almost immediately affect mortgage affordability, construction financing, and investor appetite for bricks-and-mortar assets. Understanding how these fiscal and monetary forces interact is therefore essential to interpreting past market swings and projecting the path of prices, development, and risk in the following chapters.

As monetary and financial policy both influence and are influenced by macroeconomic conditions, developments are rather cyclical than linear. This leads to real estate markets also moving in cycles. **Since 2000**, the **main global cycles** are as follows[247], [248], [249], [250], [251], [252]:

Cycle	Timeline	What was going on
Dot-com hangover	2000–2003	• Burst of the tech stock bubble hits demand while speculative development peaks in the market • Central banks cut interest rates at a fast pace
Credit & globalization boom	2004–2007	• Cheap USD/EUR funding and CMBS drive (cross-border) investment activity • Central banks hike interest rates by about 400 bp (FED)
GFC bust	2008–2009	• Lehman shock freezes credit • OECD logs steepest drop in CRE values since the 1980s
Stimulus bounce/ Euro-crisis split	2012–2013	• QE in the U.S., the U.K., JP • EU sovereign debt fears keep EUR credit tight
»Lower-for-longer« supercycle	2013–2019	• Zero (or negative) policy rates + QE flatten yields • Global volumes match pre-GFC highs
Pandemic shock	2020	• Lockdowns cut Q2 global investment -55 % YoY • Logistics demand soars, hotels collapse
Liquidity flood rebound	2021–2022 (Q1)	• Fiscal and central-bank fire hoses • 2021 sets a record with USD 809 bn global sales
Rate shock reset	2022 (Q2)–2024	• Fastest tightening in 40 yrs • MSCI all-property total return -3.8 % Q4 '22
Early-cycle thaw	2025–	• Rate cuts in the EU and U.S.; BoJ still near-zero • Prime capital values have bottomed out

Table 17: Main global cycles since 2000

247 Ruff, J., Commercial Real Estate: New paradigm or old story, Bernstein Journal: Perspectives on investing and wealth management 34–42, 2005.

248 Savills, Selling the world, 2016, https://www.savills.com/research_articles/255800/198698-0, accessed 06.08.2025.

249 Federal Reserve Bank of San Francisco, Commercial Real Estate and Low Interest Rates, 2013, https://www.frbsf.org/research-and-insights/publications/economic-letter/2013/04/commercial-real-estate-low-interest-rates/, accessed 06.08.2025.

250 CBRE, Robust Q3 Volume Puts 2021 Global Investment on Par with 2019, 2021, https://www.cbre.com/insights/briefs/robust-q3-volume-puts-2021-global-investment-on-par-with-2019, accessed 06.08.2025.

251 MSCI, Real Assets in Focus: Are We Nearly There Yet?, 2024, https://www.msci.com/research-and-insights/blog-post/real-assets-in-focus-are-we-nearly-there-yet, accessed 06.08.2025.

252 JLL, Global Real Estate Outlook 2025, https://www.jll.com/en-us/insights/market-outlook/global-real-estate, accessed 06.08.2025.

The most relevant policy decisions with lasting effects on the global real estate market followed the GFC. The »lower-for-longer« decade was the wind-tunnel that shaped today's global real estate portfolio. It inflated values, globalized capital flows, and hard-wired investors to treat property as a bond substitute. Understanding how cheap money distorted prices provides essential context for assessing both the 2022–2024 reset and the way the megatrends will interact with monetary policy cycles in the future. During the 2009–2021 »lower-for-longer« era, central bank rates at (or below) zero cut the discount rate used in real estate valuation models, mechanically inflating net present values. In addition, quantitative easing programs flattened term premia and pushed investors out of bonds into »bond-proxies,« such as core real estate. The regulation lagged the cycle: Basel III was still phasing-in, so senior CRE loans priced off rock-bottom funding costs while LTVs stayed moderate, encouraging more deals at higher prices rather than more leverage per deal. The net result was visible in real estate yields converging toward long-bond yields, sometimes leaving a risk premium of less than 250 bp – levels that seemed comfortable until rates spiked in 2022.

Cheap money reshaped real investment markets and the consequences can still be observed today. Low initial yields provide low income returns for real estate investors. To generate attractive total returns, rent growth and asset management alpha have become more important. Popular investment themes, such as »manage to core«, emerged from this market phase. Another effect of a low return environment was the broadening of investment themes. Capital spilled from traditional office and retail into alternatives such as logistics, data centers, student housing, and senior living well before their demand fundamentals were fully proven.

The sudden surge in inflation in 2022 and the following reaction by central banks' raising interest rates at a fast pace brought an end to this market cycle. The low-rate boom was less about leverage ratios and more about a duration mismatch: owners assumed that exit yields would resemble entry yields. However, when global policy rates reset 300–500 bp higher, even modest NOI growth could not offset the jump in discount rates. The repricing resulting from higher exit yields lasted over two years, and in some regions or property types, it has still not come to an end. Mark-to-market valuations were significantly impacted, with prime-asset values retracing 15–30 % in high-beta sectors (offices, CBD retail).

Refinancing gaps present challenges on the debt side of real estate investments. Loans written at 55–65 % LTVs suddenly refinance at 70–80 % LTV based on lower valuations, requiring fresh equity or rescue capital. For multi-asset portfolios, the »denominator effect« suddenly became a major factor. Falling bond and equity prices clipped real estate allocations, slowing new acquisitions. Real estate investment markets had a delayed response to rising interest rates, which led to reduced yield spreads and making real estate investments less appealing compared to alternatives, such as bonds. The disparity between sellers' valuations, expectations and actual pricing contributed to minimal market activity in 2023 and 2024. Starting in 2023, rising initial yields on real estate investments caused a significant drop in property prices, making the yields more attractive. The expected returns in this environment largely depend on rental growth expectations, which are influenced by fundamentals of the occupier market. Sectors such as industrial & logistics and residential have seen investors return more quickly compared to the office sector, where the outlook remains subdued.

Policy easing has started, but is uneven. The Fed has paused at 4.25–4.50% since June 18, 2025, waiting for inflation to fall. The ECB has cut a cumulative 100 bps to a deposit rate of 2% in 2025 Although the central bank had originally announced further cuts for the second half of 2025, further interest rate cuts are unlikely.[253] Recently, long-term interest rates have stabilized at a higher level, reflecting expectations of significantly higher government spending in the U.S. and Europe. This limits the upside for real estate markets resulting from short-term interest rate cuts by the central bank, given the reliance of the real estate sector on mid- to long-term financing.

> *Why investors should care about monetary policy:*
>
> Real estate investments are closely linked to monetary policy. On the one hand, real estate investments are in competition with other asset classes in institutional portfolios. If yields for bonds rise due to interest hikes by central banks, shrinking spreads lead to declining relative attractiveness until real estate yields rise as well. On the other hand, leverage plays an important role in the real estate market. Rising interest rates lead to higher debt costs, which reduces real estate returns. A lack of debt for real estate investments can limit market activity, as was evident during the GFC and following the interest rate hikes in 2023.

2.2.5 The influence of the economic environment on the investment market

Economic development increases property demand through five interconnected levers, and each one has hard numbers behind it

- Income and job growth: The IMF's April 2025 World Economic Outlook estimates global GDP at 3% in 2025 and 3.1% in 2026; even this »sub-trend« pace is sufficient to keep household formation and corporate leasing positive worldwide.[254]
- Sectoral change: AI, life sciences and clean manufacturing are pulling capital into specialized facilities. A good proxy is data centers: North American absorption reached 4.4 GW in 2024, while vacancy fell to 2.6% – the sharpest tightening that JLL has ever recorded, which explains why power-dense real estate now commands premium rents.[255]

253 Cut-off date is 21.10.2025.
254 World Economic Forum, Global Economy: Tenuous Resilience amid Persistent Uncertainty, 2025, https://www.imf.org/en/Publications/WEO/Issues/2025/07/29/world-economic-outlook-update-july-2025, accessed 30.07.2025.
255 JLL, North America Data Center Report Year-end 2024, 2025, https://www.jll.com/en-us/insights/market-dynamics/north-america-data-centers, accessed 30.07.2025.

- Urbanization and infrastructure development: The UN forecasts that an additional 2.4 billion people will urbanize by 2050, while the OECD calculates that the world must now channel about USD 6.9 trillion every year through 2030 into transport, energy, water, and telecommunication networks, in order for infrastructure to keep pace with economic growth and stay consistent with the Paris Agreement and the SDGs.[256]
- Global trade realignment: Near- and friend-shoring are already reprioritizing warehouse and light industrial demand. In a World Bank/MIGA survey 80% of investment-promotion agencies say that FDI relocations will benefit their markets.[257] In other words: Near- and friend-shoring is translating directly into measurable spikes in construction, take-up, and investment in a handful of gateway corridors, for example in Mexico's northern states, Poland and Czech Republic's logistics belt and India's emerging industrial hubs.
- Public investment cycles are powerful real estate accelerants, because they inject long-term, place-specific capital into transportation, energy and civic infrastructure that private schemes can leverage. The current wave of public spending is unusually broad-based and, by historic standards, enormous. The scale, thematic focus (digital, green, and resilience), and geographic spread of today's public-investment programs make them a structural demand engine for real estate markets.

> *Why investors should care about economic development:*
>
> Taken together, these metrics show why real estate investors track macro development so closely: higher output and new economic engines increase space absorption, raise rent ceilings, and widen the pool of bankable projects, while the location of growth dictates which assets will outperform in the next cycle. A negative economic development has the opposite effect: consumers are reluctant to spend additional money and the saving rates increase. Companies scale down space or go out of business, leading to vacant spaces and rental risks.

2.2.6 The influence of geopolitics and geoeconomics on the investment market

Geopolitics and geoeconomics are closely connected to globalization or deglobalization, respectively. However, some specifics have to be highlighted, as geoeconomics – i. e. the use of tariffs, subsidies, export controls and currency policy as instruments of tools – impacts real estate just as tangibly as bombs or blockades do.

256 United Nations, World Population Prospects 2024; OECD, Massive investment is needed in sustainable infrastructure to build climate change resilience, 2024, https://www.oecd.org/en/about/news/press-releases/2024/04/massive-investment-is-needed-in-sustainable-infrastructure-to-build-climate-change-resilience.html, accessed 30.07.2025.

257 World Bank Group/Multilateral Investment Guarantee Agency (MIGA), Shifting Shores: FDI Relocations and Political Risk, 2024.

First, subsidies attract bricks & mortar to new hubs. In the U.S., the Inflation Reduction Act and CHIPS Act have already triggered USD 321 billion of clean energy and semiconductor plant announcements since the second half of 2022, pushing land prices and warehouse rents up along a »battery-and-fabs belt« that stretches from Arizona to Ohio.[258] Second, tariffs and carbon levies redirect supply chains. The European Union's Carbon Border Adjustment Mechanism – final guidelines issued in July 2025 – will tax imported steel, cement, and aluminum starting in 2026, accelerating demand for low-carbon foundries and logistics parks within the EU's borders, especially in Poland, Spain, and the Nordic countries.[259] Third, export controls create sudden capacity gaps. China's 2023–2025 restrictions on gallium, germanium, and graphite have forced chip and battery manufacturers to on-shore critical mineral processing in the U.S., Japan, and Australia, driving speculative industrial parks around new refining sites.[260] At the same time, Houthi missile strikes in the Red Sea are forcing ships to circle the Cape of Good Hope, delaying the delivery of materials and raising fit-out costs for developers on three continents. War-risk insurance for Red Sea cargo now costs 0.7–1 % of hull value, roughly double last year's rate. Cap rates on logistics assets in NATO's frontline states still trade 60–80 bp wider than Western-European peers, despite full occupancy. Investors are incorporating those spreads into models – and into asking prices – every time a new headline emerges.

> *Why investors should care about geopolitics:*
>
> Geopolitical events often appear in the news as short-term developments, and it is hard to separate signal from noise. The mid- to long-term effects of these events are most relevant for real estate investors. Geopolitical tensions can lead to shifts in trade patterns that are relevant for logistics hubs. Waves of migration following wars or disasters can add pressure on housing markets and social infrastructure. Government and infrastructure spending can influence the economic development of regions or countries, changing the outlook for real estate markets as well. While short-term volatility is less important for real estate than other asset classes, long-term shifts have to be on the watch list for all long-term investors.[261]

2.2.7 Today's real estate markets

Monetary easing is finally a tailwind, but it is uneven. The Fed is on hold at 4.25–4.50 %, keeping U.S. refinancing costs elevated. In contrast, the ECB has begun cutting rates and sweetens the mix with green-finance incentives. Meanwhile, Japan's 0.5 % policy rate continues to make the

258 Clean Air Task Force, The geography of clean energy investments in the U.S., 2025, https://www.catf.us/2025/07/geography-clean-energy-investments-us/, accessed 08.09.2025.
259 EC, Carbon Border Adjustment Mechanism, https://taxation-customs.ec.europa.eu/carbon-border-adjustment-mechanism_en, accessed 30.07.2025.
260 Nath/Bean, China's Critical Mineral Export Controls: Background & Chokepoints, 2025.
261 Reuters, Red Sea insurance soars after deadly Houthi ship attacks, 2025, https://www.reuters.com/business/autos-transportation/red-sea-insurance-soars-after-deadly-houthi-ship-attacks-2025-07-10, accessed 30.07.2025.

yen the world's cheapest funding option. That said, core equity remains shy and scarce. Many core/open-end vehicles are still rebuilding liquidity and marking values. Banks are being selective due to Basel-IV in Europe and tighter underwriting in the U.S., and hedging costs deter some cross-border buyers. As a result, core capital is concentrated almost exclusively on prime, green, long-lease residential and logistics properties, while cap-ex-heavy offices struggle to clear. In contrast, there is ample value-add and opportunity »dry powder«, but most managers are waiting for fuller price discovery and a cleaner flow of motivated sales from the 2025–2027 refinancing wall before deploying at scale. In short, easing helps, but deployment lags.

(a) Transparency continues to increase

Transparency has become ever more important for investors. Transparent markets not only feel safer, but also empirically trade more, price tighter, and bounce back faster. As capital starts to redeploy in 2025, understanding the transparency map across the Americas, EMEA and APAC will be central to allocating risk, steering due diligence budgets and, ultimately, hitting target returns. Europe remains the most transparent region overall; Asia-Pacific posted the largest average two-year improvement, while the Americas are bifurcating between North American leaders and Latin American climbers. The JLL Global Real Estate Transparency Index (GRETI) improved markedly from 2000 to 2024 in many countries. The elite »Highly Transparent« tier (led by the U.K., U.S., Australia, France, Canada, Germany, etc.) now accounts for over 80 % of global investment volume. These markets benefit from abundant data, professional standards, and investor protections. In fact, the top dozen most transparent countries attracted USD 1.2 trillion of direct investment in 2022–2023, about 80 % of the global total.[262]

> *Why investors care about transparency:*
>
> Transparency pays off for investors. GRETI scores correlate positively with investment liquidity and negatively with required returns. Highly transparent markets have, on average, lower cap rates/yields than opaque markets, reflecting lower perceived risk. Empirically, improvements in transparency enable investors to underwrite deals with more confidence, which has led to compression of risk premia over time. In fact, *LaSalle Investment Management*[263] finds that transparency and liquidity factors explain a significant amount of yield variation across countries. More transparent markets tend to have yield rates that are 1–3 percentage points lower than opaque markets. This suggests that investors *price in* the higher illiquidity and information risk of opaque markets by demanding higher returns. Going forward, initiatives such as digitized land registries, open data on valuations, and sustainability disclosure are further *widening the transparency gap*: leading markets are leveraging PropTech and AI to improve data. The 2024 GRETI noted that the top countries are integrating *AI* for faster analysis of leases, valuations, and legal doc-

262 JLL, The Global Real Estate Transparency Index 2024, 2024, https://www.jll.com/en-uk/insights/global-real-estate-transparency-index, accessed 30.07.2025.

263 LaSalle Investment Management, Focus Transparency and strategy, 2024, https://www.lasalle.com/wp-content/uploads/2024/10/isa-focus-transparency-and-strategy.pdf, accessed 06.08.2025.

uments. In contrast, the least transparent markets have seen minimal improvement. For institutional investors, this means that liquidity and exit risk vary greatly by market and must be factored into portfolio strategy (e.g., via higher yield targets or lower allocations to higher-risk jurisdictions).

(b) Market liquidity under review

Higher liquidity compresses required returns (lower cap rates), reduces the risk of deals falling through and allows investors to rebalance quickly when market cycles turn. In other words, liquidity represents the ease of transacting properties at fair value. From 2000 to 2020, it improved significantly in advanced economies thanks to deeper capital markets, better data, and more standardized processes. Time-to-exit and bid-ask spreads reflect this liquidity. In seller-friendly conditions (e.g. 2015–2019), prime assets in London, Paris, or New York typically traded within 3–6 months of listing, often with multiple bidders and minimal price discounts. In contrast, in illiquid markets or periods (e.g., southern Europe during the 2012 debt crisis, or globally in late 2022), marketing periods can exceed 12 months and bid-ask spreads can widen sharply. Liquidity in 2025 is recovering, but at different rates: capital is flowing freely into highly transparent, policy-favored niches (residential properties, logistics, data centers in the U.S., Japan, the U.K., and Australia), while large swathes of secondary office and China-centric residential properties remain near illiquid. For any global real-estate investor, understanding where each region sits on the liquidity curve – and how quickly it can move when policy or sentiment shifts – is now as critical as underwriting rent forecasts or CapEx budgets.[264]

Why investors care about liquidity:

Real estate investments are considered »illiquid« and investors plan for long-term holding periods. Nevertheless, market liquidity remains an important criterion for investment decisions, as investors may need to sell their investments once the business plan is complete. Markets with lower market liquidity provide fewer capital sources as potential next buyers, limiting competition and pricing power. Additionally, more liquid markets provide more flexibility in case the business plan cannot be completed, and the investor has to sell under less favorable circumstances. Market liquidity is therefore mostly priced into yields, as reduced liquidity has to be compensated for with higher yields.

(c) Capital Flows, transaction volumes and pricing as of mid-2025

Global capital is no longer frozen, but it is highly selective. Money is flowing fastest to the most transparent and policy-favored niches – living spaces, logistics, and data-centers – especially in markets where funding is cheapest (Japan and the Eurozone) or demand is structural (U.S. reshoring and Indian industrialization). Knowing who the active buyers are, which sectors they

264 MSCI, Early Warnings of CRE Price Problems, 2025, https://www.msci.com/research-and-insights/blog-post/early-warnings-of-cre-price-problems, accessed 30.07.2025; CBRE, H2 2024 Global Real Estate Capital Flows, 2025, https://www.cbre.com/insights/reports/h2-2024-global-real-estate-capital-flows, accessed 30.07.2025.

are pursuing, and how much capital remains lets investors position their portfolios for the next phase of the economic cycle while side-stepping the remaining value traps. Across the three regions the consensus is for a »selective recovery« – quickest in the highly liquid U.S. living and logistics markets, broadening in Europe as ECB cuts take effect and pricing adjustments are completed, and two-speed in APAC, where Japan and India attract record capital while China remains in a correction period. Liquidity is back, but investors still need to price exits to a higher-for-longer rate floor and focus on sectors where structural demand will support the next phase of capital growth. MSCI notes that values bottomed in 2024 and that falling policy rates in 2025 are »allowing buyers and sellers to move closer together on pricing,« which is a prerequisite for further liquidity.[265]

Most mainstream firms do expect global real estate deal volumes, prices and lending conditions to improve in 2025–2026, none of the major industry outlooks – including those from MSCI, Savills, CBRE, PwC, and Oxford Economics – present the upturn as a straight line.[266] Oxford Economics argues that trade fragmentation could knock a full percentage point off global GDP in a downside scenario, delaying leasing and investment decisions.[267] A blog post by MSCI titled »Bumps on the Road to Recovery« underscores uneven sector performance and the sensitivity of values to small rate moves.[268] Reuters sees European CRE as »stuck in zombieland,« with Q2 2025 on track for the worst cross-border flow in a decade.

> *Why investors care about capital flows:*
>
> Market activity and capital flows are important indicators for many investors. While some investors try to be front-runners and identify new markets or act first in recovering markets, most real estate investors are more conservative. For those investors, increasing capital allocations to specific markets or sectors is an important sign to take a closer look at those markets as well and start deploying capital there. An increase in overall market activity, as most analysts expect, could therefore lead to a broader market recovery if more investors follow the first movers. On the other hand, a lack of activity by early investors can slow down market recovery.

265 MSCI, Real Estate in Focus: 2025 Trends to Watch, 2025, https://www.msci.com/research-and-insights/blog-post/real-estate-in-focus-2025-trends-to-watch, accessed 30.07.2025.

266 CBRE, 2025 Global Investor Intentions Survey, 2025, https://www.cbre.com/insights/viewpoints/2025-global-investor-intentions-survey, accessed 30.07.2025; Savills, 2025 Global Investment Outlook, 2025, https://impacts.savills.com/market-trends/2025-investment-outlook.html, accessed 30.07.2025; PwC, The global outlook for 2025 – Emerging Trends in Real Estate, 2025, https://www.pwc.com/gx/en/industries/financial-services/real-estate/emerging-trends-real-estate/etre-global-outlook.html, accessed 30.07.2025.

267 Oxford Economics, Economic Outlook 2025: Key Themes & Insights, 2025, https://www.oxfordeconomics.com/key-themes-2025/, accessed 30.07.2025.

268 MSCI, Real Estate in Focus: Bumps on the Road to Recovery, 2025, https://www.msci.com/research-and-insights/blog-post/real-estate-in-focus-bumps-on-the-road-to-recovery, accessed 30.07.2025.

2.3 Responsible investment

Björn Pfeiffer/Sabine Wieduwilt

»The future of ESG in 2025: a world divided ... But ESG goes much deeper than politics.«[269]
Dan Byrne

2.3.1 Introduction to #2.3

Responsible investment and ESG (Environmental, Social, Governance) practices have evolved within the global investment landscape in recent decades. It's 2025 (when the book is published, it's 2026) – a time to reconsider the labels we've relied on. We may question whether terms such as ›ESG‹ and ›responsible investment‹ still serve their purpose. Instead, we may be shifting focus to what lies beneath: the real drivers of sustainable value. The article »*The future of ESG in 2025: a world divided*«, portrays the global landscape as increasingly fragmented, reflecting both backlash and evolution in how environmental, social and governance principles are applied. According to *Byrne*, despite political backlash in some areas, ESG investing remains robust globally. The article predicts deepening regional divides, increased need for ESG expertise, technological advancements in ESG reporting, discrete ESG pursuits, and rising corporate activism. While certain regions are advancing ambitious sustainability agendas, others face heightened political resistance and legal challenges. Overall, the future of ESG is marked by both challenges and opportunities, with continued growth and innovation in responsible investment.[270] This subchapter #2.3 does not intend to answer that question.

#2.3 Responsible investment – terms, associations, approaches, etc.	**#2.3.1 – intro to #2.3**
	#2.3.2 – history | why + terms + concepts and tools
	#2.3.3 – (responsible) investment approaches
	#2.3.4 – institutions + bodies

Subchapter #2.3 covers a brief historical overview and the rationale behind responsible investment according to the Principles for Responsible Investment (PRI) as well as an explanation of related terms and acronyms for responsible investment with similar meaning. It gives a flavor of some of the key concepts and tools that structure sustainable and responsible investment (#2.3.2), to then focus on responsible investment approaches primarily based on the guidelines of the Global Sustainable Investment Alliance (GSIA), the

269 Byrne, Dan, The future of ESG in 2025: a world divided, Corporate Governance Institute, https://www.thecorporategovernanceinstitute.com/insights/news-analysis/the-future-of-esg-in-2025/?srsltid=AfmBOor1AP33dxY4a8ZH3tpAjU8DGEunSA5-uWt3DwaLPalsHGy6t11k, accessed 13.09.2025.

270 Byrne, Dan, The future of ESG in 2025: a world divided, Corporate Governance Institute, https://www.thecorporategovernanceinstitute.com/insights/news-analysis/the-future-of-esg-in-2025/?srsltid=AfmBOor1AP33dxY4a8ZH3tpAjU8DGEunSA5-uWt3DwaLPalsHGy6t11k, accessed 13.09.2025. For further reflections on regional developments, see chapter #6. For further reflections on the ESG debate, see chapter #1.2.

Principles for Responsible Investment (PRI), and the CFA Institute (#2.3.3), and closes with an overview of institutions, bodies and initiatives (#2.3.4).

2.3.2 History, rationale, terminology

This chapter starts with a brief recap of the history (under (a)), reasons to invest responsibly essentially based on PRI (under (b)), followed by a variety of terms and acronyms with similar meaning for responsible investment (under (c)).

(a) Historical background

The evolution from socially responsible investing (SRI) in the 1960s to today's environmental, social, and governance (ESG) practices marks a shift from exclusionary, values-based investing to a more systematic, risk-aware, and opportunity-driven approach. SRI began with negative screening – avoiding investments in sectors such as tobacco or weapons – while modern ESG integrates environmental, social, and governance factors throughout the investment process to enhance risk management and value creation. The introduction of the UN Principles for Responsible Investment (PRI) in 2006 and the Paris Agreement in 2015 accelerated this shift, embedding sustainability into mainstream finance. ESG investing now includes integration, thematic and impact investing, and active ownership. This approach is supported by global alliances such as PRI, GSIA, UNEP FI, and the Net Zero Asset Owner Alliance. The demand for standardized ESG data has given rise to new benchmarks and reporting tools, including INREV's ESG SDDS and PCAF's GHG accounting standards. The concept of fiduciary duty has also evolved, with ESG integration now seen as essential for managing long-term risks and opportunities. The variety of regional approaches underscores the global momentum and innovation in sustainable finance, with each region contributing to the advancement of ESG practices.

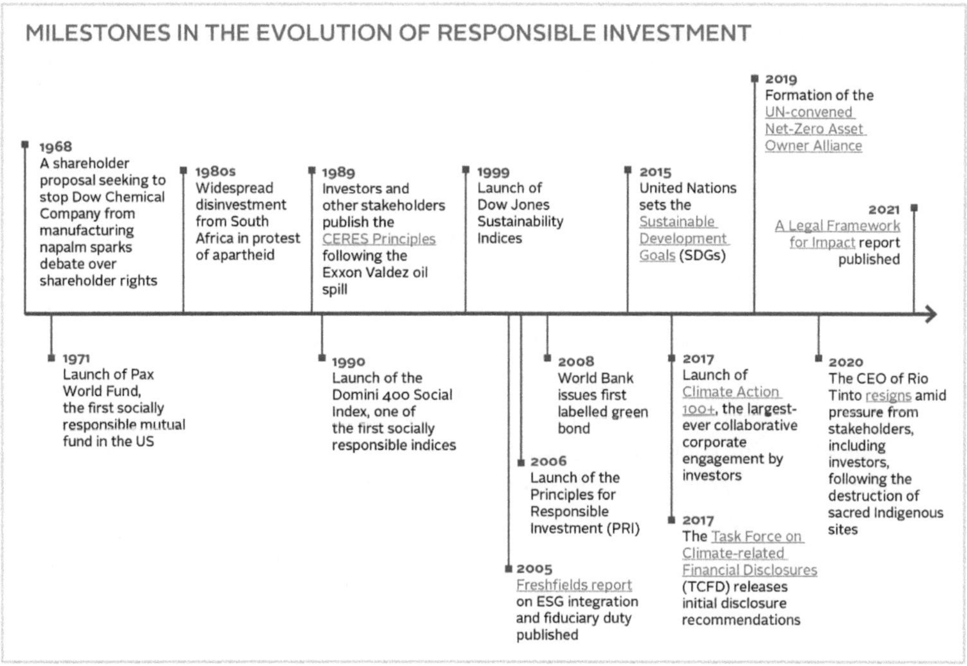

Figure 12: PRI, An introduction to responsible investment | PRI: »*Milestones in the evolution of responsible investment*« (©UNPRI)[271]

(b) Why invest responsibly?

According to *PRI*[272], the reasons to invest responsibly include: (1) financial materiality, as ESG issues can affect financial performance and risk; (2) client demand, with investors and beneficiaries seeking alignment with ESG values; (3) policy and regulation, due to increasing ESG-related rules and disclosure requirements; (4) fiduciary duties, which require consideration of ESG factors in clients' best interests; (5) sustainability outcomes, since investments have real-world impacts that should align with global goals; and (6) the Principles for Responsible Investment, with many investors adopting PRI's six principles to guide ESG integration.

According to *Martindale*[273], »*Nearly always, the primary argument in favour of responsible investment is that it contributes to superior risk-adjusted returns. In short, that a responsible investment strategy outperforms a non-responsible – or traditional – investment strategy.*« Martindale then alludes to three often-cited studies from DWS (2015), PRI (2017) and Morgan Stanley (2019). He

271 Figure: PRI, An introduction to responsible investment | PRI: »Milestones in the evolution of responsible investment« (©UNPRI), https://www.unpri.org/introductory-guides-to-responsible-investment/what-is-responsible-investment/4780.article, accessed 03.05.2025.

272 PRI, What is responsible investment?, https://www.unpri.org/introductory-guides-to-responsible-investment/what-is-responsible-investment/4780.article, accessed 03.05.2025.

273 Martindale, Will, Responsible Investment. An Insider's Account of What's Working, What's not and where next, 2024, 37, 38, 39.

also presents a range of challenges, including the inability to isolate ESG issues and to attribute financial performance; conflicting approaches all termed responsible investment, and little correlation between ESG scores and ESG data providers.

(c) Related concepts and terminology in responsible investment
Byrne, whose article is referenced in the introduction under #2.3.1 above, uses the term »responsible investment.« The same applies to the PRI when referring to the broader term. What do terms like »responsible investment« or »investment and ESG« mean, and what shapes do they take?

According to *PRI*[274], **responsible investment** is mostly used as the umbrella term, that involves considering environmental, social and governance (ESG) issues when making investment decisions and influencing companies or assets (known as active ownership or stewardship). It complements traditional financial analysis and portfolio construction techniques. Responsible investors can have different objectives. Some focus exclusively on financial returns and consider ESG issues that could impact them. Others aim to generate financial returns and to achieve positive outcomes for people and the planet, while avoiding negative ones. **Examples of ESG issues that investors can consider when investing responsibly** include:

ENVIRONMENTAL	SOCIAL	GOVERNANCE
• **Climate change** • **Circular economy** • **Biodiversity** • **Deforestation**	• **Human rights** • **Decent work** • **Diversity, equity, and inclusion**	• **Board structure** • **Executive remuneration** • **Tax fairness** • **Responsible political engagement**

Table 18: ESG issues to consider when investing responsibly (based on PRI)

Martindale[275] interviews various market participants, to then attempt a »*modern definition of responsible investment*«: »***Responsible investment** is an approach to investment that intentionally maximises real-world impact and minimizes negative real-world impact, through investment decision-making, stewardship and policy-engagement, leading to sustainable benefits to the economy, the environment and society, while optimising risk-adjusted returns.*« This definition seems close to that of impact investment.

There are **many terms with similar or slightly different connotations and meaning**, and their usage varies. Other terms include, for example: **Sustainable and Responsible Investing (SRI).**

274 PRI, What is responsible investment?, https://www.unpri.org/introductory-guides-to-responsible-investment/what-is-responsible-investment/4780.article, accessed 03.05.2025.
275 Martindale, Will, Responsible Investment. An Insider's Account of What's Working, What's not and where next, 2024, 37, 38, 39.

The industry[276] uses this term as a similar umbrella term as PRI uses »responsible investment«, but the term is used in different ways. The same applies to other terms – there are so many meanings for all of these terms that we will limit our discussion to a condensed form of one of the CFA Institute's publications. According to *CFA*[277], a slightly different term under the same acronym **Socially Responsible Investing (SRI)** refers to »*approaches that apply social and environmental criteria in evaluating companies; investors implementing SRI generally score companies using a chosen set of criteria usually in conjunction with sector specific weightings*«[278]. **Sustainable invement (SI)** »*refers to the selection of assets that contribute in some way to a sustainable economy – that is an asset that minimizes natural and social resource depletion [...]. The Term ›**sustainable investment**‹ can also be used to mean a strategy that screens out activities considered contrary to long term environmental and social sustainability such as mining or burning coal or exploring for oil in the Arctic regions*«[279]. **Social investment** »*refers to allocating capital to assets that address social challenges. These can be products that address the bottom of the pyramid (BOP). ›BOP‹ refers to the poorest 2/3 of the economic human pyramid a group of more than 4 billion people living in poverty. More broadly BOP refers to a market-based model of economic development that seeks to simultaneously alleviate poverty while providing growth and profits for businesses serving these communities. [...] Social investing can also include social impact bonds which are a mechanism to contract with the public sector. The sector pays for better social outcomes than certain services and passes on part of the savings achieved to investors.*«[280] **Ethical (or values-driven and faith-based) investment** »*refers to investing in line with certain principles often using negative screening to avoid investing in companies whose products and services are deemed morally objectionable by the investor or certain religions international declarations conventions conventions or voluntary agreements.*«[281]

In any case, regardless of the meanings attributed to the terms above, they will not be used coherently in this book, as the intention is to provide insights for implementation, not to get stuck in redefining terms.

276 On a global level, see for example some publications of UNEP FI, OECD and GSIA, but also by UNEP FI and OECD – Global Sustainable Investment Alliance, GSIA Global Sustainable Investment Review 2022, 2022, https://www.gsi-alliance.org/wp-content/uploads/2023/12/GSIA-Report-2022.pdf, accessed 03.11.2025; UN Environment Program, Investment Leadership Programme, https://www.unepfi.org/investment/investment/, accessed 13.09.2025; OECD, Finance and investment, https://www.oecd.org/en/topics/finance-and-investment.html, accessed 13.09.2025.

277 CFA Institute, Sustainable Investing Certificate Curriculum 2025, 2025 (without looking into the terms discussed under #2.3.3; or #2.5).

278 CFA, 19.

279 CFA, 20.

280 CFA, 21.

281 CFA, 22.

2.3.3 Perspectives, concepts and tools

This section aims to **link concepts and tools that structure (sustainable and) responsible investment**. It moves from intent and duties to materiality and measurement and then to capital allocation and delivery.

Clarity on **investment objectives** and the **ambition level** and **investment focus** comes first: investors specify their financial risk-return goals and the degree to which they also seek real-economy outcomes (from »*do no harm*« to »*do good*«), which then guides investment approaches, portfolio construction, stewardship, and disclosures. An investment objective is used by asset managers to determine the optimal portfolio mix for a client. Investments are chosen using the guidelines of the investment objective.[282] See for **example, on the investment objective**, a *Eurosif/University of Hamburg*[283] report that describes risks and opportunities versus impacts: »*The investment objective describes the explicit, sustainability-related goal of an investment. The investment objectives defined for this methodology describe how different categories of investments use the sustainability-related information reported by investees in their investment processes and product design. In July 2023 the European Commission published the European Sustainability Reporting Standards (ESRS), which prescribe what sustainability-related information large companies need to disclose, namely material sustainability-related risks, opportunities, and impacts (ESRS, 2023) (see also appendix B for an overview of important terms). Reflecting on this logic, our methodology* ***differentiates between four types of sustainability-related investment objectives: (1) integration of ESG factors, (2) Systematic analysis & incorporation of ESG factors, (3) Alignment with positive impacts on environment and/or society, and (4) Having a measurable contribution to positive real-world impacts.*** *The first two objectives focus on ESG risks and/or opportunities, while the latter two objectives focus on sustainability-related impacts ....*«

Fiduciary duties frame this step by requiring investors to act in the best interests of their beneficiaries, which used to be considered as a barrier to considering ESG factors in investments. However, in the modern investment system, this includes managing financially material ESG risks and opportunities[284], and, where mandates permit, pursuing specified sustainability out-

282 Chen, James (reviewed: Howard, Ebony; Fact checked Rohrs Schmitt, Kirsten), Investment Objective: Definition and Use For Portfolio Building, Investopedia, 2022, https://www.investopedia.com/terms/i/investmentobjective.asp, accessed 13.09.2025.

283 Eurosif, University of Hamburg, Sustainable Finance Research Group & Advanced Impact Research (2024) Methodology for Eurosif Market Studies on Sustainability Investments: Measuring progress of capital flows to support the sustainable transition of the real economy, Final Report, February 2024, Hamburg/Brussels: Eurosif, 2024, https://www.eurosif.org/news/methodology-market-studies-sustainability/, accessed 08.09.2025, 4, see also footnote that uses »intentionality« as the alternative term for »objective«.

284 CFA, 25; for further reading on fiduciary duties, see for example: #1.4.4(a); Martindale, Will, Responsible Investment. An Insider's Account of What's Working, What's not and where next, 2024, 41 et seq, 200 et seq; United Nations Environment Programme Finance Initiative (UNEP FI), Asset Management Working Group (AMWG), Freshfields Bruckhaus Deringer, Fiduciary Responsibilities and Responsible Investment Practices, 2005; PRI, UNEP Finance Initiative, and The Generation Foundation, Fiduciary Duty in the 21st Century: Final Report, 2019.

comes. **Systems thinking** complements fiduciary duty by widening the perspective to include how portfolio exposures interact with environmental and social systems, helping investors anticipate feedback, tipping points, and systemic risk transmission. »*You have to understand the present and future in the context of the past. Investment and indeed economics grew up with physics envy. So it got queued by solving the mathematics of markets ahead of human challenges,*« Martindale cited Roger Urwin.[285]

Ambition level and Investment focus

Ambition level refers to the degree to which an investment seeks to actively support the transition toward a more sustainable economy. It reflects how far the investment's objective, approach, and performance measurement go in aiming for positive sustainability outcomes in the real economy. The ambition level is not a measure of the actual impact achieved (impact magnitude), but rather the intent and design of the investment to contribute to sustainability goals. **Investment focus** describes the relevance and type of sustainability matters addressed by the investment – specifically, whether the focus is on financial materiality (ESG risks and opportunities), impact materiality (real-world environmental and social change), or both (double materiality).

Types of focus

Financial materiality: Focuses on sustainability issues that affect financial performance (e.g., ESG risks and opportunities).

Impact materiality: Focuses on the actual positive or negative impacts on society or the environment, regardless of financial implications.

Double materiality: Combines both financial and impact materiality, considering both financial performance and real-world outcomes. **Double materiality** provides two perspectives on relevance: financial materiality (issues that affect enterprise value) and impact materiality (the significance of an organization's effects on people and the planet). When used together, these lenses can guide the setting of objectives, research, engagement priorities and reporting, ensuring that investors manage what matters for value and for real-world outcomes.

Principal Adverse Impacts (PAIs) are standardized indicators that capture negative effects associated with investments, such as GHG emissions, biodiversity loss, and social harms. PAIs operationalize the »*impact*« side of double materiality, enabling consistent measurement, target setting, mitigation planning, and accountability across portfolios and over time.

The **capital spectrum** describes the continuum of capital, from traditional finance (risk/return only) through responsible and sustainable strategies to impact-first and concessional capital,

285 Martindale, Will, Responsible Investment. An Insider's Account of What's Working, What's not and where next, 2024, 223 et seq.

and ultimately philanthropy. The capital spectrum (sometimes called the »spectrum of capital«) highlights how capital can be deployed with different intentions and expectations for financial return and impact: The *OECD*[286] illustrates the range from finance-only investment to the other end of the capital spectrum – »*Private sector actors focusing on investing for specific social, environmental or economic outcomes include … foundations and philanthropists who have traditionally focused on using grants and are now including investment models which focus on achieving financial sustainability alongside social returns (OECD, 2015[3]). On the other end of the capital spectrum, mainstream investors have increasingly been moving from a sole focus on financial returns to seeking to mitigate environmental, social and governance risks, and, for a growing number, to pursuing investment opportunities which focus on achieving specific positive outcomes.*«

The **capital spectrum** demonstrates that responsible and sustainable investment is not a binary choice but a continuum, allowing investors to select strategies that align with their values, risk tolerance, and desired impact. See **Figure 13** for further illustration.

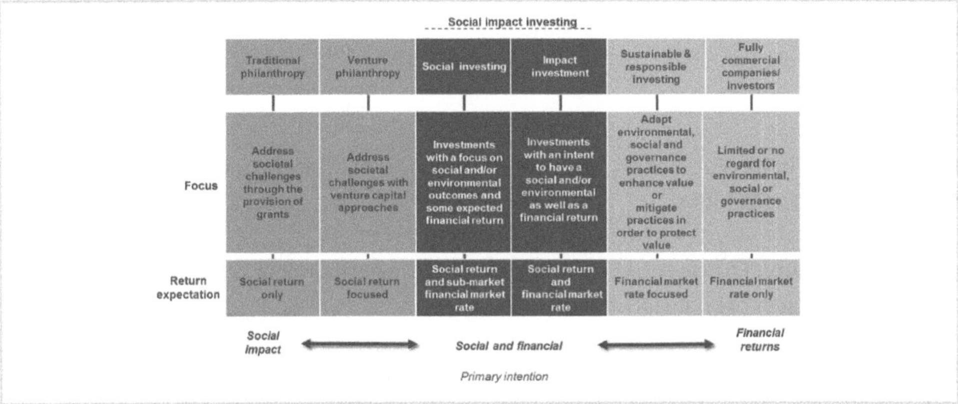

Figure 13: OECD – The spectrum of capital: Moving towards greater impact, from: OECD, Social Impact Investment 2019: The Impact Imperative for Sustainable Development (adopted from multiple sources)

Positioning a strategy on this spectrum aligns investor objectives and ambition with appropriate return expectations, instruments, and impact intent, and clarifies where transition finance and thematic allocations fit.

Investment approaches translate intent into action: exclusions and norms-based screening, ESG integration, best-in-class, thematic and solutions investing, active ownership and stewardship, impact investing, and transition finance. The choice and mix of approaches depend on the investor's objectives, capital spectrum position, mandate constraints, and theory of change.[287]

286 OECD, Social Impact Investment 2019: The Impact Imperative for Sustainable Development, 2019, https://doi.org/10.1787/9789264311299-en, accessed 10.08.2025; OECD, Social Impact Investment 2019, https://www.oecd.org/en/publications/social-impact-investment-2019_9789264311299-en.html, accessed 13.09.2025.

287 See #2.3.3 for investment approaches defined by GSIA, PRI, CFA Institute, 2023.

The **transition to ESG** refers to embedding ESG considerations into decision-making and to financing the decarbonization and improvement pathways of companies and systems. Traditional finance versus transition finance, and dedicated transition funds, distinguish capital that maintains current states from capital that enables credible shifts in high-emitting or hard-to-abate sectors via CapEx, OpEx, and business model evolution, guided by science-based pathways, interim targets, and integrity criteria.

Capital flows refer to the movement of finance across geographies, sectors, and instruments. Steering capital flows toward sustainable activities and credible transition plans is the mechanism by which investment signals influence the real economy – via primary markets (new issuance), secondary markets (pricing and cost of capital), and ownership channels (stewardship and engagement). Policies, taxonomies, and market standards help reduce friction and greenwashing, making flows more efficient and aligned.

The **results chain** – inputs, activities, outputs, outcomes, impacts – provides the causal scaffold for investment theses and stewardship plans, linking resources deployed (capital, expertise) to near-term outputs (projects financed, policies adopted) and to longer-term outcomes and impacts (emissions reduced, livelihoods improved). The results chain is a foundational framework in responsible and sustainable investment, providing a logical sequence from investment inputs to long-term impacts. It is used to clarify causality supports measurement and accountability and guides impact management. The **results chain** is visually represented in the **OECD report** (see Figure 6.3, p. 189 in the OECD report and **Figure 14** below),[288] and is widely used by both public and private actors to design, implement, and evaluate responsible and sustainable investments.

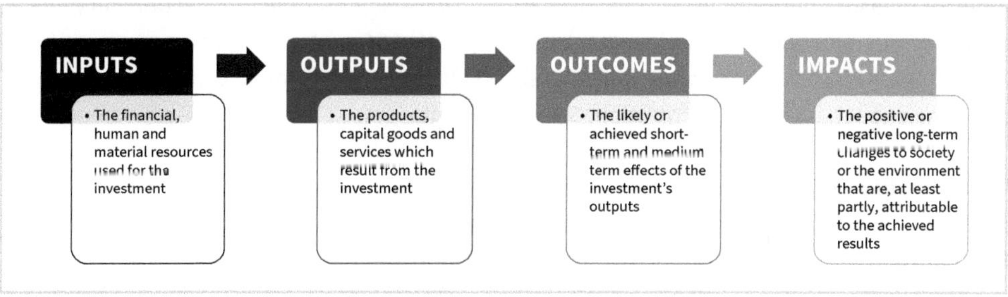

Figure 14: A visual representation of the results chain (copied from OECD report)

288 Boiardi, Priscilla, OECD, Measuring And Managing The Impact Of Sustainable Investments – A Two Axes Mapping, 2020, https://www.oecd.org/content/dam/oecd/en/publications/reports/2020/06/managing-and-measuring-the-impact-of-sustainable-investments_508e5ccf/2ff2b2f4-en.pdf, accessed 10.08.2025, with reference to: OECD, Evaluation and Aid Effectiveness No. 6 – Glossary of Key Terms in Evaluation and Results Based Management (in English, French and Spanish), 2002, https://dx.doi.org/10.1787/9789264034921-en-fr. See more recent: OECD, Effective Results Frameworks for Sustainable Development, https://www.oecd.org/en/publications/effective-results-frameworks-for-sustainable-development_aaa4bb52-en.html, accessed 10.08.2025.

The »results chain« is a widely used conceptual framework in responsible and sustainable investment to clarify how financial inputs are expected to lead to desired social, environmental, and economic impacts.
»Impact measurement frameworks help investors define the steps to follow to set up and roll out an impact measurement process, how to measure impact ex-ante and ex-post and how to report impact. Impact measurement methodologies are techniques used to measure the impact of a project, an investment, or a portfolio of investments. ... On top of clear definition of key terms, the Glossary presents the definitions of the ›results chain‹ of an investment or intervention. The causal sequence begins with inputs, moving through outputs and outcomes before culminating in impacts (see Figure 14). Another significant effort was made by the Network of Networks on Impact Evaluation (NONIE), which developed methodological guidance on impact evaluation (NONIE, 2006[34]).«

ESG or impact performance management merges ongoing performance assessment and management. This includes setting baselines, selecting KPIs and PAIs, defining targets and guardrails, measuring financial and sustainability performance, verifying data, and adapting based on evidence. The performance measurement dimension ensures that the results of the approach are tracked and reported, providing evidence of progress toward the objective. This dimension refers to how the investment's sustainability or impact performance is measured and reported. It distinguishes between measuring ESG performance (risks/opportunities) and measuring real-world impact (changes in environmental or social outcomes). Performance measurement provides evidence of whether and how the investment is achieving its stated objective. It is essential for transparency and accountability and differentiates between investments that merely consider ESG factors and those that can demonstrate real-world impact. Types of measurement discussed in a 2024 *Eurosif/University of Hamburg*[289] report on market studies on sustainability-related investments include: (1) ESG performance measurement (e.g., ESG ratings, KPIs, risk/opportunity indicators) and (2) Impact performance measurement (e.g., company impact, investor contribution, SDG alignment).

A **holistic, life-cycle approach** assesses the impacts and value drivers across the full life cycle of assets, products, and services – from raw materials and design to use and end-of-life. This approach surfaces scope 3 risks, circularity opportunities, and hidden externalities. It strengthens due diligence, scenario analysis, and engagement priorities, while improving the credibility of transition and impact claims.

289 Eurosif, University of Hamburg, Sustainable Finance Research Group & Advanced Impact Research (2024) Methodology for Eurosif Market Studies on Sustainability-related Investments: Measuring progress of capital flows to support the sustainable transition of the real economy, Final Report, February 2024, Hamburg/Brussels: Eurosif, Methodology for Eurosif Market Studies on Sustainability-related Investments, 2024, https://www.eurosif.org/news/methodology-market-studies-sustainability/, accessed 08.09.2025, 7, 8. See also the *OECD's* inverted pyramid model under #1.3.5 to categorize the landscape of impact management and measurement standards, illustrating how standards range from broad, high-level principles at the top, to specific, granular metrics at the bottom; as one moves down the pyramid, harmonization and standardization become progressively more challenging.

Investors **bring these elements together** by defining their objectives and ambitions, locating themselves on the capital spectrum, selecting investment approaches (including transition finance, when relevant), applying double materiality and PAIs to focus and measure, designing a results chain to articulate contribution, managing performance with ESG or impact performance management, and using systems thinking and a holistic, life-cycle approach to navigate complexity and align capital flows with real-economy outcomes, all while fulfilling their fiduciary duties.

2.3.4 Definitions of (responsible) investment approaches from GSIA, PRI, and the CFA Institute

In response to the growing global interest in responsible investment, there has been a demand for greater standardization of terminology to enable institutional investors, regulators, and other industry participants to communicate with precision. In November 2021, the International Organization of Securities Commissions (IOSCO) highlighted the need for the global investment industry »*to develop common sustainable finance-related terms and definitions, including relating to responsible investment approaches, to ensure consistency throughout the global asset management industry.*«[290]

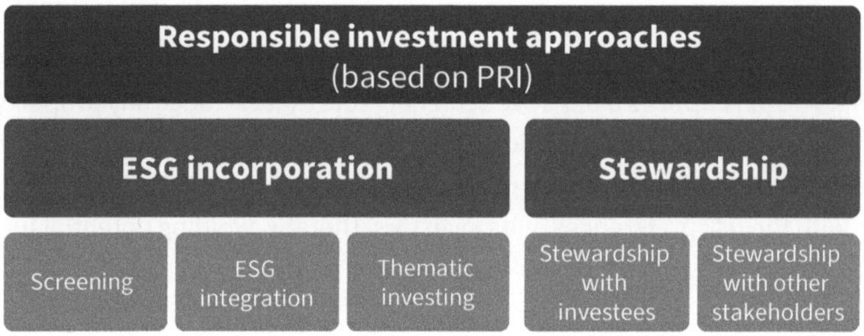

Figure 15: Responsible investment approaches (based on PRI)[291]

In 2023, the CFA Institute, GSIA, and PRI compiled definitions and concepts from various sources into a joint guide. This resource is based on an analysis of works from regional institutions and associations, offering a broader global perspective. The goal was not to provide criteria for product categorization, but rather to increase the consistency of the terminology

290 CFA/GSIA/PRI, Definitions for Responsible Investment Approaches, 2023, https://www.gsi-alliance.org/wp-content/uploads/2023/10/ESG-Terminology-Report_Online.pdf, accessed 01.05.2025; with reference to: International Organization of Securities Commissions (IOSCO), Recommendations on Sustainability-Related Practices, Policies, Procedures and Disclosure in Asset Management, www.iosco.org/library/pubdocs/pdf/IOSCOPD688.pdf, accessed 13.09.2025.

291 PRI, What is responsible investment?, https://www.unpri.org/introductory-guides-to-responsible-investment/what-is-responsible-investment/4780.article, accessed 09.06.2025.

used in responsible investment.[292] According to the CFA Institute, GSIA and PRI guide[293], »*[t]his resource is intended for investors regulators policymakers and other market participants. It describes the concepts that define each responsible investment approach rather than criteria for product labeling or categorization. The responsible investment approaches defined in this paper are not mutually exclusive and in practice are often used in combination. This resource aims to harmonise existing terms and definitions – not to create new terms or meanings.*«

See below the **definitions and concepts** from the **CFA Institute, GSIA and PRI guide**. The following section looks into the terms and their meaning based on this guide, starting with ›screening‹ (under (a)), then ›ESG integration‹ (under (b)), ›thematic investing‹ (under (c)), ›stewardship‹ (under (d)) and ‹impact investing‹ (under (e)).[294] For each term, there is a definition including essential elements, a general idea as well as some ideas about use cases, followed by an extract from the guidance.

(a) Screening[295]

Screening is the process of applying rules based on defined criteria that determine whether an investment is permissible. This can include exclusionary, negative, positive, best-in-class, and norms-based screening, each with distinct but overlapping elements.

> **Use case:**
> A real estate investment trust (REIT) decides to exclude properties located in areas prone to flooding. The REIT applies a negative screening rule that excludes any property situated in a floodplain, as defined by a specific agency. This rule is based on the defined criterion of geographical location. The screening process ensures that the REIT only includes properties that align with the risk preferences of its investors, thereby avoiding potential future losses due to flooding.
>
> **Guidance:**
> A precise, plain-language description of the process and criteria (including thresholds) used to screen a portfolio can reduce the potential for misinterpretation.
>
> Investment products characterized as implementing screens should reflect all essential elements in both the design of the screen and its implementation.

292 Eurosif, University of Hamburg, Sustainable Finance Research Group & Advanced Impact Research (2024) Methodology for Eurosif Market Studies on Sustainability Investments: Measuring progress of capital flows to support the sustainable transition of the real economy, Final Report, February 2024, Hamburg/Brussels: Eurosif, 2024, https://www.eurosif.org/news/methodology-market-studies-sustainability/, accessed 08.09.2025, 4.

293 CFA Institute, GSIA and PRI, p. 2.

294 The text under (a) to (e) is based on the resource GSIA, PRI, CFA Institute, 2023, except for the use cases.

295 CFA/GSIA/PRI, 3.

If the rules are not based on defined criteria and applied consistently, the activity should not be characterized as screening.

(b) ESG Integration[296]

ESG integration is the ongoing consideration of ESG factors within an investment analysis and decision-making process with the aim to improve risk-adjusted returns. It involves seeking out ESG information, assessing its materiality, and integrating it into investment decisions. ESG integration requires that ESG factors be considered in both the analytical and decision-making components of the investment process.

Use case

A real estate private equity firm integrates ESG factors into its investment process by evaluating the environmental impact, social practices, and governance structures of potential property investments. For example, the firm considers a building's energy efficiency, its impact on local communities, and the governance practices of property managers when analyzing its financial health and future performance. This ongoing consideration of ESG factors enables the firm make more informed investment decisions aimed at improving risk-adjusted returns.

Guidance:

When communicating to general rather than professional audiences, investors should avoid the term »ESG integration« and instead use plain language to accurately describe how ESG factors are considered in the investment process.

Investors should use the term »ESG integration« to convey the set of essential concepts described above. Although »integration« and »incorporation« are often used interchangeably in ordinary language, »ESG integration« and »ESG incorporation« have different meanings. PRI has defined »ESG incorporation« as »the assessment, review and consideration of ESG factors in existing investment practices through a combination of three approaches: integration screening and thematic investing.«

Practitioners should avoid implying that considering ESG factors will always result in a higher risk-adjusted return.

Thematic investing[297]

Thematic investing involves an investment approach focusing on long-term structural trends. This approach is based on the belief that certain economic, technological, demographic, cultural, political, environmental, social, and regulatory dynamics are key drivers of investment risk and return.

296 CFA/GSIA/PRI, 8.
297 CFA/GSIA/PRI, 12.

Use case

An investment firm launches a thematic real estate fund focused on green buildings. The fund selects assets, such as properties with green building certifications, as well as properties that utilize renewable energy solutions, like solar or geothermal systems. This strategy is anchored in the global trend toward energy efficiency and environmental responsibility. By focusing on these properties, the fund seeks to generate long-term value from the growing demand for eco-friendly and future-proof real estate.

Guidance:

Investors should not characterize their approach to asset selection as thematic investing unless they can credibly demonstrate the trends that are considered when selecting assets

They must also show how a significant portion of the assets in a portfolio are connected to those trends, and how those trends relate to economic, technological, demographic, cultural, political, environmental, social, and/or regulatory dynamics.

(d) Stewardship[298]

Stewardship refers to the use of investor rights and influence to protect and enhance overall long-term value for clients and beneficiaries. This includes the common economic, social, and environmental assets on which their interests depend.

Use case

A pension fund actively engages with the property management companies of its real estate investments to promote better environmental practices. The fund uses its influence to support initiatives on reducing energy consumption and improving waste management. Additionally, the fund's representatives meet with property managers to discuss long-term strategies for enhancing sustainability. These stewardship activities aim to protect and increase the long-term value of the fund's real estate investments by ensuring that properties adopt sustainable practices.

Guidance:

Investors should use the term »stewardship« to convey the full set of essential concepts described above. The term should not be used to refer to activities such as proxy voting and engagement unless these actions are taken to protect and enhance overall value for clients and beneficiaries.

Interactions about routine operational matters unrelated to overall long-term value should not be described as stewardship activities.

298 CFA/GSIA/PRI, 14.

(e) Impact investing[299]

Impact investing is investing with the intention to generate positive, measurable social and/or environmental impact alongside a financial return. It requires a credible explanation of the investor's contributory or catalytic role in generating improvements over the status quo.

Use case
A real estate development company invests in a project to build affordable and sustainable housing in underserved communities. The company intends to generate a positive social impact by providing safe and affordable housing while also achieving a financial return on its investment. The company measures its impact by tracking the number of housing units built and the improvements to residents' living conditions. This impact investing approach aims to create both social benefits and financial returns.

Guidance:
The term »impact investing« or its variants should not be used unless there is an intention to generate a positive, measurable social and/or environmental impact alongside a financial return.

Investors should only use the term to describe their approach if they can credibly demonstrate their contributory or catalytic role in improving environmental and social conditions.

2.3.5 Institutions, bodies and initiatives

This subchapter concludes with an overview of the institutions and regulatory or voluntary frameworks that shape, standardize, and continue to drive the global responsible investment ecosystem. **Table 19** provides a **list of institutions, associations, bodies, networks, and initiatives**, along with their definitions, presented in chronological order by their launch date. The various institutions, bodies, and initiatives are interconnected through their shared goal of promoting sustainable investment practices and integrating ESG factors into investment decision-making. For example, the PRI and UNEP FI collaborate to drive progress in responsible property investment, while the NZAOA and PCAF work towards achieving net zero GHG emissions. The WGBC and ICBC focus on sustainable building practices and climate resilience, aligning their efforts with global climate goals.

299 CFA/GSIA/PRI, 19.

Year	*Organization/Initiative and Description*
1947	**CFA Institute** – A global association of investment professionals that promotes the highest standards of ethics, education, and professional excellence for the ultimate benefit of society.
1969	**MSCI** (ESG focus: late 2000s/2010s) – A leading provider of critical decision support tools and services for the global investment community, including ESG ratings, indexes, and analytics that help investors integrate sustainability considerations.
1983	**International Organization of Securities Commissions (IOSCO)** – An international body that brings together the world's securities regulators and is recognized as the global standard-setter for securities regulation.
1992	**UN Environment Programme Finance Initiative (UNEP FI)** – A partnership between the United Nations Environment Programme and the global financial sector that aims to mobilize private sector finance for sustainable development.
1995	**International Corporate Governance Network (ICGN)** – Established by the world's most influential investors, ICGN advances high standards of corporate governance and investor stewardship worldwide.
2002	**World Green Building Council (WGBC)** – A global network of Green Building Councils that catalyzes sustainable finance and drives the sustainability agenda across the real estate industry.
2006	**Principles for Responsible Investment (PRI)** – An international network of investors working together to implement six aspirational principles for incorporating ESG issues into investment practice.
2011	**Shift** – The leading center of expertise on the UN Guiding Principles on Business and Human Rights, working to redefine corporate practices that respect human dignity.
2012	**Global Sustainable Investment Alliance (GSIA)** – A collaboration of membership-based sustainable investment organizations that promotes sustainable investment practices and provides a framework for integrating ESG factors into investment decisions.
2015	**Partnership for Carbon Accounting Financials (PCAF)** – An industry-led initiative enabling financial institutions to measure and disclose the greenhouse gas emissions associated with their financial activities.
2017	**Network for Greening the Financial System (NGFS)** – A group of central banks and supervisors aiming to enhance the role of the financial system in managing risks and mobilizing capital for green and low-carbon investments in the context of environmentally sustainable development.
2019	**Net Zero Asset Owner Alliance (NZAOA)** – A member-led initiative of institutional investors who are committed to transitioning their investment portfolios to net-zero GHG emissions by 2050.
2020	**Glasgow Financial Alliance for Net Zero (GFANZ)** – A global coalition of leading financial institutions committed to accelerating the decarbonization of the economy and achieving net-zero emissions by 2050.

Year	Organization/Initiative and Description
2021	**International Sustainability Standards Board (ISSB)** – Established by the IFRS Foundation to develop a comprehensive, global baseline of sustainability-related disclosure standards for the financial markets.
2023	**Intergovernmental Council for Buildings and Climate (ICBC)** – A council that brings governments together to collaborate on accelerating decarbonization and fostering resilience in the building sector, aligning national actions with international climate goals.

Table 19: List of institutions/associations/bodies/networks/initiatives and their definitions

2.4 Investment approaches, investor types, and cross-border investment

Rena Knöpke

2.4.1 Introduction to #2.4

The contemporary real estate investment landscape has undergone a fundamental transformation, driven by the convergence of traditional financial objectives with environmental, social, and governance imperatives. This chapter explores the relationship between investment methodologies, investor characteristics, and the complexities of cross-border capital deployment, all viewed through the lens of ESG integration.

Today, real estate investment operates within a multifaceted ecosystem where approaches range from direct ownership to sophisticated indirect vehicles, each presenting unique opportunities and challenges for ESG implementation. The diversity of investor types creates a complex web of motivations, requirements, and capabilities that fundamentally shape how ESG principles are integrated into investment decisions. Cross-border investment introduces further complexity, as investors must navigate different regulatory frameworks, cultural contexts, and ESG standards across different jurisdictions.

This chapter examines how different investment structures facilitate or constrain ESG integration, analyzes the varying ESG drivers across investor categories, and addresses the unique challenges of implementing consistent ESG standards in global real estate portfolios. The analysis reveals that successful ESG integration requires more than compliance with regulatory requirements; it requires a fundamental reimagining of how investment decisions are made, monitored, and optimized across diverse markets and stakeholder groups.

#2.4 Investment approaches, investor types, cross-border investment & ESG	
	#2.4.1 – intro to #2.4
	#2.4.2 – investment approaches and structures & ESG
	#2.4.3 – types of investors & their ESG drivers
	#2.4.4 – cross-border – global ESG complexities
	#2.4.5 – conclusion: strategic integration

In this chapter #2.4, we focus on investment approaches and structures based on different investor types and from a cross-border perspective, starting with different investment structures (#2.4.2), moving on to investor types and their ESG drivers (#2.4.3), then looking into cross-border investments and global ESG complexities (#2.4.4), and finally concluding with the strategic integration of all these parameters (#2.4.5).

2.4.2 Real estate investment approaches and structures: An ESG perspective

(a) Direct investment and ESG control

Direct real estate investment, characterized by immediate ownership and operational control of physical assets, represents the simplest way for comprehensive ESG integration. This approach enables investors to implement granular sustainability initiatives, from energy efficiency retrofits to comprehensive social impact programs, while maintaining direct oversight of governance structures and operational practices.

The fundamental **advantage** of direct ownership lies in the **investor's ability to make immediate, asset-specific ESG improvements without requiring consensus from other stakeholders or navigating complex fund structures**. The UN Principles for Responsible Investment (PRI) highlight that direct real estate ownership enables investors to incorporate ESG issues that are particularly relevant at the asset level. This approach emphasizes targeted actions, local context, and immediate response, advantages which are less accessible in indirect investment vehicles (such as funds or REITs)[300].

Direct investors can **implement comprehensive ESG strategies encompassing the entire property lifecycle**. Environmental initiatives may include installing advanced building management systems, upgrading to renewable energy sources, implementing water conservation technologies, and pursuing certifications such as LEED Platinum or BREEAM Outstanding. NEO, a pioneering real estate developer in the Philippines, demonstrates comprehensive ESG strategies throughout the property lifecycle by implementing advanced building management systems, transitioning entirely to 100% renewable geothermal energy since 2013, and achieving certifications including the International Finance Corporation's EDGE Zero Carbon and WELL Health-Safety Ratings[301]. They reached net zero carbon status four years ahead of schedule and continuously enhance sustainability through resource optimization, community engagement,

300 UNPRI, Introductory Guides to Responsible Investment, https://www.unpri.org/introductory-guides-to-responsible-investment/an-introduction-to-responsible-investment-real-estate/5628.article, accessed 29.07.2025.

301 GRESB, Elevating ESG performance in the Philippines: NEO's sustainability journey, https://www.gresb.com/nl-en/elevating-esg-performance-in-the-philippines-neos-sustainability-journey/, accessed 29.07.2025.

and industry leadership, serving as a model for proactive, asset-level environmental stewardship.

However, direct investment also poses significant **challenges** for ESG implementation. The **capital intensity required for meaningful sustainability improvements** can be substantial, particularly for older properties requiring extensive retrofitting. Owners and investors face high upfront costs for green building retrofits, and there can be uncertainty about the long-term return on investment (ROI) from energy efficiency measures, leading to resistance from some stakeholders[302].

(b) Indirect investment vehicles and ESG due diligence
Indirect real estate investment through **pooled vehicles, REITs, joint ventures, and debt instruments** provides diversification across geography, asset type, and market cycles, along with professional management capabilities. However, it also creates a more complex ESG landscape, where investors must rely on intermediaries to implement and monitor sustainability initiatives.

Real estate funds and pooled vehicles have emerged as critical vehicles for ESG integration, with fund managers increasingly recognizing that sustainability performance directly impacts long-term returns and investor attraction. High-ESG real estate portfolios perform similarly to the sector overall, but those with above-average environmental scores provide better diversification and can reduce climate impact through lower emissions[303].

Effective ESG integration in fund structures requires comprehensive assessment of the fund manager's ESG policy framework, implementation capabilities, and track record. Investors must evaluate whether the fund's ESG objectives align with their own sustainability goals and whether the manager has the necessary expertise and resources to deliver on ESG commitments.

Real estate investment trusts (REITs) offer unique advantages for ESG-conscious investors through enhanced transparency, standardized reporting, and regulatory oversight. The public nature of REIT structures creates natural incentives for strong ESG performance, as sustainability initiatives directly impact share price performance and investor perception. Leading REITs have demonstrated that comprehensive ESG integration can drive superior financial performance, with companies like Prologis achieving carbon neutrality across operations while

302 Iwuanyanwu/Gil-Ozoudeh/Okwandu/Ike, Retrofitting existing buildings for sustainability: challenges and innovations. Engineering Science & Technology Journal, 2024, 5(8), 2616–2631. https://doi.org/10.51594/estj.v5i8.1515.

303 Biasin/Delle Foglie/Giacomini, Addressing climate challenges through ESG-real estate investment strategies: An asset allocation perspective. Finance Research Letters, Volume 63, 2024, 105381.

linking ESG performance to better stakeholder value, cost efficiencies, lower capital costs (e.g., green bonds and sustainability-linked lending), tenant retention, and risk mitigation.[304]

Joint ventures present unique ESG challenges due to the need for alignment between multiple partners with potentially different sustainability objectives, risk tolerances, and implementation capabilities. Successful ESG integration in joint ventures requires clear definition of ESG roles and responsibilities, shared sustainability goals, and mechanisms for resolving conflicts between partners.

Real estate debt markets have experienced significant evolution in ESG, with lenders increasingly incorporating sustainability criteria into underwriting processes, loan terms, and ongoing monitoring requirements. Green loans and sustainability-linked loans have emerged as powerful tools for incentivizing improvements in ESG performance while providing favorable financing terms for qualifying projects[305].

Feature	Direct investment	Indirect investment (funds/REITs)
ESG due diligence focus	Asset-level physical and operational characteristics (e.g., energy audits, climate risk, tenant profiles)	Manager-level policies, processes, governance, and track record (e.g., GRESB score, ESG integration policy)
Locus of control	High. Investor makes or directly approves all major asset-level decisions	Low to moderate. Control is delegated to the fund manager; influence is exercised through engagement and governance rights
Key levers for change	Capital improvements, operational changes, tenant engagement, green leases, property manager selection	Manager selection, negotiation of fund terms (side letters), investor advisory committee participation, shareholder voting
Required expertise	In-house or contracted expertise in engineering, sustainability, property management, and local regulations	Expertise in manager due diligence, fund governance, and interpretation of ESG data and benchmarks
Cost & resources	Higher per-asset transaction costs due to detailed due diligence; significant management time required	Lower direct transaction costs; resources focused on manager selection and monitoring
Scalability of impact	Low. Impact is deep but confined to owned assets	High. A single investment can influence a manager's practices across a large, diversified portfolio
Risk of greenwashing	Low at the asset level (performance is tangible), but risk of misrepresenting performance exists	Higher. Risk that a manager's stated policies do not translate into meaningful action at the asset level

Table 20: ESG drivers and strategies by investor type – direct/indirect investments

304 Prologis, Inc., Prologis Commits to Net Zero Emissions by 2040, 22.06.2022, https://www.prologis.fr/en/insights/press-releases/prologis-commits-net-zero-emissions-2040, accessed 29.07.2025.

305 GRESB, Sustainability Linked Loans, https://www.gresb.com/nl-en/sustainability-linked-loans/, accessed 29.07.2025.

2.4.3 Typologies of real estate investors and their ESG drivers

(a) Institutional investors: fiduciary duty and long-term ESG value
Institutional investors, including pension funds, sovereign wealth funds, and insurance companies, have emerged as the **primary drivers of ESG integration** in real estate markets. Their long-term investment horizons, fiduciary responsibilities, and stakeholder accountability naturally align with sustainability objectives that extend beyond short-term financial returns.

Pension funds, in particular, face increasing pressure from beneficiaries to align investment strategies with environmental and social values while maintaining fiduciary duty to maximize long-term returns. The Dutch pension fund ABP, which manages over €600 billion in assets, has embraced a sustainable investment strategy with a strong focus on real estate to address the housing shortage in the Netherlands. ABP plans to invest €1 billion over the next five years to build 3,000 sustainable and affordable mid-market rental homes, targeting maximum rents aligned with regulated levels. Real estate is a central pillar of ABP's strategy to deliver long-term, inflation-linked returns while positively contributing to societal challenges, such as affordable housing.[306]

Sovereign wealth funds increasingly view ESG integration as essential for long-term national economic competitiveness and social stability. For example, the Government Pension Fund Global of Norway, the world's largest sovereign wealth fund, has divested from companies involved in coal production and deforestation, while increasing investments in renewable energy and sustainable real estate projects[307].

Insurance companies possess unique insights into climate-related risks and their potential impact on real estate values, making them natural advocates for comprehensive ESG integration. Their dual role as both investors and risk assessors creates incentives for supporting properties and developments that demonstrate resilience to environmental and social challenges.

(b) Private investors and high-net-worth individuals: values-driven and impact investing
High-net-worth individuals and **family offices** represent a growing segment of ESG-focused real estate investment, driven by personal values, legacy considerations, and the desire to have a positive social and environmental impact. This investor category often exhibits a strong willingness to provide patient or catalytic capital, accepting longer investment horizons or tailored risk profiles to enable meaningful ESG outcomes – thereby opening doors for innovative investment structures and impact-centered real estate projects.

306 Dutch News, ABP to invest €1bn to ease bottleneck in rental housing sector, https://www.dutchnews.nl/2025/05/abp-to-invest-e1bn-to-ease-bottleneck-in-rental-housing-sector/, accessed 05.08.2025.
307 Norges Bank Investment Management, Climate and nature disclosures 2024, https://www.nbim.no/contentassets/6fdfd333e6bf460f8e538b9b55a95bb7/gpfg-climate-and-nature-disclosures-2024.pdf, accessed 25.07.2025.

Younger generations are increasingly drawn to investment opportunities that align with their ethical principles and provide a sense of purpose beyond mere financial returns. There is a growing demand for »green« properties and impact-oriented real estate investments among this group. Impact investing, in this context, means allocating capital to projects that generate measurable social or environmental benefits alongside financial returns, such as affordable housing, green infrastructure, or community revitalization.

(c) Corporate investors: strategic ESG alignment

Corporate real estate investors, **including occupier-owners** and **strategic corporate funds**, approach ESG integration through the lens of broader corporate sustainability objectives, brand reputation management, and operational efficiency optimization. Their investment decisions often reflect commitments to corporate social responsibility, employee satisfaction goals, and stakeholder engagement requirements.

Corporate ESG drivers typically include operational cost reduction through energy efficiency improvements, employee attraction and retention through high-quality workplace environments, brand enhancement through visible sustainability commitments, and risk mitigation through investments in climate resilience. Microsoft's commitment to achieving carbon negativity by 2030 has driven significant investments in sustainable corporate real estate, including advanced building technologies and renewable energy systems[308].

(d) Public sector and government-linked entities: Leading the way on social and environmental impact

Government entities and **public sector investors** play a crucial role in establishing ESG standards, demonstrating best practices, and addressing market failures in sustainable development. They often prioritize social impact and environmental benefits over short-term financial returns in their investment decisions, creating opportunities for innovative approaches to ESG integration.

Public sector ESG initiatives typically focus on affordable housing development, urban regeneration projects, climate-resilient infrastructure, and community facility development. These entities also serve as catalysts for private sector ESG adoption through policy development, regulatory frameworks, and public-private partnership structures[309].

308 Microsoft, Reducing Embodied Carbon in Construction, https://cdn-dynmedia-1.microsoft.com/is/content/microsoftcorp/microsoft/final/en-us/microsoft-brand/documents/reducing-embodied-carbon-July-2021.pdf, accessed 29.07.2025.

309 Zhang/Nunez/English/Dehaene-Gold/Garcia Lozano, Public-Private Partnerships for Investment and Delivery of Affordable Housing in Emerging Market Economies (English). Washington, D.C.: World Bank Group.

2.4.4 Cross-border real estate investment: Navigating global ESG complexities

(a) Drivers and unique challenges of international real estate investment

Cross-border real estate investment has grown significantly, driven by objectives of portfolio diversification, capital allocation requirements, and access to emerging market opportunities. However, the integration of ESG considerations into international investment strategies presents complex challenges requiring sophisticated understanding of local regulatory frameworks, cultural contexts, and sustainability standards.

The **primary drivers** include geographic diversification to reduce portfolio concentration risk, access to higher-growth markets with attractive risk-adjusted returns, currency diversification, and exposure to different real estate cycles. However, cross-border ESG integration faces significant challenges including regulatory complexity across multiple jurisdictions, varying ESG standards and reporting requirements, cultural differences in sustainability priorities, and inconsistent data availability[310].

(b) Navigating diverse regulatory and reporting landscapes

The global ESG regulatory landscape presents a complex patchwork of requirements that varies significantly across jurisdictions. The European Union has established the world's most comprehensive ESG regulatory framework through the EU Taxonomy Regulation[311], the Sustainable Finance Disclosure Regulation (SFDR[312]), and the Corporate Sustainability Reporting Directive (CSRD)[313].

The EU Taxonomy provides specific technical screening criteria for determining whether real estate activities qualify as environmentally sustainable, including requirements for energy performance certificates, life-cycle carbon assessments, and climate adaptation measures. The SFDR requirements mandate detailed ESG disclosures for investment funds, including principal adverse impact statements and sustainability risk assessments.

In contrast, the United States ESG regulatory environment is evolving rapidly, with the Securities and Exchange Commission proposing comprehensive climate disclosure rules requiring

310 Hogan Lovells, ESG: What are the global issues for cross-border managers of real estate funds?, https://www.hoganlovells.com/en/publications/esg-what-are-the-global-issues-for-cross-border-managers-of-real-estate-funds, accessed 29.07.2025; Demers Baulne, Real estate: navigating the complexity of ESG disclosure standards and frameworks, https://www.demersbeaulne.com/en/2024/07/23/real-estate-navigating-the-complexity-of-esg-disclosure-standards-and-frameworks, accessed 29.07.2025.

311 European Parliament and Council (2020). Regulation (EU) 2020/852 on the establishment of a framework to facilitate sustainable investment (EU Taxonomy Regulation).

312 European Parliament and Council (2019). Regulation (EU) 2019/2088 on sustainability-related disclosures in the financial services sector (SFDR).

313 European Parliament and Council (2022). Directive (EU) 2022/2464 amending Directive 2013/34/EU as regards corporate sustainability reporting (CSRD).

detailed reporting of greenhouse gas emissions and climate risk assessments[314]. State-level initiatives are driving additional requirements, particularly in California and New York.

(c) Enhanced ESG due diligence in cross-border transactions

Cross-border real estate transactions require enhanced ESG due diligence processes addressing the complex interplay of local regulations, cultural contexts, and international standards. This includes comprehensive environmental liability assessments, social impact evaluations, and governance structure analyses tailored to local market conditions.

Environmental due diligence must address local climate risks, regulatory compliance requirements, and environmental liability exposure. A social impact assessment requires an understanding of local labor practices, community relations, human rights considerations, and cultural sensitivities. A governance evaluation encompasses an analysis of local legal frameworks, regulatory enforcement mechanisms, and corruption risks.

(d) Mitigating cross-border ESG risks and identifying opportunities

Successful cross-border ESG integration requires proactive risk management strategies and the identification of opportunities for positive impact that align with local development priorities and international sustainability objectives. Risk mitigation strategies include comprehensive political risk insurance, developing local partnerships, monitoring regulatory compliance, and scenario planning for potential policy changes.

Opportunity identification focuses on markets where international ESG expertise can drive significant value creation while addressing local sustainability challenges. This may include pioneering green building technologies in emerging markets, developing affordable housing solutions that address social equity concerns, or implementing circular economy principles in regions with limited waste management infrastructure.

2.4.5 Conclusion: strategic integration of investment approaches, investor types, and global context with ESG

The analysis reveals that successful ESG integration in real estate requires a sophisticated understanding of the complex interplay between investment structures, stakeholder motivations, and regulatory environments. ESG considerations are no longer optional add-ons to traditional investment analysis, but fundamental drivers of long-term value creation and risk management.

314 U.S. Securities and Exchange Commission, SEC Adopts Rules to Enhance and Standardize Climate-Related Disclosures for Investors, https://www.sec.gov/newsroom/press-releases/2024-31, accessed 02.07.2025.

Direct investment approaches offer the greatest potential for comprehensive ESG integration through immediate operational control, but they require significant capital investment and specialized expertise. Indirect investment vehicles provide diversification benefits and professional management capabilities, but they demand sophisticated due diligence and ongoing engagement to ensure that ESG objectives are met.

The diversity of investor types creates a rich ecosystem of ESG motivations and implementation approaches, from institutional investors' fiduciary-driven sustainability integration to private investors' impact strategies based on values. Cross-border investment adds layers of complexity requiring enhanced due diligence, local expertise, and adaptive implementation strategies.

The convergence of these factors points toward a future where ESG integration becomes the standard approach to real estate investment, driven by regulatory requirements, stakeholder expectations, and growing evidence that sustainability initiatives support long-term financial performance. Success in this evolving landscape requires continuous learning, adaptive strategies, and a commitment to transparency and accountability in ESG implementation and reporting.

2.5 Impact investing

Prof. Dr.-Ing. Anja Henrike Kleinke

> *«Impact investing in real estate and urban infrastructures is an exciting field of research.«*

2.5.1 Introduction to #2.5

Impact investing is a significant and growing area of sustainable finance that sets out to generate positive social or environmental impact alongside financial returns. It is more than just ESG exclusion strategies or investing in assets with a positive impact. There is an explicit contribution on the part of the investor to achieve the targeted impact. Impact investments embody core characteristics and a set of principles to be respected. Among the various frameworks for impact measurement and management, the United Nations Sustainable Development Goals serve as a normative framework with respect to impact targets, indicators and metrics. The impact investing market is relatively new but growing. However, the EU impact investing market faces some challenges regarding market standards and regulatory clarity. Impact investing in the real estate sector is gaining momentum. Relevant impact objectives in real estate range from socially beneficial to environmental aspects, offering promising perspectives regarding sector coupling, ConTech and PropTech solutions.

In this subchapter #2.5 on impact investing, we look at the classification of impact investing (#2.5.2), impact strategies and processes (#2.5.3), and finally impact measurement frameworks and positive impact in real estate (#2.5.4).

2.5.2 Classification of impact investing

There is no single, harmonized definition for impact investing. It tends to be understood as going beyond pure ESG investing due to a positive and measurable contribution to the environment and/or society.[315]

> According to the **Global Impact Investing Network (GIIN)**, impact investments are investments made with the intention of generating positive, measurable social and environmental impact alongside a financial return[316]. The Global Steering Group for Impact Investment describes that »*Impact investments aim to deliver solutions at scale to our world's biggest issues, optimising risk, return and impact to benefit people and the planet. It does so by setting specific social and environmental objectives alongside financial ones, and measuring their achievement (…)*«[317].

2.5.3 Impact investment strategies and processes

There is a range of initiatives on which investors can build to rethink their impact investment strategies and implement them in their investment processes.

Among them **two prominent high-level statements of principle** are the »*Core Characterics of Impact Investing*« drafted by the GIIN in partnership with impact investors and the »Operating Principles for Impact Management (OPIM)« convened by the IFC (International Finance Corporation, World Bank Group)[318].

---

315 European Securities and Markets Authority (ESMA), Impact investing – Do SDG funds fulfil their promises?, European Securities and Markets Authority, 2024, 4, https://data.europa.eu/doi/10.2856/444326, accessed 22.07.2025.

316 The Global Impact Investing Network (GIIN), Impact Investing: A guide to this dynamic market, 3, https://thegiin.org/publication/post/about-impact-investing/#what-is-impact-investing, accessed 22.07.2025.

317 Global Steering Group for Impact Investment (GSG Impact), https://www.gsgimpact.org/impact/impact-investment/?_gl=1*1vo56zw*_up*MQ..*, accessed 22.07.2025.

318 Global Investors for Sustainable Development Alliance (GISD), Navigator, Investors, High-level principles, https://www.gisdalliance.org/navigator, accessed 22.07.2025.

«(...) The role the investor plays in achieving non-financial objectives is other than being the provider of (secondary) capital. Impact investing is more than merely investing in positively impactful assets. There is an explicit investor's contribution to the achievement of the targeted impact. (... (This is) coupled with the active management of such targeted impact and stringent reporting. Going beyond a sustainable investment objective, impact investing requires defining a targeted impact and understanding how such impact can be achieved by the investor on the basis of an impact pathway (...)«[319].

(a) The Core Characteristics of Impact Investing

The Core Characteristics of Impact Investing, drawn up by the GIIN in partnership with impact investors, define what constitutes credible impact investing in adherence to **four high-level principles.** These characteristics complement the GIIN's definition of impact investing by helping investors understand the essential elements of impact investing, define the credibility of their practices, and evaluate the quality of potential investment partners' practices. The objective is to provide clear reference points and practical actions to establish a baseline for impact investing.[320]

(b) The Operating Principles for Impact Management (OPIM)

The Operating Principles for Impact Management (OPIM) were established in April 2019 by the IFC, following extensive consultations with industry leaders and 60 founding signatories. In 2022, the GIIN became the host.[321] According to the IFC, the **OPIM provide a reference point** against which the impact management systems of funds and institutions may be assessed. They draw on emerging best practices from a range of asset managers, asset owners, asset allocators, and development finance institutions.[322]

The OPIM *»(...) are voluntary standards that look to distinguish between ›impact investing funds‹ that have credible impact measurement and monitoring approaches in place, and those that just have the intent to do so (...)«*[323].

319 Multi-stakeholder taskforce with experts from investors, asset managers and other stakeholders under the lead of the German Alternative Investment Association (BAI) and the German Impact Investing Initiative (BIII), supported by evolutiq Impact Advisory GmbH/Frede and Herbert Smith Freehills Kramer LLP/Schmitz, Why impact investing should be recognized in the EU Sustainable Finance framework and how this could look like: Enabling the impact investing market in the EU and supporting market growth, innovation, and competition, July 2025, 4, https://bundesinitiative-impact-investing.org/publikationen/policy-paper-recognising-impact-investing-in-the-eu-sustainable-finance-framework/, accessed 22.07.2025.

320 Global Investors for Sustainable Development Alliance (GISD), Navigator, Investors, High-level principles, Core Characteristics of Impact Investing, https://www.gisdalliance.org/navigator, accessed 22.07.2025.

321 GIIN (host since 2022), Operating Principles for Impact Management, The 9 Principles, https://www.impactprinciples.org/9-principles/, accessed 22.07.2025.

322 IFC International Finance Corporation, World Bank Group, Impact investing at IFC, https://www.ifc.org/en/our-impact/impact-investing-at-ifc, accessed 22.07.2025.

323 United Nations, Inter-agency Task Force on Financing for Development, Financing for Sustainable Development Report 2023: Financing Sustainable Transformations, 2023, 72, https://developmentfinance.un.org/fsdr2023, accessed 22.07.2025.

The **OPIM's objective** is to establish a global standard around the management of investments for impact and describe the features of investment management that contribute to measurable positive social or environmental impact as well as financial returns. The **nine operating principles** are »*(...) the building blocks for a robust impact management system through the investment cycle, from strategic positioning to exit. Signatories to the principles are required to publish an annual statement in which they disclose how each principle is incorporated into their investment process. In addition, their alignment with the principles must be independently verified (...)*«.[324]

(c) Impact pathway

An impact pathway is a simplified model of complex, multifactorial relationships[325] that illustrates how impact can be achieved by an investor on the basis of an impact pathway.[326]

The impact pathway, as defined by the Impact Management Platform (IMP), is the **sequence that links organizations' actions with their effects on people and the natural environment.** It describes the relationship between an organization's inputs, activities, and outputs and their effects on people and the natural environment, especially outcomes and impact. The impact pathway is often represented graphically as step-by-step route from inputs to impacts.[327]

(d) Impact investing within the spectrum of capital

The range of investment profiles and strategies extends from finance-only to impact-only strategies. The associated financial returns as well as the potential for ESG risk mitigation, the pursuit of ESG-opportunities and the focus on measurable, high-impact solutions can differ.[328]

Impact investing, taken as a strategy intended to create concrete, measurable, and positive environmental or social impact, goes far beyond, for example, simple ESG exclusion strategies.[329]

---

324 Global Investors for Sustainable Development Alliance (GISD), Navigator, Investors, High-level principles, Operating Principles for Impact Management, https://www.gisdalliance.org/navigator, accessed 22.07.2025.

325 Impact Management Platform (IMP), impact and the impact pathway, https://impactmanagementplatform.org/impact/#:~:text=An%20impact%20pathway%20describes%20how,natural%20capital%20affect%20different%20stakeholders, accessed 27.07.2025.

326 Multi-stakeholder taskforce with experts from investors, asset managers, and other stakeholders, led by the German Alternative Investment Association (BAI) and the German Impact Investing Initiative (BIII), supported by evolutiq Impact Advisory GmbH/Frede and Herbert Smith Freehills Kramer LLP/Schmitz, Why impact investing should be recognized in the EU Sustainable Finance framework and how this could look like: Enabling the impact investing market in the EU and supporting market growth, innovation, and competition, July 2025, 4, https://bundesinitiative-impact-investing.org/publikationen/policy-paper-recognising-impact-investing-in-the-eu-sustainable-finance-framework/, accessed 22.07.2025.

327 Impact Management Platform (IMP), Impact and the impact pathway, https://impactmanagementplatform.org/impact/#:~:text=An%20impact%20pathway%20describes%20how,natural%20capital%20affect%20different%20stakeholders, accessed 27.07.2025.

328 Social Impact Investment Taskforce Working Group on Asset Allocation SIITF WGAA (2014), Fig. 1.1 A spectrum of capital in: OECD, Social Impact Investment: Building the Evidence Base, 2015, 18, http://dx.doi.org/10.1787/9789264233430-en, accessed 20.07.2025.

329 European Securities and Markets Authority (ESMA), Impact investing – Do SDG funds fulfil their promises?, European Securities and Markets Authority, 2024, 4, https://data.europa.eu/doi/10.2856/444326, accessed 22.07.2025.

Within the spectrum of capital the Social Impact Investment Taskforce (SIITF WGAA) places impact investing as being situated between ›sustainable investing‹ and ›impact-only‹ investments, with an investment profile ranging from competitive returns to below-market returns.[330]

According to the IFC, the impact investing market is relatively new, but it is growing rapidly and making progress in converging toward common frameworks for managing investments for impact[331]. The **size of the impact investing market worldwide** is estimated by the GIIN to be $1.571 trillion USD in 2024, with over 3,907 organizations worldwide that manage these impact investing assets. Of the 1,475 organizations that reported on both their assets under management (AUM) and their headquarters' location, the vast majority are based in developed markets, primarily in Western, Northern and Southern Europe, as well as the U.S. and Canada.[332] In the EU market, impact investing has gained significant traction in recent years, with market trends indicating a shift toward more intentional and measurable approaches to sustainable finance[333]. Until now, the existing EU regulations do not yet fully reflect the concept of impact investing as it has been established in the market. This lack of regulatory recognition has led to significant challenges for the EU impact industry.[334]

2.5.4 Impact measurement frameworks and positive impact in real estate

The **United Nations Sustainable Development Goals (SDG)** serve as a normative framework with respect to impact targets, indicators and metrics: »*(...) These goals span across different ESG topics (...) and are thus closely interlinked with various issues typically included in the ESG investing language (...). Not only does the SDG framework itself provide a number of metrics against which corporates can report the different goals, but various attempts have also been made by international organisations or standard setters to translate a large number of the remaining targets and metrics in such a way that corporates can integrate them into their reporting activities (...)*«.[335]

330 Social Impact Investment Taskforce Working Group on Asset Allocation SIITF WGAA (2014), Fig. 1.1 A spectrum of capital in: OECD, Social Impact Investment: Building the Evidence Base, 2015, 18, http://dx.doi.org/10.1787/9789264233430-en, accessed 20.07.2025.

331 IFC International Finance Corporation, World Bank Group, Impact investing at IFC, https://www.ifc.org/en/our-impact/impact-investing-at-ifc, accessed 22.07.2025.

332 Hand/Ulanow/Pan/Xiao, Sizing the Impact Investing Market 2024, The Global Impact Investing Network (GIIN). New York, 3ff, 2024, https://s3.amazonaws.com/giin-web-assets/giin/assets/publication/giin-sizingtheimpactinvestingmarket-2024.pdf, accessed 27.07.2025.

333 Multi-stakeholder taskforce with experts from investors, asset managers and other stakeholders under the lead of the German Alternative Investment Association (BAI) and the German Impact Investing Initiative (BIII), supported by evolutiq Impact Advisory GmbH/Frede and Herbert Smith Freehills Kramer LLP/Schmitz, Why impact investing should be recognized in the EU Sustainable Finance framework and how this could look like: Enabling the impact investing market in the EU and supporting market growth, innovation, and competition, July 2025, 5, https://bundesinitiative-impact-investing.org/publikationen/policy-paper-recognising-impact-investing-in-the-eu-sustainable-finance-framework/, accessed 22.07.2025.

334 Ibid, 4.

335 European Securities and Markets Authority (ESMA), Impact investing – Do SDG funds fulfil their promises?, European Securities and Markets Authority, 2024, 4, https://data.europa.eu/doi/10.2856/444326, accessed 24.07.2025.

The **real estate sector** is subject to impact investments – with objectives ranging from social to environmental. Impact criteria should be considered holistically, it is important to take a building's specific context into account and recognize that various criteria may be interdependent. Sustainable finance and impact investing in real estate involve green building initiatives. As a member of the UN Global Compact, the **World Green Building Council (WGBC)** reports its progress referring to the SDG. The WGBC global network has prioritized 11 SDGs where it can actively support progress, by mobilizing the building and construction sector to bring about a profound shift toward sustainable development.[336] They can be of particular relevance for real estate impact strategies.[337]

In the field of impact investing in real estate, various impact **measurement frameworks** are conceivable. Examples include the IRIS System of Global Impact Investing Network and Impact Management Norms of Impact Frontiers.[338] Some use cases can be found in the documentation and the Real Estate Impact Analysis Tool from the United Nations Environment Programme Financial Initiative (UNEP FI) and its UNEP FI Property Working Group in collaboration with RICS, Global Investor Coalition on Climate Change and PRI.[339]

The **environmental aspects** and **associated measurement criteria in real estate** are based on scientific research. Socially beneficial measures in real estate can provide a wide range of social and socio-cultural benefits to local communities and have their own set of criteria. In this regard, social criteria for real estate might be established to cover issues such as diversity, inclusion, equity, well-being, and socially responsible procurement.[340] Additional resources that address such social aspects are, for example, the WELL-Building Standard, the Living Building Challenge, the Social Impact Investing Framework of the ICG (Institute of Corporate Governance) in the German Real Estate Industry or The National TOMs Framework.[341]

336 World Green Building Council (WGBC), Sustainable built environments & the UN's Sustainable Development Goals, https://worldgbc.org/sustainable-development-goals/, accessed 25.07.2025.

337 Ibid.

338 IRIS+ System: Standards, IRIS+ is the generally accepted system for measuring, managing, and optimizing impact, https://iris.thegiin.org/standards/, accessed 20.07.2025; Impact Frontiers, Impact Management Norms. https://impactfrontiers.org/norms/, accessed 20.07.2025.

339 United Nations Environment Programme Finance Initiative (ed)/UNEP FI Property Working Group in collaboration with RICS Global Investor Coalition on Climate Change and PRI, Positive Impact Real Estate Investment Framework. A tool for holistic impact analysis. Principles for Positive Impact Finance Implementation Guidance, November 2018, https://www.unepfi.org/wordpress/wp-content/uploads/2018/11/Positive-Impact-Initiative_Real-Estate-Investment-Framework_Nov-2018.pdf, accessed 20.07.2025.

340 Zentraler Immobilienausschuss ZIA Ausschuss Büroimmobilien (ed): ESG-Leitfaden für Büroimmobilien, Januar 2024, 11, 29, https://zia-deutschland.de/project/esg-leitfaden-fur-buroimmobilien/, accessed 20.07.2025.

341 WELL Building Standard, https://standard.wellcertified.com/well, accessed 30.07.2025; International Living Future Institute: Living Building Challenge, What if every single act of design and construction made the world a better place?. https://living-future.org/lbc/, accessed 30.07.2025; ICG Institut für Corporate Governance in der deutschen Immobilienwirtschaft (ed), Social Impact Investing, Der Praxisleitfaden für die Immobilienwirtschaft, February 2021, https://icg-institut.de/en/social-impact-investing/social-impact-investing-practical-guide/, accessed 30.07.2025; National Toms Framework, https://nationaltomsframework.co.uk/social-value-portal-national-toms-calculator/, accessed 30.07.2025.

Some **potential fields of growth** for impact investments in real estate and related industries include sector coupling in real estate and urban infrastructure, as well as digital technologies such as ConTech (Construction Technology) and PropTech (Property Technology). Impact investments in sector coupling cover the integration and interaction of urban multiple energy and infrastructure systems with the aim of creating more sustainable urban environments. Impact investments in digital technologies aim to transform the construction and real estate sectors by introducing data-driven processes and innovations that improve sustainability.

Abbreviation	Full Name
GIIN	Global Impact Investing Network
GSG Impact	Global Steering Group for Impact Investment
IFC	International Finance Corporation, World Bank Group
IMP	Impact Management Platform
OPIM	Operating Principles for Impact Management
SDG	United Nations Sustainable Development Goals (SDG)
SIITF	Social Impact Investment Taskforce established under the United Kingdom's presidency of the G8
WGAA	Working Group on Asset Allocation
WGBC	World Green Building Council
UNEP FI	United Nations Environment Programme Financial Initiative

Table 21: List of abbreviations used in subchapter #2.5

2.6 Implementing ESG into real estate financing

Oliver Dreher

2.6.1 Introduction to #2.6

What is it about?

The terms »**sustainable finance**« or »**ESG finance**« stand for financings based on parameters from the areas of »environmental«, »social« and »governance«.

Integrating ESG criteria into real estate (or, come to that, any other) financing is no longer just a reflection of ethical investment strategies, but also a necessary response to the continuously increasing demand for sustainable development from various stakeholders. The goal of this subchapter is to highlight key considerations when approaching ESG-related financing.

This subchapter includes an overview of relevant financing aspects and tools (#2.6.2), key concepts for linking a financing to ESG (#2.6.3), important ESG standards that have an impact (also) on real estate financing (#2.6.4), and practical guidance for drafting ESG-linked financing clauses (#2.6.5); it also offers guidance on the risks of (involuntary) greenwashing in the context of such financing contracts (#2.6.6), an overview of »thematic bonds« (#2.6.7), closing with concluding remarks (#2.6.8).

Before we dive into the various aspects of sustainable financing, let's briefly answer the legitimate question you may have:

«Why care about sustainable financing?«

The short answer, which we will further substantiate in this chapter:

«Because sustainable finance is the operational backbone of the ESG movement.«

Without it, ESG remains a set of aspirational goals. With it, however, ESG becomes an actionable framework that redirects global capital flows toward sustainable outcomes.

Whether you like it or not, you will not be able to ignore it: the age of »soft ESG« is over. Noncompliance with reporting obligations and/or alignment increasingly leads to severe restrictions on financing conditions and options.

2.6.2 Never forget: »It's all about finance«!

(a) Every ESG financing is, first and foremost, financing

As mentioned above, ESG financing has become a major part of the financing toolbox, including in real estate. For differentiation purposes, it is generally distinguished from »conventional financing«, a term that refers to (otherwise comparable) financings without specific ESG considerations.

However, whether »sustainable« or conventional, the most important consideration when approaching ESG financing is that »*financing remains financing!*«. Therefore, despite the enthusiasm and support for ESG financing, it is important to remember that (i) the key component of any ESG financing is efficiently fulfilling the financing needs of the company and that (ii) the same economic and practical parameters largely apply to sustainable financing as to conventional financing.

(b) What types of financing? Who are they suitable for?

Prior to considering any ESG aspects, **real estate financing** can be broken down into the following typical **methods**:

Instrument	*Financing Type*	*Security*	*Lenders/Investors*
Bilateral or syndicated bank loans	• Project-/object- OR portfolio-related • Corporate balance sheet-based	• Project-related: always/first ranking • Balance sheet-based: often/first ranking	• Banks (subject to banking regulation)
Mezzanine loans or similar instruments	• Project-/object- OR portfolio-based	• Often/lower ranking	• Often funds or • other alternative lenders (not subject to banking regulation)
Bonds	• Project-/object- OR portfolio-related • Corporate balance sheet-based	• Project-/object-related: yes/lower ranking • Corporate balance sheet-based: usually not	• Project-/object-related: often special funds or • other alternative lenders (not subject to banking regulation) • Corporate balance sheet-based: broad base of institutional investors (open-ended funds, banks, insurance companies, retail investors)
Real estate asset-backed securities	• Asset-backed/real estate loan receivables	• Yes/receivables and related mortgages	• Institutional investors and financial institutions

Table 22: Comparison of financing instruments

Why is this important for ESG financings? Because the mere addition of an »ESG element« to a financing does not in itself change its key parameters.

(c) Example: the »green bond«

When discussing sustainable finance, the focus in recent years has often been on the proverbial »green bond«. However, many companies that started off to »issue a green bond« – especially smaller or medium-sized companies (SMEs) and often in respect of project or object financing – eventually ended up with a completely different financing instrument. Why is that?

- In the general market understanding, a green bond is a classic capital markets instrument – a bearer bond that
  - can be traded on the stock exchange (a so-called »liquid« financial instrument),
  - can be held in small units (partial bonds) and
  - can be held by a large number of investors (at the same time).
- The issuance of such a bond typically requires, among other things, the preparation of a securities prospectus and compliance with various trading-related follow-up obligations, including the adoption of certain accounting standards.

- Finally, the economically viable implementation of such a bond placement usually requires a relatively high issuance volume (as investors expect a realistic secondary market where they can sell their bonds to other investors if necessary).

Given these parameters, typical issuers of classic green bonds are therefore often international (development) banks, such as KfW or the EIB, or large corporations or sovereigns.

In contrast, a »green bond« (at least with the above-mentioned parameters) usually cannot and need not be the first choice for SMEs, for example:
- SMEs are often owner-managed or predominantly family-owned companies. Their typical legal forms (e.g. GmbH, the German version of a limited liability company) are mostly chosen for flexibility and owner control, which at the same time often formally restricts the tradability of shares. As a result, most SMEs worldwide are not listed on any stock exchange.
- Similarly, SME debt instruments, such as bonds, are rarely traded on stock exchanges, and many SMEs prepare their accounts in accordance with national GAAP rather than IFRS standards, which are generally required for issuers of capital market securities.
- For SMEs in particular, accessing the capital market for the first time can have a particularly dramatic impact.
- Ultimately, however, the criterion of an expected high issuance volume (e.g. EUR 50, 100 million or more) is usually the most problematic requirement for SMEs to fulfill, simply because the target figures expected by the market are not feasible (or meaningful) for them.

The basic rule to take away is:

«If you don't issue a conventional bond, you won't issue a green bond either«.

Similarly, when approaching any other type of ESG financing, you will (also) have to maneuver within the same parameters impacting all your conventional financings:

You will need access to relevant investors who are generally perceptive to a certain financial instrument and its characteristics, e.g.:
- Banks will have to generally adhere to banking regulations, which include requirements for (first-ranking) security in real estate finance.
- Insurance companies and pension funds may seek financing that can remain on their balance sheet without triggering »mark-to-market« obligations while meeting certain regulatory requirements.
- Certain alternative lenders may need to invest in »capital markets securities« for banking licensing or practical reasons.

You will need to understand the economics: while current regulations – at least in many parts of the world – continue to make ESG-related financing attractive (while increasingly »punishing« non-ESG-compliant financing), markets have recently shown significant swings against transactions labeled »ESG«. In any case, the transaction must provide an efficient financing, as well as being economically attractive to lenders and investors.

Hence, if you are considering ESG-related financing, start with the »conventional« financing you are looking for and then seek to combine it with appropriate ESG parameters.

2.6.3 «ESG is not ESG«

What types of ESG linkages exist? Which one should you choose?

Having distinguished the basic types of financing as a first step, approaching an ESG-related financing requires choosing the appropriate type of ESG linkage. As with the financing itself, the ESG linkage type must follow what the borrower (i) can provide and (ii) wants to achieve.

A basic distinction can be drawn between the following types of ESG-related financing:

a) financings where the amounts raised (or corresponding amounts) are used for purposes that meet specific ESG objectives («**ESG Frameworks**« and »**Use of Proceeds**«):
   - e.g. »green bonds«;
   - type of ESG linkage: contribution of the investment to the achievement of pre-defined environmental goals
   - type of financing: corporate balance sheet based
   - monitoring of compliance: reviewed by ESG rating agencies and confirmed by an independent second-party opinion

b) financings where the conditions (e.g., interest rates) are linked to an external rating of the company's ESG parameters («**ESG Ratings**«):
   - e.g. »ESG-linked bonds«;
   - type of ESG linkage: the conditions of the financing (such as interest rate) depend on the (changing) ESG rating of the borrower/issuer or the financed project/object (where available)
   - type of financing: corporate balance sheet based, or (still less common) project/object-related
   - control of compliance: ESG rating agencies

c) financings where the conditions (e.g., interest rate) depend on the company achieving certain ESG-related key performance indicators (KPIs) («**ESG KPIs**«):
   - e.g. »ESG-linked bonds«;
   - type of ESG linkage: financing terms (such as interest) depend on the issuer's compliance with specific ESG-related key performance indicators («KPIs«) agreed upon in the financing documentation
   - examples: »CO_2 emissions of borrower/object remain below xyz during a financial year« and »the ESG rating of issuer/portfolio improves by xyz until«
   - type of financing: corporate balance sheet-based or project/object-related

- monitoring compliance: information obligations of the borrower, as agreed upon in the contractual terms, as well as confirmation by auditors and/or other relevant experts.

2.6.4 ESG-related frameworks of relevance to ESG financing

ESG financing is »regulated« by various types of codes, laws, statutes, regulations, protocols, and other instruments of – inter alia – statutory, administrative, contractual, or voluntary nature. Their relevance to ESG financing depends not only on their legal nature, but perhaps just as much on the practical importance attributed to them by market participants. Therefore, we will rather refer to them generally as »frameworks« and demonstrate how their nature and practical application differ.

Currently, there are a number of statutory and voluntary frameworks at the national, European, and global levels that address ESG in various ways. These regulations result in specific behavioral obligations for companies and are therefore relevant for any ESG-related financing.

a) **Statutory regulations** that apply (or are expected to apply upon full implementation) **directly** to companies seeking financing, are inter alia:
   - the **EU Taxonomy Regulation**
   - the **EU Sustainability Reporting Directive (CSRD)**
   - the **EU Supply Chain Directive (CSDDD)**
   - the **SEC Climate Disclosure Rule.**
   - the **ASEAN Taxonomy**
b) In addition, there are certain statutory frameworks that, at first glance, do not directly impact companies seeking financing, but primarily address various types of financial service providers. However, these **statutory frameworks** can also have a significant – albeit **indirect** – impact on companies active in real estate, like on any other so-called »non-financial companies«, if they seek financing. These frameworks include:
   - **Parts of the EU Taxonomy Regulation** that **only affect »financial companies«**, particularly the calculation of the taxonomy-eligible and taxonomy-compliant parts of a bank's assets and investments (the so-called Green Asset Ratio (GAR) and Banking Book Taxonomy Alignment Ratio (BTAR))
   - The **EU Disclosure Regulation (SFDR) for financial companies**, particularly the determination of ESG-compliant financial products (e.g., funds) and the associated requirements for taxonomy compliance of the product's assets, for example securities in sustainable investment funds
   - **Banking supervisory laws**, which oblige supervised banks to consider ESG risks when managing their loan portfolios and granting and monitoring loans

   In order for banks, insurance companies, fund managers, and other regulated financial institutions to comply with their statutory conduct and reporting obligations, they require the necessary ESG information from the non-financial companies to which they provide

financing or investment-related services. This information is generally included in the sustainability reports provided by the companies seeking financing or by the investors.
It should also be noted that companies in one jurisdiction may also be directly or indirectly exposed to the ESG regulations of other jurisdictions via international business partners, such as banks, or through their own international activities.

c) In addition to statutory regulations, **numerous voluntary agreements or codes of conduct on ESG** have long existed. Pursuant to these agreements, companies commit to more or less precisely described ESG-compliant behavior and corresponding reports. Similar information requirements for companies can also arise from voluntary commitments by business partners, including banks, institutional investors, and others. Such frameworks include, for example:
   - United Nations Global Compact[342]
   - Net Zero Banking Alliance Germany[343]
   - Net Zero Asset Managers Initiative[344]
   - Science Based Targets Initiative (SBTi)[345] and Science Based Targets Network (SBTN)[346]

   Corresponding (voluntary) standards for sustainability reporting include, for example:
   - Global Reporting Initiative (GRI)[347]
   - IFRS Sustainability Disclosure Standards[348]
   - German Sustainability Code (DNK)[349]
   - Especially for climate gas reporting: Greenhouse Gas Protocol Standards[350]

   The treasury department of a company seeking financing should be aware of the initiatives its company has committed to and the information already published for this purpose. This can serve as a solid foundation for meeting the ESG reporting requirements of lenders and other treasury stakeholders.
   Numerous reporting standards are currently also in the process of being harmonized. Since the ESRS reporting standard, which is mandatory in the EU, is significantly more comprehensive than other comparable standards, many voluntary reports will largely be served by the ESRS in terms of data.

d) Not to be overlooked aside from statutory frameworks and general voluntary ESG related standards, are also the **voluntary sustainability standards specifically designed for the use of various financing instruments**, for example:

342 United Nations Global Compact, https://unglobalcompact.org/what-is-gc, accessed 31.08.2025.
343 The Net Zero Banking Alliance, last updated in 2024, https://climateaction.unfccc.int/Initiatives?id=Net_Zero_Banking_Alliance, accessed 31.08.2025.
344 The Net Zero Asset Managers initiative, 2025, https://www.netzeroassetmanagers.org/, accessed 31.08.2025.
345 Science-Based Targets initiative, 2025, https://sciencebasedtargets.org/, accessed 31.08.2025.
346 Science Based Targets Network, 2025, https://sciencebasedtargetsnetwork.org/, accessed 31.08.2025
347 Global Reporting Initiative, GRI, 2025, https://www.globalreporting.org/, accessed 31.08.2025.
348 The International Financial Reporting Standards Foundation, General Sustainability-related Disclosures, IFRS, 2023, https://www.ifrs.org/projects/completed-projects/2023/general-sustainability-related-disclosures/#final-stage, accessed 31.08.2025.
349 The Sustainability Code, 2025, https://www.deutscher-nachhaltigkeitskodex.de/en/, accessed 31.08.2025.
350 GHG Protocol, Standards, https://ghgprotocol.org/standards-guidance, accessed 31.08.2025.

- the Green Bond Principles (GBP) of the International Capital Market Association (ICMA)[351]
- the Green Loan Principles, the Social Loan Principles and the Sustainability-Linked Loan Principles of the Loan Market Association (LMA)[352]
- the EU Green Bond Standard (EuGBS)[353] (this standard is arguably »semi-voluntary«, as it applies when a company issues a bond called »EU Green Bond« or similar and refers to this framework)

Finally, the relevance of ESG requirements for ESG financing arises not only from such statutory and voluntary frameworks but also from contract law, where contracting parties (e.g., lending banks or the company itself) include ESG-oriented behavioral and reporting obligations in contractual texts (see #2.6.5).

2.6.5 Drafting ESG financing contracts

The most important rule for successfully drafting ESG financing contracts might sound mundane but is too often neglected, even by large, experienced, and professional companies, banks and investors.

> *«Draft the ESG elements of your financing contract with the same level of care and professionalism as its other ›conventional‹ terms.«*

As we show below, it is often the failure to follow the aforementioned paradigm that leaves even well-intentioned and honest companies at risk of being accused of »greenwashing«.

(a) What is important when drafting the ESG components of your financing contract?
When drafting ESG-related financing contracts, one main consideration is the chosen type of ESG linkage (under #2.6.2(b)). What you have to do (under #2.6.5(b)) and what can go wrong (under #2.6.6(b)) depends largely on this:

---

351 International Capital Market Association (ICMA), Green Bond Principles (GBP), 2025, https://www.icmagroup.org/assets/documents/Sustainable-finance/2025-updates/Green-Bond-Principles-GBP-June-2025.pdf, accessed 31.08.2025.

352 Loan Market Association (LMA), the Green Loans Principles, the Social Loan Principles and the Sustainability-Linked Loan Principles etc. Document index, https://www.lma.eu.com/sustainable-lending/resources, accessed 31.08.2025.

353 The EU Green Bond Standard (EuGBS), https://eur-lex.europa.eu/EN/legal-content/summary/european-green-bond-standard.html, accessed 31.08.2025.

Financing type	*Contractual clauses*	*Key components & implementation*
Use of proceeds (ESG framework) financings	• Linkage to an ESG framework • The borrower confirms the investment of an amount equal to the nominal amount of the financing, in accordance with the ESG framework. • Information obligations (including reviews by ESG rating agencies and second party opinion) to monitor compliance with the ESG framework.	• ESG framework is the key component • Takes several months to years to develop a stable, transparent framework • Cannot be implemented on an ad hoc or short-term basis
ESG ratings financing	• Linkage to an ESG rating • Financing conditions (e.g., interest rate) increase/decrease depending on ESG rating development • Information obligations (including ESG rating reports)	• ESG rating is the key component • Takes several months to years to obtain • Cannot be implemented on an ad hoc or short-term basis • Linkage between ESG rating and financing conditions requires careful structuring (see ESG KPIs linked financings)
ESG KPIs linked financing	• Financing conditions (e.g., interest rate) increase/decrease depending on compliance with ESG-related KPIs • Specifies relevant KPIs and their impact on financing conditions • Information obligations (e.g., balance sheet items, specific KPI/sustainability reports)	• ESG KPIs are the key component • May be implemented without an ESG framework, depending on business type and reporting transparency • Can be implemented on a relatively short-term basis (several weeks to a few months)

Table 23: ESG components in financing contracts

(b) Drafting and implementation – what to do/what to focus on?

- <u>**Use of proceeds (ESG framework) financing**</u>

> Prepare an ESG framework and ensure (i) it exists (in time for any financing to be linked to it); (ii) it is transparent and verifiable (in accordance with relevant standards chosen) and (iii) the related reporting can be handled by the borrower.

As mentioned above, drafting such a framework, monitoring compliance with it, and ensuring that it is properly integrated into the borrower's organization and processes is a significant piece of work. The borrower should consult with experienced advisors and service providers at an early stage to begin establishing the framework and related steps.

It will only make sense for the borrower to approach any financings linked to the framework once sufficient progress has been made in establishing it.

- **<u>ESG ratings financing</u>**

Approach ESG rating agencies to obtain a relevant ESG rating.

As with an ESG framework, obtaining and maintaining such a rating, and ensuring that its proper inclusion into the borrower's organization and processes is a significant piece of work. The borrower should consult experienced advisors/rating agencies/service providers at an early stage to approach the establishment and related steps.
Only when sufficient progress has been made in obtaining such a rating will it make sense for the borrower to approach any financings linked thereto.

The second pillar of any ESG-linked financing is the »linkage« of certain financing conditions (e.g., interest rates) to the rating. For more information, please see below (*ESG KPIs linked financing*).

- **<u>ESG KPIs linked financing</u>**
Contractual clauses: The first steps in implementing such financings are the contractual clauses, which essentially focus on two aspects:
  - the specification/definition of the »KPIs«; and
  - the specification of the link between relevant financing conditions (e.g. interest rate) and the relevant KPIs.

  The **KPIs** can largely be chosen »freely« by the borrower and the involved banks, lenders, and investors, considering the following:
  - Increasingly, regulations prescribe relevant ESG parameters that borrowers may have to measure and comply with (e.g., taxonomy regulations and related reporting obligations); accordingly, it makes sense to choose KPIs such »statutory KPIs«.
  - However, also given the individual circumstances of many borrowers and their activities, it often makes sense to specify or define KPIs individually.

In any case, borrowers must ensure the following:

☐ To specify/define the KPIs clearly

☐ To have reliable, transparent, and efficient processes in place to monitor, report, and verify the compliance with these KPIs

☐ To be able to obtain and provide information on compliance with relevant KPIs in time for the relevant clauses in the ESG financing (e.g., when will a sustainability report be available in to impact a certain interest period?)

☐ To consider the intended effects of (non-) compliance with the KPIs in a comprehensive manner. This includes:
- What are the limits and patterns of interest rate increases/decreases? (How often can the interest rate change? Can a change impact a running interest period, or only at its end? Is there an upper and/or lower limit for changes?)

- What are the consequences (if any) of noncompliance with certain KPIs – other than a change in the interest rate (e.g., an event of default in the case of a certain degree of noncompliance)?
- What are the consequences of failing to provide relevant information to assess compliance, whether by providing a sustainability report or otherwise (e.g., treatment as if the KPIs were not met or an event of default)?

2.6.6 Risks of (involuntary) greenwashing

«*The Road to hell is paved* with *good intentions.*«

(a) Why greenwashing?

Many companies seeking financing based on sustainability criteria must learn that the special attention ESG financing enjoys has not only a positive effect, but can quickly turn into the opposite. One significant advantage of »ESG financing« in comparison with an otherwise comparable »conventional« financing is its increased visibility:

- The »debut ESG-linked loan« receives much more attention than »the 17th amendment of the existing RCF.«
- However, the market and the financial press will crack down on a perceived »greenwashing« in connection with an ESG-related KPI much quicker than they would in the case of a breached or disputed financial covenant.

That said, in most cases of (alleged) greenwashing in ESG financings, there is no intentional deception or exploitation, but rather a lack of awareness of the challenges involved in implementing ESG integration and the severity of the consequences of »unsuccessful« ESG financing. This means that even »decent« companies often risk being perceived as »greenwashers« when conducting ESG financings.

We will therefore examine what causes alleged greenwashing issues in ESG financing and how to avoid these situations.

The good news is that companies can significantly reduce the related risks if they comply with the suggestions and considerations presented in #2.6.5 (*Drafting ESG Contracts*).

(b) What can go wrong?

This depends mainly on the chosen type of ESG linkage. The »DON'Ts« are nothing but the flipside of the »DOs«. For the below summary of »DON'Ts«, we compare (i) Use of Proceeds (ESG framework) financing with (ii) ESG KPIs financing.

Use of Proceeds (ESG framework) financing

For these financings, the decisive factor is the ESG framework.

The »**DON'Ts**« here are:

- There is no framework in place, even though one would be necessary to provide the basis for the relevant linkage.
- A framework exists, but it is not sufficiently clear or transparent.
- The reporting does not work, or at least not reliably and efficiently.
- The company underestimates the time and effort required to establish a proper ESG framework and informs the market generally, or possible lenders and investors, too early or – even worse – commits to financings based on a not yet (sufficiently) existing framework.

ESG KPIs linked financing

For these financings, the decisive factors are (i) the KPIs and (ii) their linkage to the conditions of the financing.

The first pillar of »**DON'Ts**« is comparable to the respective considerations set out for the ESG framework financing:

- The KPIs need to »come from somewhere« (whether you call it a »framework« or not).
- They must be measurable, and there must be assessment, reporting and verification processes in place. The considerations in this respect are similar to those of an ESG framework.
- While an ESG KPI-linked financing may be prepared and implemented more quickly than a (first) ESG framework financing, setting up and preparing for relevant ESG KPIs still requires a certain amount of time and work. This is often underestimated by companies and sometimes not properly communicated by banks or other advisors.

The second pillar of the »DON'Ts« involves contractual clauses regarding (i) the KPIs themselves and (ii) the link between financing terms and the KPIs.

Far too often, companies and banks fail to focus sufficiently on the ESG KPIs.

- The **company does not take responsibility**.
- A **paradox** persists:
  - The ESG KPIs are just as important as e.g. financial KPIs (and for reputational reasons, sometimes even more so).
  - However, the level of professionalism invested is still often far below that applied to financial covenants under the same circumstances.
- In more detail, the following are **common mistakes companies should try to avoid**:
  - KPIs are not sufficiently described (including how to measure, how to calculate).
  - It is unclear who measures, monitors, or verifies (e.g., when auditors are said to »control« or »confirm«, it is unclear whether they simply confirm the usual financial statements from which the KPIs may be taken or if they have separate instructions to assess specific KPIs, which may or may not be reflected in the financial statements).

- It is generally unclear whether KPIs are derived from financial statements, an ESG framework, or another source.
- There is no clear link between the financing contract and an eventual green framework or other basis for determining and providing the KPIs.
- KPIs are said to impact certain interest payments, yet the relevant KPIs are only available after the interest payment.
- There are no contractual consequences for noncompliance with essential obligations in the context of the ESG KPIs (e.g. failure to deliver the relevant sustainability report or confirm KPIs), which makes the KPI linkage essentially »worthless«.

Therefore, companies approaching ESG financings should seek good advice when preparing and implementing financing and not be blinded by supposed »shortcuts«. ESG financing can then become a real opportunity.

2.6.7 Thematic bonds

At the beginning of this chapter, we introduced the main features of various financial instruments (see #2.6.2), as well as of various ways to link them to ESG characteristics (see #2.6.3). With this in mind, we want to take a closer look to a particular variety of ESG financing instrument: the so-called »thematic bonds«. Remembering they are all bonds, a closer look can help us better understand the variety of instruments that have developed around the globe, which may provide inspiration for possible tools and an answer to the question: »*What is your kind of bond?*«.

(a) Green bonds

Green bonds finance projects or investments with environmental benefits, such as renewable energy, energy efficiency, clean transportation, and sustainable waste management. Technically (as addressed under #2.6.3(a)), they are so-called »use of proceeds« financings.

Prominent voluntary standards for green bonds are:

- **ICMA Green Bond Principles (GBP)** – the global baseline[354].
- **EU Green Bond Standard (EuGB)** – voluntary but legally defined under EU Regulation 2023/2631, aligning with the EU Taxonomy[355]. Not yet widely applied, but already observed closely and developing as a kind of »shadow standard«, inter alia to measure other standards against.
- **China's Green Bond Catalogue** – mandatory taxonomy for Chinese issuers that excludes »clean coal« as of 2023[356].

354 International Capital Market Association (ICMA), Green Bond Principles (GBP), 2025, https://www.icmagroup.org/assets/documents/Sustainable-finance/2025-updates/Green-Bond-Principles-GBP-June-2025.pdf, accessed 31.08.2025.

355 The EU Green Bond Standard (EuGBS), https://eur-lex.europa.eu/legal-content/EN/TXT/?uri=CELEX:32023R2631, accessed 31.08.2025.

356 Climate Bonds, China's new Green Finance Catalogue brings clarity and confidence to the market, https://www.climatebonds.net/news-events/blog/chinas-new-green-finance-catalogue-brings-clarity-confidence-market, accessed 31.08.2025.

In some jurisdictions and markets, the issuance of green bonds is subject to **external review** (e.g., second-party opinions, certification, or verification), and increasingly to **mandatory reporting** of use-of-proceeds and impact metrics.

(b) Social bonds
Social bonds fund projects aimed at improving social outcomes, such as providing affordable housing, healthcare, and education or supporting vulnerable groups. Key guidance includes:

- **ICMA Social Bond Principles (SBP)**[357].
- **ASEAN Social Bond Standards** – mandatory for regional labeling in ASEAN member states[358].

Social impact measurement is considered even more complex than environmental metrics. Legal frameworks are evolving to improve transparency and prevent »social washing.«

(c) Sustainability bonds
These bonds finance a mix of green and social projects. They are often governed by the **ICMA Sustainability Bond Guidelines**, which combine criteria from both GBP and SBP[359].

Sustainability bonds offer flexibility for issuers with diverse ESG portfolios, but are subject to similar expectations regarding the use of proceeds and post-issuance reporting.

(d) Sustainability-linked bonds (SLBs)
SLBs are structurally different from sustainability bonds in that the proceeds are not earmarked for specific investments. Instead, the financial terms (typically the coupon) are linked to the issuer's achievement of pre-defined **sustainability performance targets** (**KPIs**) – such as carbon emissions reduction or diversity goals (see #2.6.3(c) above).

- The **ICMA Sustainability-Linked Bond Principles (SLBP)** provide voluntary guidance[360].
- The **EU** has not yet created a binding SLB regime, though regulatory work is ongoing[361].

357 International Capital Market Association (ICMA), Social Bond Principles (SBP), 2025, https://www.icmagroup.org/assets/documents/Sustainable-finance/2025-updates/Social-Bond-Principles-SBP-June-2025.pdf, accessed 31.08.2025.
358 ASEAN Taxonomy Board (ATB), ASEAN Taxonomy for Sustainable Finance (ASEAN Taxonomy), Frequently Asked Questions, https://asean.org/wp-content/uploads/2024/12/ASEAN-Taxonomy-FAQ-20Dec2024.pdf, accessed 31.08.2025.
359 International Capital Market Association (ICMA), Sustainability Bond Guidelines (SBG), June 2021, https://www.icmagroup.org/assets/documents/Sustainable-finance/2021-updates/Sustainability-Bond-Guidelines-June-2021-140621.pdf, accessed 31.08.2025.
360 International Capital Market Association (ICMA), Sustainability-Linked Bond Principles (SBLP), 2024, https://www.icmagroup.org/assets/documents/Sustainable-finance/2024-updates/Sustainability-Linked-Bond-Principles-June-2024.pdf, accessed 31.08.2025.
361 EC, Platform on Sustainable Finance, https://finance.ec.europa.eu/sustainable-finance/overview-sustainable-finance/platform-sustainable-finance_en#activities, accessed 31.08.2025.

As addressed in more detail under #2.6.6(b), legal risks can arise from poorly defined KPIs, a lack of robust external verification, or misguided issuer discretion when setting targets – thereby raising potential (at least reputational) liability for greenwashing.

(e) Transition bonds

Transition bonds fund activities that are not »green« by current taxonomy standards, but contribute to decarbonization over time – e.g. retrofitting fossil fuel infrastructure with carbon capture technology. While **no universal standard** exists yet, several efforts are underway:

- **Climate Bonds Initiative (CBI) Transition Framework** and **Guidance Materials**[362].
- **UK Transition Plan Taskforce**[363] and **ASEAN+3**[364] discussions on eligible transition financing structures.

These instruments face particular scrutiny because they are seen as being placed at the intersection of climate ambition and economic realism. While they are promising for hard-to-abate sectors, they carry **significant legal and reputational risks** if not transparently structured.

2.6.8 Conclusions

The integration of ESG criteria into real estate financing is not just a trend, but an imperative for the industry, as it is for any other industry. ESG financing should be recognized as the operational backbone of sustainable finance, transforming aspirational goals into actionable frameworks. This transformation is essential for redirecting global capital flows toward sustainable and inclusive outcomes.

> ESG elements must be strategically aligned with conventional financing parameters to ensure they meet both economic viability and stakeholder expectations. The challenge lies in navigating the complexities of ESG frameworks, ratings, and KPIs, while avoiding the pitfalls of greenwashing. It is crucial for companies to adopt transparent, measurable, and verifiable ESG practices that genuinely contribute to sustainability.

Companies and banks often make dangerous mistakes when implementing such financing. These mistakes often lie in the fact that the core aspects described in this chapter are not given

362 Climate Bonds/EBRD/Green Climate Fund, Financing the corporate climate transition with bonds, November 2023, https://www.climatebonds.net/files/documents/publications/Financing-the-Corporate-Climate-Transition-with-Bonds.pdf, accessed 31.08.2025.

363 Transition plan requirements: implementation routes, 25.06.2025, https://www.gov.uk/government/consultations/climate-related-transition-plan-requirements/transition-plan-requirements-implementation-routes-accessible-webpage, accessed 31.08.2025.

364 BOAO Forum for Asia/AMRO Asean/GIC Global Institute, Financing Asia's Transition to a Net-Zero Future, March 2025, https://amro-asia.org/wp-content/uploads/2025/03/Boao-Transition-Finance-Report_Web-Version.pdf, accessed 31.08.2025.

sufficient consideration or are not implemented accordingly. Often, the attention paid to the development of the frameworks, preparation of ratings, and the drafting of the contractual clauses lags significantly behind the (later) attention paid by the market and the press. The resulting quality standard falls well short of what the same companies and banks demonstrate, for example, in the case of traditional balance sheet covenants. A »sustainability framework« is either nonexistent, poorly designed, or unclear. The requirements for a rating may no longer be met as early as next year. Contractual clauses relating to specific ESG parameters in corporate activities may be »full of holes« or missing altogether. Related corporate communications may be unclear or contradictory. The market's perception follows suit: »*That's intentional, that's greenwashing*«.

Therefore, ESG financing can quickly turn from a blessing into a curse. However, if companies prepare well and do not allow themselves to be blinded by supposed »shortcuts« during the preparation and implementation phases, sustainable financing can be a real opportunity.

3 Due diligence, valuation and users' accounting

3.1 Introduction to Chapter #3

Sabine Wieduwilt

©Judith Carla Wieduwilt (2025)

Read how others would review and value ESG risks, opportunities, and impacts. Then, think about what you would focus on and how you would value these risks, opportunities, and impacts, and why you came to that conclusion. Then, start acting on it.

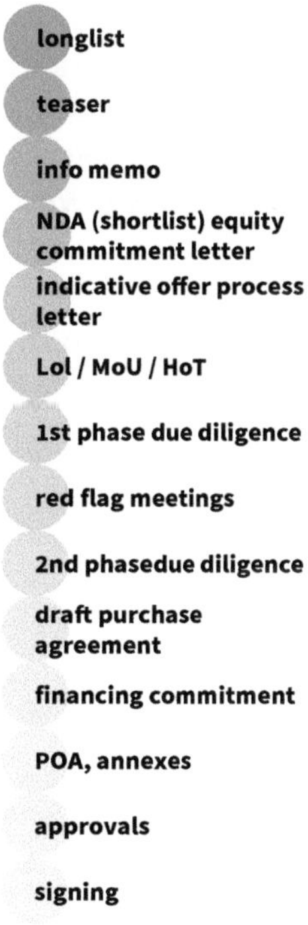

Figure 16: Process until signing – generic summary

What effect does ESG have during the investment process? How and where do I look at ESG criteria? Depending on the investment approach (#2.3, #2.5) and investor types (#2.4) this may differ, of course. This is why we are going at this from a generic perspective.

In a property transaction, the buyer typically performs financial, legal, technical, environmental, and operational due diligence. In the context of real estate acquisition, **due diligence** refers to the comprehensive process of investigating, verifying, and evaluating all relevant aspects of a property before finalizing its purchase. The primary goal is to ensure that the buyer fully understands the property's condition, legal status, financial performance, and potential risks, thereby enabling an informed investment decision. **ESG due diligence** often complements the further due diligence components. **ESG vendor due diligence** can inform the memorandum and support both parties during the transaction.

A real estate **investment memorandum** presents an investment opportunity by covering property details, financial information, legal structure, management, terms, and risks, and their mitigation strategies. Issued by investment firms, it informs investors and ensures compliance with transparency and sustainability rules. The ESG section details sustainability, social impact, and governance practices, such as energy efficiency and ethical management, and shows commitment to responsible investing by providing relevant metrics and targets. Sellers must ensure that the memorandum meets legal disclosure standards.

Sometimes, **the buyer conducts due diligence**, including ESG due diligence, following a two-step-approach. First, the properties are screened to see if they meet the criteria to continue with the investment process. If these criteria are met, the buyer continues with a more thorough due diligence (see ESG screening under #2.3, there ESG screening is described as an investment approach, less from a chronological perspective).

What's the **difference between environmental due diligence (EDD) and ESG due diligence**? What are **legal considerations**, or what would a lawyer review when conducting ESG due diligence. Would that be essentially different from that of the typical ESG due diligence being conducted in the market?

Real estate investment can be a purpose of **property valuation**. Property valuation is the process of determining the current market value of a real estate asset, such as land, a house, an apartment, or a commercial building. This assessment is typically carried out by a professional appraiser or valuer, considering various factors to estimate how much the property would likely sell for under normal market conditions. **Are ESG factors included in property valuation?** In many cases, properties are rented to tenants who have their own interests. **What's the relevance** for them?

We can also examine the **perspective of users** of the targeted assets, focusing on the integration of ESG criteria into requests for proposals (RFPs) and **accounting** practices.

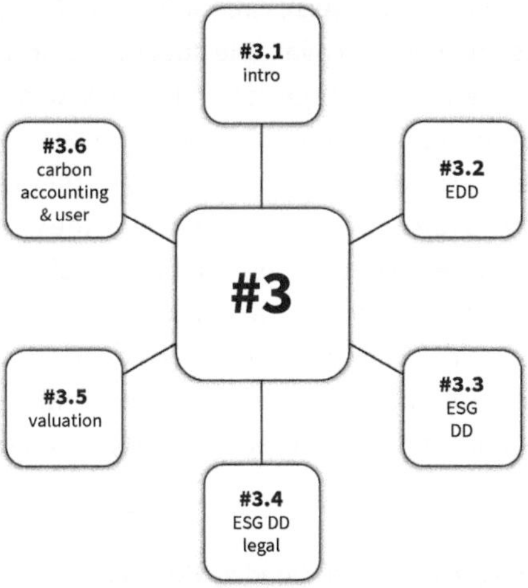

Due diligence – valuation – communication

In this chapter, we examine environmental due diligence (EDD) (#3.2), ESG due diligence (#3.3), ESG due diligence from a legal perspective (#3.4), property valuation and ESG (#3.5), and the role of carbon accounting, which is business-critical for tenants and a strategic imperative for landlords (#3.6).

3.2 Environmental due diligence (EDD) in real estate – defining standards

Sebastian Schröder/Piotr Kociołek

«A brownfield is not a candy shop, but with an EDD buying it is much sweeter.«

3.2.1 Introduction to #3.2

Today, environmental due diligence (EDD) is a crucial part of every transaction – or at least it should be. In the following, we will discuss the methods used for minimizing financial and legal risks. Those risks can result from overlooking environmental issues during the transaction phase or operation of a facility.

The **main topics an EDD should generally include** are:

a) Soil and groundwater (and ground gas, at least in some countries)
b) Hazardous building materials
c) Hazardous substances and their handling
d) Technical and environmental issues, such as drinking water, wastewater, ozone depleting substances
e) Geogenic risk factors, such as flooding, radon, earthquakes

Usually, the first step of an EDD is the **Phase I Environmental Site Assessment (Phase I ESA)**. A Phase I ESA includes site visits, interviews, as well as the review of available documents. Intrusive measurements, such as sampling, are not performed at this stage. It is important to mention that a Phase I ESA can be revised several times throughout the EDD process by different readers (stakeholders). Some of them are risk-averse, and in seller-buyer transactions, they can take advantage of unclear descriptions or conclusions to raise concerns and question the value of the property. Therefore, it is important that the EDD be carried out by reliable consultants, who can identify existing issues, even when they are not clearly visible, and discard suspicions and concerns that are not confirmed by raw data. A typical example of a report's quality is its description of building contaminants. While some consultants only mention the general possibility of hazardous materials (e.g., asbestos) in buildings based on their construction date, valuable consultants describe what they see based on experience.

Soil and groundwater issues identified in a Phase I ESA are further defined as »Recognized Environmental Conditions« (RECs). These could be either historical (HREC, already fully addressed in the past), controlled (CREC, already addressed in the past to some extent), business risks (BREC) or just simple RECs, which the surveyor identifies during the site visit.

Hazardous building materials (HBMs) and hazardous substances can only be identified during a site investigation. In the Phase I ESA, HBMs are identified by the environmental expert, then a **Phase II ESA** for HBMs (including sampling) is carried out. Laboratory analysis will ultimately determine whether a certain sample is a building contaminant. During the site visit, it is important to document the condition of installed building materials (e.g., fiber cement sheets and insulation materials) as well as the storage conditions of hazardous substances. If building materials are in poor condition (e.g., damaged insulation) or pose a risk to human health, a Phase II investigation, including sampling of materials, should be carried out.

If the storage conditions and handling of hazardous substances are found to be insufficient, the respective area of a site is designated as a REC or Area of Concern (AOC). In this case, depending on the location and the number of substances, a Phase II subsurface investigation should be carried out.

The **link between a Phase I and a Phase II ESA** is the **list of identified RECs**: issues are opened and questions are asked during the preliminary, non-intrusive step. Phase II is necessary to answer these questions and define the next steps. This could involve, for example, discussing the results with authorities and/or defining proper remediation techniques.

The following presentation will cover the different steps of a standard EDD process, from the start (purchase offer, letter of intent (LOI)) to the end (redevelopment or taking over a property). Examples will be given and common issues will be discussed.

#3.2 EDD	**#3.2.1 – intro to #3.2**	
	#3.2.2 – methodology of EDD	
	#3.2.3 – a project schedule	
	#3.2.4 – environmental topics during the redevelopment	
	#3.2.5 – ongoing site use	
	#3.2.6 – summary	

In this subchapter #3.2 on EDD in real estate – defining standards, we discuss the methodology of EDD (#3.2.2), the project schedule (#3.2.3), environmental topics during the redevelopment (#3.2.4), ongoing site use (#3.2.5), and conclude with a brief summary of our observations (#3.2.6).

3.2.2 Methodology

The **American Society for Testing and Materials (ASTM) report template** is widely accepted as a standard and used all around the world as the first step of an EDD, i. e. the Phase I Environmental Site Assessment. While the type of reporting must be adapted to the specific country's conditions and regulations, the general materials and potential issues to look at are indicated in the **ASTM standard**[365]. It should be noted that the ASTM standard is voluntary outside of the U.S. For an EDD process, local laws and regulations must always be considered. These can be significantly stricter in some cases.

The **EDD process** can be broken down into the following **steps**:

a) The **Phase I ESA** is usually carried out according to the ASTM standard, a reference document widely used and accepted. The outcome of this step is a list of RECs that have to be addressed through intrusive investigations.
b) The **Phase II ESA** is a site investigation that must take local regulations into account. Every country has its own laws, technical guidelines, and guidance documents describing how a site investigation should be carried out and providing the binding or indicative threshold values against which the results of a site investigation should be assessed. This step aims to identify major contamination and third-party liability rather than ensuring full compliance of environmental media (soil, groundwater, and ground gas) with respect to the applicable standards.
c) If the Phase II ESA confirms the existence of RECs, these must be delineated by means of a **detailed investigation**, assessed in terms of risk to human health, and addressed through a remediation plan. This process can be part of the EDD process or undertaken after the transaction under specific contractual conditions.
d) The Phase II ESA may also include an **assessment of materials (e.g., soil, artificial fill)** that will be excavated during redevelopment: can these materials be reused, or must they be disposed of based on the applicable regulations?
e) Finally, any **hazardous building materials (HBM)** in the existing buildings (if any) must be **assessed**, since their management will impact the demolition and disposal works. An HBM

365 American Society for Testing and Materials (ASTM), ASTM E1527-21 Standard Practice for Environmental Site Assessments: Phase I Environmental Site Assessment Process, 2021, https://store.astm.org/e1527-21.html, accessed 30.08.2025.

survey may be limited to a visual assessment, but it often requires specific sampling and laboratory analyses, including waste classification.

Steps (b) to (e) require detailed knowledge of valid laws and regulations and should only be undertaken by qualified (and, in some cases, registered) professionals.

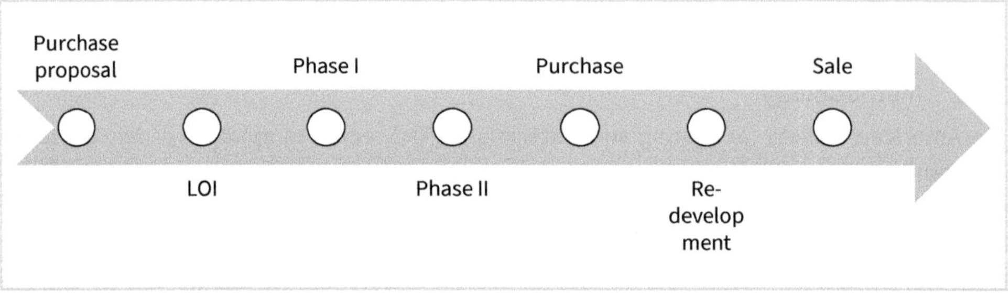

Figure 17: Standard EDD process

3.2.3 Project schedule

The first stage of a new project is when a potential buyer submits a **proposal** to the seller. If the buyer has an environmental department, this could already mark the beginning of the environmental assessment. This stage can be referred to as »**Phase 0**«. The available information is checked and a rough cost estimate for a) the EDD and b) potential cleanup costs can be estimated. In addition, a site visit helps understand the current situation.

The **second step** is signing a **letter of intent (LOI)** and, in most cases, an agreement about the timeframe of the exclusivity period. The period of exclusivity is usually estimated optimistically, as both parties want to close the deal as soon as possible. Therefore, it might be need to be extended at some point if issues requiring discussion or further investigation are identified. A proper EDD requires time, especially when it comes to brownfields.

After that, the potential buyer will **commission a consultant of choice to perform the EDD.** It is crucial to **define a level of materiality,** for example 25,000 € for common risks, whereas risks for human health are not linked to a threshold. These risks should always be mentioned and discussed. Having these agreements (LOI and approval of the consultant's proposal) in place, the consultant can begin work. Phase I ESA usually begins with a **site visit** guided by a site representative with knowledge about site-specific conditions (e.g., a technical manager). The site visit is crucial for a robust assessment, especially if the seller is not able to provide detailed documents (e.g., former investigations, reports, or test protocols). During the visit, the consultant can identify potential issues concerning soil and groundwater (e.g., poor handling of hazardous substances resulting in stains on the floor or underground storage tanks), as well as building contaminants, such as asbestos, mineral fibers, and polychlorinated biphenyls. It should be mentioned that based on the **age of a building,** a consultant should already have an idea of the building contaminants he could encounter during the site visit. Furthermore, before the visit, the consultant should research the production processes and chemicals used.

To streamline the process, it is ideal to set up a **professional data room** for the consultant. This is the most convenient way for consultants to receive data and ask **tailored questions (Q&A)**. Other methods, such as email or Q&A lists, are less convenient and pose a risk of a data loss.

A **common timeframe** for a Phase I ESA is **four weeks**. If the outcome of the Phase I ESA is to perform a soil and groundwater investigation as well as a HBM survey, **further planning** is needed.

Prior to the start of a **soil and groundwater investigation** or an **HBM survey**, all parties involved should discuss the **investigation plan**. It is the consultant's responsibility to elaborate suitable plans. The following **issues need to be considered** within the plan:

a) Accessibility of sampling points
b) Location of underground and aboveground supply lines
c) Restoration of the previous conditions (e.g., if the roof must be opened or drilling through floors with liquid-tight surfaces)
d) Distance to the REC (only for soil and groundwater)
e) Influence by unexploded ordnance (UXO) in some regions

For HBM surveys, it is very important to have **plans of the existing buildings**. This helps at a later stage to identify the areas and to remediate or demolish the buildings properly.

The **time required for an HBM survey, as well as for a soil and groundwater investigation** from start to finish is usually **6–8 weeks**. In some countries or federal states (for example in Germany), it is necessary to **inform the authorities about drilling**. This is usually done several weeks prior to the field work. **Ideally, the Phase II ESA** will address all potential issues identified in the Phase I ESA. The Phase II ESA should also include a general solution for the identified issues, as well as cost estimates for resolving them. This is also what distinguishes a good report from a poor one. In a poor report, the reader will often find standard phrases such as »additional costs for the disposal of excavated soil material can be expected«. For stakeholders who are not familiar with environmental issues, such sentences are not helpful. A good consultant should always provide at least a rough estimate. If this is not possible during the initial investigation, a more detailed investigation is the logical next step. In addition to that, the **planned use of the site** is important.

- Will the buildings be demolished?
- What will the new development be?
- What is the extent of the required earthworks?
- What risks are associated with the work and employees?

If there is a **new development on site**, it is important for a consultant to have knowledge about the **planned earthworks.** The construction of a logistics site (without a basement) differs greatly from that of an office building with an underground parking garage or technical rooms. This difference can amount to millions of Euros. It is also important to note the difference between soil protection laws and those concerning the handling of excavated fill material. While the former are connected with remediation, the handling of fill material is usually evaluated based on existing waste regulations. Threshold values for contaminants can differ.

For a **potential buyer** it is also advisable to set aside a **general budget for unexpected findings during a redevelopment phase.** Although risks have been described, identified, and evaluated in Phase I and II ESAs, surprises cannot generally be excluded. On the one hand, grid sampling is not economical; therefore the focus is on RECs. On the other hand, contamination in the soil might be localized within a radius of just a few meters, and therefore easily missed during the EDD. However, the approach of defining RECs is considered to cover significant contamination that could become deal-breakers for the entire project.

EXAMPLE 1:

During redevelopment, a bomb crater filled with building rubble was found during earthworks on a former parking lot. Since there were no indications of a REC, no drillings or analyses have been performed in the area. If a budget for unexpected events exists, it will have no influence on the project's feasibility.

A general advice for potential buyers is to include **groundwater sampling** adapted to the groundwater flow. Is my site affected by contaminated groundwater coming from upstream areas? Does contaminated groundwater leave my site? Asking these questions is important to avoid potential third-party claims in the future.

The same strategy has been proven as the best practice for **building contaminants.** Many contaminants can and will be identified in the Phase I ESA and the HBM survey. However, sometimes contaminants are hidden and cannot be accessed during limited, non-intrusive investigations. Therefore, it is also best practice to have a budget provided by the consultant and an additional budget for unexpected events. The findings of an HBM survey should be included in the offer of the demolition company (in case of redevelopment) or the offer of the chosen refurbishment company.

Once the risks associated with a property are identified, the results should be reviewed by the legal and development team and included in the purchase contract. Defining a clear interface between the responsibilities of the seller and buyer is important to avoid disputes after the purchase. It should be noted that technical topics such as drinking water quality, waste handling, type of refrigerants used in cooling machines play a more important role if the existing buildings are not going to be demolished (e.g., in the case of a lease-back agreement). In case of a redevelopment, this assessment is not of great importance, as all technical installations will be removed.

3.2.4 Environmental topics during the redevelopment

The **signing of the purchase contract** usually marks the **starting point for the redevelopment process.**

This includes the following **environmental activities:**
- Discussion of the investigation results with the authorities
- Planning of remediation (if necessary)
- Choice of demolition company
- Choice of a consultant to supervise the demolition and remediation

Ideally, the **results of the investigation can be discussed with the authorities** before signing a purchase agreement. However, the seller often does not allow the buyer to take this approach, as he may fear measurements being carried out or being left alone in case the deal will not be signed. Before any remediation work begins on site, the different parties involved need to develop an action plan and a rough timeline.

The **parties** are usually the following:
a) Buyer
b) Consultant of choice
c) Demolition or remediation company
d) General contractor

A common mistake is involving a consultant in the process at a very late stage, sometimes already too late. This can also happen during an EDD process. During the EDD, this could cause a financing party to back out from the deal. During redevelopment, it can lead to issues with the authorities. In addition, discussions may arise during the reselling of a site after development. At this stage, a consultant cannot determine how measurements and work were performed, especially when it comes to soil remediation:

EXAMPLE 2

A self-service petrol station with underground storage tanks was previously operated on the site. The Phase II soil and groundwater investigation revealed local contamination. During demolition, the tanks were removed, and the area was backfilled with soil. In the worst case, it has already been overbuilt. If a consultant is not involved, and if nothing is documented (e.g., soil sampling after removal), the current situation will remain unclear. Further measurements might be necessary. This could result in additional costs and time loss.

EXAMPLE 3

Building contaminants have been identified during the transaction phase. Although demolition companies are obliged to sort waste, they sometimes do not do so properly. This can generate massive amounts of mixed waste that is expensive to dispose of, rather than just a few tons. It is also important to have an expert confirm that the identified materials in areas *a, b, c* have been removed properly.

Summarizing, it can be stated that saving money by not commissioning a qualified environmental expert is the wrong choice and potentially costs much more in the long run. Compared to the whole transaction, these costs can be considered as minor, but they do have a major influence on the project.

Sustainability during redevelopment has been an upcoming topic in recent years. In redevelopment projects, the **reuse of crushed mineral material as a base layer for the new development, as well as the remediation of contamination and/or the permanent securing of contaminated areas** (e.g., cutting off pathways of rainfall and soil-groundwater interaction by constructing a building above) are important sustainability factors that are underestimated in all common certification programs.

EXAMPLE 4

During the demolition of a building complex 50,000 t of crushed recycled material are generated. If the material is to be disposed of, a lot of exhaust gases and traffic will be generated by the trucks transporting it to a landfill. In addition, natural resources are used to create the foundational layers of a building (for example a warehouse). This procedure is not sustainable.

3.2.5 Ongoing site use

If a site is purchased with **no plan to demolish the buildings**, the approach to ongoing use is focused on the risks for human health. For hazardous building materials, a risk assessment should be performed to **evaluate the risk to human health**. In many countries an evaluation of **asbestos**-containing materials is common. For example, a fiber cement sheet containing bounded asbestos at the façade does not pose a high risk, whereas loose fibers (e.g., in fire dampers) can pose a high risk if they are damaged. Another example is sealant joints. Before 1990, sealant joints often contained **PCBs**, which are hazardous. If these joints are exposed to building interiors, they can pose a risk to human health. In that case, indoor air measurements should be carried out. Usually, these risk assessments are done within the Phase I and Phase II ESA, and purchase remediation might be required immediately or during refurbishment.

Another **difference between ongoing use and redevelopment is the legal obligations regarding technical facilities.** These topics can be considered asset management topics. The most important here are **waste management, drinking water quality, and maintenance of cooling machines.**

3.2.6 Conclusion

Environmental due diligence plays an important role during the transaction phase and after the purchase. However, it is often not taken seriously by various stakeholders, which can lead to the major problems described above. Summarizing, a proper EDD process will help owners, buyers, future users and employees minimize the impact of environmental issues.

3.3 ESG due diligence for property transactions

Barbara Geidner-Buchelt/Giulia Peretti

3.3.1 Introduction to #3.3

Considering ESG factors (environmental, social, and governance) has become an integral part of real estate transactions and the associated due diligence processes. While environmental audits have always been part of due diligence (DD), the scope of ESG issues to be analyzed has expanded significantly due to increased social and regulatory focus, as well as developments such as rising energy prices, climate change impacts or stricter EU regulations. ESG is now understood and evaluated in a broader context. In recent years, it has become clear that the decision-makers' requirements regarding the scope and depth of ESG DD have continuously grown – from the consideration of social factors to a more detailed assessment of environmental characteristics and key figures.

Although economic, financial, technical, and legal due diligence audits are standard practice, ESG due diligence is a comparatively young discipline that is rapidly evolving in terms of content and methodology. There is still no standardized, cross-country, or cross-industry approach.

In this subchapter #3.3 on ESG due diligence, we discuss what ESG DD means (#3.3.2), how to approach an ESG DD (#3.3.3), environmental transition risks (#3.3.4), physical environmental risks (#3.3.5), social (#3.3.6), and governance (#3.3.7) transition risks, as well as our concluding remarks (#3.3.8).

3.3.2 Meaning of ESG due diligence

As an instrument of risk management in real estate transactions, due diligence serves the purpose of creating certainty about legal and actual characteristics that are relevant to purchase price determination and to identify and evaluate risks that can lead to primarily negative but possibly also positive deviations from the business case.

The following **objectives** can be derived from this **for ESG-DD,** among others:

- The review and collection of data in relation to **regulatory requirements**, such as reporting requirements under the EU Taxonomy (e.g., technical screening criteria of sustainable economic activities), EU Sustainable Finance Disclosure Regulation (SFDR) (e.g., greenhouse gas emissions, energy intensity) or EU Corporate Sustainability Reporting Directive (CSRD)[366]
- Comparison with the framework conditions of the fund documentation, contracts, or investment conditions and guidelines, such as ESG selection and exclusion criteria for investment funds with an ESG strategy (e.g., in accordance with Art. 8 of the SFDR), or an impact investing approach (e.g., in accordance with Art. 9 of the SFDR)
- Alignment with corporate policy, internal governance, risk management, and compliance framework, e.g., decarbonization strategies and ESG requirements for business partners (vendors, tenants, and suppliers), as well as the management of controversial activities with certain business partners or practices (e.g., gambling)
- Assessment of **ESG risks** and their impact on the overall economic risk of the investment (outside-in perspective). A **distinction** can be made **between transition and physical risks.** **Transition risks** result from social or political processes that entail new or changed requirements for property investments. These include in particular regulatory and legal minimum requirements for energy efficiency that are punishable by fines or a ban on use, the EU's CO_2 pricing, market requirements (e.g., decarbonization) and user preferences or consumer trends, such as changes in user behavior among tenants (occupiers) and their customers (shoppers, visitors, guests).
  Physical ESG risks have a direct physical impact on the property and location and result, among other things, from climate change, such as increasing drought and forest fire risks,

366 This applies to equivalent regulations in other regions; see for example taxonomies developed in Asia under #6.3.

heavy rain or strong wind events, or rising sea levels in the long term. However, fields of investigation that are not directly related to climate change, such as earthquakes, volcanism, landslides, flooding, soil contamination, air pollution, or noise emissions, also play an important role in DD.

- Assessment of the **property's impact on the environment and society** (inside-out perspective). This is actually a relatively new field of ESG-DD investigation that has been decisively promoted by the **UNEP FI's Responsible Property Investment Programme,** EU Taxonomy (Do-No-Significantly-Harm criteria, DNSH) and EU SFDR (Principle Adverse Impacts indicators, PAI). The aim is to identify adverse impacts and subsequently manage and limit them, as well as to avoid conflicts between different sustainability objectives. Adverse impacts can increase exposure to transition risks, e.g. through regulatory restrictions or declining user demand.
- Assessment of the potential for improving economic and ESG performance with regard to ongoing operation and subsequent sale, e.g. **opportunities for reducing CO_2 emissions through increased energy efficiency** and the **use of renewable energies**, including the necessary operating and investment costs (OpEx, CapEx) as well as possible additional income from users.

The **scope and level of detail of an ESG DD** are not formally prescribed and there is no standard catalogue. The ESG aspects are based not only on regulatory frameworks, but also on the specific sustainability requirements of the corporate and fund strategies. In addition to the energy-related aspects, they focus on detailed social and governance factors.

The **DD results** provide insight into the ESG characteristics of a property and directly impact purchase prices, CapEx requirements, business plans, clauses in the purchase agreement, valuation and financing. The DD results have a direct impact on the risk profile and medium-term performance of an investment, thereby influencing the investment decision.

3.3.3 How to approach an ESG due diligence

ESG-related due diligence can be implemented either as a stand-alone review, known as ESG DD, or integrated into the existing specialist disciplines. In practice, an **integrated approach**, in which ESG aspects are included in all areas of DD, has proven to be advantageous. This ensures that ESG is not treated as an isolated topic, but is embedded organically in the overall assessment. Many of these aspects, particularly those of a technical or energy-related nature, were already covered in traditional DD fields, but have been reassessed and reweighted due to new regulatory requirements and market standards.

Traditionally, **technical due diligence** focuses on the structural condition, comparing construction execution and actual use with the building permit, the maintenance backlog, building physics, and energy consumption. The **ESG perspective** broadens the scope of the technical DD to include the »carbon assessment«, with the aim of gaining valuable insights regarding compliance with long-term decarbonization strategies and facilitate a systematic analysis of physical climate risks at the property's location. Further additions cover, for example, waste reduction and management, biodiversity, circular economy concepts, life-cycle analysis, water consumption and greywater use.

In addition, the TDD also takes into account social aspects such as accessibility and the overall quality of stay within the building, as well as governance aspects such as green building certifications and labels.

Commercial due diligence typically examines profitability, rental income and contract structure. From an **ESG perspective**, additional topics are included, such as evaluating rental agreements with regard to green lease clauses or the analysis of the tenant structure according to ESG criteria – for example with regard to controversial sectors that may entail increased reputational risks, or are even subject to ESG exclusion criteria.

Environmental and social standards in **rental agreements** and **facility management contracts** can be meaningfully integrated into the legal due diligence.

When **sourcing properties**, ESG-relevant **basic aspects** can already be taken into account via checklists in the search profile, so that appropriate investments can be identified or sorted out in the initial phase, depending on the risk profile. Initial ESG-relevant information can often be obtained even before the actual DD begins. This includes information such as the year of construction, the energy performance certificate (EPC), building certifications (DGNB, BREEAM, LEED, HQE, Wired Score, etc.), historical consumption data, e.g. for electricity and heating, and photovoltaic (PV) installations. Depending whether the property is on-market or off-market, more or less detailed ESG information is available via investment memos.

For **subsequent DD**, specialized consultants (technical, legal, and possibly also commercial or financial) are commissioned to review the data in a data room for completeness and request additional data. They also conduct on-site inspections as part of the technical ESG analysis.

In practice, it has been shown that certain ESG-relevant **data is either unavailable or incomplete**, even in on-market processes. This applies particularly to consumption data, which is essential for valid assessments of energy consumption, and carbon intensity, as well as robust analyses based on science-based climate targets. Dealing with data gaps requires methodological compensation. In practice, missing or unclear data is often supplemented with comparative objects or cluster analyses (e.g. by building type, construction year, or use), as well as benchmarks from service providers. Conservative assumptions are also employed, particularly in the case of risks with a high potential impact on economic performance.

In the following, we focus on some important DD fields that may result in potential red flags.

3.3.4 Climate protection and other environmental transition risks

Let us recall that **transition risks** encompass a wide range of political, legal and economic changes resulting from a regulatory shift toward a sustainable, low-carbon economy at the global, European (or other regional), national, and local levels. These include, among others: carbon pricing schemes, tax burdens or subsidy cuts, bans on fossil fuel heating systems, obligations to install PV systems, charging infrastructure, ESG reporting, and new minimum energy standards under the EU Buildings Directive or similar energy performance of buildings standards. Such requirements may lead to increased investment needs, usage restrictions, and thus to reductions in value, so they must be examined in detail for specific investment locations. Systematic analysis of transition risks is therefore an integral part of ESG due diligence and should be closely interlinked with the legal and technical reviews.

These regulatory requirements are embedded in the broader context of international climate goals, particularly the Paris Agreement. Many of these European and national measures are derived from this reference framework. The **goals of the Paris Agreement** of limiting global warming and safeguarding the living conditions of humankind are behind numerous regulatory initiatives in the EU and other climate-leading countries worldwide. Consequently, the real estate industry is examining the operationalization of these goals for property investments. Analyzing current and projected CO_2 emissions and intensity to ensure conformity with the goals of the Paris Agreement provides results that can be used as a proxy for the regulatory exposure and thus for transitional risks in the field of climate protection.

This analysis is frequently conducted using the *Carbon Risk Real Estate Monitor*[367] (CRREM). CRREM breaks down the CO_2 budget that the real estate sector must adhere to in order to limit global warming to 1.5 or 2 degrees Celsius above pre industrial levels, converting them into country- and building-type-specific target pathways. The **Carbon Intensity Pathways** and the **Energy Intensity Pathways** provide a practical tool that provides orientation for comparing the conformity of individual properties with science-based climate targets – such as the 1.5° C target – and for identifying so-called »stranding points« or the ***CRREM Misalignment Year***. At the same time, it should be noted that CRREM represents a model-based approach that can only capture actual property characteristics and market developments in a simplified form. The *CRREM Misalignment Year* acts as an early-warning indicator and provides an internationally standardized guidance, i.e. an important indication for the ex-ante assessment of future climate transition risks.

367 CRREM Foundation, *Carbon Risk Real Estate Monitor*, 2025, https://crrem.org/, accessed 19.08.2025; see chapter #4.2 for additional information on CRREM.

In practice, the CRREM analysis is also increasingly being used to derive future CapEx measures, particularly regarding the decarbonization measures required to postpone stranding or misalignment points and to reduce CO_2 intensity in accordance with fund requirements.

Practical experience shows that:

- **ESG and carbon due diligence** may reveal that, in their current condition, properties are not yet (fully) aligned with the goals of the Paris Agreement, and that emissions may **exceed the CRREM thresholds**, even if the EPC indicates an apparently favorable energy efficiency class B. This could be due to the highly inconsistent implementation of EPCs across Europe, which are based on different methodologies and limit values vary country by country. There are also discrepancies between calculated and actual energy consumption.
- Specific **measures to improve energy performance** and **achieve climate targets** need to be developed and evaluated within the technical DD. These measures may include replacing fossil fuel sources such as gas boilers with heat pumps, installing refrigerant leakage detection systems, a photovoltaic system, building automation-based efficiency measures, and launching awareness campaigns. In practice, this often represents a complex optimization task where additional or reduced income, OpEx and CapEx, as well as changes in market value must be weighed against avoided CO_2 emissions. Alternative measures must be compared and optimized over the economic investment's life cycle. These upgrading measures are reflected in the business plan in order to secure financing at a later stage.
- **Energy consumption and energy efficiency classes** are key to identifying transition risks and at the same time central indicators for EU Taxonomy alignment and the Principal Adverse Impacts KPIs assessment under the SFDR. The energy performance certificate (EPC) provides an initial categorization. However, additional detailed consumption data is essential for a robust analysis of energy performance. Furthermore, the energy analysis must also include other technical components such as energy monitoring and management as well as data collection. These components play a central role in the assessment of Taxonomy and Energy Performance of Buildings Directive – for EU EPBD compliance.
- In **practice,** the assessment of emissions and energy consumption is based on data provided by the seller regarding consumption, technical building equipment, and construction of the building, as well as an on-site inspection. Monthly consumption bills (heating energy and electricity consumption) from the owner for common areas as well as from the tenant for rental areas are valuable, but are not always fully available. Therefore, consumption and other energy performance metrics – for example energy prices or CO_2 factors – need to be assessed using benchmarks from comparable properties.
- Other **transition-related environmental risks** of increasing importance are emerging in areas such as water consumption, waste management, biodiversity, the circular economy, and embodied carbon. These risks are particularly relevant for new buildings or major renovations – e.g., with regard to EU Taxonomy requirements.

3.3.5 Climate change and other physical environmental risks

Climate change and related weather phenomena, such as droughts and forest fires, are receiving significant public attention. Due to their fixed geographical location, properties cannot escape the risks of climate change or other environmental risks; they can only be protected through appropriate resilience measures. From an economic perspective, properties are particularly exposed to physical risks. Potential damage scenarios range from loss of comfort and interruption of use to destruction.

Accordingly, ESG DD includes a systematic and objective analysis of physical risks arising from current environmental risks and the projected consequences of climate change – both in terms of the probability and severity of both acute phenomena such as heat waves, droughts, strong winds, heavy rainfall, flooding, and seismic activity, and chronic phenomena, such as falling groundwater levels (subsidence effects), permanently altered wind patterns (cyclones, hurricanes, typhoons, etc.), desertification, soil erosion, and rising sea water levels. The assessment covers the geographical and geological location of the investment (macro level) and building-specific characteristics (micro level), such as construction, technical equipment, and existing protective measures. This can also include organizational measures, such as securing rooftop terraces or façade equipment against strong winds.

In practice, the results can be used to identify necessary adaptation measures (e.g. structural resilience measures, emergency plans, and technical retrofits) at an early stage, or to review the adequacy of existing measures. Thus, ESG-DD provides a reliable basis for achieving the necessary climate resilience of the property, assessing CapEx and OpEx and securing the investment's long-term value.

Best practices include a data-driven screening and evaluation process based on established forecasting models from research and practice, particularly from the insurance industry. This requires comprehensible aggregation using an in-house developed scoring tool, which enables physical risks to be systematically identified, evaluated and actively managed.

E – Data collection should **not be too narrowly defined** and **could include**, for example

- **Climate risk assessment at country level** based on established indices such as the *Global Sustainability Competitiveness Index* from Sol Ability and the *World Risk Index* from Ruhr University Bochum.
- **Location-specific climate risk analysis.** Munich Re's *Location Risk Intelligence Platform*, for example, assesses both historical risks and climate change-related risks. This analysis can be performed for an exact address and covers a wide range of natural hazards, including floods, storms, heat, drought, and earthquakes.
- Use of **scoring models for aggregation**. The individual results of the aforementioned risk analysis can be aggregated in a *physical risk scoring model* developed in-house. The weighting includes the damage potential of each risk. The result is a consolidated score for each investment, broken down into historical and future risk.

- **Individual vulnerability analyses** can be conducted where required to further investigate identified risk exposures. These include a detailed assessment of resilience in relation to selected risks, e.g., heatwaves, water stress, and changing wind patterns. Among other factors, historical damage events, the potential impact on building structures, technical equipment, and business continuity are evaluated in more detail, and suitable technical and organizational measures appropriate to the projected climate change impacts are discussed.

In practice, protection against groundwater and surface water is of particular importance for real estate. Taking into account factors such as groundwater depth, the permeability of the geology on the property and in the surrounding area, the distance to surface water, and the existing protective measures on the property and in the vicinity, the vulnerability is assessed and set in relation to the potential damage to the property. The identified countermeasures are highly relevant for CapEx planning, insurance coverage, and organizational measures that the purchaser must take, e.g., the preparation for possible flooding of an underground car park.

3.3.6 Social risks

While environmental risks are closely linked to technical DD, social risks are **traditionally more connected with commercial DD** (i. e. particularly with regard to sustainable cash flow generation) **and legal DD** (e.g. in the case of subsidized housing). When analyzing social risks, it can be useful to distinguish between regulatory or market-driven changes (comparable to transition risks) and event-related risks (comparable to physical risks). In practice, the latter only causes physical damage to the property in exceptional cases, but usually results in economic losses, such as reputational damage or rent defaults. A particular challenge lies in the measurability and quantitative assessment of certain social risks.

S – Typical areas of investigation in an ESG DD include:

- **Socio-demographic development:** trends such as an aging population, gentrification, loss of income or education, the presence of critical sectors and population groups (e.g., gambling and prostitution), and declining public safety (evaluation of crime statistics, press reports, historical incidents, and signs of vandalism and neglect). On-site inspections of the surrounding area are also required.
- **Access to** public and private services: Absolute and relative changes in areas such as access to education, healthcare, culture, retail and gastronomy, sports, and leisure activities are decisive for the quality of the location.
- **Infrastructure: The** Quality of current connections and foreseeable changes regarding private transportation, including pedestrians, bicyclists, car-sharing, cars, and delivery traffic, as well as local and long-distance public transportation. Access to high-speed internet and mobile services.
- **Restrictive regulation and public implementation gaps**: This includes potential restrictions on the use of land through restrictive rent regulation in the residential sector as well as restrictions on conversions and densification due to local political decision-making processes. It also includes increasing public opposition or administrative implementation shortcomings in the development of public infrastructure, e.g. protests against the construction of power lines, transport routes, or educational facilities.

- **Living and working conditions:** Compliance with local legal regulations regarding the design and equipment of residential and working spaces, as well as thermal, visual and acoustic indoor quality.
- **Social integration and mixed use**: e.g. socially balanced residential use, offers for vulnerable groups, as well as the presence of special features and additional services.
- **Accessibility and inclusiveness**: In new developments and conversions requiring authorization, barrier-free accessibility is a legal requirement in many cases. Therefore, its implementation is not automatically an ESG-related added value, but rather a minimum compliance requirement. In the ESG DD, however, accessibility counts as ESG added value if it goes beyond legal obligations or if it is systematically addressed in existing properties.

The areas of assessment for social risks can vary depending on the investment strategy. For example, it is evident that logistics investments are exposed to different social risks than residential or retail properties. If the investment strategy includes additional social investment criteria or even a social impact strategy, the fields covered by ESG DD can expand considerably.

3.3.7 Governance risks

As part of the ESG DD of real estate the governance review focuses less on the property itself and more on the associated legal entities, i.e. primarily sellers, occupiers, suppliers and service providers. The objective is to ensure that the transaction environment is in line with the principles of good governance, so that the transaction and the subsequent management of the property can take place without compromising the ESG objectives.

For investments made under the EU Taxonomy, the »Minimum Safeguards« under Article 18 of the EU Taxonomy Regulation represent a key area of review. They are designed to prevent conflicts between environmental objectives and minimum social and governance standards. Article 18 requires companies to comply with internationally recognized guidelines, particularly with regard to the protection of human rights and labor rights as well as the implementation of corporate due diligence obligations in areas such as anti-corruption, fair competition, and taxation.

G – With regard to **business partners**, the scope of legal DD may include the following in-depth analyses of the **ESG governance environment**:

- **Green leases or clauses**, e.g. in rental agreements with provisions for data exchange, green electricity procurement, environmentally friendly materials or cleaning practices.
- **Controversial business activities:** screening for exclusion criteria, e.g. excluding tenants from sectors such as fossil fuels, weapons, or tobacco; screening for past involvement in criminal activities or signs of aggressive tax practices.
- Review of **ESG reports** from business partners subject to disclosure requirements covering strategies, objectives, measures, incidents (e.g. accidents), and **certifications and labels** as an additional source of data and external validation.

3.3.8 Conclusion

The **audience** for ESG-relevant information in the context of real estate transactions **has expanded**: Not only technical asset managers, but also institutional investors, banks, credit assessors, or ESG rating agencies demand transparent and reliable ESG information. Against this backdrop, ESG due diligence serves as a key instrument to establish clarity in the legal and actual characteristics of a property that are relevant to determining the purchase price, while at the same time identifying and assessing ESG risks. As the demand for information and statutory reporting requirements increase, so do the expectations of ESG DD and its documentation.

> **ESG due diligence is no longer a detached, voluntary additional check**, but rather a **prerequisite** for investments, financing and regulatory reporting obligations. It is not a separate task, but generally fully integrated into the classic DD process. Specialists in commercial, financial, legal and technical DD are expected to integrate all relevant ESG risks into their risk identification and assessment programs, as well as to consider and evaluate mitigating measures. The boundaries between traditional DD topics are increasingly fluid. For the investment manager coordinating the DD process, this means that the various components of ESG DD must subsequently be consolidated, and the interactions must be recognized and managed similarly to those between the traditional DD disciplines.

Key environmental criteria such as the contribution to climate change mitigation (through energy efficiency, carbon emissions, and decarbonization) and resilience to environmental risks, especially the consequences of climate change (climate change adaptation), are currently among the most important assessment factors for investors, valuation experts and financing banks due to their significant and growing economic relevance. They are regularly assessed during transactions and financing, directly influencing the value of a property, financing conditions, overall return, and even the investment decision itself.

The tasks of the ESG DD have **gained a firm and prominent role**. While the analyses of climate change mitigation and adaptation already draw on well-developed, widely recognized methods, other DD areas are still developing and will require further deepening and specialization. Increasing regulatory influence is expected, particularly in the areas of freshwater and wastewater management, waste management, biodiversity, the circular economy, and embodied carbon. The requirements for DD to comply with minimum social and governance standards will also continue to grow, driven by (EU) regulation.

3.4 ESG due diligence in real estate investment/legal perspective

Jordi Ventura

«What was once voluntary is now vital: ESG is the license to operate.«
- World Economic Forum, 2021

3.4.1 Introduction to #3.4

Environmental, social, and governance (ESG) considerations have evolved from aspirational goals to enforceable standards in real estate investment. For legal practitioners, ESG due diligence now represents a critical component of risk assessment, shaping decisions regarding acquisitions, financing, and long-term asset management. Beyond environmental compliance, ESG due diligence examines a property's social impact, such as tenant and community relations, as well as its governance structures, including ownership transparency and anti-bribery safeguards.

The stakes are high: regulatory scrutiny, reputational exposure, and financial penalties for ESG lapses can derail deals, reduce asset value, and invite litigation. This subchapter explores the meaning, scope, risks, and practical tools for integrating ESG into legal due diligence for real estate transactions worldwide.

#3.4	**#3.4.1 – intro to #3.4**
ESG due diligence / legal perspective	**#3.4.2 – meaning and scope**
	#3.4.3 – legal risks and red flags
	#3.4.4 – practical example
	#3.4.5 – tools and strategies
	#3.4.6 – conclusion

In this subchapter #3.4 on ESG due diligence in real estate investment from a legal perspective, we will discuss the meaning and scope (#3.4.2), legal risks and red flags (#3.4.3), a practical example (#3.4.4), tools and strategies (#3.4.5), and close with concluding remarks (#3.4.6).

3.4.2 Meaning and scope of ESG due diligence in real estate

ESG due diligence goes beyond the traditional checklist of title verification, zoning, and contractual review. Rather, it requires a **holistic assessment of risks and obligations** across **three dimensions**:

- Environmental: Compliance with building codes, energy efficiency mandates, climate risk exposure, waste management, and legacy contamination liabilities.

- Social: Respect for tenant rights, non-discrimination in leasing, labor conditions on development projects, and community engagement obligations.
- Governance: Ownership transparency, anti-money laundering compliance, conflict of interest prevention, and operational integrity.

International frameworks shape investor expectations. The Organization for Economic Co-operation and Development (OECD) Guidelines for Multinational Enterprises, United Nations Principles for Responsible Investment (UNPRI), and EU measures like the Taxonomy and Sustainable Finance Disclosure Regulation (SFDR) all influence due diligence standards. Industry benchmarks, such as the Global Real Estate Sustainability Benchmark (GRESB) and the Task Force on Climate-related Financial Disclosures (TCFD), also guide disclosure and climate risk assessment.

In **real estate,** these standards **give rise to practical legal questions**: Is the property vulnerable to climate-related zoning restrictions? Are there unresolved land claims by Indigenous People? Might opaque ownership structures pose anti-money laundering (AML) or sanctions risks?

Please see **Figure 18 ESG Risk Matrix for Real Estate Transactions** for further illustration.

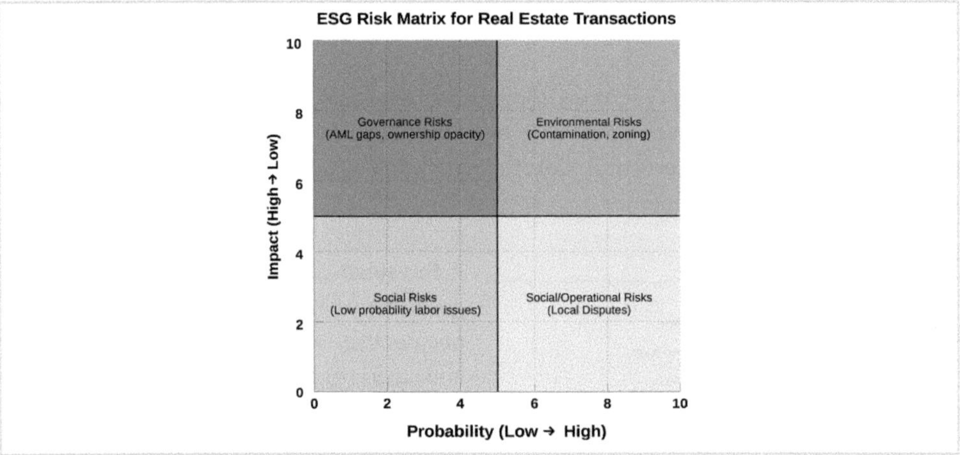

Figure 18: ESG Risk Matrix for Real Estate Transactions

Interpretation of the matrix:
Top-right quadrant (High Impact/High Probability): Immediate red flags (e.g., contamination liability, lack of free, prior and informed consent – FPIC).
Bottom-left quadrant (Low Impact/Low Probability): Monitor with low urgency (e.g., minor disclosure gaps).
Mid-risk zones: Require targeted contractual protections and insurance.

3.4.3 Legal risks and red flags

Legal risks can be related to environmental, social and governance aspects. Please see **Figure 19 ESG – legal risks** for further illustration.

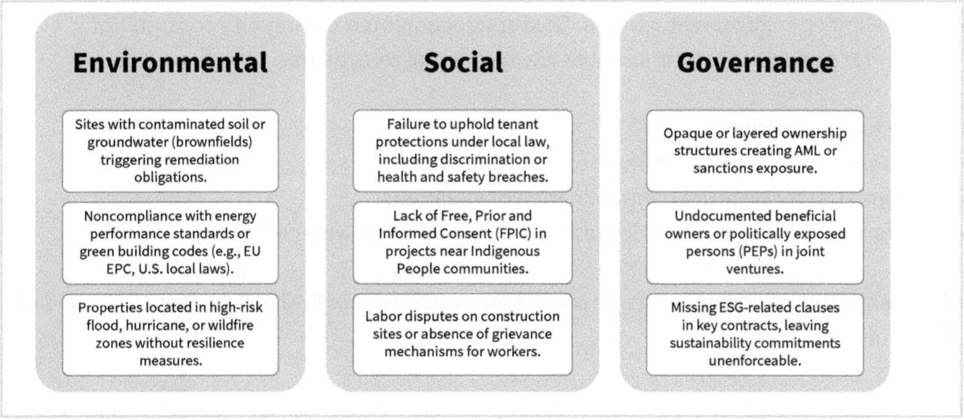

Figure 19: ESG – legal risks

3.4.4 Practical example

In recent years, the acquisition of a Latin American mixed-use site by a European investment fund was significantly delayed when indigenous peoples initiated litigation over an insufficient title review and a lack of free, prior and informed consent (FPIC). The litigation – which echoed the precedent set by cases such as *Maya Q'eqchi' Agua Caliente v. Guatemala,*[368] where operations were halted due to missing FPIC, resulted in financial losses and reputational damage. Proactive ESG due diligence, including verifying Indigenous title and ensuring truly informed consent, would likely have prevented this outcome.

The **top five legal red flags in ESG due diligence** are:

	Red flag	Why it matters
1	Contaminated land or pending remediation claims	Triggers cleanup liability and delays in development
2	Noncompliance with green building or energy codes	Risk of fines, retrofits, and regulatory enforcement
3	Lack of FPIC or stakeholder consultation	Exposure to litigation, injunctions, and reputational harm
4	Opaque ownership or PEP involvement	AML, corruption, and sanctions compliance issues
5	Absence of ESG clauses in key contracts	No enforceable basis for sustainability commitments

Table 24: Top 5 legal red flags in ESG DD

368 Corte Interamericana de Derechos Humanos, Sentencia de 16 de mayo de 2023 en el caso Comunidad Indígena Maya Q'eqchi' Agua Caliente vs. Guatemala, Fondo, Reparaciones y Costas, Serie C No. 488, párrs. I–VIII, 178–188.

3.4.5 Key due diligence tools and strategies

Legal advisors can integrate ESG into the transaction lifecycle through:

- Enhanced questionnaires and checklists: Incorporate ESG-specific queries on environmental permits, labor practices, supply chains, and governance protocols.
- Stakeholder engagement reviews: Confirm documented community consultations, especially for projects involving social or environmental sensitivities.

Contractual protections:

- Representations and warranties for ESG compliance.
- Indemnities for historical contamination or violations.
- Performance-based clauses in leases tied to energy and water efficiency.

Alignment with frameworks: Ensure consistency with investor ESG policies (e.g., SFDR and PRI commitments).

Technology tools: Use data analytics for carbon benchmarking, climate risk mapping, and ownership verification.

Quick checklist for legal teams:

☐ Is the asset compliant with environmental and building codes?

☐ Are there environmental liens or pending remediation claims?

☐ Are ownership and control structures fully transparent?

☐ Has stakeholder consultation been documented?

☐ Are ESG representations, warranties, and indemnities included in the purchase agreement?

3.4.6 Conclusion

ESG due diligence in real estate is not a peripheral concern, but rather a legal and financial imperative. Integrating ESG considerations into the transaction process mitigates regulatory, operational, and reputational risks while preserving asset value. Legal practitioners must expand beyond conventional due diligence and adopt tools and frameworks that address climate resilience, human rights, and governance integrity.

In short, ESG is no longer a »soft« risk – it is central to defining materiality, shaping contractual protections, and ensuring long-term investment performance.

Recommended reading:

PRI, Principles for Responsible Investment, 2022, https://www.unpri.org/about-us/what-are-the-principles-for-responsible-investment, accessed on 27.07.2025.

RICS, *Professional Statement: ESG in Real Estate*, Royal Institution of Chartered Surveyors, London, 2022.

TCFD, *Guidance on Climate-Related Legal Risks for Companies, Directors, and Investors*, Task Force on Climate-Related Financial Disclosures, 2021, https://www.tcfdhub.org, accessed 27.07.2025.

3.5 ESG valuation: A status assessment in uncertain times

Peter Salostowitz

3.5.1 Real estate investment and valuation on a global scale. Introduction to #3.5

ESG is currently the buzzword for investment-grade buildings in the EU. Real estate investors must therefore ask themselves whether ESG has or could have an impact on valuation if the building is to be fully investment-grade. Outside the EU, the situation is very different. However, as non-ESG-compliant armaments are steadily gaining ground in the EU and, in combination with poorer economic prospects, are overshadowing the issue of climate change and diverting public funds, the question arises as to how far ESG criteria will be watered down and in what direction, and whether there are already initial signs of this happening. The following chapter explores these issues.

#3.5	**#3.5.1 – intro to #3.5**
ESG valuation / assessment in uncertain times	**#3.5.2 – status update – summer 2025**
	#3.5.3 – framework conditions
	#3.5.4 – building regulations & FM/AM
	#3.5.5 – valuation approach
	#3.5.6 – ESG in valuation methodologies
	#3.5.7 – conclusion

In this subchapter #3.5 on valuation, we provide a status update on the summer of 2025 (#3.5.2), examine framework conditions (#3.5.3) and building regulations (#3.5.4), to then proceed with the valuation approach (#3.5.5), and the integration of ESG factors into valuation methodologies (#3.5.6). We conclude with closing remarks (#3.5.7).

3.5.2 ESG valuation: A brief status update, summer of 2025

ESG and sustainability considerations are increasingly recognized – particularly within the European Union – as decisive factors in investment and lending decisions. They directly influence asset performance, market opportunities, and the risk of obsolescence. This trend is largely driven by the binding commitment of EU member states to the Paris Climate Agreement, although each nation has flexibility in translating these objectives into national legislation.

Outside Europe, however, ESG requirements are applied far less stringently, and there are currently no clear indications that other regions will adopt EU-level standards in the foreseeable future.

Due to the global nature of capital markets, developments in the United States under the Trump administration are expected to have short- to medium-term impacts on ESG-related investment trends. The U.S. Environmental Protection Agency (EPA) is planning to revoke a landmark legal finding that underpins virtually all of its climate regulations, including limits on greenhouse gas emissions from vehicles and power plants. According to EPA Administrator Lee Zeldin, this would constitute »*the largest deregulatory action in U.S. history*« if finalized[369].

The withdrawal of major institutional investors – including BlackRock, Munich RE, Swiss RE, and JPMorgan Chase – from key United Nations climate pacts such as the *Net Zero Asset Managers Initiative* and *Climate Action 100+* is also unlikely to strengthen the EU's ESG agenda[370, 371]. Currently, the ultimate impact of these developments on EU ESG policies remains unclear. Nevertheless, ESG and sustainability considerations are expected to continue influencing property valuations in Europe in the near future.

Notably, the EU's latest five-year plan shifts its primary focus from climate goals to economic growth[372] (Die Welt, 24 January 2025, *The End of the Green Deal – The New Agenda for Europe's Competitiveness*). This is unsurprising, given the rising implementation costs of stricter environmental standards for property owners, who often cannot pass these costs on to tenants. National governments have increasingly resorted to subsidy programs to facilitate compliance, particularly in sectors such as residential construction, where projects are financially viable only with state support.

Furthermore, ESG criteria are subject to rapid changes in geopolitical contexts. For instance, the defense industry was long considered non-ESG-compliant. However, following Russia's invasion of Ukraine, this classification shifted dramatically, opening buildings previously consid-

369 Spring, Jake/Mathur, Anusha, EPA moves to end climate regulation under Clean Air Act, Washington Post, 29.07.2025, https://www.washingtonpost.com/climate-environment/2025/07/29/epa-endangerment-finding-clean-air-act/?utm_source=alert&utm_medium=email&utm_campaign=wp_news_alert_revere&location=alert, accessed 29.07.2025.

370 Werner, Reinhard, Munich Re kehrt ESG-Initiativen den Rücken – Rückzug aus vier Klimabündnissen, Epoch Times, https://www.epochtimes.de/wirtschaft/munich-re-kehrt-esg-in...pr7DECBhhzGdKezz7FssFYPdlr4maBhB7CFDdQXTQviCOMIExHFnw%3D%3D, accessed 13.06.2025.

371 Ozimek, Tom/Signus, Oliver, BlackRock steigt aus Klimapakt der Vereinten Nationen aus, Epoch Times, https://www.epochtimes.de/wirtschaft/munich-re-kehrt-esg-in...pr7DECBhhzGdKezz7FssFYPdlr4maBhB7CFDdQXTQviCOMIExHFnw%3D%3D, accessed 11.01.2025.

372 Beutelsbacher, Stefan, Das Ende des Green Deal – die neue Agenda für den Standort Deutschland, Die Welt, https://www.welt.de/wirtschaft/plus255235456/Das-Ende-des-Green-Deal-die-neue-Agenda-fuer-den-Standort-Europa.html?source=puerto-reco-2_ABC-V44.0.B_maximize_engagement, accessed 24.01.2025.

ered unsuitable for such occupiers to new tenant groups. This volatility introduces significant uncertainty for ESG-based property valuation: just as certain tenant groups are newly admitted to the market, others may be excluded in the future, even if they hold long-term leases.

A review of existing literature on ESG factors in property valuation reveals that publications typically stem from:

- Industry associations, seeking to provide their members with broadly applicable guidance; or
- Market participants promoting proprietary tools that are often built on weak or inconsistent data foundations, with projections that fail to account for future regulatory changes and evolving subsidy landscapes.

The absence of robust, standardized analysis underscores the limitations of current ESG valuation models and the challenges appraisers encounter when attempting to forecast long-term impacts.

(a) Previously neglected considerations

The fundamental challenge of integrating ESG criteria into real estate valuations lies in the **limited availability of reliable data** and the inherent **uncertainties surrounding future political developments.** In all honesty, two crucial factors are practically impossible to predict. For instance, while calculations may include sustainably achievable rents, there is no such certainty regarding sustainably achievable subsidies[373]. While it is straightforward to incorporate periodic replacements – such as windows or heating systems along with corresponding CO_2 reductions – into valuation models, the ongoing availability of subsidies to finance these replacements cannot be guaranteed. Recent experience demonstrates clearly that entire sectors like residential construction in Germany can rapidly collapse or renovations simply halt altogether once financial incentives are withdrawn. Alternatively, less sustainable systems, such as gas heating, may replace planned heat pumps. The first scenario distorts the supply side, leading to higher rents and increased property values, while the second scenario worsens the CO_2 balance, which will soon be subject to cost-sharing rules. There is also the question of whether increasingly restrictive regulations could mandate replacing heating systems every eight instead of every ten years, rendering detailed long-term planning obsolete.

The **electricity issue** further complicates matters. Countries such as the Netherlands have begun to ration electricity,[374] while at the same time, the EU is moving towards exclusive approval of electric vehicles. Paradoxically, certain municipalities are prohibiting the installation of new

373 Pezzei, Kristina, Katherina Reiche will Mittel für energetische Sanierung drastisch kürzen, Immobilienzeitung, https://www.iz.de/politik/news/-katherina-reiche-will-mittel-fuer-energetische-sanierung-drastisch-kuerzen-2000036348?utm_source=%2Fmeta%2Fnewsletter%2Fizaktuell&utm_medium=newsletter&utm_campaign=nl2510-abonnent&utm_term=eff3e668ceccb7eab6eda8876c3063a2, accessed 30.08.2025.

374 Hancock, Alice/Bounds Andy, Netherlands rations electricity to ease power grid stresses, Financial Times, https://www.ft.com/content/9c7560ec-a220-4150-a35e-a79db70c0c07, accessed 19.07.2025.

charging infrastructure in buildings due to fire safety regulations. What will happen to the existing infrastructure in these cases? Will residents of these buildings be forced to walk everywhere, and will such buildings become more or less marketable? One thing is certain: this will not remain value-neutral.

This also raises questions around **underground car parks**. Following the collapse of the Soviet Union, subsidies for bunker-equipped underground garages, which were available exclusively for new buildings, ended abruptly. Should such subsidies return – until the early 1990s, these practically covered the entire construction cost of underground garages – the question remains about the amount and distribution of these potential incentives.

Another critical development is emerging in some EU countries (e.g., the Netherlands and France), where governments are **prohibiting property owners from renting buildings that fall below specified energy efficiency ratings**. Such regulations could immediately render a fully occupied building nearly worthless. This scenario raises the question: Who will bear this loss in value? Should such occurrences become more frequent, what impact would this have on the balance sheets of credit institutions, and where would displaced tenants relocate to? If tenants move to slightly better and more expensive properties, this would greatly increase the value of these properties due to increased demand. Conversely, if tenants become insolvent due to affordability constraints, this initially leaves the quality of the properties unaffected, at least temporarily.

A further consideration that has not been extensively covered in existing literature is **whether users can afford these increasing costs**. In commercial real estate, tenants can avoid stricter regulations and associated costs through insolvency, increased home office use, or relocating operations abroad. Rising vacancy rates, especially in peripheral office locations, the conversion of office buildings into residential properties, and ongoing deindustrialization trends provide early indicators in this direction. In the residential sector, however, government subsidies support tenants. An equivalent trend is not yet evident in commercial real estate, except perhaps concerning industrial electricity.

Added to this is the **punitive treatment of entire sectors** – such as the defense industry, mentioned earlier – even though it is currently experiencing a renaissance that significantly benefits warehouse markets. If tenants from these industries fail to appear, or worse, are actively barred from renting spaces, vacancy rates will inevitably rise. In such cases, the financial resources required for necessary renovations could become scarce, financing might become difficult to secure, and individual property companies could become insolvent due to vacancies. The ESG concept was conceived at a time when vacancy rates were considerably lower, and the term »deindustrialization« was not yet common.

These considerations are currently missing from standard valuation models. This raises fundamental questions about the usefulness and validity of existing models and their forecasts. As the German newspaper *Die Welt* humorously summarized it in its headline regarding the summer weather of 2025: »*The forecasts were correct – but the weather didn't cooperate.*«[375]

(b) Implications for valuation

Until now, ESG considerations have primarily been assessed at the individual building level, which is an inherently logical approach within real estate valuation. To support this, deriving property-specific performance indicators is essential.

However, given the changing regulatory landscape, it is necessary to reconsider whether this method remains practical or if broader economic and geographic aspects should receive more attention. In other words, given these evolving conditions, will certain buildings still have a realistic chance of market viability? This question could profoundly affect the balance sheets and business models of local banks, including smaller savings and cooperative banks, in their commercial and residential sides of their real estate lending. Additionally, considering the increased prevalence of remote work, new living patterns may emerge, potentially driving population shifts away from urban areas and influencing urban housing and land markets. Consequently, one must ask whether detailed modeling – such as precisely simulating when each building component will require replacement and at what cost – may now be overly ambitious or even impractical.

Given these escalating uncertainties, adopting a »less is more« approach might be more pragmatic. This could partially explain the retreat of international investors from certain markets, a factor that should now be explicitly incorporated into valuations. It may also be prudent to reorient valuation methods to anticipate potential disruptions and their market impacts – for instance, assessing whether office properties in peripheral urban locations will remain rentable, or if costly conversions into residential spaces might become necessary. This perspective increasingly aligns with property developers' views rather than those of traditional appraisers. This is particularly relevant when considering that Western Europe currently leads global statistics in large-scale corporate bankruptcies.[376]

Another crucial aspect is the unintended consequences of politically promoted technological systems. Recent developments suggest that these systems may soon face regulatory restrictions due to unforeseen environmental consequences. For example, on 26 July 2025[377] the Berlin-based newspaper *Berliner Zeitung* reported that district heating and ground-based heat exchangers have significantly increased groundwater temperatures in some city areas.

375 Bojanowski, Alex, Die Prognosen waren korrekt – nur das Wetter hat nicht mitgespielt, Die Welt, https://www.welt.de/debatte/plus688484330e680a76f4e96135/Sommer-2025-Die-Prognosen-waren-korrekt-nur-das-Wetter-hat-nicht-mitgespielt.html, accessed 28.07.2025.

376 Allianz Trade, Insolvenz-Update Mai 2025, https://www.allianz-trade.de/content/dam/onemarketing/aztrade/allianz-trade_de/dokumente/2025-05-27-allianz-trade-insolvenz-update-mai-2025.pdf, accessed 24.06.2025.

377 Maritta Adam-Tkalec, Berliner Grundwasser doppelt so warm wie normal. Was sagt der Senat dazu, https://www.berliner-zeitung.de/mensch-metropole/berliner-grundwasser-doppelt-so-warm-wie-normal-was-sagt-der-senat-dazu-li.2341291, accessed 27.07.2025.

3.5.3 Framework conditions

(a) Public-law framework conditions

Appraisers evaluating properties under ESG criteria must now – this is a relatively new development – be well-informed about existing and upcoming regulations and their potential impact on a building's usability and economic viability.

In addition, fiscal incentives, such as tax benefits for renovations, CO_2 reduction, or new developments that align with current ESG requirements, as well as penalties, such as carbon taxes or regulatory fines, can significantly influence a property's market value. Therefore, subsidies and incentive programs must be explicitly considered in the valuation process. Without these financial supports, ESG-compliant buildings often prove to be economically infeasible – a fact implicitly acknowledged by the very existence of such programs.

(b) Technical framework conditions

A new and increasingly essential component of valuation is the assessment of a property's ESG performance. Various systems and frameworks have emerged to support appraisers in this task, such as:

- **LEED, BREEAM, DGNB:** Certification schemes focusing on environmental performance and energy efficiency.
- **GRESB:** An ESG benchmark specifically designed for real estate portfolios.
- **CRREM:** A tool for assessing decarbonization pathways.
- **EU Taxonomy, ISO 14001, TCFD:** Additional relevant standards and frameworks.

While certifications can serve as useful indicators, they should not be used as the sole basis for determining value. When considering certificates, appraisers must pay particular attention to their issuance date, market acceptance, and the transparency of the underlying assessment methodology.

Furthermore, some investors and tenants now require properties to meet certain minimum certification standards. The absence of these credentials can negatively impact a property's market price, while high-quality certifications can increase demand and tenants' willingness to pay more. However, appraisers must critically evaluate whether achieving the highest certification levels is truly economically viable, as the associated construction costs often outweigh potential gains. Ultimately, appraisers must determine whether a given ESG certificate is genuinely market-relevant and value-enhancing.

3.5.4 Building regulations and facility/asset management

Planning regulations, zoning requirements, and sustainability targets at both municipal and national levels have a direct and often substantial impact on project development. These requirements may include mandatory green roofs, façade greening, or the installation of photovoltaic systems. ESG criteria are increasingly influential in the issuance of building permits, change-of-use approvals, and revitalization projects.

Appraisers must therefore carefully assess project developments in light of the following considerations:

- Compliance with ESG standards: Which specific ESG criteria must be met to obtain a building permit? Could adherence to these standards potentially accelerate the permitting process?
- Required investments: What additional capital expenditures will be necessary to meet these ESG requirements?
- Economic feasibility: Will these investments realistically lead to an increase in value, or might they reduce overall profitability?

When a valuation involves development potential, ESG factors introduce new layers of risk and cost. Appraisers must decide if they can address these issues independently or if they need to involve external specialists, such as planners or cost estimators.

Sustainability strategies also influence the operational phase of a property's lifecycle. Key measures to improve ESG performance may include the following:

- Modernizing technical systems well before the end of their lifecycle
- Replacing inefficient materials, which may require refurbishing entire façades
- Strategic facility management approaches, designed to improve environmental performance over time

Appraisers must assess whether they can analyze these factors in-house or if they should engage expert consultants.

An additional consideration is the role of »green leases« – contracts that define ESG-related responsibilities between landlords and tenants. These agreements may stipulate cost-sharing arrangements for renovations or establish operational obligations for sustainability measures. Such clauses can directly impact rent levels, affect demand, and shift ESG-related risks between contractual parties. Appraisers must understand these nuances when assessing value implications.

Finally, location accessibility has always been a key value driver in real estate appraisal, and this aspect is becoming increasingly relevant under ESG frameworks. When analyzing location factors, appraisers should pay particular attention to the following:

- Proximity to public transportation (bus, rail, metro)
- Options for freight transfer to rail in logistics and warehouse contexts
- Potential restrictions due to traffic routing or limited road access
- Availability of bicycle parking and electric vehicle charging stations

- Accessibility for disabled persons
- Parking availability (private vs. public) and, for logistics properties, adequate truck parking and driver facilities

These considerations become more valuable when ESG-conscious tenants specifically seek these features or when mobility options influence demand patterns or operational costs. For example, low-income workers depend on public transportation, and insufficient parking creates operational inefficiencies.

(a) Social aspects

ESG considerations encompass more than environmental issues; the social dimension is becoming increasingly important in real estate valuation. This aspect relates to how buildings contribute to the health, comfort, and overall well-being of their users. **Key factors include**:

- Spatial design, natural light, and indoor air quality to create healthy and productive environments
- Quality of communal areas, such as canteens, lounges, or relaxation zones for employees and visitors
- Sanitary and fitness facilities, including provisions for truck drivers in logistics properties
- Health promotion measures in the workplace, enhancing both productivity and employee retention
- Façade design, such as green façades on residential or office buildings, or visually appealing, color-accented façades on industrial and logistics facilities

These features can positively influence a property's marketability, long-term tenant retention, and overall image. Appraisers should evaluate the extent to which such measures add tangible value for the target tenant group and whether they might even be a prerequisite for obtaining planning approval in certain municipalities.

The concept of »social value«, although not yet globally defined in a standardized manner, is gaining traction, particularly in urban development projects and public-sector contracts. **Social value refers to**:

- The societal benefits of a property for both users and nonusers – for example, rooftop bars open to the public or the transformation of previously inaccessible areas into community spaces
- Positive impacts on the surrounding community, such as improved public amenities, the creation of green spaces, or access to waterfront areas

As of mid-2025, it is likely that new definitions of social value will soon include publicly accessible shelters or bunkers, particularly in light of recent geopolitical events.

(b) Governance

Within the ESG framework, governance relates to managing sustainability requirements and adhering to regulatory standards. **This includes**:

- The integration of ESG-related obligations into contracts, operational processes, and organizational structures
- Disclosure, measurement, and monitoring of ESG-related information to ensure compliance and transparency

From the author's perspective, evaluating governance aspects often requires legal expertise rather than traditional valuation skills. Many of these elements pertain more to regulatory compliance and corporate governance practices than to the physical or economic attributes of the property itself. Therefore, appraisers must be cautious not to exceed their area of professional competence when assessing governance-related factors and should potentially rely on external legal specialists.

3.5.5 Valuation approach

As **with traditional property valuation,** the scope and depth of the analysis must be clearly defined within the valuation mandate if ESG factors are to be considered. Specific sustainability-related characteristics, such as energy efficiency, choice of building materials, refurbishment needs, or exposure to climate risks (e.g., flooding), should be explicitly examined as part of the assignment.

Appraisers must ensure that they have access to the information and expertise necessary to professionally evaluate ESG-relevant attributes of a property. Where limitations exist – such as incomplete data, unclear regulations, or uncertainties about future government support – they must be clearly documented in both the report and the engagement agreement.

> If the appraiser does not delegate the evaluation of ESG-related information to a specialized consultant, they are responsible for **obtaining relevant data directly from**:
>
> - the client,
> - external service providers, or
> - publicly accessible sources (e.g., certification bodies, regulatory agencies).
>
> Data sources may include energy performance certificates, environmental benchmarks, or recognized sustainability certifications. The timeliness of the data is crucial because outdated or historical information may no longer reflect current market or regulatory conditions, thus compromising the reliability of the valuation.

Therefore, the **integration of ESG factors into the valuation approach requires**:
- a transparent documentation of all relevant assumptions and data sources
- a realistic assessment of the appraiser's own expertise and limitations

Clear delineation of responsibilities is necessary, particularly when the assignment intersects with ESG consultancy services that go beyond pure valuation tasks.

3.5.6 Integration of ESG into valuation methodologies

In order to **future-proof property valuations** within the EU, appraisers must increasingly assess the sustainability factors and ESG-related risks associated with a given asset. Only by identifying these elements can their influence on market value be reliably and transparently determined.

This process requires a comprehensive property inspection, combined with the evaluation of all available information relevant to the building's environmental, social, and governance profile. It is important to recognize that sustainability considerations affect nearly every valuation parameter. While sustainable construction methods have historically influenced development costs, net rents, and tenant operating expenses, they now also significantly impact future modernization costs. Older certifications, for example, may become obsolete as certain tenant groups increasingly demand the latest ESG-compliant buildings. This shift affects pricing and can alter the capitalization rate (yield) applied in a valuation.

3.5.7 Selection of valuation method

(a) Methodology

Within the limits of legal and professional standards, appraisers can select the methodology best suited to the specific property and market in question. Broadly speaking, two categories can be distinguished: implicit and explicit models. See **Figure 20** for further details.

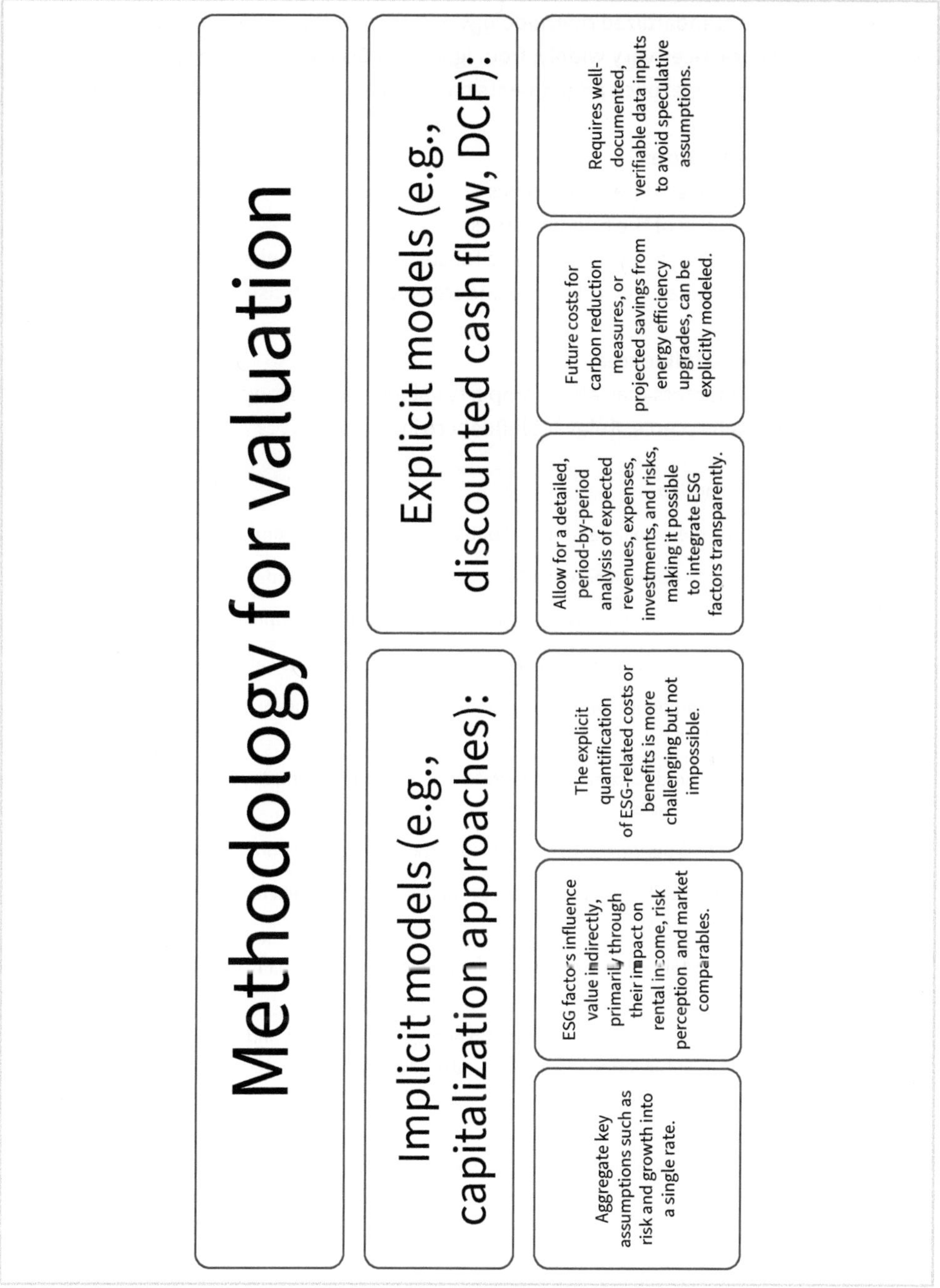

Figure 20: Methodology for valuation

Currently, there is no standardized methodology for incorporating ESG criteria into real estate valuations. Market practices vary widely, from ignoring ESG factors entirely, to implicitly embedding them to applying explicit adjustments based on a property's specific ESG status.

Key challenges include:
- Lack of standardized data and metrics
- High heterogeneity of the building stock
- Complex and uncertain cost estimates for sustainability-related refurbishments, which are not typically included in standard valuation exercises

(b) Specific ESG-related influences
Although various ESG factors may affect property values, reliable long-term data for quantifying their impact remains scarce. Relevant influences include:

Title	Description
Land acquisition	Some municipalities only sell public land to buyers committing to ESG measures.
Building permits	Easier to obtain if certain ESG or social criteria are voluntarily addressed.
Leasing potential	Certain tenant groups now exclusively occupy ESG-compliant buildings.
Marketing period	Properties with poor ESG performance may face longer sales or leasing times.
Rental growth	ESG-compliant buildings can command premium rents or enjoy stronger demand dynamics.
Incentives and concessions	ESG-related risks may necessitate longer rent-free periods or other concessions to attract tenants.
Risk premiums	Poor ESG performance may increase the required discount rate or capitalization yield.
Exit yield	At the end of a DCF projection, properties with ESG deficiencies may have lower resale values.
Value depreciation	Non-sustainable assets may suffer accelerated obsolescence and a faster decline in market value.
Decarbonization requirements	Appraisers should gather data on energy consumption and CO_2 emissions, particularly in anticipation of »net zero« objectives. Self-generated energy (e.g., solar power) may offer additional income streams but usually requires substantial upfront investment.
Refurbishment and modernization	Upgrades related to heating, insulation, water efficiency, and related sustainability can significantly affect value. Importantly, investment costs do not automatically translate into proportional value increases. Market acceptance and regulatory context determine the value effect.
Physical climate risks	Increased exposure to floods, storms, or wildfires can impact property values and insurance costs.

Title	Description
Transition risks	Regulatory changes may restrict usage or even prohibit letting certain properties (e.g., as seen in the Netherlands).
Market accept-ance	Different markets react at different speeds to ESG factors. Prime institutional markets are typically the first to price ESG attributes into transactions. Appraisers must under-stand buyer expectations and the minimum ESG standards relevant to the asset's target market.

Table 25: Specific ESG-related influences

3.5.8 Conclusion

Sustainability and ESG considerations have become integral components of professional real estate valuation, provided the assignment explicitly requires their inclusion. Key insights can be summarized as follows:

- The impact of ESG criteria on market value depends significantly on market maturity, property quality, intended use, and prevailing regulatory frameworks.
- Investment decisions driven by ESG-focused investors or funds may diverge from established market value definitions and should be reflected in investment value assessments, rather than generalized as market-wide effects.

It should be noted that properties with modern specifications, no maintenance backlog, and strong transportation access have always achieved higher rents, better occupancy rates, and higher valuations compared to inferior assets. Similarly, sustainability certifications have historically been implemented primarily in investor-focused, higher-quality buildings, rather than universally across all asset classes.

For this reason, valuation assignments must be based on clearly defined assumptions, documented within the mandate. A distinction should always be made between market value, fair value, and investment value to ensure that ESG considerations are applied only where they are genuinely value-relevant. Advanced valuation tools, such as DCF models with scenario analysis and sensitivity testing can capture ESG risks and opportunities. However, the lack of robust, standardized data often limits the predictive reliability of these models.

Ultimately, ESG-related valuation adjustments should not be assumed to automatically lead to higher property values. In many cases, ESG-compliant buildings command premiums primarily because they are newer, more modern, and located in superior areas, rather than due to ESG factors alone. Maintaining this »modern standard« requires continuous investment, such as the regular replacement of building systems and finishes – a process that is only financially sustainable when supported by strong tenant demand and adequate funding. Extended vacancies or prolonged lease-up periods can rapidly erode expected returns.

Furthermore, subsidies and tax incentives currently play a significant role in making ESG-compliant developments financially viable. The future availability of such support is uncertain, which adds further complexity to long-term forecasting.

In conclusion, although ESG considerations are increasingly important and must be transparently documented in valuation reports, they do not fundamentally change the core principles of sound real estate appraisal.

ESG integration primarily introduces:
- a greater emphasis on data-driven analysis,
- a need for external ESG expertise, and
- heightened sensitivity to regulatory and market uncertainties.

The future of ESG in valuation will likely depend less on abstract principles and more on the availability of reliable data, evolving regulatory landscapes, and sustained demand from financially capable tenants. Currently, ESG in property valuation is often »*talked about more than it is practically implemented,*« and its true market impact remains dynamic and uncertain.

3.6 Why carbon accounting is business-critical for tenants, and a strategic imperative for landlords

Aragon St. Charles

3.6.1 Introduction to #3.6

Across global real estate markets, sustainability has moved from the margins to the mainstream. What was once considered a matter of corporate social responsibility has become a strategic business issue that affects how companies operate, how they compete, and how they choose commercial real estate. At the heart of this change lies carbon accounting – the systematic measurement and disclosure of a company's greenhouse gas emissions.

For tenants in commercial buildings, carbon accounting is no longer optional. It is increasingly mandated by law, demanded by clients, and scrutinized by investors. For landlords, the issue is equally urgent. They are being asked not only to provide emissions data to their tenants, but also to demonstrate that their buildings are on a credible pathway to net zero.

This chapter explores why carbon accounting is becoming business-critical for commercial tenants, why it matters (or should matter) just as much to landlords, and how both parties must work together if they are to remain competitive and compliant. The focus is on Europe and the

United Kingdom, where regulatory frameworks are advancing most quickly, but we will also look at examples from North America and Australia.

#3.6 **Carbon accounting – for tenants & landlords**	**#3.6.1 – intro to #3.6**
	#3.6.2 – carbon accounting & tenants
	#3.6.3 – implications for landlords
	#3.6.4 – interdependencies & a shared path forward
	#3.6.5 – conclusion

In this subchapter #3.6 on the role of carbon accounting, we discuss the role for tenants (#3.6.2), the implications for landlords (#3.6.3), interdependencies which call for a shared path forward (#3.6.4), finishing up with concluding remarks (#3.6.5).

3.6.2 Carbon accounting and tenants: Regulatory, client, and market pressures

For tenants, the pressure to measure and report carbon emissions now comes from three main sources: statutory obligations, voluntary disclosure systems, and client demand. Together, these forces are making carbon accounting part of the »license to operate« for any serious business.

The regulatory environment in Europe illustrates just how broad the requirements have become. The **Corporate Sustainability Reporting Directive (CSRD)**[378] (notwithstanding recent directives that are watering down the reporting requirements) expands the number of companies that must publish detailed climate information, including Scope 1, 2, and 3 emissions. Even companies not directly in scope may still be required to report emissions if they are subsidiaries of larger groups, meaning that thousands of tenants in European buildings will now need office-level emissions data.

Similarly, the revised **Energy Performance of Buildings Directive (EPBD)**[379], published in May 2024, requires member states to establish a plan for achieving zero-emission buildings by 2050. This will entail more stringent energy performance standards, clearer renovation requirements, and better sub-metering. These changes underscore the importance of tenants engaging with their landlords on energy and carbon data.

The UK has taken a very similar path. The **Streamlined Energy and Carbon Reporting (SECR)** framework requires large companies to publish their annual energy usage and emissions, while the **Energy Savings Opportunity Scheme (ESOS)** also mandates regular audits. More signifi-

378 European Commission, Corporate Sustainability Reporting Directive (CSRD), 2023, https://finance.ec.europa.eu/capital-markets-union-and-financial-markets/company-reporting-and-auditing/company-reporting/corporate-sustainability-reporting_en, accessed 30.08.2025.

379 Council of the EU, Revision to the Energy Performance of Buildings Directive (EPBD), 2024, https://www.consilium.europa.eu/en/press/press-releases/2022/10/25/fit-for-55-council-agrees-on-stricter-rules-for-energy-performance-of-buildings/, accessed 30.08.2025.

cantly for leasing markets, the **Minimum Energy Efficiency Standards (MEES)**[380] make it unlawful to lease commercial spaces with an EPC rating below »E« (unless specific exemptions have been granted), forcing landlords to retrofit noncompliant buildings or face having unrentable properties. For tenants, MEES significantly increases the importance of choosing buildings that will remain compliant in the medium and long term, rather than being caught up in the disruption of forced retrofits.

Beyond regulatory compliance, voluntary frameworks have established powerful new norms. The **Science Based Targets initiative (SBTi)**[381] has become the de facto standard for corporate climate ambition, requiring companies to cover at least 67 % of Scope 3 emissions in their short-term targets, rising to 90 % for long-term net zero targets. For tenants, this raises the immediate question of how to account for »leased asset emissions.« According to the Greenhouse Gas Protocol, emissions from rented space are divided depending on who controls the building systems. Tenants may need to report them under Scope 1 and 2 if they directly control energy use or under Scope 3 Category 8, if the landlord controls the plant (GHG Protocol, 2011)[382]. In either case, tenants require reliable building data in order to comply.

Client expectations add a further, and sometimes more compelling, layer of obligation. Large and medium-sized companies increasingly use platforms such as **CDP** and **Ecovadis** as part of their supply chain management systems to request emissions (and broader ESG) information from their suppliers. If a tenant is part of the supply chain for a major manufacturer, retailer, or government agency, they may be asked to submit emissions data as part of the RFP or procurement processes. In the UK, the public sector has gone even further: **Procurement Policy Note (PPN)**[383] **06/21** requires suppliers bidding on central government contracts above £5 million to submit a detailed Carbon Reduction Plan that includes current emissions and reduction targets. For professional service-sector tenants, such as law firms, consultancies, IT companies etc., these requirements often mean that, without accurate building data, they cannot bid on new business or are at a disadvantage in the procurement process.

The combination of regulatory pressure, voluntary frameworks, and client expectations has made carbon accounting a matter of both compliance and market competitiveness. Tenants increasingly understand that accurate emissions data is not simply an ESG add-on but a prerequisite for winning contracts, retaining customers, and avoiding reputational risk. Commercial

380 UK Government, Minimum Energy Efficiency Standards: Non-domestic Private Rented Property, 2023, https://www.gov.uk/guidance/non-domestic-private-rented-property-minimum-energy-efficiency-standard-landlord-guidance, accessed 30.08.2025.

381 Science Based Targets initiative, Near-term Criteria and Recommendations, 2022, https://sciencebasedtargets.org/blog/explained-minor-revisions-resources, accessed 30.08.2025.

382 GHG Protocol, Corporate Value Chain (Scope 3) Accounting and Reporting Standard, 2011, https://ghgprotocol.org/corporate-value-chain-scope-3-standard, accessed 30.08.2025.

383 UK Cabinet Office, Procurement Policy Note 06/21: Taking account of Carbon Reduction Plans, 2021, https://www.gov.uk/government/publications/procurement-policy-note-0621-taking-account-of-carbon-reduction-plans-in-the-procurement-of-major-government-contracts, accessed 30.08.25.

leasing decisions are increasingly influenced by a building's ability to supply the necessary data and demonstrate credible low-carbon credentials.

3.6.3 Implications for landlords: Data, buildings, and value

While tenants increasingly demand carbon data to remain compliant with regulatory requirements and stay competitive in business, landlords must be the ones to provide it. Most of the relevant information – such as base building electricity, data for common areas, central plant fuel use, refrigerant leakage, district heating allocations etc. – sits primarily with the landlord, not the occupier. In multi-tenant offices, it is common for tenants to have only a sub-meter for their direct consumption, while the bulk of heating and cooling is managed centrally. Without landlord cooperation, tenants will not be able to meet their reporting obligations and may need to consider whether they can remain in such a building.

This creates a powerful commercial incentive for landlords to invest in metering, monitoring, and transparent data sharing. Forward-thinking owners are already developing »tenant carbon packs«: monthly or quarterly reports detailing energy use, emissions factors, and renewable energy certificates formatted to align with SECR, CSRD, CDP, or SBTi requirements. By institutionalizing data flows, landlords are not only helping tenants but also strengthening their own attractiveness to institutional investors.

The real estate sector accounts for approximately 40% of global carbon emissions (11% during construction, and 28% during day-to-day operations). As a result, investors and lenders are increasingly focused on the climate performance of real estate assets. The **EU Taxonomy** for sustainable finance requires owners to prove that their buildings meet energy performance thresholds to be considered environmentally sustainable. The **Sustainable Finance Disclosure Regulation (SFDR)** requires asset managers to disclose the environmental performance of their portfolios, which in turn motivates them to demand credible emissions data from landlords. Buildings that cannot clearly demonstrate their carbon emissions profile will find it harder to attract capital, refinance, or achieve premium valuations and rents.

Beyond measurement, landlords face growing pressure to actually reduce emissions from the day-to-day operations of the building. In the UK, MEES has already rendered thousands of assets noncompliant, and a future tightening of the EPC thresholds is anticipated. In Europe, the EPBD's trajectory toward zero-emission buildings will necessitate deep retrofits. For landlords, this means planning capital expenditure commitments well ahead of deadlines, focusing on the building fabric, HVAC upgrades, electrification of heating and cooling, and renewables integration. Delays in these upgrades carry the risk of forced, expensive retrofits under regulatory duress.

Green certification systems can provide a structured route forward. **BREEAM** in the UK, and **LEED** and **WELL** internationally all offer frameworks to measure, improve, and communicate a building's sustainability credentials. For existing assets, certifications such as **LEED for Operations and Maintenance** provide a framework for optimizing building performance in areas like energy and water consumption, waste management, and indoor environmental quality. Importantly, certifications also function as market signals: tenants competing for government contracts or multinational clients often prefer to occupy certified buildings, which simplifies their own sustainability reporting and strengthens their brand.

The economic rationale is becoming clear. Energy-efficient buildings can hedge against volatile energy prices, reduce service-charge shocks, and deliver more predictable net operating income. Tenants are more likely to renew leases in buildings that support their sustainability goals, reducing vacancy risks. Investors value assets with clear decarbonization pathways, as they are less exposed to regulatory and reputational risks. In short, landlords should recognize that greener, more energy-efficient buildings and measuring and reducing carbon emissions are essential strategies for protecting the value of real estate assets, not just compliance exercises.

3.6.4 A shared path forward

The dynamic between landlords and tenants is rapidly evolving into one of mutual interdependence. Tenants cannot report their emissions without relevant data from landlords; and landlords cannot maintain the value of their buildings without high-quality tenants who are compliant with statutory requirements and competitive in their markets. This interdependence calls for new collaboration models.

One approach that is gaining traction is the increased use of **green lease clauses**, which set out mutual obligations regarding data sharing, energy efficiency measures, and improvement works. The Better Buildings Partnership's Green Lease Toolkit[384] provides practical guidance, model clauses, and best practice recommendations to encourage collaboration between landlords and tenants to improve the environmental performance of buildings. These provisions can, for example, require tenants to install efficient lighting during a fit-out, oblige landlords to provide sub-metering, or commit both parties to share the costs and benefits of renewable energy procurement. Crucially, they move sustainability from informal cooperation into the legally binding core of the lease.

Practical collaboration also means designing data flows »by default.« In new developments, landlords can install smart meters and energy management systems that automatically gen-

384 Better Buildings Partnership, Green Lease Toolkit, 2024, https://www.betterbuildingspartnership.co.uk/green-lease-toolkit-0, accessed 30.08.2025.

erate tenant-ready reports. For existing assets, retrofitting sub-meters and creating standardized reporting templates is becoming a priority. The most sophisticated landlords are already providing dashboards where tenants can log in and download data aligned with their chosen reporting framework.

Financial innovation will inevitably play a role too. Energy-service models, on-bill financing, and shared-savings contracts can help fund upgrades without imposing unmanageable capital costs. In some cases, landlords can recover costs through an increased service charge, provided they can demonstrate clear efficiency benefits to tenants. Over time, it is likely that sustainability-linked leases and performance-based contracting will become more common, aligning financial incentives with emissions outcomes.

International experience suggests a consistent direction across markets. In California, new legislation (SB 253 and SB 261)[385] requires large companies to disclose Scope 1, 2, and 3 emissions and to publish biennial climate-risk reports. In Australia, the NABERS rating system has driven substantial improvements in building performance by requiring the disclosure of operational energy intensity. Canada is following similar pathways at the provincial level. The message is simple for global tenants: wherever you operate, you will be asked to account for your carbon footprint, and you will invariably need your landlords to provide a significant part of that data.

3.6.5 Conclusion

Carbon accounting and statutory reporting requirements are rapidly becoming operational necessities for companies in most jurisdictions, particularly in Europe, the UK, and parts of the U.S. and Canada. Voluntary reporting frameworks, such as CDP, Ecovadis, and SBTi, have raised expectations among clients and investors and are increasingly being used as part of sophisticated supply chain management protocols of large companies. For commercial real estate tenants, accurate emissions data is essential not just for compliance but also for winning contracts, retaining customers (and personnel), and maintaining market competitiveness.

The implications for landlords are equally profound. A building that cannot provide reliable carbon data or demonstrate a credible path to decarbonization risks becoming unlettable and unfinanceable – effectively, a stranded asset. Conversely, assets that are energy-efficient, data-rich, and certified under recognized frameworks can, and regularly do, command stronger demand, higher rents and better valuations.

> The future of sustainable real estate lies in stronger collaboration. Landlords and tenants have to move beyond traditional transactional relationships and recognize their shared

385 State of California, SB 253 and SB 261 Climate Accountability Package, 2023, https://www.dentons.com/en/insights/alerts/2023/october/19/new-climate-reporting-requirements-to-take-effect-in-california, accessed 30.08.2025.

interest in carbon transparency and reduction. Emissions data reporting must be seen as a must-have, rather than a nice-to-have. Green lease clauses must become standard market practice, and retrofits must be planned as value-creating investments rather than as regulatory burdens.

In short, carbon accounting is no longer a peripheral ESG exercise. It is the new currency of commercial leasing as statutory reporting requirements increase and tenants demand robust and certified emissions data in order to meet their own reporting requirements and to maintain market competitiveness. Landlords need to protect asset value, and those who act early and decisively will not only meet their statutory obligations but also strengthen their competitive position in a marketplace that increasingly rewards sustainability.

4 ESG deep dives: CRREM, water, brownfields, insurance, and AI

4.1 Introduction to Chapter #4

Sabine Wieduwilt

«The activist is not the man who says the river is dirty. The activist is the man who cleans up the river.«
– Ross Perot

4.1.1 Content of Chapter #4

The details concerning environmental, social and governance issues under review may differ from region to region and from investment to investment. For example, chapter #6 refers to indigenous rights highlighted in certain regions, but not in others. There is the – seemingly constant – change of laws for every region, which is not always focused and thus not very sustainably managed by the regulators, if we look at the stress and impact this constant change causes for companies. All regions are facing severe stress due to extreme weather events (severe flooding, fires, heat waves). Even in regions where the reporting requirements seem to be simplified, there is a monetary unit connected to the use of energy and resources, as for example with the emissions trading systems (ETS). The real estate community together with the regulators will find more solutions to promote circularity in design, construction, the use and treatment of waste as a resource or product, also in the built environment. The history of unlimited growth and linear production gives way to circularity in our designs and in our thinking. Also, the real estate community and regulators will find solutions to push more capital into refurbishment of existing buildings instead of constructing new ones in order to further reduce embodied carbon and be mindful of use of resources.

Thinking about the long lifespan of a building and the unlimited nature of real estate, an investor will want to be forward-looking and think sustainably, regardless of where regulators in a given market are currently heading. There are not only tons of definitions of sustainability/CSR/ESG; there is also a wide array of topics you can dive into in relation to real estate investment and ESG. In this chapter we delve into some of those details that we believe may be relevant to any real estate investor at some point.

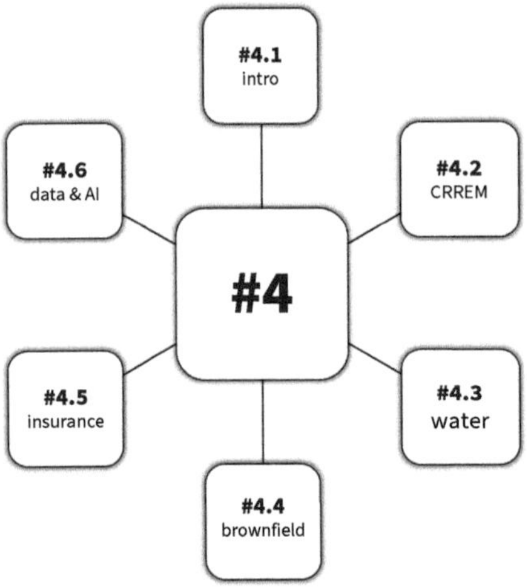

In this chapter #4, after a brief overview of ESG details for real estate (#4.1.2), we proceed to review the Carbon Risk Real Estate Monitor (CRREM) (#4.2), water management (#4.3), brownfield investment (#4.4), insurance and climate adaptation (#4.5), as well as data and AI including some of the regulatory considerations (#4.6).

Before you continue reading, think about the following: Do these topics affect you and are they part of your ESG strategy?

This is not an exhaustive list of topics you can tend to.

4.1.2 ESG details for real estate: Topics overviews

The following is to give you ideas for further reading.[386]

(a) Topics we will be touching upon under #4.2 to #4.6:

Term	Shortened definition	Standards & sources used on a global scale
Carbon Risk Real Estate Monitor (CRREM)	A tool that helps real estate owners assess and reduce carbon risks by aligning property emissions with climate targets.	CRREM Initiative; GRESB; Science Based Targets initiative (SBTi)
Embodied carbon	The total amount of greenhouse gas emissions from producing, transporting, and disposal of building materials, excluding emissions during use.	World Green Building Council, GHG Protocol, ISO 14067 (see for example for the EU: Level(s))
Water management	Strategies and practices for using, conserving, and protecting water resources efficiently and sustainably.	UN Water, World Bank, ISO 14046[387] (see for example for the EU: EU Water Framework Directive, European Environment Agency)

386 Footnotes to the tables are non-exhaustive and serve only as examples.

387 Environmental management – Water footprint – Principles, requirements and guidelines (ISO 14046:2014); German and English version EN ISO 14046:2016, https://www.dinmedia.de/en/standard/din-en-iso-14046/249457985, accessed 14.09.2025; Ruhlin, What is ISO 14046 Water Footprint Evaluation?, 08.07.2025, https://www.rmagreen.com/rma-blog/bid/91696/what-is-iso-14046-water-footprint-evaluation, accessed 08.09.2025; Amar, Omer, The ISO 14000 Standards Family: A Complete Guide, 02.09.2025, https://www.arbor.eco/blog/iso-14000-standards, accessed 08.09.2025.

Term	Shortened definition	Standards & sources used on a global scale
Brownfield investments	Investments in redeveloping previously used or contaminated land, often for new construction or urban renewal.	World Bank[388], UNEP[389] (see regional examples: US EPA, EU Brownfield Policy, European Environment Agency, EIB and EC[390])
Climate adaptation and insurance	Adjusting to climate impacts and using insurance to manage risks from extreme weather and environmental changes.	IPCC[391], UNFCCC[392], Geneva Association (see EU example: EU Climate Adaptation Strategy, Insurance Europe)
Resilience (physical and social)	The ability of buildings and communities to withstand and recover from environmental, social, and economic shocks and stresses.	UNDRR (UN Office for Disaster Risk Reduction), ISO 22301[393] (see EU example: EU Climate Adaptation Strategy, Resilience4EU)
Climate risk assessment	Evaluating the exposure of real estate assets to climate-related risks, such as flooding, heatwaves, and sea level rise.	TCFD (Task Force on Climate-related Financial Disclosures), IPCC, UNEP FI (see EU example: EU Sustainable Finance Disclosure Regulation (SFDR), EU Taxonomy)
Data and artificial intelligence (AI)	Using digital data and AI technologies to analyze, predict, and optimize sustainability and business processes.	OECD AI Principles, ISO/IEC JTC 1/SC 42 (see EU example: EU AI Act, European Data Strategy)

Table 26: Overview: ESG details under #4.2 to #4.6

388 World Bank Group, The management of brownfields redevelopment: a guidance note (English), 2008, https://documents.worldbank.org/en/publication/documents-reports/documentdetail/754171468295822120/the-management-of-brownfields-redevelopment-a-guidance-note, accessed 13.09.2025.

389 UNEP-WCMC, Brownfield Sites: Achieving net gain through their biodiversity potential, 2021, https://www.proteuspartners.org/content//uploads/2021/09/Proteus-Technical-Brief-Brownfield-Sites.pdf, accessed 13.09.2025.

390 EIB/EC, Investing in nature-based solutions. State-of-play and way forward for public and private financial measures in Europe, 2023, https://www.eib.org/attachments/lucalli/20230095_investing_in_nature_based_solutions_en.pdf, accessed 13.09.2025.

391 IPCC, Climate Change 2022: Impacts, Adaptation and Vulnerability, 2022, https://www.ipcc.ch/report/ar6/wg2/, accessed 13.09.2025.

392 Agata Bator and Agnieszka Borek, Adaptation to Climate Change under Climate Change Treaties, International Community Law Review, 2021, https://brill.com/view/journals/iclr/23/2-3/article-p158_4.xml, accessed 13.09.2025.

393 United Nations Office for Disaster Risk Reduction (UNDRR), Reducing Risk & Building Resilience of SMEs to Disasters, 2020, https://www.undrr.org/media/48692/download?startDownload=20250908, accessed 08.09.2025; Bevan, Tony nqa, ISO 22301:2019 Business Continuity Standard Implementation Guide, 2019, https://www.nqa.com/medialibraries/NQA/NQA-Media-Library/PDFs/NQA-ISO-22301-Implementation-Guide.pdf, accessed 08.09.2025; DIN Media, DIN EN ISO 22301:2020-06, Security and resilience – Business continuity management systems – Requirements (ISO 22301:2019); EN ISO 22301:2019, https://www.dinmedia.de/de/norm/din-en-iso-22301/311095091, accessed 14.09.2025; UNDRR, Reducing risk and building resilience to SMEs to disasters, https://www.undrr.org/publication/reducing-risk-and-building-resilience-smes-disasters, accessed 14.09.2025.

(b) Additional topics (in addition to those in #4.2 to #4.6):

Term	Shortened definition	Standards & sources used on a global scale
Biodiversity and ecosystems in the built environment	Integrating and protecting natural habitats and species within urban development to support ecological health.	UN Environment Programme, Convention on Biological Diversity (CBD), ISO 17298, CDP-TNFD (see EU/UK example: EU Biodiversity Strategy, CIEEM (UK/EU))
Carbon leakage and carbon sinks	Carbon leakage occurs when emissions shift to laxer jurisdictions due to stricter local climate policies; carbon sinks are systems that absorb more carbon than they emit.	IPCC, UNFCCC, Kyoto Protocol (see EU example: EU Emissions Trading System (EU ETS), Carbon Border Adjustment Mechanism (CBAM))
Circularity/waste hierarchy	Circularity keeps resources in use as long as possible; the waste hierarchy ranks waste management from prevention to disposal.	Ellen MacArthur Foundation, ISO 14040, ISO 14044 (see EU example: EU Waste Framework Directive, Ellen MacArthur Foundation (EU))
Cradle to cradle (C2C)	A design approach in which products are made for continuous reuse or safe return to nature, thus eliminating waste.	Cradle to Cradle Certified™, McDonough & Braungart, ISO 14021 (see EU/U.S. examples: C2C Certified (EU/U.S.), EU Circular Economy Action Plan)
Energy benchmarking and disclosure	Comparing and publicly reporting the energy performance of buildings to drive improvements and transparency.	ENERGY STAR Portfolio Manager (U.S./Global), GRESB, ISO 50001 (see EU/UK examples: EU Energy Efficiency Directive, UK Energy Savings Opportunity Scheme (ESOS))
Energy performance certificates (EPCs)	Official documents that rate the energy efficiency of buildings, often required by law, providing information on energy use and recommendations for improvement.	ISO 52000 series, International Energy Agency (IEA) (see EU/UK example: EU Energy Performance of Buildings Directive, UK Government)
Environmental product declarations (EPDs)	Verified documents showing a product's environmental impact throughout its life cycle, based on life cycle assessment.	ISO 14025, ISO 21930 (see EU example: EN 15804 (EU), EPD International (EU))
Green building materials	Use of materials with low environmental impact, high recycled content, and responsible sourcing in construction and renovation.	Cradle to Cradle Certified™, FSC, PEFC, ISO 14021 (see regional examples: EU Ecolabel, EN 15804, BRE Green Guide)
Green governance	Policies and practices ensuring environmental responsibility and sustainability in organizations or governments.	OECD, UN Global Compact, ISO 26000 (see EU example: EU Green Deal, EU Taxonomy Regulation)

Term	Shortened definition	Standards & sources used on a global scale
Green infrastructure	Networks of natural and semi-natural areas designed to deliver ecosystem services, such as green roofs, parks, and urban forests.	IUCN, UNEP, Convention on Biological Diversity (CBD) (see EU examples: EU Green Infrastructure Strategy, Natura 2000)
Green leases	Lease agreements that include sustainability obligations for landlords and tenants, such as energy efficiency, waste reduction, and reporting.	UNEP FI Principles for Responsible Property Investment, GRESB (see UK example: Better Buildings Partnership (UK), Green Lease Toolkit (UK))
Health and well-being in buildings	Design and operation practices that promote occupant health, comfort, and productivity, including air quality, lighting, and access to nature.	WELL Building Standard, Fitwel, WHO Healthy Buildings Guidelines
Life cycle costing (LCC)	Assessment of the total cost of ownership of a building or asset throughout its entire life cycle, including construction, operation, maintenance, and disposal.	ISO 15686-5, ISO 15686-2 (see EU example: EN 16627 (EU), Level(s) (EU))
Net zero carbon buildings	Buildings that balance the amount of carbon emitted with the amount removed or offset, achieving net zero emissions over the course of a year.	WorldGBC Net Zero Carbon Buildings Commitment, SBTi Net Zero Standard, ISO 14068 (see EU/UK example: EU Renovation Wave, Level(s) (EU))
Rating and building certifications	Third-party verified standards that assess and certify the sustainability, energy efficiency, and environmental performance of buildings (e.g., LEED, BREEAM, DGNB, WELL).	LEED (U.S./Global), WELL (IWBI), EDGE (IFC/World Bank), Green Star (Australia), GRESB, ISO 21929 (see UK/EU example: BREEAM (UK/EU), DGNB (Germany/EU), HQE (France))
Responsible supply chain/procurement	Ensuring that materials and services used in real estate are sourced ethically and sustainably, considering environmental and social impacts.	ISO 20400, UN Global Compact, GRI Standards (see EU examples: EU Public Procurement Directive, EU Green Public Procurement)
Social value in real estate	The positive social impact generated by real estate projects, such as community benefits, affordable housing, and local employment.	UN SDGs, GRESB Social Impact Module (see UK/EU examples: UK Social Value Act, EU Social Economy Action Plan)
Sustainable finance/ green bonds	Financial instruments and investments specifically aimed at funding environmentally sustainable projects, including green buildings.	ICMA Green Bond Principles, Climate Bonds Initiative (see EU example: EU Green Bond Standard, EU Taxonomy Regulation)

Term	Shortened definition	Standards & sources used on a global scale
Sustainable land use/urban sprawl	Planning and development practices that minimize land consumption, protect natural habitats, and promote compact and efficient urban growth.	UN Habitat, New Urban Agenda, ISO 37101 (see EU examples: EU Urban Agenda, European Spatial Development Perspective)
Sustainable urban mobility	Transportation systems and infrastructure that reduce environmental impact, promote active travel, and improve accessibility.	UN Habitat, Sustainable Mobility for All (SuM4All) (see EU examples: EU Urban Mobility Framework, CIVITAS Initiative)
Tenant engagement/Occupant behavior	Strategies to involve building users in sustainability initiatives, such as energy conservation, recycling, and wellness programs.	GRESB, WorldGBC, WELL Building Standard (see UK/EU examples: UK Green Building Council (UKGBC) Guidance, EU Green Week)

Table 27: Overview: Additional ESG details beyond #4.2 to #4.6

4.2 Transition risks in real estate: The role of CRREM in investment strategies

Sebastian Leutner

«Decarbonization in real estate is not only about doing good – it's about doing well by staying ahead of regulation and capital market expectations.«

4.2.1 Introduction to #4.2

Relying on government action to determine a corporate sustainability strategy is a risky approach. Capital markets have already surpassed regulators, imposing stricter and faster requirements than most current regulations. To meet these rising market expectations and make more informed investment decisions, investors require forward-looking analytical frameworks such as the Carbon Risk Real Estate Monitor (CRREM). Used in over 40 countries, CRREM facilitates practical action toward achieving climate goals across global real estate markets by aligning asset performance with transition risk pathways.

#4.2 Transition risks, CRREM and investment strategies	**#4.2.1 - intro to #4.2**
	#4.2.2 - transition risks - definition & market dynamics
	#4.2.3 - carbon in real estate operations, CRREM basics
	#4.2.4 - CRREM in practice: application and limitations

In this subchapter #4.2, we review the definition and market dynamics of transition risks (#4.2.2), the role of carbon in real estate operations and CRREM basics (#4.2.3), and the application and limitations of CRREM in practice (#4.2.4).

4.2.2 Transition risks: Definition and market dynamics

Real estate differs from most asset classes in terms of climate risk due to its immobility and limited ability to adapt quickly to climate-related influences as a long-term investment. As an asset class, it is not only particularly exposed to climate-related risks but is also responsible for over one-third of global energy consumption and CO_2 emissions.[394]

Beyond physical climate risks, which are the direct effects of climate change on properties and their surroundings, **transition risks** represent the second major category of climate risk. These risks generally encompass financial risks that could result from transitioning to a lower-carbon economy. The effects of transition risks on real estate throughout the investment cycle are highly multifaceted, complex, and subject to significant uncertainty. While it is difficult to list all transition risks, the Task Force on Climate-related Financial Disclosures (TCFD) has defined four major risk categories: **policy and legal risks, technology risks, market risks, and reputation risks.**[395] **Table 28** illustrates the **core risks and their potential impact on real estate markets**.

Transition risk	Impact on real estate markets
Policy and legal risks Climate-related litigation claims and policies that limit climate-harming activities or promote climate adaptation	• Carbon taxes on building emissions • Stricter energy efficiency laws • Zoning and land-use reforms • Fines for noncompliance with ESG disclosure standards • Litigation for climate adaptation and mitigation failure
Technology risks New technology can disrupt or displace existing systems	• Renewable energy technologies are making fossil fuel-based energy sources economically obsolete • Subsidy phase-outs for high-emission and less efficient heating, ventilation, and air conditioning (HVAC) systems • Legacy system vulnerabilities such as critical spare parts shortages

394 Hamilton, Ian, Global Status Report for Buildings and Construction, 2020, https://globalabc.org/resources/publications/2020-global-status-report-buildings-andconstruction, accessed 25.06.2025.

395 Task Force on Climate-related Financial Disclosures, Recommendations of the Task Force on Climate-related Financial Disclosures, 2017, https://assets.bbhub.io/company/sites/60/2021/10/FINAL-2017-TCFD-Report.pdf, accessed 25.06.2025.

Transition risk	Impact on real estate markets
Market risks Climate-related changes in supply and demand	• Value and rent depreciation of carbon-intensive or energy-inefficient assets • Lower investor and tenant demand • Constrained access to debt and equity markets
Reputation risks Climate-related changes in customer or community perceptions	• Market opposition to non-resilient companies • Tenant backlash against high-emission landlords • Fund divestment from carbon-intensive or energy-inefficient real estate portfolios

Table 28: Overview of transition risks and their impacts on real estate markets

A key concept frequently associated with transition risks in real estate is that of the **»stranded asset«**. First coined by the Carbon Tracker Initiative, the term refers to investments *»which, at some time prior to the end of their economic life, are no longer able to generate an economic return, as a result of changes in the market and regulatory environment«.*[396] However, it is important to note, that the term »stranded asset« has not been exclusively linked to climate discourse; historically, it has been applied across various industries. As such, definitions can vary, and may refer to partial impairments, total loss of value, or even situations where an asset becomes a financial burden.

As a physically immobile yet adaptable asset, real estate typically retains some residual value even in adverse conditions. Properties facing regulatory or market-driven impairments do not become permanently obsolete; rather, they can be repositioned through retrofitting, repurposing, or operational improvements. Consequently, viewing assets through a binary lens – classifying them as either »stranded« or »non-stranded« – tends to oversimplify the reality and may even be misleading. Reflecting this complexity, the **global real estate industry is increasingly moving away from using the term »stranded asset«** and adopting a more nuanced approach to assessing transition risk exposure (see **»CRREM Misalignment Year«** in #4.2.3).

4.2.3 Carbon in real estate operations and CRREM basics

Real estate emissions are generally **classified into two categories**: embodied and operational carbon. While **embodied carbon**, which arises from a building's construction, maintenance, and demolition, can account for a substantial share of total lifecycle emissions, transition risk considerations have traditionally focused on **operational carbon**.

To accurately determine a building's full transition risk exposure from a carbon perspective, it is essential to account for both *direct emissions* and *indirect emissions*. Direct emissions are those occurring within the site boundary, such as from on-site fuel combustion or refrigerant

396 Carbon Tracker Initiative, Unburnable Carbon – Are the World's Financial Markets Carrying a Carbon Bubble?, 2011.

leakage and *indirect emissions*, which are generated off-site during the production of energy carriers like electricity or district heating but are ultimately consumed within the building.

> Unlike the accounting and reporting of carbon emissions from real estate operations, the **assessment of transition risks is not based on a company's organizational boundaries** (such as equity share, financial control, or operational control), emission scopes (1, 2, or 3), or lease type (operating, finance, or capital lease). Instead, the building is considered a single, integrated unit in terms of its total energy consumption – a principle referred to as the »**whole-building approach**«.[397]

This approach recognizes that operational carbon emissions stem directly from energy usage, with **energy use intensity (EUI)** serving as the primary transition risk metric over carbon intensity in several real estate markets globally. This is partly because a building's carbon footprint can heavily depend on the carbon intensity of the local electricity grid – a regional factor largely beyond the owner's control. While reducing emissions is the ultimate goal, relying too heavily on market-based instruments, such as green tariffs or energy certificates, can obscure operational inefficiencies if they don't result in actual energy savings. In this context, energy intensity can serve as a **valuable metric for assessing a building's environmental performance**, especially in regions where carbon factors fluctuate significantly.

> CRREM was developed in response to these challenges, and to support a science-based assessment of transition risks. **CRREM is the leading global initiative that helps the real estate industry manage and reduce operational carbon emissions**. At its core, the CRREM methodology **provides decarbonization pathways that define the annual emissions and energy intensity thresholds which buildings must meet to remain aligned with a 1.5°C climate scenario.**

The methodology begins by allocating global or regional **carbon budgets** derived from climate scenarios (e.g., for limiting global warming to 1.5°C or 2°C). These budgets represent the maximum allowable greenhouse gas emissions over time to remain within specific temperature thresholds. From there, a portion of this budget is allocated to the real estate sector and then disaggregated further by building type (e.g., residential, office, or retail) and geography. The result is a set of dynamic carbon and energy intensity pathways that decrease over time in line with climate targets.[398]

---

397 For detailed accounting and reporting guidance for commercial real estate aligned with the GHG Protocol and the PCAF GHG accounting standard methodologies, see: PCAF/GRESB/CRREM, Accounting and reporting of GHG emissions from real estate operations: Technical guidance for the financial industry (Version 1.0), 2023, https://crrem.org/wp-content/uploads/2025/05/PCAF-GRESB-CRREM-GHG_emissions_real_estate_guidance_1.0.pdf, accessed 26.06.2025.

398 For more details on CRREM and its methodology, see www.crrem.org.

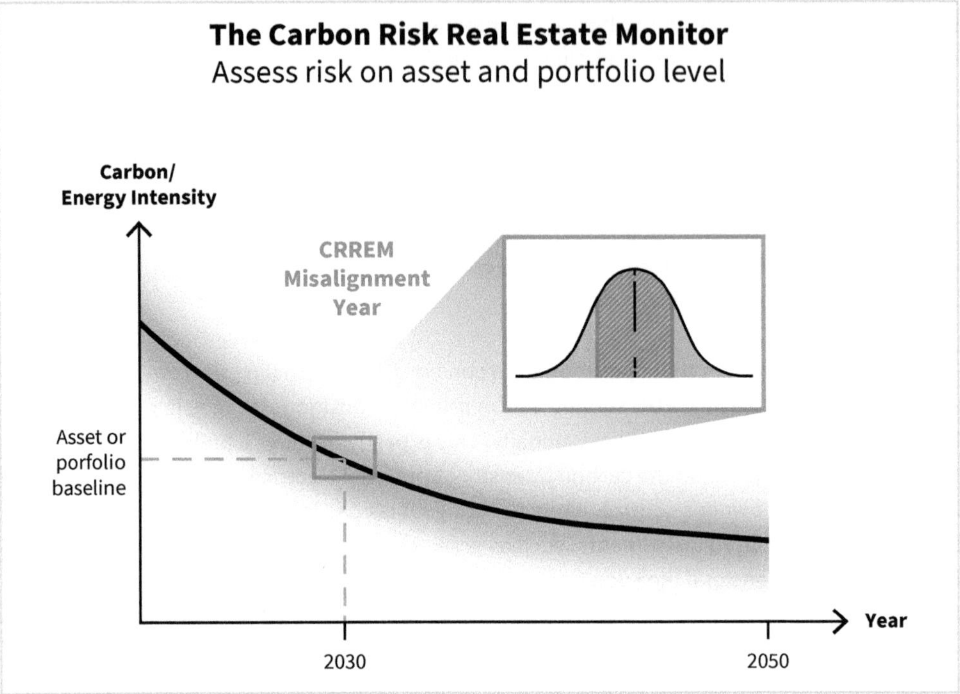

Figure 21: Illustration of CRREM risk assessment. Source: Own illustration, © 2025 CRREM Foundation

The core application of the CRREM Pathways lies in identifying an asset's »**CRREM Misalignment Year**«, which is defined as the first year in which a building's carbon or energy intensity exceeds the corresponding CRREM threshold (see **Figure 21**).

The CRREM Misalignment Year is an **early warning system** and an important piece of information to help investors identify transition risks. However, just as an investment manager would never consider one key valuation metric in isolation, it is advisable to complement the CRREM risk assessment with additional asset-specific and market-based analyses for a more comprehensive view. It is essential to **place an asset's CRREM performance within the broader context** of local regulations, tenant demand, lease structure and length, capital market conditions, and how the asset itself differs from the market average due to atypical use patterns or other potential causes of deviation.

> The **CRREM Pathways reflect the market average** for a given asset type and region (see asset level input sheet, **Figure 22**). This information should be considered when making a judgment about the transition risk of an asset. This additional supportive context is what helps turn isolated CRREM results into meaningful transition risk assessments.

4.2.4 CRREM in practice: Application and operational considerations

The **practical application of the CRREM Pathways** can be found not only in the tools developed by CRREM Partners, but also in the free, Excel-based **CRREM Risk Assessment Tool**.[399] The tool visualizes projected building emissions and energy intensity against the CRREM Pathways over time. It factors in future conditions, such as the decarbonization of electricity grids, making it easier to identify retrofitting needs, explore energy alternatives, and plan interventions that keep buildings aligned with long-term climate goals.

399 The CRREM Risk Assessment Tool is available for free download at: https://crrem.org/crrem-risk-assessment-tool/.

ASSET LEVEL INPUT

The asset level input sheet serves as main section for entering data on individual assets that is necessary to conduct the CRREM transition risk analysis.
Users may employ the plus- and minus-signs above column headers to collapse and expand data groups.

Please note: All input and output parameters in square metre [m²] and Euro [$]

		General information						General information
Asset ID	Inclusion	Asset Name	Reporting year	Gross Asset Value (GAV)	Reporting period		Entity	
					Starting month	Months of data		
Pre-filled		Mandatory	Mandatory	Optional (required for calculating certain risk indicators)	Mandatory	Mandatory	Optional (for further possibilities of aggregation)	
	Dropdown	Text	Year	[$]	Drop-down	Number of Months	Text	
ID	*INC*	*NAME*	*AS.YR*	*GAV*	*AS.MON*	*AS.LENG*	*ENT*	
1	Include	Asset 1	2024	35.526.000	January	12		
2	Exclude		2024		January	12		
3	Exclude		2024		January	12		

Building characteristics									Total energy procurement				
					Property type	Air conditioning	Asset size		Whole building total energy procurement Combined energy procurement of Common Areas + Tenant Space Energy procured by tenants and base building services to lettable/leasable and common spaces. This should include all energy supplied to the building				
Country	City	Zip Code / HDD & CDD Code	Address	Pathway			Total gross internal area (IPMS 2)	Average annual vacant area	Grid Electricity			Natural gas	
									Usage	Data Coverage	Maximum Coverage	Usage	Data Coverage
Mandatory	Optional (only to be displayed in results)	Mandatory	Optional (only to be displayed in results)	automatically chosen by ZIP mapping	Mandatory	Optional	Mandatory	Mandatory		Mandatory if usage ≠ 0	Mandatory if usage ≠ 0		Mandatory if usage ≠ 0
Drop-down *COUN*	Text *CITY*	Text/Numbers *ZIP/ CODE*	Text *Address*		Type of use *AS.TY*	Drop-down AC.YN	[m²] TO.FL	[m²] BSR_OC.AN	[kWh] EL.GRID	[m²] EL.DC	[m²] EL.MC	[kWh] NG.CON	[m²] NG.DC
USA	Chicago	60616	Michigan Ave	RFCWc_Cool_5A	Office	No	17.692	-	1.942.382	17.692	17.692	1.486.720	17.692

Figure 22: Screenshot from the CRREM Risk Assessment Tool – Asset Level Input sheet

By entering data such as building characteristics and energy consumption (see **Figure 22**), users can generate CRREM key performance indicators (KPIs), including the estimated »**CRREM Misalignment Year**«, which indicates the first year in which the building's carbon or energy intensity exceeds the corresponding CRREM threshold (see **Figure 23**). This signals when a property may experience increased transition risk if no improvement measures are taken.

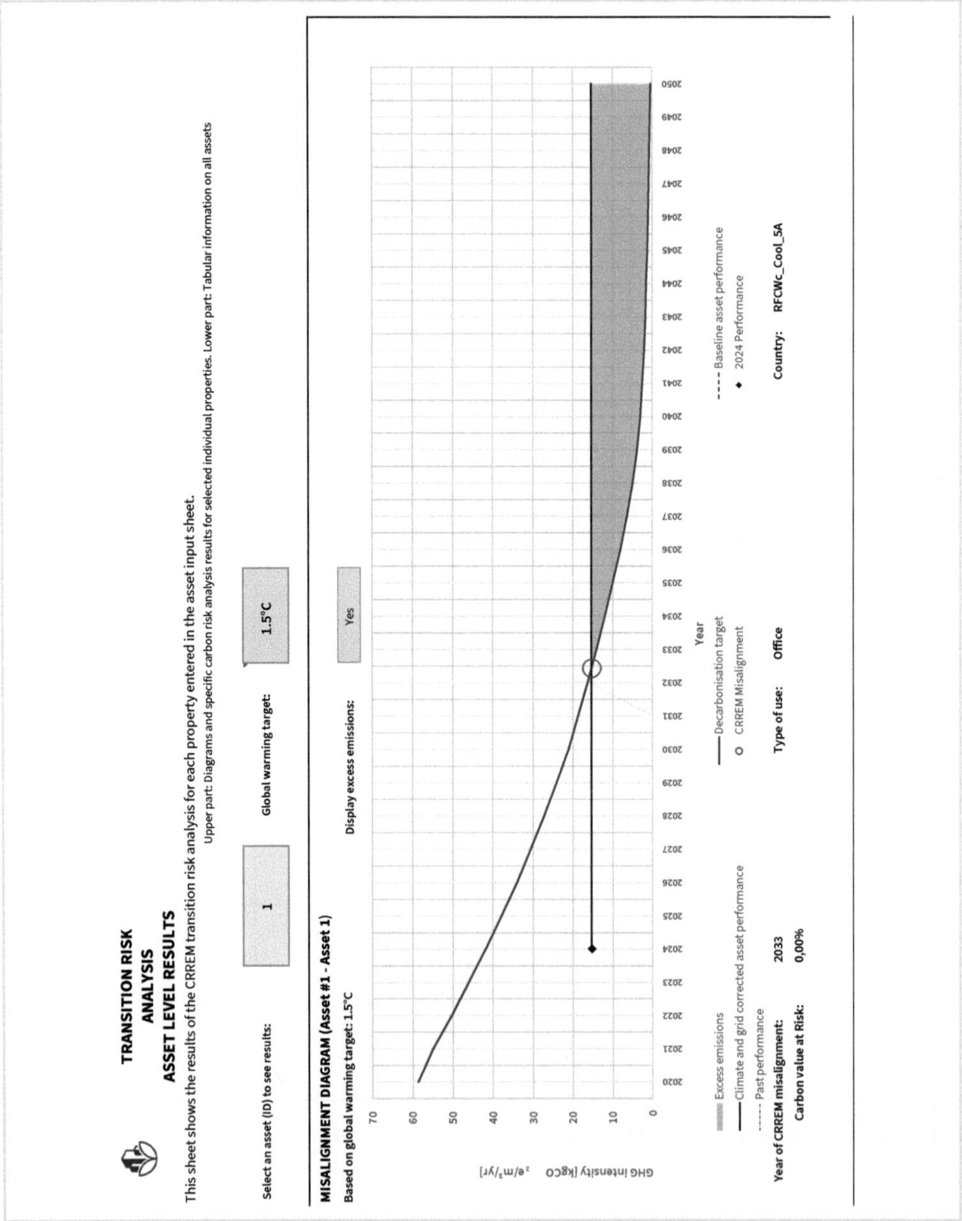

Figure 23: Screenshot from the CRREM Risk Assessment Tool – Misalignment Diagram

To obtain meaningful results from a CRREM analysis, asset data should be entered **comprehensively and be representative of normal operating conditions**. However, in many cases, only some of the required data is available, and certain input parameters are inherently difficult to estimate. As a result, working with the CRREM Risk Assessment Tool may involve certain considerations regarding the input data. **Table 29 provides an overview of common input-related questions and offers guidance on how to address them.**

Input-related question	Recommended approach
Whole-building energy data Neither metered data available, nor submetering of individual areas in available.	Recommended hierarchy for data: (1) Estimated building energy consumption per floor area based on official building energy labels **(consumption EPC)** AND the floor area (2) Estimated building energy consumption per floor area based on official building energy labels **(demand EPC)** AND the floor area (3) Estimated building energy consumption per floor area based on building type and location-specific statistical data AND the floor area (4) Estimated building energy consumption per building based on building type and location-specific statistical data, AND the number of buildings
Atypical energy consumption Energy consumption is not representative of typical asset usage, and/or cannot be attributed to the carbon budget of the building sector.	Energy use can be normalized for carbon risk management (note: GHG accounting and reporting allows less flexibility). This includes, for example, EV charging or industrial processes within a building, but not amenities typical of the asset class, such as a swimming pool for the asset class hotel. Although the tool doesn't support considering process-specific loads, such uses can be documented separately. Creating a »second asset« within the tool can help explain why an efficient building may appear misaligned.
Asset type not covered by CRREM The asset type is not yet represented by a specific CRREM pathway or is not clearly assignable.	Asset types not explicitly covered by CRREM (e.g., student housing or life sciences) can be approximated using blended pathways within the tool's »mixed-use« function – for instance, by combining the multi-family residential and lodging/leisure pathways for student housing, or the office and healthcare pathways for life sciences properties.
Floor area covered by CRREM How to treat areas that represent a large share of floor space but a small share of energy use	All gross internal area (GIA) should generally be included in CRREM analysis. However, it is advisable to proportionally exclude extensive areas with minimal energy consumption such as parking garages or large basement areas to avoid distorting energy and carbon intensity results.

Table 29: Guidance for handling typical data inputs in CRREM assessments

The CRREM analysis serves as an **early-warning system for transition risks** and provides the foundation to quantify their financial impact. Translating this technical gap into investment valuations allows investors to understand the costs and benefits associated with different mitigation strategies.

In direct and non-listed real estate markets – where more detailed data on asset characteristics and energy performance is typically available – transition risks are often reflected explicitly, for example through adjustments to income projections, operating costs, or capital expenditures. In contrast, listed markets tend to rely on the implicit integration of CRREM results, with transition risk exposure priced into higher return requirements or adjustments to the weighted average cost of capital (WACC). In either case, care must be taken to avoid double-counting risk factors across multiple valuation inputs.

Nevertheless, mitigating transition risks is not just a technical challenge. It also depends on having the right data to translate findings into investment decisions. Only risks supported by robust, asset-specific information can be credibly quantified and priced. **Figure 24** illustrates **one possible approach to converting a CRREM analysis into an investment valuation**, which bridges the gap between risk assessment and investment action.

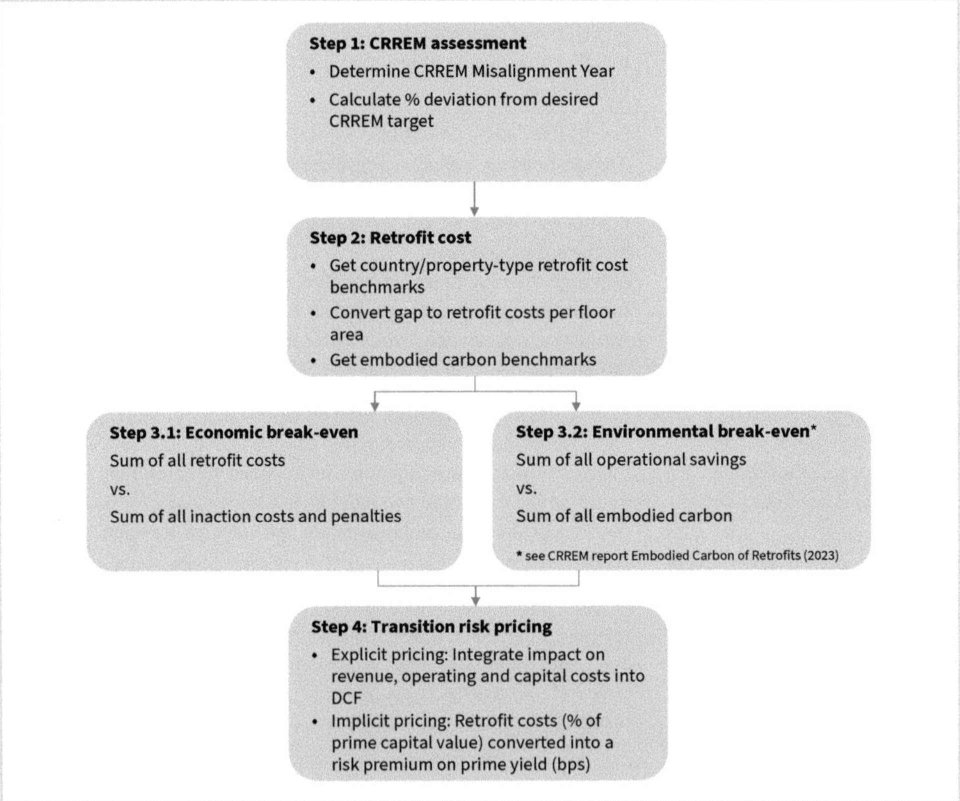

Figure 24: Integrating the results of a CRREM assessment into asset valuation. Source: Own illustration, © 2025 CRREM Foundation

4.3 More than operations: Deep dive into water

Astrid Wunderle

> *«All is here. … Not in the mind, because the mind will either follow illusions, or either follow the heart. The mind is the decoder, that decides how to treat information. Information comes either from an external source or from the heart vortex. Truth is found throughout the mid-vortex, the heart, for it connects to the whole universe. You see, emotions are fluids, like an invisible water.«*[400]
>
> – Elena Danaan

4.3.1 Vortex, water, wealth. Introduction to #4.3

In the years leading up to 2030, no stone will be left unturned. There will be no standstill or balance. New companies will appear on the scene, and established ones will disappear. New goods will be produced, existing ones will be modified or disappear from the market, just as new production methods will emerge.

In the course of this dynamic, the structure of the economy will constantly change, and what was valid yesterday will no longer be valid today. This means that there are always new opportunities for newcomers. In a market economy, the cards are constantly being reshuffled. The same happens during economic crises when asset prices fall. These times of crisis open up new opportunities for new companies with new ideas.

My wish for us is that instead of lamenting the crises, we understand them for what they are: phases of economic transformation. Time for orientation – let's make the best of it by moving in harmony with the laws of nature.

#4.3	**#4.3.1 – intro to #4.3**
VORTEX WATER	**#4.3.2 – my WHY – vortex**
WEALTH	**#4.3.3 – the FUTURE – water and life force**
	#4.3.4 – the PRESENT
	#4.3.5 – the HOW – forces of nature

In this subchapter #4.3, under the category of WHY, we review the laws of nature (#4.3.2), under the category of FUTURE, we look into where (impact) investments should be made (#4.3.3), in the category of PRESENT, we discuss a project that has been realized (#4.3.4) and with HOW we discuss examples of future technologies (#4.3.5).

400 Danaan, Elena, The Seeders: The Return Of The Gods, 2022, https://www.elenadanaan.org/the-seeders-return-of-the-gods, accessed 31.08.2025.

4.3.2 My WHY

Cosmic cycles can never be reversed, and the next cycles can no longer be stopped with the old paradigms. Through my deep understanding of both economic and natural growth cycles, I have realized the connection between our planet's water and our bodily waters (cell water). Our health and inFORMation are not only a matter of purity and oxygen content, but also follow the natural laws of life.

#Water's spiritual and energetic properties
#Water's potential to store memory and consciousness
#Water's ability to respond to intentions and frequencies

I would like to invite you to imagine the current geopolitical chaos as a vortex that, thanks to our trained consciousness, can be steered in a meaningful way that promotes life.

Vortex: Why vortex formation brings cooling
The concept of water with vortex formation became popular and internationally known through the work of the legendary Austrian natural scientist Viktor Schauberger. Schauberger spent much of his life researching water. This led him to the conviction that water gains a special »vitality« when it flows in the form of whirlpools.

A century ago, Schauberger followed Rudolf Steiner, whose fields of activity included *»biodynamic agriculture«*. To this day, farmers and fruit growers value swirling water and can produce harvests of astonishing abundance without fertilizer (food with a demonstrably high bioavailability).

Today, Gerald Pollack is one of the researchers offering us groundbreaking discoveries. Pollack has succeeded in making the vortex phenomenon measurable. Swirling brings water into constant contact with oxygen from the bubbles below. As a result, the water is constantly mixed with oxygen.

Vortex technology is being used successfully in a number of international projects. Even though it is ancient knowledge that is now accepted as fundamental wisdom, chemicals are still being used, and the natural order has not yet received its due appreciation. This is already different in Middle Eastern countries. Due to the reconstruction work that always follows geopolitical cycles, we will see the largest and most effective investments here.

4.3.3 The FUTURE

Why should we be concerned about the quality of water? Water exists in four phases: solid, liquid, vapor, and liquid crystalline water (fourth phase water), also called »exclusion zone« or »EZ« water. The core meaning of water's importance to our health is nothing new, but it has been progressively forgotten. With various schools of science emphasizing molecular, atomic, and even subatomic levels, we have lost sight of what happens when all the pieces/elements come together to form a larger, more holistic entity. The whole may indeed exceed the sum of its parts. 99% of those parts are water molecules. To think that 99% of our molecules merely bathe the »more important« molecules of life ignores centuries of evidence to the contrary. Water plays a central role in all aspects of life.

Until recently, our understanding of water's properties was limited by the common misconception that water has three phases. We now know it has four. Taking this fourth phase into account allows many of water's »anomalies« to vanish, turning them into predictable features. Water becomes more understandable, and so do entities made largely of water, such as oceans, clouds, and human beings.[401]

4.3.4 The PRESENT – We are on the threshold of the greatest upheaval in living memory

The next step is to examine experience with water cleaning. The press release for the flagship project on the biological cleaning of polluted water from oil production, which was awarded by the United Nations (UN) and others, reads as follows:

> «World's largest reed bed treatment plant in operation for 10 years
> After ten years of operation, a total of approx. 1.275 million tons of CO_2 emissions have been saved – according to estimates, by the end of operations in 2044, it will save 4.5 million tons of CO_2.

Nimr, Oman – In the middle of a desert landscape in Oman, BAUER Nimr LLC, a local subsidiary of BAUER Resources GmbH, has now been operating the world's largest commercial reed bed treatment plant for ten years. With an area of 13.5 km^2, it is roughly the size of 1,600 football fields. It can even be seen on satellite images. The plant is a multi-award-winning flagship project for the biological cleaning of polluted water from oil production at the Nimr oil field in the south of the country, with the first phase of the project completed by Bauer Nimr in 2011. After just three weeks, the plant achieved its first milestone: »We were able to significantly outperform the contractually agreed cleaning capacity of 45,000 m^3 per day,« reports Ulrich Emmer,

401 Pollack, Gerald, the fourth phase of water, Compendium Volume 2 Number 2, January 2019, https://bio4climate.org/article/water-isnt-what-you-think-it-is-the-fourth-phase-of-water-by-gerald-pollack/, accessed 24.06.2025.

Managing Director of Bauer Nimr. Construction work was successfully completed in 2019 with the third and final expansion. At peak times, up to 175,000 m^3 of polluted water currently runs through the plant in one day, and a total of 370 million m^3 of water has been cleaned with excellent results so far: By the end of the process, a hydrocarbon content of less than 0.5 mg/l is achieved. Nearly 95% of the crude oil in the water can be removed or recovered without using energy or chemicals. What makes this innovatively constructed wetland one-of-a-kind is not only its size and remarkable cleaning performance, but also the new standards it sets for sustainability: By treating contaminated water using natural flow processes in the form of graduated settling pits and reusing the purified waste water on the surface, it is no longer necessary to use energy-intensive pumps for circulation or for discharging residual amounts into the subsoil. »After ten years of operation, a total of approx. 1.275 million tons of CO_2 emissions have been saved – according to estimates, by the end of operations in 2044, it will save 4.5 million tons of CO_2,« explains Dr. Roman Breuer, Managing Director of BAUER Resources GmbH.

«In addition to this, with approx. 1.5 billion reed plants, the former desert landscape also provides a habitat for more than 140 animal species including numerous birds, fish and reptiles.

With an order volume of roughly 600 million US dollars over its entire period of operation, the reed bed treatment plant in Oman is one of the most significant projects run by Bauer Resources and we will continue operation for another 23 years,« concludes Dr. Roman Breuer.[402]

4.3.5 The HOW – Using the forces of nature

We are all aware that clean water is vital – it is a force of life. Up until now, we have tolerated the pollution of our environment, including our water sources. If you're reading this, it's no accident – you're one of the **New 1%**, the quiet revolutionaries and vibrational architects of a reborn world.

You've felt it: the old systems are creaking and groaning as they collapse, but we don't flinch. We don't panic. We ***pivot.*** Because we're not here to play by the outdated rules of a dying world – we're here to **rebuild it**, radiant and renewed.

Out with the old. In with the aligned.

At **awas fee GmbH, research and development** are based on contemporary considerations involving natural physical processes.[403]

402 Bauer Group, World's largest reed bed treatment plant in operation for 10 years, Press Release 26.01.2021, https://resources.bauer.de/en/media/1092/download?inline, accessed 24.06.2025.

403 Abscheider zum Trennen eines Zweiphasen-Flüssigkeitsgemisches in Leichtflüssigkeit und Schwerflüssigkeit, Patent EP 0 960 643 A1, 01.12.1999 Patentblatt 1999/48, Erfinder: Heinz Ihne, www.awas-fee.de.

The new spiral shape developed for the **Vortex Separator System** is derived from the motion mechanism of the galaxies – mechanisms which cause light bodies to move inward toward the center and heavy bodies to move outward.

The task of the invention is to provide a separator that improves the separation of the two-phase liquid mixture into light liquid and heavy liquid, particularly in the case of oil-contaminated and possibly sludge-bearing water, possibly with small inflow quantities.

The asymmetrical design of the lower partition wall allows floated particles, micelles, and light liquid droplets, which may remain in the heavy liquid escaping at the bottom, to rise in the separator on the side of the inlet pipe, i. e. as far away as possible from the outlet pipe, so that they do not immediately exit but remain in the separator and can be trapped.

During prolonged operation, a circular flow also forms in the separator tank under the influence of the circular flow in the collector. This allows the final suspended particles, micelles, and droplets to be retained by a baffle and returned to the collector from an upper area of the baffle.

Four different laws of nature have been harmoniously implemented in a single system, in which the only source of energy needed is a drop height of about 10 cm.

> ***1. Centrifugal and centripetal forces:*** *While heavy particles move outwards centrifugally towards the baffles and are deposited, light liquids simultaneously flow inwards towards the inner walls, i. e. centripetally.*
>
> *The result: A dual effect for the purification of waste water.*
>
> ***2. The pulsating force:*** *The baffles in the spiral are spaced at different distances apart. As a result, the flowing motion is slower in some places and faster in others. This produces the desired pulsating flow, which optimally supports the coalescence effect (fine separation) of the oil droplets.*
>
> *A point worth noting is the non-clogging passage, with a width of ≥ 60mm.*
>
> ***3. The adhesive force:*** *Whereas the outer walls of the spiral system are designed to be oil-repellent («**oleophobic**«), the inner wall is coated with composite material which attracts oil.*
>
> *A self-cleaning system.*
>
> ***4. Coalescence induced by circulation and vortex action:*** *In these GALAXIE separator systems, the oil accumulates at the center as a result of the slow circulatory flow. It is precisely there that the oils are removed from the surface via the funnel that is located there.*

> *The vortex-induced suction energy draws even the finest of oil films toward the center.*
>
> *Due to the flow, oil droplets detach from the baffle and float toward the center.*

Why can the observation of the investment have such a great value to us? This builds on a huge project that is 100 % aligned with all aspects of sustainability/ESG and was implemented at a time when sustainability/ESG was not yet mainstream. Without a doubt, water is essential for all life. When the water stops moving within us (which is the blood), life ends essentially. It is time for realignment. Let's make the most of it by moving in harmony with the laws of nature.

We are at a turning point where we have the constant interface between sustainability / ESG, ESG, disruption and AI. Each one of us can ask ourselves: Is this a process of creative destruction or a process of creative facilitation?

4.4 Brownfield investments: Forward-looking opportunities and challenges

Raphael Thießen

«Sustainability starts with the ground – not just with the building itself.«
– Raphael Thießen

4.4.1 Introduction to #4.4

The future of brownfield investments is closely tied to political and economic developments. A clear distinction between brownfields and other construction activities and political support through targeted incentives are crucial. A well-structured contractual framework and the involvement of experienced experts can ensure the success of brownfield projects. Despite the challenges, brownfield investments offer great opportunities for sustainable urban development and responsible resource management. Moreover, they are the future – without a doubt.

#4.4	**#4.4.1 – intro to #4.4**
Brownfield investments	**#4.4.2 – definition of a brownfield**
	#4.4.3 – political classification of brownfields
	#4.4.4 – the myth of land scarcity
	#4.4.5 – incentives & implementation into contracts

This subchapter #4.4 covers the definition (#4.4.2) and political classification of brownfields (#4.4.3), the myth of land scarcity (#4.4.4), as well as opportunities through incentives and contractual solutions (#4.4.5).

4.4.2 Definition of a brownfield

According to the **German Brownfield Association (Deutscher Brownfield Verband, DEBV)**, a brownfield refers to a previously used plot of land that exists with or without structural facilities, regardless of its location, and whose reuse may be hindered by structural conditions or existing contamination. Such plots require material or immaterial investments for new development. These areas are usually already developed and have planning permissions.[404] The definition of the DEBV aligns with the US-Environmental Protection Agency's (EPA) common definition and is also agreed upon by other European brownfield stakeholders.[405]

The importance of differentiation: It is necessary to make a clear distinction between brownfield development and building on existing structures. While brownfield development often requires soil interventions, this is not usually the case with building on existing structures. Both concepts are distinct topics, with brownfield development requiring more intensive planning and development.

4.4.3 Political classification of brownfields

Sustainability strategies and political goals: The development of brownfields is politically significant. Without this development, achieving the set sustainability goals will not be possible. The German sustainability strategy calls for reducing the daily increase in settlement and traffic areas to less than 30 hectares per day by 2030 and achieving net-zero consumption by 2050. This demand underscores the importance of revitalizing brownfields. The goal of reducing new land sealing is not just a purely German issue, but one demanded at the entire EU level. Similar discussions are currently taking place in Austria, Belgium, and France, and the UK.[406]

Recent data shows that the average daily land consumption in Germany between 2019 and 2022 was still around 52 hectares – far from the 2030 goal of less than 30 hectares per day.[407]

404 DEBV, Wie definiert der DEBV ein Brownfield?, https://deutscherbrownfieldverband.de/media/site/5a169a257d-1718194962/debv_rubrik-erklaerbaer_brownfield_01.pdf, accessed 31.08.2025.

405 EPA, Brownfield Overview and Definition, https://19january2017snapshot.epa.gov/brownfields/brownfield-overview-and-definition_.html, accessed 31.08.2025.

406 Bundesministerium für Umwelt, Klimaschutz, Naturschutz und nukleare Sicherheit (BMUKN), Flächenverbrauch – Worum geht es?, https://www.bmuv.de/themen/nachhaltigkeit/strategie-und-umsetzung/reduzierung-des-flaechenverbrauchs, accessed 31.08.2025.

407 BMUKN, Flächenverbrauch, According to the World Green Building Council (WGBC), regenerating brownfield sites can also provide social value to people in the community: World Green Building Council (WGBC), Beyond The Business Case – Why You Can't Afford Not To Invest in a Sustainable Built Environment, https://worldgbc.org/wp-content/uploads/2022/08/WorldGBC-Beyond-the-Business-Case.pdf, accessed 31.08.2025.

The EU confirmed its goal of net-zero land use by 2050 through the 2021 Soil Strategy, although it remains non-binding.[408]

EU taxonomy and political direction: The EU taxonomy also reflects the political pressure to promote sustainable development and highlights the necessity of revitalizing brownfields. Whether the goal of zero-hectare consumption by 2050 will be achieved remains to be seen, but the direction is clearly set.

4.4.4 The myth of land scarcity

As of 2025, Austria will introduce a national brownfield funding scheme. The Altlastenfonds (contaminated site fund) was expanded by a 2024 legal amendment to also support less-contaminated sites. Private developers can receive subsidies of 20–40 % of remediation costs.[409]

Land scarcity is a myth: There is often discussion about land scarcity in Germany and other European countries. The German Brownfield Association has taken initial steps with a nationwide AI-supported potential land registry to inventory potential areas, especially in the commercial sector. This shows that there are numerous areas, but they are often not located in the agglomeration areas preferred by project developers. Nevertheless, these areas offer numerous opportunities. It is important to find suitable concepts and users for them.

A model similar to that of the DEBV is currently being rolled out in Austria. Unlike the models in Germany, all potential brownfields are to be recorded by the end of 2024 and made accessible to the public. The DEBV also intends to take a similar path. All members will be allowed to access the data collection.

France launched the »Fonds Friches« program, providing €750 million between 2021 and 2022 to reactivate over 1,000 hectares of brownfield sites. This initiative continues under the »fonds vert« through 2025.[410]

---

408 Communication From the Commission to the European Parliament, the Council, the European Economic and Social Committee and the Committee of the Regions EU Soil Strategy, https://eur-lex.europa.eu/legal-content/DE/TXT/?uri=CELEX%3A52021DC0699, accessed 31.08.2025.

409 Federal Ministry Agriculture and Forestry, Climate and Environmental Protection, Regions and Water Management, Contaminated site management, https://www.bmluk.gv.at/en/topics/climate-environment/waste-and-circular-economy/contaminated-site-management.html, accessed 31.08.2025.

410 Ministère de la Transition écologique, Recyclage des friches: lancement de la 3e édition du fonds friches, https://www.ecologie.gouv.fr/actualites/recyclage-friches-lancement-3e-edition-du-fonds-friches, accessed 31.08.2025.

4.4.5 Incentives and implementation into contracts

Subsidies and political incentives: Currently, there are few incentives in Germany for the development of brownfields compared to greenfields (e.g. undeveloped land, typically in a rural or suburban area). The existing subsidies are inconsistently coordinated and insufficient at the municipal and national levels. Many developers also find the bureaucratic effort too high. One positive example, though only accessible to municipalities, is the Contaminated Sites Association («Verband für Flächenrecycling und Altlastensanierung«, AAV) in North Rhine-Westphalia (NRW)[411], which supports municipalities in developing municipal brownfield sites. They can apply for subsidies to revitalize areas that are difficult to sell. Additionally, the AAV, with its expertise, takes over the tendering and supervision of the work if needed. Opening the association to the private sector would be desirable. The authority's expertise is unique and could help accelerate approval processes, as the individual small municipalities would not have to maintain specialized personnel. However, the prerequisite would be that the municipalities allow themselves to be supported by the authority.[412]

EU level: At the EU level, there are funds available, such as those from the European Investment Bank, but most of these funds flow to France. A remarkable model exists in Belgium with the Covenant Act of OVAM, which provides subsidies for companies that want to develop brownfields. These models could serve as examples for Germany. Here, project developers are assigned a fixed project manager from the administration who ensures that the development is completed on time and meets the goals for all parties. This model has proven immensely successful in recent years.[413]

Importance of a clear contractual framework: A well-structured contractual framework is essential for successfully developing brownfields. Transparent communication between project developers, municipalities, and former owners are crucial. A transparent contractual framework ensures that all parties know what to expect and enables smooth project development.

Involvement of experts: Involving appraisers and experienced service providers from the beginning is important to minimize risks and ensure well-founded planning. All parties must work openly and cooperatively to create a win-win situation.

Long-term financing perspective: Currently, brownfield investments in Germany (still) do not offer better financing conditions than greenfield projects, although this has been discussed repeatedly in recent years. It would be desirable for sustainable investments to be financed

411 NRW is one of 16 federal states in Germany.

412 AAV, Deshalb braucht NRW den AAV, https://www.aav-nrw.de/hintergrund.html, accessed 31.08.2025.

413 European Investment Bank (EIB), Brownfields Redevelopment Fund, https://www.eib.org/de/products/equity/funds/brownfields-redevelopment-fund, accessed 31.08.2025, OVAM, Brownfieldconvenant, https://www.vlaio.be/nl/subsidies-financiering/brownfieldconvenant/, accessed 31.08.2025, Interreg Europe, Brownfieldcovenants as an instrument to revitalize former landfill sites, 2019, https://www.interregeurope.eu/good-practices/brownfieldcovenants-as-an-instrument-to-revitalize-former-landfill-sites, accessed 31.08.2025.

preferentially in the future to increase political and societal acceptance of brownfield developments. Additionally, the authorities could introduce a fast-track process for projects that prefer brownfields or building on existing structures over greenfields. This could encourage more actors to engage with this topic.

Model from Canada: One example of a successful incentive model comes from Canada, where companies are encouraged to develop brownfields through tax breaks and other financial incentives. Such models could also be implemented in Germany to promote brownfield development. One option would be to waive the property tax for a set number of years. Thus, the project developer does not receive subsidies in the traditional sense, but rather earns a return later. They also help with the settlement of (preferably) high-quality commercial and residential areas to generate a corresponding return. The municipality thus receives a completed development including users, which promises corresponding tax revenues in the long term.[414]

4.5 Insurance and climate adaptation

Romy Tenbieg

Insurance is not just protection – it's a catalyst for climate-resilient real estate investment.

4.5.1 Introduction to #4.5

Climate change has increased the frequency and intensity of extreme weather events, highlighting the critical role of insurance in managing climate risks. This chapter examines how insurance can help mitigate financial losses, promote recovery, and support climate adaptation efforts. The chapter discusses the challenges that insurers face due to rising climate risks and emphasizes the need for collaboration across sectors. It also explores how insurance can incentivize investments in climate-resilient infrastructure and real estate.

#4.5	**#4.5.1 – intro to #4.5**
Insurance & climate adaptation	**#4.5.2 – insurance in climate risk management**
	#4.5.3 – challenges & need for collaboration
	#4.5.4 – adaptation measures

This subchapter #4.5 follows the headlines: the role of insurance in climate risk management (#4.5.2), challenges to insurability and the need for collaboration (#4.5.3), and the role of adaptation measures (#4.5.4).

414 City of Calgary, Brownfield Tax Incentive Program, https://www.calgary.ca/environment/programs/brownfield-tax-incentive.html#:~:text=The%20Brownfield%20Tax%20Incentive%20Program,from%20increased%20assessed%20property%20value, accessed 31.08.2025; government of Ontario, Brownfields financial tax incentive program, https://www.ontario.ca/page/brownfields-financial-tax-incentive-program, accessed 31.08.2025.

The discussion emphasizes the urgency of integrating insurance with effective adaptation strategies to ensure long-term resilience in the face of climate change.

What do we mean by **climate adaptation**, what do we mean by **insurance and insurance types in property investment**? Please see **Table 30** for a brief illustration.

Topic	Meaning (in a nutshell)
Climate adaptation	Adjusting to climate impacts
Insurance & real estate investment	Risk transfer for property loss to mitigates financial risks
Insurance types:	
Property insurance	Covers damage to buildings (often includes natural hazard insurance)
Natural hazard insurance	Covers damages from natural hazards (often includes flood insurance)
Flood insurance	Protects against flood losses
Title insurance	Secures ownership rights
Liability insurance	Covers third-party legal claims or injuries
Environmental insurance	Covers environmental damage risks
Rent loss insurance	Compensates for lost rental income

Table 30: Climate adaptation, insurance in property investment & insurance types

4.5.2 The role of insurance in climate risk management

Insurance plays a critical role in mitigating the financial losses caused by climate-driven extreme weather events, such as floods, storms, and wildfires. As these events become increasingly frequent and intense due to climate change, they put increasing pressure on the broader economy.[415] By absorbing these losses, insurance facilitates recovery, enhances resilience, and contributes to economic stability.[416] It provides the flow of capital necessary for communities and infrastructure to recover quickly from disasters. In the absence of adequate coverage, the financial burden of recovery falls primarily on individuals, governments, or aid organizations. This can strain public budgets and create significant economic and social challenges for those affected. Countries with higher levels of insurance coverage tend to recover more swiftly from disasters, and governments are increasingly recognizing the value of insurance in transferring disaster-related risks.[417]

415 Swiss Re Institute, The economics of climate change: no action not an option, 2021, 22.
416 IPCC, Summary for Policymakers, 2022, p. 9.
417 Swiss Re Institute, The economics of climate change: no action not an option, 2021, 22; Jarzabkowski/Chalkias/Clarke/Iyahen/Stadtmueller/Zwick, Insurance for climate adaptation: Opportunities and limitations, 2019.

Insurance not only helps with recovery and fosters a deeper understanding of climate change risks. It plays a key role in promoting measures that individuals, businesses, and communities can implement to improve their protection against disasters driven by climate change. For instance, insurance companies' risk assessment expertise can provide economic benefits for implementing flood protection measures or modifying construction practices, such as where and how buildings are constructed to better withstand future climate impacts.[418] Without access to adequate insurance, the ability to recover from climate-related disasters would be severely limited, potentially exacerbating economic instability.[419]

The importance of insurance is also recognized in the United Nations' Sustainable Development Goals (SDGs), where it is acknowledged as a key mechanism for strengthening societal resilience and ensuring sustainable development.[420] Additionally, international frameworks, such as the Paris Agreement, are increasingly influencing how insurers assess risks and support climate adaptation strategies on a global scale.[421]

4.5.3 Challenges to insurability and the need for collaboration

However, rising natural disaster damages, cumulative risks, and escalating costs are increasingly burdening the insurance industry.

> In fact, insured losses from extreme weather events have surged by as much as 250 % over the last 30 years.[422] From 2000 to 2019, total global insured losses from extreme weather amounted to US $2.86 trillion, averaging US $143 billion per year.[423]

In many high-risk areas, some risks are becoming uninsurable due to constraints on both the supply of coverage (availability of insurance) and the demand for it (affordability of premiums). This challenge is particularly evident with regard to flood insurance in regions such as Europe, the United States, and parts of Sub-Saharan Africa, where poor land use practices, inadequate building regulations, and the intensification of climate change effects are driving up insurance premiums and reducing the availability of coverage.[424]

---

418 Jarzabkowski/Chalkias/Clarke/Iyahen/Stadtmueller/Zwick, Insurance for climate adaptation: Opportunities and limitations, 2019.
419 Swiss Re Institute, The economics of climate change: no action not an option, 2021, 22.
420 United Nations, Transforming our world: the 2030 Agenda for Sustainable Development, 2015, p. 20.
421 Golnaraghi/Bresch/Höppe/Löffler/Nagamura/Rauch, COP 21 Paris Agreement: What Does It Mean for the (Re) insurance Sector?, 2016, 1–2.
422 Gupta/Venkataraman, Insurance and climate change, in: Environmental Sustainability, Volume 67, 2024.
423 Newman/Noy, The global costs of extreme weather that are attributable to climate change, *at Commun* 14, 6103, 2023, 3.
424 Prudential Regulation Authority and Bank of England, The impact of climate change on the UK insurance sector, 2015; Swiss Re Institute, The economics of climate change: no action not an option, 2021, 22.

Given the rapid evolution of climate change risks, it is crucial for insurance markets to enhance their ability to effectively signal risks and develop strategies to mitigate the economic impact of these losses.[425]

As certain risks become uninsurable, collaboration between reinsurers, insurers, government and other stakeholders becomes essential to maintaining insurance as a crucial tool for managing climate risks. This collaboration is vital to maintain the insurability of high-risk areas and strengthen climate resilience across sectors, including real estate. Reinsurers, in particular are already collaborating closely with clients to support the transition to a low-carbon economy. They accomplish this by incorporating insurance and investment strategies that promote sustainability, encourage behavioral changes, adjust risk prices, and develop new, innovative products to address emerging risks.[426] These efforts not only aim to mitigate the impacts of climate change and protect real estate investments by enhancing resilience.[427] The expertise of the insurance industry in identifying risks can be highly beneficial for local communities, governments, and real estate investors, especially when engaging with emerging markets where such risk data and strategies have not traditionally been used.[428]

4.5.4 The role of adaptation measures

Sustainable management of climate risks requires a multi-faceted approach, as part of a comprehensive climate adaptation strategy. It combines insurance, preventive measures, such as building regulations and climate adaptation strategies, and robust government regulation. Together, these efforts help close the insurance gaps and ensure that high insurance penetration is maintained, which is crucial for stabilizing real estate asset values. Adaptation measures, such as enforcing building codes, improving flood protection, and discouraging settlement in high-risk areas, complement insurance by reducing risk and preventing damage.[429]

> For instance, the **Netherlands** provides a valuable example of successful climate adaptation. Through collaboration between the government, the private sector, and the insurance industry, the country has developed comprehensive flood protection strategies, such as wet floodproofing, which limits the potential damage once water has entered a building, and dry floodproofing, which attempts to prevent water from entering a building. Additionally, sustainable urban planning, and an insurance framework that ensures high-risk properties remain insurable have been implemented.

425 Gupta/Venkataraman, Insurance and climate change, in: Environmental Sustainability, Volume 67, 2024.
426 Gupta/Venkataraman, Insurance and climate change, in: Environmental Sustainability, Volume 67, 2024; EIOPA, Policy measures to reduce climate-related insurance protection gaps, 2023.
427 Swiss Re Institute, The economics of climate change: no action not an option, 2021, 22.
428 Jarzabkowski/Chalkias/Clarke/Iyahen/Stadtmueller/Zwick, Insurance for climate adaptation: Opportunities and limitations, 2019.
429 Swiss Re Institute, Changing climates: the heat is (still) on, 2024, 15.

Australia's National Flood Insurance Program is another example of the positive effects of insurance and climate adaption. Designed to reduce flood risks and promote resilience, it offers policyholders discounted premiums for buildings that incorporate flood-resistant features.[430]

Similarly, **Japan**'s urban resilience programs integrate disaster-resistant infrastructure into their insurance policies. These efforts focus on reducing damage from earthquakes and floods, by combining government regulation, insurance incentives, and disaster preparedness[431].

These proactive risk management approaches have reduced the economic impact of extreme weather events in the region. Each of these measures will have different costs and levels of effectiveness and can provide economic benefits ranging from a 2:1 to an 11:1 cost-effectiveness ratio, demonstrating their cost-effectiveness and long-term value.[432]

One such approach is the »Building Back Better« philosophy, which integrates risk reduction into the reconstruction process after disasters. This philosophy views the aftermath of disasters as an opportunity to improve resilience by rebuilding structures that can better withstand future climate risks and by incorporating technologies like remote sensing. Ideally, these improvements in resilience should account for the potential climate changes over a building's lifespan, which may span several decades. This approach requires long-term, forward-thinking construction regulations that »future-proof« buildings against the evolving impacts of climate change.[433]

Furthermore, preventive strategies such as zoning, retrofitting buildings, and strengthening infrastructure can significantly reduce vulnerability to extreme weather events. For existing buildings, retrofitting to prevent flooding and wind damage can offer up to six times the return on investment, further underscoring the importance of proactive measures.[434]

Given the lengthy lead times associated with adaptation projects, it is crucial to take action today to mitigate future risks and safeguard current and prospective real estate investments. In this context, the Swiss Re Institute states the obvious: »no action is not an option.«[435]

---

430 Insurance Council of Australia, Local Government and Insurance Flood Insurance Pricing, 2025, 1–2.

431 Ishiwatari/Kawakami/Sasaki/Sakamoto/Nakayama, Enhancing Disaster Resilience for Sustainable Urban Development: Public–Private Partnerships in Japan, in: Sustainability, 2024, 16.

432 Hudson/Wouter Botzen/Feyen/Aerts, Incentivising flood risk adaptation through risk based insurance premiums: Trade-offs between affordability and risk reduction, in: Ecological Economics, Volume 125, 2016; Aerts, Jeroen C. J. H., A review of cost estimates for flood adaptation. Water (Switzerland) 10(11), 2018, 1–33; Swiss Re Institute, Changing climates: the heat is (still) on, 2024, 2.

433 Jarzabkowski/Chalkias/Clarke/Iyahen/Stadtmueller/Zwick, Insurance for climate adaptation: Opportunities and limitations, 2019.

434 Swiss Re Institute, Changing climates: the heat is (still) on, 2024, 16.

435 Swiss Re Institute, The economics of climate change: no action not an option, 2021, 26.

4.6 Data and AI

Verena Reichstein

4.6.1 Introduction to #4.6

Although still in its early stages, artificial intelligence (**AI**) is more and more frequently used in the real estate sector. As the pressure to meet environmental targets grows, leveraging AI can become a game-changer in improving efficiency and help to achieve ESG goals. For instance, AI can be used to predict maintenance needs, optimize buildings and their use, identify high-risk assets in terms of climate exposure or social vulnerabilities, generate property valuations and price forecasts, analyze investment opportunities, and automatically prepare ESG compliance reports. However, the use of AI is accompanied by significant legal challenges that should not be underestimated. To ensure regulatory compliance and minimize legal risks, a thorough review should be conducted on a case-by-case basis.

#4.6 Data and AI	**#4.6.1 – intro to #4.6**
	#4.6.2 – FM platforms
	#4.6.3 – legal challenges

This subchapter #4.6 covers data and AI with a focus on facility management platforms (#4.6.2) and legal challenges (#4.6.3).

4.6.2 Example: Facility management platforms

For example, AI powered facility management platforms like *Verdigris*[436] show considerable potential for optimizing efficiency.

The implementation of connected sensors (e.g., on building circuit panels) allows for the automatic collection and storage of real-time consumption or usage data (for example, on electricity, heating or water consumption, air quality, or comfort preferences) on a platform. Connected sensors can also be attached to equipment, such as pumps for early detection of failures or malfunctions. Additional data can be extracted from various other sources, including IT system interfaces (e.g., occupancy management software), publicly available sources (e.g., weather and climate data or market data), and manual input (e.g., on maintenance work that has been carried out). AI then assesses and analyzes such data, taking into account external factors, such

436 Reference to platform is used as example for illustrative purposes only and is not to be understood as recommendation or advertisement.

as weather or occupancy, to uncover valuable insights in real time. AI can quickly identify irregularities, such as sudden spikes in energy use, equipment malfunctions, or changes in air quality, and issue alerts. Furthermore, AI can recommend or automatically implement corresponding actions, for example adjustments of the heating, ventilation, and air conditioning (**HVAC**) system settings for energy efficiency. For example, *Verdigris* advertises that its platform identified up to 50 % savings potential in energy usage and heating costs for a client.[437]

4.6.3 Legal challenges

While the potential benefits of using AI in facility management are significant, using AI raises legal challenges, in particular regarding data protection, data economy, cybersecurity, liability, and regulatory compliance, and the responsive use of AI. Therefore, a comprehensive and detailed contractual framework is required.

(a) Data protection and data economy
In the context of facility management, data collected and processed may include personal data, i. e., data that, either directly on its own or indirectly when combined with other data, can be linked back to identified or identifiable tenants, employees or other individuals. This is, for example, the case where data on energy usage or on occupancy patterns can be linked back to an individual using a facility, either directly or indirectly. Storage and processing of personal data are subject to various national or regional data protection regulations, for example, the European General Data Protection Regulation (GDPR),[438] the California Consumer Privacy Act (CCPA) or the Chinese Personal Information Protection Law (PIPL). The applicable regulatory requirements must be identified and complied with. Even if a facility management platform provided by a third-party provider is used, the user usually remains responsible for ensuring that the provider complies with applicable data protection laws.

Where feasible, it is generally recommended to anonymize data, i. e., by removing or altering personal identifiers from data sets so that individuals cannot be identified (directly or indirectly in combination with other data), whereas requirements of anonymization slightly differ in worldwide regulations and must be assessed on a case-by-case basis.

Even if no personal data is processed, regulatory requirements related to the processing or storage of data may still apply. For example, the EU Data Act,[439] largely applicable as of Sep-

437 See Verdigris Case Study, https://www.verdigris.co/case-studies/jabil-video-case-study, accessed 30.07.2025.

438 Regulation (EU) 2016/679 of the European Parliament and of the Council of 27 April 2016 on the protection of natural persons with regard to the processing of personal data and on the free movement of such data, and repealing Directive 95/46/EC (General Data Protection Regulation), https://eur-lex.europa.eu/eli/reg/2016/679/oj/eng, accessed 31.07.2025.

439 Regulation (EU) 2023/2854 of the European Parliament and of the Council of 13 December 2023 on harmonised rules on fair access to and use of data and amending Regulation (EU) 2017/2394 and Directive (EU) 2020/1828 (Data Act), https://eur-lex.europa.eu/eli/reg/2023/2854/oj/eng, accessed 31.07.2025.

tember 12, 2025, applies when user data is collected by connected products – irrespective of whether such data is personal data – inter alia granting users of connected products (e.g., users of a smart air conditioning system) the right to access, use, and share data generated by their use of connected products and imposing obligations on providers to promote interoperability and enable switching between cloud services. Potentially applicable data economy regulations and options to comply with such regulations (e.g., regarding data access) need to be assessed.

(b) Cybersecurity

The reliance on real-time data from multiple sources makes facility management particularly vulnerable to cyber threats. Cyberattacks can lead to unauthorized access to sensitive information, and, in consequence, legal action, regulatory penalties, reputational damage, and operational disruption, which can cause significant financial loss. According to existing legal concepts in various jurisdictions, executive (or management) board members may be held personally liable for organizational negligence regarding cybersecurity.

To address these risks, a comprehensive, risk-based approach to cybersecurity should be taken, including state-of-the-art technical, organizational, and governance measures. Recognized cybersecurity standards, such as ISO/IEC 27001[440] or the recommendations of competent authorities or other recognized entities, like the cybersecurity framework developed by the U.S. National Institute of Standards and Technology (NIST)[441], can provide helpful guidance.

Additionally, sector-specific regulations setting out mandatory cybersecurity requirements may apply to sensitive environments, such as critical infrastructure, as outlined in the European NIS-2 Directive[442] or the North American Electric Reliability Corporation (NERC) Critical Infrastructure Protection (CIP) standards and Presidential Policy Directive 21 (PPD-21).

(c) Liability

Facility management based on AI-driven decisions or actions raises additional challenges in terms of liability. When a decision of the AI solution is inaccurate or otherwise causes damage, it must be determined whether the AI's developers, deployers, operators, or other involved parties can be held responsible.

Cross-jurisdictionally, liability in connection with AI widely relies on existing liability frameworks, such as tort and contract law, which usually require at least simple negligence, and product liability law, which potentially includes strict liability, regardless of fault, for high-risk

440 ISO.org: ISO/IEC 27001:2022 Information security, cybersecurity and privacy protection — Information security management systems — Requirements, 2022, https://www.iso.org/standard/27001, accessed 02.11.2025.

441 National Institute of Standards and Technology, Cybersecurity Framework, https://www.nist.gov/cyberframework/getting-started-csf-11, accessed 30.07.2025.

442 Directive (EU) 2022/2555 of the European Parliament and of the Council of 14 December 2022 on measures for a high common level of cybersecurity across the Union, amending Regulation (EU) No 910/2014 and Directive (EU) 2018/1972, and repealing Directive (EU) 2016/1148 (NIS 2 Directive), https://eur-lex.europa.eu/eli/dir/2022/2555/oj/eng, accessed 30.07.2025.

applications. The European Commission published a first draft of an AI liability directive in 2022,[443] but withdrew it in February 2025 due to a lack of consensus on core issues.[444] However, it reserved the option to table another proposal or choose a different approach. Likewise, other major jurisdictions like the U.S. and the U.K. have not adopted specific AI liability legislation. As a result, AI liability remains a dynamic and evolving legal topic.

Meanwhile, allocating liability among developers, the deployer, operators, and other involved parties poses considerable difficulty. The same applies to proving causation, given that AI is referred to as a not fully explainable »blackbox«, making it difficult to trace faults and failures. Dedicated contractual liability provisions and allocations are essential to mitigating liability risks. Before using an AI solution, the risks associated with unauthorized access, misuse, and inaccuracies in AI-generated results (including their consequences) should be assessed, and measures for prevention or mitigation should be implemented. Obtaining suitable insurance coverage can also reduce overall risk.

(d) Compliance with AI regulation and governance

When AI solutions adjust HVAC settings or lighting, it can impact occupant comfort. Considering the potential risks associated with use of AI, especially when AI makes decisions that impact individuals or may have significant consequences, a growing number of international initiatives and regulations have emerged to define standards for the responsible development and use of AI, aiming to ensure the safety, transparency, fairness, and accountability of AI-systems. In 2019, the OECD's council on AI adopted the first intergovernmental standard on the responsible use of AI (including recommendations), which is currently adhered to by 48 governments.[445] While these recommendations are not legally binding, they demonstrate a political commitment to the principles they contain and entail an expectation that adherents will strive to implement them. Meanwhile, binding regulations exist in some states. These include China's Interim Measures for the Management of Generative Artificial Intelligence Services, which came into effect on August 15, 2023,[446] and the EU AI Act,[447] which establishes a risk-based approach to AI regulation by prohibiting several categories of AI classified as unacceptable risk and establishing a detailed regulatory framework for AI classified as *high-risk*. As noncompliance with

443 Proposal for a directive of the European Parliament and of the Council on adapting non-contractual civil liability rules to artificial intelligence (AI Liability Directive), COM/2022/496 final, https://eur-lex.europa.eu/legal-content/EN/TXT/?uri=celex:52022PC0496, accessed 31.07.2025.

444 European Commission, 2025 Commission work programe – annexes, p. 26, https://commission.europa.eu/strategy-and-policy/strategy-documents/commission-work-programme/commission-work-programme-2025_en, accessed 30.07.2025.

445 See for details on recommendations and adherents: Organisation for Economic Co-operation and Development (OECD), Recommendation of the Council on Artificial Intelligence, OECD/LEGAL/0449, https://legalinstruments.oecd.org/en/instruments/OECD-LEGAL-0449#adherents, accessed 30.07.2025.

446 Interim Measures for the Management of Generative AI Services, https://www.cac.gov.cn/2023-07/13/c_1690898327029107.htm, accessed 30.07.2025.

447 Regulation (EU) 2024/1689 of the European Parliament and of the Council of 13 June 2024 laying down harmonised rules on artificial intelligence and amending Regulations (EC) No 300/2008, (EU) No 167/2013, (EU) No 168/2013, (EU) 2018/858, (EU) 2018/1139 and (EU) 2019/2144 and Directives 2014/90/EU, (EU) 2016/797 and (EU) 2020/1828 (Artificial Intelligence Act), https://eur-lex.europa.eu/eli/reg/2024/1689/oj/eng, accessed 31.07.2025.

these regulations may result in significant fines, legal action, operational disruption, or reputational damage, it is essential to ensure compliance with applicable regulations. Even where no binding regulation exists, it is advisable to establish a comprehensive AI governance framework to ensure responsible use. Technical and organizational measures should be implemented, including the establishment of human oversight for AI-generated decisions that may have significant consequences as well as the training of personnel.

(e) Contractual framework

When AI solutions are obtained from an external provider, a comprehensive and detailed contractual framework tailored to the individual case is required. The contents of the contract should typically include a clear and detailed description of the AI solution to be provided, including its capabilities and limitations, as well as provisions clearly allocating liability and solid rules on confidentiality, data governance, and data protection. Regarding intellectual property, the contract should specify ownership of the input and the rights to use it (including whether it can be used for further training of the AI solution), ownership of results generated by AI as well as rights to use them. Furthermore, contracts should clearly define support standards, including the scope and frequency of system updates and routine maintenance, to ensure continued accuracy and relevance. Additionally, system availability and detailed support and incident management procedures should be established, including response and resolution times and escalation paths. Warranties on compliance with laws may be essential. Specific termination and exit strategy terms should also be included to address noncompliance with evolving regulations, data handling after termination, and to ensure a smooth transition.[448]

448 The required contents vary on a case-by-case basis. This list is not comprehensive.

5 Contracts and words – legalese: Deal-specifics, procurement, funds, antitrust and management

5.1 Introduction to Chapter #5

Sabine Wieduwilt

«Sustainability is a mindset, a way of life, and a path to success.«
– Liz Brenna

5.1.1 Content of Chapter #5

What aspects might be of interest when it comes to understanding the legal aspects of ESG and real estate investment? Anything that avoids risks and also has a commercial impact, and since we're talking about sustainability/ESG, anything that might make a difference in sustainable investment practices.

©Judith Carla Wieduwilt (2025)

Chapter #5 is written from a legal point of view, and provides food for thought for practitioners, without regard for completeness.

There are various dimensions or approaches related to legal topics. Two of these are: (1) What are the regulatory frameworks (in relation to ESG), thus we come up with different disciplines. Then, (2) what do we do with our real estate (investment) projects, including these regulatory frameworks and other sustainability/ESG-related aspects? We begin with the practical part (related to the second dimension), which involves contracts related to the acquisition itself.

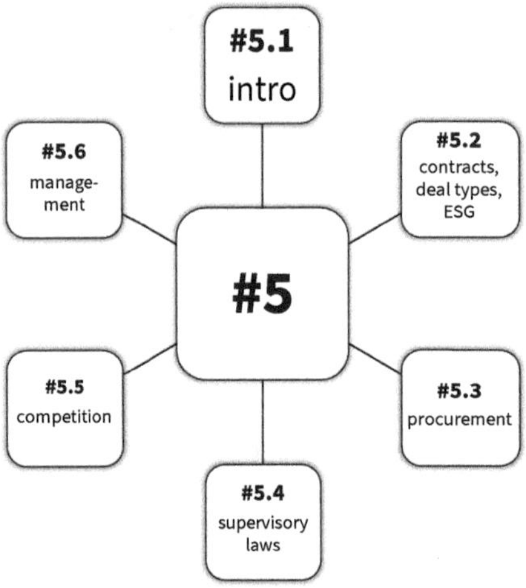

In this chapter, we start with different deal types, (real estate) contracts, cross-border-deals, sustainability/ESG in (real estate) contracts (#5.2), proceed with ESG and procurement (#5.3), supervisory laws, fund management and investing (#5.4), competition (#5.5), and real estate management (#5.6).
The focus is on selected legal aspects relevant to transactional practice and investment structuring, rather than on providing an exhaustive treatment of all possible legal issues related to ESG in real estate.

5.1.2 Legal perspective: Further food for thought

This chapter does not cover the full spectrum of regulatory frameworks that may impact ESG considerations in real estate investment, such as

- tax law,
- environmental litigation,
- employment law,
- construction law/design and build contracts,
- leases,

or the full spectrum of regulatory frameworks that may impact ESG considerations in real estate investment, these being, for example

- anti-money laundering regulations,
- anti-corruption laws,
- health and safety standards,
- zoning and land use regulations, building codes,
- energy efficiency requirements,
- data protection and privacy laws,
- financial reporting and disclosure obligations,
- tenant protection statutes, and
- international ESG reporting standards.

For further study, the following sources and related chapters provide additional insights and practical guidance[449]:

Davies, Paul (ed.), The Global ESG Handbook: A Guide for Practitioners, 2024.

Franklin, Aaron, Structuring Sustainable Finance Transactions: A Practical Guide to the Legal and Financial Considerations of Green Finance Instruments, 2025.

Hölkemöller/Koch/Thomer/Wieduwilt, »Social Impact Investing« im Lichte des Immobilienwirtschafts- und Immobiliensteuerrechts, BB 2025, 1047, also accessible via: https://www.dentons.com/de/insights/articles/2025/may/6/social-impact-investing-in-the-light-of-real-estate-business-and-real-estate-tax-law, accessed 02.11.2025.

International Capital Market Association (ICMA), Sustainable Finance, https://www.icmagroup.org/sustainable-finance/, accessed 14.09.2025.

International Corporate Governance Network (ICGN), Publications, https://www.icgn.org/publications, accessed 14.09.2025.

Maslow/Snyder, Contracts for Responsible and Sustainable Supply Chains. Model Contract Clauses, Legal Analysis, and Practical Perspectives, 2023.

Nykitenko, Rostyslav, Renewable Energy Law & Investment: A Global Legal Guide for Solar, Wind, Hydrogen, and Green Power Projects: Legal, Permits, PPAs, ESG Compliance, Green Hydrogen, and Project Finance Strate, 2025.

PRI, Selecting, appointing and monitoring investment managers, 2021, https://www.unpri.org/introductory-guides-to-responsible-investment/an-introduction-to-responsible-investment-selecting-appointing-and-monitoring-investment-managers/7093.article#:~:text=asset%20owner%20guide-,Appointment,engagement%20practices%20and%20human%20rights, accessed 14.09.2025.

The Chancery Lane Project (TCLP), 2025, https://chancerylaneproject.org/clauses/, accessed 02.11.2025.

United Nations Principles for Responsible Investment (UN PRI)[450] – UN PRI, Global Policy, https://www.unpri.org/policy/global-policy.

449 For example #1.4 litigation risks, ABC, #1.5 ABC, AML and sanctions, #2.6 financing, greenwashing, #3.4 legal ESG due diligence, #4.6 data and AI, and then the various legal frameworks under #6.2–#6.6 within different regions.

450 PRI, Investment Manager Appointment Guide: ESG Clauses, 2020, https://dwtyzx6upklss.cloudfront.net/Uploads/l/i/j/pri_assetownertechnicalguide_appointment_clauses_428793.pdf, accessed 15.08.2024.

Wieduwilt, Sabine (ed.), Implementing ESG into Real Estate Contracts: A guide and toolkit for practitioners from a European perspective, 2025.

Wieduwilt/Taghiyeva/Dalton/Danismant/Doherty et al., Green leases crossing borders – ESG and Real Estate – a European Perspective #2, 2024, https://www.dentons.com/en/insights/articles/2024/may/8/green-leases-crossing-borders-esg-and-real-estate-a-european-perspective, accessed 16.08.2025.

5.2 Asset deals/share deals and joint ventures/structuring cross-border deals/legalese

Sona Taghiyeva/Sabine Wieduwilt

«Progress is impossible without change, and those who cannot change their minds cannot change anything.«
– George Bernard Shaw

5.2.1 Introduction to #5.2

At the core, this subchapter #5.2 is about the transaction documents and legal issues surrounding them. We are taking a very generic approach to the types of clauses and the basic approach to deals.

When investing in or divesting real estate, not all ESG-related topics find their way into the contracts and other transaction documents. Depending on the investment approach and due diligence of the investor, ESG-related topics may be resolved by the parties separately from the documents, or they may lead to the parties not signing the documents at all. Depending on the situation, the approach to this can be addressed in preliminary documents[451].

If ESG-related topics are dealt with in the transaction documents, how can we include ESG into our contracts?

#5.2 ESG in purchase contracts, legalese	**#5.2.1 – intro to #5.2**
	#5.2.2 – legalese for real estate investment, cross-border
	#5.2.3 – sustainability / CSR / ESG and contracts

In this subchapter #5.2, we review how cross-border real estate transactions are structured, the advantages and disadvantages of different transaction forms, the applicable law

451 For details regarding the preliminary agreements, see Wieduwilt, Sabine in: Wieduwilt, Sabine, Implementing ESG into Real Estate Contracts. A guide and toolkit for practitioners from a European perspective, 2025, #2.2, 160.

based on the principles of conflict of laws, how to approach cross-border deals (#5.2.2), as well as the types of ESG-related clauses included in different deal types, namely asset deals, share deals, forward deals, joint ventures (JV), portfolio and cross-border deals (#5.2.3).

5.2.2 Legalese for cross-border real estate investments

Real estate investment transactions employ different structures depending on the type and geographical location of the assets, the parties involved, the availability of financing, and future plans. Most commonly, investors opt for one of three types of transactions: asset transactions, share transactions, and joint ventures, each having its own distinct advantages and disadvantages.

(a) Heads of terms/LOI

Establishing comprehensive Heads of Terms or a Letter of Intent is essential in cross-border real estate transactions to ensure that buyers and sellers agree on fundamental commercial terms before incurring substantial legal costs and drafting definitive transaction documents. This preliminary agreement significantly reduces the risk of major disputes during the documentation phase while protecting buyers through an exclusivity period that prevents sellers from disposing of the asset to competitors during due diligence. This exclusivity window, typically ranging from 30–90 days, provides buyers with the necessary time and security to conduct thorough investigations without facing commercial pressure from competing bids.

(b) Primary transaction structures

Asset Acquisition Transactions

An asset transaction allows the investor to acquire specific real estate assets free from the liabilities of the property company owner. However, this structure may be associated with costs for asset registration, transfer of licenses, and tax issues.

Share Transactions

In contrast, a share transaction involves the acquisition of shares in the company that owns the real estate asset. In my experience, this is the preferred method for acquiring assets in several jurisdictions, as it allows for the seamless acquisition of multiple assets without needing to change company structures through a holding company acquisition. It also eliminates the need to transfer licenses and avoids registration issues.

However, this scenario requires thorough legal, technical, environmental, and financial due diligence to ensure that no significant red flags (e.g., debts, taxes, environmental liabilities, golden parachutes for key employees, pension schemes, or disputes) are transferred to the buyer. There are often issues regarding latent capital gain.

Structural considerations for buyers

In both asset and share transaction structures, different issues must be considered, depending on which party you represent. The primary concern for buyers is the transaction structure. They want to ensure that the target fits into the buyer's current legal and organizational structure and can be easily managed, preferably in a tax-friendly and less regulated jurisdiction.

This can be achieved either by establishing a separate special purpose vehicle or through acquisition by an existing entity. For European real estate transactions involving European or U.S. players, Luxembourg, Malta, Cyprus, the Netherlands, Jersey, or other countries with relatively flexible corporate and tax regimes are typically chosen. The decision on the acquisition structure is interlinked with capital flow (both inbound and outbound) and compliance with various financial regulations and tax regimes.

It is never too early to consider antitrust clearances and structure the transaction accordingly (e.g., EU: Council Regulation (EC) No 139/2004 (EU Merger Regulation), Arts. 1–3 (thresholds and notification requirements).

Risk management through insurance

In many transactions, sellers prioritize receiving payment with certainty rather than providing extensive guarantees to buyers. Insurance becomes crucial when buyers want to avoid taking on financial risks after closing a deal. Instead of holding back part of the sale price in an escrow account to cover potential future claims, various insurance products can offer protection.

The market offers several types of coverage, including:
- Title insurance
- Warranty and indemnity insurance
- Tax liability insurance
- Environmental insurance
- Contingent liability or litigation insurance

Warranty and indemnity insurance typically covers unknown risks, while tax and contingent liability insurance can also cover some known risks if certain conditions are met. Using insurance not only transfers risk but also accelerates negotiations for both sale agreements and financing documents.

Joint venture structures are preferred,[452] when a project requires multiple stakeholders due to insufficient funding or expertise, when synergy and partnerships are essential, or when a seller wishes to retain some of its ownership equity. However, before entering joint venture arrangements, investors must carefully consider regulatory restrictions.

Regulatory considerations – These restrictions include:

Foreign ownership limitations: Many countries restrict foreign ownership of real estate, requiring careful legal structuring.

Investment approval requirements: Many countries have established comprehensive foreign investment approval regimes that mandate government authorization for overseas real estate acquisitions exceeding specified monetary thresholds or involving particular property categories. These regulatory frameworks typically require foreign investors to obtain prior approval (in some cases prior notification) from designated government authorities before completing property transactions.

The approval processes often require detailed disclosure of investment purposes, funding sources, and beneficial ownership structures. Threshold amounts vary significantly between jurisdictions and may differ based on factors such as property type, location sensitivity, or the investor's country of origin. Noncompliance typically results in severe penalties, including forced divestiture, substantial financial penalties, and potential criminal sanctions.

Licensing and registration: When the target company holds multiple properties across different jurisdictions, each location may have distinct registration procedures, transfer taxes, stamp duties, and disclosure obligations that must be satisfied before legal title can be transferred. Additionally, some jurisdictions mandate registration with specific regulatory bodies or the obtaining of special permits before completing property-related aspects of the transaction.

A prime example is the proposed change to Switzerland's Lex Koller law, which significantly restricts foreign investors by allowing commercial property purchases only for their own business operations, effectively eliminating investment-only acquisitions.[453]

---

452 The ideas for this have been inspired, among other, by: Harrison, David, Key structuring considerations for crossborder acquisitions and joint ventures, 27.02.2019, https://uk.practicallaw.thomsonreuters.com/w-019-4151?transitionType=Default&contextData=(sc.Default)&firstPage=true, accessed 01.09.2025; special thanks to Stewart Middleman (Partner at Dentons) for his ideas and comments.

453 Müller/Johner/Serag/Eugster/Jacaccia, Another Foray Into Amending the Swiss Lex Koller, https://chambers.com/rankings/real-estate-switzerland-europe, accessed 10.06.2025.

Practical challenges in emerging markets

The key issue is determining not only the legal framework but also actual practices, especially if assets are located in countries in Africa, Latin America, Central Asia, or the Caucasus. While it is relatively easy to establish a company, including a joint venture, it is very difficult to repatriate revenue and/or initial capital contributions, even if the law does not prevent it.

This difficulty arises when the law is ineffective, and judges follow internal instructions to protect the local economy by preventing investment outflow. For example, they may simply not allow insolvency or bankruptcy. Numerous challenges are created by unwritten currency control rules, which impose artificial barriers preventing foreign investors from taking their legally distributed profits as shareholders. The situation is further complicated by the fact that insurance companies are unwilling to provide coverage in these emerging jurisdictions.

Exit structure planning is a critical component that must be meticulously planned from the outset. It should incorporate clear mechanisms for partner withdrawal, forced sale provisions, drag-along and tag-along rights, and valuation methodologies to prevent future disputes and ensure smooth transitions when partnership objectives are achieved or circumstances change.

Equally important is establishing robust governance frameworks and profit distribution structures that clearly delineate decision-making authority, operational responsibilities, capital contribution requirements, and revenue sharing arrangements, whilst accounting for the risk appetites, investment horizons, and strategic objectives of different partners.

Tax is unavoidable, but it can definitely be optimized while observing legal compliance, making it a cornerstone of every transaction. **Tax optimization** is a critical value point, encompassing double taxation treaties, transfer pricing, stamp duties, and other considerations.

Double taxation treaties are bilateral or multilateral agreements between countries that can provide relief from withholding taxes, establish rules for the taxation of cross-border services, and allocate taxing rights. Some countries offer systems of tax credit and exemptions that allow for similar tax optimization, whereby taxes paid in one country might reduce the tax burden in another.

Transfer pricing encompasses the valuation and pricing mechanisms applied to transactions involving loans between affiliated entities operating within a multinational corporate group. The accurate establishment and determination of these transfer prices (for which market interest rates are used when loans are involved) represents a fundamental requirement for maintaining tax regulatory compliance while simultaneously ensuring that all intercompany transactions adhere to arm's length principles and standards. Transfer pricing involves the interest rate charged for intercompany loans, which is subject to market pricing.

Sale-and-leaseback transactions

Sale-and-leaseback has emerged as a preferred business strategy, providing easy access to money for operating companies that own real estate but need capital for investment or operations. This structure, originating from the U.S. and widely used in the U.K., is now prevalent throughout Europe.

A sale-and-leaseback is an arrangement in which the company that sells an asset can lease back that same asset from the purchaser. The details of the arrangement, such as lease payments and lease duration, are determined immediately after the sale of the asset. The seller of the asset becomes the lessee, and the purchaser becomes the lessor.[454] By converting real estate assets into cash, companies can improve their balance sheet, potentially enhancing their creditworthiness and financial ratios.

(c) Cross-border legal consideration

One specific legal issue in cross-border transactions is the need to develop relatively harmonized sales and purchase agreements for various countries. Each country has its own specific requirements regarding the sale and lease of real property. For example, in Germany and Spain, the lease part of the agreement must be written in a specific way to be acceptable for notarization and subsequent registration with the authorities.

In some jurisdictions, sale and leaseback arrangements may be reclassified as secured financing rather than true sales, which affects the intended legal and tax treatment. Clear allocation of responsibility for property expenses, taxes, insurance, and maintenance is crucial, especially since local laws may impose mandatory obligations regardless of contractual terms.

(d) Applicable law and dispute resolution

Choice of law

The majority of investors, irrespective of asset location, prefer to apply the laws of jurisdictions with well-established legal systems in share transactions, e.g., U.S. (typically New York or Delaware laws) or U.K. law. European transactions are usually governed by UK (and sometimes Luxembourg) law, even if the connection of the parties and assets to the UK or Luxembourg is minimal.

However, when dealing with asset transactions, the imperative norms of the country where the asset is located shall apply. In property law, most jurisdictions apply the lex situs rule: the law of the location of the property governs rights in real estate. This principle is nearly universal, with limited exceptions. For example, a dispute over land in Germany will be governed by

454 Tardi, Carla, Leaseback (or Sale-Leaseback): Definition, Benefits, and Examples, https://www.investopedia.com/terms/l/leaseback.asp, accessed 19.06.2024.

German property law, even if the parties are based in the U.S. and the contract is governed by New York law.

Dispute resolution

In cross-border real estate transactions, establishing clear and enforceable dispute resolution clauses becomes paramount to managing potential conflicts effectively. International arbitration has emerged as the preferred mechanism for resolving cross-border real estate disputes, with parties frequently choosing well-established institutional rules, such as those administered by the International Chamber of Commerce (ICC), the London Court of International Arbitration (LCIA), or the Singapore International Arbitration Centre (SIAC).

The benefits of using institutional arbitration include clear procedural frameworks, experienced arbitrator panels with real estate expertise, and established enforcement mechanisms that provide greater certainty and efficiency compared to traditional litigation in multiple jurisdictions.

The choice of arbitration rules should consider the countries involved in the transaction perimeter, the flexibility the parties want in the process, and the complexity of any future disputes. The ICC rules are often chosen for their strong case management, the LCIA rules for their efficiency and cost-effective. The SIAC rules are becoming popular for deals in the Asia-Pacific region because of their modern approach and local expertise.

(e) Approaching cross-border deals
Team assembly

Every successful project starts with the right team. Regardless of the ultimate goal, location, or structure of the transaction, investors must have trusted legal, tax, financial, environmental, and technical specialists to analyze the overall transaction and conduct due diligence on each asset. The team should consist of both international experts and local advisers who understand how the system works on the ground.

Time is of the essence when investors participate in a bidding process, especially in emerging markets with few sophisticated local experts, as they might already be hired by other bidders.

Due diligence considerations

Conducting thorough due diligence is essential for understanding regulations (such as environmental, employment, or tax rules), the target business, and compliance with laws. This includes examining government concessions, permits, and any employee approval requirements that could affect the transaction structure.

Although materiality thresholds are frequently used in due diligence processes to eliminate minor issues, even seemingly minor issues, such as the existence of a trade union in countries like France, could delay the entire deal in the absence of compliance with consent/consultation requirements, even if the transaction does not take place at the level of a French entity standing far below the acquired target company.

5.2.3 Sustainability/CSR/ESG and contracts

This section outlines how ESG, CSR, and sustainability requirements can be embedded into various types of real estate deals, providing practical guidance and examples for asset deals (under (a)), share deals (under (b)), forward deals (under (c)), joint ventures (JVs) (under (d)), portfolio transactions (under (e)), and cross-border investments (under (f)).

ESG, CSR, and sustainability can have an impact on pricing (amount, retention, reduction, earn-out, etc.), representations and warranties and limitations, contract penalties, incentives, compliance, covenants, undertakings, remediation, on information, reporting, and disclosure, as well as monitoring. These are typical clauses in transaction documents. Some topics have historically been included in transaction documents (which some will not attribute to ESG), such as environmental representations, warranties, limitations, and indemnities, energy performance certificates (EPCs), and green building certifications. Other topics attributed to sustainability/CSR/ESG, such as compliance with EU and other taxonomy requirements, the integration of sustainability reporting and disclosure, or supply chain laws and standards, are not that common in transaction documents. For these topics, transparency tools may be preferable to hard sanctions or even incentives (transparency being a mechanism of enforcement) – depending on the risks for the companies involved and the information available. Also, depending on the deal types and issues to be resolved, some might not be resolved in a short period of time. This is why, in forward deals, forward funding or JVs, issues can be resolved as part of the immediate fulfillment of the deal, but for other, more-short term contractual arrangements, the parties need to make a risk assessment. Then, they can either leave the risk with the buyer, possibly in connection with a price adjustment, or address it with representations and warranties.

Concerning the topics to include, there are topics historically integrated into real estate transaction documents and more recent »ESG« topics that have evolved for M&A and real estate M&A. These clauses may include specific commitments to sustainable practices, such as renewable energy usage, waste management protocols, and adherence to industry-specific sustainability certifications. Environmental topics include addressing the redevelopment of contaminated sites with sustainability in mind (brownfield sites) and implementing strategies for environmental restoration (soil remediation). Social topics focus on ensuring ESG compliance throughout the supply chain, including ethical sourcing and labor practices, as well as developing policies that support sustainable development goals. Governance topics involve leveraging data analytics for ESG performance tracking, utilizing ESG ratings to evaluate investment potential, and establishing key performance indicators to measure ESG impact.[455]

These examples and clause types aim to give a starter kit for practitioners seeking to embed responsible business practices into the fabric of real estate transactions across asset classes and jurisdictions. These are merely exemplary to gather ideas and food for thought. They need to be aligned with the mandatory and voluntary standards relevant for the parties and other content in the transaction documents. Also, with regard to the ESG content, they need to be »as specific as necessary«, meaning the content shouldn't be too specific, so as not to omit the key requirements, or too broad so as not to overburden the seller. Therefore, the wording cannot simply be copy-pasted from the examples below.

(a) Asset deal

An asset deal involves the purchase of specific assets of a company, rather than the company itself. This type of transaction is common in real estate, where the buyer acquires properties, equipment, and other tangible assets. For a **timeline of the asset deal**, see **Figure 25**.

455 For further topics and ideas of contract types, see other chapters of the book. See for example ideas for impact investing (subchapter #2.5) in TCLP, Matteo's Clause, Climate and Nature Impact Investing Terms, https://chancerylaneproject.org/clauses/climate-and-nature-impact-investing-terms/, accessed 22.06.2025; Hölkemeier/Koch/Thomer/Wieduwilt, »Social Impact Investing« im Lichte des Immobilienwirtschafts- und Immobiliensteuerrechts, BB 2025, 1047–1056, also retrievable via https://www.dentons.com/de/insights/articles/2025/may/6/-/media/2ef46b16ef2147dcbadd2e164eb770de.ashx,, accessed 03.11.2025.

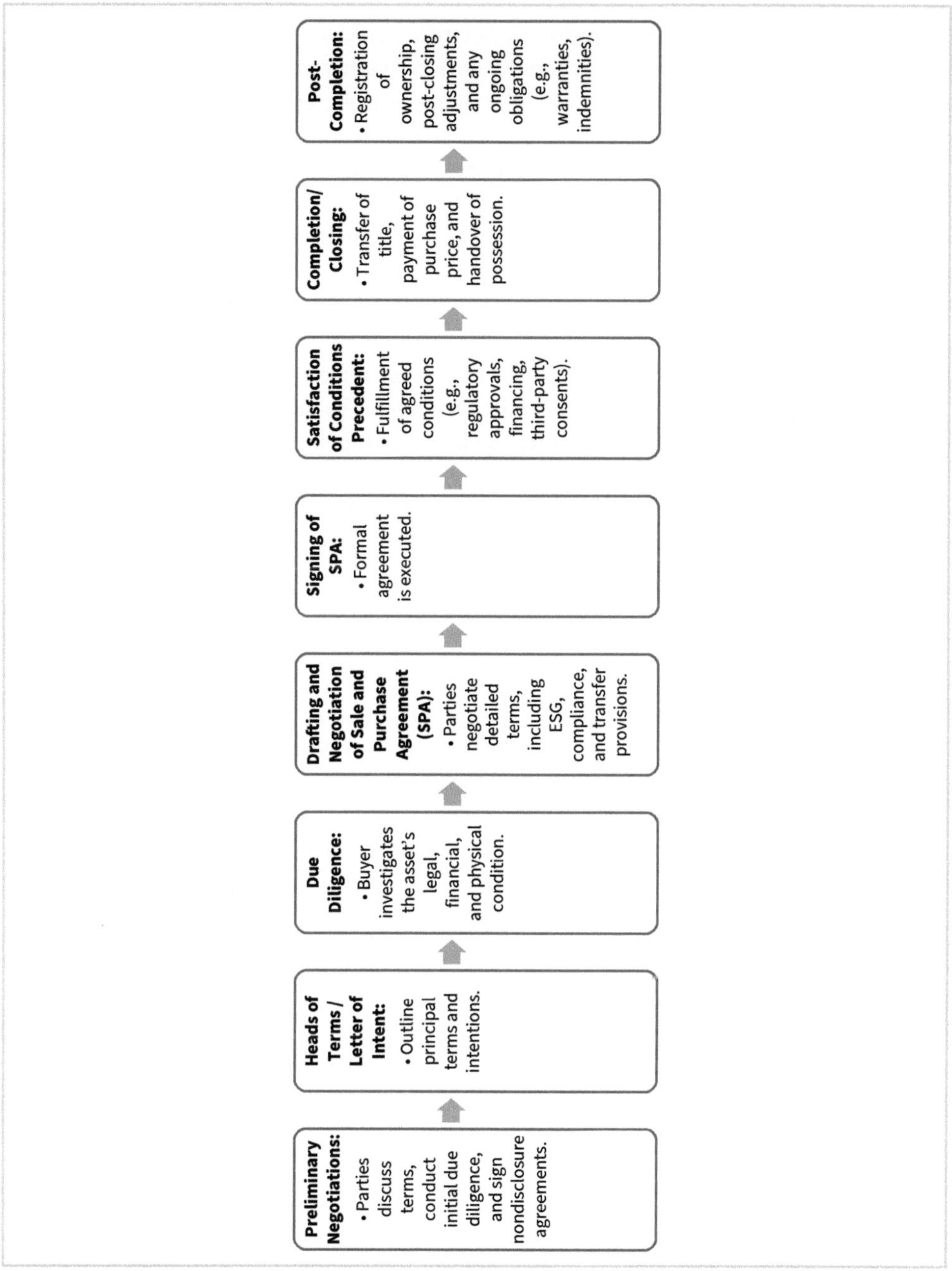

Figure 25: Timeline asset deal

The purchase agreement includes the following types of clauses:

- **Object of sale:** Description of the property (including other assets) being acquired.
- **Purchase price:** Amount of purchase price and payment conditions; condition and terms of payment.
- **Handover/transfer of rights and obligations:** Transfer of possession, with transfer of rights and obligations (including contracts, such as leases).
- **Representations and warranties:** Assurances regarding the condition and ownership of assets.
- **Indemnities:** Provisions for compensation in case of breaches or losses (e.g., in case of third-party claims).
- **Transfer of title:** Legal process for transferring ownership of the property.
- **Historically, purchase agreements tend to include for example:** Specific clauses related to environmental compliance, property condition, and zoning regulations.

The integration of ESG criteria can affect the valuation and due diligence processes, particularly when assessing environmental liabilities and compliance with sustainability standards. In asset deals, the direct transfer of real estate assets provides an opportunity to incorporate additional ESG requirements into the transaction documentation. See **examples of clauses/ clause types** below:[456]

> **Disclosure of ESG information:** The Seller must provide all available Carbon Risk Real Estate Monitor (CRREM) analyses, energy performance certificates (EPCs), transition risk assessments, and life cycle assessments (LCAs) for the property.
>
> **Sustainability reporting data:** The Seller will supply the Buyer with all necessary digital data and documents for (asset-specific) sustainability reporting up to closing, including energy, water, waste, and environmental certifications, within a set timeframe.
>
> **Payment condition/condition precedent (green leases):** The payment of the purchase price depends on the Seller amending or entering into leases with all tenants to include green lease terms, covering energy, water efficiency, waste, data sharing, and sustainability cooperation (as per a schedule to be attached).
>
> **Retention (ESG):** The Buyer withholds a specified amount from the purchase price in escrow for a set period to cover potential ESG liabilities post-closing. The funds are released to the Seller if no ESG claims arise; otherwise, they are used to resolve such claims. The Buyer may audit the Seller's ESG practices during this period, and disputes are resolved as agreed.

456 The ideas for clauses have been inspired, among other, by: Lauer, Jörg, Due Diligence im gewerblichen Immobiliengeschäft, ZfIR 2022, 467; see also overview under: Pfeiffer/Wieduwilt/Dalton, in: Wieduwilt, Implementing ESG into Real Estate Contracts, A guide and toolkit for practitioners from a European perspective, 2025, #2.4, 182, 195.

Green Lease: A portion of the purchase price is held back and is only released once the Seller proves that all tenants have signed green lease clauses within a specified period.

Earn-out payments: The Seller can earn additional payments if the property meets the agreed ESG targets (e.g., carbon reduction, waste diversion) within a defined period. Payments are made after the targets have been verified, with dispute resolution procedures in place.

Improvement covenants: The Seller commits to completing specific ESG upgrades (e.g., energy efficiency, waste systems) by a set deadline, ensuring compliance with all laws and standards.

Ongoing reporting: The Seller must provide regular (e.g., quarterly) reports to the Buyer on ESG performance and improvements until a specified end date, including relevant metrics.

Remedies: If the Seller fails to meet ESG obligations or reporting requirements, the Buyer may seek remedies such as specific performance, damages, or contract termination, following written notice and the lapse of a reasonable cure period

Warranties: The Seller confirms that the property holds the specified building certifications (e.g., LEED, BREEAM).

Representations: The Seller states that the property meets all required energy efficiency and sustainability standards and that all certifications are current and valid.

(b) Share deal

A share deal involves the purchase of shares in a company, thereby acquiring ownership and control of the company and its assets. Share deals involve the transfer of shares in a company that owns real estate, rather than the direct transfer of the asset itself. For a **timeline of a share deal**, see **Figure 26**.

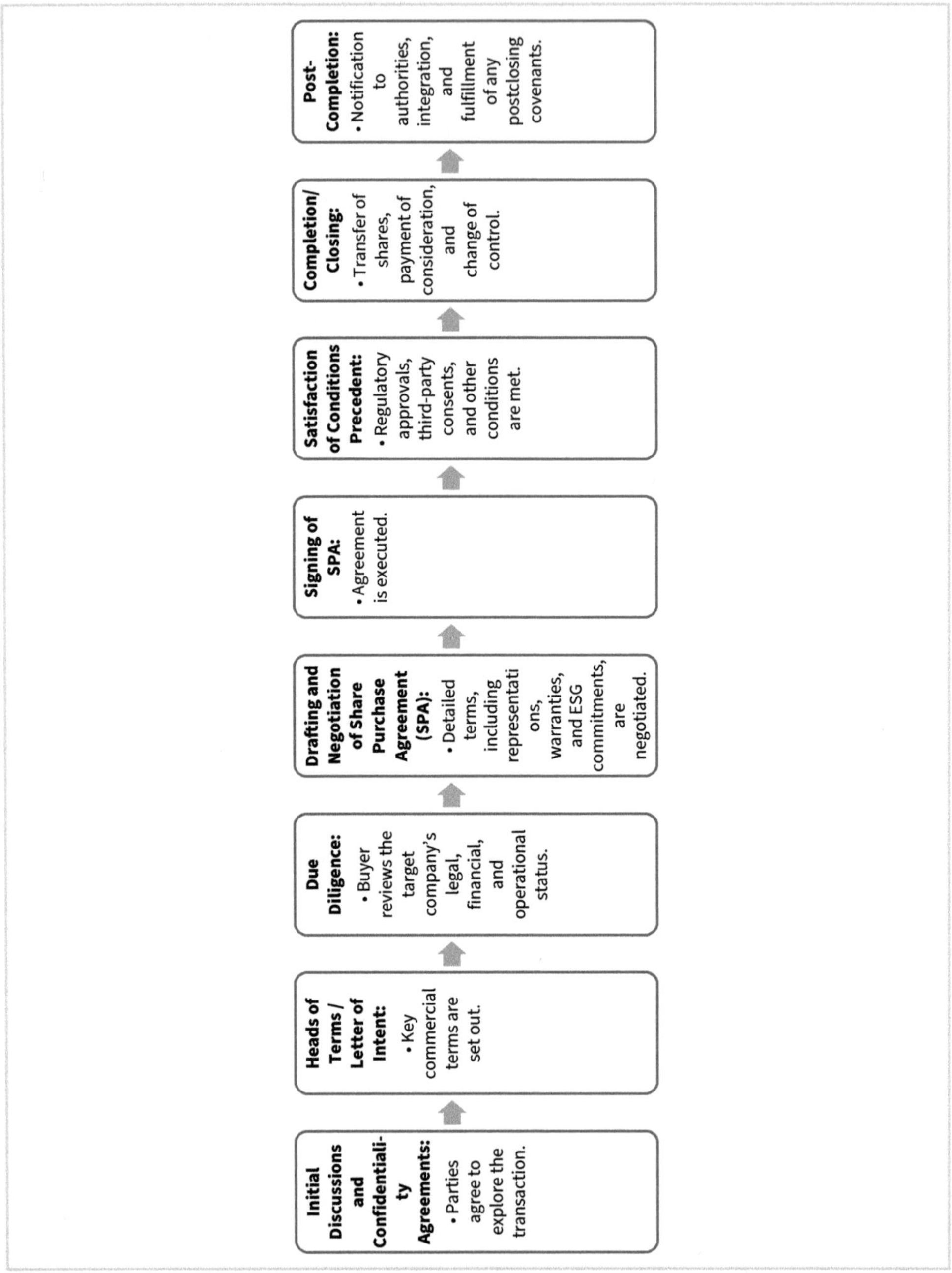

Figure 26: Timeline share deal

The purchase agreement (share purchase agreement, SPA) includes the following types of clauses:

- **Object of sale:** Description of the shares being acquired and the target company.
- **Purchase price:** Terms of payment and share price.
- **Representations and warranties:** Assurances regarding the financial health and legal status of the company.
- **Closing conditions:** Requirements that must be met before the transaction is finalized.
- **Indemnities:** Provisions for compensation in case of breaches or losses.
- **Transfer of shares:** Legal process for transferring ownership of shares.
- **Historically, SPAs tend to include for example (with regard to sustainability/CSR/ESG):** Historically, aspects, purchase agreements tend to include, for example, specific clauses related to corporate governance, shareholder rights, and financial disclosures.

In share deal transactions, ESG clauses can, in addition to the compliance and performance of the asset/property, focus on the company's policies, historical compliance, and future commitments. See the examples of clauses and clause types that may be included in the share purchase agreements (SPA)[457] below[458]:

> **Closing conditions:** Requirements before closing, including positive (e.g., adoption of ESG policies, obtaining permits/certifications, and conducting ESG due diligence) and negative (e.g., no new ESG investigations, no material breaches, no new code violations) conditions.

457 Not reviewed (food for thought for further reading): Where ESG considerations influence other agreements, such as shareholder agreements, with a focus on ensuring corporate governance aligns with sustainability goals.

458 The ideas for clauses have especially been inspired by: Seibt/Alles, M&A-Transaktionen als Teil nachhaltiger Unternehmensführung (ESG) – Praxishinweise zur Prozessstrukturierung und Vertragsgestaltung, DB 2024, 370–381 (to review also for further concepts: carve-out, ring-fencing, signing condition, price reduction, post-closing-measure; post-merger-integration measure by buyer; contract penalty; W&I insurance, etc.); Hollerung, Lukas, Sustainable Mergers & Acquisitions – eine Bestandsaufnahme, ZHR 2024, 148–175; Quill, Tobias, ESG und Unternehmensbewertung: partei- und phasenspezifische Besonderheiten im M&A-Prozess, DB 2024, 2645–2651; Wagner, Florian/Mumme, Fabian/Schuler, Florian, ESG und Post-M&A-Streitigkeiten – (Wie) passt das zusammen?, ZIP 2024, 1363–1369; Louven, Christoph, ESG: Der Umgang mit Chancen und Risiken beim Unternehmenskauf, BB 2022, 2178–2197; Katharina Mareike Franitza/Berrit Roth-Mingram, ESG-Faktoren in M&A Transaktionen – nachhaltige Verhandlungen, 19.11.2024, https://www.cmshs-bloggt.de/rechtsthemen/sustainability/sustainability-corporate-governance-risk-compliance/esg-faktoren-in-ma-transaktionen-nachhaltige-verhandlungen/, accessed 25.06.2025; Jamie Nowak/Julia Grünberg/Manuel Gleich, ESG: Dealing with sustainability risks in the company purchase agreement, November 2023, https://www.nortonrosefulbright.com/en-de/knowledge/publications/b6715168/esg-dealing-with-sustainability-risks-in-the-company-purchase-agreement, accessed 25.06.2025; Jaletzke/Henle M&A/Henle, Share Purchase Agreement in englischer Sprache mit Anmerkungen in deutscher Sprache, Henle, Jaletzke/Henle, M&A Agreements in Germany, 2. Aufl. 2020, II. 8., accessed 25.06.2025; TCLP, Justin's Clause, SPA/APA/Investment Agreement: Representations, Warranties and Covenants Re: Disclosure of Climate Change Plans – The Chancery Lane Project, 2023, https://chancerylaneproject.org/clauses/spa-apa-investment-agreement-representations-warranties-and-covenants-re-disclosure-of-climate-change-plans/, accessed 15.06.2025: This clause ties seller-provided information to contractually enforceable representations, warranties and covenants, giving a buyer access to truthful climate-related information. See also: TCLP, Zack's Clause, SPA/Investment Agreement: Disclosure of Climate Change Plans, https://chancerylaneproject.org/clauses/spa-investment-agreement-disclosure-of-climate-change-plans/, accessed 22.06.2025.

Closing actions: Actions taken at closing, such as delivering compliance certificates, transferring ESG policies, audit reports, supply chain documentation, and green building certifications.

Pre-closing covenants: Seller obligations before closing such as maintaining ESG standards, not altering policies or disposing of permits, not making layoffs or appointing new suppliers without ESG checks, and not making unauthorized property changes.

Post-closing covenants: Ongoing obligations after closing, e.g., buyer to implement ESG management systems, maintain certifications, continue reporting, uphold community and supplier commitments, or seller to assist with transition.

Undertakings: Ongoing commitments by buyer or seller, such as implementing ESG policies, publishing reports, remediating issues, providing training, or disclosing risks.

Representations: Statements of fact regarding ESG compliance, absence of violations, valid permits, lack of ongoing investigations, and adherence to standards.

Warranties: Assurances of ESG compliance, including remedies if untrue, covering legal, industry, and self-imposed standards, historical compliance, and the absence of specific violations.

Bring down: Seller reaffirms ESG warranties at closing.

Indemnities: Seller compensates the buyer for losses from ESG risks, fines, remediation costs, or undisclosed issues.

Material adverse change (MAC): Allows the buyer to withdraw if significant ESG-related events occur pre-closing (e.g., regulatory changes, major violations, loss of certifications).

Earn-out clause: Part of price tied to future ESG performance (e.g., achieving certifications, emissions reduction, meeting diversity goals).

Escrow arrangement: Portion of price held to cover ESG-related claims post-closing (e.g., remediation, fines, certification delays).

Other clauses: Retention of key ESG staff, non-compete and non-solicitation (protecting ESG data and relationships), and confidentiality of sensitive ESG information.

(c) Forward deals, forward purchase, forward funding

Forward deals involve agreements to purchase property or assets at a future date, often contingent on certain conditions being met. Forward funding refers to financing provided in advance for the development of a property. For a **timeline for forward deals/forward funding**, see **Figure 27**.

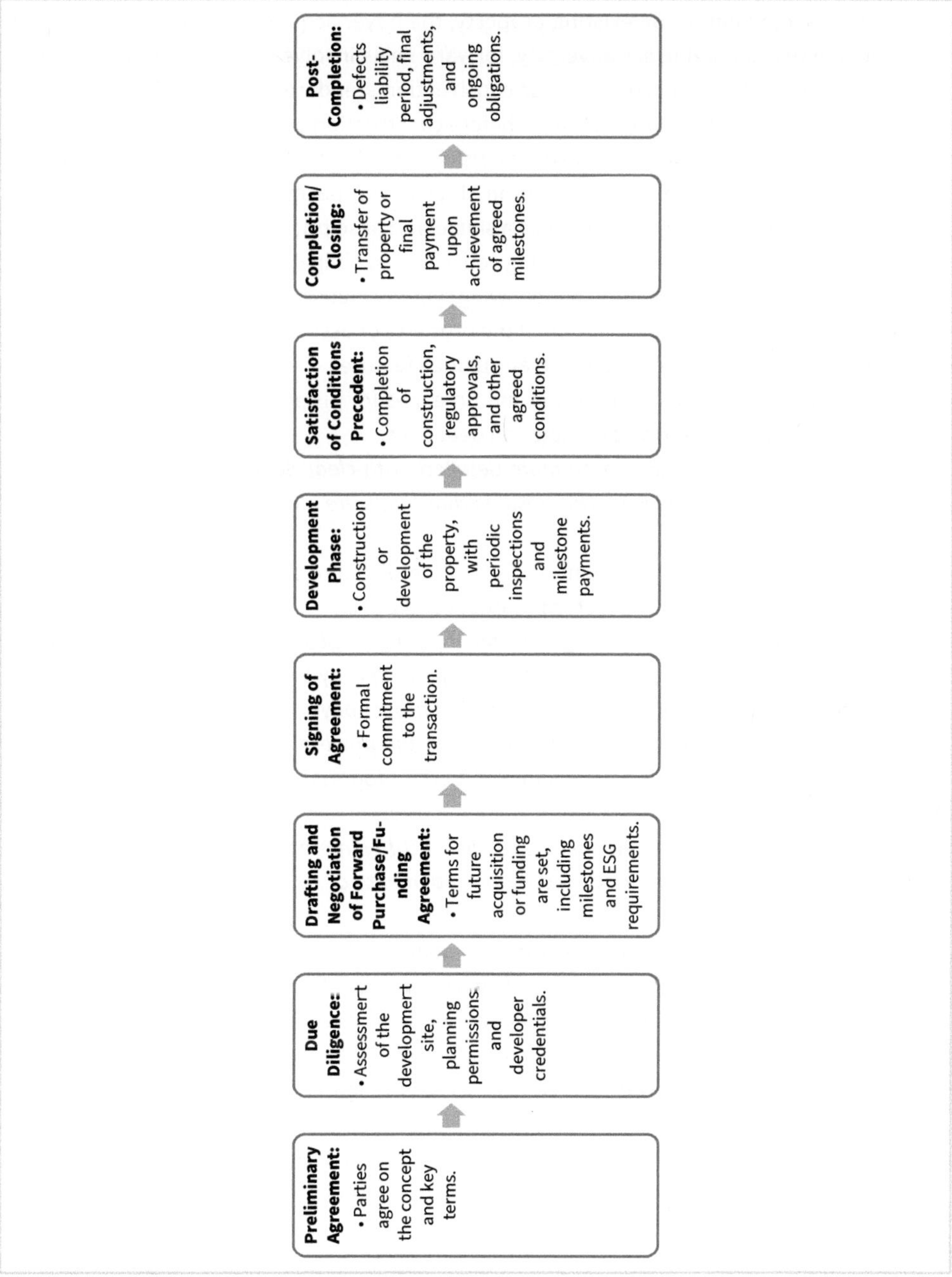

Figure 27: Timeline forward deals/forward funding

In a purchase agreement for an existing property, the buyer acquires a completed asset with immediate possession and use. Conversely, forward deals involve future delivery upon completion and require detailed provisions for construction standards and timelines.[459] Forward deals differ in that they secure the purchase before construction begins, necessitating detailed contractual elements to manage construction risks and obligations. Forward funding involves financing the construction of the property in stages, with payments made as construction progresses. Forward deals typically involve a single purchase price agreed upon upfront, with completion contingent on the seller fulfilling construction obligations. Forward deals and forward funding arrangements include the following types of clauses:

- **Object of sale:** A detailed description of the property or assets to be constructed and sold, including specifications, location, and any unique features.
- **Development milestones:** Conditions and timelines for property development, outlining key stages of construction and completion deadlines.
  [Forward funding: These should be more detailed, with clear definitions of the stages that correspond to funding releases. This ensures that funds are allocated appropriately as construction progresses.]
- **Purchase price:** Terms of payment and valuation of future assets, including any adjustments based on construction costs or market conditions.
  [Forward funding: Instead of a single payment upon completion, forward funding involves staged payments aligned with construction progress. Specify the schedule and conditions for each disbursement, including the milestones that trigger payments.
  Funding disbursement: Includes clauses detailing the process for requesting and releasing funds, including documentation required to verify progress and compliance with agreed standards.
  Security interests: Forward funding may require security interests or collateral to protect the lender's investment. Specify any security arrangements or guarantees that ensure project completion.
  Adjustment mechanisms: Include provisions for adjusting funding amounts based on changes in construction costs or unforeseen circumstances to ensure flexibility in financial planning.
  Monitoring and reporting: Introduce clauses that require regular reporting on construction progress and financial expenditures, allowing for oversight and adjustments as needed.]
- **Representations and warranties:** Assurances regarding the future condition and compliance of assets, including quality standards and legal requirements.
- **Closing conditions:** Requirements to be met before the transaction is finalized, such as obtaining necessary permits, completion of construction, and fulfillment of contractual obligations.
- **Indemnities:** Provisions for compensation in case of breaches or losses, to protect parties against unforeseen liabilities or defects.
- **Contracts include, for example**: Specific clauses related to detailed building specifications, construction standards, project timelines, tenant/lease agreement structure and

459 Developer contracts focus on the construction and sale of properties by developers.

specific requirements, funding disbursement, and allocation of responsibilities among parties involved in the development process.[460]

Forward deal and forward funding arrangements, where assets are acquired before completion or construction, present opportunities to embed ESG requirements from the outset. **ESG factors may impact future development plans, requiring a commitment to sustainable building practices and energy-efficient designs.** See the examples of clauses and clause types below:[461]

> **Design and build/construction standards:** The Developer must design and build the Property according to the standards listed in Schedule […], such as achieving specific energy and carbon performance targets (e.g., CRREM 1.5°C pathway), obtaining building certifications, applying for EPC ratings, using renewable energy, incorporating circular design and materials, and ensuring supply chain compliance at the time of Practical Completion.
>
> **Sustainable supply chain:** The Seller must ensure that all construction materials and services are sourced through a responsible and transparent supply chain, following sustainable sourcing, ethical practices, transparency, risk management, and reporting requirements.
>
> **Use of building information modeling (BIM):** The Seller is required to use BIM technology throughout the project to improve design precision, construction processes, and collaboration. The Buyer must be given access to BIM data for decision-making and quality control purposes.
>
> **Post-completion environmental assessment (e.g., LCA):** After construction, the Seller must carry out a full life cycle assessment (LCA) to analyze the environmental impact of the Property's construction, operation, and eventual decommissioning. The LCA should cover material, energy, and water use, as well as environmental impacts such as carbon footprint, resource efficiency, and waste generation. The Seller must provide a detailed LCA report to the Buyer within a specified period after completion, including recommen-

460 Depending on the contract, the investor must bear varying degrees of the risks associated with project development: Söhnchen/Zentis/Berka/Eichler/Huperz, BB 2018, 1090–1096. For forward deals, see the investment law perspective, especially for forward funding: Geier/Strauch, RdF 2020, 92–96. Typical buyers considering forward deals now also include capital management companies acting on behalf of an investment fund they manage.

461 Slightly different setting, but nevertheless with parallel topics (parties to review whether commitments can be upheld): TCLP, Sam's Clause, Net Zero Land Development, https://chancerylaneproject.org/clauses/net-zero-land-development/, accessed 22.06.2025: A clause which can be added to a development agreement between a municipality and a developer to promote net zero development. See for further details in relation to the construction and planning: For details regarding the preliminary agreements, see Staniszewski/Wieduwilt, in: Wieduwilt, Implementing ESG into Real Estate Contracts, A guide and toolkit for practitioners from a European perspective, 2025, #2.3, p. 168; Wieduwilt, in: ESG-Property Development – Legal Requirements to construction and planning contracts, in: Veith/Conrads/Hackelberg, ESG and Real Estate, 2021 (English 2022), p. 525.

dations for further sustainability improvements. The Buyer can use this report to check compliance and guide future operations.

ESG monitoring and reporting: Both Buyer and Seller will jointly appoint a third-party auditor to perform regular ESG compliance audits according to the established schedule and milestones.

ESG certification milestones, green lease clauses, and payment conditions: The Seller/Developer must achieve at least the minimum required building certification (e.g., BREEAM »Excellent«), a specified EPC rating, and ensure that all leases include the ESG terms listed in Schedule [...]. Proof of these achievements must be provided to the Buyer before completion, as a condition for payment or final payment.

Funding linked to ESG performance: The Buyer will fund the development project only if the Seller provides quarterly ESG performance reports, verified by a third-party expert or auditor. If the project deviates from the agreed ESG standards, funding may be delayed or adjusted.

Warranties on future performance: After completion, an independent assessment must confirm that the Property meets minimum energy performance standards, LCA requirements, and the CRREM pathway. If these standards are not met, the Seller/Developer must pay for any necessary remediation.

(d) Joint Ventures (JVs)

A joint venture is an agreement between two or more parties to collaborate on a specific project or business activity, sharing risks, rewards, and control. A real estate joint venture agreement outlines the terms of a partnership between two or more parties to undertake a specific real estate project, such as development, acquisition, or management. For a **joint venture timeline**, see **Figure 28**.

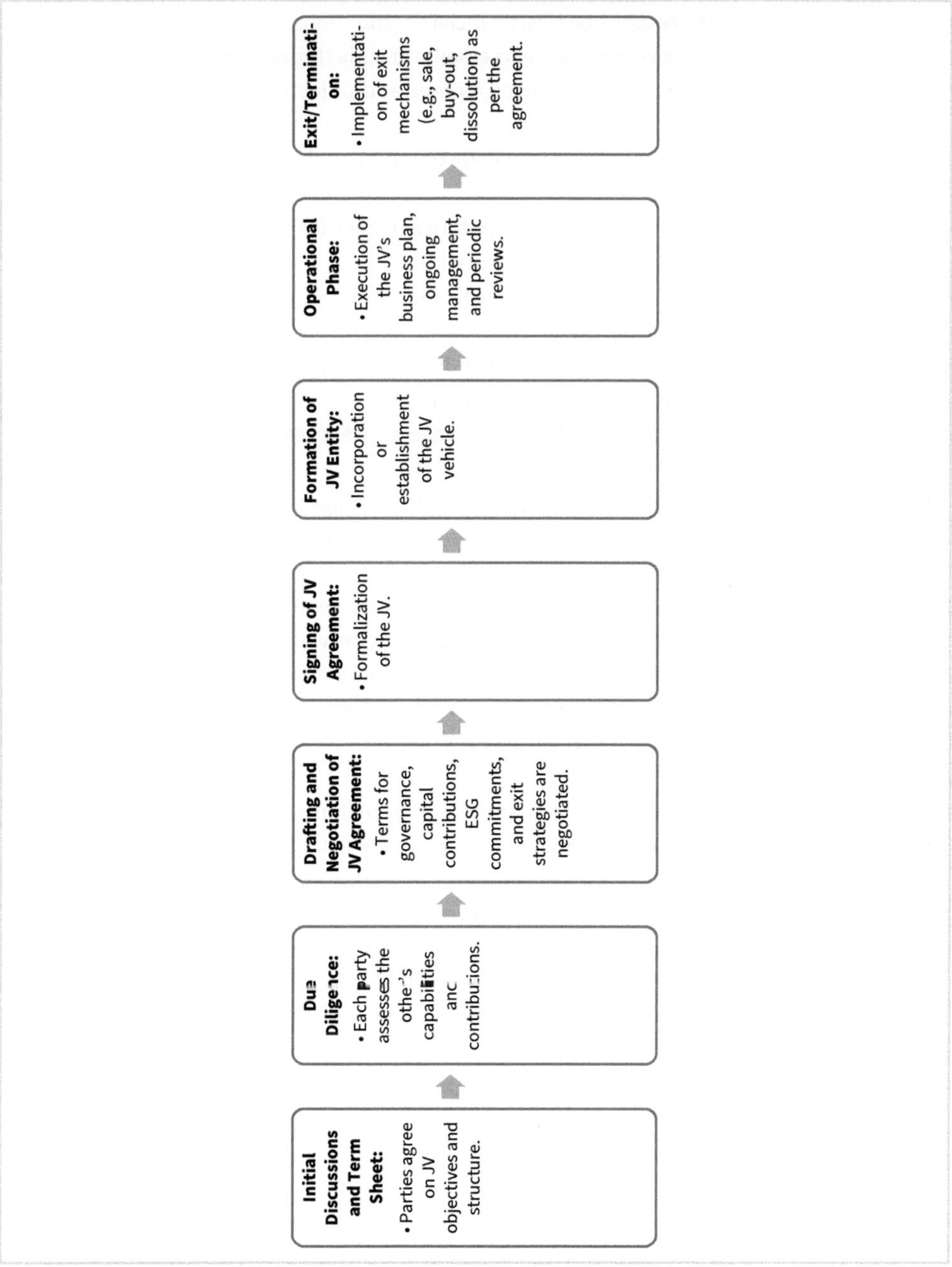

Figure 28: Timeline joint ventures (JV)

These agreements detail the responsibilities, financial contributions, profit-sharing, and exit strategies among the parties. Joint venture (JV) agreements include the following types of clauses[462]:

- **Introduction:** Description of the JV arrangement and objectives, outlining the strategic goals and expected outcomes.
- **Capital contributions:** Terms of financial investment by each party, initial and subsequent funding obligations.
- **Management and control:** Governance structure and decision-making processes, detailing the roles and responsibilities of each JV partner.
- **Profit and loss sharing:** Allocation of financial outcomes, including the distribution of profits and losses among the JV partners.
- **Exit strategies:** Provisions for terminating the JV or withdrawing parties, including detailed procedures for dissolution and asset distribution.
- **Indemnities:** Provisions for compensation in case of breaches or losses to ensure protection against liabilities and unforeseen events.
- **Contracts may include for example:** Specific clauses related to project management, dispute resolution, and performance metrics to ensure clarity in operational execution.

Joint ventures allow parties to collaborate on real estate projects to align ESG objectives and responsibilities from the start. JVs can require alignment between partners on sustainability strategy. **ESG requirements may serve to align the strategic objectives of JV partners toward sustainable investment outcomes.** Clauses may set out shared commitments and governance. See examples of clauses and clause types below[463]:

> **ESG principles and reporting:** JV Partners recognize their mandatory ESG obligations and whether they are signatories to frameworks such as the UNPRI. They comply with both required and voluntary ESG reporting standards (e.g., UNPRI, ISSB, SASB, GRI, GRESB, TCFD, TCND, etc.). The JV or Company [...] will obtain relevant building certifications (e.g., BREEAM, LEED) and manage assets according to CRREM pathways where appropriate. The partners will monitor changes to the ESG framework, cooperate with third parties, share information on risks, and implement measures to address ESG issues.
>
> **Joint ESG policy and improvement plan:** The partners will jointly develop and implement an ESG plan, adopt group-wide ESG policies, integrate them into compliance systems, and pursue specific sustainability targets (e.g., reducing emissions, promoting diversity, and ob-

462 Note that there are variations in how JVs are structured, as well as in their legal form (where relevant), depending on the project type and the constraints of the parties. For further general information on the JV agreement, see, for example: Volkmann, Frederike, Joint Venture – Gemeinsame Chancen, geteiltes Risiko?, BB 2023, 771; Wittneben: Joint-Venture-Verträge in der Immobilien-Projektentwicklung, ZfIR 2009, 846; EquityMultiple, Glossary for Investors, Joint Venture Real Estate, https://equitymultiple.com/glossary/joint-venture-real-estate, accessed 22.06.2025; Blakes, Tips for Building Resilient Real Estate Partnerships, 2024, https://www.blakes.com/insights/tips-for-building-resilient-real-estate-partnerships/, accessed 22.06.2025.

463 To review and exchange, where adequate, for example: roles of the parties involved and use of the terms JV partners/ JV/Company X/Y/Z; ESG requirements and considerations, especially review to align and further specify them, where necessary.

taining green certifications). These policies will be updated regularly to meet or exceed the standards of any partner, ensuring compliance with all relevant ESG laws and commitments.

Investment criteria: No acquisition or development will proceed without ESG screening (e.g., CRREM assessment) and approval from the JV Board.

ESG carve-outs: Partners may exclude or separately manage assets or activities with high ESG risks, with distinct management and reporting.

ESG compliance and reporting: Partners will jointly invest in green infrastructure. The JV will provide regular ESG performance reports, and each partner may conduct or commission ESG audits.

ESG disclosure and remediation: The JV will maintain up-to-date ESG records, promptly disclose significant ESG incidents, and conduct annual ESG audits. If assets fall out of alignment with ESG standards, a remediation plan will be agreed within a set timeframe.

ESG breach: If a material ESG breach occurs, partners will notify each other and cooperate to implement corrective actions, which may include suspending activities or replacing noncompliant suppliers.

ESG committee: An ESG Committee with representatives from each partner will oversee ESG policy development, implementation, and monitoring, and advise the JV Board.

Consent for ESG matters: Certain actions – such as entering ESG-sensitive sectors, investing in non-sustainable assets, or selling to noncompliant parties – require either unanimous partner consent or ESG Committee approval.

ESG-linked incentives: Management incentives may be tied to achieving ESG targets, such as reducing environmental impact or improving diversity.

ESG exit restrictions: Partners cannot transfer JV interests to parties that do not meet minimum ESG standards or that are on restricted lists unless all partners agree.

ESG dispute resolution: The JV has a structured process for resolving ESG disputes, starting with negotiation, then moving on to mediation, and, if needed, arbitration, to maintain ESG commitments.

(e) Portfolio[464]

A portfolio deal involves the acquisition of a group of assets or properties that are often diversified across different locations or types. For a **timeline for a portfolio deal**, see **Figure 29**.

464 See subchapter #5.6 for (investment) management.

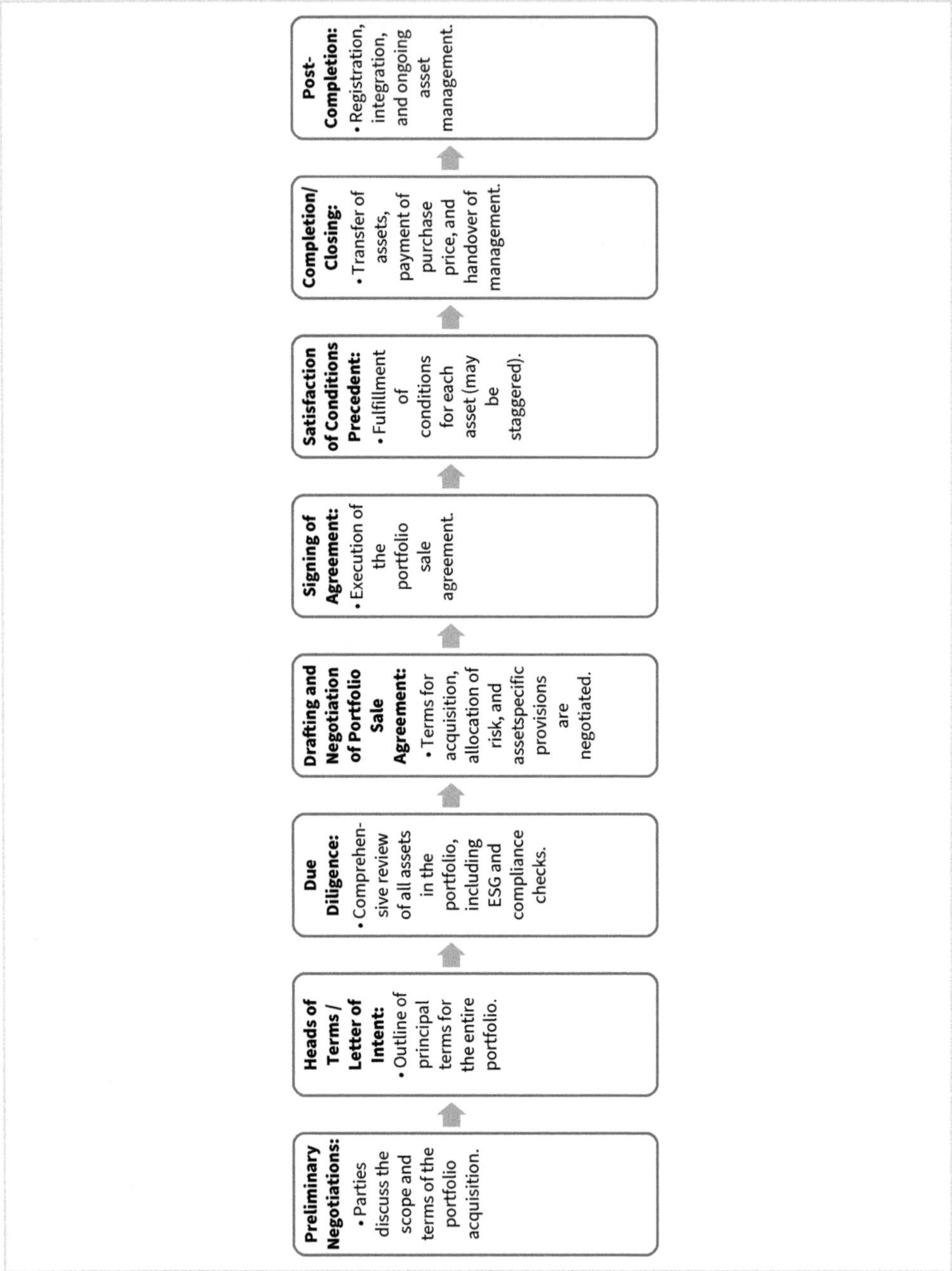

Figure 29: Timeline portfolio deal

Portfolio transactions involve multiple assets, often with varying performance characteristics. The purchase and framework agreements for portfolio deals include the following types of clauses:

- **Object of sale/portfolio description:** Description of the portfolio and its components and any associated rights.
- **Aggregate purchase price:** Terms of payment and valuation of portfolio assets, as well as the total purchase price for the portfolio and its allocation across properties.
- **Cross-collateralization clause:** May link the financing or obligations across multiple properties.
- **Representations and warranties:** Assurances regarding the condition and ownership of the portfolio assets.
- **Closing conditions:** Requirements that must be met before the (portfolio) transaction is closed.
- **Indemnities:** Provisions for compensation in case of breaches or losses.
- **Transfer of title:** The legal process for transferring ownership of portfolio assets.
- **Special provisions:** Clauses relating to models for handling acquisition obstacles in real estate portfolio transactions[465], differentiation for individual properties, performance benchmarks for single assets or the overall portfolio, asset management, diversification, and risk mitigation.

Real estate portfolio transactions may involve selling a few large properties or many residential units, often with no internal connection between them. The agreements should allow for the transaction to cover all, some, or specific properties, and provide for the completion or reversal of individual assets as needed. Each property's completion conditions must be met, and the contract should allow for the partial completion or rescission of specific properties.[466]

Portfolio transactions require coordinated ESG integration across diverse assets and jurisdictions. ESG due diligence is key to assessing risks and compliance with sustainability standards. Transaction documents may include the following clauses:

465 Conradi, Johannes, in: Eilers/Koffka/Mackensen/Paul/Josenhans Private Equity, 4. Aufl., 2022, III. 2. Rn. 94–96: The text discusses three specific models for handling acquisition obstacles in real estate portfolio transactions. The Total Portfolio model views the portfolio as a single unit, where any disruption causes a complete withdrawal. The Individual Portfolio model treats each property independently, allowing only affected properties to be withdrawn. The Core and Fringe Portfolio model defines essential properties as a core, with disruptions in fringe properties leading to partial withdrawal while core disruptions affect the entire transaction. It emphasizes the need for detailed contractual arrangements, such as individual pricing for each property and adjustments to liability limitations, to manage purchase price changes and legal encumbrances, ensuring the transaction remains viable even if certain properties fall out of the portfolio.

466 BeckM&A-HdB/v. Bismarck/Freytag/Kress, 2. Aufl. 2022, § 74 Rn. 234; see also: Tschammler, in: Schäfer/Conzen, Praxishandbuch Immobilieninvestition, 4. Aufl., 2020, 621.

ESG portfolio assessment and disclosure: The seller must provide a CRREM-based risk assessment or specific ESG data (e.g., energy ratings, waste management) for each asset by a set date.

Material adverse change (MAC) clause: The Buyer can renegotiate or terminate if the condition of the properties significantly deviates from the agreed ESG standards.

Purchase price retention for ESG benchmarks: The Buyer may withhold a portion of the purchase price if less than a specified percentage of the properties meet ESG criteria (e.g., EU Taxonomy, CRREM, EPC rating). Release of funds depends on independent verification, with costs borne by the Seller.

Sustainability reporting undertaking: The Seller must provide all documents needed for sustainability reporting (e.g., GRI, SASB) before and after closing to ensure standardized documentation and full cooperation.

ESG representations and warranties: The Seller guarantees that all assets meet the minimum energy efficiency or CRREM standards, as verified by a third party. Noncompliant assets require a remediation plan with costs allocated as agreed.

ESG warranty (ratings): The Seller warrants that the property manager complies with ISO 14001 and maintains a minimum MSCI ESG rating. Breaches trigger indemnification.

Remedies for ESG underperformance: The Buyer monitors ESG performance (e.g., CR-REM) and reports annually to investors.[467]

(f) Cross-border

Cross-border deals involve transactions between parties in different countries and require consideration of international laws and regulations. For a **timeline for a cross-border deal**, see **Figure 30**.

467 This only makes sense, if the Seller continues to have a stake (for example, due to a put option or equity participation of the Seller).

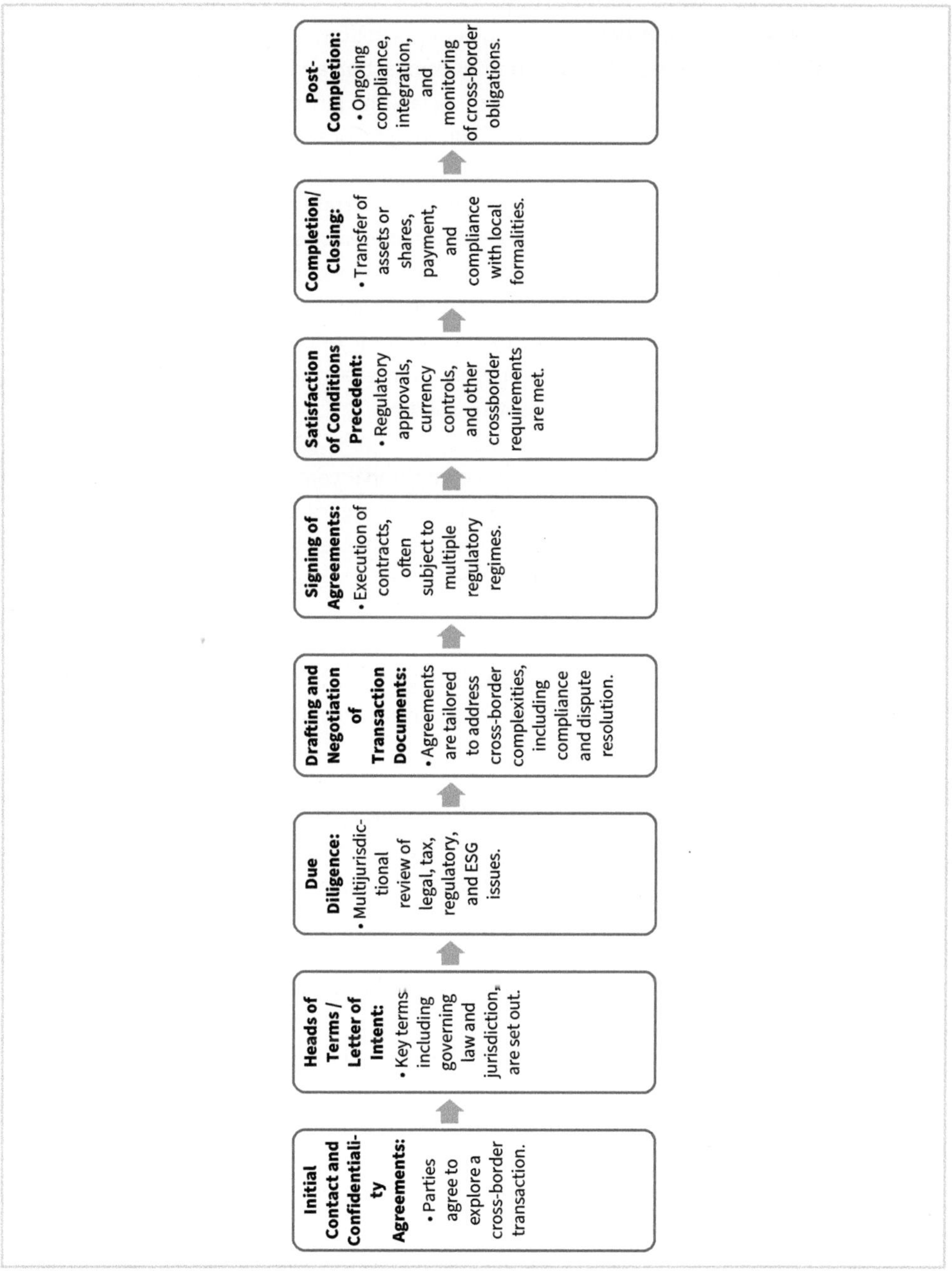

Figure 30: Timeline cross-border deal

Purchase agreements for cross-border deals include the following types of clauses:

- **Introduction:** Description of the cross-border transaction and the jurisdictions involved.
- **Applicable law:** Determination of the governing law and jurisdiction.
- **Regulatory compliance:** Requirements for adhering to local and international regulations.
- **Representations and warranties:** Assurances regarding compliance and legal status.
- **Closing conditions:** Requirements to be met before the transaction is finalized.
- **Indemnities:** Provisions for compensation in case of breaches or losses.
- **Special provisions:** Specific clauses addressing carve-outs, jurisdictional challenges, varying employee participation rights across jurisdictions, staggered closing, locked box transactions and purchase price adjustments, currency exchange, citation suggestions, references to various legal handbooks and comments relevant to transaction structuring, tax implications, and international dispute resolution.

Cross-border real estate transactions introduce additional complexity due to differing legal systems, regulatory standards, and cultural expectations regarding ESG. **ESG compliance may vary by jurisdiction, necessitating a thorough analysis of international sustainability standards and practices.** Cross-border deals must address differing regulatory regimes. See examples of clauses and clause types below[468]:

> **Harmonization of ESG standards across jurisdictions**: All assets will be assessed and managed according to either the CRREM decarbonization pathway or a local EPC benchmark above [...]% for each jurisdiction.
>
> **Disclosure of regulatory risks:** The Seller must disclose all known or expected ESG-related risks, including compliance with local laws, potential social and governance liabilities, and any upcoming regulatory changes that could affect the deal.
>
> **Cross-border ESG compliance, representation, and warranty:** The Seller confirms that all properties meet the ESG standards listed in Schedule [...] for each jurisdiction (e.g., LEED, BREEAM, or local equivalents; accessibility and ethical management verified by local auditors). Any noncompliance triggers the agreed indemnification.
>
> **Adaptation of ESG requirements to local frameworks:** The Seller warrants that each asset complies with local energy efficiency laws and has been assessed against the CRREM pathway or the latest mandatory requirements.
>
> **Adaptation of ESG requirements for cross-border JV:** The joint venture includes a process to update ESG policies as local laws change.

468 In cross-border deals, ESG standards may differ significantly between jurisdictions, making it challenging to ensure consistent compliance across all regions involved.

Choice of law and arbitration for ESG disputes: ESG-related disputes will be governed by the laws of [...] and resolved by arbitration under [...] rules, with the seat and language specified.

5.3 The evolution of EU public procurement: From a focus on sustainability to strategic autonomy in the ESG era

Dr. Peter Braun

5.3.1 Introduction to #5.3

The European Union's public procurement landscape is undergoing a fundamental transformation that reflects broader shifts in EU policy priorities and evolving global dynamics. The process began as compliance-heavy and price-focused and is now being reimagined as a strategic lever for economic resilience, sustainability, and industrial innovation. With an annual volume of approximately €2.3 trillion – roughly 15% of EU GDP – public procurement represents one of the most significant policy tools at the EU's disposal. Additionally, public procurement is responsible for approximately 10% of the EU's greenhouse gas emissions. Recent developments, however, suggest a notable shift away from the sustainability-first approach that characterized earlier reforms. This shift raises important questions about the future of environmental, social, and governance (ESG) considerations in public procurement.

#5.3 Evolution of EU public procurement - from sustainability to strategic autonomy	**#5.3.1 - intro to #5.3**
	#5.3.2 - development of policies
	#5.3.3 - current reform landscape
	#5.3.4 - recommendations for ESG integration
	#5.3.5 - conclusion

Subchapter #5.3 focuses on the evolution of EU public procurement, we explore the development of sustainable procurement policies (#5.3.2), the current reform landscape (#5.3.3), and recommendations for legislators regarding ESG integration (#5.3.4), concluding with final remarks (#5.3.5).

5.3.2 The development of sustainable procurement policies

In the **1990s, sustainability criteria** were **often dismissed as »non-procurement criteria«** – meaning they were not considered legitimate factors under the prevailing legal interpretation for the award of public contracts. The main criteria at that time were price and quality, while environmental and social aspects were largely ignored.

A significant turning point came with the European Court of Justice (ECJ) ruling in the **Concordia Bus Finland case.**[469] The ECJ ruled that **sustainability criteria can be included** in procurement under certain conditions. These conditions include that the criteria are related to the subject matter of the contract, are transparent and non-discriminatory, and are announced in advance. The same applies to social criteria.[470]

The 2014 procurement reform package[471] expressly incorporated the possibility of providing for sustainability criteria into European procurement law. This idea is reflected in the preamble to Directive 2014/24/EU on public procurement:

> *«Nothing in this Directive should prevent the imposition or enforcement of measures necessary to protect public policy, public morality, public security, health, human and animal life, the preservation of plant life or other environmental measures, in particular with a view to sustainable development, provided that those measures are in conformity with the TFEU.«*

In **2016**, the **third version of the handbook »Buying green!«** was published by the European Commission containing guidelines and opportunities for greening public procurement. In February **2023**, the **Manifesto on Socially Responsible Procurement** was published, supported by more than 90 public and semi-public organizations. The manifesto focuses on encouraging ambitious socially responsible procurement and purchasing.

Although the implementation of sustainable criteria is **generally not mandatory** for contracting authorities and entities, there are a few **exceptions**. For instance, contracting authorities must ensure that bidders comply with **national minimum wage rules.**[472] The Clean Vehicles Directive (EU) 2019/1161 was enacted for public purchases of vehicles to provide a mandatory framework for contracting authorities and utilities in Europe to purchase clean and energy-efficient road vehicles and thereby to achieve the environmentally binding policy goals such as the Paris Climate Agreement.[473] In view of the significant share of public and utilities procurement expenditures in the overall economic performance of a country, the CVD was meant to serve as a deliberate signal for the relevant economic sectors and markets that acceptance of clean vehicles is to be increased, as well as competitiveness promoted.[474]

---

469 ECJ, judgment of 17.09.2002, Case C-513/99, Concordia Bus Finland Oy Ab v Helsingin kaupunki and HKL-Bussiliikenne [2002] ECR I-7213, para 69.

470 ECJ, Judgment of 20.09.1988, Case 31/87, Gebroeders Beentjes BV v State of the Netherlands.

471 Directive 2014/23/EU of the European Parliament and of the Council of 26.02.2014 on the award of concession contracts, Directive 2014/24/EU of the European Parliament and of the Council of 26.02.2014 on public procurement, Directive 2014/25/EU of the European Parliament and of the Council of 26.02.2014 on procurement by entities operating in the water, energy, transport and postal services sectors.

472 ECJ, judgment of 17.11.2015, C-346/06 Regio Post; ECJ, judgment of 03.04.2008, C-549/13 Rüffert.

473 Preamble, 10 Directive 2019/1161/EU.

474 Preamble 7 of Directive 2019/1161/EU.

ESG considerations, particularly those related to sustainability, can be **strategically integrated throughout multiple phases of the public procurement process**.

- During the **initial procurement phase**, contracting authorities should conduct market consultations where appropriate before launching the tender, particularly when defining the subject matter of the contract. This preliminary step enables the identification of innovative, sustainable solutions available in the market and facilitates more accurate life-cycle cost assessments.
- Subsequently, where legally permitted, the strategic application of **award criteria and variants** (particularly within negotiation procedures) can effectively promote more sustainable procurement outcomes.
- Throughout the **procurement evaluation process**, violations of environmental law or labor and employment laws constitute valid **grounds for bidder exclusion**. Furthermore, **sustainability-based selection criteria** may be established, provided they satisfy **three fundamental requirements**: (i) non-discriminatory application, (ii) direct relation to the contract's subject-matter, and (iii) proportionality to the scope of the contract. Examples include environmental management requirements for contract performance that are environmentally essential (such as ISO 14001 certification for asbestos removal) or specialized personnel training for green building construction. However, contracting authorities must consider that such criteria may limit the pool of eligible bidders, and they must possess the resources necessary to verify compliance with these specifications.
- **Life-cycle cost analysis** serves as a valuable tool for sustainability assessment in procurement. While legitimate, this criterion may not always provide a neutral evaluation, as incumbent bidders (particularly those with previous similar contracts) face reduced placement costs compared to other bidders.

The **current Directive's failure to mandate Green Public Procurement (GPP)** rather than merely allow it has been one of the main reasons for the uneven levels of GPP across EU member states, as confirmed by the European Commission's 2025 evaluation of the 2014 Public Procurement Directives.[475] According to the 2025 evaluation, on average across 14 Member States, just under 25% of contracts include green criteria by number and about 37% by value, though this varies significantly – from Lithuania's 89.3% of procurement value dedicated to green initiatives, to Denmark's 59.9% in 2022, and Finland's 48.3% in 2023, while other Member States lag considerably behind. According to **incomplete data** from the Public Procurement Data Space, only 15% of procurement contracts above EU thresholds integrate environmental criteria, highlighting the persistent gap between policy ambitions and implementation.[476]

475 Commission Staff Working Document, Evaluation of Directive 2014/23/EU on Concessions, Directive 2014/24/EU on Public Procurement and Directive 2014/25/EU on Utilities (SWD(2025) 333 final).

476 Public Procurement Data Space. Indicator 5 Award criteria based on price alone, https://api.public-procurement-data-space.europa.eu/superset/dashboard/smsindicator5/?standalone=true, accessed 01.09.2025.

The voluntary nature of GPP **undermines healthy competition** for green public tenders and limits procurers' ability to achieve value for money. Without a clear demand signal, businesses have little incentive to offer green products, services, and infrastructure or to decarbonize supply chains.

The EU Procurement Directives fail to create the required **legal certainty** on GPP, which hinders the implementation of ambitious, consistent, and legally sound green requirements throughout the procurement process – a finding reinforced by the 2025 Commission evaluation which identified the absence of harmonized definitions and standards as a key barrier. Procurers frequently raise concerns about unclear legal definitions, the lack of binding sustainable procurement targets, and diverging national interpretations. This legal uncertainty poses the risk of slowing down procurement processes and makes procurement authorities much more reluctant to implement sustainable procurement on a large scale.

Furthermore, the current EU Public Procurement Directives fail to create a **coherent framework** that promotes sustainability. The EU has also introduced obligations for public procurement in other legal instruments[477]. Some EU sectoral legislation introduces binding Green Public Procurement (GPP) targets in areas such as energy efficiency, building performance, clean vehicles, net-zero products and technologies, and packaging waste. Additionally, the transposition and implementation at member state level of the Directives has been inconsistent regarding GPP, which has led to fragmented outcomes[478]. The 2025 Commission evaluation confirmed this regulatory fragmentation, noting that the proliferation of sectoral and horizontal legislation with green requirements has increased complexity and sometimes led to legal incoherence, making it harder for contracting authorities to apply ESG criteria consistently.

This **fragmentation** is evident in the varying levels of GPP implementation across EU member states. The 2025 Commission evaluation highlighted that data collection and monitoring of GPP uptake remain inconsistent and challenging, with the lack of standardised reporting and voluntary nature of many data fields meaning that available statistics may not accurately reflect the real level of green procurement or its effectiveness.[479] Time and capacity constraints within procurement agencies for implementing GPP further complicate navigation of this legal landscape.

477 Directive 2023/1791 on Energy Efficiency, https://eur-lex.europa.eu/eli/dir/2023/1791/oj/eng, accessed 01.09.2025, Directive 2024/1275 on Energy Performance of Buildings, https://eur-lex.europa.eu/eli/dir/2024/1275/oj/eng, accessed 01.09.2025, Directive 2019/1161 on Clean and Energy-Efficient Road Transport Vehicles, https://eur-lex.europa.eu/eli/dir/2019/1161/oj/eng, accessed 01.09.2025, Regulation 2024/1735 Net-Zero Industry Act, https://eur-lex.europa.eu/eli/reg/2024/1735/oj/eng, accessed 01.09.2025, Regulation 2025/40 on Packaging and Packaging Waste, https://eur-lex.europa.eu/eli/reg/2025/40/oj/eng, accessed 01.09.2025.

478 International Institute for Sustainable Development, How Reforming the European Union's Public Procurement Directive Can Help Drive a Green Transition, 2025.

479 European Commission, Implementation and best practices of national procurement policies in the Internal Market, COM(2021) 245 final, https://eur-lex.europa.eu/legal-content/EN/TXT/?uri=celex:52021DC0245, accessed 01.09.2025.

5.3.3 The current reform landscape: The European Commission's strategic vision

The European Commission's 2025 Communication »A Competitiveness Compass for the EU« includes a proposal for revision of the Public Procurement Directives.[480] The revision aims to reinforce technological security and domestic supply chains, simplify and modernize the rules, particularly for startups and innovative companies. The revision also seeks to protect and promote clean technology and decarbonized manufacturing in the EU.[481] The Commission proposes introducing a European preference for public procurement in strategic sectors and technologies.[482]

These proposals come at a time when the EU is prioritizing increased action on defense and climate, viewing procurement as a policy tool that expands and complements a wide range of actions and policies, including the Net Zero Industry Act (NZIA), ecodesign rules, the proposed Security Action for Europe (SAFE) initiative, and the Carbon Border Adjustment Mechanism (CBAM). However, these various procurement reforms are unlikely to produce tangible results before the end of the decade, which will delay the impact on climate action and the scaling up of European industries, but it could also offer businesses time to adapt.

The European Parliament has taken a **proactive stance on the future of public procurement through its Internal Market and Consumer Protection Committee (IMCO)**, which adopted an initiative report on 7 July 2025 aimed at influencing the Commission's upcoming legislative proposals. The Parliament's diagnosis is clear: The current procurement framework too often favors the cheapest bid over value, quality, and innovation, weakening Europe's ability to use public procurement as a lever for strategic autonomy.

The Parliament's recommendations include moving beyond price-only awards by strengthening the use of **Most Economically Advantageous Tender (MEAT) criteria** , introducing price review clauses in contracts to accommodate inflation and commodity price fluctuations, digitizing procurement procedures using interoperable platforms with specific attention to SME access, and encouraging, but not mandating, the use of social and environmental criteria to promote sustainability.

480 European Commission, A Competitiveness Compass for the EU, COM(2025) 30 final, https://eur-lex.europa.eu/legal-content/EN/TXT/?uri=celex:52025DC0030, accessed 01.09.2025.

481 European Court of Auditors, Special report 28/2023: Public procurement in the EU – Less competition for contracts awarded for works, goods and services in the 10 years up to 2021, https://www.eca.europa.eu/en/publications/SR-2023-28, accessed 02.09.2025.

482 Council of the European Union, Public procurement – strategic goals and way forward. Discussion Paper, Brussels, 22.05.2025, https://data.consilium.europa.eu/doc/document/ST-8638-2025-INIT/en/pdf, accessed 02.09.2025.

(a) The shift from sustainability to strategic autonomy: Influence of the Letta and Draghi reports

The reform trajectory has been significantly shaped by two influential reports: the Letta report, »Much More Than a Market«, on the Single Market,[483] and Mario Draghi's report, »The Future of European Competitiveness«.[484] Both reports reference the role of public procurement in relation to the future of the EU internal market. With public procurement market representing approximately 15 % of EU GDP, it has become an indispensable tool for achieving EU strategic objectives.[485]

The **Letta report** proposes fundamentally redefining the objectives of public procurement legislation, suggesting the establishment of »a smaller, more precise set of objectives that are both clear and measurable« to facilitate efficient realization of desired outcomes. However, this approach appears to prioritize productivity, resilience, and supply chain security over traditional sustainability concerns.

What emerges from those recent policy documents reveals a stark contrast to the European approach under the first von der Leyen Commission, which was mainly driven by environmental concerns through the EU Green Deal. Although strategic procurement is frequently mentioned, »strategic« in this context seems to primarily refer to values other than sustainability, such as productivity, supply security, and strategic autonomy.

The sustainability perspective appears marginalized in the current vision for European public procurement reform. Even though proposals related to circularity and raw materials may have sustainability angles, they appear to be driven mainly by considerations related to security of supply and strategic autonomy rather than environmental protection. This represents a significant **departure from the 2011 Green Paper** on modernizing public procurement, which placed sustainability in the spotlight by dedicating 39 out of 114 questions to environmental and social considerations.

(b) Opportunities for reform and ESG integration: Mandatory Green Public Procurement

Moving from voluntary to mandatory GPP could take many forms, such as GPP targets, product-specific requirements, or minimum requirements. Critically, shifting from voluntary to mandatory GPP would decrease complexity by reducing legal fragmentation and uncertainty for both procurers and companies. A clear definition of mandatory requirements ensures clarity regarding expectations, necessary proof, and equivalent certifications.

483 Letta, Enrico, Much more than a market, 2024, https://www.consilium.europa.eu/media/ny3j24sm/much-more-than-a-market-report-by-enrico-letta.pdf, accessed 31.08.2025.

484 The Draghi report on EU competitiveness, https://commission.europa.eu/topics/eu-competitiveness/draghi-report_en, accessed 31.08.2025.

485 European Commission. Single market and competitiveness scoreboard, https://single-market-scoreboard.ec.europa.eu/business-framework-conditions/public-procurement_en, accessed 31.08.2025.

To foster green innovation in the internal market and enhance competitiveness, reform efforts to »buy European« must be tied to environmental requirements. Since procurement is already predominantly local – with 40 % of winning bidders in 2021 registered in the same region as the contracting authority – and particularly high local procurement in transport services (73 %) and construction (55 %), adding GPP requirements is an opportunity to increase competition based on environmental performance in the EU internal market.[486]

Effective public procurement reform requires better monitoring at the EU level and in member states to track GPP progress and identify strategic areas for intervention. Better monitoring and data systems improve the transparency and accountability of public spending. The 2025 Commission evaluation confirmed these monitoring deficiencies, noting that some Member States have developed more robust monitoring systems, but overall, the ability to assess the impact of GPP on environmental outcomes remains limited. Future systems must be designed to track and quantify the contribution of procurement to climate goals and other sustainability objectives. The evaluation suggests that further harmonization, clearer definitions, and improved monitoring could help increase the uptake and effectiveness of GPP across the EU.

EU policymakers face the challenge of reconciling the legitimate need for strategic autonomy with environmental and social objectives. The current approach risks creating a false dichotomy between competitiveness and sustainability when, in fact, these objectives can be mutually reinforcing. As noted in recent policy documents, joint procurement can offset some of the cost increases that introducing non-pricing criteria might produce through economies of scale and better negotiating power.

The revision of public procurement directives is expected in late 2026 and the Commission is currently preparing its proposal. This timeline presents both challenges and opportunities. While it may delay the implementation of sustainability measures, it also allows stakeholders time to develop comprehensive approaches that integrate ESG considerations with strategic autonomy objectives.

5.3.4 Recommendations for ESG integration: Strengthening legal framework

To address current challenges, several legislative changes merit consideration. First, contracting authorities should be given more discretion to include environmental and social considerations, requiring careful consideration of the optimal balance between market integration principles and sustainability objectives. Second, policymakers should review the types of sustainable public procurement that are currently prohibited, such as including CSR policies in

486 European Commission, Single market and competitiveness scoreboard, https://single-market-scoreboard.ec.europa.eu/business-framework-conditions/public-procurement_en, accessed 31.08.2025.

award criteria. Third, policymakers should consider how mandatory requirements can increase the uptake of sustainable public procurement.

Different sectors require tailored approaches to ESG integration. In healthcare, energy, and security, targeted procurement models that prioritize long-term value and resilience should be developed. For the biotech sector, innovation-led procurement models with stronger IP protections and joint procurement arrangements should be promoted.

The digitization of procurement procedures using interoperable platforms that specifically address SME access represents a crucial opportunity to embed ESG criteria more systematically. Digital systems can facilitate better monitoring of sustainability outcomes and reduce administrative burdens associated with ESG compliance.

5.3.5 Conclusion

The evolution of EU public procurement represents a pivotal moment in the integration of ESG considerations into public policy. Although recent reforms have shifted the focus toward strategic autonomy and competitiveness, this does not necessarily mean the abandonment of sustainability objectives. Rather, it presents an opportunity to develop more sophisticated approaches that recognize the interconnected nature of environmental, social, and governance challenges with economic competitiveness and security concerns.

The success of future reforms will depend on the EU's ability to create a coherent framework that addresses fragmentation, provides legal certainty, and mandates rather than merely permits sustainable procurement practices. With public procurement representing approximately 15% of EU GDP and responsible for around 10% of the EU's greenhouse gas emissions, the stakes are too high to treat sustainability as a secondary consideration.

> As the legislative process continues toward the 2026 deadline, stakeholders must ensure that ESG considerations remain central to the reform agenda. The challenge is not choosing between sustainability and strategic autonomy but rather developing innovative approaches that advance both objectives simultaneously. Only through this integration can the EU achieve its ambitious goal of becoming a competitive, resilient, and sustainable economy by 2050.

Continued engagement from all stakeholders – including policymakers, procurement authorities, industry, and civil society – is required to ensure that the next generation of public procurement rules delivers on the promise of driving innovation, reducing emissions, and promoting sustainability, all while maintaining the EU's strategic autonomy and competitiveness in an increasingly complex global environment.

5.4 Real estate investment funds and ESG

Vivien Teu[487]

5.4.1 Introduction to #5.4

Real estate investment funds pool capital from multiple investors to acquire, manage, and profit from property-related assets, which may include office, residential, industrial, logistics and retail real estate. There are also numerous secondary sectors, including hospitality, self-storage, student accommodation, retirement housing, and other special purpose buildings. The establishment and operation of real estate investment funds enable investors to gain exposure to real estate markets without owning physical properties, offering diversification, professional management, and potentially lower entry barriers compared to buying real estate outright.

There are different types or forms of vehicles for channeling capital into the real estate market, each tailored to investor type, liquidity needs, and regulatory requirements. Most real estate funds in the market are private equity real estate («**PERE**«) funds, which are structured as limited partnerships with the promoter as general partner and investors subscribing for fund interests as limited partners, or other corresponding structures understood as such. As further discussed below, PERE funds are typically available to a select, limited number of investors on a private placement basis. Another common form of real estate investment fund is the real estate investment trust («**REIT**«), which is listed on stock exchanges and accessible to retail investors. In the public markets, REITs offer an alternative or complementary way to gain exposure to the real estate sector besides investing in the listed securities of real estate groups.

#5.4 real estate investment funds & ESG	**#5.4.1 - intro to #5.4**
	#5.4.2 - strategies of real estate investment funds
	#5.4.3 - PERE and REITs
	#5.4.4 - real estate investment funds' ESG

This subchapter #5.4 on **real estate investment funds and ESG** covers strategies of real estate investment funds (#5.4.2), Private Equity Real Estate («PERE«) and Real Estate Investment Trusts («REITs«) (#5.4.3), as well as real estate investment funds ESG (#5.4.4).

487 Please see chapter #6.3 on Asia, including deeper dive into examples of real estate investment funds ESG initiatives in Asia.

5.4.2 Strategies of real estate investment funds

Real estate funds vary across a spectrum, ranging from the low-risk, income-focused »**core funds**« to the high-risk, development-driven »**opportunistic**« strategies. Core funds tend to hold anchor portfolios, investing mainly in existing income-producing buildings. They use low leverage and have no or very low development exposure and generate a high proportion of returns through income. At the other end of the spectrum, development funds may seek outsized gains by building from scratch or repositioning properties. Development funds typically employ higher leverage and are exposed to development risks, as well as risks relating to existing buildings requiring significant improvements and asset management. Such funds aim to deliver returns primarily in the form of capital appreciation. Each point on the spectrum has its own profile of asset quality, cash flow stability, return expectations, holding period and investor suitability.

A report published by Realfin[488] suggests that the first half of 2025 saw the lowest number of real estate fund launches and the lowest amount of targeted capital since 2017. This continues the negative trend that started in the wake of the recent pandemic. However, opportunistic fundraising recorded the highest level since the first half of 2023, with general partners attracting $43.9 billion in limited partner commitments. It is also worth noting that **real estate debt funds** recorded the biggest increase in private real estate capital raising, which is consistent with a global growth trend in private credit, while core funds attracted only $2.7 billion of capital commitments in the first half of 2025, which is the lowest figure in the last 10 years.

5.4.3 Private Equity Real Estate («PERE«) and Real Estate Investment Trusts («REITs«)

As mentioned previously, PERE funds and REITs are the two main types of real estate investment funds. These can be considered as offering investors complementary paths to real estate exposure.

PERE funds are predominantly closed-end vehicles that pool capital from institutional and high-net-worth investors seeking active value creation and higher return targets in exchange for long-term, illiquid investment and greater concentration risk, to acquire, develop, and reposition property assets. Managers typically call committed capital over a defined investment period (often three to five years) and fund a term of between seven and[489] twelve years to execute opportunistic strategies. PERE funds also usually employ significant leverage to enhance equity returns, which amplifies downside risk if asset values decline, presenting a risk-return profile that is more appropriate for sophisticated institutional or professional investors.

488 Realfin State of the Market Report Global Real Estate H1 2025.
489 GRESB, GRESB Public Results, https://www.gresb.com/nl-en/gresb-public-results/, accessed 01.09.2025.

REITs are publicly offered vehicles that own, operate, or finance income-producing real estate across sectors such as retail, office, industrial, and residential. By pooling capital from retail investors and investing across various property sectors, REITs offer broad diversification and professional management, offering access to real estate investment opportunities to investors without having to buy or manage buildings directly. In Hong Kong, REITs authorized by the Securities and Futures Commission must distribute at least 90 % of their audited annual income after tax each year, as required by the Code on Real Estate Investment Trusts. A defining feature of REITs is liquidity, which allows investors to buy or sell shares daily, capturing dividend yields (commonly 4–8 %) plus any appreciation in market price.

5.4.4 Real estate investment funds' ESG

Since its launch in 2009 with three original investor members, GRESB has been growing in membership of real estate companies, fund managers and asset operators, institutional investors, asset owners, as well as consultants and industry bodies, covering 208,250 real estate assets and 3,145 infrastructure facilities in more than 80 markets in 2024. It is generally considered as the authoritative ESG benchmark for real estate, while its adoption and use have been largely voluntary, representing industry best practice.

Under the EU Green Deal and the EU Taxonomy, the introduction of the **EU Sustainable Finance Disclosure Regulation (SFDR)** has imposed mandatory disclosure and reporting requirements on the sustainability practices of investment managers and funds as financial market participants, including real estate investment managers and funds within scope. The convergence of market standards and regulatory requirements in this area is well illustrated by GRESB's support of the industry through its Real Estate Assessment methodology aligning with international reporting frameworks (such as TCFD, GRI and PRI), along with its SFDR Real Estate Assessment tool for reporting on sustainability data and the **Principal Adverse Impacts (PAIs)** to comply with SFDR.

However, there are concerns in the industry that the SFDR's implementation has proven to be complex and costly and there is a lack of legal clarity on key concepts, which poses particular challenges in the real estate industry due to its sector-specific complexities, such as issues linked to data availability, inadequate accommodation of environmental, or impact-focused transition strategies. There is a need for a more tailored application of the rules.[490] Overall, sustainability and long-term resilience are integral to the real estate sector. Investor and stakeholder expectations may drive the ESG focus more than regulations. Arguably, regulatory requirements should not create an unnecessary compliance burden for real estate investment managers and funds or add to the difficulties of additional compliance costs borne by fund investors.

490 INREV, Response to European Commission Call for Evidence on the Sustainable Finance Disclosure Regulation (SFDR), https://www.inrev.org/system/files/2025-06/INREV-Response-to-European-Commission-Call-for-Evidence-on-SFDR.pdf, accessed 01.09.2025.

5.5 ESG and antitrust

Dr. Bertold Bär-Bouyssière, LL.M.[491]

5.5.1 Introduction to #5.5

The concept of antitrust was invented in America (the U.S.) in the late 19th century, culminating in the Sherman Act, a fundamental piece of Federal legislation.[492] It **prohibits (1) anticompetitive agreements** and **(2) unilateral conduct that monopolizes or attempts to monopolize the relevant market.** This marked the beginning of a new legal philosophy that spread around the world like a virus. Most antitrust laws follow the bifocal approach of the Sherman Act.

A consequence of the broad and general nature of antitrust law is that it can mean whatever the incumbent government or administration wants it to mean. In the 1950s, big was bad; in the 1980s, however, big was not big enough.

> At the core of antitrust is the idea of **consumer welfare**. This concept refers to our wallets. Assuming the market price for real estate agency services is a 3 % commission, an agreement or arrangement among agencies to artificially inflate the commission to 5 % would hurt our wallet.

#5.5 ESG & antitrust	**#5.5.1 – intro to #5.5**
	#5.5.2 – meaning of ESG and antitrust
	#5.5.3 – two trends
	#5.5.4 – conclusion

In this subchapter, we cover the meaning of ESG and antitrust (#5.5.2), two trends that shape ESG and antitrust (#5.5.3), followed by concluding remarks (#5.5.4).

5.5.2 The meaning of ESG and antitrust

ESG encompasses many things, and the concept has arguably become overinflated in recent years, turning into a religion of its own. There is a healthy pushback these days, but core issues won't disappear just because of politics. Climate change is one of them. Tsunamis, hurricanes, and wildfires – no need to explain. The scenario of insurers refusing to provide coverage for entire geographic regions is looming on the horizon. Another term for environmental preservation is »sustainability«, the »S« in ESG. This is where the link to antitrust pops up.

491 The author is a Germany and New-York qualified Antitrust specialist with more than 30 years of relevant experience in the EU Brussels Bubble. He initiated the »ESG-Alliance« between Dentons and the Maharashtra National law University (Mumbai) and services as advisor to the President of the African Center for Competitive Intelligence (ACCI).

492 The Sherman Antitrust Act of 1890 (26 Stat. 209, 15 U.S.C. §§ 1–7).

Responsible real estate operators consider the environment. Ideally, they would *produce* only green cement, but it comes to a cost, and what if the competition does not follow the idea? So, cement producers stick their heads together and come up with an alliance for green steel production, agreeing on a common sales price.

As laudable as the initiative may be, it technically restricts competition, and hurts our wallet. Luckily, antitrust law is not blind and allows for justifications: efficiencies that somewhat outweigh the restriction of competition or balancing under the rule of reason test. Were the above example about organic chicken, consumers would pay a dollar more for their poultry but would receive a yummy and drug-free feed in return.

The producers would have to demonstrate and quantify the benefits in one way or the other. Of course, not all cases are that straightforward, and antitrust regulators are wary of »greenwashing«. The lesson here is: Good intentions alone won't keep you out of trouble.

In the example given, we saw a collaboration between competing cement *producers* regarding *sales* prices. Now, imagine the same type of collaboration one level down in the supply chain: competing construction companies form an alliance to only *use* green cement. This would be restrictive as well, even though the collaboration affects the purchase market.

Antitrust law is not limited to »horizontal« collaborations between competitors, it also applies »vertically« to collaborations between economic operators at different market levels, i. e. seller and buyers/resellers. A commercial mall operator may want to impose restrictive covenants on tenants, such as »exclusivity«, »preferential«, »non-compete« or »non-solicitation« (of personnel) clauses.[493] These restrictions may be justified under the rule of reason or efficiency tests, but this has to be considered in advance, even when such restrictive covenants are motivated by laudable sustainability considerations. For example, a mall operator specializing in food may require all tenants to source organic cooking oil from a supplier specified by the operator. There may be less restrictive means to achieve a similar result.

Antitrust law applies to all industries and types of economic activity. Therefore, it must always be on everybody's radar. Failure to comply can result in significant penalties, litigation, reputational loss, and a drop in share price.

Note that **consumer welfare is not only about price but also about buyers having alternatives of choice, product or service quality, and innovation**. In the field of sustainability, an agreement between competing operators to adhere to a specific innovation standard and not exceed it is as anticompetitive as a collaboration affecting price. Standard setting must follow strict, transparent protocols.

493 Non-solicitation agreements between employers harm workers.

5.5.3 Two trends that shape ESG and antitrust

Two important developments or trends should be briefly mentioned: The **first trend** is about the **politicization of antitrust**. In the early decades of the 20th century, antitrust was often influenced by social and industrial policies other than consumer welfare, such as job preservation, the creation of national champions, and more. In the wake of the U.S. Reagan administration and pushed by the OECD, a global consensus emerged that antitrust should be a **market-focused and politically neutral discipline**. Even Communist China adhered to it, even more than some others. However, this consensus has fallen apart. Industrial policy and geopolitically driven economic nationalism are playing a greater role again, reducing the foreseeability of administrative decision-making. While this sounds threatening, it can also be an opportunity. Antitrust is a strategic weapon. Not only regulators use it, but private operators can use it too – by way of administrative complaints or judicial claims.

The **second trend** is still in **the process of emerging** – and I confess to have co-invented it based on the intuition of a Turkish law student who made **the connection between »consumer welfare« and »consumer well-being«.** As you have seen in the above examples, **sustainability is sitting in the backseat of antitrust**, and only operates defensively as a justification. **How can we bring it to the forefront**, so that we can use it as a weapon against unsustainable competition? Should antitrust regulators authorize collaborations that reduce prices but harm the environment? Admittedly, many countries have environmental protection laws and authorities, but antitrust enforcement is a strategic weapon that can overcome legislative loopholes or administrative inefficiency. You can decide to file a complaint with the regulator or go directly to court whenever you have a strong case. If you and others do the right thing, you may want to fight those who undercut you because they do not. After all, does the competitive level-playing field not deserve green grass, fresh air and clean water? Think about it.

5.5.4 Conclusion

You don't need to be an antitrust expert. It's enough to keep it in mind and activate it early enough in the process to ensure project feasibility or maximize your options. It could mean millions, no matter what your currency is.

5.6 Management

Bogdan Papandopol

»The world has enough for everyone's need, but not for everyone's greed.«
– Mahatma Ghandi

5.6.1 Not an introduction

© Bogdan Papandopol, 2025

When I was invited to contribute to this chapter, I initially thought it might be overly technical, leading readers to simply bypass it. However, during my research, I realized there is a lack of studies on the importance of integrating ESG post-mergers and within management agreements. This realization motivated me to create this summary, hoping that even a small step might help raise awareness about this topic.[494]

While searching for the perfect motto for my chapter, I found myself drawn to a frequently cited quote from *Mahatma Gandhi* that I had even encountered on Facebook. Its profound message resonates deeply with me and fits my section perfectly: *»The world has enough for everyone's need, but not for everyone's greed«.* Read this chapter to see why this perfectly matches my topic.

Now, moving away from rhetoric, I was tasked with writing this chapter from a legal perspective. Despite the children's book author within me encouraging a less conventional introduction, I hope you appreciate the summary along with the sketch I've drawn to highlight my chapter.

Finally, as a tech enthusiast who embraces AI and similar creative tools to enhance human work, I admit that AI was used only to refine certain phrases. I wonder how readers will perceive this in three, five, or even ten years from now, when I may assume AI will be like Windows XP.

494 Bogdan Papandopol leads Dentons' real estate practice in Romania and is the author and illustrator of several children's books. His works include »I Love My Friends: A Book for Kids Only«, which received a 2020 Mom's Choice Award, »Look At the Skies«, honored with a 2020 Purple Dragonfly Book Award, »Zina and the Brave«, which garnered both a 2020 Mom's Choice Award and a 2020 Royal Dragonfly Book Award, and »Alfabeta«, a vibrant alphabet book.

5.6.2 Introduction to #5.6

Currently, there is no comprehensive global study examining the integration of Environmental, Social, and Governance (ESG) principles in the post-acquisition phase of companies. This period is notably challenging for both new and existing managers, as they must integrate the acquired company into the parent organization and ensure alignment with various policies, including ESG principles. It's a complex task. Thus, the question arises: Are companies today prioritizing the integration of ESG principles and policies following mergers and within management agreements? Although we lack specific metrics or indicators to gauge this trend, it is evident that ESG principles have gained importance in the post-acquisition phase, indicating a move toward sustainable and ethical governance.

This shift is largely motivated by global trends favoring responsible investment and the growing demand for climate action, which has evolved from being a voluntary initiative to a business necessity. Beyond this general notion, the application of ESG principles post-acquisition or post-merger is indeed influenced by the business strategy. Existing studies suggest that ESG considerations can yield economic advantages, such as higher premiums paid by acquiring firms[495].

#5.6 Management	**#5.6.1 – not an introduction**
	#5.6.2 – intro to #5.6
	#5.6.3 – ESG in management agreements
	#5.6.4 – post-merger integration
	#5.6.5 – practical studies
	#5.6.6 – my practical example
	#5.6.7 – conclusion

In subchapter #5.6, we explore various aspects of ESG factors, including their role in management agreements (#5.6.3), post-merger integration (#5.6.4), practical studies (#5.6.5), and a practical example (#5.6.6), and conclude with final remarks (#5.6.7).

5.6.3 ESG in management agreements

We touched upon the significance of ESG in management agreements, but **why is it so crucial,** and **what do these agreements entail**?

> Essentially, when an investor acquires a company, it must be integrated to align with the policies of the parent company. This is achieved by implementing a robust set of ESG principles established by the acquiring company. It involves ensuring that the ESG principles of the acquired company are in harmony with those of the parent company and,

495 Herman Falkenberg & Jakob Vogt, supervised by Charlotte Østergaard, The effect of ESG-performance on M&A premiums – An Empirical Analysis of ESG in M&A's, 2022.

importantly, securing post-acquisition management agreements in key areas. Henceforth, the post-acquisition management agreements must evolve to effectively incorporate ESG principles.

But, **what are the key management agreements**? Briefly, these agreements can be categorized as **operational, strategic**, or **financial management agreements,** with each focusing on different aspects of business operations.

Post-acquisition management agreements are crucial for ensuring a smooth transition and successful integration of companies after a merger or acquisition[496]. They may be classified as follows:

a) **Operational management agreements,** which concentrate on the daily operations of the acquired (absorbed) entity. These agreements are designed to incorporate ESG principles into routine activities, as follows:
   Environmental focus: Adopting measures such as energy conservation and waste reduction.
   Social responsibility: Developing fair labor practices, employee welfare, and community involvement.
   Governance practices: Promoting transparency, accountability, and ethical conduct in the acquired company.
   Environmental initiatives: Commitments to reduce energy consumption, implementing waste recycling programs, and utilizing renewable energy sources.
   Practical examples may include: setting criteria for choosing suppliers who comply with ESG standards, educating employees on ESG practices, creating initiatives that promote employee involvement in community service, and setting systems to consistently track and report ESG metrics.
b) **Strategic management agreements** outline the company's long-term objectives and direction following an acquisition. These agreements integrate ESG principles to ensure that business strategies align with sustainable development goals and policies.
   Environmental focus: Establishing targets to lower carbon emissions and invest in sustainable technologies.
   Social responsibility: Creating initiatives to strengthen stakeholder relationships and enhance corporate social responsibility.
   Governance practices: Enhancing the governance framework to support strategic decision-making and manage risks effectively.
   Practical examples may include: establishing long-term objectives to reduce the company's carbon emissions, creating programs to enhance stakeholder relationships, including regular dialogues to collect feedback and improve corporate social responsibility, adopting a risk management approach that facilitates strategic decision-making committed to ESG standards, directing resources toward sustainability-focused projects, creating plans to

496 Arjona/Cornet/Degen/Krebs, ESG Integration in Contracts: Trends and Opportunities, 2025.

boost diversity and inclusion within the company, with specific goals for diverse leadership representation.

c) **Financial management agreements** address the financial aspects of the acquired company, ensuring that ESG principles are reflected in financial planning and reporting.
   Environmental focus: Allocating resources for environmental projects and assessing the financial impact of sustainability initiatives.
   Social responsibility: Investing in social programs that support employee development and community growth.
   Governance practices: Enhancing financial transparency and accountability through robust reporting and compliance measures.
   Practical examples may encompass: creating guidelines for investment choices that focus on ESG-compliant projects, adopting financing strategies that promote eco-friendly projects, creating detailed reporting frameworks that reveal ESG-related financial performance, incorporating ESG factors into risk evaluations to identify potential financial risks associated with ESG, and adopting procurement guidelines that favor suppliers with strong ESG credentials.

Now that we are familiar with the key management agreements, we should discuss **why they are important to secure the proper integration of an acquired company**. In fact, management agreements are critical to set forth the roles, responsibilities, and expectations of the parent and the acquired company, as well as their managers, as follows:

- **Securing ESG integration**: The inclusion of ESG clauses in management agreements secures the aligning of the business practices of the acquired company with the ESG policies of the parent company.
- **Enhancing the corporate profile**: Adopting ESG principles in management agreements can enhance corporate reputation, attract investors, and foster long-term growth.
- **Ensuring a smooth post-merger integration**: An effective integration of ESG strategies can align the merged entity's objectives with sustainable practices, ensuring compliance and risk mitigation (see below).
- **Risk mitigation**: Addressing ESG factors in management agreements helps mitigate risks associated with regulatory compliance, environmental liabilities, and reputational damage.
- **Strategic alignment**: Management agreements should be strategically aligned with the ESG goals of the absorbing company.

I believe it is clear that integrating ESG principles into post-acquisition management agreements is vital for achieving sustainable business growth and enhancing corporate reputation. Categorizing these agreements into operational, strategic, and financial management areas, companies can ensure a comprehensive approach to ESG integration, ultimately leading to improved financial performance and stakeholder trust[497].

497 Arjona/Cornet/Degen/Krebs, ESG Integration in Contracts: Trends and Opportunities, 2025.

5.6.4 Post-merger integration of ESG principles

In post-merger integration, aligning ESG standards is critical for ensuring operational continuity, stakeholder trust, and long-term sustainability. This is because, as outlined above, mergers and acquisitions often bring together companies with differing ESG policies, sometimes from different countries and cultures. Harmonizing these elements helps mitigate various risks and generally secures the following integrations between the absorbed company and its parent company:

- **Environmental alignment** ensures compliance with local and international regulations, reduces liabilities, and supports sustainability goals[498].
- **Social integration** fosters employee engagement, diversity, and community relations.
- **Health policies integration** protects workforce well-being, reduces absenteeism, and enhances performance, especially in industries with high safety risks[499].
- **Remediation of ESG due diligence findings conducted prior to acquisition.** This process includes identifying weaknesses and implementing corrective measures to improve ESG scores. Key strategies include enhancing governance structures, promoting social responsibility initiatives, and improving environmental practices, which collectively mitigate risks and enhance the company's reputation and increase its long-term value. Effective ESG integration also signals responsible governance to investors and regulators, enhancing post-merger value creation and resilience[500]. For more details on ESG due diligence, please refer to chapters #3.2, #3.3 and #3.4.

5.6.5 Practical studies

As outlined above, there is no global study. Hence, there are a few practical studies suggesting the importance of ESG integration post-merger and in management agreements. I found the following examples interesting and thought it would be useful to outline a few conclusions from those existing studies:

North America and Europe. An already cited study[501] explores the impact of Environmental, Social, and Governance (ESG) performance on the premiums paid in Mergers and Acquisitions (M&A) transactions. Using an analysis of 1,498 transactions from North America and Europe, the study found that the M&A premiums generally reflect the ESG performance of the target firm. However, results vary across industries due to differing stages of ESG integration, leading

498 Epstein, Mark J, Making Sustainability Work: Best Practices in Managing and Measuring Corporate Social, Environmental, and Economic Impacts, 2014.

499 World Health Organization (WHO), 2010.

500 Herman Falkenberg & Jakob Vogt, supervised by Charlotte Østergaard, The effect of ESG-performance on M&A premiums – An Empirical Analysis of ESG in M&A's, 2022.

501 Herman Falkenberg & Jakob Vogt, supervised by Charlotte Østergaard, The effect of ESG-performance on M&A premiums – An Empirical Analysis of ESG in M&A's, 2022.

to ambiguous outcomes in some sectors. The study highlights the importance of ESG in M&A decision-making, suggesting that improving ESG scores can enhance premiums.

Another study[502] investigates how ESG performance impacts acquisition premiums in M&A transactions. By analyzing 509 deals in the United States and Europe between 2002 and 2021, the study found that higher overall ESG scores and better governance performance positively affect acquisition premiums. The research also highlights the growing importance of ESG factors in M&A valuations.

ESG reporting. One notable summary[503] examines the importance of ESG reporting in investor decisions during mergers and acquisitions. The study found that companies with high levels of ESG reporting achieved better financial outcomes post-merger, gaining greater investor trust, improved financing terms, and financial stability. However, the author acknowledges limitations, such as regional differences in ESG regulations and a lack of data from certain sectors.

Nordic Countries. Another interesting study[504] investigates the impact of ESG factors on valuation models used in mergers and acquisitions involving Nordic companies. The authors integrate ESG as a risk component into established models, such as the Capital Asset Pricing Model (CAPM) and the Fama & French multi-factor model. They analyze the relationship between ESG scores and financial metrics, such as return on invested capital (ROIC) and enterprise value, in Denmark, Finland, Sweden, and Norway. The conclusion is that ESG factors are crucial in investment decisions, particularly in M&A transactions, and emphasize the importance of corporate governance in these processes.

The research demonstrates the real impact of ESG integration on businesses in M&A decisions to support sustainable development within ecosystems.

5.6.6 My practical example

Imagine an investor purchasing a target company and carrying out ESG due diligence, which reveals challenges such as weak governance practices and insufficient environmental policies. Following the acquisition, the investor implements a thorough plan to address these issues, which involves appointing a diverse board to enhance governance and initiating projects to lower the company's carbon emissions. These strategies are executed via updated ESG policies and new key management agreements post-acquisition. Through these measures, the acquired company aligns with the parent company's ESG standards, boosts its market value, and reduces the risk of damages and fines.

502 Tintin Almqvist and Fredrik Wendt, supervised by Mussa Hussaini, ESG Performance – Effect on Acquisition Premium, 2022.
503 Danuta Kozłowska-Makóś, The Role of ESG Reporting in Mergers and Acquisitions, 2024.
504 Klitskov/Kiknadz, How Do Nordic Companies' ESG Attributes Impact Their Valuation Models Used in M&A?, 2021.

5.6.7 Conclusion

My conclusion is simple. The post-acquisition period is crucial for integrating ESG principles into management agreements and operations. By addressing ESG due diligence findings and adopting responsible investment strategies, investors can enhance the value and sustainability of their acquisitions, aligning with broader market expectations and contributing to long-term success.

Therefore, if your business strategy as an investor is to acquire and integrate an existing company on a market, you should focus on ESG integration. Successful integration in those two areas would pave the way to success of the newly integrated business and may also result in a higher bonus for the responsible management. This equals prosperity for a company that is keen or at least focused on improving our world. Thus, to paraphrase Ghandi, ESG integration post-merger and in key management agreements *»is about meeting everyone's needs, not being driven by greed«.*

6 Mapping the continents & deep dives into regional/country/local perspectives

6.1 Introduction to Chapter #6

Sabine Wieduwilt

»*Toast to Freedom*«[505]
– listen and understand

6.1.1 Content of Chapter #6

When it comes to cross-border and portfolio deals, we want to know what drives ESG standards. What are recent developments? From an investment standpoint, what should we consider when developing investment approaches?

In this chapter #6, we delve into different continents and geographies.

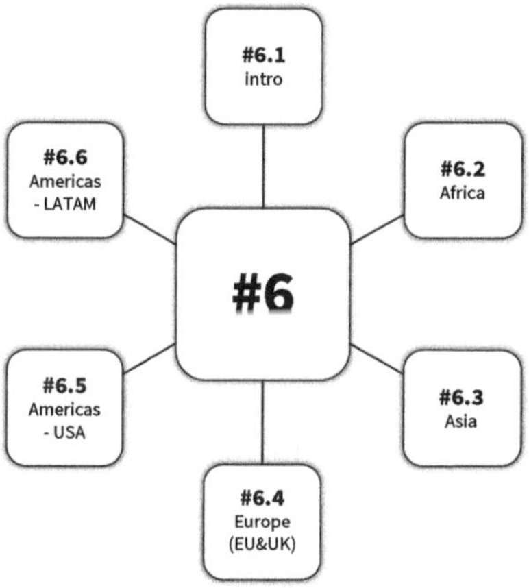

We started with Africa, the cradle of humanity, and reframed it as a destination for sustainable real estate investment (#6.2). Then we continued in the order this planet was inhabited according to historians with Asia (#6.3), followed by Europe, specifically the European Union (EU) and the UK (#6.4). Then we moved on to North America, specifically the U.S. (#6.5) and finally, South America, or more specifically, Latin America (#6.6).

How do we map the continents in the context of real estate investment and ESG? What are the questions we have asked ourselves from a regional perspective? The experts based in these regions have focused on all or part of the following: different bodies, standards, and regulatory requirements for sustainability and ESG in real estate investments,

505 Carlton/Campbell, youtube, 2012, https://www.youtube.com/watch?v=EBLHwtGBUAE, accessed 22.07.2025. The song »Toast To Freedom« is dedicated to human rights activism around the world. Nearly 50 artists contributed to celebrate Amnesty International's 50th Anniversary. Toast To Freedom was written by music veterans Carl Carlton and Larry Campbell.

with different spotlights either on specific countries, ESG finance and disclosure, regional regulatory developments, and practical implications and strategies for investors.

We're aware that we have left out important regions, for example Canada and Australia, among others, and with this approach we will not be able cover all countries, regions, communities.

Figure 31: The Mercator projection

The **Mercator projection** of the world map shown in **Figure 31** against other projections, for example from Gall-Peters (see under #6.2.1) reveals that there are many perspectives to view our world.
As we know, focusing on a continent in a few pages does not do justice to the details within a country, especially the local specifics. Also, the political and economic connections and common standards are not always defined by continental borders.

Also, bodies and associations that set standards often have a global reach, such as the OECD. However, they do not cover many countries.

However, we strive to understand the nuances of different continents in order to better understand how to handle sustainability and ESG within an investment setting, whether within regions or for international portfolio investments, and also to learn from each other.

In my opinion, listening to and trying to understand each other is a »*toast to freedom*«.

6.1.2 Further reading

We know that no book can be complete, so please see the sources below **for further reading** including insights on regional perspectives, in addition to the further chapters of this book. The sources are exemplary, not exhaustive:

CRREM, EPRA, Green Governance, 2024, https://www.crrem.eu/green_governance/, accessed 06.09.2025.

Davies, Paul (ed.), The Global ESG Handbook: A Guide for Practitioners, 2024.

GSIA, GSIA-Report 2022, https://www.gsi-alliance.org/wp-content/uploads/2023/12/GSIA-Report-2022.pdf; accessed 06.09.2025, GSIA Responsible Investment Definitions 2023, https://

www.gsi-alliance.org/wp-content/uploads/2023/10/ESG-Terminology-Report_Online.pdf, accessed 06.09.2025.

Martindale, Will, Responsible Investment. An Insider's Account of What's Working, What's not and where next, 2024.

Sarmento/Herman, Global Handbook of Impact Investing. Solving Global Problems via Smarter Capital Markets Towards a More Sustainable Society, 2021.

The Chancery Lane Project (TCLP), https://chancerylaneproject.org/, accessed 06.09.2025.

UN PRI, INREV, Urban Land Institute, Mapping ESG: A landscape review of certifications, reporting frameworks and practices, 2023, https://www.unpri.org/real-estate/mapping-esg-a-landscape-review-of-certifications-reporting-frameworks-and-practices/11348.article, accessed 06.09.2025.

UN PRI, Policy reports, https://www.unpri.org/policy/policy-reports, accessed 06.09.2025.

UNEP FI, UNEP FI, PRI and Climate Bonds Initiative join forces to support taxonomy efforts around the world, 2024, https://www.unepfi.org/news/unep-fi-pri-and-climate-bonds-initiative-join-forces-to-support-taxonomy-efforts-around-the-world/, accessed 06.09.2025.

UNEP FI, UNPRI, Updated position paper on Governmental Carbon Pricing, 2024, https://www.unepfi.org/industries/net-zero-asset-owner-alliances-updated-position-on-governmental-carbon-pricing/, accessed 06.09.2025.

United Nations Principles for Responsible Investment (UN PRI), https://www.unpri.org/, accessed 06.09.2025.

World Green Building Council (WGBC), Global Directory of Green Building Councils, https://worldgbc.org/global-directory-of-green-building-councils/, accessed 06.09.2025.

6.2 Africa

Dr. Dephney Ramaphosa

»Africa, despite being the second largest continent by landmass and population, has long been misinterpreted in global narratives, often been portrayed as a continent of poverty, political conflict and underdevelopment. … For Africa to realize its true potential, this narrative needs to shift.«

6.2.1 Introduction to #6.2

Africa stands at a pivotal moment in its development trajectory, with urbanization, demographic growth, and the need for climate resilience reshaping its real estate landscape. This chapter explores the evolving narrative of Africa as a compelling destination for sustainable real estate investment, driven by global interest in Environmental, Social, and Governance (ESG) principles. It provides country-specific spotlights on: South Africa, Kenya, Ghana, and Nigeria, offering insights into regulatory frameworks maturity, ESG financing mechanisms, and disclosure practices. The goal is to equip investors, policymakers, and sustainability professionals with a nuanced understanding of Africa's readiness and potential for ESG-aligned real estate investment.

Despite being the second largest continent by landmass and population, Africa has long been misinterpreted in global narratives, often been portrayed as a continent of poverty, political conflict and underdevelopment.

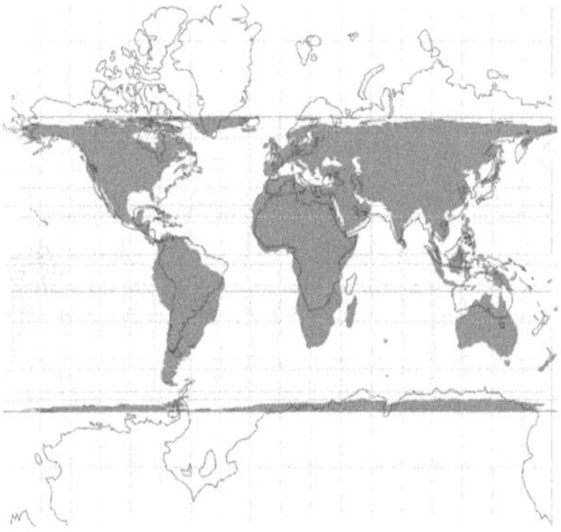

Figure 32: Gall-Peters Projection vs. Mercator Projection Map[506]

This narrative is partly rooted in the historical distortion of Africa's size and scale on the world maps, as shown on **Figure 32**, in the **Mercator projection and Gall-Peter's projection**[507]. This cartographic distortion has contributed to the continent's undervaluation, leading to underinvestment in infrastructure, real estate, and technology, as well as limited access to capital and a high perceived risk among global investors.

For Africa to realize its true potential, this narrative must change.

#6.2 Mapping Africa	**#6.2.1 – intro to #6.2**
	#6.2.2 – reframing Africa
	#6.2.3 – spotlight South Africa
	#6.2.4 – spotlight Kenya
	#6.2.5 – spotlight Ghana
	#6.2.6 – spotlight Nigeria
	#6.2.7 – conclusion

In this subchapter #6.2, we introduce Africa as a destination for sustainable real estate investment (#6.2.2), giving special attention to South Africa (#6.2.3), Kenya (#6.2.4), Ghana (#6.2.5), and Nigeria (#6.2.6), to then close with concluding remarks (#6.2.7).

506 Jung, Tobias, CC BY-SA 4.0, http://creativecommons.org/licenses/by-sa/4.0), via map-projections.net.
507 Monmonier, Mark, Rhumb Lines and Map Wars: A Social History of the Mercator Projection, 2004, https://press.uchicago.edu/ucp/books/book/chicago/R/bo3634012.html, University of Chicago Press, accessed 14.08.2025.

6.2.2 Reframing Africa as a destination for sustainable real estate investment

As the world rapidly moves towards sustainable development, it is necessary to reframe Africa as a continent with vast potential, and not merely as a continent of problems. Sectors such as real estate present genuine opportunities in African countries such as South Africa, Kenya, Ghana and Nigeria to mention a few. The growth of the middle class and government reforms in these markets have created demand for housing, offices, and retail spaces. Coupled with investors seeking opportunities that align with ESG principles, growing regulatory support and overall heightened awareness of sustainability issues, a window of opportunity for growth in sustainable real estate investment is opening. Unlike saturated markets, Africa provides a blank canvas for smart cities, which could allow the continent to bypass legacy systems and adopt cutting-edge sustainable technologies from the ground up[508].

Historically, real estate in Africa was not seen as an attractive investment option by institutional investors due to poor or lack of regulatory support. The introduction of the African Continental Free Trade, poised to significantly influence real estate investment across Africa by shaping the economic and regulatory landscape is a step in the right direction insofar as driving infrastructure investment across the continent[509]. It should be noted that Africa's real estate regulations vary significantly by country, with some markets offering more mature and transparent systems, while others still face bureaucratic hurdles and inconsistent enforcement. Below is a spotlight on a few countries, highlighting some of the key laws governing real estate investments and ESG integration.

6.2.3 Spotlight: South Africa

(a) Regulatory Framework

The South African real estate sector is governed by a robust legal framework that includes national legislation, municipal bylaws and sector-specific regulations. The Deeds Registries Act (No. 47 of 1937) and the Land Titles Adjustment Act (No. 111 of 1993) oversee the registration, correction, and adjustment of land titles, ensuring legal certainty and transparency in property ownership and transactions. The Sectional Titles Act (No. 95 of 1986) and the Sectional Titles Schemes Management Act (No. 8 of 2011), respectively[510], regulate ownership and management of sectional title properties. Collectively, these acts establish a comprehensive governance framework for real estate in South Africa. They ensure that land and property ownership is legally recorded, secure, and transparent. These laws provide mechanisms for correcting or

508 World Economic Forum, 2025, Africa is harnessing technology to leapfrog towards growth, https://www.weforum.org/stories/2025/07/africa-leapfrog-moment-harnessing-technology-green-growth-and-regional-integration-for-global-value-chains/, accessed 23.07.2025.

509 South Centre, Assessing Five Years of the AfCFTA: Recalibrating the Path to Africa's Economic Transformation. South Centre Research Paper 215, 2025, https://www.southcentre.int/wp-content/uploads/2025/01/RP215_Assessing-Five-Years-of-the-AfCFTA_EN.pdf, accessed 23.07.2025.

510 Southern African Legal Information Institute, 2025, https://www.saflii.org/, accessed 23.07.2025.

formalizing land titles and set out clear rules for the management and administration of sectional title schemes through body corporates.

Additionally, South Africa also has legal instruments that govern the environmental and social aspects of real estate development. These include the Spatial Planning and Land Use Management Act, No. 16 of 2023 (SPLUMA), the National Environmental Management Act, No 107 of 1998 (NEMA), the Carbon Tax Act, No 15 of 2019, and the Green Building Council South Africa (GBCSA). These instruments collectively embed ESG principles into South Africa's real estate sector, ensuring that land use and development are environmentally sustainable, socially inclusive, and governed by transparent standards. SPLUMA promotes integrated and equitable spatial planning; NEMA mandates Environmental Impact Assessments (EIA) and accountability; the Carbon Tax Act incentivizes low-carbon building practices; and the GBCSA provides measurable green building certifications[511]. Together, they create a regulatory and market environment that supports responsible investment and aligns real estate development with global ESG expectations.

(b) ESG Finance

In South Africa, sustainable finance instruments for real estate investments have evolved significantly, aligning with global ESG standards and national climate goals. Key instruments include green bonds, sustainability-linked loans (SLLs), blended finance, impact investment funds, and green real estate investment trusts (REITs). Green bonds are used to finance environmentally friendly real estate projects, such as energy-efficient buildings and solar installations, which are subject to third-party verification[512]. SLLs are tied to a borrowers' achievement of predefined sustainability performance targets. Blended finance combines concessional capital from development finance institutions, such as the Development Bank of South Africa, with private investment to reduce the risk of high-impact real estate projects and support affordable developments aligned with the Just Energy Transition[513] (JET). Green REITs and social and impact investment funds offer financing that focuses on measurable social outcomes within real estate portfolios[514].

(c) ESG Disclosure

South Africa requires non-financial reporting under the Companies Act and promotes ESG integration through the Johannesburg Stock Exchange's Sustainability Disclosure Guidelines[515] and the SA REIT Association's Sustainability Disclosure Framework, which aligns with global

511 Southern African Legal Information Institute, 2025.

512 Standard Bank of South Africa, The South African real estate sector defies trends to reflect greenshoots, 2025, https://corporateandinvestment.standardbank.com/cib/global/insights/the-south-african-real-estate-sector-defies-trends-to-reflect-greenshoots, accessed 28.07.2025.

513 National Treasury of South Africa, Report highlights key steps to strengthen South Africa's Green Finance Taxonomy, 2025, https://www.treasury.gov.za/comm_media/press/2025/2025032601%20Media%20Statement%20-%20Green%20Finance%20Taxonomy.pdf, accessed 12.07.2025.

514 South African Real Estate Investment Trust, Association, (SA REITs) 2025, https://sareit.co.za/, accessed 28.07.2025.

515 Johannesburg Stock Exchange (JSE), Sustainability Disclosure Guidance, 2022, https://www.jse.co.za/sites/default/files/media/documents/JSE%20Sustainability%20Disclosure%20Guidance_1.pdf, accessed 07.08.2025.

standards, such as International Financial Reporting Standards (IFRS) S1 and S2. The Financial Sector Conduct Authority[516] and the Prudential Authority have also issued guidance to financial institutions regarding climate-related disclosures and governance[517].

6.2.4 Spotlight: Kenya

(a) Regulatory Framework

Similar to South Africa, Kenya has a comprehensive legal framework governing real estate. Kenya's real estate sector ensures secure land ownership, structured development, and environmental sustainability. The Constitution of Kenya (2010) lays the foundation by recognizing land as a national resource and guaranteeing equitable access to it and its sustainable use[518]. The Land Act (Cap 280) and the Land Registration Act (Cap 300) provide mechanisms for land administration and secure title registration. The Community Land Act (Cap 287) protects communal land rights. The Physical and Land Use Planning Act (Cap 303) ensures that developments align with national and county spatial plans. The Sectional Properties Act (Cap 286) facilitates individual ownership within multi-unit developments, which is critical for urban housing and commercial real estate[519].

From an ESG perspective, Kenya has also integrated sustainability into its legal and financial systems. The Environmental Management and Coordination Act (Cap 387) (EMCA) mandates Environmental Impact Assessments (EIAs) for real estate projects, while the Climate Change Act (Cap 387A) requires climate resilience to be factored into planning and investments[520].

(b) ESG Finance

Kenya has a growing sustainable finance market that supports real estate investment. Much like in South Africa, Kenya has green bonds, green REITs, mezzanine financing and climate-aligned infrastructure funding. Green bonds are earmarked for climate and environmental projects; green REITs pool capital to invest in environmentally sustainable real estate assets. Mezzanine financing is a hybrid debt and equity instrument often tied to sustainability-linked per-

516 Financial Sector Conduct Authority (FSCA), Strengthening South Africa's sustainable finance framework. Moonstone Information Refinery, 2025, https://www.moonstone.co.za/strengthening-south-africas-sustainable-finance-framework/, accessed 10.07.2025.

517 Davis/Novotny, ESG disclosure requirements for financial institutions in South Africa: A 2025 update, 2025, https://www.polity.org.za/article/esg-disclosure-requirements-for-financial-institutions-in-south-africa-a-2025-update-2025-07-16, accessed 28.07.2025.

518 Republic of Kenya/ Parliament of Kenya, The Constitution of Kenya, 2010,, https://parliament.go.ke/sites/default/files/2025-04/The_Constitution_of_Kenya_2010.pdf, accessed 18.07.2025.

519 National Land Commission of Kenya, Land Laws, 2025, https://landcommission.go.ke/land-laws/, accessed 02.07.2025.

520 Republic of Kenya, 2010.

formance targets, while climate aligned infrastructure funding targets climate resilience and mitigation efforts[521].

(c) ESG Disclosure

In Kenya, ESG disclosure is supported by the Capital Markets Authority's Code of Corporate Governance[522] and the Nairobi Securities Exchange (NSE) ESG Disclosure Manual[523], which mandates ESG reporting for listed companies. The Central Bank of Kenya has introduced the Climate Risk Disclosure Framework and Green Finance Taxonomy to guide financial institutions in managing and reporting climate-related risks[524].

6.2.5 Spotlight: Ghana

(a) Regulatory Framework

Ghana's real estate sector is undergoing significant reforms aimed at enhancing transparency, investor protection, and sustainable development. A key component of this transformation is the 2020 Land Act (Act 1026), which aims to consolidate and modernize Ghana's land laws and introduces compulsory land registration, formalizes dispute resolution mechanisms; and supports the digitization of land records to reduce registration timelines and improve transparency[525]. Ghana also enacted the Real Estate Agency Act of 2020, (Act 1047), which through its Real Estate Agency Council (REAC), licenses and regulates real estate brokers and agents[526]. Starting in 2025, all intermediaries must be registered with the REAC, and unlicensed practice will be subject to prosecution. This act will professionalize the real estate sector and reduce fraud. Additionally, Ghana has strengthened anti-money laundering (AML) compliance in real estate transactions by aligning with global standards and requiring the reporting of suspicious transactions, especially those involving foreign buyers or large cash payments[527].

In terms of ESG, Ghana has several sector-specific laws and regulatory initiatives that support ESG integration. The Environmental Protection Act, 1994 (Act 490) and Environmental Assess-

521 Institute of Certified Securities of Kenya, Funding Sustainable Projects through Green Financing in Kenya. Institute of Certified Secretaries, 2025, https://www.ics.ke/2025/01/28/funding-sustainable-projects-through-green-financing-in-kenya/, accessed 28.07.2025.

522 Capital Markets Authority, Code of Corporate Governance Practices for Issuers of Securities to the Public, 2015, https://cma.or.ke/wp-content/uploads/2023/03/Code-of-Corporate-Governance-Practices-for-Issuers-of-Securities-to-the-Public-2015-Code-8.pdf, accessed 04.07.2025.

523 Nairobi Securities Exchange (NSE), ESG Disclosures Guidance Manual, 2021, https://www.nse.co.ke/wp-content/uploads/NSE-ESG-Disclosures-Guidance-Manual.pdf, accessed 14.07.2025.

524 MMAN Advocates, Environmental, Social and Governance (ESG) Landscape in Kenya: Key Considerations for Listed and Non-Listed Entities, 2021, https://www.mman.co.ke/sites/default/files/Environmental%20Social%20and%20Governance%20%28ESG%29%20Landscape%20in%20Kenya_0.pdf, accessed 28.07.2025.

525 Lands Commission of Ghana, Land Act, 2020 (Act 1036): Notice of Application for Deeds Registration, 2025, https://www.lc.gov.gh/2025/07/22/land-act-2020-act-1036-notice-of-application-for-deeds-registration-4/, accessed 28.07.2025.

526 Real Estate Agency Council (REAC), Regulating the Ghana Real Estate Agency Sector, 2025, https://reac.gov.gh/, accessed 28.07.2025.

527 Real Estate Agency Council (REAC), 2025.

ment Regulations, 1999 (L.I. 1652) require Environmental Impact Assessments (EIAs) for real estate and infrastructure projects[528], while social compliance is embedded in laws such as the Federal Competition and Consumer Protection Act (2018), Factories Act (2004), and Employees' Compensation Act (2010), which protect consumer rights, workplace safety, and fair labor practices[529]. The Bank of Ghana has implemented Sustainable Banking Principles and is piloting a Climate-Related Financial Risk Directive to ensure that financial institutions integrate climate risk into their governance and investment decisions.[530]

(b) ESG Finance

Similar to South Africa and Kenya, Ghana is also actively promoting sustainable finance instruments that integrate ESG through its Capital Market Master Plan. The country offers green bonds, sustainability-linked loans, and social bonds to finance real estate projects. Green bonds target financing or refinancing real estate projects with clear environmental benefits. Social bonds and loans target those that deliver positive social outcomes. Sustainability-linked bonds and loans are tied to overall sustainability performance[531]. All instruments in Ghana's framework adhere to international standards, including the International Capital Markets Association Green and Social Bond Principles, Sustainability Bond Guidelines, and Sustainability-Linked Loan Principles, ensuring credibility and investor confidence[532].

(c) ESG Disclosure

Ghana has adopted ESG disclosure through the Ghana Stock Exchange's ESG Disclosure Guidelines and the Securities and Exchange Commission's Green Bond Guidelines[533]. These frameworks encourage listed companies to report on their sustainability performance, while the Bank of Ghana's Sustainable Banking Principles promote ESG integration in financial institutions.[534]

528 Environmental Protection Agency (EPA), Ghana's Framework on International Carbon Markets and Non-Market Approaches, 2022, https://cmo.epa.gov.gh/wp-content/uploads/2022/12/Ghana-Carbon-Market-Framework-For-Public-Release_15122022.pdf, accessed 10.07.2025.

529 Environmental Protection Agency (EPA), Final ESMP – Northern Ecological Zone, 2025, https://glrssmp.epa.gov.gh/wp-content/uploads/2025/07/Final_ESMP_NSZ_GLRSSMP.pdf, accessed 28.07.2025.

530 Bank of Ghana, Climate-Related Financial Risk Directive, 2024, https://www.bog.gov.gh/wp-content/uploads/2024/11/BOG-Climate-Related-Financial-Risks-Directive.pdf, accessed 28.07.2025.

531 Securities and Exchange Commission Ghana, Ghana Capital Market Master Plan. Accra: SEC, 2020, https://sec.gov.gh/wp-content/uploads/Press-Release/SEC_CMMP.pdf, accessed 28.07.2025.

532 Ministry of Finance and Economic Planning of Ghana, Ghana Sustainable Financing Framework. Accra: Government of Ghana, 2021, https://www.mofep.gov.gh/sites/default/files/news/Ghana-Sustainable-Financing-Framework.pdf, accessed 21.07.2025

533 Ghana Stock Exchange, ESG Disclosures Guidance Manual, 2022, https://gse.com.gh/market-news/esg-disclosures-guidance-manual/, accessed 18.06.2025; Securities and Exchange Commission Ghana, 2024, Securities Industry (Green Bond) Guidelines 2024, https://sec.gov.gh/wp-content/uploads/Final-Regulatory-Laws/Guidelines/Green_Bond_Guidelines_2024.pdf, accessed 28.07.2025.

534 Bank of Ghana, Sustainable Banking Principles and Sector Guidance Notes, 2019, https://www.bog.gov.gh/wp-content/uploads/2019/12/Ghana-Sustainable-Banking-Principles-and-Guidelines-Book-1.pdf, accessed 04.07.2025.

6.2.6 Spotlight: Nigeria

(a) Regulatory Framework

In Nigeria, the real estate sector is regulated by a combination of statutory, customary, and case law. Serving as the cornerstone is the Land Use Act of 1978 which grants ownership of all land in each state to the governor, who holds this land in trust for the people, and provides for the issuance of Certificates of Occupancy (C of O) as proof of land rights. Additionally, the Property and Conveyancing Law (PCL), the Registration of Titles Law, and the Stamp Duties Act are also key to real estate investment in Nigeria. Investors must obtain the governor's consent for any land transaction to be valid. The PCL establishes the legal framework for transferring property rights through contracts, leases, and deeds, ensuring that transactions are valid and enforceable, particularly in the southwestern states. The Registration of Titles Law mandates the formal registration of land titles in designated areas, such as Lagos Island and Ikoyi, offering legal certainty and protecting investors from fraudulent claims or disputes[535].

In terms of the integration of environmental and social principles into investments, the 1992 Environmental Impact Assessment Act (Cap E12 LFN 2004) mandates EIAs for projects that are likely to have environmental impact. while the 2021 Climate Change Act establishes Nigeria's legal framework for transitioning to a low-carbon economy[536].

(b) ESG Finance

Nigeria also has sustainable finance instruments, however not widely implemented due to challenges such as weak regulatory frameworks, limited institutional capacity, and low public awareness. These instruments include green bonds, social bonds, and sustainability-linked bonds. To unlock long term value in the real estate sector[537], experts recommend strengthening ESG and sustainability-related regulations.

(c) ESG Disclosure

In Nigeria, although ESG disclosure is still largely voluntary, it is gaining momentum. In 2019, the Nigerian Stock Exchange (NSE) issued Sustainability Disclosure Guidelines, and the Financial Reporting Council (FRC) is leading efforts to adopt the IFRS sustainability disclosure standards. Nigeria aims to be an early adopter of these standards, signaling a shift toward more structured ESG reporting.

535 Resolution Law Firm, Overview of the Laws Regulating Real Estate in Nigeria, 2023, https://www.resolutionlawng.com/overview-of-the-laws-regulating-real-estate-in-nigeria/, accessed 28.07.2025.

536 Tunde & Adisa Legal Practitioners, Navigating ESG compliance in Nigeria: How Nigerian entities can leverage ESG compliance for competitive advantage, 2025, https://tundeadisa.com/media_insights/navigating-esg-compliance-in-nigeria-how-nigerian-entities-can-leverage-esg-compliance-for-competitive-advantage/, accessed 28.07.2025.

537 Imoisi/Okoro, Advancing sustainable finance in Nigeria: A policy-oriented analysis of challenges and opportunities. International Journal of Advanced Studies in Economics and Public Sector Management, 13(1), 2025, pp. 245–263, https://internationalpolicybrief.org/wp-content/uploads/2025/05/ARTICLE-20.pdf, accessed 08.08.2025.

6.2.7 Conclusion

Africa's real estate sector is undergoing a transformative shift as countries adopt ESG principles across their legal, financial, and operational systems, supported by reforms and global standards. From South Africa to Nigeria, Ghana, and Kenya, a growing body of laws and regulations are establishing a structured, transparent environment for real estate investment. These frameworks enhance investor confidence by ensuring title security, promoting sustainable development, and enabling participation in property governance. Financial innovation is accelerating as well, with instruments such as green bonds, sustainability-linked loans, and sovereign green bonds providing access to ESG aligned capital. These tools mitigate environmental and social risks while providing competitive advantages for developers and investors. Moreover, the rise of ESG disclosure guidelines signals a continent-wide commitment to transparency and accountability. Together, these developments position Africa as a resilient and attractive destination for sustainable real estate investment.

6.3 Asia: Sustainable finance and real estate ESG

Vivien Teu

6.3.1 Introduction to #6.3

Unlike the EU, Asia Pacific does not have a single common framework, but most jurisdictions in Asia are seeking to align with international standards in order to build resilience and maintain the competitiveness of their domestic companies and markets. Regulators as well as investors increasingly expect companies to adopt strong ESG practices and sustainable supply chains. This shift is also driven by the growing recognition in Asia, particularly the Global South and emerging markets, that sustainability is essential for long-term success and that addressing climate change is a necessity.

The real estate industry is a key sector in Asia's transition to a low-carbon economy. Buildings contribute significantly to greenhouse gas (GHG) emissions, resource consumption (particularly energy and water), and also waste generation in the built environment. In response, governments, financial institutions, investors and real estate developers across Asia are aligning with global initiatives in addressing climate risks and climate change, through the development of sustainable finance frameworks to accelerate the green transformation of real estate and infrastructure, and the establishment of more concrete green policies, regulations, and best practices.

#6.3	#6.3.1 – intro to #6.3
Mapping Asia – sustainable finance & real estate	#6.3.2 – taxonomies and policy support
	#6.3.3 – green bonds and real estate financing
	#6.3.4 – real estate investment funds & REITs
	#6.3.5 – real estate transition finance
	#6.3.6 – Asia data center green initiatives
	#6.3.7 – real estate ESG contract clauses
	#6.3.8 – conclusion & outlook

In this subchapter #6.3, we introduce Asia with a focus on sustainable finance and real estate, looking into taxonomies and policy support (#6.3.2), green bonds and real estate financing (#6.3.3), real estate investment funds and REITs (#6.3.4), real estate transition finance (#6.3.5), data center green initiatives (#6.3.6), real estate ESG contract clauses (#6.3.7), to then close with concluding remarks and an outlook (#6.3.8).

6.3.2 Taxonomies and policy support

(a) Introduction to taxonomies in Asia

One of the cornerstones of sustainable finance in Asia is the development of **taxonomies** that define what qualifies as sustainable economic activity. The **International Platform on Sustainable Finance (IPSF)** has published the **Common Ground Taxonomy (CGT)** which aligns the EU Taxonomy with **China's Green Bond Endorsed Project Catalogue (2021 edition),** while countries such as Singapore, Malaysia and the ASEAN region have made significant progress in formulating green taxonomies that align with international standards, as well as local or regional economic and environmental contexts.

(b) Examples for real estate

The following examples from selected taxonomies provide guidance to developers, lenders and investors around green real estate, facilitating greater flows of capital in the market into green buildings and infrastructure:

> **China's Green Bond Endorsed Project Catalogue (2021 edition)** emphasizes low-carbon buildings, green urban infrastructure, and energy-efficient retrofitting.
>
> **The Hong Kong Taxonomy, published by the Hong Kong Monetary Authority (HKMA) in May 2024,** initially covers four sectors and 12 economic activities, including construction and renovation of buildings for energy efficiency, green buildings and climate change mitigation.
>
> **Singapore's Green Finance Industry Taskforce (GFIT)** has launched a taxonomy for environmental sustainability that includes the construction and real estate sectors.
>
> **The ASEAN Taxonomy for Sustainable Finance,** supported by regional finance ministries and regulators, is emerging as a harmonizing tool across Southeast Asia.

(c) Multi-jurisdiction evolution (M-CGT)

In November 2024, an expanded version of the CGT – the **Multi-Jurisdiction Common Ground Taxonomy (M-CGT)** was released, bridging the EU, China, and Singapore's (Singapore-Asia Taxonomy) frameworks. This extension supports greater interoperability in cross-border investment flows across real estate and construction sectors by mapping the comparability of included activities and assessing overlaps in criteria.

The **table 31** below provides a brief **comparative summary of the Hong Kong Taxonomy and the CGT/M-CGT** regarding construction and real estate activities. This information can help investors and developers assess regional and global alignment.

Comparative summary		
Feature	**Hong Kong Taxonomy**	**Common Ground Taxonomy (CGT/M-CGT)**
Includes real estate?	Yes – under construction/renovation sector	Yes – via construction sector (aligned with ISIC codes)
Detail level	Moderate – broad sector with supplemental guidance	Analytical – compares technical criteria across taxonomies
Environmental scope	Focused on climate mitigation (with adaptation in development)	Climate mitigation only (no DNSH/ minimal safeguards)
Goal	Encourage green finance in Hong Kong and reduce greenwashing	Facilitate interoperability across the EU, China, and Singapore taxonomies
Cross-border alignment	Designed for interoperability	Core purpose: taxonomy alignment

Table 31: Comparative summary of the Hong Kong Taxonomy and the CGT/M-CGT

(d) ASEAN taxonomy – technical screening criteria for real estate, classification of buildings

For Asia, it is also important to consider the **ASEAN Taxonomy for Sustainable Finance**[538], which provides detailed coverage of the real estate sector. The **ASEAN Taxonomy Version 3**, effective 20 December 2024, extends its Plus Standard (PS) by adding Construction and Real Estate as one of its Focus Sectors alongside Transportation & Storage.[539]

The taxonomy's **Technical Screening Criteria (TSC)** for this sector explicitly cover:

- Construction of new buildings (ISIC 410)
- Renovation of existing buildings (ISIC 410)
- Demolition and site preparation (ISIC 431)

538 Asean Taxonomy Board, Asean Taxonomy for Sustainable Finance Version 3, 2024, https://asean.org/wp-content/uploads/2024/12/ASEAN-Taxonomy-Finalised-Version-3-4.pdf, accessed 06.09.2025.

539 https://keuanganberkelanjutan.ojk.go.id/keuanganberkelanjutan/en/newsmedia/detailpressconference/3481/asean-taxonomy-board-atb-menerbitkan-asean-taxonomy-for-sustainable-finance-version-3-untuk-sektor-transportation-storage-dan-construction-real-estate.

- Acquisition and ownership of buildings (ISIC 681)

Also included are measures such as building-level EV charging, energy-efficient equipment, building management systems (BMS)/measurement and control, on-site renewables, and early-warning systems.

The ASEAN Taxonomy employs a multi-tiered **»traffic-light« system**, in which the »Green« tier encompasses activities that meet rigorous environmental thresholds and are aligned with recognized international green building certifications (e.g., LEED, BEAM Plus), whereas the »Amber« tier covers transitional activities that are gradually moving toward green standards.

Additionally, the **updated annexes of the ASEAN Taxonomy** now include:
- Life Cycle Assessment (LCA) worked examples
- Climate Risk and Vulnerability Assessment (CRVA) examples
- Updated national environmental and social regulations for certain ASEAN member states (AMS), such as Indonesia, Malaysia, and the Philippines.

These additions highlight ASEAN's commitment to directing capital toward sustainable real estate development throughout the region.

Classification of buildings (Green and Amber)

Version 3 (**ASEAN Taxonomy**) introduces improved definitions and a non-exhaustive list of local and global green building certifications, and more clarity on the criteria that qualify an activity for the Green Tier.

ASEAN Taxonomy – classification of buildings (Green and Amber)		
	Green (Tier 1)	**Amber (Tier 2)**
Acquisition & ownership of buildings (ISIC 681) under Climate Change Mitigation (EO1):	• If built before December 31, 2023, the building has an advanced level of certification from a recognized GBC program; or • If built after December 31, 2023: the building meets the criteria specified under Tier 1 (Green) in »Construction of New Buildings« criteria; and • For large non-residential buildings (HVAC or combined system > 290 kW), there is energy performance monitoring and assessment in operation.	• If the building was built before December 31, 2023, it has certification from a recognized GBC program, and • An Energy Efficiency Improvement Plan that will reduce Energy Use Intensity (EUI) when implemented.

ASEAN Taxonomy – classification of buildings (Green and Amber)		
	Green (Tier 1)	**Amber (Tier 2)**
Acquisition & ownership of buildings under Climate Change Adaptation (EO2):	• Material physical climate risks are addressed via adaptation solutions, as evidenced by an advanced GBC adaptation category, and/or • A CRVA is performed according to the guidance in the Annex, and/or • The assessment of climate risks and impacts is based on best practices and available guidance, and/or • The adaptation solutions do not adversely affect the effectiveness and climate resilience of other stakeholders, • The implemented adaptation solutions are consistent with local or national strategies, and/or • The adaptation solutions ensure monitoring and measurement against pre-defined indicators, and remedial action is considered where the indicators are not met.	
Construction of New Buildings (ISIC 410) under Climate Change Mitigation:	• The building is certified under a national GBC program recognized by an AMS or the relevant industry association in that jurisdiction, and achieves an advanced level of certification applicable to climate change mitigation, or • The building is certified under an internationally recognized GBC program (e.g., LEED, BREEAM), and has achieved an advanced level of certification specifically applicable to climate change mitigation.	• The building is certified under a national GBC program recognized by an AMS or relevant industry association in that jurisdiction that includes criteria relevant to climate change mitigation, or • The building is certified under one of the internationally recognized GBC programs, and • An Energy Efficiency Improvement Plan for the building has been prepared and provided that, upon implementation, will lead to a reduction of the current EUI.

Table 32: ASEAN Taxonomy – classification of buildings (Green and Amber)

Definitions: Recognized GBC and Advanced Level of Certification

A »**recognized GBC program**« refers to national and international GBC programs that are credible and accepted, such as Green Mark and LEED.

An »**advanced level of certification**« means achieving a performance level that is above average in a country within a given recognized GBC program, or lower as long as the building in question represents a marked improvement on common practices in the country and is explicitly above the lowest available tier.

6.3.3 Green bonds and real estate financing

The issuance of **green bonds** by real estate developers has expanded rapidly across Asia. In particular, the Hong Kong Monetary Authority's (HKMA) Green and Sustainable Finance Grant Scheme has incentivized green and sustainable finance, by providing subsidies to costs related to the structuring, issuance, and assurance (including legal, audit, listing, arrangement fees, and pre-issuance or post-issuance external review expenses) of eligible green and sustainable loans or bonds, extended in May 2024 to cover transition bonds and loans. Notable issuers and borrowers in the real estate industry include Link REIT, Swire Properties, New World Development and Greentown China Holdings Ltd. By far, most bond issuances are use-of-proceeds green bonds, but there has also been growing use of sustainability-linked loans besides green loans in the market.

For example, Link REIT issued the first green bond in Hong Kong in 2016, becoming the first property issuer to tap into green financing in the Asia Pacific region.[540] Link REIT is a constituent of the Hong Kong securities market benchmark, the Hang Seng Index, and is recognized for its sustainability efforts as a component of the Dow Jones Sustainability Asia Pacific Index, the FTSE4Good Index Series, and the Hang Seng Corporate Sustainability Index. The use-of-proceeds requirements for its green bonds issued in 2016 and 2019 covered green building certification, energy efficiency, pollution prevention and control, sustainable water management and wastewater management, and clean transportation, and renewable energy to improve climate change resilience. Regarding sustainability-linked loans, the Sustainable Finance Framework[541] requires all such transactions to include, at a minimum, one target under each of the environmental, social and governance aspects, intended to support the organization's broader sustainability goals, including achieving net-zero carbon emissions by 2035.

Another notable example is the Green SRI Sukuk, valued at up to RM2 billion, which was issued by PNB Merdeka Ventures Sdn Bhd to fund the construction of the Merdeka 118 Tower, now recognized by the Council on Tall Buildings and Urban Habitat as the second tallest building in the world.[542] The Merdeka Green SRI Sukuk was successfully issued on December 27, 2017, as the first adopter of the ASEAN Green Bond Standards and it also met the requirements of the Sustainable Responsible Investment Sukuk Framework of the Malaysia Securities Commission. The building stands at 678.9 meters with 118 stories, a development area of 19 Acres and a

540 LinkReit.com, Sustainable Finance, https://www.linkreit.com/en/sustainability/sustainability-governance/sustainable-finance/, accessed 06.09.2025.

541 LinkReit.com, Sustainable Finance Framework, 2022, https://www.linkreit.com/-/media/linkreit/sustainability/sustainability-governance/sustainable-finance/link-sf-framework_web_final.pdf?rev=dce6ef2b6a544b2eaefe7eebadafecbd, accessed 06.09.2025.

542 Council on Tall Buildings and Urban Habitat (CTBUH), Merdeka 118, https://www.skyscrapercenter.com/building/merdeka-118/10115, accessed 06.09.2025.

built-area of 3.1 million square feet. It achieved LEED Platinum certification. Its framework emphasizes sustainability features, including sustainable site planning and management, water efficiency, optimization of energy performance and atmosphere, material resource conservation, indoor environmental quality and sustainable construction.[543]

According to the OECD's Asia Capital Markets Report 2025[544], most corporate green bonds in Asia are use-of-proceeds instruments. This allows issuers to direct funds toward new or existing eligible green projects, and the practice commonly includes refinancing existing green assets.

Importantly, many bond prospectuses and green or sustainable finance frameworks explicitly permit refinancing via green bonds.

As the use-of-proceeds remains the dominant structure, real estate developers channel green bonds or loan funds toward eligible assets. Refinancing is fully permitted and common, and **frameworks often tie proceeds to certified green buildings or developments.** As issuers disclose environmental performance and restrict proceeds within green frameworks, transparency is increasingly expected, and its quality and rigor are rising, thereby reinforcing investor trust while aligning with ICMA guidelines.

Merdeka 118 Sustainability

Targeting the first »**Triple Green Platinum**« Certification in Malaysia

Sustainability features

- High-performance façade glazing
- District cooling plant
- Smart air recycling in the car park
- Rainwater harvesting system
- Reuse of rainwater and gray water
- Hotel hot water generated from rooftop solar panels
- Solar cells on the foyer roof

Targeting »**WELL**« Certification

543 Onsite visit to Merdeka II8 and immersive learning opportunity in July 2025 organized by the Malaysia Securities Industry Development Corporation.

544 OECD, Asia Capital Markets Report 2025, 2025, https://www.oecd.org/en/publications/asia-capital-markets-report-2025_02172cdc-en/full-report/sustainable-bonds_21e9a353.html, accessed 06.09.2025.

6.3.4 Real estate investment funds and REITs

While central banks and supervisory bodies, including the efforts of the **Network for Greening the Financial System (NGFS)**, continue to develop climate- and environment-related risk management strategies to mobilize mainstream finance for the transition to a sustainable economy[545], investors, including asset owners (sovereign wealth funds, pension funds, insurance companies) and in this connection the investment management industry as asset managers are increasingly attracted to sustainable real estate assets, driven by ESG mandates and risk mitigation concerns around climate impacts and regulatory compliance. In addition to regulatory expectations, such as the requirements of the **Hong Kong Securities & Futures Commission** that licensed fund managers incorporate climate-related risks into their governance, strategy, risk management, metrics, and targets using a TCFD-aligned framework, and the Guidelines on Environmental Risk Management for Asset Managers[546] issued by the **Monetary Authority of Singapore**, it is particularly apparent in the real estate investment sector that the industry has long recognized the critical importance of the resilience to physical climate risks in real estate assets, adopting voluntary frameworks, such as GRESB and/or the PRI in its guides or tools for real estate.[547] The investment management industry has also responded to climate-related opportunities through sustainability efforts enhancing real estate value.

There are numerous examples of Asian real estate investment funds using GRESB, as outlined below and extracted from publicly available information:

- Keppel Capital's Alpha Asia Macro Trends Fund III, Keppel Asia Macro Trends Fund IV, and Keppel Education Asset Fund submitted to GRESB 2024 and achieved GRESB »Green Star« status. Its listed vehicles (Keppel REIT, Keppel DC REIT) also achieved this status.[548]
- Gaw Capital Partners (Hong Kong) participates in GRESB to report fund sustainability performance and aligns monthly asset-level reporting with GRESB performance indicators across its Gateway Asia funds.[549]
- ESR Group (Hong Kong), one of Asia's largest global real estate investment managers, has 49 participating entities (up from 45 in 2023) comprising its listed REITs and private funds, with 66 submissions (up from 56 in 2023). According to ESR[550] its average GRESB score and rating are 84.24 out of 100 and 3.41 out of 5 respectively, which exceed the targets set in the Group's ESG 2030 Roadmap.

---

545 Network of Central Banks and Supervisors for Greening the Financial System (NGFS), https://www.ngfs.net/en, accessed 06.09.2025.

546 Monetary Authority of Singapore, Guidelines on Environmental Risk Management for Asset Managers, https://www.mas.gov.sg/regulation/guidelines/guidelines-on-environmental-risk-management-for-asset-managers, accessed 06.09.2025.

547 Please refer to #5.4.

548 Keppel Ltd., Keppel's sustainability performance recognized at GRESB 2024, https://www.keppel.com/media/keppels-sustainability-performance-recognised-at-gresb-2024/, accessed 06.09.2025.

549 GAW Capital Partners, Responsible Investment Policy, https://www.gawcapital.com/srdisclosure/responsible-investment-policy/, accessed 06.09.2025.

550 ESR Group, ESR Group achieves outstanding performance across global ESG benchmarks, https://www.esr.com/news/esr-group-achieves-outstanding-performance-across-global-esg-benchmarks/, accessed 06.09.2025.

- CapitaLand Investment (Singapore) reports that its platform and listed business trusts achieved leading positions in the 2024 GRESB and that it has also pegged sustainability-linked loans to GRESB rankings.[551]

Another example is the Invesco Real Estate Asia Fund (FCP-SIF)[552], which is Invesco's »Asia Core Real Estate Strategy«, which was launched in 2014. The fund has been benchmarked against GRESB, achieving a 5-Star, #1 ranking for ESG+Resilience. This highlights its sustainable real estate management, through embedding due diligence and ongoing monitoring processes in its investment lifecycle. While the fund does not qualify as Article 9 under the SFDR due to the absence of an explicit sustainable investment objective, the fund is commited to achieving **net-zero carbon emissions by 2050 or sooner**, through adoption of the **IIGCC Paris Aligned Investment Initiative (PAII)** framework for real estate. Adopting the IIGCC PAII suggests a forward-looking decarbonization pathway consistent with industry best practices and meaningful net-zero alignment, while the fund is integrated into Invesco's global ESG operational framework and is intended to support long-term transition goals.

In Singapore, the UOB APAC Green REIT ETF tracks the iEdge-UOB APAC Yield Focus Green REIT index, an index which highlights the performance of Real Estate Investment Trusts (REITs) that are listed across the Asia-Pacific and Oceania regions, with a specific focus on yield-based selection process and a weighting method that favors the environmental attributes of real estate assets.[553]

Several prominent REITs in Asia have adopted concrete sustainability frameworks and standards, aligning their financing and reporting practices with global benchmarks. Apart from Link REIT referred to above, other examples include Keppel REIT (Singapore), Fortune REIT (Hong Kong and Singapore), and Star Asia REIT (Japan). Star Asia has crafted a Green Finance Framework targeting environmentally beneficial projects, including the acquisitions or refinancing of green-certified real estate, aligning use of proceeds accordingly.[554]

According to the Fortune REIT's 2024 ESG Report[555], over 60% of its loan portfolio consists of sustainability-linked loans due to extensive use. Under these agreements, Fortune REIT earns interest-rate reductions by meeting ESG performance benchmarks, and it has reported a 41.3%

551 PR Newswire, CapitaLand Investment advances Sustainability leadership in 2024 by progressing toward decarbonization milestones and recognition in leading global indexes, https://en.prnasia.com/releases/apac/capitaland-investment-advances-sustainability-leadership-in-2024-by-progressing-toward-decarbonisation-milestones-and-recognition-in-leading-global-indexes-474468.shtml, accessed 06.09.2025.

552 Invesco, Invesco Real Estate Asia Fund FCP-SIF (the »Fund«), https://www.invesco.com/content/dam/invesco/emea/en/real-estate-sustainability-disclosures/invesco-real-estate-asia-fund-fcp-sif-invesco-sustainability-full-disclosure.pdf, accessed 06.09.2025.

553 Singapore Exchange, iEdge-UOB APAC Yield Focus Green REIT Index [SGD] (NTR), https://www.sgx.com/indices/products/agreitsn, accessed 06.09.2025.

554 Starasia, Green Finance Framework, https://starasia-reit.com/en/esg/greenfinance.html, accessed 06.09.2025.

555 Fortune Reit, Environmental, Social and Governance Report 2024, https://www.fortunereit.com/wp-content/uploads/2025/04/ESG-Report_EW00778.pdf, accessed 06.09.2025.

reduction in Scope 1 & 2 emissions in 2024 versus a 2019 baseline. It has set science-based targets to cut emissions by 46% by 2030 (Scope 1 & 2) and engages tenants via green lease clauses to reduce Scope 3 emissions. Furthermore, the Report is produced in accordance with the ESG Reporting Guide of the Hong Kong Stock Exchange for listed companies and aligns with the IFRS S2 disclosure standard and the GRI.[556]

Meanwhile, the local regulatory infrastructure for sustainability reporting varies across the region. Some countries have had mandatory disclosure and reporting requirements on environmental, social, and governance issues for some time, such as the stock exchange rules of Hong Kong and Taiwan. These rules reflect international guidelines like the TCFD[557] and GRI, whereas others are less prescriptive. However, following the issuance of the ISSB standards, which are intended to serve as a global baseline for corporate sustainability reporting, Asia has trended towards adopting and adapting them into local requirements. As companies in Asia are required to comply with the ISSB standards for sustainability reporting, the market should see corporations more concretely and strategically assessing climate-related risks and opportunities in their business models, activities, and value chains. Companies should adopt more robust climate risk management, specific decarbonization metrics, and target settings that support the transition to a low-carbon economy.

6.3.5 Real estate transition finance

Transition finance supports high-carbon sectors with credible, time-bound plans to decarbonize. In real estate, this covers existing building portfolios that may not yet meet »green« standards, but which can transition through staged upgrades, such as low-carbon materials and retrofitting. Existing buildings in Asia are a major source of emissions, and as many assets cannot be replaced immediately, retrofitting and operational improvements are the main decarbonization strategies. Transition finance provides capital for upgrading brown assets, and eligibility is not limited to those that are already green-certified, often with interim performance targets.

In Asia, the **retrofitting of existing buildings** is gaining momentum, especially in dense urban centers where demolition and reconstruction are costly and disruptive. Retrofitting and adaptive reuse create direct and indirect business benefits, including lower acquisition costs and an attractive investment case for sustainability-minded investors. In response to the 2025/2026 Budget of the Hong Kong government, which commits to developing a green city and promoting Hong Kong's green industries, the Hong Kong Green Building Council (HKGBC) has launched the »HKGBC Retrofitting Guidebook«, and is in the process of creating an online Retrofitting and

556 Global Reporting Initiative, https://www.globalreporting.org/, accessed 06.09.2025.
557 Task Force on Climate-related Financial Disclosures, https://www.fsb-tcfd.org/, accessed 06.09.2025.

Technology Hub at the time of this writing. The Council aims to incorporate green technologies to formulate retrofitting strategies and scale up applications across existing buildings.[558]

Furthermore, the construction industry is increasingly adopting **low-carbon building materials** such as **low-emission cement and concrete, or** alternatives like fly ash, slag, **recycled steel, timber, and sustainable prefabricated components**, which reduce onsite waste and energy use. The Malaysian government has promoted the implementation of green practices, specifically incorporating sustainable building products and the principles of the circular economy within the construction sector[559], ultimately aiming to increase the number of buildings certified under the Green Building Index (GBI) since its introduction in 2009. In particular, the Penang Green Council (PGC) published the »Penang Green Agenda 2030« in 2020, recommending that all new buildings in Penang be GBI certified by 2030, to make green buildings or townships mandatory for certain types of development, encourage the use of recycled materials and modular building practices.[560] In 2025, it was also announced that all new buildings in Penang must meet Building Energy Intensity (BEI) requirements and new mandatory requirements were introduced for public buildings to increase the use of renewable energy.[561] These regulations mark significant strides in Malaysia's journey to achieving its sustainability goals.

In **Japan**, major developers have committed to using carbon-neutral concrete[562], while **South Korea** has expanded the adoption of renewable energy sources, through incentives in the form of subsidies for the installation of solar panels and hydrogen fuel cells, More than 1500 public buildings are to be retrofitted by 2050 under the Green Remodelling Project.[563] Finally, India is promoting the use of fly ash bricks[564], as well as active remodeling, through its Smart Cities initiative.[565]

As outlined above, the ASEAN Taxonomy Version 3 includes »Amber« tiers for construction and real estate, where assets are on a path to meet, but have not yet achieved »Green« criteria (e.g., non-advanced GBC certification plus energy improvement plan). Japan's Green Bond and

558 Hong Kong Green Building Council, Hong Kong Green Building Council's Response to 2025/26 Budget, https://www.hkgbc.org.hk/eng/news-events/news/2025/20250226.jsp, accessed 06.09.2025.
559 MGTC, Steady increase of ›green buildings‹, https://www.mgtc.gov.my/2024/12/steady-increase-of-green-buildings/, accessed 06.09.2025.
560 Penang Green Council, PENANG GREEN AGENDA 2030, 2020, https://www.pgc.com.my/2020/wp-content/uploads/2020/09/6_PGA-Sectoral-Formatted-Final-Report_GBT.pdf, accessed 06.09.2025.
561 https://www.penangpropertytalk.com/2025/03/new-public-buildings-in-penang-to-adopt-renewable-energy-by-requirement/.
562 The Government of Japan, Carbon-Negative Concrete: A Game Changer for a Sustainable Future, https://www.japan.go.jp/kizuna/2022/08/carbon-negative_concrete.html, accessed 06.09.2025.
563 Local Governments for Sustainability, Promoting Renewable Energy Consumption. The Cases of Kitakyushu and Seoul, https://eastasia.iclei.org/wp-content/uploads/2023/12/Promoting-Renewable-Energy-Consumption-1205.pdf, accessed 06.09.2025.
564 NBCC (India) Limited, Use of Fly Ash, https://nbccindia.in/webEnglish/FlyAsh, accessed 06.09.2025.
565 Government of India Ministry of Housing and Urban Affairs, Vision Of Smart Cities Mission, https://smartcities.gov.in, accessed 06.09.2025.

Sustainability-Linked Bond Guidelines (2024) identify green retrofitting and construction as eligible green projects if the align with national carbon neutrality targets.[566]

Transition finance is poised to fill a key gap for Asia's large number of non-green certified buildings, especially in markets with aggressive net-zero targets but limited green asset supply. Both use-of-proceeds instruments and sustainability-linked loans or bonds can be adopted for transition finance. Common forms include sustainability-linked loans with interest rates linked to improvements in energy intensity, certification levels, or carbon footprints; while transition bonds apply proceeds toward a defined decarbonization roadmap for a building or portfolio. Hybrid structures may involve features such as applying the first tranche of proceeds toward an initial retrofit, with subsequent tranches contingent on meeting agreed-upon milestones or targets.

For example, Japanese developers such as Mitsubishi Estate and Nomura Real Estate, use transition-linked loans, sustainability bonds, and green bonds backed by Japanese banks to finance multi-year retrofits.[567] These products support the electrification and decarbonization of businesses, ultimately aiming to achieve carbon neutrality.[568] Mapletree (Singapore) uses sustainability-linked loans for industrial and logistics assets, tying KPIs to achieving Green Mark or LEED improvements over time.[569]

To enhance credibility and avoid greenwashing, transition finance frameworks should incorporate science-based targets (e.g., SBTi for buildings)[570], set concrete milestones such as measurable percentage improvements in EUI, emissions, or certification level within 3–5 years with technical or technological feasibility. These targets should be coupled with robust disclosure, reporting and verification, encompassing requirements of annual reporting, third-party assurance, and linking finance terms to actual performance.

The following **tables 33 to 35** provide **examples of transition finance for real estate in Asia**, consider relevant instruments, KPIs and covenants, drawing on real-world examples from publicly available information. The tables also show how these may align with regional taxonomies and guidance.

566 Ministry of the Environment Japan, Green Bond and Sustainability Linked Bond Guidelines. Green Loan and Sustainability Linked Loan Guidelines, 2024, https://greenfinanceportal.env.go.jp/pdf/greenbond_guideline_eng.pdf, accessed 06.09.2025.

567 Mitsubishi Heavy Industries, Transition Bonds, https://www.mhi.com/finance/stock/esg/transitionbond.html, accessed 06.09.2025.

568 Nomura Real Estate Holding, Sustainable Finance, https://www.nomura-re-hd.co.jp/english/sustainability/finance/#section02, accessed 06.09.2025.

569 Mapletree, Stewarding Sustainability, https://www.mapletree.com.sg/uploads/2025/07/MIPL_SR25_Final-July-14-1.pdf, accessed 06.09.2025.

570 Science Based Targets, Buildings, https://sciencebasedtargets.org/sectors/buildings, accessed 06.09.2025.

(a) Instrument map

Instrument	Use case	Deal features	When to use
Sustainability-Linked Loan (SLL)	Portfolio-wide retrofit programs and stepwise energy/carbon intensity reductions	Margin ratchets tied to KPIs (e.g., EUI ↓, GHG ↓, certification upgrades); annual testing; external verification	Brown-to-green journeys where assets are not yet eligible for »green« use-of-proceeds financing
Transition loan/bond	CapEx for deep retrofits (HVAC replacement, envelope upgrades, electrification, on-site renewables) under a published roadmap	Use-of-proceeds governed by a transition finance framework; interim milestones; failure leads to step-up margin/coupon	Whole-building pathways with clear, multi-year decarbonization plans
Hybrid facilities (Tranche A green/ Tranche B transition)	Blend of already-green assets and to-be-improved assets	Allocation reporting split by tranche; harmonized KPIs at portfolio level	Mixed portfolios with staggered readiness levels
Sustainability-Linked Derivatives (SLDs)	Hedge linked to ESG performance to reinforce incentives	Coupon/settlement adjustments based on KPI outcomes	To complement SLLs/ transition bonds where hedging is needed

Table 33: Transition finance for real estate in Asia – instruments

(b) Illustrative Asia transactions and programs

Sponsor/Market	Asset type	Instrument	Transition use of funds/KPI focus	Notes
Fortune REIT (HK)	Retail malls	SLL portfolio facilities	Energy intensity reduction vs. the 2019 baseline; green lease rollout; waste diversion improvements	The majority of loans SLL; supports progressive retrofits and tenant engagement
Mapletree (SG/Asia)	Logistics & industrial	SLLs/hybrid structures	Achieve BCA Green Mark/LEED upgrades; LED & HVAC replacement; submetering and BMS installation	Portfolio program with supplier/tenant data-sharing covenants
Mitsubishi Estate/ Nomura Real Estate(JP)	Offices (legacy stock)	Transition loans	ZEB Ready targets; electrification and heat pump conversion; façade/insulation upgrades	Bank-led frameworks aligned with national transition guidelines

Table 34: Transition finance for real estate in Asia – transactions and programs

(c) Typical KPIs, testing, and covenants

KPI/Covenant	Indicative thresholds (Examples)	Measurement & assurance
Energy Use Intensity (EUI) reduction	−10–15 % by Year 3; −25–35 % by Year 5 (vs. 2019/2022 baseline)	Utility metering/submetering; independent engineer verification; annual audit
GHG emissions intensity reduction ($kgCO_2e/m^2$)	−20–30 % by Year 5; alignment to SBTi buildings pathway	Supplier-specific emission factors where available; third-party assurance
Green building certification upgrade	Achieve/maintain BEAM Plus Gold/BCA Green Mark GoldPLUS/LEED Gold; or one-tier uplift	Certification body award/annual surveillance reports
Electrification milestones	x% of boilers replaced with heat pumps by Y3; gas intensity ↓ ≥50 % by Y5	Completion certificates; commissioning reports
Renewable energy adoption	≥10–20 % onsite/contracted green electricity by Y3; 100 % by Y10 (market dependent)	REC/IGA documentation; PPA records
Waste & water performance	≥70 % waste diversion; water intensity ↓ ≥10–20 % by Y5	Waste hauler statements; water bills; sampling protocols

Table 35: Transition finance for real estate in Asia – KPIs, testing and covenants

6.3.6 Asia data center green initiatives

With unprecedented growth in cloud computing and artificial intelligence technologies over recent years, data center facilities have experienced a surge in global demand to support the booming digital economy.[571] Alongside the current global push to protect the environment, considerable focus has been placed on making traditionally energy-intensive data centers more sustainable. This approach is reflected in Asia's data center sector, which has seen an increase in green initiatives spanning renewable energy, efficiency technologies, and policy frameworks.

There has been a steady flow of large deals involving sustainable debt to finance new data center facilities in Asia, indicating a promising commitment to sustainability. For example, Singtel secured a S$643 million (~$476 million) five-year green loan that is backed by major banks to develop the 58-megawatt DC Tuas data center in Singapore. This move aligns with the corporation's goal of reducing its carbon footprint and achieving their net zero.[572] Meanwhile, tech giant

571 World Economic Forum, This is the state of play in the global data centre gold rush, 2025, https://www.weforum.org/stories/2025/04/data-centre-gold-rush-ai/, accessed 06.09.2025.

572 Reuters, SingTel secures $476 million green loan to develop data centre, 2025, https://www.reuters.com/sustainability/sustainable-finance-reporting/singtel-secures-476-million-green-loan-develop-data-centre-2025-02-06/, accessed 06.09.2025.

Google is set to invest a record $6 billion in a 1-gigawatt data center in India, of which $2 billion is committed to building renewable energy infrastructure that will power the facility.[573]

The practice of incorporating on-site renewable energy infrastructure reflects a growing trend among new data center facilities, particularly those in Malaysia. For example, AirTrunk (Malaysia) installed a 1-megawatt rooftop solar generation system at its Johor Bahru data center facility as part of its larger 30-megawatt virtual power purchase agreement (VPPA). This is the first time that data centers have achieved this level of renewable energy under Malaysia's corporate green energy scheme.[574] Additionally, a RM15 billion project by YTL Green Data Centre Park (Malaysia) in Johor features the first solar-powered data center campus (500 MW) in Malaysia. This will be is particularly attractive to customers looking for green data centers in the region.[575]

Furthermore, new data center facilities in the region are adopting energy-efficient and innovative cooling technologies to become more sustainable. For example, Digital Edge has launched green-ready colocation sites in Manila and Jakarta using Statepoint® liquid cooling, which is a state-of-the-art membrane-based evaporative cooling technology that significantly lowers both annual power and water use.[576] Meanwhile, the Infocomm Media Development Authority in Singapore introduced the Green Data Centre (DC) Roadmap to support the growth of sustainable data centers. This initiative aims to improve energy efficiency (PUE of 1.3 or lower) at both hardware and software levels while accelerating the adoption of green energy by data centers. For example, it involves tusing best-in-class technologies to provide liquid cooling solutions, allowing energy savings and operating temperatures to be safely increased.[577]

At the regional ASEAN level, there has been sector collaboration and policy support among the Southeast Asian countries. For example, the recent Innovative Finance Clinic for Green Data Centers held in Singapore brought together policymakers, financiers, operators, and technology providers from seven Southeast Asian governments to promote energy efficiency, water use, and renewable energy in regulatory frameworks and financial structures in Southeast Asia. A key aim of the event was to encourage collaboration between the public and private sectors in

573 Varadhan, Sudarshan, Google to invest $6 billion in southern India data centre, sources say, https://www.reuters.com/sustainability/boards-policy-regulation/google-invest-6-billion-southern-india-data-centre-sources-say-2025-07-30/, accessed 06.09.2025.

574 Airtrunk, AirTrunk and Pekat Solar to develop rooftop solar at AirTrunk's Johor Bahru data centre, JHB1, 2024, https://airtrunk.com/airtrunk-and-pekat-solar-to-develop-rooftop-solar-at-airtrunks-johor-bahru-data-centre-jhb1/, accessed 06.09.2025.

575 YTL Beyond, YTL Green Data Center Park launches in Johor, the First Integrated Data Center Park Powered by Renewable Solar Energy in Malysia, https://www.ytl.com/press-releases/ytl-green-data-center-park-launches-in-johor-the-first-integrated-data-center-park-powered-by-renewable-solar-energy-in-malaysia-2/, accessed 06.09.2025.

576 Digital Edge DC, Construction of Green Data Centers in Asia, https://www.digitaledgedc.com/construction-of-green-data-centers-in-asia/, accessed 06.09.2025.

577 Infocomm Media Development Authority, Charting green growth pathways at scale for data centres in Singapore, 2024, https://www.imda.gov.sg/resources/press-releases-factsheets-and-speeches/factsheets/2024/charting-green-growth-for-data-centres-in-sg, accessed 06.09.2025.

advancing sustainable data center development.[578] Meanwhile, governments across Southeast Asia are offering grants, tax incentives (e.g., the Philippines), and selective approval processes (e.g., Singapore's DC-CFA scheme) that favor energy-efficient, green-powered data center projects. These initiatives work hand-in-hand with lower construction costs and electricity tariffs, fueling the ASEAN region's growing market as a global data center hotspot and attracting giant tech firms such as Google, Amazon Web Services, and Microsoft.[579]

Evidently, Asia's data center sector is steadily advancing its environmental footprint by blending renewable energy, energy-efficient technology, and targeted green financing. Its future greatly depends on the success of grid decarbonization, smarter load balancing, and the widespread adoption of best-in-class technologies to ensure the sustainability of digital infrastructure.

However, many data centers in Southeast Asia remain heavily reliant on fossil fuel-based grids. For instance, Singapore's grid was around 92% (53 TWh) gas-powered in 2023, complicating true carbon reductions.[580] Even with an increased renewable energy supply, greater deployment of battery storage and AI-led energy optimization is needed to support intermittent clean energy usage.[581]

6.3.7 Real estate ESG contract clauses in Asia

(a) Role of contracts

Contracts are a pivotal mechanism for embedding sustainability into real estate development and financing. Key developments include **construction contracts with low-carbon procurement obligations** and waste diversion and water reuse targets, as well as **performance-based design-build contracts**. They also include incentives for contractors to exceed green performance benchmarks, **green lease clauses** that require tenants to comply with energy targets or share sustainability data, and, as outlined above, **sustainability-linked loan terms** that tie interest rates to ESG performance indicators.

Sustainability and related legal frameworks in Asia are gradually evolving to recognize and enforce these obligations. It is worth noting the growing interest in the climate contract clauses of The Chancery Lane Project (TCLP). While not limited to the real estate industry, this chapter focuses on its relevance in real estate contracts in Asia. The increased use of climate clauses

578 Southeast Asia Development Solutions (SEADS), Data Centers and the Sustainability Challenge, 2025, https://seads.adb.org/articles/data-centers-and-sustainability-challenge, accessed 06.09.2025.

579 EMBER, ASEAN's data centres electricity demand keeps growing, https://ember-energy.org/chapter/setting-the-scene/, accessed 06.09.2025.

580 Seyawati/Lolla, Regional grids key to Singapore's energy future, 2024, https://ember-energy.org/latest-insights/regional-grids-key-to-singapores-energy-future/, accessed 06.09.2024.

581 Fernandez, Hannah Alcoseba, A third of Southeast Asia's data centres could be powered by renewable energy by 2030: study, 2025, https://www.eco-business.com/news/a-third-of-southeast-asias-data-centres-could-be-powered-by-renewable-energy-by-2030-study/, accessed 06.09.2025.

and fostering of legal innovation for sustainability through contracts were highlighted by the Global Alliance of Impact Lawyers (GAIL) Asia Pacific in 2022, when it hosted two panel discussions. The first was with TCLP on bringing together a collaborative initiative of international lawyers to create contractual clauses that enable solutions to climate change. The second was with Hong Kong University's interdisciplinary and experiential program to foster Law, Innovation, Technology and Entrepreneurship (LITE Lab). The panelists discussed how practitioners can utilize TCLP resources and get involved to improve their skills and develop knowledge of sustainability and impact law in the Asia-Pacific region. Since then, a number of working groups have been established and led by LITE Lab, while being supported by private practice and in-house lawyers in Hong Kong, Singapore, and Malaysia. These groups consider and adapt selected TCLP climate clauses to local contexts and develop local toolkits.[582]

The recently published ESG Resource Library by the Law Society of Singapore compiles a collection of resources and tools for lawyers to incorporate sustainability considerations and goals into businesses. Among others, TCLP is included as part of climate-aligned legal clauses to drive environmental action.[583]

While there is no public record yet of TCLP clauses being formally embedded in real estate contracts in Asia, the project is actively localizing and promoting awareness through translated resources and practitioner networks. For real estate lawyers or ESG-focused firms across the region, adapting these clauses can push legal drafting toward more climate-responsible norms.

(b) Real estate-specific TCLP clauses

While not specifically drafted for Asia, TCLP offers several real estate-relevant clauses that can be adapted regionally. Depending on the context, appropriate references should be made to applicable local laws, such as Hong Kong's **Buildings Energy Efficiency Ordinance**[584] or Singapore's **Building Control (Environmental Sustainability) Regulations**[585]. **Measurable targets should also be aligned with relevant local green building certification requirements.**

582 The author of this chapter, Vivien Teu, is a founding member of GAIL Asia Pacific and currently a global and regional board member. She is also a working group member and contributor to-date of the LITE Lab-TCLP climate contracting working groups for green capital markets, green loans, green buildings and construction and as lead coordinator for the green investment funds working group.

583 The Law Society of Singapore, ESG Resource Library, https://www.lawsociety.org.sg/esg-hub/esg-resource-library/

584 Hong Kong e-Legislation, Buildings Energy Efficiency Ordinance, https://www.elegislation.gov.hk/hk/cap610, accessed 06.09.2025.

585 Singapore Statutes Online, Building Control Act, 2008, https://sso.agc.gov.sg/SL/BCA1989-S199-2008, accessed 06.09.2025.

Clause	Application	Localization Opportunity
Commercial lease: Alterations (improve environmental performance) (Rosie's Clause)	The landlord must not unreasonably withhold consent for tenant green fit-outs	Tie consent criteria to local certifications (e.g., BEAM Plus, Green Mark) and city building codes
Green residential lease clauses (Emma's Clause)	Residential lease: tenant to operate unit efficiently, reduce emissions	Integrate with utility data-sharing requirements and incentives under the Singapore BCA Green Lease Toolkit or HK landlord schemes
Report on title: Commercial real estate (Marni's Clause)	Conveyance: disclose building's climate risk and energy performance	Embed references to local risk databases (e.g., HKMA Climate Risk Assessment, SG PUB flood maps)

Table 36: TCLP clauses (real estate) – localization opportunities

EXAMPLES OF LOCALIZED CLAUSES

Localized Emma's Clause – Singapore (Residential lease): »The Tenant shall operate the Premises in a manner that optimizes energy and water efficiency, including by maintaining air-conditioning temperature settings between 24°C and 26°C, using appliances with at least 3-tick NEA Energy Labels, and separating recyclables in accordance with the National Environment Agency's guidelines. The Landlord may offer a monthly rental rebate of 2 % if the Tenant achieves an annual energy consumption at least 10 % lower than the baseline measured in the first month of tenancy.«

Localized Rosie's Clause – Hong Kong (Commercial lease): »The Landlord shall not unreasonably withhold or delay consent to any alterations proposed by the Tenant that are intended to improve the environmental performance of the Premises, including measures to achieve or maintain BEAM Plus Gold or higher certification. The Tenant shall provide sufficient technical details for the Landlord's approval and ensure that any such works comply with the Buildings Energy Efficiency Ordinance (Cap. 610) and other applicable legislation.«

Localized Marni's Clause– Hong Kong (Commercial/Residential real estate): »The Seller's legal counsel shall include in the Report on Title a summary of (a) the Building's BEAM Plus or equivalent green building certification status; (b) any available energy efficiency ratings under the Buildings Energy Efficiency Ordinance (Cap. 610); and (c) known material physical climate risks affecting the Property, including a reference to the Hong Kong Climate Adaptation and Resilience Assessment Map, if available.«

Localized Green Fit-Out Guide Clause – Hong Kong & Singapore (Commercial lease): »The Tenant shall comply with the Landlord's Green Fit-Out Guide (as amended from time to time), which specifies approved materials, energy-efficient equipment, and waste separation requirements for all fit-out and alteration works. In Hong Kong, compliance shall include the ›Code of Practice on Separating, Collecting and Transporting Food Waste to Organic Resources Recovery Centre Phase 1‹ and in Singapore, the Resource Sustainability Act 2019. Any deviations from the Guide require prior written consent from the Landlord.«

(c) Introduction of ESG clauses by developers and REITs

There are numerous **examples of real estate developers and REITs in Asia** that have introduced explicit green requirements into tenancy agreements (›**green leases**‹), Below are selected examples with reference to publicly reported clauses and initiatives.

City Developments Limited – CDL (Singapore): CDL has been an industry pioneer in green lease partnerships[586], providing green fitting-out kits to tenants since 2009. Under its longstanding program, it is reported that by May 2015, more than 80% of CDL's commercial tenants have signed the Green Lease Memorandum of Understanding. More recently, CDL launched the City Green Tenant Bonus Programme (2024) as an extension of its green lease initiative to incentivize tenant energy reductions (Scope 3).[587] The requirements focus on monitoring, managing and reducing energy, as well as broader sustainable practices.

Swire Properties (Hong Kong): In 2022, Swire Properties introduced the Green Performance Pledge (GPP), as well as a dedicated green clause in its standard tenancy agreement in Hong Kong. A major office lease renewal at Pacific Place in 2024 included this clause. Typical requirements span fit-out and operations, with targets related to energy, water and waste.[588]

Link REIT (Hong Kong): Link REIT updated its tenancy document suite to include green lease clauses based on international best practices. Its 2024/2025 sustainability report shows the continued rollout (including to new market tenants). The clauses cover landlord and tenant requirements, as well as ongoing engagement and education.[589]

CapitaLand Investment (CLI)/Ascendas (in Singapore and the region): CLI has expanded green tenant leases and »standardising green lease implementation requirements.«[590] Media coverage notes

586 Triplepundit, A new lease of life for sustainability, https://triplepundit.com/2015/new-lease-life-sustainability/, accessed 06.09.2025.

587 City Development Linited, CDL pilots first-of-its-kind decarbonisation initiative City Green Tenant Bonus Programme for Republic Plaza tenants, https://www.cdl.com.sg/newsroom/cdl-pilots-first-of-its-kind-decarbonisation-initiative-city-green-tenant-bonus-programme-for-republic-plaza-tenants, accessed 06.09.2024.

588 Swire Properties, Green Performance Pledge, https://sd.swireproperties.com/2024/en/partners/tenants/environment, accessed 06.09.2025.

589 Link Real Estate Investment Trust, From Strength to Strategy: SHAPING TOMORROW, TODAY, https://www.linkreit.com/-/media/linkreit/investor-relations/financial-reports-and-presentations/financial-report/2024/annual-report-2324-e-book-3.pdf, accessed 06.09.2025.

590 Srivastava, Vinamra, CLI Sustainability Strategy – The Way Forward, 2024, https://ir.capitalandinvest.com/newsroom/20241028_063535_9CI_3IXKOP9RIAK67EIA.1.pdf, accessed 06.09.2025.

green lease penetration has risen to 57% of tenants in China and Singapore by the end of 2023.[591] CapitaLand Ascendas REIT's sustainability reporting suggests use of clauses to support the group-wide pathway, including clauses on data-sharing, efficiency measures, and fit-out guidance.[592]

Mapletree (Singapore; logistics/industrial portfolios across Asia): The Mapletree Group's sustainability report for the period from April 1, 2024 to March 31, 2025, describes the active implementation of green lease clauses with tenants. These include utility, Scope 3 data sharing, waste minimization and recycling, use of green materials/services, and sustainable operations guidance. Recent updates reaffirm the portfolio-wide adoption across logistics and industrial assets.[593]

GLP J-REIT (Japan): GLP Japan Inc. is committed to include green lease clauses in all new contracts starting in fiscal year 2025, and to work with existing tenants on reducing energy/water consumption and waste, collaborating on green building certifications, and also undertaking co-financed retrofits (solar and wind power generation, LED installation, and HVAC upgrades).

At GLP Shinkiba, a dedicated facility for DHL Japan, GLP and DHL Japan renewed the lease. Through close collaboration between the two parties, both were able to contribute to sustainable environmental and social development. Specifically, GLP Japan installed solar panels and supported the installation of LED lighting. These improvements contribute to DHL's global carbon neutrality initiatives and enable DHL Japan to reduce its electricity costs. In addition, the proposal to switch facility management to GLP Japan will enable more efficient facility operations and reduce operating costs by leveraging GLP Japan's nationwide network and expertise.[594]

6.3.8 Conclusion and outlook

The outlook is that growing market and stakeholder expectations will lead real estate developers and managers to adopt holistic frameworks which integrate material ESG considerations throughout the business and operational life cycle. By way of example, as illustrated by CLI's sustainability strategy (October 2024)[595], sustainability is intended to be integrated by tailoring ESG strategies to real estate fund product development, capital raising while taking into account investors' ESG concerns and transparent disclosure of ESG risks and opportunities. Additionally, this includes conducting environmental, health and safety impact assessments for investments

591 The Straits Times, CapitaLand Investment pushes ahead with disclosures from suppliers, more green leases, 2024, https://www.straitstimes.com/business/capitaland-investment-pushes-ahead-with-disclosures-from-suppliers-more-green-leases, accessed 06.09.2025.

592 Capital Ascendas Reit, INTEGRATED SUSTAINABILITY REPORT 2022, https://investor.capitaland-ascendasreit.com/newsroom/20230406_060107_A17U_ECIMIIRIYBFHU7YI.1.pdf, accessed 06.09.2025.

593 Mapletree STEWARDING SUSTAINABILITY, 2025, https://www.mapletree.com.sg/uploads/2025/07/MIPL_SR25_Final-July-14-1.pdf, accessed 06.09.2025.

594 GLP, Environmental Activities (E), https://www.glpjreit.com/en/esg/environment.html, accessed 06.09.2025.

595 Srivastava, Vinamra, CLI Sustainability Strategy – The Way Forward, 2024, https://ir.capitalandinvest.com/newsroom/20241028_063535_9CI_3IXKOP9RIAK67EIA.1.pdf, accessed 06.09.2025.

and developing asset-level ESG plans that cover operational and asset management expertise, while participating in internationally recognized ESG frameworks, namely GRESB.

> Asia's real estate industry is at the forefront of a major sustainability shift, supported by evolving sustainable finance frameworks, material innovation, and green policy incentives. As capital markets, developers, and regulators align, the integration of sustainability into real estate development will become the norm rather than the exception. Through the right use of taxonomies, financial instruments, and legally enforceable sustainability obligations, Asia is well-positioned to construct the low-carbon cities of tomorrow.

6.4 Europe (EU & UK)

Laura Gowing/Sabine Wieduwilt

6.4.1 Introduction to #6.4

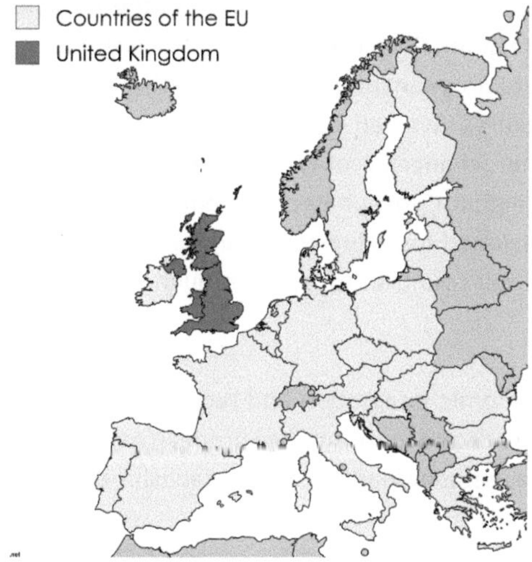

We will continue our overview with Europe, concentrating on the European Union (EU) (#6.4.2) and the United Kingdom (UK) (#6.4.3).[596]

596 Several countries in Europe are neither members of the European Union (EU) nor part of the United Kingdom (UK). These include: Norway, Iceland, Liechtenstein, Switzerland, Albania, Bosnia and Herzegovina, Serbia, Montenegro, North Macedonia, Kosovo, Moldova, Ukraine, Belarus, Russia, Turkey, Andorra, Monaco, San Marino, Vatican City (Holy See). Some of these countries (such as Norway, Iceland, Liechtenstein, and Switzerland) are part of the European Economic Area (EEA) or have other agreements with the EU, but are not EU members. Microstates like Andorra, Monaco, San Marino, and Vatican City are independent and not in the EU.

6.4.2 European Union (EU): Focus on ESG drivers, including frameworks, laws, and standards

Sabine Wieduwilt

»In varietate concordia (›United in diversity‹) is the official motto of the European Union (EU), adopted in 2000.«[597]

(a) The European Union (EU). Introduction to #6.4.2

The European Union (EU) is a political and economic union of 27 member states in Europe. It is one of the world's largest single markets. The EU's real estate investment landscape is shaped by its diverse property markets. The EU has developed an extensive sustainability agenda and regulatory framework, which are currently being remodeled.

The European Union (EU), as it is known today, was formally established by the Maastricht Treaty, signed in 1992 and effective in 1993. However, the roots of the EU go back further, to the creation of the European Economic Community (EEC) in 1957 with the signing of the Treaty of Rome[598]. The EEC was founded by six countries: Belgium, France, Germany, Italy, Luxembourg, and the Netherlands, building on earlier efforts at European integration by countries that had previously been adversaries in war. Prominent figures involved in the founding of these early European communities included Konrad Adenauer (chancellor of West Germany), Charles de Gaulle (president of France), Paul-Henri Spaak (Belgium), Joseph Bech (Luxembourg), and Joseph Luns (the Netherlands). These leaders envisioned fostering economic cooperation and preventing future conflicts in Europe by binding their countries together through shared institutions and policies.

The primary focus of these founders was on economic integration and reconstruction after World War II, with the broader aim of promoting peace and unity among European nations. The process of integration evolved over the decades, eventually leading to the establishment of the European Union in 1993.

The architects of European integration recognized that lasting peace and unity required a stable, prosperous, and cohesive society – one in which economic progress would be accom-

597 Wikipedia, Motto of the European Union, https://en.wikipedia.org/wiki/Motto_of_the_European_Union, accessed 25.05.2025. The motto »United in diversity« is inspired by its Latin-language version coined by the Italian Nobel prize winner Ernesto Teodoro Moneta – »In varietate concordia« or »In varietate unitas« – which is also used as a compromise. According to the European Commission, »It signifies how Europeans have come together, in the form of the EU, to work for peace and prosperity, while at the same time being enriched by the continent's many different cultures, traditions and languages.« – EC, EU Motto, https://european-union.europa.eu/principles-countries-history/symbols/eu-motto_en#:~:text=%22United%20in%20diversity%22%2C%20the,in%20all%20official%20EU%20languages, accessed 27.07.2025.

598 Treaty of Rome, Document 02016ME/TXT-20160901, https://eur-lex.europa.eu/legal-content/EN/TXT/?uri=celex%3A02016ME%2FTXT-20160901, accessed 02.08.2025.

panied by social advancement and mutual support among member states. This vision was formalized in the Treaty of Rome (1957), which established the EEC and set out objectives such as harmonizing economic activities, achieving a high degree of economic convergence, and raising the standard of living[599].

As the EEC evolved, this broader vision began to manifest itself in the development and revision of its foundational treaties. Over time, the scope of European integration expanded to address not only market efficiency and economic growth, but also the well-being of citizens, the protection of the environment, and the promotion of responsible business practices. This evolution is reflected in successive treaty amendments and policy initiatives, such as the Single European Act (1986)[600], which introduced environmental protection as a Community objective[601], and the Maastricht Treaty (1992)[602], which explicitly included social policy and sustainable development among the Union's aims[603], as well as made the environment an official EU policy area[604]. The Treaty of Amsterdam (1997)[605] further reinforced these commitments by integrating environmental protection requirements into the definition and implementation of all Community policies[606], as well as sustainable development as an explicit objective of the Union[607].

Consequently, the EU's foundational treaties and subsequent policy developments have consistently emphasized not only economic integration but also the promotion of social welfare, environmental protection, and responsible business conduct. This commitment is evident in the current Treaty on the Functioning of the European Union (TFEU)[608], which mandates a high level of protection and improvement of the quality of the environment[609], the promotion of social justice and protection[610], and the encouragement of sustainable development[611]. These principles have shaped the trajectory of sustainability and ESG frameworks across the region, including their application to real estate investments. The EU's journey from a primarily economic union to a multifaceted community with strong social and environmental dimensions

599 Treaty of Rome, OJ C 202, 07.06.2016, https://eur-lex.europa.eu/legal-content/EN/TXT/?uri=celex%3A02016ME%2FTXT-20160901, accessed 02.08.2025 – Treaty of Rome, Article 2; Treaty establishing the EEC and Euratom (Treaty of Rome), 25 March 1957, OJ 27, 30.10.1962; OJ C 325, 24.12.2002, https://eur-lex.europa.eu/legal-content/EN/TXT/?uri=celex%3A12016A%2FTXT, accessed 02.08.2025.

600 Single European Act (1986), OJ L 169, 29.06.1987, https://eur-lex.europa.eu/resource.html?uri=cellar:a519205f-924a-4978-96a2-b9af8a598b85.0004.02/DOC_1&format=PDF, accessed 30.07.2025.

601 Single European Act, Article 130r.

602 Maastricht Treaty, OJ C 191, 29.07.1992, https://eur-lex.europa.eu/legal-content/EN/TXT/PDF/?uri=CELEX:11992M/TXT&from=EN, accessed 30.07.2025.

603 TEU, OJ C 191, 29.07.1992, https://eur-lex.europa.eu/legal-content/EN/TXT/PDF/?uri=CELEX:11992M/TXT&from=EN, accessed 30.07.2025 – TEU, Article 3.

604 TEU, Article 2; TFEU, Articles 191–193.

605 Treaty of Amsterdam amending the TEU, the Treaties establishing the ECs (Treaty of Amsterdam), 2 October 1997, OJ C 340, 10.11.1997, https://eur-lex.europa.eu/eli/treaty/ams/sign/eng, accessed 30.07.2025.

606 Treaty of Amsterdam, Article 6 EC, now Article 11 TFEU.

607 Treaty on European Union, Article 3(3); see also later: Treaty on the Functioning of the European Union, Article 11.

608 Treaty on the Functioning of the European Union (TFEU), OJ C 202, 7.6.2016, https://eur-lex.europa.eu/legal-content/EN/TXT/?uri=celex%3A12016ME%2FTXT, accessed 30.07.2025.

609 Article 191 TFEU.

610 Article 151 TFEU.

611 Article 3 TEU.

illustrates how its foundational goals have broadened to encompass a holistic approach to sustainable development.

What issues does the EU have to face? An abundant sustainability/CSR/ESG agenda, local developments in parallel, retrofit needs, an aging building stock that presents challenges and opportunities for sustainable retrofitting, opportunities for cross-sectoral innovation and technology, green technology, smart buildings, and ESG data reporting to offer new investment opportunities.

To better understand the investment approach in the EU, we deem reasonable to explore (an extract of) the regulatory structure and agenda.

#6.4.2 Mapping Europe – EU	**(a) – intro to #6.4.2**
	(b) – Sustainable Finance Action Plan & EU Green Deal
	(c) – sustainability/sustainable finance/CSR/ESG
	(d) – energy, climate and environmental laws and the social and governance agenda
	(e) – urban development and built environment
	(f) – developments since September 2024
	(g) – EU policy documents, bodies, institutions, associations

In this subchapter #6.4.2, we will focus on EU frameworks, starting with two milestones, the Sustainable Finance Action Plan and the EU Green Deal (under (b)), then dive into details concerning sustainability/CSR/ESG/sustainable finance (under (c)), energy, climate and environmental laws and the social and governance agenda (under (d)), urban development and built environment (under (e)), following up with recent developments since September 2024 (under (f)), to close with an overview of terms used for policy documents, bodies, institutions and associations (under (g)).

(b) Two Milestones with EU Sustainable Finance Action Plan in 2018 (updated 2021) and EU Green Deal in 2019

In the wake of the Paris Agreement and the Agenda 2030, two milestone frameworks followed in the EU: The **Sustainable Finance Action Plan (SFAP) and the EU Green Deal**. Both Sustainable Finance Action Plan and EU Green Deal each include a wide array of policy action plans.

The 2018 »**Action Plan: Financing Sustainable Growth**«[612] (»**Sustainable Finance Action Plan**« or »**SFAP**«) identifies **three main objectives**: redirecting capital flows towards sustainable investments, mainstreaming sustainability into risk management, and fostering transparency and long-termism. It proposes **ten actions** to achieve these objectives, such as establishing an EU classification system for sustainable activities (the EU Taxonomy), creating standards and labels for green financial products, incorporating sustainability in financial advice and prudential requirements, and strengthening sustainability disclosure and accounting rule-making.[613]

612 Communication from the Commission to the European Parliament, the European Council, the Council, the European Central Bank, the European Economic and Social Committee and the Committee of the Regions Action Plan: Financing Sustainable Growth, COM/2018/097 final, https://eur-lex.europa.eu/legal-content/EN/TXT/?uri=celex:52018DC0097, accessed 21.07.2025.

613 Sustainable Finance Action Plan (SFAP).

An EU Commission Communication from **2021 »EU Strategy for Financing the Transition to a Sustainable Economy«** updated the 2018 Action Plan of and identified four main areas for further action: developing a more comprehensive framework, improving inclusiveness, enhancing financial sector resilience, and fostering global ambition.

The **European Green Deal (EGD)**[614] of 2019 is again a Communication from the EU Commission and covers a new growth strategy that aims to transform the EU into a fair and prosperous society, with a modern, resource-efficient and competitive economy, where there are no net greenhouse gas emissions by 2050 and where economic growth is decoupled from resource use. It also aims to protect, conserve, and enhance the EU's natural capital, and to protect the health and well-being of citizens from environment-related risks and impacts. The EGD covers all sectors of the economy, particularly transport, energy, agriculture, buildings, and industries such as steel, cement, ICT, textiles and chemicals. It sets out a roadmap of key policies and measures to achieve the transition.

(c) Details: EU sustainable development, CSR, and sustainable finance frameworks

The **European Union's approach to sustainable development, corporate social responsibility (CSR), and sustainable finance has evolved over time.**

Sustainable development and CSR (2000–2011). Early this century, the **Lisbon Strategy (2000)**, established sustainability as a core pillar of EU economic and social policy. Building on this, the **European Sustainable Development Strategy (EU SDS) of 2001** sought to integrate economic, social, and environmental considerations into all EU policies, emphasizing the need for continuous improvement in quality of life and responsible resource management. The 2006 revision of the EU SDS specifically highlighted the importance of energy efficiency in buildings, foreshadowing later real estate-specific sustainability measures. In parallel, the **European Commission's Green Paper on CSR (2001)** launched a broad debate on how to promote responsible business conduct, encouraging companies to voluntarily integrate social and environmental concerns into their operations. This was further developed in **the Renewed EU Strategy for CSR (2011)**, which redefined CSR as the responsibility of enterprises for their impacts on society and set out concrete actions to improve transparency, stakeholder engagement, and the integration of CSR into business practices.

Non-financial and sustainability reporting (2014–2023). A major step was the introduction of mandatory reporting requirements. The **Non-Financial Reporting Directive (NFRD, 2014)** required large companies to disclose information on environmental, social, and governance matters, marking the mainstreaming of ESG reporting in the EU. This was significantly expanded by the **Corporate Sustainability Reporting Directive (CSRD, 2022)**, which broadened the

614 Communication from the Commission to the European Parliament, the European Council, the Council, the European Economic and Social Committee and the Committee of the Regions – The European Green Deal (EGD), 2019, https://eur-lex.europa.eu/legal-content/EN/TXT/?uri=celex%3A52019DC0640, accessed 06.09.2025.

scope to include more companies and introduced detailed reporting standards through the **European Sustainability Reporting Standards (ESRS, 2023).**

Defining sustainable activities: the EU taxonomy and related regulations (2020–2023). To provide clarity and consistency in what constitutes a sustainable economic activity, the EU Taxonomy Regulation (2020) established a classification system for environmentally sustainable activities. This regulation, along with its Delegated Acts, sets out technical screening criteria for six environmental objectives, directly impacting real estate investment by defining which building and renovation activities qualify as sustainable. Companies subject to the CSRD must also report on their taxonomy eligibility and alignment, further integrating sustainability into financial and investment decision-making. The Taxonomy Regulation serves as a reference point for other legislative acts, such as the EU Green Bond Standard and the EU Benchmark Regulation, ensuring that financial products and benchmarks align with the EU's sustainability objectives.

Integrating sustainability into financial markets: SFDR, MiFID II, etc. The **Sustainable Finance Disclosure Regulation (SFDR, 2019)** introduced harmonized rules for financial market participants, including real estate funds, requiring them to disclose how they integrate sustainability risks and consider adverse impacts in their investment processes. The SFDR's Regulatory Technical Standards provide detailed templates and methodologies for these disclosures. At the same time, the **Markets in Financial Instruments Directive II (MiFID II, 2014)** and the **Markets in Financial Instruments Regulation (MiFIR, 2014)** have enhanced transparency and investor protection, including the requirement for financial advisors to consider clients' sustainability preferences when offering investment products. These measures aim to ensure that sustainability is embedded in the advice and products offered to investors, including those in the real estate sector.

Expanding Corporate Responsibility: due diligence and value chains (2024). One of the most recent developments is the Corporate Sustainability Due Diligence Directive (CSDDD, 2024), which requires large companies to identify, prevent, and mitigate adverse impacts on human rights and the environment throughout their value chains. The directive applies to real estate operations and investments, obliging companies to integrate due diligence into their policies, assess risks, engage stakeholders, and report on their actions.

(d) Details: EU energy, climate, and environmental laws, social and governance agenda
Below is an overview of laws that may affect compliance and risk management. Investors and developers must meet binding targets and standards and manage regulatory and market risks. There are also requirements for energy efficiency, renewables, and environmental protection that need to be integrated, and aim to drive market transformation by encouraging innovation and best practices.

Climate targets, overarching climate commitments. The EU aims to achieve climate neutrality by 2050. The EU Climate Law (2021) legally binds the EU to these goals, which include achieving climate neutrality by 2050 and a 55% reduction in greenhouse gas emissions by 2030 (from 1990 levels). The »Fit for 55« package introduces legislative measures to achieve these targets, influencing all sectors, including real estate.

Climate change and energy transition. The EU's climate and energy policy is based on several directives and regulations:

- The **Renewable Energy Directive (RED)**: Since 2001, the RED has set binding targets for renewable energy use, driving the shift to clean energy sources.
- **Energy Efficiency Directive (EED)**: Introduced in 2012, the EED mandates energy-saving and efficiency measures, including those for buildings.
- **Energy Performance of Buildings Directive (EPBD)**: Establishes minimum energy performance standards and certification for buildings, directly impacting real estate.

Market-based climate tools. To reduce emissions efficiently, the EU employs market mechanisms:

- The **EU Emissions Trading System (EU ETS)**: Launched in 2005, this »cap and trade« system limits emissions from key sectors and allows trading of emission allowances.
- The **EU ETS2 (from 2027)**: Expands emissions trading to buildings and road transport, further affecting real estate.
- The **Carbon Border Adjustment Mechanism (CBAM)**: Ensures that imported goods face a carbon price similar to that of EU-produced goods, thereby supporting climate goals.

Environmental protection laws. The EU has enacted a series of laws to protect natural resources. To name just a few: The Drinking Water Directive (DWD, 1980) sets EU-wide water quality standards; the Water Framework Directive (WFD, 2000) promotes sustainable water use and protects aquatic environments; the REACH Regulation (2006) regulates chemicals to ensure safety in construction and real estate; the Waste Framework Directive (2008) defines principles for waste management, emphasizing recycling and environmental protection; the Eco-Design and Sustainable Products Regulation (ESPR, 2024) sets requirements for product sustainability, circularity, and durability; the Repair Directive (2024) promotes repair over replacement to reduce waste; the Nature Restoration Regulation (2024) targets restoration of 30% of land and sea by 2030; the EU Soil Preservation Law (proposed 2023) aims to protect and restore soil health.

Environmental governance and assessment. Environment Action Programmes (EAPs): Since 1973, these multiannual strategies have guided EU environmental policy, introducing principles like »polluter pays.« The Environmental Impact Assessment (EIA) Directive (1985, as amended) requires major projects to assess and mitigate environmental impacts before approval.

Social and governance agenda. The EU has a wide-reaching social and governance agenda, including **building fairness and inclusion** (e.g. the European Pillar of Social Rights; EU Charter of Fundamental Rights); **health and safety** (e.g. Framework Directive; EU Accessibility Act; Consumer Rights Directive); **accountability and transparency** (e.g. Shareholder Rights Directive; NFRD; CSRD; **corruption and financial crime** (Anti-Money Laundering Directives – AMLDs, Whistleblower Protection Directive); **data protection** (e.g. General Data Protection Regulation – GDPR).

Standards and voluntary frameworks: guiding best practices. Beyond binding legislation, the EU real estate sector benefits from a range of standards and voluntary frameworks that promote best practices in financial and sustainability reporting. The European Public Real Estate Association's (EPRA) Best Practices Recommendations provide guidelines for listed real estate companies, while the European Association for Investors in Non-Listed Real Estate Vehicles (INREV) Guidelines offer a benchmark for non-listed real estate investments. These European standards complement global frameworks such as GRESB, the UN Principles for Responsible Investment (PRI), and the OECD Guidelines for Multinational Enterprises, supporting a harmonized approach to ESG integration.

(e) Details: urban development and built environment
Urban development and territorial cohesion: This century, the EU has committed to sustainable urban development through several declarations and charters that establish a vision for integrated, balanced, and sustainable cities, such as the **Budapest Declaration (2003)**, the **Leipzig Charter (2007, updated 2020)**, the **Pact of Amsterdam, and Urban Agenda for the EU (2016)**. The **New European Bauhaus (NEB, 2021, investment guidelines from 2024)** connects sustainability, aesthetics, and inclusion in the built environment. The NEB initiative encourages innovative, people-centered approaches to urban transformation.

Laws and frameworks for the built environment: The EU has enacted a series of directives and frameworks that establish binding standards for the energy performance, sustainability, and quality of buildings:

- **Renovation Wave (2020)**: As part of the European Green Deal, this Commission Communication seeks to double the rate of building renovations, enhance energy efficiency, and cut emissions across the EU's building stock.
- **Energy Performance of Buildings Directive (EPBD): Energy efficiency** and related policies drive renovation, decarbonization, and smart technology adoption. First adopted in 2002 and revised several times, the EPBD sets minimum energy performance standards for both new and existing buildings. It requires regular energy certification (Energy Performance Certificates, EPCs) and promotes the integration of renewable energy sources. The latest recast (2024) aims for a zero-emission building stock by 2050, with a strong focus on renovating existing buildings to improve energy efficiency and reduce greenhouse gas emissions.

- **Construction Products Regulation (CPR, 2011, as revised in 2024**[615]**)**: Establishes harmonized rules for the marketing of construction products, providing a common technical language for assessing product performance and ensuring reliable information for professionals and consumers.[616]

Voluntary schemes and certification: driving market transformation: In addition to mandatory regulations, the EU has promoted voluntary schemes and certifications to encourage best practices in sustainable construction and building management: **EU Ecolabel (1992) and EMAS (Eco-Management and Audit Scheme, 1993)**, which are EU-managed voluntary schemes that provide recognition for products and organizations demonstrating superior environmental performance. EMAS, in particular, enables organizations to evaluate, report, and improve their environmental impact. Also, the **Level(s) Framework (2017)** was developed as a common European framework for assessing and reporting on the sustainability performance of buildings throughout their life cycle. Level(s) is supported by European standards and provides a shared language for sustainability in the built environment. Last, but not least, **green building certifications** are notable: While the EU has its own voluntary schemes, the market is also shaped by widely used, non-EU, or non-state-managed certifications, such as BREEAM, LEED, DGNB, HQE, Minergie, and PassivHaus. These schemes, primarily used for commercial buildings, assess a range of environmental and energy criteria, though their differing baselines and indicators can make direct comparisons challenging.

(f) Further wave of changes in the EU – updates end of 2024/as of 2025 and beyond

The avalanche of laws, especially those related to extensive reporting and disclosure requirements (often parallel for similar topics), has caused distress, especially for businesses, due to the vast amount of resources used to implement them, given their complexity. The EU responded – for example by commissioning the **Draghi report**,[617] which included an industrial strategy identifying three necessities for the EU to boost its competitiveness: Closing the innovation gap, decarbonizing the economy and reducing dependencies with key goal of an industrial strategy driving innovation, decarbonization, competitiveness, while increasing security and reducing dependencies.[618]

615 Regulation (EU) 2024/3110 of the European Parliament and of the Council of 27 November 2024 laying down harmonized rules for the marketing of construction products and repealing Regulation (EU) No 305/2011, https://eur-lex.europa.eu/legal-content/EN/TXT/?uri=OJ:L_202403110, accessed 27.07.2025.

616 Not covered, for example, procurement, for example Green Public Procurement (GPP).

617 The Draghi report on EU competitiveness, 09.09.2024, https://commission.europa.eu/topics/eu-competitiveness/draghi-report_en: Mario Draghi – former European Central Bank President and one of Europe's great economic minds – was tasked by the European Commission to prepare a report on his personal vision for the future of European competitiveness. The report examines the challenges faced by the industry and companies in the Single Market. It outlines how Europe will no longer be able to rely on many of the factors that have supported growth in the past and lays out a clear diagnosis and provides concrete recommendations to put Europe onto a different trajectory.

618 Communication from the Commission to the European Parliament, the European Council, the Council, the European Economic and Social Committee and the Committee of the Regions a Competitiveness Compass for the EU, COM(2025) 30 final, IMMC.COM%282025%2930%20final.ENG.xhtml.1_EN_ACT_part1_v7.docx, accessed 21.07.2025. See also: Competitiveness Compass – extract from factsheet (EC) of 29.01.2025 – EC, A Competitiveness Compass for the EU, Factsheet, January 2025, Factsheet – Competitiveness Compass.pdf, https://ec.europa.eu/commission/presscorner/api/files/attachment/880290/Factsheet%20-%20Competitiveness%20Compass.pdf, accessed 29.06.2025.

The Commission's **Competitiveness Compass**[619] identifies **five horizontal enablers** to **reinforce competitiveness across all sectors**. One of these enablers is **simplification**, a **flagship action** for simplification being the **omnibus packages** starting with **proposals for regulatory revisions** end of February 2025.

The EU launched these initiatives while maintaining, or at least striving to maintain, the strategic objectives of the European Green Deal (EGD) and the Sustainable Finance Action Plan (SFAP) from the last decade.

The **initial (Omnibus I) proposals**[620] included changes to the **Corporate Sustainability Reporting Directive (CSRD)**, along with targeted changes to the **accounting directive**, (ii) the disclosure regime (delegated acts) under the **EU taxonomy regulation**, (iii) the **Corporate Sustainability Due Diligence Directive (CSDDD** or **CS3D)**, and (iv) the **Carbon Border Adjustment Mechanism (CBAM)**[621], covering (among other):

619 EC, A Competitiveness Compass for the EU, 29.01.2025, COM(2025) 30 final, https://commission.europa.eu/topics/eu-competitiveness/competitiveness-compass_en, accessed 29.06.2025; Communication from the Commission to the European Parliament, the European Council, the Council, the European Economic and Social Committee and the Committee of the Regions. A Competitiveness Compass for the EU, COM/2025/30 final, https://eur-lex.europa.eu/legal-content/EN/TXT/?uri=celex:52025DC0030, accessed 29.06.2025.

620 EC, Proposal for a directive, Commission simplifies rules on sustainability and EU investments, delivering over €6 billion in administrative relief, 26 February 2025, https://finance.ec.europa.eu/publications/commission-simplifies-rules-sustainability-and-eu-investments-delivering-over-eu6-billion_en, accessed 29.06.2025; EC, EU taxonomy for sustainable activities, What the EU is doing to create an EU-wide classification system for sustainable activities, https://finance.ec.europa.eu/sustainable-finance/tools-and-standards/eu-taxonomy-sustainable-activities_en, accessed 29.06.2025.

621 Changes to CBAM published: Regulation (EU) 2025/2083 of the European Parliament and of the Council of 8 October 2025 amending Regulation (EU) 2023/956 as regards simplifying and strengthening the carbon border adjustment mechanism, https://eur-lex.europa.eu/legal-content/EN/TXT/?uri=OJ%3AL_202502083, accessed 27.10.2025.

- a »**stop the clock**« proposal for delay of certain reporting requirements for **CSRD** and **CSDDD**[622],
- »**content**« **proposals** which included changes to simplify reporting under the **CSRD** and the reporting standards **ESRS**, especially substantially reducing the number of data points, clarify unclear provisions and improve consistency with other legislation and enhance interoperability with international standards, moving 80% of companies from the scope of the CSRD, and introduce a voluntary standard (developed by EFRAG for SMEs, the »VSME«)[623], and
- changes to the **taxonomy delegated acts**, especially to simplify and standardize (Article 8) reporting requirements, including a materiality concept and simplification of templates[624].

> The Draghi report estimates that the **EU is facing an annual investment gap of 750–800 billion euros** to meet its decarbonization and competitiveness targets.

In the context of the Omnibus I simplification initiative, **Eurosif**, which works as a partnership of Europe-based national Sustainable Investment Fora (SIFs)[625], coordinated a joint statement from 295 organizations, including over 200 businesses and investors, to call attention to the investors, companies, banks, and other financial institutions across our economy that support preserving the core elements of the CSRD/ESRS and CS3D, to achieve the EU's wider sustainability, growth and competitiveness ambitions, by contributing to reorienting investment toward the technologies and sectors that support the goals of the Clean Industrial Deal and can reinforce harmonization efforts for EU capital markets, as set out in the Savings and Investment Union. The signatories of this statement consider that **regulatory simplification can be achieved without compromising the substance of sustainability rules** or their significant benefits to businesses across the EU.[626]

The EU also intends to improve the **Sustainable Finance Disclosure Regulation (SFDR).** In November 2025, the European Commission tabled a proposal to revise the SFDR. The initiative seeks to simplify and streamline sustainability disclosures, improve comparability for investors, and more effectively prevent greenwashing. Core elements include the deletion of

622 »Stop the clock« (regarding CSRD and CS3D) published: Directive (EU) 2025/794 of the European Parliament and of the Council of 14 April 2025 amending Directives (EU) 2022/2464 and (EU) 2024/1760 as regards the dates from which Member States are to apply certain corporate sustainability reporting and due diligence requirements, https://eur-lex.europa.eu/eli/dir/2025/794/oj/eng, accessed 27.10.2025.

623 »Content proposal« (CSRD) were tabled for Trilogue discussions, which started 18.11.2025, after the Council adopted its negotiating position in June, the EP in November, informal trilogue negotiations between Comission, EP and Council; after trilogue, the Directive needs to be formally adopted by EP and Council, then published in the Official Journal to enter into force. The aim is to finalize the legislation by the end of 2025. For further update, cf.: EP, Legislative Observatory, 2025/0045(COD), Certain corporate sustainability reporting and due diligence requirements, https://oeil.secure.europarl.europa.eu/oeil/en/procedure-file?reference=2025/0045(COD), accessed 30.11.2025.

624 Changes to taxonomy delegated acts not (yet) published: EU, Commission to cut EU taxonomy red tape for companies, https://finance.ec.europa.eu/publications/commission-cut-eu-taxonomy-red-tape-companies_en, accessed 27.10.2025: adopted by EC 04.07.2025, under scrutiny of Council and EP.

625 GSIA, Eurosif, the European Sustainable Investment Forum, 2025, https://www.gsi-alliance.org/alliance-members/eurosif/, accessed 29.06.2025, with the direct support of their network, which spans over 400 Europe-based organizations drawn from the sustainable investment industry value chain. These organizations include institutional investors, asset managers, financial services, index providers and ESG research and analysis firms.

626 Eurosif, Communication, Investor and business joint statement on Omnibus initiative, 18 July 2025, https://www.eurosif.org/news/investor-and-business-joint-statement-on-omnibus-initiative/, accessed 22.08.2025.

entity-level »principal adverse impacts« disclosures and a substantial reduction of product-level templates, coupled with the introduction of a three-tier product categorization regime distinguishing »sustainable,« »transition,« and »ESG basics« products. The review also replaces the current definition-driven concept of »sustainable investment« with category-specific criteria, aiming to align the framework more closely with the EU Taxonomy on a voluntary-use basis and with EU Climate Benchmarks where relevant.[627]

Part of the recent initiatives of the European Commission is the **Clean Industrial Deal (2025)**, which sets out concrete actions to make decarbonization a driver of growth and competitiveness. It includes measures to ensure affordable energy and lower energy bills, create quality jobs, and provide the right conditions for businesses to invest and thrive. The Deal focuses on two closely linked areas – energy-intensive industries and the clean-tech sector – with circularity as a priority. It also aims to maximize the use of the EU's limited resources, reduce over-dependencies on third-country suppliers by diversifying supply chains for critical raw materials, and ensure a competitive and resilient European market.[628]

Despite what legislative changes will bring or the impact they will have (e.g., if you believe impact measurement depends on missing data points), we can continue to focus on real-world impacts.

There's a lot to look out for.

(g) Terms used in EU policy documents; bodies, institutions and associations (extract)
There is a lot going on in the EU. The EU has to deal with regulatory complexity, as it has overarching rules for more than one state and includes the lawmaking and enforcement of laws by member states, such as member states' policy areas or execution of EU laws and EU directives adopted through member states' transposition, etc.

Regarding terms used for **EU policy making**, see **Table 37** including a brief description to differentiate between some of the **terms used** for EU laws, frameworks, policy initiatives:

627 EC, Commission simplifies transparency rules for sustainable financial products, 20.11.2025, https://finance.ec.europa.eu/publications/commission-simplifies-transparency-rules-sustainable-financial-products_en, accessed 30.11.2025: incl. link to SFDR-proposal of 20.11.2025, COM(2025) 841 final, 2025/0361 (COD).

628 EP, Environment policy: general principles and basic framework – Fact Sheets on the European Union – European Parliament, https://www.europarl.europa.eu/factsheets/en/sheet/71/environment-policy-general-principles-and-basic-framework, accessed 20.07.2025; European Commission. The Clean Industrial Deal: A Joint Roadmap for Competitiveness and Decarbonisation. COM(2025) 85 final. Communication from the Commission to the European Parliament, the Council, the European Economic and Social Committee and the Committee of the Regions. Brussels, 26 February 2025, https://eur-lex.europa.eu/legal-content/EN/TXT/?uri=celex:52025DC0085, accessed 27.10.2025; European Commission. Delivering on the Clean Industrial Deal. COM(2025) 378 final. Communication from the Commission to the European Parliament, the Council, the European Economic and Social Committee and the Committee of the Regions. Brussels, 2 July 2025, https://commission.europa.eu/publications/delivering-clean-industrial-deal-i_en, accessed 27.10.2025.

Term	Meaning and example (in brief)
Primary vs. secondary law	**Primary** = consists mainly of the treaties, such as the Treaty on European Union (TEU) and the Treaty on the Functioning of the European Union (TFEU). **Secondary** = Legal acts adopted on the basis of the treaties, such as regulations, directives, and decisions (Article 288 TFEU).
EU regulations vs. directives	**Regulations** = are binding in their entirety and directly applicable in all member states. **Directives** = set goals for member states to achieve, requiring them to adapt national laws to meet those goals.
Level 1, 2, 3	**Level 1 = Legislative acts (Article 289 TFEU)** are legal acts adopted through ordinary or special legislative procedure. ***Examples: EPBD – Directive (EU) 2024/1275 (EPBD 2024); Taxonomy Regulation; SFDR.*** **Level 2 = Delegated acts (Article 290 TFEU)** are non-legislative acts adopted by the European Commission to supplement or amend non-essential elements of legislative acts (Article 290 TFEU). The objectives, content, scope, and duration of the delegation of power are defined in the legislative act. *Example: Climate Delegated Act to EU Taxonomy Regulation.* **Level 3 = Implementing acts (Article 291 TFEU)** are generally adopted by the Commission, which is competent to do so when uniform conditions are required for the implementation of legally binding acts. Implementing acts are the responsibility of the Council only in specific cases which are duly justified and in areas of common foreign and security policy. ***Example: Implementing acts under the SFDR*** *(Article 13).*
Further (usually) non-binding documents	**Communication** – (usually issued by the European Commission) to set out its policy intentions or explain how it interprets EU law. *Examples: EU Green Deal; EU Finance Action Plan.* **Strategy** – A high-level plan or approach adopted by the EU to achieve specific long-term objectives in a particular policy area. *Example: Lisbon Strategy.* **Programme** – A coordinated set of actions or initiatives, often with allocated funding, to implement EU policy objectives over a defined period. *Example: Environment Action Programmes (EAPs).* **Green Paper** – A consultative document published by the European Commission launch a public debate and consultation on a particular policy area, outlining the current situation and potential future directions. *Example: Green Paper on CSR.*

Table 37: Terms used for EU policy documents

For **bodies, institutions and associations** see **Table 38**, which summarizes **EU bodies, institutions, and associations related to real estate investment and ESG** that influence policy, set standards, provide data and research, and foster collaboration among stakeholders to advance sustainable and responsible real estate practices.

Category	Organizations/Institutions
European Union institutions and regulatory bodies	European Commission (EC), European Parliament (EP), Council of the European Union (Council), European Banking Authority (EBA), European Securities and Markets Authority (ESMA), European Insurance and Occupational Pensions Authority (EIOPA), European Central Bank (ECB), European Investment Bank (EIB).
EU agencies and initiatives	European Environment Agency (EEA), Joint Research Centre (JRC), European Energy Efficiency Platform (E3P).
Pan-European and industry associations	European Public Real Estate Association (EPRA), European Association for Investors in Non-Listed Real Estate Vehicles (INREV), Urban Land Institute (ULI), Europe, Royal Institution of Chartered Surveyors (RICS), Europe, European Property Federation (EPF), European Mortgage Federation (EMF), Green Building Councils (GBCs) in Europe, GRESB (Global Real Estate Sustainability Benchmark).
Other relevant organizations and networks	Climate Bonds Initiative (CBI) Europe, European Sustainable Investment Forum (Eurosif), Building Performance Institute Europe (BPIE), Madaster Foundation.

Table 38: Bodies, institutions, associations

6.4.3 ESG in UK real estate investment

Laura Gowing

»In the decade ahead, businesses must compete not just for market share but for the future itself.«

– Lindsay Hooper, CEO for the Cambridge Institute for Sustainability Leadership[629]

(a) Introduction to subchapter #6.4.3

ESG considerations have become central to real estate investment decision-making in the United Kingdom. Investors, developers, and advisors are increasingly required to navigate a com-

629 Hooper, Lindsay, ESG is dead. Long live ESG, We must urgently address the tension between profitability and sustainability, Financial Times, 19.09.2024, https://www.ft.com/content/47b334a9-69eb-4cd0-af22-6ad0b92c0ef6, accessed 04.08.2025.

plex landscape of regulatory requirements, voluntary standards, and market expectations. This chapter explores the UK's regulatory and standards framework for ESG in real estate, its relationship with global and EU standards, common building certifications, and recent developments.

The UK's approach to ESG in real estate investment is characterized by a strong regulatory foundation, alignment with global standards, and a dynamic market environment. Practitioners must stay abreast of evolving requirements, engage with standard-setting bodies, and integrate ESG considerations into all stages of the investment lifecycle. Although regional variations exist, the overarching trend is toward greater consistency and ambition in sustainable real estate.

#6.4.3 Mapping Europe – UK	**(a) – intro to #6.4.3**
	(b) – regulatory requirements for sustainable finance, reporting and disclosure
	(c) – standard-setting bodies

In this subchapter #6.4.3 on the United Kingdom (UK), we review regulatory requirements for sustainable finance, reporting, and disclosure (under (b)), as well as standard-setting bodies (under (c)).

(b) Regulatory requirements for sustainable finance, reporting, and disclosure

Overview of the UK regulatory framework

The UK has implemented, or is in the process of implementing, a range of regulatory requirements aimed at promoting sustainable finance and enhancing ESG-related disclosures. Key regulations include:

Task Force on Climate-Related Financial Disclosures (TCFD) and International Sustainability Standards Board (ISSB): The UK was the first G20 country to make TCFD-aligned disclosures mandatory for large companies and financial institutions, including listed Real Estate Investment Trusts (REITs) and asset managers.

The UK government has been a strong supporter of the ISSB since its launch at COP26 in Glasgow, and views its work as consistent with the UK government's aim to make the UK a global center for sustainable finance.

As part of this initiative, the UK government conducted a consultation on exposure drafts of UK versions of IFRS S1 and IFRS S2 standards, which built upon and incorporated TFCD recommendations (respectively called UK SRS S1 and UK SRS S2) until 17 September 2025, ahead of publishing finalized versions for voluntary use. Subsequently, the government and the Financial Conduct Authority (FCA) will consider whether to introduce mandatory requirements for certain UK entities to report against these standards.

Sustainable Disclosure Requirements (SDR)[630]**:** The UK SDR aims to streamline and strengthen ESG disclosure obligations, building on TCFD and aligning with international standards to provide sustainability labeling for funds and anti-greenwashing rules (although currently only applicable to financial actors within the UK). Currently, the UK SDR and the EU SFDR share various features, including mandating product- and entity-level disclosures. However, the UK SDR does not include the concepts of double materiality or cross-product asset-level definitions, such as »sustainable investment«, including the concept of »do no significant harm«, which exist in the EU SFDR. The UK SDR also does not mandate specific disclosure templates that must be completed to adhere to the disclosure requirements. The UK SDR does, however, explicitly introduce new sustainability labels and related conditions, such as an evidence-based standard that is an absolute measure of environmental and/or social sustainability.

Streamlined Energy and Carbon Reporting (SECR)[631]**:** Large companies are required to publicly report on their energy use, carbon emissions, and energy efficiency actions.

Applicability to real estate

These requirements apply to a broad range of real estate market participants, including listed property companies, institutional investors, and large private firms. Smaller entities may be indirectly affected through investor expectations or supply chain obligations.

UK-based entities marketing to or serving EU investors or operating in the EU, may need to comply with both UK and EU regimes, leading to dual reporting and compliance challenges.

(c) Relevant bodies

Standard-setting bodies for sustainable finance and ESG reporting

Several bodies set the standards for ESG reporting and sustainable finance in the UK:

- **Financial Conduct Authority (FCA):** The FCA regulates disclosures for listed companies and asset managers, including ESG-related information.
- **Financial Reporting Council (FRC):** Oversees corporate governance and reporting standards, including ESG integration.
- **HM Government:** Sets policy direction and oversees the development of the UK SDR.
- **International Sustainability Standards Board (ISSB):** The UK government has committed to adopting ISSB standards, which aim to harmonize global sustainability reporting.
- **Task Force on Climate-related Financial Disclosures (TCFD):** Provided the framework for climate-related disclosures.

630 UK Government policy paper Sustainability Disclosure Requirements: Implementation Update 2024, https://www.gov.uk/government/publications/sustainability-disclosure-requirements-implementation-update-2024, accessed 04.08.2025.

631 Companies (Directors' Report) and Limited Liability Partnerships (Energy and Carbon Report) Regulations 2018/1155 https://www.legislation.gov.uk/uksi/2018/1155/contents/made, accessed 04.08.2025.

Bodies Defining and Promoting Sustainable/Responsible Investment

There are also numerous organizations that promote the sustainable agenda, including:

- **UK Sustainable Investment and Finance Association (UKSIF):** Promotes sustainable investment across the UK financial sector.
- **Principles for Responsible Investment (PRI):** A global initiative with strong UK participation, setting voluntary standards for responsible investment.
- **Global Sustainable Investment Alliance (GSIA):** An umbrella organization promoting sustainable investment globally, with UKSIF as a member.
- **Better Buildings Partnership (BBP):** A collaboration of leading property owners who are working together to improve the sustainability of commercial buildings.
- **The Chancery Lane Project (TCLP):** A charity helping organizations reduce emissions using legal documents and processes.

Building ratings, certifications, and real estate toolkits

There are multifarious building ratings and certifications used by real estate players in the UK. Some of these are government requirements, whilst others can be used voluntarily to attract investors, funders, and tenants:

EPCs (Energy Performance Certificates) play a prominent role in UK real estate transactions, because they must be produced whenever a property is marketed for sale or lease, and since 2023 it has been unlawful to rent out a property with an EPC rating below E (unless certain exemptions apply). This rule applies to all types of leases, encompassing both new and existing agreements. There have been proposals to increase this minimum required level up to a B rating by 2030, which will require significant investment into energy efficiency improvements across real estate sectors.

BREEAM: Launched back in 1990, BREEAM (the Building Research Establishment's Environmental Assessment Method) is the world's longest-established green building certification system and is commonly used in the UK. It assesses buildings based on a range of criteria, including energy and water use, pollution, transport, materials, waste, ecology, management processes, and health and well-being.

LEED (Leadership in Energy and Environmental Design) provides a framework for designing, constructing, and operating sustainable buildings, with levels of certification ranging from Certified to Platinum. Developed originally in the U.S., it is also increasingly used in the UK.

NABERS UK, unlike design-based energy ratings, measures and rates the actual energy use of offices, helping building owners to accurately track and communicate the energy performance of their buildings. It also helps identify areas for savings and improvements.

The WELL Building Standard is a performance-based system for certifying buildings based on their impact on human health and well-being. It focuses on aspects such as air quality, water, nourishment, fitness, and comfort.

The Net Zero Carbon Building Standard (NZCBS) is a new framework designed to standardize how buildings achieve net-zero carbon status in the UK. It aims to provide clear, consistent rules for defining and verifying net-zero carbon buildings, reducing confusion and promoting genuine carbon reduction. The standard covers both operational and embodied carbon, emphasizing energy efficiency, renewable energy, and responsible material selection. The standard is free-to-access and voluntary. It applies to new and existing buildings with a particular emphasis on retrofitting, due to its potential for reducing embodied carbon and increasing sustainable resource use.

The BPP Green Lease Toolkit is a UK-based resource that provides guidance and model clauses to help landlords and tenants incorporate sustainability provisions into commercial leases. It aims to encourage collaboration and improve the environmental performance of buildings through a more sustainable approach to property management. The toolkit offers different levels of detail to accommodate varying levels of experience and ambition in green leasing, and sets out »Green Lease Essentials« providing guidance on the minimum level of expectation for a green lease.

(d) Regional variations within the UK

While the UK's regulatory framework is largely consistent across England, Scotland, Wales, and Northern Ireland, there are some differences:

- **Devolved powers:** Planning, building regulations, and certain environmental policies are devolved. For example, Scotland has targeted net zero emissions by 2045, ahead of 2050 for the UK as a whole.
- **Local initiatives:** Cities such as London and Manchester have introduced their own sustainability requirements for new developments, with often higher standards in areas like carbon reduction, biodiversity, and urban greening.
- **Market practice:** Investor expectations and market maturity may vary, but the direction of travel is towards greater alignment.

6.5 The Americas: United States Perspective

Jordi Ventura

»The business of America is business.«
– Calvin Coolidge

6.5.1 Introduction to #6.5

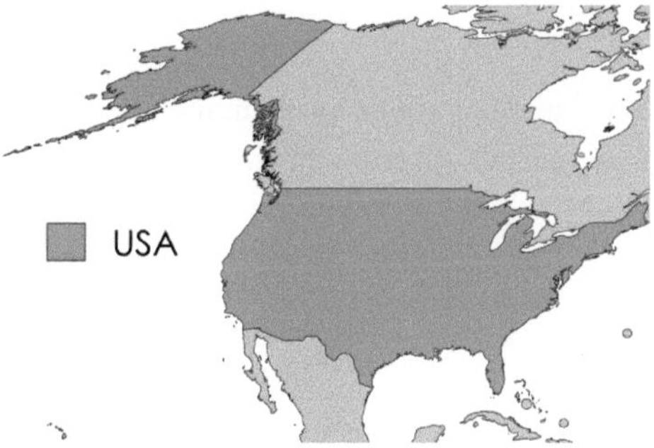

The United States occupies a paradoxical position in the global ESG real estate investment landscape. It is home to the world's largest asset managers and some of the most sophisticated sustainability disclosure frameworks – yet it is also the epicenter of a fierce political backlash against ESG. For real estate investors, the U.S. represents both opportunities and risks: robust urban sustainability initiatives coexist with regulatory uncertainty and growing anti-ESG sentiment. Understanding these dynamics is critical for cross-border investors, portfolio managers, and legal practitioners structuring deals.

#6.5 Mapping US	**#6.5.1 – intro to #6.5**
	#6.5.2 – trends and regulatory landscape
	#6.5.3 – investment trends
	#6.5.4 – practical implications for real estate
	#6.5.5 – strategies for investors
	#6.5.6 – looking ahead

In this subchapter #6.5, we dive into ESG trends and regulatory landscape (#6.5.2) and investment trends (#6.5.3), practical implications for real estate (#6.5.4), strategies for investors (#6.5.5), and finish up with an outlook (#6.5.6).

6.5.2 ESG trends and regulatory landscape

Unlike the European Union, the United States lacks a comprehensive federal ESG regime. Instead, regulation is fragmented:

(a) Federal level
The SEC's proposed Climate-Related Disclosure Rule[632] would require public companies to disclose Scope 1 and Scope 2 emissions and, in some cases, Scope 3. However, political pushback has delayed implementation.

The Inflation Reduction Act (IRA) provides tax credits and incentives for renewable energy and building decarbonization – affecting valuation for green-certified assets.

(b) State and city level
New York City's Local Law 97,[633] part of the Climate Mobilization Act, imposes greenhouse gas emission caps on buildings over 25,000 square feet, starting in 2024, with penalties of $268 per metric ton of CO_2-equivalent emissions for buildings exceeding the annual limit. Compliance deadlines escalate in 2030 as the caps become stricter.

California SB 253 and SB 261[634] impose climate disclosure obligations on companies doing business in California, including real estate owners above certain revenue thresholds.

For investors, this patchwork requires property-level compliance checks across multiple jurisdictions.

6.5.3 ESG investment trends – from surge to scrutiny

The U.S. was an early driver of ESG adoption. Following BlackRock's landmark 2020 statement that »climate risk is investment risk« and its commitment to integrate sustainability into investment decisions, institutional investors channeled billions into ESG real estate funds. By 2022, global ESG assets had reached $30 trillion, with U.S. managers holding a significant share. However, the momentum has shifted. Anti-ESG legislation, political investigations, and heightened greenwashing liability now shape the risk environment.

> By 2025, the tone of U.S. financial giants had shifted dramatically. After years of positioning sustainability as central in fiduciary duty, even BlackRock – the emblem of ESG's rise – quietly removed references to »climate,« »net zero,« and »ESG« from its annual flagship letter. This rhetorical retreat underscores the growing political and legal risks associated with sustainability language in the U.S.

632 SEC, Proposed Rule: Enhancement and Standardization of Climate-Related Disclosures for Investors, 2022.
633 Local Law 97 of 2019, New York City Climate Mobilization Act, § 28-320.3.2, https://www.nyc.gov/assets/buildings/local_laws/ll97of2019.pdf, accessed 22.07.2025.
634 Senate Bill 253 (Climate Corporate Data Accountability Act) requires U.S.-based entities with more than $1 billion in annual revenue doing business in California to report Scope 1 and 2 emissions beginning in 2026 and Scope 3 emissions in 2027; SB 261 (Climate-Related Financial Risk Act) requires U.S.-based entities with over $500 million in annual revenue doing business in California to disclose climate-related financial risks by January 1, 2026, with biennial updates.

> *»Fink's 2025 letter underlines BlackRock's backpedaling in those areas and U.S. financial firms' wider retreat from publicly touting … ESG … corporate sustainability as we once knew it is dead.«* – Barron's (2025)

(a) Anti-ESG laws
More than 20 states (and in some reports over 23) have enacted or proposed laws restricting the use of ESG factors in public pension fund investment decisions.[635] Texas' Senate Bill 13[636] blacklists firms perceived as »boycotting« fossil fuels, affecting real estate funds marketed as climate-aligned.

(b) Political investigations
A coalition of state attorneys general launched antitrust inquiries into whether ESG alliances (e.g., Climate Action 100+) constitute collusion. Subpoenas specifically targeted major asset managers, creating significant reputational and legal risk.[637]

6.5.4 Practical implications for real estate

Key risk areas for investors

> Disclosure and Reporting: Pending SEC rules could impose costly compliance obligations. Failure to anticipate these requirements may lead to enforcement action or investor litigation.
>
> Energy Performance Standards: Noncompliance with local laws, such as Local Law 97 in New York City can result in fines and reduce asset liquidity.
>
> Greenwashing liability is on the rise in the U.S.: class action claims frequently target funds – and, increasingly, Real Estate Investment Trusts (REITs) – marketed as »sustainable« despite lacking robust metrics, creating legal and reputational risks.

635 Soares, Kristen, Webinar Recap: Anti-ESG Legislation – Why It Matters and What States Can Do, 2023, https://climate-xchange.org/2023/07/anti-esg-legislation-why-it-matters-and-what-states-can-d/, accessed 03.11.2025: in 2023 alone, 165 bills across 37 states included measures aimed at curbing ESG in state contracting and pension fund investments; 14 passed in 2023, and 42 bills in 2024 were in states including Iowa, Oklahoma, and South Carolina.

636 Texas Senate Bill 13 (87th La.), Chapter 809: Prohibition on Investment in Financial Companies That Boycott Certain Energy Companies, Government Code, effective 01.09.2021, https://capitol.texas.gov/tlodocs/87R/billtext/pdf/SB00013F.pdf, accessed 24.07.2025.

637 Dial, Lance C. & L'Hommedieu, Anna E., The ESG Debate Heats Up: State AGs Investigating Asset Manager Involvement in ESG Initiatives and Related Proxy Voting, K&L Gates Client Alert, 25 May 2023, https://www.klgates.com/The-ESG-Debate-Heats-Up-State-AGs-Investigating-Asset-Manager-Involvement-in-ESG-Initiatives-and-Related-Proxy-Voting-5-25-2023, accessed 24.07.2025.

6.5.5 Strategies for investors

Enhanced Due Diligence: Verify compliance with city and state energy laws, labor standards, and governance frameworks. Include ESG reps and warranties in purchase agreements.

Political risk mapping: For portfolios in states such as Texas or Florida, assess anti-ESG regulations that could restrict access to public funds or trigger investigations.

Contractual protection: Embed measurable ESG targets into leases (e.g., energy-use intensity) and construction contracts.

Transparency: Align reporting with TCFD and GRESB benchmarks to mitigate greenwashing claims.

6.5.6 Looking ahead

Despite the political pushback, structural trends such as climate risk, investor demand for resilient assets, and tenant expectations ensure ESG remains material for U.S. real estate. However, ESG in the U.S. will be litigation-heavy, politically charged, and disclosure-driven. Investors must strike a balance between sustainability commitments and regulatory risk management.

Checklist for U.S. Real Estate ESG Due Diligence

- ☐ Confirm that the property complies with local energy and emissions laws (e.g., LL97).
- ☐ Assess state-level anti-ESG legislation exposure.
- ☐ Review environmental permits and remediation liabilities.
- ☐ Verify stakeholder engagement where Indigenous or community claims may arise (e.g., FPIC for renewable or pipeline projects intersecting real estate).
- ☐ Include ESG-specific reps, warranties, and indemnities in contracts.

6.6 The Americas: Latin American perspective

Anderson Moura

> *»Latin America neither wants, nor has any reason, to be a pawn without a will of its own.«*
> — Gabriel García Márquez

6.6.1 Introduction to #6.6

Latin America is a region of great potential, but also of great complexity, where opportunity and risk walk side by side. Its historical political instability affects regulatory predictability, which is certainly a challenge for investors. Yet the region is seen as a promising investment opportunity[638].
Many of the complex challenges of the region offer fertile ground for ESG-oriented real estate investment.

#6.6 Mapping Latin America	**#6.6.1 – intro to #6.6**
	#6.6.2 – ESG & real estate investment in Latin America
	#6.6.3 – regulatory landscape
	#6.6.4 – practical risks and opportunities for real estate investors
	#6.6.5 – risk mitigation mechanisms

In this subchapter #6.6, we introduce ESG and real estate investment in Latin America (#6.6.2), the regulatory landscape in the region (#6.6.3), practical risks and opportunities for real estate investors (#6.6.4), to then close the chapter and the book with risk mitigation mechanisms (#6.6.5).

638 BlackRock, A decade of promise for long-term investing in Latin America, https://www.blackrock.com/uk/solutions/investment-trusts/our-range/blackrock-latin-american-investment-trust/trust-information/insights/exciting-decade-ahead-for-long-term-investing-in-latin-america, accessed 25.07.2025.

6.6.2 ESG and real estate investment in Latin America

Latin America has a combination of social challenges, indigenous peoples, abundant natural resources and is one of the world's richest regions in terms of biodiversity. This complex combination is fairly related to ESG aspects that may be opportunities for real estate projects.

The region's social challenges are connected to its increasing demand for housing and infrastructure projects, while its environmental aspects create great opportunities for carbon offsetting projects (as mentioned under #6.6.5).

In addition, while indigenous territories and environmentally protected areas are a challenge for real estate projects in general, they also offer opportunities for positive social and environmental impacts for ESG-oriented real estate investments.

6.6.3 ESG regulatory landscape

ESG regulations are evolving in Latin America and different levels of regulatory development can be found across the countries of the region, as in the examples below.

(a) Argentina
Although ESG reporting is not yet mandatory in Argentina, the country's National Securities Commission has published its Guidelines for Voluntary ESG Reports[639].

In the financial sector, the Central Bank of Argentina has been working on Argentina's Sustainable Finance National Strategy[640].

Argentina has also implemented its regulations on climate change, such as the law on minimum budgets for adaptation and mitigation to global climate change (Law No. 27,520/2019)[641].

(b) Brazil
The Brazilian Securities and Exchange Commission (CVM) rule on ESG disclosures[642] and the Federal Council of Accounting (CFC) rules on sustainability reports[643] require publicly-held

639 National Securities Commission of Argentina, Guide for the voluntary reporting and disclosure of environmental, social, and governance (ESG) information, 2023, https://www.argentina.gob.ar/sites/default/files/guia_informacion_asg-_2023.pdf, accessed 31.07.2025.

640 Central Bank of Argentina, Argentina's Sustainable Finance National Strategy, https://www.bcra.gob.ar/Pdfs/SistemasFinancierosYdePagos/Sustainable%20Finance%20National%20Strategy.pdf, accessed 31.07.2025.

641 Law No. 27,520/2019 on minimum budgets for adaptation and mitigation to global climate change, https://www.argentina.gob.ar/normativa/nacional/ley-27520-333515, accessed 01.08.2025.

642 Resolution No. 193/2023, Securities and Exchange Commission (CVM), https://conteudo.cvm.gov.br/legislacao/resolucoes/resol193.html, accessed 23.06.2025.

643 Resolution No. 1017/2023, Federal Council of Accounting (CFC), https://www.in.gov.br/en/web/dou/-/resolucao-cfc-n-1.710-de-25-de-outubro-de-2023-520669405, accessed 23.06.2025.

companies, investment funds, securitization companies, and all companies that disclose sustainability reports (whether voluntarily or not) to disclose sustainability-related financial information in accordance with the ISSB standards IFRS S1 (general requirements for disclosure of sustainability-related financial information) and IFRS S2 (climate-related disclosures), starting in 2026.

The Brazilian Central Bank (BCB) Resolution No. 139/2021[644] requires financial institutions to disclose reports on social, environmental, and climate-related risks and opportunities.

The Superintendency of Private Insurance (SUSEP) Ordinance No. 666/2022[645] provides sustainability requirements for the insurance sector, including aspects relating to climate, environmental and social risks.

The country also has a national framework on climate change, including a National Policy on Climate Change (Law No. 12,187/2019)[646], the Brazilian Emission Trading System (Law No. 15,042/2024)[647], and other applicable regulations.

(c) Chile

The Chilean Financial Market Commission (CMF) General Rule No. 461[648] requires that listed companies and other financial market entities, such as banks, insurers, and issuers of securities, integrate ESG data into their annual reports.

The Chilean Financial Market Commission (CMF) General Rule No. 519[649] requires that annual reports to adopt ISSB standards IFRS S1 and IFRS S2.

Law No. 21,595[650] improved Chile's criminal liability system by addressing economic and environmental crimes.

Chile also has a national framework on climate change, set by Law No. 21,455[651].

644 Resolution No. 139/2021, Brazilian Central Bank (BCB), https://www.bcb.gov.br/estabilidadefinanceira/exibenormativo?tipo=Resolu%C3%A7%C3%A3o%20BCB&numero=139, accessed 23.06.2025.

645 Ordinance No. 666/2022, Superintendency of Private Insurance (SUSEP), https://www2.susep.gov.br/safe/scripts/bnweb/bnmapi.exe?router=upload/26128, accessed 23.06.2025.

646 Law No. 12,187/2019 on Brazil's National Policy on Climate Change, https://www.planalto.gov.br/ccivil_03/_ato2007-2010/2009/lei/l12187.htm, accessed 23.06.2025.

647 Law No. 15,042/2024 on the Brazilian Emission Trading System, https://www.planalto.gov.br/ccivil_03/_ato2023-2026/2024/lei/L15042.htm, accessed 23.06.2025.

648 General Rule No. 461 on the structure and content of the annual report of securities issuers, https://www.cmfchile.cl/normativa/ncg_461_2021.pdf, accessed 27.07.2025.

649 General Rule No. 519 on integrated annual report, https://www.cmfchile.cl/normativa/ncg_519_2024.pdf, accessed 27.07.2025.

650 Law No. 21,595 of 2023, Economic Crimes Law, https://bcn.cl/3enf9, accessed 27.07.2025.

651 Law No. 21,455, Framework Law on Climate Change, https://bcn.cl/32l1s, accessed 27.07.2025.

(d) Colombia

External Circular 031 of 2022[652] provides instructions on sustainability reporting, including climate issues, for entities under the supervision of the Colombian Financial Superintendency.

External Guideline No. 100-000002-2025[653], issued by Superintendence of Companies, addresses the submission of non-financial information, which includes promoting voluntary sustainability reporting.

Law No. 2169 of 2021[654] promotes the country's low-carbon development by establishing minimum goals and measures in the areas of carbon neutrality and climate resilience.

(e) Mexico

The Ministry of Finance and Public Credit of Mexico published the country's Sustainable Taxonomy[655].

The resolution issued by the National Banking and Securities Commission[656] modifies the general provisions applicable to participants in the securities market, bringing about the obligation to prepare annual sustainability reports aligned with the ISSB standards IFRS S1 and IFRS S2.

Mexico has also enacted and updated a General Law on Climate Change[657].

652 External Circular 031 of 2022, Financial Superintendency, https://www.superfinanciera.gov.co/loader.php?lServicio=Tools2&lTipo=descargas&lFuncion=descargar&idFile=1057619, accessed 30.07.2025.

653 External Guideline No. 100-000002-2025, Superintendence of Companies, https://www.supersociedades.gov.co/documents/107391/8611340/Circular+Externa+100-000002+de+14+de+marzo+de+2025.pdf/82dc3c0b-1695-295b-ad37-3327ab2d683b, accessed 30.07.2025.

654 Law 2169 of 2021 on minimum carbon neutrality and climate resilience targets and measures, http://www.secretariasenado.gov.co/senado/basedoc/ley_2169_2021.html, accessed 30.07.2025.

655 Sustainable Taxonomy, The Ministry of Finance and Public Credit of Mexico, 2023, https://www.finanzassostenibles.hacienda.gob.mx/work/models/finanzassostenibles/recursos/documentos/TaxonomyEV_2024_V1.pdf, accessed 30.07.2025.

656 Resolution on general provisions applicable to securities issuers and other securities market participants, the National Banking and Securities Commission, https://www.cnbv.gob.mx/Normatividad/Disposiciones%20de%20car%C3%A1cter%20general%20aplicables%20a%20las%20emisoras%20de%20valores.pdf, accessed 30.07.2025.

657 General Law on Climate Change of 2012, https://climate-laws.org/documents/general-law-on-climate-change-2023-amended-text_3db4, accessed 30.07.2025.

6.6.4 Practical risks and opportunities for real estate investment

(a) Key opportunities for investors

Increasing demand for housing: Due to urbanization and population growth, the Latin American real estate market is expected to grow significantly from 2025 to 2030[658].

Increasing demand for infrastructure projects: Latin America is expected to require an investment of approximately USD 2.2 trillion by 2030, to ensure the necessary infrastructure to meet the Sustainable Development Goals[659].

Great potential for carbon offsets: Agriculture, Forestry and Other Land Uses (AFOLU) projects offer significant decarbonization opportunities[660], and Latin America has great potential for such projects, as the region is home to 23% of the world's forests[661]. Major players in the global economy are already investing in decarbonization projects in the region[662].

(b) Key risks for investors

Protected areas: Latin America is one of the most biodiverse regions in the world, being home to the Amazon rainforest, the Andes Mountains, Patagonia, and other crucial regions and biomes. For this reason, an average of 24.5% of its territory consists of protected areas[663], that may restrict or prevent certain uses of a property.

Indigenous territories: Indigenous peoples represent nearly 8% of the population in Latin America[664], and the legal protection of their territories may restrict or prevent certain uses of properties within or around their borders. Also, many countries in the region have ratified the

---

658 Market Data Forecast, Latin America Real Estate Market Report, https://www.marketdataforecast.com/market-reports/latin-america-real-estate-market, accessed 30.07.2025; Grand View Research, Latin America Real Estate Market Size & Outlook – 2024–2030, https://www.grandviewresearch.com/horizon/outlook/real-estate-market/latin-america, accessed 30.07.2025; Mordor Intelligence, Latin America Residential Real Estate Market Size & Share Analysis – Growth Trends & Forecasts (2025–2030), 2025, https://www.mordorintelligence.com/industry-reports/residential-real-estate-market-in-latin-america, accessed 30.07.2025.

659 Allianz Global Investors, Financing Growth with Infrastructure in Latin America, https://www.allianzgi.com/en/insights/outlook-and-commentary/financing-growth-with-infrastructure-in-latin-america, accessed 01.08.2025.

660 Intergovernmental Panel on Climate Change (IPCC), IPCC Sixth Assessment Report, Chapter 7: Agriculture, Forestry, and Other Land Uses (AFOLU), https://www.ipcc.ch/report/ar6/wg3/chapter/chapter-7/, accessed 31.07.2025.

661 Organisation for Economic Co-operation and Development (OECD), Environment at a Glance in Latin America and the Caribbean: Spotlight on Climate Chang, https://www.oecd.org/content/dam/oecd/en/publications/reports/2023/07/environment-at-a-glance-in-latin-america-and-the-caribbean_97fe557f/2431bd6c-en.pdf, accessed 31.07.2025.

662 LEAF Coalition, Press Release: Pará signs $180 m LEAF Coalition deal – first in Brazil, https://emergentclimate.com/wp-content/uploads/2024/09/Para-ERPA-announcement-Emergent-Final.pdf, accessed 27.06.2025; Microsoft, Enabling a sustainable future, https://www.microsoft.com/pt-br/maisbrasil/habilitando-um-futuro-sustentavel, accessed 27.06.2025; Apple, Apple's restore fund cultivates new roots in the Atlantic forest, https://www.apple.com/br/newsroom/2024/03/apples-restore-fund-cultivates-new-roots-in-the-atlantic-forest/, accessed 27.06.2025.

663 Protected Planet, data on protected areas in Latin America and the Caribbean, https://www.protectedplanet.net/region/SA, accessed 28.07.2025.

664 The World Bank, Indigenous Latin America in the Twenty-First Century, 2015, https://documents1.worldbank.org/curated/en/145891467991974540/pdf/Indigenous-Latin-America-in-the-twenty-first-century-the-first-decade.pdf, accessed 28.07.2025.

Indigenous and Tribal Peoples Convention (C169)[665], of the International Labour Organization (ILO) (such as Argentina, Bolivia, Brazil, Chile, Colombia, Mexico, Peru, and many others). ILO C169 requires countries to obtain the free, prior, and informed consent of indigenous peoples for projects that may impact their lives and territories.

Land title problems: Problems such as lack of legal titles, overlapping titles and lack of digital land records are persistent across Latin America, which brings significant legal uncertainty for real estate investors, especially for large-scale projects.

6.6.5 Risk mitigation mechanisms

- ☐ **Legal due diligence:** Carry out a complete assessment of land titles, protected areas, and indigenous territories, along with other usual legal due diligence standards, to map, prevent and mitigate potential restrictions, conflicts and legal compliance issues.
- ☐ **Free and prior informed consent (FPIC):** Verify local laws on how to formally implement FPIC to assure legal compliance and avoid social conflicts.
- ☐ **ESG reporting:** Consider aligning reporting standards with ISSB standards IFRS S1 and IFRS S2 in anticipation of the adoption of these global standards by important Latin American economies.
- ☐ **Contracts:** Implement contractual mechanisms that properly allocate social and environmental risks between contracting parties. Consider reasonable guarantees in light of each local environmental liability regime, to protect investors, shareholders and landlords from potential joint and several liability.

665 International Labour Organization (ILO), Indigenous and Tribal Peoples Convention (C169), https://normlex.ilo.org/dyn/nrmlx_en/f?p=NORMLEXPUB:55:0::NO::P55_TYPE,P55_LANG,P55_DOCUMENT,P55_NODE:REV,en,C169,/Document, accessed 27.06.2025.

Bibliography

AAV, Deshalb braucht NRW den AAV, https://www.aav-nrw.de/hintergrund.html, accessed 31.08.2025.

Abscheider zum Trennen eines Zweiphasen-Flüssigkeitsgemisches in Leichtflüssigkeit und Schwerflüssigkeit, Patent EP 0 960 643 A1, 01.12.1999 Patentblatt 1999/48, Erfinder: Heinz Ihne, www.awas.de.

Achtelik, Olaf, in: Herzog/Achtelik, Money Laundering Act, section 15.

Achtelik, Olaf, The new EU legislation to combat money laundering and terrorist financing, BKR 2024, 353.

Adam-Tkalec, Maritta, Berliner Grundwasser doppelt so warm wie normal. Was sagt der Senat dazu?, Berliner Zeitung, https://www.berliner-zeitung.de/mensch-metropole/berliner-grundwasser-doppelt-so-warm-wie-normal-was-sagt-der-senat-dazu-li.2341291, accessed 27.07.2025.

Aerts, Jeroen C. J. H., A review of cost estimates for flood adaptation. Water (Switzerland) 10(11), 2018, 1–33.

Airtrunk, AirTrunk and Pekat Solar to develop rooftop solar at AirTrunk's Johor Bahru data centre, JHB1, 2024, https://airtrunk.com/airtrunk-and-pekat-solar-to-develop-rooftop-solar-at-airtrunks-johor-bahru-data-centre-jhb1/, accessed 06.09.2025.

Allianz Global Investors, Financing Growth with Infrastructure in Latin America, https://www.allianzgi.com/en/insights/outlook-and-commentary/financing-growth-with-infrastructure-in-latin-america, accessed 01.08.2025.

Allianz Trade, Insolvenz-Updeate Mai 2025, https://www.allianz-trade.de/content/dam/onemarketing/aztrade/allianz-trade_de/dokumente/2025-05-27-allianz-trade-insolvenz-update-mai-2025.pdf, accessed 24.06.2025.

Almqvist/Wendt, supervised by Mussa Hussaini, ESG Performance – Effect on Acquisition Premium, 2022.

Amar, The ISO 14000 Standards Family: A Complete Guide, 02.09.2025, https://www.arbor.eco/blog/iso-14000-standards, accessed 08.09.2025.

Apple, Apple's restore fund cultivates new roots in the atlantic forest, https://www.apple.com/br/newsroom/2024/03/apples-restore-fund-cultivates-new-roots-in-the-atlantic-forest/, accessed 27.06.2025.

Arjona/Cornet/Degen/Krebs, ESG Integration in Contracts: Trends and Opportunities, 2025.

Asean Taxonomy Board, Asean Taxonomy for Sustainable Finance Version 3, https://asean.org/wp-content/uploads/2024/12/ASEAN-Taxonomy-Finalised-Version-3-4.pdf, accessed 06.09.2025.

ASTM E1527-21 Standard Practice for Environmental Site Assessments: Phase I Environmental Site Assessment Process, https://store.astm.org/e1527-21.html, accessed 30.08.2025.

BAFIN, Preparing for DORA: »We've stepped it up a notch«, 28.02.2025, https://www.bafin.de/SharedDocs/Veroeffentlichungen/EN/Fachartikel/2025/fa_250117_Interview_Obermoeller_en.html?cms_expanded=true, accessed 01.05.2025.

Bank of Ghana, 2024, Climate-Related Financial Risk Directive, https://www.bog.gov.gh/wp-content/uploads/2024/11/BOG-Climate-Related-Financial-Risks-Directive.pdf, accessed 28.07.2025.

Bank of Ghana, Sustainable Banking Principles and Sector Guidance Notes, 2019, https://www.bog.gov.gh/wp-content/uploads/2019/12/Ghana-Sustainable-Banking-Principles-and-Guidelines-Book-1.pdf, accessed 04.07.2025.

Barbier, Edward, The Concept of Sustainable Economic Development, 1987, in: Environmental Conservation, vol. 14, issue2, 101–110.

Bartek, Michal, UN PRI, PRI Blog, Part III: ESG factors and returns – a review of recent research, 2024, https://www.unpri.org/pri-blog/part-iii-esg-factors-and-returns-a-review-of-recent-research/12728.article, accessed 07.09.2025.

Barzuza/Curtis/Webber, Shareholder Value(s): Index Fund ESG Activism and the New Millennial Corporate Governance, Southern California Law Review 93, no. 6 (2020), https://southerncalifornialawreview.com/2020/09/01/shareholder-values-index-fund-esg-activism-and-the-new-millennial-corporate-governance-article-by-michal-barzuza-quinn-curtis-david-h-webber/, accessed 14.09.2025, 1243–1296.

Basler, Ernst, »Our living space is finite, but our capacity for innovation is not.«, https://www.ebp.global/ch-de/about-ebp/unsere-geschichte, accessed 06.09.2025.

Basler, Ernst, Strategy of Progress: Environmental Pollution, Habitat Scarcity and Future Research, 1973, (originally, Strategie des Fortschritts: Umweltbelastung Lebensraumverknappung and Zukunftsforschung, 1973).

Bator/Borek, Adaptation to Climate Change under Climate Change Treaties, International Community Law Review, 2021, https://brill.com/view/journals/iclr/23/2-3/article-p158_4.xml, accessed 13.09.2025.

Bauer Group, Press Release 26.01.2021, World's largest reed bed treatment plant in operation for 10 years, 2021, https://resources.bauer.de/en/media/1092/download?inline, accessed 24.06.2025.

Bauerfeind/Hille, The future of money laundering supervision, GWR 2024, 33, 34.

Belsom, Toby, UN PRI, PRI Blog, ESG factors and equity returns – a review of recent industry research, 2021, https://www.unpri.org/pri-blog/esg-factors-and-equity-returns-a-review-of-recent-industry-research/7867.article, accessed 07.09.2025.

Bernard-Rau/Busch/Kaiser/Weber in: Bundesinitiative Impact Investing/Sustainable Finance Research Group an der Universität Hamburg/Advanced Impact Research (AIR)/Zentrum für Europäische Wirtschaftsforschung (ZEW), Impact Investing in Deutschland: Marktstudie 2022, https://bundesinitiative-impact-investing.org/publikationen/impact-investing-in-deutschland-2022-marktstudie/, accessed 22.07.2025.

Better Buildings Partnership, Green Lease Toolkit, 2024, https://www.betterbuildingspartnership.co.uk/green-lease-toolkit-0, accessed 30.08.2025.

Beutelsbacher, Stefan, Das Ende des Green Deal – die neue Agenda für den Standort Deutschland, Die Welt, https://www.welt.de/wirtschaft/plus255235456/Das-Ende-des-Green-Deal-die-neue-Agenda-fuer-den-Standort-Europa.html?source=puerto-reco-2_ABC-V44.0.B_maximize_engagement, accessed 24.01.2025.

Bevan, Tony, nqa, ISO 22301:2019 Business Continuity Standard Implementation Guide, 2019, https://www.nqa.com/medialibraries/NQA/NQA-Media-Library/PDFs/NQA-ISO-22301-Implementation-Guide.pdf, accessed 08.09.2025.

Biasin/Delle Foglie/Giacomini, Addressing climate challenges through ESG-real estate investment strategies: An asset allocation perspective. Finance Research Letters, Volume 63, 2024, 105381.

BlackRock, A decade of promise for long-term investing in Latin America, https://www.blackrock.com/uk/solutions/investment-trusts/our-range/blackrock-latin-american-investment-trust/trust-information/insights/exciting-decade-ahead-for-long-term-investing-in-latin-america, accessed 25.07.2025.

Blakes, Tips for Building Resilient Real Estate Partnerships, 2024, https://www.blakes.com/insights/tips-for-building-resilient-real-estate-partnerships/, accessed 22.06.2025.

Boiardi, Priscilla, OECD, Measuring And Managing The Impact Of Sustainable Investments – A Two Axes Mapping, 2020, https://www.oecd.org/content/dam/oecd/en/publications/reports/2020/06/managing-and-measuring-the-impact-of-sustainable-investments_508e5ccf/2ff2b2f4-en.pdf, accessed 10.08.2025.

Bojanowski, Alex, Die Prognosen waren korrekt – nur das Wetter hat nicht mitgespielt, Die Welt, https://www.welt.de/debatte/plus688484330e680a76f4e96135/Sommer-2025-Die-Prognosen-waren-korrekt-nur-das-Wetter-hat-nicht-mitgespielt.html, accessed 28.07.25.

Bolognesi/Dreassi/Migliavacca/Paltrinieri, Mapping sustainable investing: Exploring ambiguities and consistencies among sustainable indices, Journal of Environmental Management, Volume 367, 2024, 122081, https://doi.org/10.1016/j.jenvman.2024.122081, accessed 10.08.2025.

Brokmann/Dißmann in: Bundesverband Alternative Investments e. V. (BAI)/Bundesinitiative Impact Investing e. V. (BIII), Position Paper: Impact Investing in Infrastructure. Turning Potential into Practice: What does it take to implement Impact Investing in Infrastructure, May 2025, https://bundesinitiative-impact-investing.org/publikationen/position-paper-05-impact-investing-in-infrastructure-turning-potential-into-practice-what-does-it-take-to-implement-impact-investing-in-infrastructure/, accessed 22.07.2025.

Bundesinitiative Impact Investing, Position Paper #02: Impact Investing in Real Estate, October 2023, https://bundesinitiative-impact-investing.org/wp-content/uploads/2025/02/250115_BIII_PP2_eng_D2.pdf, accessed 22.07.2025.

Bundesinitiative Impact Investing, Position Paper #03: Impact Due Diligence Principles, February 2024, https://bundesinitiative-impact-investing.org/wp-content/uploads/2024/02/240226_BIII_PP3_IDD_eng.pdf, accessed 22.07.2025.

Bundesministerium für Umwelt, Klimaschutz, Naturschutz und nukleare Sicherheit (BMUKN), Flächenverbrauch – Worum geht es?, https://www.bmuv.de/themen/nachhaltigkeit/strategie-und-umsetzung/reduzierung-des-flaechenverbrauchs, accessed 31.08.2025.

Byrne, Dan, The future of ESG in 2025: A world divided, Corporate Governance Institute, https://www.thecorporategovernanceinstitute.com/insights/news-analysis/the-future-of-esg-in-2025/?srsltid=AfmBOor1AP33dxY4a8ZH3tpAjU8DGEunSA5-uWt3DwaLPalsHGy6t11k, accessed 13.09.2025.

Cabeza/Bai/Bertoldi/Kihila/Lucena/Mata/Mirasgedis/Novikova/Saheb, Buildings. In IPCC, 2022: Climate Change 2022: Mitigation of Climate Change. Contribution of Working Group III to the Sixth Assessment Report of the Intergovernmental Panel on Climate Change.

Cao/Chantana/Chen/Fermo/Fu/Ho/Lan/Wang, S./Wang, Z/Wynn, Financing Asia's Transition to a Net-Zero Future, https://amro-asia.org/wp-content/uploads/2025/03/Boao-Transition-Finance-Report_Web-Version.pdf, accessed 31.08.2025.

Capital Ascendas Reit, Integrated Sustainability Report 2022, https://investor.capitaland-ascendasreit.com/newsroom/20230406_060107_A17U_ECIMIIRIYBFHU7YI.1.pdf, accessed 06.09.2025.

Capital Markets Authority, Code of Corporate Governance Practices for Issuers of Securities to the Public, 2015, https://cma.or.ke/wp-content/uploads/2023/03/Code-of-Corporate-Governance-Practices-for-Issuers-of-Securities-to-the-Public-2015-Code-8.pdf, accessed 04.07.2025.

Carbon Tracker Initiative, Unburnable Carbon – Are the World's Financial Markets Carrying a Carbon Bubble?, 2011.

Carlowitz, Hanns Carl von, Sylvicultura oeconomica, 1713.

Carroll, Archie B, Carroll's pyramid of CSR: taking another look. International Journal of Corporate Social Responsibility, International Journal of Corporate Social Responsibility, 2016, https://jcsr.springeropen.com/articles/10.1186/s40991-016-0004-6#citeas, accessed 29.10.2025.

Carson, Rachel, Silent Spring, 1962.

Cato, Scott, Green Economics, 2009.

CBRE, 2025 Global Investor Intentions Survey, 2025. https://www.cbre.com/insights/viewpoints/2025-global-investor-intentions-survey, accessed 08.09.2025

CBRE, AI Boom Drives Data Centre Demand Amid Supply and Power Challenges, 2025, https://www.cbre.com/press-releases/ai-boom-drives-data-centre-demand-amid-supply-and-power-challenges-cbre, accessed 30.07.2025.

CBRE, H2 2024 Global Real Estate Capital Flows, 2025, https://www.cbre.com/insights/reports/h2-2024-global-real-estate-capital-flows, accessed 30.07.2025.

CBRE, Robust Q3 Volume Puts 2021 Global Investment on Par with 2019, 2021, https://www.cbre.com/insights/briefs/robust-q3-volume-puts-2021-global-investment-on-par-with-2019, accessed 06.08.2025.

Central Bank of Argentina, Argentina's Sustainable Finance National Strategy, https://www.bcra.gob.ar/Pdfs/SistemasFinancierosYdePagos/Sustainable%20Finance%20National%20Strategy.pdf, accessed 31.07.2025.

CFA Institute, Sustainable Investing Certificate Curriculum 2025, 2025.

CFA/GSIA/PRI, Definitions for Responsible Investment Approaches, 2023, https://www.gsi-alliance.org/wp-content/uploads/2023/10/ESG-Terminology-Report_Online.pdf, accessed 01.05.2025.

CFI Team, Friedman Doctrine, https://corporatefinanceinstitute.com/resources/equities/friedman-doctrine/, accessed 13.09.2025.

Cheever/Campbell-Mohn, environmental law, in: Brittanica, https://www.britannica.com/topic/environmental-law, accessed 07.06.2025.

Chen, James (reviewed: Howard, Ebony; Fact checked Rohrs Schmitt, Kirsten), Investment Objective: Definition and Use for Portfolio Building, Investopedia, 2022, https://www.investopedia.com/terms/i/investmentobjective.asp, accessed 13.09.2025.

City of Calgary, Brownfield Tax Incentive Program, https://www.calgary.ca/environment/programs/brownfield-tax-incentive.html#:~:text=The%20Brownfield%20Tax%20Incentive%20Program,from%20increased%20assessed%20property%20value, accessed 31.08.2025.

Clean Air Task Force, The geography of clean energy investments in the U.S., 2025, https://www.catf.us/2025/07/geography-clean-energy-investments-us/, accessed 08.09.2025.

Climate Club, The History of Climate Conferences in 10 minutes, Part 2, YouTube, 2024, https://www.youtube.com/watch?v=Hi8xPSK4AWE, accessed 08.06.2025.

Climate Club, The History of Climate Conferences in 13 minutes, YouTube, 2024, https://www.youtube.com/watch?v=aPV2nVcflo4, accessed 08.06.2025.

Coleman, James. S, Social Capital in the Creation of Human Capital, https://www.jstor.org/stable/2780243, accessed 13.09.2025.

Conrads/Serode/Sauer/Tauberschmitt, Vier Grundprinzipien der ESG-Transformation als Basis der teleologischen Auslegung – Teil 1, 2023, 168.

Conrads/Wilke/Sauer, Vier Grundprinzipien der ESG-Transformation als Basis der teleologischen Auslegung – Teil 2, 2023, 292.

Council on Tall Buildings and Urban Habitat (CTBUH), Merdeka 118, https://www.skyscrapercenter.com/building/merdeka-118/10115, accessed 06.09.2025.

CRREM Foundation, Carbon Risk Real Estate Monitor, 2025, https://crrem.org/, accessed 19.08.2025.

CRREM, EPRA, Green Governance, 2024, https://www.crrem.eu/green_governance/, accessed 06.09.2025.

CSR, (initiative by) German Federal Ministry of Labour and Social Affairs, Sustainability and CSR, https://www.csr-in-deutschland.de/EN/CSR/Background/Sustainability-and-CSR/sustainability-and-csr.html, accessed 29.07.2025.

Danaan, Elena, The Seeders: The Return Of The Gods, 2022, https://www.elenadanaan.org/the-seeders-return-of-the-gods, accessed 31.08.2025.

Dathe, T/Helmhold/Dathe, R/Dathe, I, Implementing Environmental, Social and Governance (ESG) Principles for Sustainable Businesses, 2024.

Davies, Paul (ed.), The Global ESG Handbook: A Guide for Practitioners, 2024.

Davis/Novotny, ESG disclosure requirements for financial institutions in South Africa: A 2025 update, 2025, https://www.polity.org.za/article/esg-disclosure-requirements-for-financial-institutions-in-south-africa-a-2025-update-2025-07-16, accessed 28.07.2025.

DEBV, Wie definiert der DEBV ein Brownfield?, https://deutscherbrownfieldverband.de/media/site/5a169a257d-1718194962/debv_rubrik-erklaerbaer_brownfield_01.pdf, accessed 31.08.2025.

Del Sarto, Nicola, ESG Factors and Financial Outcomes in Banks. Quantitative Insights into the ESG-Cost of Debt Relationship, 2025.

Demers Baulne, Real estate: navigating the complexity of ESG disclosure standards and frameworks, https://www.demersbeaulne.com/en/2024/07/23/real-estate-navigating-the-complexity-of-esg-disclosure-standards-and-frameworks, accessed 29.07.2025.

Department for Energy Security & Net Zero (UK), Transition plan requirements: implementation routes, https://www.gov.uk/government/consultations/climate-related-transition-plan-requirements/transition-plan-requirements-implementation-routes-accessible-webpage, accessed 31.08.2025.

Dial/L'Hommedieu, The ESG Debate Heats Up: State AGs Investigating Asset Manager Involvement in ESG Initiatives and Related Proxy Voting, K&L Gates Client Alert, 25.05.2023, https://www.klgates.com/The-ESG-Debate-Heats-Up-State-AGs-Investigating-Asset-Manager-Involvement-in-ESG-Initiatives-and-Related-Proxy-Voting-5-25-2023, accessed 24.07.2025.

Digital Edge DC, Construction of Green Data Centers in Asia, https://www.digitaledgedc.com/construction-of-green-data-centers-in-asia/, accessed 06.09.2025.

DIN Media, DIN EN ISO 22301:2020-06, Security and resilience – Business continuity management systems – Requirements (ISO 22301:2019); EN ISO 22301:2019, https://www.dinmedia.de/de/norm/din-en-iso-22301/311095091, accessed 14.09.2025.

Dutch News, ABP to invest €1bn to ease bottleneck in rental housing sector, https://www.dutchnews.nl/2025/05/abp-to-invest-e1bn-to-ease-bottleneck-in-rental-housing-sector/, accessed 05.08.2025.

EC, Communication from the Commission, A Competitiveness Compass for the EU, Factsheet, 2025, https://ec.europa.eu/commission/presscorner/api/files/attachment/880290/Factsheet%20-%20Competitiveness%20Compass.pdf, accessed 29.06.2025.

EC, Corporate sustainability and responsibility, https://single-market-economy.ec.europa.eu/industry/sustainability/corporate-sustainability-and-responsibility_en, accessed 03.08.2025;

Eccles/Stroehle, Exploring Social Origins in the Construction of ESG Measures, SSRN, 12.07.2018. https://papers.ssrn.com/sol3/papers.cfm?abstract_id=3212685, accessed 14.09.2025.

Edmans, Alex, The End of ESG, European Corporate Governance Institute (ECGI) Working Paper No. 847, 2022, https://papers.ssrn.com/sol3/papers.cfm?abstract_id=4221990, accessed 14.09.2025.

EIB/EC, Investing in nature-based solutions State-of-play and way forward for public and private financial measures in Europe, 2023, https://www.eib.org/attachments/lucalli/20230095_investing_in_nature_based_solutions_en.pdf, accessed 13.09.2025.

Eilers/Koffka/Mackensen/Paul/Josenhans, Private Equity, 2022.

EIOPA, Policy measures to reduce climate-related insurance protection gaps, 2023.

EMBER, ASEAN's data centres electricity demand keeps growing, https://ember-energy.org/chapter/setting-the-scene/, accessed 06.09.2025.

Enabling the impact investing market in the EU and supporting market growth, innovation, and competition, July 2025, https://bundesinitiative-impact-investing.org/publikationen/policy-paper-recognising-impact-investing-in-the-eu-sustainable-finance-framework/, accessed 22.07.2025.

Environmental Protection Agency (EPA), Final ESMP – Northern Ecological Zone, 2025, https://glrssmp.epa.gov.gh/wp-content/uploads/2025/07/Final_ESMP_NSZ_GLRSSMP.pdf, accessed 28.07.2025.

Environmental Protection Agency (EPA), Ghana's Framework on International Carbon Markets and Non-Market Approaches, 2022, https://cmo.epa.gov.gh/wp-content/uploads/2022/12/Ghana-Carbon-Market-Framework-For-Public-Release_15122022.pdf, accessed 10.07.2025.

EPA, Brownfield Overview and Definition, https://19january2017snapshot.epa.gov/brownfields/brownfield-overview-and-definition_.html, accessed 31.08.2025.

Epstein, Mark J, Making Sustainability Work: Best Practices in Managing and Measuring Corporate Social, Environmental, and Economic Impacts, 2014.

Equator Principles, The Equator Principles – Equator Principles, https://equator-principles.com/about-the-equator-principles/, accessed 07.08.2025.

EquityMultiple, Glossary for Investors, Joint Venture Real Estate, https://equitymultiple.com/glossary/joint-venture-real-estate, accessed 22.06.2025;

ESMA, International Cooperation, https://www.esma.europa.eu/about-esma/international-cooperation, accessed 01.05.2025.

ESR Group, ESR Group achieves outstanding performance across global ESG benchmarks, https://www.esr.com/news/esr-group-achieves-outstanding-performance-across-global-esg-benchmarks/, accessed 06.09.2025.

European Investment Bank (EIB), Brownfields Redevelopment Fund, https://www.eib.org/de/products/equity/funds/brownfields-redevelopment-fund, accessed 31.08.2025.

European Union, The Draghi report on EU competitiveness, https://commission.europa.eu/topics/eu-competitiveness/draghi-report_en, accessed 31.08.2025.

Eurosif, Communication, Investor and business joint statement on Omnibus initiative, 18 July 2025, https://www.eurosif.org/news/investor-and-business-joint-statement-on-omnibus-initiative/, accessed 22.08.2025.

Eurosif, University of Hamburg, Sustainable Finance Research Group & Advanced Impact Research (2024) Methodology for Eurosif Market Studies on Sustainability Investments: Measuring progress of capital flows to support the sustainable transition of the real economy, Final Report, February 2024.Hamburg/Brussels: Eurosif, 2024, https://www.eurosif.org/news/methodology-market-studies-sustainability/, accessed 08.09.2025.

Eurostat, Household composition statistics, 2025, https://ec.europa.eu/eurostat/statistics-explained/index.php/Household_composition_statistics, accessed 30.07.2025.

Eurostat, Population structure and ageing, 2025, https://ec.europa.eu/eurostat/statistics-explained/index.php/Population_structure_and_ageing, accessed 30.07.2025.

External Circular 031 of 2022, Financial Superintendency, https://www.superfinanciera.gov.co/loader.php?lServicio=Tools2&lTipo=descargas&lFuncion=descargar&idFile=1057619, accessed 30.07.2025.

External Guideline No. 100-000002-2025, Superintendence of Companies, https://www.supersociedades.gov.co/documents/107391/8611340/Circular+Externa+100-000002+de+14+de+marzo+de+2025.pdf/82dc3c0b-1695-295b-ad37-3327ab2d683b, accessed 30.07.2025.

Falkenberg/Vogt, supervised by Charlotte Østergaard, The effect of ESG-performance on M&A premiums – An Empirical Analysis of ESG in M&A's, 2022.

Federal Ministry Agriculture and Forestry, Climate and Environmental Protection, Regions and Water Management, Contaminated site management, https://www.bmluk.gv.at/en/topics/climate-environment/waste-and-circular-economy/contaminated-site-management.html, accessed 31.08.2025.

Federal Reserve Bank of San Francisco, Commercial Real Estate and Low Interest Rates, 2013, https://www.frbsf.org/research-and-insights/publications/economic-letter/2013/04/commercial-real-estate-low-interest-rates/, accessed 06.08.2025.

Fernandez, Hannah Alcoseba, A third of Southeast Asia's data centres could be powered by renewable energy by 2030: study, 2025, https://www.eco-business.com/news/a-third-of-southeast-asias-data-centres-could-be-powered-by-renewable-energy-by-2030-study/, accessed 06.09.2025.

Figura, Julia, in: Herzog/Achtelik, Money Laundering Act, 5. Ed. 2023, section 10.

Financial Sector Conduct Authority (FSCA), Strengthening South Africa's sustainable finance framework. Moonstone Information Refinery, 2025, https://www.moonstone.co.za/strengthening-south-africas-sustainable-finance-framework/, accessed 10.07.2025.

Fink, Larry, Larry Fink's 2017 Letter to CEOs, BlackRock, https://www.blackrock.com/corporate/investor-relations/2017-larry-fink-ceo-letter, accessed 14.09.2025.

FNG – Forum nachhaltige Geldanlagen, Marktbericht Nachhaltige Geldanlagen 2025.

Fortune Reit, Environmental, Social and Governance Report 2024, https://www.fortunereit.com/wp-content/uploads/2025/04/ESG-Report_EW00778.pdf, accessed 06.09.2025.

Freer Spreckley, Social Enterprise Planning Toolkit, https://locallivelihoods.com/wp-content/uploads/2020/06/Social-Enterprise-Planning-Toolkit.pdf, accessed 13.09.2025.

GAW Capital Partners, Responsible Investment Policy, https://www.gawcapital.com/srdisclosure/responsible-investment-policy/, accessed 06.09.2025.

General Law on Climate Change of 2012, https://climate-laws.org/documents/general-law-on-climate-change-2023-amended-text_3db4, accessed 30.07.2025.

General Rule No. 461 on the structure and content of the annual report of securities issuers, https://www.cmfchile.cl/normativa/ncg_461_2021.pdf, accessed 27.07.2025.

General Rule No. 519 on integrated annual report, https://www.cmfchile.cl/normativa/ncg_519_2024.pdf, accessed 27.07.2025.

Ghana Stock Exchange, ESG Disclosures Guidance Manual, 2022, https://gse.com.gh/market-news/esg-disclosures-guidance-manual/, accessed 18.06.2025.

GHG Protocol, Corporate Value Chain (Scope 3) Accounting and Reporting Standard, 2011, https://ghgprotocol.org/corporate-value-chain-scope-3-standard, accessed 30.08.2025.

GHG Protocol, Standards, https://ghgprotocol.org/standards-guidance, accessed 31.08.2025.

GIIN, Operating Principles for Impact Management, The 9 Principles, https://www.impactprinciples.org/9-principles/, accessed 22.07.2025.

Global Climate Action (NAZCA), The Net Zero Banking Alliance, 2024, https://climateaction.unfccc.int/Initiatives?id=Net_Zero_Banking_Alliance, accessed 31.08.2025.

Global Investors for Sustainable Development Alliance (GISD), Navigator, Investors, High-level principles, Operating Principles for Impact Management, https://www.gisdalliance.org/navigator, accessed 22.07.2025.

Global Reporting Initiative (GRI), Our Mission and History, https://www.globalreporting.org/about-gri/mission-history/, accessed 14.09.2025.

Global Reporting Initiative, GRI, 2025, https://www.globalreporting.org/, accessed 31.08.2025.

Global Steering Group for Impact Investment (GSG Impact), https://www.gsgimpact.org/impact/impact-investment/?_gl=1*1vo56zw*_up*MQ..*_ga*OTc3ODE0MTc5LjE3NTM0NjAzNjM.*_ga_782VKK04HX*czE3NTM0NjAzNjIkbzEkZzAkdDE3NTM0NjAzNjIkajYwJGwwJGgw, accessed 22.07.2025.

Global Sustainable Investment Alliance, GSIA Global Sustainable Investment Review 2022, 2022, https://www.gsi-alliance.org/wp-content/uploads/2023/12/GSIA-Report-2022.pdf, accessed 03.11.2025.

GLP, Environmental Activities (E), https://www.glpjreit.com/en/esg/environment.html, accessed 06.09.2025.

Golnaraghi/Bresch/Höppe/Löffler/Nagamura/Rauch, COP 21 Paris Agreement: What Does It Mean for the (Re)insurance Sector?, 2016, 1.

Government of India Ministry of Housing and Urban Affairs, Vision of Smart Cities Mission, https://smartcities.gov.in, accessed 06.09.2025.

Government of Otario, Brownfields financial tax incentive program, https://www.ontario.ca/page/brownfields-financial-tax-incentive-program, accessed 31.08.2025.

Grand View Research, Latin America Real Estate Market Size & Outlook – 2024–2030, https://www.grandviewresearch.com/horizon/outlook/real-estate-market/latin-america, accessed 30.07.2025.

Greenwood, Christopher, Sources of International Law: An Introduction, https://legal.un.org/avl/pdf/ls/greenwood_outline.pdf, accessed 07.06.2025.

GRESB, Elevating ESG performance in the Philippines: NEO's sustainability journey, https://www.gresb.com/nl-en/elevating-esg-performance-in-the-philippines-neos-sustainability-journey/, accessed 29.07.2025.

GRESB, GRESB Public Results, https://www.gresb.com/nl-en/gresb-public-results/, accessed 01.09.2025.

GRESB, Sustainability Linked Loans, https://www.gresb.com/nl-en/sustainability-linked-loans/, accessed 29.07.2025.

Grunwald/Kopfmüller, Nachhaltigkeit, 3., aktualisierte und erweiterte Auflage, Frankfurt/New York, 2022.

Grützner/Behr, in: Momsen, Carsten, WirtschaftsSteuerStrafR-HdB, 2. Ed. 2020, section 30.

GSIA Responsible Investment Definitions 2023, https://www.gsi-alliance.org/wp-content/uploads/2023/10/ESG-Terminology-Report_Online.pdf, accessed 06.09.2025.

GSIA, Eurosif, the European Sustainable Investment Forum, 2025, https://www.gsi-alliance.org/alliance-members/eurosif/, accessed 29.06.2025.

GSIA, GSIA-Report 2022, https://www.gsi-alliance.org/wp-content/uploads/2023/12/GSIA-Report-2022.pdf, accessed 06.09.2025.

Gupta/Venkataraman, Insurance and climate change, in: Environmental Sustainability, Volume 67, 2024.

Haak, Andreas, Unternehmerische Zusammenarbeit in der öffentlichen Auftragsvergabe, https://www.vdz.org/vergabe-beschaffung/unternehmerische-zusammenarbeit-der-oeffentlichen-auftragsvergabe, accessed 15.08.2025.

Hamilton, Ian, Global Status Report for Buildings and Construction, 2020, https://globalabc.org/resources/publications/2020-global-status-report-buildings-andconstruction, accessed 25.06.2025.

Hancock/Bounds, Netherlands rations electricity to ease power grid stresses, Financial Times, https://www.ft.com/content/9c7560ec-a220-4150-a35e-a79db70c0c07, accessed 19.07.2025.

Hand/Ulanow/Pan/Xiao, Sizing the Impact Investing Market 2024, in: The Global Impact Investing Network (GIIN). New York, 2024, 3ff, https://s3.amazonaws.com/giin-web-assets/giin/assets/publication/giin-sizingtheimpactinvestingmarket-2024.pdf, accessed 27.07.2025.

Harrison, David, Key structuring considerations for crossborder acquisitions and joint ventures, 27.02.2019, https://uk.practicallaw.thomsonreuters.com/w-019-4151?transitionType=Default&contextData=(sc.Default)&firstPage=true, accessed 01.09.2025

Haufellner/Haffke/Heinrichs, Current developments in money laundering law, BKR 2025, 392.

Herzog, Felix, in: Herzog/Achtelik, Money Laundering Act, sections 7 and 8.

Hogan Lovells, ESG: What are the global issues for cross-border managers of real estate funds?, https://www.hoganlovells.com/en/publications/esg-what-are-the-global-issues-for-cross-border-managers-of-real-estate-funds, accessed 29.07.2025.

Hölkemeier/Koch/Thomer/Wieduwilt, »Social Impact Investing« im Lichte des Immobilienwirtschafts- und Immobiliensteuerrechts, BB 2025, 1047, also retrievable via: https://www.dentons.com/de/insights/articles/2025/may/6/-/media/2ef46b16ef2147dcbadd2e164eb770de.ashx, accessed 03.11.2025.

Hong Kong Green Building Council, Hong Kong Green Building Council's Response to 2025/26 Budget, https://www.hkgbc.org.hk/eng/news-events/news/2025/20250226.jsp, accessed 06.09.2025.

Hooper, Lindsay, ESG is dead. Long live ESG, We must urgently address the tension between profitability and sustainability, Financial Times, 19.09.2024, https://www.ft.com/content/47b334a9-69eb-4cd0-af22-6ad0b92c0ef6, accessed 04.08.2025.

Hudson/Wouter Botzen/Feyen/Aerts, Incentivising flood risk adaptation through risk based insurance premiums: Trade-offs between affordability and risk reduction, in: Ecological Economics, Volume 125, 2016.

Human Rights Council, Report of the Special Representative of the Secretary General on the issue of human rights and transnational corporations and other business enterprises, John Ruggie. Guiding Principles on Business and Human Rights: Implementing the United Nations »Protect, Respect and Remedy« Framework, 2011, https://www.ohchr.org/sites/default/files/Documents/Issues/Business/A-HRC-17-31_AEV.pdf, accessed 06.09.2025.

ICG Institut für Corporate Governance in der deutschen Immobilienwirtschaft (ed): Social Impact Investing, Der Praxisleitfaden für die Immobilienwirtschaft, February 2021, https://icg-institut.de/en/social-impact-investing/social-impact-investing-practical-guide/, accessed 30.07.2025.

ICGN Investor Viewpoint – Artificial Intelligence – An engagement guide, 2024, https://www.icgn.org/sites/default/files/2024-03/ICGN%20Investor%20Viewpoint%20-%20Artificial%20Intelligence%20-%20An%20engagement%20guide%20%282%29.pdf, accessed 03.05.2025.

IDRC Digital Library/Bibliothèque numérique du CRDI, Brundtland Commission/Commission Brundtland (WCED), https://hdl.handle.net/10625/53401, accessed 11.09.2025.

IFC International Finance Corporation, World Bank Group, Impact investing at IFC, https://www.ifc.org/en/our-impact/impact-investing-at-ifc, accessed 22.07.2025.

Imoisi/Okoro, Advancing sustainable finance in Nigeria: A policy-oriented analysis of challenges and opportunities. International Journal of Advanced Studies in Economics and Public Sector Management, 13(1), 2025, https://internationalpolicybrief.org/wp-content/uploads/2025/05/ARTICLE-20.pdf, accessed 08.08.2025, 245.

Impact Frontiers, Impact Management Norms, https://impactfrontiers.org/norms/, accessed 20.07.2025.

Impact Management Platform (IMP), Impact and the impact pathway, https://impactmanagementplatform.org/impact/#:~:text=An%20impact%20pathway%20describes%20how,natural%20capital%20affect%20different%20stakeholders, accessed 27.07.2025.

Infocomm Media Development Authority, Charting green growth pathways at scale for data centres in Singapore, 2024, https://www.imda.gov.sg/resources/press-releases-factsheets-and-speeches/factsheets/2024/charting-green-growth-for-data-centres-in-sg, accessed 06.09.2025.

Initiative Climate Bonds, China's new Green Finance Catalogue brings clarity and confidence to the market, https://www.climatebonds.net/news-events/blog/chinas-new-green-finance-catalogue-brings-clarity-confidence-market, accessed 31.08.2025.

Initiative Climate Bonds, Financing the Corporate Climate Transition with Bonds, https://www.climatebonds.net/files/documents/publications/Financing-the-Corporate-Climate-Transition-with-Bonds.pdf, accessed 31.08.2025.

INREV, Response to European Commission Call for Evidence on the Sustainable Finance Disclosure Regulation (SFDR), https://www.inrev.org/system/files/2025-06/INREV-Response-to-European-Commission-Call-for-Evidence-on-SFDR.pdf, accessed 01.09.2025.

Institute of Certified Securities of Kenya, Funding Sustainable Projects through Green Financing in Kenya. Institute of Certified Secretaries, 2025, https://www.ics.ke/2025/01/28/funding-sustainable-projects-through-green-financing-in-kenya/, accessed 28.07.2025.

Insurance Council of Australia, Local Government and Insurance Flood Insurance Pricing, 2025, https://www.floods.asn.au/client_images/1787680.pdf, accessed 11.08.2025.

Intercontinental Exchange, Sustainable Bond Analysis, 2024, https://www.ice.com/insights/sustainable-bond-report-2024, accessed 30.07.2025.

Intergovernmental Panel on Climate Change (IPCC), IPCC Sixth Assessment Report, Chapter 7: Agriculture, Forestry, and Other Land Uses (AFOLU), https://www.ipcc.ch/report/ar6/wg3/chapter/chapter-7/, accessed 31.07.2025.

Interim Measures for the Management of Generative AI Services, https://www.cac.gov.cn/2023-07/13/c_1690898327029107.htm, accessed 30.07.2025.

International Capital Market Association (ICMA), Green Bond Principles (GBP), 2025, https://www.icmagroup.org/assets/documents/Sustainable-finance/2025-updates/Green-Bond-Principles-GBP-June-2025.pdfm, accessed 31.08.2025.

International Capital Market Association (ICMA), Social Bond Principles (SBP), 2025, https://www.icmagroup.org/assets/documents/Sustainable-finance/2025-updates/Social-Bond-Principles-SBP-June-2025.pdf, accessed 31.08.2025.

International Capital Market Association (ICMA), Sustainability Bond Guidelines (SBG), June 2021, https://www.icmagroup.org/assets/documents/Sustainable-finance/2021-updates/Sustainability-Bond-Guidelines-June-2021-140621.pdf, accessed 31.08.2025.

International Capital Market Association (ICMA), Sustainability-Linked Bond Principles (SBLP), 2024, https://www.icmagroup.org/assets/documents/Sustainable-finance/2024-updates/Sustainability-Linked-Bond-Principles-June-2024.pdf, accessed 31.08.2025.

International Capital Market Association (ICMA), Sustainable Finance, https://www.icmagroup.org/sustainable-finance/, accessed 14.09.2025.

International Corporate Governance Network (ICGN), Publications, https://www.icgn.org/publications, accessed 14.09.2025.

International Energy Agency (IEA), Energy demand from AI, 2025, https://www.iea.org/reports/energy-and-ai/energy-demand-from-ai, accessed 30.07.2025.

International Institute for Sustainable Development, How Reforming the European Union's Public Procurement Directive Can Help Drive a Green Transition, 2025.

International Labour Organization (ILO), Indigenous and Tribal Peoples Convention (C169), https://normlex.ilo.org/dyn/nrmlx_en/f?p=NORMLEXPUB:55:0::NO::P55_TYPE,P55_LANG,P55_DOCUMENT,P55_NODE:REV,en,C169,/Document, accessed 27.06.2025.

International Living Future Institute, Living Building Challenge, What if every single act of design and construction made the world a better place?, https://living-future.org/lbc/, accessed 30.07.2025.

International Organization of Securities Commissions (IOSCO), Recommendations on Sustainability-Related Practices, Policies, Procedures and Disclosure in Asset Management, www.iosco.org/library/pubdocs/pdf/IOSCOPD688.pdf, accessed 13.09.2025.

Interreg Europe, Brownfieldcovenants as an instrument to revitalize former landfill sites, 2019, https://www.interregeurope.eu/good-practices/brownfieldcovenants-as-an-instrument-to-revitalize-former-landfill-sites, accessed 31.08.2025.

Invesco, Invesco Real Estate Asia Fund FCP-SIF (the »Fund«), https://www.invesco.com/content/dam/invesco/emea/en/real-estate-sustainability-disclosures/invesco-real-estate-asia-fund-fcp-sif-invesco-sustainability-full-disclosure.pdf, accessed 06.09.2025.

IPCC, Climate Change 2022: Impacts, Adaptation and Vulnerability, 2022, https://www.ipcc.ch/report/ar6/wg2/, accessed 13.09.2025.

IPCC, Climate Change 2022: Mitigation of Climate Change. Contribution of Working Group III to the Sixth Assessment Report of the Intergovernmental Panel on Climate Change, 2022.

IRIS+ System, Standards, IRIS+ is the generally accepted system for measuring, managing, and optimizing impact, https://iris.thegiin.org/standards/, accessed 20.07.2025.

Ishiwatari/Kawakami/Sasaki/Sakamoto/Nakayama, Enhancing Disaster Resilience for Sustainable Urban Development: Public–Private Partnerships in Japan, in: Sustainability, 2024.

ISO.org: ISO/IEC 27001:2022 Information security, cybersecurity and privacy protection — Information security management systems — Requirements, 2022, https://www.iso.org/standard/27001, accessed 02.11.2025.

Iwuanyanwu/Gil-Ozoudeh/Okwandu/Ike, Retrofitting existing buildings for sustainability: challenges and innovations. Engineering Science & Technology Journal, 2024, 5(8), 2616, https://doi.org/10.51594/estj.v5i8, accessed 14.09.2025.

Jarzabkowski/Chalkias/Clarke/Iyahen/Stadtmueller/Zwick, Insurance for climate adaptation: Opportunities and limitations, 2019.

JLL, EMEA Data Centre Report Q4 2024, 2024, https://www.jll.com/en-de/insights/emea-data-centre-report, accessed 30.07.2025.

JLL, Global Real Estate Outlook 2025, https://www.jll.com/en-us/insights/market-outlook/global-real-estate, accessed 06.08.2025.

JLL, Global Real Estate Perspective, May 2025, 2025. https://www.jll.com/en-us/insights/market-perspectives/global, accessed 29.07.2025.

JLL, North America Data Center Report Year-end 2024, 2025, https://www.jll.com/en-us/insights/market-dynamics/north-america-data-centers, accessed 30.07.2025.

JLL, Record-low data center vacancy fuels modern-day »gold rush«, 2025, https://www.jll.com/en-us/newsroom/record-low-data-center-vacancy-fuels-modern-day-gold-rush, accessed 30.07.2025.

JLL, Sustainability remains a key driver for European real estate investors, 2025, https://www.jll.com/en-belux/insights/sustainability-remains-a-key-driver-for-european-real-estate-investors, accessed 30.07.2025.

JLL, The Global Real Estate Transparency Index 2024, 2024, https://www.jll.com/en-uk/insights/global-real-estate-transparency-index, accessed 30.07.2025.

Johannesburg Stock Exchange (JSE), Sustainability Disclosure Guidance, 2022, https://www.jse.co.za/sites/default/files/media/documents/JSE%20Sustainability%20Disclosure%20Guidance_1.pdf, accessed 07.08.2025.

Keilich, Jochen, ESG reporting obligations and their impact on labour law, SPA 2024, 73.

Keppel Ltd., Keppel's sustainability performance recognised at GRESB 2024, https://www.keppel.com/media/keppels-sustainability-performance-recognised-at-gresb-2024/, accessed 06.09.2025.

Klitskov/Kiknadz, How Do Nordic Companies' ESG Attributes Impact Their Valuation Models Used in M&A?, 2021.

Kozłowska-Makóś, Danuta, The Role of ESG Reporting in Mergers and Acquisitions, 2024.

Labowitz/Baumann-Pauly, Business as usual is not an option: Supply chains and sourcing after Rana Plaza, https://bhr.stern.nyu.edu/publication/business-as-usual-is-not-an-option-supply-chains-and-sourcing-after-rana-plaza/, accessed 11.08.2025.

Lands Commission of Ghana, Land Act, 2020 (Act 1036): Notice of Application for Deeds Registration, 2025, https://www.lc.gov.gh/2025/07/22/land-act-2020-act-1036-notice-of-application-for-deeds-registration-4/, accessed 28.07.2025.

LaSalle Investment Management, Focus Transparency and strategy, 2024, https://www.lasalle.com/wp-content/uploads/2024/10/isa-focus-transparency-and-strategy.pdf, accessed 06.08.2025.

Layna Mosely, Labor Rights and Multinational Production, Cambridge University Press, https://scispace.com/pdf/labor-rights-and-multinational-production-390o8as1aa.pdf, accessed.08.08.2025.

LEAF Coalition, Press Release: Pará signs $180 m LEAF Coalition deal – first in Brazil, https://emergentclimate.com/wp-content/uploads/2024/09/Para-ERPA-announcement-Emergent-Final.pdf, accessed 27.06.2025.

LeBaron, Genevieve, Subcontracting Is Not Illegal, But Is It Unethical? Business Ethics, Forced Labor, and Economic Success, in The Brown Journal of World Affairs Vol. 20, No. 2, 237.

Letta, Enrico, Much more than a market, 2024, https://www.consilium.europa.eu/media/ny3j24sm/much-more-than-a-market-report-by-enrico-letta.pdf, accessed 31.08.2025.

Letta, Enrico, Much more than a market, https://www.consilium.europa.eu/media/ny3j24sm/much-more-than-a-market-report-by-enrico-letta.pdf, accessed 31.08.2025.

Link Real Estate Investment Trust, From Strength to Strategy: Shaping Tomorrow, Today, https://www.linkreit.com/-/media/linkreit/investor-relations/financial-reports-and-presentations/financial-report/2024/annual-report-2324-e-book-3.pdf, accessed 06.09.2025.

LinkReit.com, Sustainable Finance Framework, 2022, https://www.linkreit.com/-/media/linkreit/sustainability/sustainability-governance/sustainable-finance/link-sf-framework_web_final.pdf?rev=dce6ef2b6a544b2eaefe7eebadafecbd, accessed 06.09.2025.

LinkReit.com, Sustainable Finance, https://www.linkreit.com/en/sustainability/sustainability-governance/sustainable-finance/, accessed 06.09.2025.

Loan Market Association (LMA), the Green Loans Principles, the Social Loan Principles and the Sustainability-Linked Loan Principles etc. Document index, https://www.lma.eu.com/sustainable-lending/resources, accessed 31.08.2025.

Local Governments for Sustainability, Promoting Renewable Energy Consumption. The Cases of Kitakyushu and Seoul, https://eastasia.iclei.org/wp-content/uploads/2023/12/Promoting-Renewable-Energy-Consumption-1205.pdf, accessed 06.09.2025.

Lund, Dorothy S, Asset Managers as Regulators, University of Pennsylvania Law Review 171, no. 1, 2022, https://scholarship.law.upenn.edu/penn_law_review/vol171/iss1/2, accessed 14.09.2025, 77.

Lund/Pollman, The Corporate Governance Machine. Columbia Law Review 121, no. 7 2021, https://columbialawreview.org/content/the-corporate-governance-machine/, accessed 14.09.2025, 2563–2625.

Mapletree Stewarding Sustainability, 2025, https://www.mapletree.com.sg/uploads/2025/07/MIPL_SR25_Final-July-14-1.pdf, accessed 06.09.2025.

Market Data Forecast, Latin America Real Estate Market Report, https://www.marketdataforecast.com/market-reports/latin-america-real-estate-market, accessed 30.07.2025.

Martindale, Will, Responsible Investment. An Insider's Account of What's Working, What's not and where next, 2024.

Maslow/Snyder, Contracts for Responsible and Sustainable Supply Chains. Model Contract Clauses, Legal Analysis, and Practical Perspectives, 2023.

McKinsey & Company, The cost of compute: A $7 trillion race to scale data centers, 2025, https://www.mckinsey.com/industries/technology-media-and-telecommunications/our-insights/the-cost-of-compute-a-7-trillion-dollar-race-to-scale-data-centers, accessed 30.07.2025.

Meadows, D. H/Meadows, D. L./Randers/Behrens, The Limits to Growth. A report for the Club of Rome's project on the predicament of mankind, 1972, https://www.donellameadows.org/wp-content/userfiles/Limits-to-Growth-digital-scan-version.pdf, accessed 03.08.2025.

MGTC, Steady increase of ›green buildings‹, https://www.mgtc.gov.my/2024/12/steady-increase-of-green-buildings/, accessed 06.09.2025.

Microsoft, Enabling a sustainable future, https://www.microsoft.com/pt-br/maisbrasil/habilitando-um-futuro-sustentavel, accessed 27.06.2025.

Microsoft, Reducing Embodied Carbon in Construction, https://cdn-dynmedia-1.microsoft.com/is/content/microsoftcorp/microsoft/final/en-us/microsoft-brand/documents/reducing-embodied-carbon-July-2021.pdf, accessed 29.07.2025.

Ministère de la Transition écologique, Recyclage des friches: lancement de la 3e édition du fonds friches, https://www.ecologie.gouv.fr/actualites/recyclage-friches-lancement-3e-edition-du-fonds-friches, accessed 31.08.2025.

Ministry of Finance and Economic Planning of Ghana, Ghana Sustainable Financing Framework, 2021, https://www.mofep.gov.gh/sites/default/files/news/Ghana-Sustainable-Financing-Framework.pdf, accessed 21.07.2025

Ministry of the Environment Japan, Green Bond and Sustainability Linked Bond Guidelines. Green Loan and Sustainability Linked Loan Guidelines, 2024, https://greenfinanceportal.env.go.jp/pdf/greenbond_guideline_eng.pdf, accessed 06.09.2025.

Mitsubishi Heavy Industries, Transition Bonds, https://www.mhi.com/finance/stock/esg/transitionbond.html, accessed 06.09.2025.

MMAN Advocates, Environmental, Social and Governance (ESG) Landscape in Kenya: Key Considerations for Listed and Non-Listed Entities, 2021, https://www.mman.co.ke/sites/default/files/Environmental%20Social%20and%20Governance%20%28ESG%29%20Landscape%20in%20Kenya_0.pdf, accessed 28.07.2025.

Monetary Authority of Singapore, Guidelines on Environmental Risk Management for Asset Managers, https://www.mas.gov.sg/regulation/guidelines/guidelines-on-environmental-risk-management-for-asset-managers, accessed 06.09.2025.

Monmonier, Mark, Rhumb Lines and Map Wars: A Social History of the Mercator Projection, 2004, https://press.uchicago.edu/ucp/books/book/chicago/R/bo3634012.html, University of Chicago Press, accessed 14.08.2025.

Mordor Intelligence, Latin America Residential Real Estate Market Size & Share Analysis – Growth Trends & Forecasts (2025–2030), 2025, https://www.mordorintelligence.com/industry-reports/residential-real-estate-market-in-latin-america, accessed 30.07.2025.

MSCI, Early Warnings of CRE Price Problems, 2025, https://www.msci.com/research-and-insights/blog-post/early-warnings-of-cre-price-problems, accessed 30.07.2025.

MSCI, EBA Solutions for Banks, https://www.msci.com/data-and-analytics/sustainability-and-climate-regulatory-toolkit/eba-solutions-for-banks?utm_source=google&utm_medium=cpc&utm_campaign=sustainb_eba_regulatory_pp_consid&utm_content=sustainb_eba_regulatory_pp_consid_plfm_ban_emea_theme-eba&utm_term=esg%20for%20banks&creative=765923091100, accessed 13.09.2025.

MSCI, Real Assets in Focus: Are We Nearly There Yet?, 2024, https://www.msci.com/research-and-insights/blog-post/real-assets-in-focus-are-we-nearly-there-yet, accessed 06.08.2025.

MSCI, Real Estate in Focus: 2025 Trends to Watch, 2025, https://www.msci.com/research-and-insights/blog-post/real-estate-in-focus-2025-trends-to-watch, accessed 30.07.2025.

MSCI, Real Estate in Focus: Bumps on the Road to Recovery, 2025, https://www.msci.com/research-and-insights/blog-post/real-estate-in-focus-bumps-on-the-road-to-recovery, accessed 30.07.2025.

Müller/Johner/Serag/Eugster/Jacaccia, Another Foray Into Amending the Swiss Lex Koller, https://chambers.com/rankings/real-estate-switzerland-europe, accessed 10.06.2025.

Nairobi Securities Exchange (NSE), ESG Disclosures Guidance Manual, 2021, https://www.nse.co.ke/wp-content/uploads/NSE-ESG-Disclosures-Guidance-Manual.pdf, accessed 14.07.2025.

Nath/Bean, China's Critical Mineral Export Controls: Background & Chokepoints, 2025.

National Institute of Standards and Technology, Cybersecurity Framework, https://www.nist.gov/cyberframework/getting-started-csf-11, accessed 30.07.2025.

National Land Commission of Kenya, Land Laws, 2025, https://landcommission.go.ke/land-laws/, accessed 02.07.2025.

National Securities Commission of Argentina, Guide for the voluntary reporting and disclosure of environmental, social, and governance (ESG) information, 2023, https://www.argentina.gob.ar/sites/default/files/guia_informacion_asg-_2023.pdf, accessed 31.07.2025.

National Toms Framework, https://nationaltomsframework.co.uk/social-value-portal-national-toms-calculator/, accessed 30.07.2025.

National Treasury of South Africa, Report highlights key steps to strengthen South Africa's Green Finance Taxonomy, 2025, https://www.treasury.gov.za/comm_media/press/2025/2025032601%20Media%20Statement%20-%20Green%20Finance%20Taxonomy.pdf, accessed 12.07.2025.

Natour, Faris, Respecting Human Rights in the On-Demand Economy: Closing the New Governance Gap, https://www.cambridge.org/core/services/aop-cambridge-core/content/view/D449DF0A9E34E3D56A3C2361551DB551/S2057019816000079a.pdf/respecting-human-rights-in-the-on-demand-economy-closing-the-new-governance-gap.pdf, accessed 13.08.2025, 317.

NBCC (India) Limited, Use of Fly Ash, https://nbccindia.in/webEnglish/FlyAsh, accessed 06.09.2025.

Neshat/Patkar/Hariharan, MSCI Real Estate Market Size Report – The size of the professionally managed global real estate investment market in 2024, 2025.

Network of Central Banks and Supervisors for Greening the Financial System (NGFS), https://www.ngfs.net/en, accessed 06.09.2025.

Nidumolu/Ellison/Whalen/Billman, The Collaboration Imperative for Sustainable Business Practices, https://hbr.org/2014/04/the-collaboration-imperative-2, accessed 29.05.2025.

NISM, What is a security market, https://www.nism.ac.in/what-is-securities-market/, accessed 01.05.2025.

Nomura Real Estate Holding, Sustainable Finance, https://www.nomura-re-hd.co.jp/english/sustainability/finance/#section02, accessed 06.09.2025.

Norges Bank Investment Management, Climate and nature disclosures 2024, https://www.nbim.no/contentassets/6fdfd333e6bf460f8e538b9b55a95bb7/gpfg-climate-and-nature-disclosures-2024.pdf, accessed 25.07.2025.

Nowak/Grünberg/Gleich, ESG: Dealing with sustainability risks in the company purchase agreement, November 2023, https://www.nortonrosefulbright.com/en-de/knowledge/publications/b6715168/esg-dealing-with-sustainability-risks-in-the-company-purchase-agreement, accessed 25.06.2025.

OECD, Asia Capital Markets Report 2025, 2025, https://www.oecd.org/en/publications/asia-capital-markets-report-2025_02172cdc-en/full-report/sustainable-bonds_21e9a353.html, accessed 06.09.2025.

OECD, Effective Results Frameworks for Sustainable Development, https://www.oecd.org/en/publications/effective-results-frameworks-for-sustainable-development_aaa4bb52-en.html, accessed 10.08.2025.

OECD, Finance and investment, https://www.oecd.org/en/topics/finance-and-investment.html, accessed 13.09.2025.

OECD, Global Outlook on Financing for Sustainable Development 2025: Towards a More Resilient and Inclusive Architecture, 2025, https://doi.org/10.1787/753d5368-en, accessed 22.07.2025.

OECD, Massive investment is needed in sustainable infrastructure to build climate change resilience, 2024, https://www.oecd.org/en/about/news/press-releases/2024/04/massive-investment-is-needed-in-sustainable-infrastructure-to-build-climate-change-resilience.html, accessed 30.07.2025.

OECD, Members and partners, https://www.oecd.org/en/about/members-partners.html, accessed 13.09.2025.

OECD, OECD Guidelines for Multinational Enterprises on Responsible Business Conduct, 2023, https://www.oecd.org/en/publications/oecd-guidelines-for-multinational-enterprises-on-responsible-business-conduct_81f92357-en.html, accessed 30.08.2025, 33, 35.

OECD, Responsible Business Conduct, https://www.oecd.org/en/topics/responsible-business-conduct.html, accessed 12.09.2025.

OECD, Social Impact Investment 2019, 2019, https://www.oecd.org/en/publications/social-impact-investment-2019_9789264311299-en, html, accessed 13.09.2025.

OECD, Social Impact Investment 2019: The Impact Imperative for Sustainable Development, 2019, https://doi.org/10.1787/9789264311299-en, accessed 22.07.2025.

OECD, Social Impact Investment: Building the Evidence Base, 2015, http://dx.doi.org/10.1787/9789264233430-en, accessed 22.07.2025.

OECD, Strengthening Sustainable Investment through International Investment Agreements, 2024, https://www.oecd.org/content/dam/oecd/en/publications/reports/2024/10/strengthening-sustainable-investment-through-international-investment-agreements_b8772cb7/a8729c98-en.pdf, accessed 24.07.2025.

OECD/UNDP, OECD – UNDP Impact Standards for Financing Sustainable Development, 2021, https://doi.org/10.1787/744f982e-en, accessed 22.07.2025.

OECD/UNDP, OECD UNDP Impact Standards for Financing Sustainable Development: Implementation Guidance Note for Standard 1 – Impact Strategy (Unclassified), 11.01.2023, https://one.oecd.org/document/DCD(2022)39/en/pdf, accessed 22.07.2025.

Glance in Latin America and the Caribbean: Spotlight on Climate Change, https://www.oecd.org/content/dam/oecd/en/publications/reports/2023/07/environment-at-a-glance-in-latin-america-and-the-caribbean_97fe557f/2431bd6c-en.pdf, accessed 31.07.2025.

Organisation for Economic Co-operation and Development (OECD), Recommendation of the Council on Artificial Intelligence, OECD/LEGAL/0449 https://legalinstruments.oecd.org/en/instruments/OECD-LEGAL-0449#adherents, accessed 30.07.2025.

Organisation for Economic Co-operation and Development. OECD Guidelines and Corporate Social Responsibility in a Global Economy. Paris: OECD, 2001.

OVAM, Brownfieldconvenant, https://www.vlaio.be/nl/subsidies-financiering/brownfieldconvenant/, accessed 31.08.2025.

Oxford Economics, Economic Outlook 2025: Key Themes & Insights, 2025, https://www.oxfordeconomics.com/key-themes-2025/, accessed 30.07.2025.

Ozimek/Signus, BlackRock steigt aus Klimapakt der Vereinten Nationen aus, Epoch Times, https://www.epochtimes.de/wirtschaft/munich-re-kehrt-esg-in…pr7DECBhhzGdKezz7FssFYPdlr4maBhB7CFDdQXTQviC0MIExHFnw%3D%3D, accessed 11.01.2025.

PCAF/GRESB/CRREM, Accounting and reporting of GHG emissions from real estate operations: Technical guidance for the financial industry (Version 1.0), 2023, https://crrem.org/wp-content/uploads/2025/05/PCAF-GRESB-CRREM-GHG_emissions_real_estate_guidance_1.0.pdf, accessed 26.06.2025.

Penang Green Council, PENANG GREEN AGENDA 2030, 2020, https://www.pgc.com.my/2020/wp-content/uploads/2020/09/6_PGA-Sectoral-Formatted-Final-Report_GBT.pdf, accessed 06.09.2025.

Pezzei, Kristina, Katherina Reiche will Mittel für energetische Sanierung drastisch kürzen, Immobilienzeitung, https://www.iz.de/politik/news/-katherina-reiche-will-mittel-fuer-energetische-sanierung-drastisch-kuerzen-2000036348?utm_source=%2Fmeta%2Fnewsletter%2Fizaktuell&utm_medium=newsletter&utm_campaign=nl2510-abonnent&utm_term=eff3e668ceccb7eab6eda8876c3063a2, accessed 30.08.2025.

Philippines Urban Population, 2023, https://www.macrotrends.net/global-metrics/countries/phl/philippines/urban-population, accessed 30.07.2025.

Policy Department for Citizens' Rights and Constitutional Affairs, Liability in Subcontracting Chains: National Rules and the Need for a European Framework, https://www.europarl.europa.eu/RegData/etudes/STUD/2017/596798/IPOL_STU(2017)596798_EN.pdf, accessed 19.08.2025, 19.

Pollack, Gerald, The fourth phase of water, Compendium Volume 2 Number 2, January 2019, https://bio4climate.org/article/water-isnt-what-you-think-it-is-the-fourth-phase-of-water-by-gerald-pollack/, accessed 24.06.2025.

Pollman, Elizabeth, The Making and Meaning of ESG, Harvard Business Law Review 14, 2024, https://ssrn.com/abstract=4219857, accessed 14.09.2025, 404–453.

Popescu/Dissanayake/Mansi/Stancu, Eco Breakthroughs: Sustainable Materials Transforming the Future of Our Planet, in: Sustainability 16 23, 10790, https://www.mdpi.com/2071-1050/16/23/10790, accessed 25.05.2025.

PR Newswire, CapitaLand Investment advances Sustainability leadership in 2024 by progressing toward decarbonisation milestones and recognition in leading global indexes, https://en.prnasia.com/releases/apac/capitaland-investment-advances-sustainability-leadership-in-2024-by-progressing-toward-decarbonisation-milestones-and-recognition-in-leading-global-indexes-474468.shtml, accessed 06.09.2025.

PRI, Investment Manager Appointment Guide: ESG Clauses, 2020, https://dwtyzx6upklss.cloudfront.net/Uploads/l/i/j/pri_assetownertechnicalguide_appointment_clauses_428793.pdf, accessed 15.08.2024.

PRI, Principles for Responsible Investment, 2022, https://www.unpri.org/about-us/what-are-the-principles-for-responsible-investment, accessed 27.07.2025

PRI, Selecting, appointing and monitoring investment managers, 2021, https://www.unpri.org/introductory-guides-to-responsible-investment/an-introduction-to-responsible-investment-selecting-appointing-and-monitoring-investment-managers/7093.article#:~:text=asset%20owner%20guide-,Appointment,engagement%20practices%20and%20human%20rights, accessed 14.09.2025.

PRI, UNEP Finance Initiative, and The Generation Foundation, Fiduciary Duty in the 21st Century: Final Report, 2019.

PRI, What is responsible investment?, https://www.unpri.org/introductory-guides-to-responsible-investment/what-is-responsible-investment/4780.article, accessed 03.05.2025.

Prologis, Inc, Prologis Commits to Net Zero Emissions by 2040, 2022, https://www.prologis.fr/en/insights/press-releases/prologis-commits-net-zero-emissions-2040, accessed 29.07.2025.

Protected Planet, data on protected areas in Latin America and the Caribbean, https://www.protectedplanet.net/region/SA, accessed 28.07.2025.

Prudential Regulation Authority and Bank of England, The impact of climate change on the UK insurance sector, 2015.

Public Procurement Data Space. Indicator 5 Award criteria based on price alone, https://api.public-procurement-data-space.europa.eu/superset/dashboard/smsindicator5/?standalone=true, accessed 01.09.2025.

PWC, A global thought leadership report on nature-positive strategies for the built environment, June 2025, https://www.pwc.de/en/real-estate/pwc-study-real-estate-and-biodiversity-a-critical-nexus.pdf, accessed 29.06.202.

PwC, The global outlook for 2025 – Emerging Trends in Real Estate, 2025, https://www.pwc.com/gx/en/industries/financial-services/real-estate/emerging-trends-real-estate/etre-global-outlook.html, accessed 30.07.2025.

Quellen zur Geschichte der Menschenrechte, The Sullivan Principles, https://www.geschichte-menschenrechte.de/fileadmin/editorial/download/Sullivan_Principles.pdf, accessed 13.09.2025.

Real Estate Agency Council (REAC), Regulating the Ghana Real Estate Agency Sector, 2025, https://reac.gov.gh/, accessed 28.07.2025.

Realfin State of the Market Report Global Real Estate H1 2025, 2025, https://www.withintelligence.com/insights/realfin-state-of-the-market-report-global-real-estate-h1-2025/, accessed 03.11.2025.

Redvers/Aubrey/Celidwen/Hill, Indigenous Peoples: Traditional knowledges, climate change, and health, 2023, https://pmc.ncbi.nlm.nih.gov/articles/PMC10575522/, accessed 11.09.2025.

Republic of Kenya, 2010, The Constitution of Kenya, 2010. Parliament of Kenya, https://parliament.go.ke/sites/default/files/2025-04/The_Constitution_of_Kenya_2010.pdf, accessed 18.07.2025.

Resolution Law Firm, Overview of the Laws Regulating Real Estate in Nigeria, 2023, https://www.resolutionlawng.com/overview-of-the-laws-regulating-real-estate-in-nigeria/, accessed 28.07.2025.

Resolution No. 1017/2023, Federal Council of Accounting (CFC), 2023, https://www.in.gov.br/en/web/dou/-/resolucao-cfc-n-1.710-de-25-de-outubro-de-2023-520669405, accessed 23.06.2025.

Resolution No. 139/2021, Brazilian Central Bank (BCB), 2021, https://www.bcb.gov.br/estabilidadefinanceira/exibenormativo?tipo=Resolu%C3%A7%C3%A3o%20BCB&numero=139, accessed 23.06.2025.

Resolution on general provisions applicable to securities issuers and other securities market participants, the National Banking and Securities Commission, https://www.cnbv.gob.mx/Normatividad/Disposiciones%20de%20car%C3%A1cter%20general%20aplicables%20a%20las%20emisoras%20de%20valores.pdf, accessed 30.07.2025.

Reuters, International, domestic insurers push into catastrophe-hit US property markets, 2024, https://www.reuters.com/markets/us/international-domestic-insurers-push-into-catastrophe-hit-us-property-markets-2024-12-16; accessed 30.07.2025.

Reuters, Red Sea insurance soars after deadly Houthi ship attacks, 2025, https://www.reuters.com/business/autos-transportation/red-sea-insurance-soars-after-deadly-houthi-ship-attacks-2025-07-10; accessed 30.07.2025.

Reuters, SingTel secures $476 million green loan to develop data centre, 2025, https://www.reuters.com/sustainability/sustainable-finance-reporting/singtel-secures-476-million-green-loan-develop-data-centre-2025-02-06/; accessed 06.09.2025.

Reuters, World military spending hits $2.7 trillion in record 2024 surge, 2025, https://www.reuters.com/business/aerospace-defense/world-military-spending-hits-27-trillion-record-2024-surge-2025-04-27; accessed 30.07.2025.

RICS Professional Statement: ESG in Real Estate. RICS, Professional Statement: ESG in Real Estate, Royal Institution of Chartered Surveyors, 2022.

Ritchie, Hannah, Are We the Last Generation, or the First Sustainable One, TED, YouTube, https://www.youtube.com/watch?v=Kl3VVrggKz4; accessed 16.08.2025.

Roeder/Werthmüller/Schlutz/Havlik, Compliance (due diligence) in the context of transactions – ESG due diligence, CCZ 2024, 13;

Ruff, Jon, Commercial Real Estate: New paradigm or old story, Bernstein Journal: Perspectives on investing and wealth management, 2005, 34.

Ruggie, John Gerard, The United Nations and Globalization: Patterns and Limits of Institutional Adaptation, Global Governance 9, no. 3, 2003, https://www.jstor.org/stable/27800413, accessed 14.09.2025, 301.

Ruhlin, Doug, What is ISO 14046 Water Footprint Evaluation?, 08.07.2025, https://www.rmagreen.com/rma-blog/bid/91696/what-is-iso-14046-water-footprint-evaluation, accessed 08.09.2025.

S&P Global, Green bond issuance by US REITs picks up in 2024, 2025, https://www.spglobal.com/market-intelligence/en/news-insights/articles/2025/1/green-bond-issuance-by-us-reits-picks-up-in-2024-87195777, accessed 30.07.2025.

Sandberg, Nina Holck, et al. Large potentials for energy saving and greenhouse gas emission reductions from large-scale deployment of zero emission building technologies in a national building stock, 2021.

Sarmento/Herman, Global Handbook of Impact Investing. Solving Global Problems via Smarter Captial Markets Towards a More Sustainable Society, 2021. Eurostat, Population structure and ageing, 2025, https://ec.europa.eu/eurostat/statistics-explained/index.php/Population_structure_and_ageing, accessed 30.07.2025.

Savills, 2025 Global Investment Outlook, 2025, https://impacts.savills.com/market-trends/2025-investment-outlook.html, accessed 08.09.2025.

Savills, Selling the world, 2016, https://www.savills.com/research_articles/255800/198698-0, accessed 06.08.2025.

Schoop/Ballo, in: Volk/Beukelmann, Munich Lawyers' Handbook: Defence in Commercial and Tax Criminal Matters, 3rd edition 2020, section 20 corruption.

Science Based Targets Initiative, Buildings, https://sciencebasedtargets.org/sectors/buildings, accessed 06.09.2025.

Science Based Targets Initiative, Near-term Criteria and Recommendations, 2022, https://sciencebasedtargets.org/blog/explained-minor-revisions-resources, accessed 30.08.2025.

SEC, Proposed Rule: Enhancement and Standardization of Climate-Related Disclosures for Investors, 2022.

Securities and Exchange Commission Ghana, 2020, Ghana Capital Market Master Plan. Accra: SEC, https://sec.gov.gh/wp-content/uploads/Press-Release/SEC_CMMP.pdf, accessed 28.07.2025.

Securities and Exchange Commission Ghana, Securities Industry (Green Bond) Guidelines 2024, 2024, https://sec.gov.gh/wp-content/uploads/Final-Regulatory-Laws/Guidelines/Green_Bond_Guidelines_2024.pdf, accessed 28.07.2025.

See Verdigris Case Study, https://www.verdigris.co/case-studies/jabil-video-case-study, accessed 30.07.2025.

Seyawati/Lolla, Regional grids key to Singapore's energy future, 2024, https://ember-energy.org/latest-insights/regional-grids-key-to-singapores-energy-future/, accessed 06.09.2024.

Shaw, Malcolm, International law, in: Brittanica, https://www.britannica.com/topic/international-law, accessed 07.06.2025; UN, International Law and Justice, https://www.un.org/en/global-issues/international-law-and-justice, accessed 07.06.2025.

Singapore Exchange, iEdge-UOB APAC Yield Focus Green REIT Index [SGD] (NTR), https://www.sgx.com/indices/products/agreitsn, accessed 06.09.2025.

Singapore Statutes Online, Building Control Act, 2008, https://sso.agc.gov.sg/SL/BCA1989-S199-2008, accessed 06.09.2025.

Soares, Kristen, Webinar Recap: Anti-ESG Legislation – Why It Matters and What States Can Do, 2023, https://climate-xchange.org/2023/07/anti-esg-legislation-why-it-matters-and-what-states-can-d/, accessed 03.11.2025.

SOMO and CCC, Fatal Fashion – Analysis of recent factory fires in Pakistan and Bangladesh: a call to protect and respect garment workers' lives, https://www.somo.nl/fatal-fashion-2/, accessed 10.08.2025.

SOMO, Fact Sheet, Hidden subcontracting in the garment industry, Zooming in on the role of buying companies, https://www.somo.nl/wp-content/uploads/2015/09/Hidden-subcontracting.pdf, accessed 20.08.2025, 3.

South African Real Estate Investment Trust, Association, (SA REITs) 2025, 2025, https://sareit.co.za/, accessed 28.07.2025.

South Centre, Assessing Five Years of the AfCFTA: Recalibrating the Path to Africa's Economic Transformation. South Centre Research Paper 215, 2025, https://www.southcentre.int/wp-content/uploads/2025/01/RP215_Assessing-Five-Years-of-the-AfCFTA_EN.pdf, accessed 23.07.2025.

Southeast Asia Development Solutions (SEADS), Data Centers and the Sustainability Challenge, 2025, https://seads.adb.org/articles/data-centers-and-sustainability-challenge, accessed 06.09.2025.

Southern African Legal Information Institute, 2025, https://www.saflii.org/, accessed 23.07.2025.

Spießhofer, § 5 Corporate Social Responsibility – neue Formen normativer Steuerung im globalen Ordnungsrahmen, in: Burgi/Habersack, Handbuch Öffentliches Recht des Unternehmens, 1. Auflage 2023.

Spießhofer, Birgit, Corporate Political Responsibility – Handel nur mit Freunden, IWRZ 2024, 259.

Spießhofer, Birgit, Sustainable Corporate Governance, NZG 2022, 435.

Spring/Mathur, EPA moves to end climate regulation under Clean Air Act, Washington Post, 29.07.2025, https://www.washingtonpost.com/climate-environment/2025/07/29/epa-endangerment-finding-clean-air-act/?utm_source=alert&utm_medium=email&utm_campaign=wp_news_alert_revere&location=alert, accessed 29.07.2025.

Srivastava, Vinamra, CLI Sustainability Strategy – The Way Forward, 2024, https://ir.capitalandinvest.com/newsroom/20241028_063535_9CI_3IXKOP9RIAK67EIA.1.pdf, accessed 06.09.2025.

Standard Bank of South Africa, The South African real estate sector defies trends to reflect greenshoots, 2025, https://corporateandinvestment.standardbank.com/cib/global/insights/the-south-african-real-estate-sector-defies-trends-to-reflect-greenshoots, accessed 28.07.2025.

Staniszewski/Wieduwilt, Property Development, in: Wieduwilt, Sabine, Implementing ESG into Real Estate Contracts. A guide and toolkit for practitioners from a European perspective, 2025.

Starasia, Green Finance Framework, https://starasia-reit.com/en/esg/greenfinance.html, accessed 06.09.2025.

Statista, USA: Militärausgaben von 2008 bis 2024, 2025, https://de.statista.com/statistik/daten/studie/183059/umfrage/militaerausgaben-der-usa/, accessed 30.07.2025.

Steinmüller, Thomas, ESG is out, GSE is in, May 2025, https://www.linkedin.com/feed/update/urn:li:activity:7331911204061200384/, accessed 31.05.2025.

Sustainable Taxonomy, The Ministry of Finance and Public Credit of Mexico, 2023, https://www.finanzassostenibles.hacienda.gob.mx/work/models/finanzassostenibles/recursos/documentos/TaxonomyEV_2024_V1.pdf, accessed 30.07.2025.

Swire Properties, Green Performance Pledge, https://sd.swireproperties.com/2024/en/partners/tenants/environment, accessed 06.09.2025.

Swiss Federal Department of Foreign Affairs/United Nations, Who Cares Wins. Connecting Financial Markets to a Changing World, https://documents1.worldbank.org/curated/en/280911488968799581/pdf/113237-WP-WhoCaresWins-2004.pdf, accessed 07.09.2025

Swiss Re Institute, Changing climates: the heat is (still) on, 2024, 2.

Swiss Re Institute, The economics of climate change: no action not an option, 2021, 26.

Tardi, Carla, Leaseback (or Sale-Leaseback): Definition, Benefits, and Examples, https://www.investopedia.com/terms/l/leaseback.asp, accessed 19.06.2024.

Task Force on Climate-related Financial Disclosures (TCFD), https://www.fsb-tcfd.org/, accessed 06.09.2025.

TCFD, Guidance on Climate-Related Legal Risks for Companies, Directors, and Investors, Task Force on Climate-Related Financial Disclosures, 2021, https://www.tcfdhub.org, accessed 27.07.2025.

TCLP, Sam's Clause, Net Zero Land Development, https://chancerylaneproject.org/clauses/net-zero-land-development/, accessed 22.06.2025.

TCLP, Zack's Clause, SPA/Investment Agreement: Disclosure of Climate Change Plans, https://chancerylaneproject.org/clauses/spa-investment-agreement-disclosure-of-climate-change-plans/, accessed 22.06.2025.

The Chancery Lane Project (TCLP), 2025, https://chancerylaneproject.org/clauses/, accessed 02.11.2025.

The Chancery Lane Project (TCLP), Matteo's Clause, Climate and Nature Impact Investing Terms, https://chancerylaneproject.org/clauses/climate-and-nature-impact-investing-terms/, accessed 22.06.2025.

The Convention on Biological Diversity, Ad Hoc Open-ended Working Group on Benefit-sharing from the Use of Digital Sequence Information (DSI) on Genetic Resources, 2024, https://www.cbd.int/conferences/wgdsi-2, accessed 10.08.2024.

The Economic Times, Healthy inflows into India to continue in 2025, 2025, https://economictimes.indiatimes.com/markets/stocks/news/inflows-into-india-to-continue-in-2025/articleshow/116649887.cms, accessed 30.07.2025.

The Economist, Measure Less, But Better, 21.07.2022, https://www.economist.com/special-report/2022/07/21/measure-less-but-better, accessed 14.09.2024.

The Global Impact Investing Network (GIIN), Impact Investing: A guide to this dynamic market, 2025, https://thegiin.org/publication/post/about-impact-investing/#what-is-impact-investing, accessed 22.07.2025.

The Government of Japan, Carbon-Negative Concrete: A Game Changer for a Sustainable Future, https://www.japan.go.jp/kizuna/2022/08/carbon-negative_concrete.html, accessed 06.09.2025.

The Guardian, UK and Australia sign Aukus treaty to build nuclear submarines as Lammy downplays US doubts, 2025, https://www.theguardian.com/australia-news/2025/jul/26/uk-and-australia-sign-aukus-treaty-to-build-nuclear-submarines-as-lammy-downplays-us-doubts, accessed 30.07.2025.

The Intergovernmental Panel on Climate Change, https://www.ipcc.ch/, accessed 14.08.2025.

The International Financial Reporting Standards Foundation, General Sustainability-related Disclosures, IFRS, 2023, https://www.ifrs.org/projects/completed-projects/2023/general-sustainability-related-disclosures/#final-stage, accessed 31.08.2025.

The Law Society of Singapore, ESG Resource Library, https://www.lawsociety.org.sg/esg-hub/esg-resource-library/, accessed 14.09.2025.

The Net Zero Asset Managers initiative, 2025, https://www.netzeroassetmanagers.org/, accessed 31.08.2025.

The Origin of »Limits to Growth« – Interview with Dennis Meadows, YouTube, 14.07.2016, https://www.youtube.com/watch?v=U7Z6h-U4CmI, accessed 12.09.2025.

The Rockefeller Foundation, Global Impact Investing Network (GIIN), https://www.rockefellerfoundation.org/bellagio-bulletin/from-the-archives/global-impact-investing-network-giin/, accessed 22.07.2025.

The Straits Times, CapitaLand Investment pushes ahead with disclosures from suppliers, more green leases, 2024, https://www.straitstimes.com/business/capitaland-investment-pushes-ahead-with-disclosures-from-suppliers-more-green-leases, accessed 06.09.2025.

The Wall Street Journal, Bracing for Tariffs, Logistics Operators Stand by Their Border Investments, 2025, https://www.wsj.com/articles/bracing-for-tariffs-logistics-operators-stand-by-their-border-investments-3b1b1054, accessed 30.07.2025.

The World Bank, Indigenous Latin America in the Twenty-First Century, 2015, https://documents1.worldbank.org/curated/en/145891467991974540/pdf/Indigenous-Latin-America-in-the-twenty-first-century-the-first-decade.pdf, accessed 28.07.2025.

Thérien/Pouliot, The Global Compact: Shifting the Politics of International Development?, Global Governance 12, no. 1, 2006, https://www.jstor.org/stable/27800613, accessed 14.09.2025, 55.

Thoms, Anahita in: Moosmayer/Lösler, Corporate Compliance, § 17. ESG – Legal and Regulatory Foundations, margin note 26.

Thürer, Daniel, Soft Law, in: Oxford Public International Law, 2009, https://opil.ouplaw.com/display/10.1093/law:epil/9780199231690/law-9780199231690-e1469, accessed 07.06.2025.

thwink.org, Finding and Resolving the Root Causes of the Sustainability Problem, The Malthusian Trap, https://www.thwink.org/sustain/glossary/MalthusianTrap.htm, accessed 11.09.2025.

Trading Economics, Indonesia – Urban Population Growth in %, 2024, https://tradingeconomics.com/indonesia/urban-population-growth-annual-percent-wb-data.html, accessed 14.09.2025.

Triplepundit, A new lease of life for sustainability, https://triplepundit.com/2015/new-lease-life-sustainability/, accessed 06.09.2025.

Tschammler, Timo, in: Schäfer/Conzen, Praxishandbuch Immobilieninvestition, 4. Ed., 2020.

Tunde & Adisa Legal Practitioners, Navigating ESG compliance in Nigeria: How Nigerian entities can leverage ESG compliance for competitive advantage, 2025, https://tundeadisa.com/media_insights/navigating-esg-compliance-in-nigeria-how-nigerian-entities-can-leverage-esg-compliance-for-competitive-advantage/, accessed 28.07.2025.

U.S. Securities and Exchange Commission, SEC Adopts Rules to Enhance and Standardize Climate-Related Disclosures for Investors, https://www.sec.gov/newsroom/press-releases/2024-31, accessed 02.07.2025.

UN Climate Change, Chronological Overview of Key Climate Conferences and Agreements: UNFCCC, Past conferences overview, https://unfccc.int/process-and-meetings/conferences/past-conferences/past-conferences-overview, accessed 21.04.2025.

UN documents on Climate Change:, Decisions, https://unfccc.int/decisions?gad_source=1&gclid=EAIaIQobChMIjafvzLDHhwMVFKKDBx2ANANpEAAYASABEgLn1_D_BwE, accessed 27.07.2024.

UN Environment Program, Investment Leadership Programme, https://www.unepfi.org/investment/investment/, accessed 13.09.2025.

UN Environment Programme, Global Status Report for Buildings and Construction, https://wedocs.unep.org/bitstream/handle/20.500.11822/45095/global_status_report_buildings_construction_2023.pdf, accessed 14.08.2025, 17.

UN PRI, Fiduciary Duty in the 21st Century, https://www.unepfi.org/investment/history/fiduciary-duty/, accessed 03.05.2025.

UN PRI, INREV, Urban Land Institute, Mapping ESG: A landscape review of certifications, reporting frameworks and practices, 2023, https://www.unpri.org/real-estate/mapping-esg-a-landscape-review-of-certifications-reporting-frameworks-and-practices/11348.article, accessed 06.09.2025.

UN PRI, Policy reports, https://www.unpri.org/policy/policy-reports, accessed 06.09.2025.

UN, OHCR, Complaints about human rights violations, Treaty Bodies, https://www.ohchr.org/en/treaty-bodies/complaints-about-human-rights-violations, accessed 21.04.2025.

UN, OHCR, International Human Rights Law, https://www.ohchr.org/en/instruments-and-mechanisms/international-human-rights-law, accessed 21.04.2025.

UN, OHCR, The Core International Human Rights Instruments and their monitoring bodies, https://www.ohchr.org/en/core-international-human-rights-instruments-and-their-monitoring-bodies, accessed 08.06.2025.

UN, OHCR, Understanding international agreements, 2024, https://www.unep.org/news-and-stories/video/understanding-international-agreements, accessed 21.04.2025.

UN, OHCR, What are human rights, https://www.ohchr.org/en/what-are-human-rights, accessed 21.04.2025.

UN, Statute of the International Court of Justice, https://www.un.org/en/about-us/un-charter/statute-of-the-international-court-of-justice, accessed 01.06.2025.

UN, Vienna Convention on the Law of Treaties, 1969, https://legal.un.org/ilc/texts/instruments/english/conventions/1_1_1969.pdf, accessed 13.09.2025.

UNCED, Agenda 21: Program of Action for Sustainable Development, 1992, https://sustainabledevelopment.un.org/outcomedocuments/agenda21, accessed 03.08.2025.

UNCTAD, International Investment Agreements Navigator, Trade and Development, https://investmentpolicy.unctad.org/international-investment-agreements, accessed 30.08.2025.

UNDRR, Reducing risk and building resilience to SMEs to disasters, https://www.undrr.org/publication/reducing-risk-and-building-resilience-smes-disasters, accessed 14.09.2025.

UNEP FI, A legal framework for the integration of environmental, social and governance issues into institutional investment, 2005, https://www.unepfi.org/wordpress/wp-content/uploads/2022/07/Freshfields-A-legal-framework-for-the-integration-of-ESG-issues-into-institutional-investment.pdf, accessed 24.07.2025.

UNEP FI, UNEP FI, PRI and Climate Bonds Initiative join forces to support taxonomy efforts around the world, 2024, https://www.unepfi.org/news/unep-fi-pri-and-climate-bonds-initiative-join-forces-to-support-taxonomy-efforts-around-the-world/, accessed 06.09.2025.

UNEP FI, UNPRI, Updated position paper on Governmental Carbon Pricing, 2024, https://www.unepfi.org/industries/net-zero-asset-owner-alliances-updated-position-on-governmental-carbon-pricing/, accessed 06.09.2025.

UNEP, Secretariats and Conventions (MEAs), https://www.unep.org/about-un-environment/why-does-un-environment-matter/secretariats-and-conventions#global, accessed 08.06.2025.

UNEP-WCMC, Brownfield Sites: Achieving net gain through their biodiversity potential, 2021, https://www.proteuspartners.org/content//uploads/2021/09/Proteus-Technical-Brief-Brownfield-Sites.pdf, accessed 13.09.2025.

UNFCC, Documents and decisions, https://unfccc.int/decisions?gad_source=1&gclid=EAIaIQobChMIjafvzLDHhwMVFKKDBx2ANANpEAAYASABEgLn1_D_BwE, accessed 08.06.2025.

UNFCCC, What are United Nations Climate Change Conferences?, https://unfccc.int/process-and-meetings/what-are-united-nations-climate-change-conferences, accessed 21.04.2025.

UNGPs, Commentary to Principle 17, https://www.ohchr.org/sites/default/files/documents/publications/guidingprinciplesbusinesshr_en.pdf, accessed 20.08.2025.

United Nations Academic Impact (UNAI), Sustainability, https://www.un.org/en/academic-impact/sustainability, accessed 29.07.2025.

United Nations Environment Program Finance Initiative (ed)/UNEP FI Property Working Group in collaboration with RICS Global Investor Coalition on Climate Change and PRI, Positive Impact Real Estate Investment Framework. A tool for holistic impact analysis. Principles for Positive Impact Finance Implementation Guidance, November 2018, https://www.unepfi.org/wordpress/wp-content/uploads/2018/11/Positive-Impact-Initiative_Real-Estate-Investment-Framework_Nov-2018.pdf, accessed 20.07.2025.

United Nations Environment Programme Finance Initiative (UNEP FI), Asset Management Working Group (AMWG), Freshfields Bruckhaus Deringer, Fiduciary Responsibilities and Responsible Investment Practices, 2005.

United Nations Global Compact, Our Mission, https://www.unglobalcompact.org/what-is-gc/mission, accessed 14.09.2025.

United Nations Office for Disaster Risk Reduction (UNDRR), Reducing Risk & Building Resilience of SMEs to Disasters, 2020, https://www.undrr.org/media/48692/download?startDownload=20250908, accessed 08.09.2025.

United Nations Principles for Responsible Investment (UN PRI), https://www.unpri.org/, accessed 06.09.2025.

United Nations Treaty Collection, VCLT, https://treaties.un.org/pages/ViewDetailsIII.aspx?src=TREATY&mtdsg_no=XXIII-1&chapter=23&Temp=mtdsg3&clang=_en, accessed 01.06.2025.

United Nations, Climate Action, The Paris Agreement, https://www.un.org/en/climatechange/paris-agreement, accessed 03.08.2025.

United Nations, Conferences, Environment and Sustainable Development, United Nations Conference on the Human Environment, 5–16 June 1972, Stockholm, https://www.un.org/en/conferences/environment/stockholm1972, accessed 03.08.2025.

United Nations, Inter-agency Task Force on Financing for Development, Financing for Sustainable Development Report 2023: Financing Sustainable Transformations, New York: United Nations, 2023, 72, https://developmentfinance.un.org/fsdr2023, accessed 22.07.2025.

United Nations, Millenium Development Goals and Beyond 2015, https://www.un.org/millenniumgoals/bkgd.shtml, accessed 03.08.2025.

United Nations, Report of the World Commission on Environment and Development: Our Common Future, 1987.

United Nations, Transforming our world: the 2030 Agenda for Sustainable Development, https://sdgs.un.org/2030agenda, accessed 12.09.2025;

United Nations, UN Sustainable Development Goals, https://www.un.org/sustainabledevelopment/, accessed 29.07.2025.

United Nations, World Population Prospects 2024, 2024.

United States Census Bureau, Sun Belt Cities and Towns Led Nation in Population Growth, 2024. https://www.census.gov/library/stories/2024/05/sun-belt-cities-and-towns.html, accessed 30.07.2025.

United States Census Bureau, Sun Belt Cities and Towns Led Nation in Population Growth, 2024, https://www.census.gov/library/stories/2024/05/sun-belt-cities-and-towns.html, accessed 30.07.2025.

Università di Macerata, What is Sustainability?, https://www.unimc.it/farminc/en/mod4/unit4.html, accessed 11.09.2025;

UNPRI, Introductory Guides to Responsible Investment, https://www.unpri.org/introductory-guides-to-responsible-investment/an-introduction-to-responsible-investment-real-estate/5628.article, accessed 29.07.2025.

Varadhan, Sudarshan, Google to invest $6 billion in southern India data centre, sources say, https://www.reuters.com/sustainability/boards-policy-regulation/google-invest-6-billion-southern-india-data-centre-sources-say-2025-07-30/, accessed 06.09.2025.

Vienna Convention on the Law of Treaties, 1969, https://legal.un.org/ilc/texts/instruments/english/conventions/1_1_1969.pdf, accessed 07.06.2025, Art. 2(1)(a).

Volk/Beukelmann/Schoop/Ballo, section 20 corruption.

Volkmann, Frederike, Joint Venture – Gemeinsame Chancen, geteiltes Risiko?, BB 2023, 771.

WCW Future Proof? »Outcomes of the Who Cares Wins Initiative 2004–2008: Future Proof? Embedding Environmental, Social and Governance Issues in Investment Markets.« United Nations Global Compact, 2008, https://documents1.worldbank.org/curated/en/476811468158704493/pdf/476600WP0Futur10Box338858B01PUBLIC1.pdf, accessed 14.09.2025.

WELL Building Standard, https://standard.wellcertified.com/well, accessed 30.07.2025.

Werner, Reinhard, Munich Re kehrt ESG-Initiativen den Rücken – Rückzug aus vier Klimabündnissen, Epoch Times, https://www.epochtimes.de/wirtschaft/munich-re-kehrt-esg-in…pr7DECBhhzGdKezz7FssFYPdlr4maBhB7CFDdQXTQviC0MIExHFnw%3D%3D, accessed 13.06.2025.

Wettstein/Dey/Schaefers/Bahlmann, in: Feri Cognitive Finance Institute/Institut für Wirtschaftsethik Universität St. Gallen, Impact Investing: Konzept, Spannungsfelder und Zukunftsperspektiven. Eine Orientierung für private und institutionelle Investoren, 2019.

Wieduwilt, Sabine (ed.), Implementing ESG into Real Estate Contracts, A guide and toolkit for practitioners from a European perspective, 2025.

Wieduwilt, Sabine, in: ESG-Property Development – Legal Requirements to construction and planning contracts,» in: Veith/Conrads/Hackelberg, ESG and Real Estate, 2021 (English 2022).

Wieduwilt/Taghiyeva/Dalton/Danismant/Doherty and others, Green leases crossing borders – ESG and Real Estate – a European Perspective #2, 2024, https://www.dentons.com/en/insights/articles/2024/may/8/green-leases-crossing-borders-esg-and-real-estate-a-european-perspective, accessed 16.08.2025.

Wintermeyer, Lawrence, Time to Get Real On Real Estate Net Zero With Talent, Technology, And Tokenization,» https://www.forbes.com/sites/lawrencewintermeyer/2024/05/02/time-to-get-real-on-real-estate-net-zero-with-talent-technology-and-tokenization/, accessed 14.08.2025.

Wittneben, Mirko, Joint-Venture-Verträge in der Immobilien-Projektentwicklung, ZfIR 2009, 846.

Wolfram/Peukert, Impact of the ›new‹ Section 299 of the German Criminal Code (StGB) on compliance practice, NZWiSt 2017, 200.

Wolfrum, Rüdiger, Sources of International Law, Oxford Public International Law: Sources of International Law, May 2011, https://opil.ouplaw.com/display/10.1093/law:epil/9780199231690/law-9780199231690-e1471, accessed 07.06.2025.

World Bank Group, Population ages 65 and above (% of total population), 2025. https://data.worldbank.org/indicator/SP.POP.65UP.TO.ZS, accessed 30.07.2025.

World Bank Group, Public-Private Partnerships for Investment and Delivery of Affordable Housing in Emerging Market Economies, 2020, https://www.thegpsc.org/sites/default/files/public-private-partnerships-for-investment-and-delivery-of-affordable-housing-in-emerging-market-economies.pdf, accessed 03.11.2025.

World Bank Group, The management of brownfields redevelopment: a guidance note (English), 2008, https://documents.worldbank.org/en/publication/documents-reports/documentdetail/754171468295822120/the-management-of-brownfields-redevelopment-a-guidance-note, accessed 13.09.2025.

World Bank Group/Multilateral Investment Guarantee Agency (MIGA), Shifting Shores: FDI Relocations and Political Risk, 2024.

World Commission on Environment and Development (WCED), Our Common Future, 1987, https://sustainabledevelopment.un.org/content/documents/5987our-common-future.pdf, accessed 03.08.2025.

World Economic Forum, Africa is harnessing technology to leapfrog towards growth, 2025, https://www.weforum.org/stories/2025/07/africa-leapfrog-moment-harnessing-technology-green-growth-and-regional-integration-for-global-value-chains/, accessed 23.07.2025.

World Economic Forum, Global Economy: Tenuous Resilience amid Persistent Uncertainty, 2025, https://www.imf.org/en/Publications/WEO/Issues/2025/07/29/world-economic-outlook-update-july-2025, accessed 30.07.2025.

World Economic Forum, More than 1 in 10 people in Japan are aged 80 or over. Here's how its ageing population is reshaping the country, 2023, https://www.weforum.org/stories/2023/09/elderly-oldest-population-world-japan, accessed 30.07.2025.

World Economic Forum, This is the state of play in the global data centre gold rush, 2025, https://www.weforum.org/stories/2025/04/data-centre-gold-rush-ai/, accessed 06.09.2025.

World Green Building Council (WGBC), Global Directory of Green Building Councils, https://worldgbc.org/global-directory-of-green-building-councils/, accessed 06.09.2025.

World Green Building Council (WGBC), Global Policy Principles for a sustainable Built Environment, 12.04.2023, https://build-up.ec.europa.eu/sites/default/files/content/worldgbc-global-policy-principles_final.pdf, accessed 22.07.2025.

World Green Building Council (WGBC), Sustainable built environments & the UN's Sustainable Development Goals, https://worldgbc.org/sustainable-development-goals/, accessed 25.07.2025.

World Green Building Council, Beyond The Business Case – Why You Can't Afford Not To Invest in A Sustainable Built Environment, https://worldgbc.org/wp-content/uploads/2022/08/WorldGBC-Beyond-the-Business-Case.pdf, accessed 31.08.2025.

World Green Building Council, Bringing Embodied Carbon Upfront, https://worldgbc.s3.eu-west-2.amazonaws.com/wp-content/uploads/2022/09/22123951/WorldGBC_Bringing_Embodied_Carbon_Upfront.pdf, accessed 14.08.2025.

WTO, The Doha mandate on multilateral environmental agreements (MEAs), https://www.wto.org/english/tratop_e/envir_e/envir_neg_mea_e.htm, accessed 30.08.2025.

YTL Beyond, YTL Green Data Center Park launches in Johor, the First Integrated Data Center Park Powered by Renewable Solar Energy in Malysia, https://www.ytl.com/press-releases/ytl-green-data-center-park-launches-in-johor-the-first-integrated-data-center-park-powered-by-renewable-solar-energy-in-malaysia-2/, accessed 06.09.2025.

Zentraler Immobilienausschuss ZIA Ausschuss Büroimmobilien (ed.), ESG-Leitfaden für Büroimmobilien, January 2024, https://zia-deutschland.de/project/esg-leitfaden-fur-buroimmobilien/, accessed 20.07.2025.

Zhang/Nunez/English/Dehaene-Gold/Cazel/Garcia Lozano/Glickman, real estate investor, from: Realty Mogul, 20 Famous Real Estate Investing Quotes, https://www.realtymogul.com/knowledge-center/article/20-famous-real-estate-investing-quotes, accessed 10.08.2025.

Legal sources

Commission Delegated Regulation (EU) 2023/2772 of 31 July 2023 supplementing Directive 2013/34/EU of the European Parliament and of the Council as regards sustainability reporting standards, https://eur-lex.europa.eu/legal-content/en/TXT/?uri=CELEX:32023R2772, accessed 02.11.2025. European Commission (2025), A Competitiveness Compass for the EU, COM(2025) 30 final, https://eur-lex.europa.eu/legal-content/EN/TXT/?uri=celex:52025DC0030, accessed 01.09.2025.

Commission of the European Communities, Green Paper Promoting a European framework for Corporate Social Responsibility, 18.07.2001, https://eur-lex.europa.eu/LexUriServ/LexUriServ.do?uri=COM:2001:0366:FIN:en:PDF, accessed 06.09.2025.

Commission Staff Working Document, Evaluation of Directive 2014/23/EU on Concessions, Directive 2014/24/EU on Public Procurement and Directive 2014/25/EU on Utilities (SWD(2025) 333 final).

Communication from the Commission to the European Parliament, the European Council, the Council, the European Central Bank, the European Economic and Social Committee and the Committee of the Regions Action Plan: Financing Sustainable Growth, COM/2018/097 final, https://eur-lex.europa.eu/legal-content/EN/TXT/?uri=celex:52018DC0097, accessed 21.07.2025.

Communication from the Commission to the European Parliament, the European Council, the Council, the European Economic and Social Committee and the Committee of the Regions — The European Green Deal (EGD), 2019, https://eur-lex.europa.eu/legal-content/EN/TXT/?uri=celex%3A52019DC0640, accessed 06.09.2025.

Communication from the Commission to the European Parliament, the Council, the European Economic and Social Committee and the Committee of the Regions EU Soil Strategy, https://eur-lex.europa.eu/legal-content/DE/TXT/?uri=CELEX%3A52021DC0699, accessed 31.08.2025.

Communication from the Commission to the European Parliament, the European Council, the Council, the European Economic and Social Committee and the Committee of the Regions. A Competitiveness Compass for the EU, COM/2025/30 final, https://eur-lex.europa.eu/legal-content/EN/TXT/?uri=celex:52025DC0030, accessed 29.06.2025.

Communication from the Commission to the European Parliament, the European Council, the Council, the European Economic and Social Committee and the Committee of the Regions. A Competitiveness Compass for the EU, COM(2025) 30 final, IMMC.COM%282025%2930%20final.ENG.xhtml.1_EN_ACT_part1_v7.docx, accessed 21.07.2025.

Communication from the Commission to the European Parliament, the European Council, the European Economic and Social Committee and the Committee of Regions, A Competitiveness Compass for the EU COM/2025/30 final, https://eur-lex.europa.eu/legal-content/EN/TXT/?uri=celex:52025DC0030, accessed 02.11.2025.

Companies (Directors' Report) and Limited Liability Partnerships (Energy and Carbon Report) Regulations 2018/1155 https://www.legislation.gov.uk/uksi/2018/1155/contents/made, accessed 04.08.2025.

Corte Interamericana de Derechos Humanos, Sentencia de 16 de mayo de 2023 en el caso Comunidad Indígena Maya Q'eqchi' Agua Caliente vs. Guatemala, Fondo, Reparaciones y Costas, Serie C No. 488, párrs. I–VIII, 178–188.

Council of the EU, Revision to the Energy Performance of Buildings Directive (EPBD), 2024, https://www.consilium.europa.eu/en/press/press-releases/2022/10/25/fit-for-55-council-agrees-on-stricter-rules-for-energy-performance-of-buildings/, accessed 30.08.2025.

Council of the European Union, Public procurement – strategic goals and way forward. Discussion Paper, Brussels, 22.05.2025, https://data.consilium.europa.eu/doc/document/ST-8638-2025-INIT/en/pdf, accessed 02.09.2025.

Directive (EU) 2019/1161 on Clean and Energy-Efficient Road Transport Vehicles, https://eur-lex.europa.eu/eli/dir/2019/1161/oj/eng, accessed 01.09.2025.

Directive (EU) 2019/1161 on Clean and Energy-Efficient Road Transport Vehicles, https://eur-lex.europa.eu/eli/dir/2019/1161/oj/eng, accessed 01.09.2025.

Directive (EU) 2022/2464 of the European Parliament and of the Council of 14 December 2022 amending Regulation (EU) No 537/2014, Directive 2004/109/EC, Directive 2006/43/EC and Directive 2013/34/EU, as regards corporate sustainability reporting, https://eur-lex.europa.eu/eli/dir/2022/2464/oj/eng, accessed 02.11.2024.

Directive (EU) 2022/2555 of the European Parliament and of the Council of 14 December 2022 on measures for a high common level of cybersecurity across the Union, amending Regulation (EU) No 910/2014 and Directive (EU) 2018/1972, and repealing Directive (EU) 2016/1148 (NIS 2 Directive), https://eur-lex.europa.eu/eli/dir/2022/2555/oj/eng, accessed 30.07.2025.

Directive (EU) 2023/1791 on Energy Efficiency, https://eur-lex.europa.eu/eli/dir/2023/1791/oj/eng, accessed 01.09.2025.

Directive (EU) 2023/1791 on Energy Efficiency, https://eur-lex.europa.eu/eli/dir/2023/1791/oj/eng, accessed 01.09.2025.

Directive (EU) 2024/1275 on Energy Performance of Buildings, https://eur-lex.europa.eu/eli/dir/2024/1275/oj/eng, accessed 01.09.2025.

Directive (EU) 2024/1275 on Energy Performance of Buildings, https://eur-lex.europa.eu/eli/dir/2024/1275/oj/eng, accessed 01.09.2025.

Directive 2014/23/EU of the European Parliament and of the Council of 26 February 2014 on the award of concession contracts, https://eur-lex.europa.eu/eli/dir/2014/23/oj/eng, accessed 02.11.2025.

Directive 2014/24/EU of the European Parliament and of the Council of 26 February 2014 on public procurement and repealing Directive 2004/18/EC, https://eur-lex.europa.eu/eli/dir/2014/24/oj/eng, accessed 02.11.2025.

Directive 2014/25/EU of the European Parliament and of the Council of 26 February 2014 on procurement by entities operating in the water, energy, transport and postal services sectors and repealing Directive 2004/17/EC, https://eur-lex.europa.eu/eli/dir/2014/25/oj/eng, accessed 02.11.2025.

EC, Corporate sustainability and responsibility, https://single-market-economy.ec.europa.eu/industry/sustainability/corporate-sustainability-and-responsibility_en, accessed 03.08.2025.

EC, Newsletter 21 May 2025 Directorate-General for Financial Stability, Financial Services and Capital Markets Union, Sustainable Finance, https://finance.ec.europa.eu/news/sustainable-finance-2025-05-21_en, accessed 21.07.2025.

ECJ, judgment of 17.09.2002, Case C-513/99, Concordia Bus Finland Oy Ab v Helsingin kaupunki and HKL-Bussiliikenne [2002] ECR I-7213, para 69.

ECJ, judgment of 17.11.2015, C-346/06 Regio Post; ECJ, judgment of 03.04.2008, C-549/13 Rüffert.

ECJ, Judgment of 20.09.1988, Case 31/87, Gebroeders Beentjes BV v State of the Netherlands.

EP, Interactive timeline. A guide to climate change negotiations – infographic containing a timeline listing milestones and key initiatives in the global fight against climate change. EP, Interactive timeline. A guide to climate change negotiations, https://www.europarl.europa.eu/topics/en/article/20180404STO00910/infographic-timeline-of-climate-change-negotiations, accessed 21.04.2025.

EP, Women in peace building: why and how to increase their role, 2025, https://www.europarl.europa.eu/topics/en/article/20250227STO27080/women-in-peace-building-why-and-how-to-increase-their-role, accessed 21.04.2025.

European Commission, 2025 Commission work programme – annexes, 2025, https://commission.europa.eu/strategy-and-policy/strategy-documents/commission-work-programme/commission-work-programme-2025_en, accessed 30.07.2025, 26.

European Commission, A Competitiveness Compass for the EU, COM(2025) 30 final, https://eur-lex.europa.eu/legal-content/EN/TXT/?uri=celex:52025DC0030, accessed 01.09.2025.

European Commission, Carbon Border Adjustment Mechanism, https://taxation-customs.ec.europa.eu/carbon-border-adjustment-mechanism_en, accessed 30.07.2025.

European Commission, Corporate Sustainability Reporting Directive (CSRD), 2023, https://finance.ec.europa.eu/capital-markets-union-and-financial-markets/company-reporting-and-auditing/company-reporting/corporate-sustainability-reporting_en, accessed 30.08.2025.

European Commission, Directorate-General for Employment, Social Affairs & Inclusion Directorate D — Labour Mobility, Unit Unit D-1: Free movement of Workers and EURES, European Platform tackling undeclared work, Glossary of Terms, October 2018, https://www.ela.europa.eu/sites/default/files/2021-09/Glossary%20v6-final_0.pdf, accessed 20.08.2025, 5.

European Commission, Implementation and best practices of national procurement policies in the Internal Market, COM(2021) 245 final, https://eur-lex.europa.eu/legal-content/EN/TXT/?uri=celex:52021DC0245, accessed 01.09.2025.

European Commission, Nearly-zero energy and zero-emission buildings, 2025, https://energy.ec.europa.eu/topics/energy-efficiency/energy-performance-buildings/nearly-zero-energy-and-zero-emission-buildings_en, accessed 30.07.2025.

European Commission, Single market and competitiveness scoreboard, https://single-market-scoreboard.ec.europa.eu/business-framework-conditions/public-procurement_en, accessed 31.08.2025.

European Commission, Single market and competitiveness scoreboard, https://single-market-scoreboard.ec.europa.eu/business-framework-conditions/public-procurement_en, accessed 31.08.2025.

European Commission. Single market and competitiveness scoreboard, https://single-market-scoreboard.ec.europa.eu/business-framework-conditions/public-procurement_en, accessed 31.08.2025.

European Court of Auditors, Special report 28/2023: Public procurement in the EU – Less competition for contracts awarded for works, goods and services in the 10 years up to 2021, https://www.eca.europa.eu/en/publications/SR-2023-28, accessed 02.09.2025.

European Parliament, European defence industrial strategy, 2025, https://www.europarl.europa.eu/RegData/etudes/BRIE/2024/762402/EPRS_BRI%282024%29762402_EN.pdf, accessed 30.07.2025.

European Securities and Markets Authority (ESMA), Impact investing – Do SDG funds fulfil their promises?, European Securities and Markets Authority, 2024, https://data.europa.eu/doi/10.2856/444326, accessed 22.07.2025.

Hong Kong e-Legislation, Buildings Energy Efficiency Ordinance, https://www.elegislation.gov.hk/hk/cap610, accessed 06.09.2025.

Law 2169 of 2021 on minimum carbon neutrality and climate resilience targets and measures, 2021, http://www.secretariasenado.gov.co/senado/basedoc/ley_2169_2021.html, accessed 30.07.2025.

Law No. 12,187/2019 on Brazil's National Policy on Climate Change, https://www.planalto.gov.br/ccivil_03/_ato2007-2010/2009/lei/l12187.htm, accessed 23.06.2025.

Law No. 15,042/2024 on the Brazilian Emission Trading System, https://www.planalto.gov.br/ccivil_03/_ato2023-2026/2024/lei/L15042.htm, accessed 23.06.2025.

Law No. 21,455, Framework Law on Climate Change, https://bcn.cl/32l1s, accessed 27.07.2025.

Law No. 21,595 of 2023, Economic Crimes Law, https://bcn.cl/3enf9, accessed 27.07.2025.

Law No. 27,520/2019 on minimum budgets for adaptation and mitigation to global climate change, https://www.argentina.gob.ar/normativa/nacional/ley-27520-333515, accessed 01.08.2025.

Proposal for a Directive of the European Parliament and of the Council on combating corruption, replacing Council Framework Decision 2003/568/JHA and the Convention on the fight against corruption involving officials of the European Communities or officials of Member States of the European Union and amending Directive (EU) 2017/1371 of the European Parliament and of the Council (Anti-Corruption Directive (2023/0135(COD)) – proposal), https://eur-lex.europa.eu/legal-content/EN/TXT/?uri=celex%3A52023PC0234, accessed 29.10.2025.

Proposal for a Directive of the European Parliament and of the Council on adapting non-contractual civil liability rules to artificial intelligence (AI Liability Directive), COM/2022/496 final, https://eur-lex.europa.eu/legal-content/EN/TXT/?uri=celex:52022PC0496, accessed 31.07.2025.

Regulation (EU) 2016/679 of the European Parliament and of the Council of 27 April 2016 on the protection of natural persons with regard to the processing of personal data and on the free movement of such data, and repealing Directive 95/46/EC (General Data Protection Regulation), https://eur-lex.europa.eu/eli/reg/2016/679/oj/eng, accessed 31.07.2025.

Regulation (EU) 2019/2088 of the European Parliament and of the Council of 27 November 2019 on sustainability-related disclosures in the financial services sector, https://eur-lex.europa.eu/eli/reg/2019/2088/oj/eng, accessed 02.11.2025.

Regulation (EU) 2020/852 of the European Parliament and of the Council of 18 June 2020 on the establishment of a framework to facilitate sustainable investment, and amending Regulation (EU) 2019/2088, https://eur-lex.europa.eu/eli/reg/2020/852/oj/eng, accessed 07.06.2025.

Regulation (EU) 2023/2854 of the European Parliament and of the Council of 13 December 2023 on harmonised rules on fair access to and use of data and amending Regulation (EU) 2017/2394 and Directive (EU) 2020/1828 (Data Act), https://eur-lex.europa.eu/eli/reg/2023/2854/oj/eng, accessed 31.07.2025.

Regulation (EU) 2024/1689 of the European Parliament and of the Council of 13 June 2024 laying down harmonised rules on artificial intelligence and amending Regulations (EC) No 300/2008,

(EU) No 167/2013, (EU) No 168/2013, (EU) 2018/858, (EU) 2018/1139 and (EU) 2019/2144 and Directives 2014/90/EU, (EU) 2016/797 and (EU) 2020/1828 (Artificial Intelligence Act), https://eur-lex.europa.eu/eli/reg/2024/1689/oj/eng, accessed 31.07.2025.

Regulation (EU) 2024/1735 Net-Zero Industry Act, https://eur-lex.europa.eu/eli/reg/2024/1735/oj/eng, accessed 01.09.2025.

Regulation (EU) 2024/1735 Net-Zero Industry Act, https://eur-lex.europa.eu/eli/reg/2024/1735/oj/eng, accessed 01.09.2025.

Regulation (EU) 2024/3110 of the European Parliament and of the Council of 27 November 2024 laying down harmonised rules for the marketing of construction products and repealing Regulation (EU) No 305/2011, https://eur-lex.europa.eu/legal-content/EN/TXT/?uri=OJ:L_202403110, accessed 27.07.2025.

Regulation (EU) 2025/40 on Packaging and Packaging Waste, https://eur-lex.europa.eu/eli/reg/2025/40/oj/eng, accessed 01.09.2025.

Report from the Commission, Implementation and best practices of national procurement policies in the Internal Market, https://eur-lex.europa.eu/legal-content/EN/TXT/?uri=celex:52021DC0245, accessed 01.09.2025.

Senate Bill 253 (Climate Corporate Data Accountability Act).

Special report 28/2023: Public procurement in the EU – Less competition for contracts awarded for works, goods and services in the 10 years up to 2021, https://eur-lex.europa.eu/eli/C/2023/1259/oj/eng, accessed 02.11.2025.

State of California, SB 253 and SB 261 Climate Accountability Package, 2023, https://www.dentons.com/en/insights/alerts/2023/october/19/new-climate-reporting-requirements-to-take-effect-in-california, accessed 30.08.2025.

Superintendency of Private Insurance (SUSEP), Ordinance No. 666/2022, https://www2.susep.gov.br/safe/scripts/bnweb/bnmapi.exe?router=upload/26128, accessed 23.06.2025.

Texas Senate Bill 13 (87th La.), Chapter 809: Prohibition on Investment in Financial Companies That Boycott Certain Energy Companies, Government Code, effective 01.09.2021, https://capitol.texas.gov/tlodocs/87R/billtext/pdf/SB00013F.pdf, accessed 24.07.2025.

The Draghi report on EU competitiveness, https://commission.europa.eu/topics/eu-competitiveness/draghi-report_en, accessed 31.08.2025.

The EU Green Bond Standard (EuGBS), https://eur-lex.europa.eu/legal-content/EN/TXT/?uri=CELEX:32023R263, accessed 31.08.2025.

The European Union's New Circular Economy Action Plan, COM/2020/98 final, https://eur-lex.europa.eu/legal-content/EN/TXT/?uri=celex:52020DC0098, accessed 07.09.2025.

The Sherman Antitrust Act of 1890 (26 Stat. 209, 15 U.S.C. §§ 1–7).

The Single European Act, https://eur-lex.europa.eu/EN/legal-content/summary/the-single-european-act.html, accessed 30.07.2025.

Treaty establishing the EEC and Euratom (Treaty of Rome), 25.03.1957, https://eur-lex.europa.eu/legal-content/EN/TXT/?uri=celex%3A12016A%2FTXT, accessed 02.08.2025.

Treaty of Amsterdam amending the TEU, the Treaties establishing the ECs (Treaty of Amsterdam), 2 October 1997, OJ C 340, 10.11.1997, https://eur-lex.europa.eu/eli/treaty/ams/sign/eng, accessed 30.07.2025.

Treaty on European Union, https://eur-lex.europa.eu/eli/treaty/teu/sign/eng, accessed 02.11.2025.

Treaty on the Functioning of the European Union (TFEU), OJ C 202, 07.06.2016, https://eur-lex.europa.eu/legal-content/EN/TXT/?uri=celex%3A12016ME%2FTXT, accessed 30.07.2025.

UK Cabinet Office, Procurement Policy Note 06/21: Taking account of Carbon Reduction Plans, 2021, https://www.gov.uk/government/publications/procurement-policy-note-0621-taking-account-of-carbon-reduction-plans-in-the-procurement-of-major-government-contracts, accessed 30.08.25.

UK Government policy paper Sustainability Disclosure Requirements: Implementation Update 2024, 2024, https://www.gov.uk/government/publications/sustainability-disclosure-requirements-implementation-update-2024, accessed 04.08.2025.

UK Government, Minimum Energy Efficiency Standards: Non-domestic Private Rented Property, 2023, https://www.gov.uk/guidance/non-domestic-private-rented-property-minimum-energy-efficiency-standard-landlord-guidance, accessed 30.08.2025.

Index

About the editor and co-authors

About the editor

Sabine Wieduwilt

Sabine Wieduwilt is a real estate partner in Dentons' Frankfurt office. She has been an attorney since 2005 and joined Dentons in April 2014. Prior to joining Dentons, she worked for US and UK law firms. She specializes in the purchase, sale, asset management and project development of commercial properties. Sabine advises national and global/multinational companies on leasing, ongoing advisory, execution, and other real estate matters. As Co-Head of Dentons' Real Estate ESG Steering Committee Europe, Sabine works with lawyers across 15 countries to implement ESG in real estate. She is also a member of the committees Logistics Real Estate and Corporate Real Estate of the ZIA Zentraler Immobilien Ausschuss e.V.

About the co-authors[666]

Dr. Bertold Bär-Boussière

Dr. Bertold Bär-Bouyssière, LL.M., a Germany- and New York-qualified attorney and one of the world's leading antitrust lawyers with over 30 years of experience in the »Brussels EU Bubble«. Bertold advises global companies on complex antitrust matters. With his keen sense of the policy dynamics of competition law, he is a creative developer of novel concepts that push the boundaries of the law. Bertold is a prolific writer in German, English, and French, embracing the world in its ever-increasing complexity. He initiated the »ESG Alliance« between Dentons and Maharashtra National Law University (Mumbai) and serves as advisor to the president of the African Center for Competition Intelligence in Yaoundé. Since 2005, Bertold's family has run a revolving financial adoption program for two children in Ethiopia.

666 In alphabetical order.

Dr. Peter Braun

Dr. Peter Braun is a partner in the Dentons' Frankfurt office and member of the German Public Procurement group. He specializes in national and international matters of public procurement law, privatizations, public-private partnerships (PPP) and compliance. He regularly advises public sector authorities, such as federal agencies and municipalities, on the structuring of complex public procurement processes, predominantly in the IT sector. He is also experienced in litigating procurement matters on behalf of public sector institutions or private sector companies before review chambers in Germany. Peter regularly defends clients before the World Bank Sanctions Board against allegations of corrupt practices in World Bank procurement, advising in relation to international financial institutions (EBRD, EIB, EU, etc.) to avoid debarment and cross-debarment and on the structured disclosure of past misconduct.

Dr. Matthias Brockhaus

Dr. Matthias Brockhaus has been a lawyer since 2005 and a partner at VBB Rechtsanwälte since 2013. He advises and defends individuals and companies in matters related to white-collar and tax criminal law, focusing on asset, corruption, and capital market offenses as well as medical criminal law. Dr. Brockhaus is experienced in complex criminal proceedings and provides preventive compliance advice to businesses. He is regularly recommended by peers and clients and is recognized by the trade press as a leading white-collar crime lawyer. Dr. Brockhaus is also the author of numerous publications and a lecturer at the NRW Judicial Academy, a member of the IHK committee, an honorary judge, and a board member of the German Ombudsman Association.

Dr. Tobias Dichtl

Dr. Tobias Dichtl is Head of Data & Foresight at neoshare AG. The company sees itself as a pioneer of digital transformation in the property and finance industries. As a leading AI-supported platform, neoshare AG acts as a unique interface between the two industries. Previously, Dichtl was Senior Director and Co-Head of Market Intelligence & Foresight at Colliers. As Head of Research & Strategy Real Assets at Helaba Invest between 2016 and 2022, he was responsible for market analysis and fund strategy for the European and international real asset portfolios. Dichtl started his career in real estate market research at Colliers International in 2013.

Oliver Dreher

Oliver Dreher, LL.M. (King's College), is a partner at Dentons' Frankfurt office and Head of the Debt Capital Markets (DCM) practice group in Germany. His main areas of expertise include corporate, bank, and sovereign bonds, MTN-, CP- and structured issuance programs, structured finance products, Schuldschein loans and registered bonds (Namensschuldverschreibungen), derivatives and advising on financial infrastructure, such as the clearing and settlement of financial instruments. A key area of his work for years has been sustainable financings and financial instruments. Oliver Dreher regularly advises on green sovereign, bank, and corporate bonds, sustainable Schuldschein loans, and other ESG-related financings.

Barbara Geidner-Buchelt

Barbara is Head of the International Investment Management and a member of the Investment Committee at Real I.S. She is responsible for deal origination, due diligence, and transactions involving office, logistics, residential, hotel, and retail properties in all European markets and Australia. Barbara is also involved in product development and fundraising for institutional investment funds and mandates. With over 20 years of experience in the investment market, she has a proven track record encompassing core, value-add, opportunistic and ESG strategies. Before joining Real I.S., she worked for Henderson Global Investors (Nuveen). Barbara is a member of the Royal Institution of Chartered Surveyors (MRICS) and holds degrees in Real Estate Economics and Architecture.

Laura Gowing

Laura is a partner in Dentons' Real Estate practice based in London. She has extensive experience of advising UK and overseas clients on investment, finance, and development transactions. She acts for a variety of property companies, developers, funds and banks across a wide range of sectors, but with a particular focus on the »beds« (BTR, student accommodation, and hospitality) and office sectors. As part of Dentons' Greater Europe ESG Taskforce, BBP's Green Lease Toolkit Legal Working Group, and the ULI UK Sustainable Development Product Council, Laura advises on green leasing and sustainability within the built environment.

Prof. Dr. Anja Henrike Kleinke

Dr.-Ing. Anja Henrike Kleinke (MBA, M.Arch) is a professor at the Jade University of Applied Sciences in Oldenburg and at TH Aschaffenburg University of Applied Sciences, Germany. She teaches sustainable project development, smart city strategies (Jade University of Applied Sciences), and project management (TH Aschaffenburg). Before she was appointed as professor, she worked in Hamburg, London, Berlin and Wiesbaden in international real estate asset management, development, transactions, project management and planning. Her research focuses on sustainable real estate project development, taking an interdisciplinary approach to ESG, impact investing, smart cities, and sector coupling. She is a member of the Institute for Corporate Governance in the German Real Estate Industry (ICG) and the German Federal Initiative for Impact Investing (BIII).

Rena Knöpke

Rena Knöpke has over two decades of experience in investment management, with a focus on real estate funds for institutional investors. Her work has centered on investor relations, fundraising, marketing, product development, and navigating regulatory frameworks. As Head of Business Development at Savills Investment Management, she managed institutional client relationships across German-speaking markets and contributed to the development and management of real estate funds with a strong focus on ESG integration. She previously held senior positions at Warburg-HIH, Henderson Global Investors, and M.M.Warburg & CO. Bilingual in German and English, she brings a broad perspective on investor needs, investment approaches, and cross-border real estate strategies.

Piotr Kociołek

Piotr Kociołek is a chemistry graduate from the University of Turin. After spending a few years broadening his knowledge of laboratory analysis, environmental regulations and industrial processes, he joined Golder Associates in 1991, where he spent 25 years dealing with environmental engineering (EDD, remediation of contaminated land, environmental permitting, REACH, ISO 14001, EMAS). He started as a junior environmental auditor and left as a Principal of the global consultancy company (now part of WSP). In 2016, he joined Panattoni Europe, a leading developer of warehouses and industrial real estate, as Environmental Director, gradually expanding the environmental team as the company increased its operations from 3 to the current 18 countries across Europe and Asia. Panattoni's environmental team manages pre-acquisition environmental matters (assessment of the environmental risks presented by the properties of interest) as well as post-acquisition matters (remediation, demolition, relationships with public administrations, investors, banks and insurance companies) to ensure that Panattoni projects are environmentally safe.

Sebastian Leutner

Sebastian is a Ph.D. candidate at the IRE|BS International Real Estate Business School, University of Regensburg, specializing in sustainable real estate finance and investment. He works for the CRREM Foundation, where he recently led the CRREM North America project in collaboration with the Urban Land Institute (ULI) and the Lawrence Berkeley National Laboratory (LBNL). Prior to joining CRREM, Sebastian worked at the Institute for Real Estate Economics under the direction of Prof. Dr. Sven Bienert, focusing on real estate valuation and portfolio advisory services. He holds a double Master's degree in real estate investment from IRE|BS, University of Regensburg, and Bayes Business School in London.

Alexander McGregor

Alex is a litigation partner in Dentons' London office. He advises on a wide range of commercial disputes and contentious regulatory matters, with a particular focus on ESG litigation and product liability issues. He has worked on cross-border claims, group/class actions and regulatory investigations for clients in the energy and resources, automotive, manufacturing, technology, and healthcare sectors. Alex has spent time on secondment to one of the world's largest energy companies, a major consumer goods company and a multinational metals and mining corporation. He is a qualified solicitor in England and Wales, and was admitted as a barrister and solicitor of the Supreme Court of Western Australia. Alex has an LLM in environmental, product and regulatory law.

Eriphyle Mitakidou-Ghabel

Eriphyle Mitakidou-Ghabel, LL.M. (Georgetown), has an academic and professional background in ESG, with a focus on regulatory compliance and corporate sustainability. She works in the Compliance & Human Rights Department of a global company, advising on ESG-related legal matters. Eriphyle holds a Master of Laws from Georgetown University Law Center in Washington, D.C., where she received the CALI Excellence for the Future Award and was named to the Dean's List for her outstanding academic performance in business and human rights. She is currently pursuing her doctoral research at Leuphana University in Lüneburg, Germany, focusing on human rights and corporate accountability.

Anderson Moura

Anderson Moura is a partner in environmental law, litigation & arbitration at Vella Pugliese Buosi e Guidoni Advogados. He has over 15 years of experience in environmental law and disputes. He guides clients through contamination claims, pollution control, licensing, waste management, forestry and indigenous issues, water management, climate change, and other sustainability matters. He has represented major players in the mining, steel, energy, automotive, chemical and petrochemical, food, agribusiness, infrastructure, and financial services industries. His work includes providing strategic advice, participating in court and administrative proceedings, engaging in complex negotiations with regulators, and offering support on transactions and projects. Anderson also counsels on Brazilian regulatory regimes for biotechnology, food and agribusiness. He is ranked by The Legal 500, Who's Who Legal and Análise Advocacia.

Bogdan Papandopol

Partner Bogdan Papandopol leads the Real Estate practice at Dentons in Romania. He advises leading domestic and international investors on real estate matters across all major asset classes, with a strong focus on the energy, retail, office, and logistics sectors. His experience includes structuring and negotiating high-value acquisitions, developments, and lease transactions for landmark office buildings, major retail projects, and large-scale logistics parks. Bogdan has represented institutional investors, developers, and funds in both greenfield and brownfield projects, guiding them through all stages of the real estate lifecycle. With over 20 years of experience, he is known for navigating complex real estate M&A deals, often involving cross-border elements and financing from local and international banks. He frequently coordinates the real estate workstreams in transactions and due diligence processes, particularly for renewable energy projects. Bogdan is also closely involved in advising clients on ESG and sustainability aspects of their real estate investments, helping them align with evolving regulatory frameworks and market expectations. He provides strategic insight into how environmental performance, green certifications, and social impact considerations influence long-term value in the real estate sector.

Giulia Peretti

Giulia Peretti is Head of Sustainability at Real I.S. in Munich, BayernLB's fund service provider for real estate investments. Since joining in 2021, she has led the sustainability and ESG strategies and implementation across company and product levels, focusing on ESG-regulation, decarbonization, climate protection, corporate sustainability, and reporting. With nearly 20 years of experience in the building sector, including as a team leader at the renowned engineering firm Werner Sobek, she combines deep sustainability expertise with practical experience in building design and implementation. Peretti holds a degree in architecture with a specialization in sustainable design and is a DGNB auditor.

Björn Pfeiffer

Björn Pfeiffer began his career in real estate with BEOS AG in Hamburg, where he progressed from Project Manager to Senior Project Manager, specializing in investment and asset management across Germany. In January 2021, he joined Swiss Life Asset Managers UK as an Assistant Portfolio Manager, was promoted to Portfolio Manager in February 2022, and advanced to Senior Portfolio Manager in April 2023. In his current role, he leads the performance and strategy of a pan-European logistics and light industrial fund.Björn holds an MSc in Real Estate from Henley Business School at the University of Reading, and is a Certified ESG Analyst (CESGA).

Dr. Dephney Ramaphosa

Dr. Dephney Ramaphosa is a Corporate Sustainability and ESG Leader with a doctorate in business leadership and a master's in environmental management. She is the Global Sustainability Senior Manager at Dentons, leading environmental sustainability across the company's global jurisdictions, and serves as an external examiner for several universities in South Africa on ESG and Sustainability related topics. Her expertise spans ESG advisory, strategy, assurance, and reporting, with experience in climate change, occupational health and safety, stakeholder engagement, sustainable finance, and investor relations. She has worked in the health, logistics, engineering, municipal services, and energy systems sectors. Dr. Ramaphosa has led diverse teams and initiatives that drive ESG value at strategic, tactical, and operational levels. Her work supports a »just and equitable transition,« promoting sustainable investment, community resilience, and nature-positive economies.

Verena Reichstein

Verena Reichstein is a senior associate in Dentons' Düsseldorf office. She specializes in advising national and international companies on legal issues related to information technology law, in particular digital transformation projects and the outsourcing of IT services and business processes, as well as European digital regulation. Verena has extensive practical experience in advising on complex, large-scale IT projects for multinational companies in the automotive, finance, and insurance industries. She is also an expert in providing legal advice on artificial intelligence and the Internet of Things.

Peter Salostowitz

Peter Salostowitz is a certified civil and industrial engineer with postgraduate studies in Real Estate Finances from the Frankfurt School of Finance and Management. He is a Fellow of the Royal Institution of Chartered Surveyors (FRICS) and a RICS-certified appraiser. From 2014 to 2022, he taught logistics, trade, and real estate management at Fresenius University of Applied Sciences. With over 20 years of experience in real estate research and valuation, he has been the managing partner of IndustrialPort since 2012, specializing in European industrial and logistics real estate, and owns the only scientific rental price index for this sector. In 2023, he published »Rating of Industrial Real Estate« and has authored several professional contributions. Since 2024, he is co-spokesperson for the »Trends and Innovations in Logistics Real Estate« group of the German Logistics Association (BVL).

Sebastian Schröder

Sebastian Schröder has studied geology at the University of Mainz (Dipl. Geologe). He worked as an environmental consultant between 2014–2020 (Valteq, CBRE Preuss Valteq, CBRE) and joined Panattoni in 2020. He is currently the Head of the Environmental Department at Panattoni Germany, he is responsible for evaluating environmental tasks during the purchase and redevelopment phases in Germany and Austria. He is also a so-called Radon Fachperson (radon specialist), certified by the Bauakademie Sachsen, and a member of the advisory board of the German Brownfield Association (DEBV).

Aragon St-Charles

Aragon serves as Dentons' inaugural Global ESG Officer, responsible for designing, implementing, and leading the firm's global ESG strategy. He works closely with the global leadership team and board to align initiatives and is a member of the Global ESG Steering Committee. As a dedicated advocate for sustainability, Aragon drives stakeholder engagement and advances key issues across all organizational levels. With his extensive experience in ESG, sustainability, and business operations, he has a proven track record of delivering performance targets, operational efficiencies, and transformative change within the legal industry. As part of this and previous roles, he ensures that commercial real estate portfolios and office refits meet or exceed sustainable building standards.

Sona Taghiyeva

Sona Taghiyeva is Partner in Dentons' Prague office. Sona focuses on corporate and real estate law. She has particular expertise in project management of multi-country deals, real estate M&A, title insurance, W&I insurance, and complex due diligence processes. She also has broad experience in energy and infrastructure, banking and finance, compliance, real estate law, construction, licensing and hospitality issues. Sona also advises clients on the development and implementation of ESG strategies across the real estate sector and serves as co-head of Dentons' Real Estate ESG Steering Committee Europe. She was admitted to the New York Bar in January 2011. She is also registered as a foreign lawyer in the Czech Bar Association since July 2018.

Romy Tenbieg

Romy Tenbieg is Managing Director of Aventus Düsseldorf (Insurance Broker). She began her career in industrial insurance and gained extensive experience in international insurance programs at Allianz Commercial. She later managed such programs on the client side. After several years in the insurance industry, she transitioned to the real estate sector, working as an investment manager with a focus on ESG, further strengthening her expertise in sustainable asset development. Her professional expertise lies in risk management and the structuring of international insurance programs. She holds a Bachelor's degree in Industrial Insurance and a Master's degree in Economics.

Vivien Teu

Vivien Teu is a lawyer with over 25 years of experience in capital markets, asset management, financial institutions, funds, investment transactions and financial regulation, with a market-leading focus on ESG law. Since launching her ESG and impact practice in 2018, she has advised on sustainable finance across asset classes, markets, institutions, and structures, while shaping standards and frameworks for sustainability and impact. Demonstrating her commitment, she founded the Vivien Teu Law Practice, an impact firm dedicated to financial services, asset and wealth management, funds, sustainable and impact finance, and philanthropy. Vivien previously held senior roles at Invesco, Clifford Chance and other global firms, and was a partner and Head of Asset Management & ESG at Dentons Hong Kong, where she also sat in global leadership for ESG, sustainable finance, financial institutions, and funds.

Raphael Thießen

Raphael Thießen is key account manager for site development and brownfields at SIERA. Before joining SIERA in November 2025, Raphael Thießen was with Brownfield24 from 2017, since 2021 as Managing Director. Previously, he worked in asset management for Hagedorn Revital GmbH. The graduate geographer and real estate specialist has many years of experience in the real estate sector. He has worked for METRO AG, METRO PROPERTIES and BNP Paribas Real Estate, among others. Since 2021, Mr. Thießen has also been Managing Director of the German Brownfield Association, which was founded on the initiative of Bronwfield24.

Andreas Trumpp

Andreas Trumpp is Head of Market Intelligence & Foresight at PTXRE GmbH, a wholly owned subsidiary of neoshare AG, which sees itself as a pioneer of digital transformation in the property and finance industries Trumpp is a Fellow of the Royal Institution of Chartered Surveyors (FRICS). Previously, he was a Managing Director and the Head of Market Intelligence & Foresight at Colliers, where he led a research team of 20 analysts. As Head of Research & Strategy Europe at Savills Investment Management between 2015 and 2022, he worked on the investor side and led a team of five international analysts. Between 2006 and 2015, he held various positions at Colliers, most recently as Head of Research Germany. Trumpp has more than 20 years of experience in property market research and analysis and is he lectures at the ADI Akademie der Immobilienwirtschaft as well as a volunteer at gif e.V.

Jordi Ventura

Jordi specializes in the mining industry and has decades of experience in the Americas. He is a native Spanish and English speaker with extensive experience in domestic and cross-border M&A, joint ventures, and strategic alliances. He negotiates and drafts agreements in both languages, including purchase and sale, earn-in, farm-out, commercial mining, property option, off-take, and joint operating agreements. Jordi is recognized for his expertise in international mining due diligence, especially regarding environmental, social, and governance (ESG) issues. He has led numerous legal and ESG due diligence projects and audits of mining operations throughout the Americas. Before joining Dentons, Jordi was Country General Counsel for multinational mining and industry leaders in Latin America, including Barrick Gold (Peru), Firestone Ventures, Ventana Mining (Guatemala), and Chiquita Brands International (Ecuador, Honduras).

Astrid Wunderle

myESG_My Life is about HEALING. I landed on this planet in 1962 in the middle of the Ruhr Area in Germany – improving human and environmental health. Toxic pollution was the order of the day, industrial waste was repeatedly found in important waterways. Fortunately, German inventors have been able to develop environmental engineering technologies that are essential for the health of our families and they will become even more important in the near future. My professional career has taken me through asset management, M&A, technical & environmental due diligence, impact investing and bioenergetic remediation of buildings, people and organizations. Today, I am dedicated to enhancing health of people and the planets.

After credit scene...

©Judith Carla Wieduwilt (2025)

The dinosaurs will return.